An Apology for the Life of
Mr Colley Cibber,
Comedian and Late Patentee
of the Theatre Royal

Colley Cibber was one of the most derided men in eighteenth-century London. Mocked for his work in the theatre and as Poet Laureate, he was nevertheless a successful actor and playwright, and co-managed the Theatre Royal Drury Lane for twenty-four years. His response to his critics, *An Apology for the Life of Mr Colley Cibber*, is often described as the first theatrical autobiography, and even as the first secular autobiography in English. But what kind of text is it? Intimate confession or cunning pose? History of the stage or political polemic? Rambling or purposeful? Or perhaps, even, the first celebrity memoir? Including comprehensive notes and a detailed scholarly introduction, this modernized text makes Cibber's enigmatic literary landmark accessible to a wide readership for the first time and allows both specialists and general readers to explore Cibber's extraordinary career against the rich, turbulent background of London theatre in the eighteenth century.

DAVID ROBERTS is Professor of English at Birmingham City University. His book *Thomas Betterton* (Cambridge University Press, 2010) was a finalist for the Freedley Award. His other scholarly editions include *Lord Chesterfield's Letters* (1992) and William Congreve's *The Way of the World* (2019). His essay on Beethoven and Shakespeare was Editor's Choice in the June 2019 issue of *The Cambridge Quarterly*.

FRONTISPIECE. Engraving of Colley Cibber and a young woman by
Edward Fisher of the portrait by Jean Baptiste van Loo, from the first
edition of the *Apology*.

AN

APOLOGY

for the LIFE of

Mr COLLEY CIBBER,

COMEDIAN and Late PATENTEE of the

THEATRE ROYAL

A Modernized Text

Edited with an Introduction by

DAVID ROBERTS

Birmingham City University

CAMBRIDGE
UNIVERSITY PRESS

CAMBRIDGE
UNIVERSITY PRESS

University Printing House, Cambridge CB2 8BS, United Kingdom

One Liberty Plaza, 20th Floor, New York, NY 10006, USA

477 Williamstown Road, Port Melbourne, VIC 3207, Australia

314–321, 3rd Floor, Plot 3, Splendor Forum, Jasola District Centre,
New Delhi – 110025, India

103 Penang Road, #05-06/07, Visioncrest Commercial, Singapore 238467

Cambridge University Press is part of the University of Cambridge.

It furthers the University's mission by disseminating knowledge in the pursuit of
education, learning, and research at the highest international levels of excellence.

www.cambridge.org
Information on this title: www.cambridge.org/9781009098366
DOI: 10.1017/9781009093019

First published 2022

Printed in the United Kingdom by TJ Books Limited, Padstow Cornwall

A catalogue record for this publication is available from the British Library.

ISBN 978-1-009-09836-6 Hardback

To Evie

CONTENTS

FIGURES

ACKNOWLEDGEMENTS

Previous editors of the *Apology* – Edmund Bellchambers, Robert W. Lowe, B. R. S. Fone, and John Maurice Evans – built the foundations on which this new edition rests. Its footnotes express better than any acknowledgements page my debt to the magnificent resources created by the editors of *The London Stage* and, above all, by Professors Judith Milhous and Robert D. Hume. For early encouragement to pursue this project, I thank Professors Peter Holland and Tiffany Stern; for answers to specific queries, Dr Mark Darlow of Christ's College, Cambridge, Mr Francis Firth of Birmingham City University, Ms Faye McLeod of the Bodleain Library, and Ms Suzanne Foster of Winchester College. Professor David Hopkins of Bristol University kindly secured me a copy of the second edition of Cibber's *Apology* and offered wise counsel about copy texts. Dr Izabela Hopkins has provided invaluable assistance with searches and many other tasks. A parallel commission from Professor Graham Saunders at the University of Birmingham encouraged me to look further into Cibber's reflections on censorship. I first encountered Cibber during my doctoral studies and take this opportunity to pay tribute to the wisdom and kindness of my late supervisor, Professor Emrys Jones of New College, Oxford. Professor Robert D. Hume's generosity has saved me from a number of errors. Any that remain are mine or, as the footnotes explain, Cibber's.

I am very grateful to my editor at Cambridge, Bethany Thomas, for her faith and guidance, and to George Laver, Liz Davey, Dr Chris Jackson, Mr Denesh Shankar, and the production team for their characteristically expert support. The advice of the Press's two anonymous readers was impeccably thorough as well as instrumental in the decision to produce a modernized text, which it is to be hoped will open up this landmark work to a wider readership. One day, perhaps, it may even be read by the latest addition to my ever-loving family, who by happy chance was delivered in the same month as the revised manuscript for this edition: a first grandchild, Evelyn Rose, to whom this book is fondly dedicated.

LIST OF FREQUENTLY CITED WORKS

Aston: Anthony Aston, *A Brief Supplement to Colley Cibber, Esq; his lives of the famous actors and actresses* (London: Anthony Aston, 1747). Reprinted in Lowe (see below), II.297–318.

Barker: Richard Hindry Barker, *Mr Cibber of Drury Lane* (New York: Columbia University Press, 1939)

Bellchambers: Colley Cibber, *An Apology for the Life of Mr Colley Cibber*, ed. Edmund Bellchambers (London: Simpkin and Marshall, 1822)

Biographia Dramatica: David Erskine Baker, *Biographia Dramatica; or, a Companion to the Playhouse*, 2 vols. (London: Rivingtons, 1782)

BL: British Library (followed by collection and reference number)

Boswell: James Boswell, *The Life of Samuel Johnson, LL.D.*, 2 vols. (London: Dent, 1906)

Buckingham: George Villiers, 2nd Duke of Buckingham, *Plays, Poems and Miscellaneous Writings associated with George Villiers, Second Duke of Buckingham*, ed. Robert D. Hume and Harold Love, 2 vols. (Oxford: Clarendon Press, 2007)

Burnet: Gilbert Burnet, *Bishop Burnet's History of His Own Time*. 2 vols. (London: Thomas Ward, 1724–34)

C: Chancery legal actions, followed by class, bundle, and piece numbers

Chetwood: William Rufus Chetwood, *A General History of the Stage* (London: W. Owen, 1749)

Cibber, *Letter*: Colley Cibber, *A Letter from Mr Cibber to Mr Pope* (London: W. Lewis, 1742)

Collier: Jeremy Collier, *A Short View of the Immorality and Profaneness of the English Stage* (London: S. Keble, 1698)

Comparison: Anon., *A Comparison Between the Two Stages* (London, 1702); sometimes attributed to Charles Gildon

Congreve, *Letters*: William Congreve, *Letters and Documents*, ed. John C. Hodges (London: Macmillan, 1964)

Congreve, *Works*: William Congreve, *The Works of William Congreve*, ed. D. F. McKenzie, 3 vols. (Oxford: Clarendon Press, 2011)

CSPD: *The Calendar of State Papers Domestic 1660–1714.* The National Archives, online at https://tna.koha-ptfs.co.uk/cgi-bin/koha/opac-detail. pl?biblionumber=52196

Davies: Thomas Davies, *Dramatic Miscellanies Consisting of Critical Observations on Several Plays of Shakespeare*, 3 vols. (London: Thomas Davies, 1784)

DNB: *Dictionary of National Biography*, ed. Leslie Stephen and Sidney Lee, 22 vols. (Oxford: Oxford University Press, 1917)

Document Register: Judith Milhous and Robert D. Hume, eds., *A Register of English Theatrical Documents, 1660–1737*, 2 vols. (Carbondale and Edwardsville: Southern Illinois University Press, 1991)

Downes: John Downes, *Roscius Anglicanus*, ed. Judith Milhous and Robert D. Hume (London: Society for Theatre Research, 1987)

Dryden: John Dryden, *The Poems and Fables of John Dryden*, ed. James Kinsley (Oxford: Oxford University Press, 1970)

Egotist: Colley Cibber, *The Egotist: or, Colley upon Cibber* (London: W. Lewis, 1743)

Evans: *A Critical Edition of* An Apology for the Life of Mr Colley Cibber, Comedian, ed. John Maurice Evans (New York and London: Garland Publishing, 1987)

Evelyn, Diary: John Evelyn, *The Diary of John Evelyn*, ed. E. S. Beer, 6 vols. (Oxford: Clarendon Press, 1955)

Faber: Harald Faber, *Caius Gabriel Cibber* (Oxford: Clarendon Press, 1924)

Farquhar, Works: George Farquhar, *The Works of George Farquhar*, ed. Shirley Strum Kenny, 2 vols. (Oxford: Clarendon Press, 1988)

Fawcett: Julia H. Fawcett, *Spectacular Disappearances: Celebrity and Privacy, 1696–1801* (Ann Arbor: University of Michigan Press, 2016)

Fielding, Plays: Henry Fielding, *Plays*, ed. Thomas Lockwood, 3 vols. (Oxford: Clarendon Press, 2011)

Fone: Colley Cibber, *An Apology for the Life of Mr Colley Cibber*, ed. B. R. S. Fone (Ann Arbor: University of Michigan Press, 1968)

Genest: John Genest, *Some Account of the English Stage, From the Restoration in 1660 to 1830*, 10 vols. (Bath: H. E. Carrington, 1832)

Hotson: Leslie Hotson, *The Commonwealth and Restoration Stage* (Cambridge, MA: Harvard University Press, 1928)

Howe: Elizabeth Howe, *The First English Actresses* (Cambridge: Cambridge University Press, 1992)

Hume, 'Aims': 'The Aims and Genre of Colley Cibber's *Apology* (1740)', *Studies in Philology* vol. 14, no. 3 (summer 2017), 662–95

Hume, *Development*: Robert D. Hume, *The Development of English Drama in the Late Seventeenth Century* (Oxford: Clarendon Press, 1976)

Hume, *Fielding*: Robert D. Hume, *Henry Fielding and the London Theatre, 1728–37* (Oxford: Clarendon Press, 1988)

Johnson, *Lives*: Samuel Johnson, *The Lives of the English Poets*, ed. Roger Lonsdale, 4 vols. (Oxford: Clarendon Press, 2006)

Koon: Helene Koon, *Colley Cibber: A Biography* (Lexington: University Press of Kentucky, 1986)

Laureate: Anon., *The Laureate: or, the right side of Colley Cibber, Esq* (London: John Roberts, 1740); sometimes attributed to Henry Fielding

LC: Lord Chamberlain's Papers. The National Archives, online at https://discovery.nationalarchives.gov.uk/details/r/C10232

Leacroft: Richard Leacroft, *The Development of the English Playhouse* (London: Methuen, 1973)

London Encyclopaedia: Ben Weinreb and Christopher Hibbert, eds., *The London Encyclopaedia* (London: Macmillan, 1983)

Lowe: Colley Cibber, *An Apology for the Life of Mr Colley Cibber*, ed. Robert W. Lowe, 2 vols. (London: John Nimmo, 1889)

LS1: William Van Lennep, ed., *The London Stage Part 1, 1660–1700* (Carbondale: Southern Illinois University Press, 1965)

LS2: Emmett L. Avery, ed., *The London Stage Part 2, 1700–1729* (Carbondale: Southern Illinois University Press, 1960)

LS2a: Judith Milhous and Robert D. Hume, eds., *The London Stage, 1660–1800: A New Version of Part 2 (1700–11)*. Adam Matthew Digital, 2021, at www.eighteenthcenturydrama.amdigital.co.uk/#

LS3: Arthur H. Scouten, ed., *The London Stage Part 3, 1729–1747*, 2 vols. (Carbondale: Southern Illinois University Press, 1961)

Luttrell: Narcissus Luttrell, *A Brief Historical Relation of State Affairs, 1678–1714*, 6 vols. (Oxford: Oxford University Press, 1857)

McGirr: Elaine M. McGirr, *Partial Histories: A Reappraisal of Colley Cibber* (London: Palgrave Macmillan, 2016)

Milhous, *Management*: Judith Milhous, *Thomas Betterton and the Management of Lincoln's Inn Fields, 1695–1708* (Carbondale: Southern Illinois University Press, 1979)

Milhous and Hume, *Publication*: Judith Milhous and Robert D. Hume, *The Publication of Plays in London, 1660–1800* (London: The British Library, 2015)

Nicoll, *History*: Allardyce Nicoll, *A History of English Drama 1660–1800, Volume II: Early Eighteenth Century Drama*, 3rd ed. (Cambridge: Cambridge University Press, 1955)

Nicoll, *Restoration*: Allardyce Nicoll, *Restoration Drama*, 3rd ed. (Cambridge: Cambridge University Press, 1940)

OED: *Oxford English Dictionary*. Online edition: www.oed.com

Pepys: Samuel Pepys, *The Diary of Samuel Pepys*, ed. Robert Latham and William Matthews, 11 vols. (London: Bell & Hyman, 1971–83)

Pope, *Poems*: Alexander Pope, *The Poems of Alexander Pope*, ed. John Butt (London: Methuen, 1963)

PSGB: Anon., *The Political State of Great Britain* (London: John Baker, 1711–40)

Schoch: Richard Schoch, *Writing the History of the British Stage, 1660–1900* (Cambridge: Cambridge University Press, 2016)

Stern: Tiffany Stern, *Rehearsal from Shakespeare to Sheridan* (Oxford: Clarendon Press, 2000)

Thomas and Hare: David Thomas and Arnold Hare, eds., *Restoration and Eighteenth-Century English Theatre: A Documentary History* (Cambridge: Cambridge University Press, 1988)

Tilley: Morris Tilley, *A Dictionary of the Proverbs in England in the Sixteenth and Seventeenth Centuries* (Ann Arbor: University of Michigan Press, 1950)

Wanko: Cheryl Wanko, *Roles of Authority: Thespian Biography and Celebrity in Eighteenth-Century Britain* (Lubbock: Texas Tech University Press, 2003)

Winn: James Anderson Winn, *John Dryden and His World* (New Haven: Yale University Press, 1987)

Except where adaptations are concerned, references to Shakespeare are to the *Complete Works*, ed. Jonathan Bate and Eric Rasmussen (Basingstoke: Macmillan, 2007). References to Latin works are as follows:

Horace: *The Complete Odes* and *Epodes*, ed. David West (Oxford: Oxford University Press, 2008)

'A Letter to Augustus' and 'The Art of Poetry', in *Classical Literary Criticism*, ed. D. A. Russell and M. Winterbottom (Oxford: Oxford University Press, 1989), pp.91–110

Satires, Epistles, The Art of Poetry, ed. and trans. H. Rushton Fairclough. Loeb Classical Library 194 (Cambridge, MA: Harvard University Press, 1926)

Juvenal: *Juvenal and Persius*, ed. and trans. Susanna Morton Braund. Loeb Classical Library 91 (Cambridge, MA: Harvard University Press, 2004)

Lucretius: *On the Nature of Things*, trans. W. H. D. Rouse, rev. Martin F. Smith. Loeb Classical Library 181 (Cambridge, MA: Harvard University Press, 1924)

Martial: *Martial. Epigrams*, ed. and trans. D. R. Shackleton Bailey, 3 vols. Loeb Classical Library 94–6 (Cambridge, MA: Harvard University Press, 1993)

Ovid: *Metamorphoses*, ed. and trans. Frank Justus Miller, rev. G. P. Goold, 2 vols. Loeb Classical Library 42–3 (Cambridge, MA: Harvard University Press, 1916)

Persius: *Juvenal and Persius*, ed. and trans. Susanna Morton Braund. Loeb Classical Library 91 (Cambridge, MA: Harvard University Press, 2004)

Terence: *The Woman of Andros. The Self-Tormentor. The Eunuch*, ed. and trans. John Barsby. Loeb Classical Library 22 (Cambridge, MA: Harvard University Press, 2001)

Virgil: *Aeneid*, ed. and trans. H. R. Fairclough, rev. G. P. Goold, 2 vols. Loeb Classical Library 63–4 (Cambridge, MA: Harvard University Press, 2000)

INTRODUCTION

A Theatrical Life

One hundred and forty-eight roles, at least; many thousands of stage appearances spanning the six decades from his debut in 1690; twenty-six dramatic entertainments with more eighteenth-century outings than any playwright other than Shakespeare;[1] nearly a quarter of a century co-managing London's leading playhouse: the theatrical career of Colley Cibber (1671–1757) was in variety and volume a match for any before or since. The same may be said for the vitriol Cibber attracted, whether as actor, writer, or manager. Yet none of his achievement would be quite as significant, or criticism of him quite so bruising, had he not become more than a subject of theatre history – had he not, that is, become a pioneering author of it.

An Apology for the Life of Mr Colley Cibber (1740) is often described as the first theatrical autobiography; one recent critic goes so far as to label it 'the first secular autobiography in English'.[2] Landmark text it certainly is, but precisely what kind of text, and why Cibber wrote it, remain contested. Confession or crafted pose? History or polemic? Ramblingly digressive or purposefully organized? The memoir of a 'peacock strutting on the public stage', the 'impudently titled' work of a 'publicity hound'?[3] Or a 'sober history' of London theatre by an 'opinionated' but 'remarkably accurate' reporter who, against the odds, wrote a work of 'something like genius'?[4] Or perhaps an attempt at self-definition that presents the 'illusion of interiority only to expose it as an illusion'?[5] The full title of the work poses many possibilities. *An Apology for the Life of Mr Colley Cibber, Comedian and late Patentee of the Theatre-Royal. With an Historical View of the Stage during his Own Time. Written by Himself*: the promise of autobiography, self-justification, objective history, and eye-witness memoir is complemented by the diverse guises in which the author appears, at once actor ('comedian'), owner-manager ('patentee'), and historian. Even that is an underestimate. No mention is made on the title page of Cibber as playwright or even Poet Laureate, the post he occupied from 1730 to his death twenty-seven years later.

---

1   Based on the estimates of Robert D. Hume, 'Reevaluating Colley Cibber and Some Problems in Documentation of Performance, 1690–1800', *Eighteenth-Century Life* vol. 43, no. 3 (September 2019), 101–14.
2   Fawcett, p.2.   3 Schoch, p.230.   4 Hume, 'Aims', 687, 690, 695.   5 Fawcett, p.3.

In its abundance and elusiveness, the *Apology* is a fitting counterpart to the disconcertingly lifelike bust of its author in London's National Portrait Gallery (cover illustration), probably crafted to celebrate the book's instant notoriety.[6] Brightly coloured, smoothly self-assured: the thin-lipped smile suggests an amused thought withheld, the piercing blue eyes averted so that the viewer has to lean and bend to catch their gaze. At first, it seems as though the man is really there, but that shock dissolves into an unsettling puzzle, the decoding of an ironic wink frozen in time. Unmistakably it is the image of a man comfortably retired in his black turban cap, the gold embroidered waistcoat announcing membership of the *beau monde*. Who made it is aptly enigmatic. It used to be thought the work of Louis-François Roubiliac, sculptor of Shakespeare and Handel; now it is tentatively attributed to the less celebrated Sir Henry Cheere and his brother John, sculptor and plasterer respectively.[7]

If the form of Cibber's *Apology* and his reasons for writing it resist easy definition, its distinctiveness is not in doubt. No previous work had offered such insight into the daily business of acting and theatre management; none had attempted to chart in such detail the relationships between licensed companies and the agencies of state; none had featured a mere actor placing himself so comprehensively in the sightlines of readers. Without the *Apology*, our knowledge of London theatre from 1690 to 1732 would be drastically diminished. Recalling the great actors of his time, Cibber developed a critical language of performance of unprecedented vividness and subtlety. Rather than setting forth the gestural and rhetorical conventions thought by some to underpin good acting as they did other kinds of public speaking, the *Apology* examines the individual qualities of actors and their impact on audiences, allowing readers a glimpse of what it was like to witness first-hand the greats of the Restoration stage.[8] This, the first theatrical autobiography, therefore also ranks as the first body of theatre criticism.[9] Not content with observation, Cibber asks us to re-evaluate his profession,

---

6   Notes published by the National Portrait Gallery give the date of the bust as 'circa 1740'. See www.npg.org.uk/collections/search/portrait/mw01301/Colley-Cibber (last accessed 12 October 2021).

7   See John Kerslake, *Early Georgian Portraits* (London: HMSO, 1977), p.54.

8   Compare, for example, John Downes's *Roscius Anglicanus* (1708), which had represented great acting as an imitation of predecessors' practice, while Charles Gildon's *The Life of Mr Thomas Betterton* (1710) included a lengthy treatise on the rhetorical and gestural language of acting, said to be useful for actors, lawyers, and clergymen alike. See Wanko, pp.38–48.

9   See, for example, Stanley Wells, ed., *Shakespeare in the Theatre* (Oxford: Oxford University Press, 1997), p.18, which includes Cibber's appreciation of Thomas Betterton as the first piece of theatre criticism in the language.

identifying in the best performers an art equal to any playwright's, composer's, or painter's.

A Life in Brief

Colley Cibber lived through part or all of the reigns of six monarchs: Charles II, James II, William III (with Mary II), Anne, George I, and George II. Unlike most of the major playwrights to emerge in the Restoration period (depending on definitions, 1660–1714), he was a Londoner by birth and, when it came to representing city life, less disposed to satire than many of his contemporaries.[10] His heritage was European and artistic. Born in 1671, he was the son of the distinguished Danish sculptor Caius Gabriel Cibber and his second wife Jane, née Colley.

Caius Gabriel's commissions meant an itinerant childhood; young Colley attended school in Lincolnshire. He missed out on scholarships to Winchester College and therefore Oxford University, episodes he describes in the *Apology*. After a brief spell in military service, in 1690 he joined what was at the time London's only licensed theatre company, playing minor roles and seeing his name recorded in the cast lists of printed editions as, variously, 'Sibber', 'Zibber', 'Colly' and 'Zybars':[11] as if he needed reminding, clumsy signals that he was the child of an immigrant father, bearing a foreign-sounding name that attracted derision throughout his career.[12] It is little wonder that he offered his credentials as a self-made man ('the weight of my pedigree will not add an ounce to my intrinsic value'),[13] that he craved respectability, and settled for integration when others preferred rebellion.

10 Of the more prolific dramatists to emerge in the period, only Cibber and John Crowne (1641–1712) were Londoners. William Congreve (1670–1729) was from a Shropshire family and attended Trinity College Dublin. John Dryden (1631–1700) was a Northamptonshire boy who went to Cambridge; Thomas Durfey (1653–1723) was from Devon, while Sir George Etherege (1636–92) grew up in Berkshire and came to London to study law. George Farquhar (1677–1707), of Scots planter heritage, went to school in Londonderry and university in Dublin (like Cibber, he was apt to see his unfamiliar name gratuitously misspelled). Thomas Otway (1652–85) was born in Sussex and failed to complete his degree at Oxford; Thomas Shadwell (1641–92) grew up in Norfolk and went to school in Bury St Edmunds. Like Congreve and Farquhar, Thomas Southerne (1660–1746) and Nahum Tate (1652–1715) attended Trinity College Dublin. Sir John Vanbrugh (1664–1726) spent most of his childhood in Chester; William Wycherley (1641–1715) was baptized in Hampshire but had family roots in Shropshire. Little is known of the early life of Aphra Behn (1640–89) other than that she probably spent some time in Surinam.
11 See lists of dramatis personae for Thomas Durfey, *Bussy d'Ambois* (1691, 'Sibber') and *The Marriage-Hater Matched* (1692, 'Colly'); Nicholas Brady, *The Rape* (1692, 'Zibber'); and Elkanah Settle, *The Ambitious Slave* (1694, 'Zybars').
12 For example, *Apology*, pp.328–9 n.51. 13 *Apology*, p.14.

Initially he worked under the penny-pinching, bullying management of the lawyer and theatre-owner Christopher Rich. In 1695, when a group of senior actors left with Thomas Betterton to form a new company at Lincoln's Inn Fields, Cibber remained behind and ended up assisting Rich. The two men evidently socialized, but in the *Apology* Cibber distances himself from the relationship; it did not fit a narrative that promotes the union of art and lucre, Rich's interests having embraced only the latter.[14] Doubtless for the same reason, Cibber skates over the many later occasions when he proved himself, in turn, a managerial penny-pincher.[15]

The 1695 division of companies created opportunities for Rich's younger actors, but to achieve his breakthrough Cibber had to take a first step in the project of self-authoring whose peak is the *Apology*. He created the foppish Sir Novelty Fashion in his own *Love's Last Shift* (January 1696), itself a landmark in the evolution of comedy, showing a penitent hero who learns to entertain generous feeling at the expense of aggressive lust and wit.[16] The following November he repeated the role, now ennobled as Lord Foppington, in Sir John Vanbrugh's *The Relapse*, and then again in his own play, *The Careless Husband*, in 1704. The association of actor and role stuck. In a series of post-retirement benefit performances during the 1740s Cibber was still playing it, serving up living relics of his career to a nostalgic audience. He was even painted in the role by Giuseppe Grisoni (Figure 7). It is arguable whether he plays up to it in the *Apology*.[17] What is clear is that he devotes little space to discussing it. If he knew the association would be taken for granted, he also had more important, less obvious, and less personal topics to write about.

While other fop roles featured prominently in his repertoire (Osric in *Hamlet*, Tattle in Congreve's *Love for Love*, Sparkish in Wycherley's *The Country Wife*, and Sir Fopling Flutter in Etherege's *The Man of Mode*), he was a highly versatile performer, with character roles including Captain Brazen in Farquhar's *The Recruiting Officer*, Ben the Sailor in Congreve's *Love for Love*, and Justice Shallow in *2 Henry IV*. Middling classical roles such as Gloucester in *King Lear*, Syphax in Addison's *Cato*, and Worcester in *1 Henry IV* were staples. Villains are almost as conspicuous in his career as fops: he played Richard III, Iago, and Volpone; in more recent work, Renault in Otway's *Venice Preserved* and Young Woudbe in Farquhar's *The Twin Rivals*, a role that drew on the success of both his Richard III and

---

14 *Apology*, p.171. 15 *Apology*, p.285 n.30.

16 For an account of the different comic elements in *Love's Last Shift*, see Hume, *Development*, pp.411–12.

17 See below, pp.lvii–lviii.

his Lord Foppington. Still, he was accused of disliking villain roles because audiences came to believe he was really playing himself – a charge he rebuts in the *Apology*.[18] Tragic heroes and romantic leads were, he admits, beyond him; he was very much the 'comedian' of the title page rather than a trage-dian.[19] Relishing the chance to send himself up (in *The Egoist* he admits to an 'utter insensibility of being ridiculous'), he played the hapless playwright Bayes in Buckingham's *The Rehearsal* and the unfunny Witwoud in Con-greve's *The Way of the World*, a role he may well have inspired: the essence of that character is captured in Congreve's devastating summary that *Love's Last Shift* 'had only in it a great many things that were like wit, that in re-ality were not wit'.[20]

That put-down was a further instance of Cibber's being felt not quite to belong, while his cheerful recycling of Congreve's verdict suggests that, like Witwoud, he was happy to play along with occasional humiliation if it kept him near the centre of things (on more than one occasion, it might be added, Congreve's words are no less true of the *Apology* than of *Love's Last Shift*). He was as critical as anyone of his own plays, which were as diverse as his portfolio of roles. Tragedy, comedy, burlesque, Shakespear-ean adaptation, Molière imitation, masque, pastoral interlude, ballad opera: he attempted them all between 1696 and 1730. When he came to publish a collected two-volume edition in 1721, only half of his existing dramatic output featured. He knew he was not a great originator but largely retained an instinct for what would work in the theatre with a particular company of actors. His best plays – particularly *Love's Last Shift* and *The Careless Husband* – were repertory standards long after his death, and his modern editors aptly summarize his dramaturgic strengths: 'plots that involved the standard formulas of his day' and 'the presentation of memorable charac-ters'.[21] Just as importantly, he understood the relationship between com-mercial viability and political loyalty.

As a manager – a period lasting formally from 1708 to 1732 – Cibber was at pains to portray himself as a cautious, mollifying intermediary. He gained his managerial apprenticeship in the late 1690s and early 1700s, as buffer between the financially driven Christopher Rich and his discontent-

---

18 As reported by Steele in *Town-Talk*, no.2; see *Document Register* no.2638. In the *Apology*, Cibber states that some actors declined villain roles for the same reason, a practice he mocks as 'theatrical prudery' (*Apology*, p.99).

19 *Apology*, p.127. Compare the title of Charles Gildon's 1710 *Life of Mr Thomas Betterton, the Late Eminent Tragedian*.

20 *Apology*, p.150; *Egotist*, p.34.

21 *The Plays of Colley Cibber, Volume I*, ed. Timothy J. Viator and William J. Burling (Cran-bury, NJ, and London: Associated University Presses, 2001), p.12.

ed actors. As one of the Drury Lane triumvirate with Robert Wilks and Barton Booth – the latter from 1713 – he was apparently the umpire, caught between contrasting talents and temperaments; in the *Apology* he misses no opportunity to mention Wilks's short fuse. Cibber's diplomatic skills were further tested in contractual disputes with other partners such as Thomas Doggett and Sir Richard Steele.[22] Whether they were tested beyond their limit is an open question. During his years in management he was involved in at least eight significant legal disputes relating to theatre governance; a further case pursued him for years after.[23] His retirement was calculating but messy. In July 1731 a patent was drafted to enable Cibber, Wilks, and Booth to run Drury Lane for a further twenty-one years, effective from September the following year.[24] Before it could come into effect, Booth sold half his interest to John Highmore; soon after, Wilks died.[25] Cibber assigned his own share to his son Theophilus for the duration of the 1732–3 season in return for a one-off rental reported to be worth £442, plus a further 12 guineas a week for acting.[26] Theophilus proved a disastrous manager, and in March 1733 Cibber sold his entire interest to Highmore for a reported 3,000 guineas.[27]

An appetite for reasonable accommodation served him well enough during his lifetime but has hardly helped his reputation since. A loyal supporter of Sir Robert Walpole's Whig government (1721–42), he became Poet Laureate partly on the strength of his Molière adaptation, *The Non-Juror*, which transformed the hypocritical priest Tartuffe into the rapacious Jacobite Dr Wolf, another role he wrote for himself. The *Apology* occasionally disguises his partisanship, attributing the success of Addison's *Cato* to its pleasing rival Whig and Tory factions equally, but for his detractors his name continued to give the game away: like the Hanoverian dynasty

---

22 For Cibber's account, *Apology*, pp.303–7 (Doggett) and 333–41 (Steele).
23 As recorded in *Document Register* nos.2026 (Christopher Rich), 2120 (Owen Swiney), 2228 (Thomas Doggett), 2526 (William Collier), 2831 (John and Christopher Mosyer Rich), 3283 (Richard Steele), 3298 (Francis Henry Lee, Master of the Revels), 3525 (Josias Miller). In 1736, along with other parties with a current or former interest in Drury Lane, Cibber was pursued for money owed to James Calthorpe (C11/1268/13, in *Document Register* no.4008).
24 LC 5/202, pp.407–9, in *Document Register* no.3568, and C66/3586, no.5, in *Document Register* no.3623.
25 *Daily Courant*, 13 July 1732, in *Document Register* no.3639.
26 Barker, p.167.
27 *Daily Post*, 27 March 1733, in *Document Register* no.3695; for alternative figures, see *Apology*, p.197 n.73. For 3,000 guineas, the Bank of England inflation calculator suggests an equivalent current value of £760,073. For an account of Theophilus's brief period in charge, including a dispute with Highmore, see Barker, pp.169–73.

he supported or his own Tarfuffian incarnation, he was an intruder in the house who had snatched the keys.[28]

When the *Apology* covers the foremost regulatory controversies affecting the theatre, Cibber advertises his moderation. Jeremy Collier's 1698 diatribe, *A Short View of the Immorality and Profaneness of the English Stage*, led to a pamphlet war and the prosecution of actors and playwrights; Cibber himself was tried but acquitted.[29] In his plays he observed standards of moral decency appropriate for the post-Collier age, while the *Apology* stresses the need for performers to live unimpeachable private lives – an assertion some early readers found questionable given Cibber's reputation (how far warranted it is hard to tell) for gambling and womanizing.[30] When Walpole's government introduced a Licensing Act in 1737, the culmination of several years when anti-Whig satire (much of it from the pen of Henry Fielding) had proliferated alongside a growth in theatre buildings, Cibber was robust in his defence of new measures that restricted the number of licensed theatres to two. The arguments about artistic quality he advances in the *Apology* were underwritten by seasoned understanding of the commercial advantage that accrued to managers of theatrical monopolies or (at worst) duopolies, the system in which he gained his own stage apprenticeship. But where money was involved, compliance had its limits. He was evidently proud of refusing to pay the Master of the Revels a licensing fee demanded merely by convention rather than statute, although the *Apology* conveniently fails to mention the adverse consequences.[31] Even so, it is easy to characterize Cibber as a classically dislikeable establishment figure: an upholder of bourgeois morality who welcomed state censorship as long as he did not incur it; who gained office by deference; who sat in judgment on the work of playwrights and actors more talented than himself; who drew handsome profits from the theatre while squeezing pennies owed to dressmakers and scene-painters.

Family matters are thinly represented in the *Apology*, but the youngest of Cibber's six children to survive infancy stretched his capacity for harmonious co-existence well past breaking-point. Charlotte – actress, baker, sausage merchant, playwright, transvestite, and autobiographer – outraged her father by mocking him in performance and by her convention-defying

---

28 *Apology*, pp.327–8.
29 Report in *The Post Boy*, 24–6 February 1702, of Drury Lane actors summoned for 'some immoral expressions contained in the plays acted by them' (*Document Register* no.1683).
30 As documented and challenged by McGirr, pp.145–80.
31 *Apology*, pp.185 and 332 n.2.

lifestyle.[32] Her *Narrative of the Life of Mrs Charlotte Charke* was published in 1755, two years before her father's death. It reflects on the difficulties of their relationship and appears to ask for forgiveness, which duly came in insultingly small measure via Cibber's will. His granddaughters, Jenny and Betty, received £1,000 each; Charlotte, a mere £5. Even her wayward brother Theophilus was allowed £50. Neither child is mentioned by name in the *Apology*, but two awkward children do not necessarily make a bad parent. In Elaine M. McGirr's recent study, Cibber is painted as the man depicted by Jean Baptiste van Loo (see frontispiece) to coincide with plans for the *Apology*: at ease over his writing desk, attended to by a young woman McGirr argues is one of his granddaughters. Cibber's forty-one-year marriage to Katherine Shore, McGirr claims, 'seems to have stepped from the boards of one his comedies: genteel, affectionate and productive'.[33] If only we could be sure.

The pursuit of gentility characterized Cibber's life after the *Apology* and the critical furore it provoked. He was 68 when the book appeared but, in Richard Hindry Barker's words, continued to behave 'like a much younger man' with a social life and an interest in much younger women to match, Katherine having died in 1734.[34] He befriended the actress Peg Woffington, the author Laetitia Pilkington, and the society belle Elizabeth Chudleigh. The Laureateship opened doors that might have been closed to a mere retired actor, but reports of his behaviour are at odds with the more pious protestations of the *Apology*. He did not impress Samuel Johnson, who thought it 'wonderful that a man who for forty years had lived with the great and the witty should have acquired so ill the talents of conversation', adding that 'one half of what he said was oaths'.[35] Cibber continued to write. *The Character and Conduct of Cicero* was published in 1747 and *The Lady's Lecture* the year after. In 1751 he published *A Rhapsody upon the Marvellous, Arising from the First Odes of Horace and Pindar*. The title pages of all three works identify him either as 'Servant to His Majesty' or 'P.L.' (i.e. Poet Laureate), so reminding the public that he was no mere actor, playwright, manager, or theatrical apologist.

Among his literary acquaintance the foremost was Samuel Richardson, who in 1740 had also published a groundbreaking book. Fielding skewered both the *Apology* and Richardson's *Pamela* in his 1741 spoof, *An Apology for the Life of Mrs Shamela Andrews*, advertising it as the work of 'Conny Keyber' and 'necessary to be had in all families'. Both Pamela and Colley, he alleged, were attention-seeking upstarts who drew readers into a taw-

---

32 See below, pp.lviii–lix n.201.   33 McGirr, p.150. 34 Barker, p.233.
35 Boswell, I.542.

dry, linguistically inept world of obsessive selfhood. Cibber took a close
interest in the evolution of Richardson's subsequent masterpiece, *Clarissa*;
according to Laetitia Pilkington he was horrified when he learned of the
dire fate that awaited its heroine. His reaction ('he shuddered – nay, the
tears stood in his eyes') was that of the ideal sentimental reader; he concluded that 'he should no longer believe Providence, or eternal wisdom, or
goodness governed the world, if merit, innocence, and beauty were to be
so destroyed'.[36] Cibber's relationship with Richardson and his circle ran
into greater difficulties when he proposed that the pure-hearted hero of *Sir
Charles Grandison* should prove his moral worth by first taking a mistress
and then forsaking her, as though reborn into virtue like the hero of *Love's
Last Shift*. Richardson's correspondent, Rachel, Lady Bradshaigh, was horrified, complaining that Cibber was 'the most finished coxcomb that ever
humanity produced' and asked never again to hear the name of 'that irre-
claimable sinner of seventy-nine'.[37]

By then, Cibber had identified an unlikely successor for the Laureateship. Henry Jones was an Irish bricklayer and poet who had been brought
to London by the Lord Lieutenant of Ireland, Lord Chesterfield, whom
Cibber describes admiringly in the *Apology*.[38] Warming to the idea of another self-made man rising to literary celebrity, Cibber encouraged Jones
and in 1753 assisted him with what turned out to be a popular play, *The Earl
of Essex*. Falling dangerously ill, Cibber sent a message to Charles Fitzroy,
Duke of Grafton and Lord Chamberlain, proposing that Jones become the
new Laureate. But Cibber recovered; Jones offended Chesterfield, took to
drink, and died in a workhouse.[39] Without showing any more sign of being
equipped for the task than he had in 1730, Cibber continued to write the
celebratory odes required of a Laureate up to his death on 11 December 1757.
Soon after, his troublesome son Theophilus, disappointed in the provisions
of Cibber's will, accepted an engagement in Dublin but drowned en route,
shipwrecked off the Scottish coast. The Laureateship went to the Cam-
bridge-educated playwright and poet William Whitehead, whose poetic
gifts were, it is fair to say, not far removed from Cibber's.

Apologies, Lives, Memorials

Apology: 'the pleading off from a charge or imputation, whether expressed,
implied, or only conceived as possible; defence of a person, or vindication

---

36 Letter from Pilkington to Richardson of 1745, cited in Barker, p.251.
37 Rachel, Lady Bradshaigh, Letter to Richardson of 1750, cited in Barker, p.255.
38 *Apology*, pp.20–22 and n.25.   39 For further details see Barker, pp.255–7.

of an institution, etc., from accusation or aspersion'; thus the Oxford English Dictionary defines the word as it was used from the sixteenth to the middle of the nineteenth century. As a literary genre, the Apology has a much older history, beginning with Plato's *The Apology of Socrates*, which records a defence mounted in 399 BC against charges of corruption. Cibber's basic classical education may have introduced him to the work; he twice refers to Socrates in the *Apology*.[40] If he also knew the two foremost examples of English Apologies, Philip Sidney's *An Apology for Poetry* (1595, also known as *A Defence of Poetry*) and Thomas Heywood's *An Apology for Actors* (1612), both would have appealed to his sense of the moral and civic role of the arts.

The hundreds of Apologies published between 1612 and 1740 embraced a far wider group of people, institutions, trades, books, ideas, and belief systems. Often the subjects were religious: witness two works published in the year of *The Non-Juror* (1717), *A Brief Apology in behalf of the people in derision called Quakers*, and *An Apology for the foreign Protestant churches having no episcopacy*. Such appeals on behalf of the underdog or the socially marginal were common: Catholics and Baptists, debtors and usurers, younger brothers, and those disgraced in office were all the subjects of Apologies. The promise was a defence of conduct undertaken in the public realm, or such as to raise questions about the public realm's assumptions, conventions, and expectations. It follows that a 1740 Apology for a *Life* did not quite herald what today would be classed as an autobiography. Instead, it pointed to what was already in the public domain: a defence less of a life than of a career.

Cibber goes out of his way to declare personal matters off limits, but with inconsistent results. Of his fellow managers, he writes, 'whatever might be our personal errors, I shall think I have no right to speak of them farther than where the public entertainment was affected by them'.[41] When it comes to actors, he is just as forthright:

If therefore, among so many, some particular actors were remarkable in any part of their private lives that might sometimes make the world merry without doors, I hope my laughing friends will excuse me if I do not so far comply with their desires or curiosity as to give them a place in my history.[42]

Considered in that light, the *Apology*'s aims might seem clear enough. It is plainly the self-justification of one of the most frequently and virulently derided men in early eighteenth-century London: a man who stood up

---

40 *Apology*, pp.24 and 35.   41 *Apology*, p.288.   42 *Ibid*.

staunchly for what was still a widely maligned species (he refers to 'that disgrace and prejudice which custom has thrown upon the profession of an actor').[43] It is unquestionably an account of a career in which acting, writing, and theatrical management were for four decades so all-consuming an obsession as to make private life a luxury. So emphatic is Cibber's search for professional as opposed to private justification that he is prone to lapse into smugness, or digression, or simply an excess of optimism. Making his own work the centre of his narrative, he is inclined to be a little catty about former associates, but only as long as they are dead; the book concludes at the point he fears depicting 'some persons living in a light they possibly might not choose to be seen in'.[44] Conscious of his own longevity, he is sombre in marking the passing of his former colleagues, and by so honouring their memory he seeks to exonerate himself from being thought a mere gossip.

Beyond his fractious relationships with Theophilus and Charlotte, family miseries such as his father's intermittent periods in the Marshalsea prison, a feud with an uncle, an arrest for assault, and what appears to be an accusation of rape, are entirely omitted.[45] Robert D. Hume's rough statistical analysis lays bare the gaps: a mere 17 per cent of the text is 'personal', of which less than one-third might be described as 'strictly autobiographical'.[46] It is, Hume concedes, not quite that simple for a work significantly made up of eye-witness testimony, but the conclusion is hard to dispute: Cibber had no intention of laying bare his emotions or personal relationships. Whether there were precedents for doing so is debatable. Hume cites studies of sixteenth- and seventeenth-century writing about the self by Paul Delany and Meredith Skura that give priority to the organization of worldly experience over any exploration of inner life.[47] A more recent study by Kathleen Lynch offers an alternative perspective, albeit in the context of religious narratives largely alien to Cibber's purpose, whatever his occasional nods towards 'Providence'.[48]

---

43 *Apology*, p.56.   44 *Apology*, p.370.
45 For Caius Gabriel Cibber, his debts, and his feud with his brother-in-law, Edward Colley, see Faber, pp.17–21; for Cibber's brief detention in prison during April 1697 at the suit of Jane Lucas, see *Document Register* no.1553; for allegations against him by Mary Osborne, see McGirr, pp.154 and 182 n.24; for his relationships with Theophilus Cibber and Charlotte Charke, see McGirr, pp.160–73.
46 Hume, 'Aims', 662.
47 Paul Delany, *British Autobiography in the Seventeenth Century* (London: Routledge & Kegan Paul, 1969); Meredith Skura, *Tudor Biography: Listening for Inwardness* (Chicago: University of Chicago Press, 2008). See also Adam Smyth, *Autobiography in Early Modern England* (Cambridge: Cambridge University Press, 2010).
48 Kathleen Lynch, *Protestant Autobiography in the Seventeenth-Century Anglophone World* (Oxford: Oxford University Press, 2012).

Those who have visited the *Apology* hoping for prolonged introspection have therefore tended to leave disappointed, while some prefer to find its gaps psychologically significant. According to Donald A. Stauffer, the book reveals the enigmatic emptiness of its author.[49] Leonard R. N. Ashley bemoans its want of existential despair or even self-doubt.[50] J. Paul Hunter claims the *Apology* for the tradition of Puritan confessional literature in which 'no secrets [are] wilfully kept [and] no flaws unmentioned', only to blame Cibber for failing to shape up: he was not, Hunter concludes, 'an especially perceptive viewer of himself'.[51] In recent criticism, performance has often taken the place of introspection. If the text reveals little of Cibber the private man, it must be because the *Apology* is a studiously contrived pose, or perhaps catalogue of poses: either an outsize version of Lord Foppington or a series of performances depending on the topic, like roles selected from an actor's repertoire. Cibber himself tantalized his readers with the idea that the book might excite 'the curiosity of his spectators to know what he really was when in nobody's shape but his own', only to insist that it is his 'theatrical character' that is on display (leaving open the question of whether that was the same thing as his managerial character).[52] At the start of the final chapter, he invites us to imagine him in another persona entirely, that of a plaintiff in Chancery: 'let the scene open, and at once discover your comedian at the Bar!'[53]

Although the *Apology* is silent on many aspects of Cibber's private life, its opening chapters give an account of his childhood which explains, in classic autobiographical fashion, how the child was father to the man: 'I remember I was the same inconsistent creature I have been ever since.'[54] Typically, self-deprecation is a route to self-celebration. He recalls how he was whipped by his teacher for writing poorly but in the same instant told that 'what was good of it was better than any boy's in the form', an anticipation of what he later admits are the sunny uplands and muddy swamps of his playwriting.[55] Professing a naivety that makes him still, at the age of 68, incredulous that anyone could be 'capable of envy, malice, or ingratitude', he admits that a loose tongue and a habit of joking at others' expense continue to land him in trouble.[56] If those are diversionary tactics designed to show that no criticism of him can be as accurate as his own, they are

49 Donald A. Stauffer, *The Art of Biography in Eighteenth-Century England* (Princeton, NJ: Princeton University Press, 1941), p.38.
50 Leonard R. N. Ashley, *Colley Cibber* (New York: Twayne, 1965).
51 J. Paul Hunter, *Before Novels: The Cultural Contexts of Eighteenth-Century British Fiction* (New York: Norton, 1990), p.330.
52 *Apology*, p.12.   53 *Apology*, p.333.   54 *Apology*, p.17.   55 *Apology*, pp.17–18.
56 *Apology*, p.18.

folded into a scheme of reflection typically characterized in literary history as 'sentimental'. *Love's Last Shift* is often described as the first sentimental comedy, and the *Apology* bathes in its warm principles. 'Wit is not always a sign of intrinsic merit', pleads Cibber, partly in self-reproach, and partly as a defence against those who doubted he had any wit at all; 'so the want of that readiness is no reproach to a man of plain sense and civility'.[57]

This notably non-confessional *Life* nonetheless invites reading as an instance of what Jacques Derrida described as 'circumfession': a life reconstructed not from introspection but from circles of friendship and professional acquaintance.[58] Here, it is male relationships and their vicissitudes that preoccupy Cibber, from a school friend who turned against him, to his father; from Lord Chesterfield, to the patentees Christopher Rich and Henry Brett; from Master of the Revels Charles Killigrew, to the actor-managers Robert Wilks, Thomas Doggett, and Barton Booth; and finally to Sir Richard Steele, a legal dispute with whom, following a long period of 'agreeable amity', is described as 'painful'.[59] One brief mention of his marriage aside, Cibber is silent on relationships with women, a charitable explanation of which is that he paid actresses the compliment of treating them purely as professionals (even as he admits to having been somewhat unprofessionally dismissive of the young Anne Oldfield).[60] His focus is on his ability to reconcile his fellow managers and to please or occasionally defy men in positions of greater influence. Reference is made to the institutions of male society that lay beyond the theatre: to coffee houses and the less salubrious establishments apparently enjoyed by Christopher Rich.[61] In particular, Cibber is drawn to anecdotes, personal and otherwise, that blur hierarchies between men. The composer Corelli elegantly corrects a patron and, in an episode remarkable only for blending schoolboy japes with suppressed eroticism, Cibber swaps shirts with his soon-to-be-master, Henry Brett.[62] His dedication of the *Apology* to a man believed to be the politician Henry Pelham is rapturous to a degree unusual even in that overheated genre. 'When I see you lay aside the advantages of superiority', he writes, 'then 'tis I taste you! Then, life runs high! I desire! I possess you!'[63] As will be seen, the *Apology* may owe its very existence to evenings that combined friendship with patronage in a way that crystallized Cibber's craving for respectability.

---

57 *Apology*, p.19.
58 Jacques Derrida, 'Circumfession', in Derrida and Geoffrey Bennington, *Jacques Derrida* (Chicago: University of Chicago Press, 1993), pp.3–315.
59 *Apology*, p.333.   60 *Apology*, p.202.   61 *Apology*, p.171.
62 *Apology*, pp.365 and 245.   63 *Apology*, p.5.

So much for the *Life* of its title: what sort of *Historical View* does the *Apology* offer? Richard Schoch argues that its roots lie in Gilbert Burnet's *History of his own time* (1724–34), a text Cibber quotes, the 'key advantage' of which was Burnet's 'privileged access to great people and...important events'.[64] Burnet's plain style communicated the vividness of personal experience. His highly individual perspective meant he felt no obligation to write about what immediate observation did not tell him: 'Where I was in the dark, I passed over all', he wrote.[65] With Burnet as Cibber's model, the *Apology* becomes 'history [understood] as coterminous with the historian', but with a catch: the Cibberian historian is 'a figure so outsized that it risks eclipsing the very knowledge to which he claims privileged access'.[66]

Hume extends the field of reference (as well as diminishing the risk of Schoch's 'eclipsing') by referring to the many 'secret histories' published between 1660 and 1750. He counts no fewer than 448 of them: some devoted to unsubstantiated and occasionally smutty rumours, but all concerned with opening up to a reading public forbidden spaces, whether personal or institutional.[67] It is an appealing context for a book that charts the jealousies and machinations of off-stage life. Nevertheless, when it comes to detailing some of his more sensitive transactions, such as multiple series of legal actions involving patentees and fellow managers, or adverse orders from the Lord Chamberlain that might have ended his career altogether, Cibber is no more forthcoming than he is about his family life.[68] If this is a secret history of the theatrical state, the author maintains tight control over which state secrets to leak, often according to whether they show him in a good light.

How well Cibber organized his history is no less debatable. He confesses he is inclined to favour the 'mere effect of chance or humour' over 'policy' even as he aspires to 'the fidelity of an historian'.[69] That preference finds voice in digressions that recall the asides when actor confides in audience; at one point Cibber even compares his digressions to a dance between the acts of a play.[70] For Schoch, as for most critics, the effect is to create a 'rambling', poorly structured narrative thrown together from the three ingredients of autobiography, stage history, and 'a gathering of anecdotes

---

64 Schoch, p.228; also *Apology*, pp.14 n.8, 26 n.41, 52 n.33, 342–3 ns.29 and 31.
65 Burnet, I: B IV, cited in Schoch, p.228.   66 Schoch, pp.247–8.
67 Hume, 'Aims', 682–3.
68 See, for example, the lawsuits involving Christopher Rich in 1709 (*Document Register* no.2026) and Owen Swiney in 1711 (*Document Register* no.2120), and his suspension from acting and managing by Lord Chamberlain Newcastle in 1719 (*Document Register* no.2957).
69 *Apology*, pp.248 and 318.   70 *Apology*, p.326.

and comments upon actors and acting'. Sometimes, Schoch adds, the three 'follow sequentially but other times they are jumbled and frequently overlap'.[71] The digressions are there, Schoch argues, to satisfy readers' yearning for familiar, foppish Colley. In the *Apology* Cibber agrees with the need for such a leavening, foreseeing a mixed audience of 'the wise and learned' as well as 'readers of no more judgment than some of my *quondam* auditors'.[72]

However, the summary of chapters that appears at the beginning of the *Apology* does not immediately suggest disorganization. In fact, reading the book in its entirety supports the idea that Cibber set out with a plan. For the first three chapters, he describes his aims and method, and charts his life before he became an actor in 1690. Chapters 4 and 5 cover the London stage and its performers between 1660 and 1690, while Chapter 6 moves on to Cibber's first years as an actor and playwright, describing the breaking up of the United Company in 1695. Chapter 7 is largely concerned with growing indiscipline in the breakaway company, with a digression on Cibber's failed attempt to imitate the much later success of *The Beggar's Opera*. In Chapter 8, he turns back to his own company and to the impact of Jeremy Collier's *A Short View*. The opening of the Haymarket Theatre in 1704, and the vicissitudes of ownership, regulation, and technology that followed, dominate Chapters 9 to 11, with Chapter 10 featuring a series of reflections on censorship. Since the Haymarket became the prime venue for performing opera, Cibber's mistrust of that genre looms large in Chapter 12, alongside a review of further changes in management and personnel, including Cibber's rise to leadership. Christopher Rich's acquisition of the old Lincoln's Inn Fields Theatre in 1709 introduces further observations about competition and regulation in Chapter 13, while the final three chapters are devoted largely to Cibber's experience of co-managing the Theatre Royal Drury Lane, including an account of a dispute in the mid 1720s with Richard Steele, who had been awarded a patent in 1715. If that falling out of friends propels the narrative forward at speed in its final chapter, it is only a sign that Cibber felt he had important business to settle for both professional and personal reasons. The same may be said for his concluding reflections on his managerial colleagues, Booth and Wilks.

Cibber's basic chronological plan is not, of course, either exhaustive or consistent. He can glide forwards from the reopening of Lincoln's Inn Fields in 1714 to attacks on him in *Mist's Journal* from 1717, and occasionally – whether knowingly or not – he reverses the order of events.[73] 'About this time' is a preferred, conveniently non-committal linking device. There is

71 Schoch, p.237. 72 *Apology*, p.326. 73 *Apology*, pp.280–1, n.16.

only so much autobiographical material as is needed to fill the gap between his birth and the point at which he began his theatrical career; it made sense to deal with his early life first before tracking back to explain how his first theatre company came into being eight years before he joined it as an 18-year-old. From start to finish he is clear about the scope of his history, his penultimate sentence referring us back to what was advertised on the title page:

> What commotions the stage fell into the year following, or from what provocations the greatest part of the actors revolted and set up for themselves in the little house in the Haymarket, lies not within the promise of my title page to relate.[74]

Hume goes a step further in defending the book's structure: while the *Apology* 'seems like rambling free association', it is really 'a focused discussion of regulatory issues' and a 'seriously thought-out attempt to tell theatre history and draw conclusions from it'.[75] Cibber's digressions are better understood as moments where key concerns are reviewed: the civic and moral role of theatre, the most and least favourable styles of management, the ideal regulatory environment, questions about his own conduct as a manager and performer, and what it is that counts as excellence in acting. Those are Schoch's 'overlapping and interwoven purposes' of the *Apology* as Hume construes them. The result: not a rambling series of reminiscences, but a more or less linear history of theatre that constitutes 'an utterly astonishing and unprecedented enterprise for its time'.[76] Cibber's own statements about his method, self-indulgent as they may seem, do not necessarily contradict that verdict. He declares that he can 'no more put off [his] follies, than [his] skin'; he admits that his 'frequent digressions may have entangled [the reader's] memory' and makes no claim to a 'regular method'; variants of the word 'digress' appear throughout the book.[77] We might expect a 'focused discussion of regulatory issues' to show more development and less repetition than Cibber bestows on the principles of theatre regulation and management: 'I believe I may have said something like this in a former chapter' he admits at one point; half-way through he fears he has bitten off more than he can chew.[78] Yet the very use of such language suggests, paradoxically, that Cibber was confident of his material, that he knew when he needed to move from core narrative to topic-based reflection and back again, but wanted (as any actor might) to re-create the atmosphere of a live audience.

---

74 *Apology*, p.370.   75 Hume, 'Aims', 680–1.   76 Hume, 'Aims', 684 and 681.
77 *Apology*, pp.13 and 198.   78 *Apology*, pp.284 and 198.

Hume further defends Cibber's historical method by speculating that he may have been allowed access to the records of Drury Lane and Covent Garden by their respective managers, Charles Fleetwood and John Rich.[79] On that question Cibber is clear: he states that he relied on memory. From that 'repository alone', he declares, 'every article of what I write is collected'.[80] Like many people advanced in years, he remembered distant events more sharply than some more recent ones. His errors are explained in the footnotes to this edition. Depending on what is counted, there are approximately fifty of them. Sometimes he gives the wrong year; sometimes he conflates separate events or reverses the order in which they happened; sometimes he misquotes. But the error count includes secondhand reports, such as stories about the early Restoration period relayed to him by senior members of the United Company. He evidently did pay attention to the 'veracity' or otherwise of his sources.[81] In short, there is nothing in the *Apology*'s history of the stage to suggest Cibber ventured an idle boast in claiming to have relied on memory (a faculty which, after all, he had honed during five decades of acting), or indeed to undermine the view that the book is, when all is said, the astonishing, deceptively coherent, and accurate feat celebrated by Hume.

Occasions of Writing

So why did he write it? It is easy to imagine that the *Apology* was conceived from Cibber's desire once and for all to answer those who had attacked him for being either an undeserving Poet Laureate, an indifferent actor, an unsympathetic manager, a peremptory judge of new scripts, a toady of the Walpole government, a supporter of the Licensing Act, a social climber, a plagiarist, a defacer of Shakespeare, or all of the above. His appointment to the Laureateship in 1730, from a list that included only those loyal to the government, sparked widespread mockery. One newspaper declared after the announcement, 'there is a report the renowned Keyber is learning to spell', the reference to foreign provenance compounding the indignation.[82] His acting was not universally praised. A hostile witness to one of his signature roles, Richard III, recalled that 'when he was killed by Richmond, one might plainly perceive that the good people were not better pleased that so execrable a tyrant was destroyed than that so execrable an actor was

---

79 Hume, 'Aims', 690.   80 *Apology*, p.294.   81 *Apology*, p.351.
82 *Fog's Weekly Journal*, 12 December 1730. For Cibber and the Laureateship, *Apology*, pp.39–42.

silent', and went on to claim that 'the general taste was against him'.[83] Cibber incurred the wrath of playwrights whose work he judged flawed or too subversive, while his eye for popular success deserted him when for reasons of political sensitivity he rejected the single most transformative play of the eighteenth century, John Gay's *The Beggar's Opera*; the error was compounded by Cibber's botched attempt to mimic its success with his own rather less impressive *Love in a Riddle*.[84] *The Non-Juror* annoyed opponents of the government and, to make things worse, earned him royal favour.[85] Throughout his twenty-four years of theatre management he retained a vested interest in securing the highly controlled environment that would come into being with the Licensing Act (even 'two sets of actors, tolerated in the same place, have constantly ended in the corruption of the theatre', he claims).[86] As a playwright he was often accused of plagiarism, and the new connections opened up by the Laureateship made others despise the pretensions of this mere actor (even those who, like Alexander Pope, had admired Thomas Betterton). On top of all that, Cibber had been the butt of Pope's withering irony in the 1728 *Dunciad Variorum*, classed among those with '[l]ess human genius than God gives an ape'; in the 1743 version of the same poem, he would be installed as the sleeping epitome of dullness.[87]

The text of the *Apology* contains warrant for all those motives for self-justification. Sometimes the defence is indirect. Cibber's reflections on the Licensing Act and the principles of good acting and management suggest he thought of this as both a topical book, useful for future generations, and one that would make readers yearn for times past. In the event, it was times past that formed the best education for the future; he had considered writing 'a select dissertation upon theatrical action', but found that describing Betterton's performances did the job for him.[88] Whatever the initial motive, impetus for the project as it eventually turned out was, as befits a work of circumfession, supplied by friendship. The dedication tells us Cibber had stayed with a man believed to be Henry Pelham, former Secretary to Lord

---

83 McGirr, pp.118–20, assesses this often-quoted extract from *The Laureate* and concludes it may have been prompted by one of Cibber's comeback performances in the 1730s rather than when he was in his prime as an actor.
84 The antagonism with Fielding may date from Cibber's rejection of his *Don Quixote in England* (1729) and/or *The Temple Beau* (1730). See also below, p.190 n.49. For a comprehensive account see Fielding, *Plays*, I.101–4. John Dennis accused Cibber of obstructing the hoped-for success of *The Invader of his Country* (1720); *Apology*, p.146 n.76. On Cibber judging new scripts, see Stern, pp.207–11.
85 *Apology*, pp.327–9. 86 *Apology*, p.324.
87 Alexander Pope, *The Dunciad Variorum*, I.236, and *The Dunciad* (1743), IV.20, in Pope, *Poems*, pp.368 and 767.
88 *Apology*, p.88.

Chamberlain Newcastle, and reminisced to him for three days about his career in the theatre. Pelham exercised 'several hours of patience' in listening to Cibber reading the manuscript aloud and commenting on it as 'a lover of the stage (and one of those few good judges who know the use and value of it)'.[89] The text of the *Apology* bears the mark of this genial origin, with 'sir' used as a term of address several times, but with diminishing frequency as patron morphs gradually into reader, the latter addressed sometimes proprietorially ('my reader'), sometimes in a more cautionary manner ('a good-natured reader' or 'a sensible reader'), and always, as befits this survey of male friendships, as a man. Throughout, Cibber attempts to re-create the feeling of a live exchange: 'now I have shot my bolt, I shall descend to talk more like a man of the age'; 'you may naturally suspect that I am all this while leading my own theatrical character into your favour'; 'if there you are not as fond of seeing, as I am of showing myself in all my lights, you may turn over two leaves together, and leave what follows to those who have more curiosity and less to do with their time than you have'.[90] He even stages momentary lapses of memory: 'Let me see – ay, it was in that memorable year …'.[91] Those and a host of other moments of feigned intimacy mimic the presence of a living voice while seeking to pre-empt, manipulate, or provoke the reader's response. His hesitations and digressions anticipate the meanderings of Sterne's *The Life and Opinions of Tristram Shandy* (1759–67); partly the accident of a written style lacking in formal elegance, they are also key to his project of self-defence. We may be reassured that in the course of this exchange between celebrity author and curious reader we are at our 'own liberty of charging the whole impertinence of it either to the weakness of my judgment or the strength of [Cibber's] vanity', but we are constantly made to feel our debt.[92] The *Apology* ushers us to the Pelham fireside, inviting us to eavesdrop. Opening the door to the green room of the theatre, it simultaneously invites us into a community of refined taste, with its vision of what an appreciation of theatre might look like in times when 'the general taste' is not 'vulgar' or 'insulted by the noise and clamour of … savage spectators'.[93] Cibber's snobbery can be excruciating (no more so than when he reflects without irony on the honour of being the butt of Lord Chesterfield's jokes),[94] but it is a component of the genre which the *Apology* foreshadows: the *bildungsroman*, in this case a story of unpromising beginnings followed by self-improvement to a life of fame, connections, and ultimately leisure. *Otium cum dignitate* – leisure with honour – was one

---

89 See *Apology*, pp.3–4. In 1754 Cibber would publish 'Verses to the Memory of Mr Pelham'. For Pelham's country home, Esher Place, see Figure 1.
90 *Apology*, pp.239, 144, and 26. 91 *Apology*, p.199. 92 *Apology*, p.340.
93 *Apology*, pp.302 and 158. 94 *Apology*, p.21.

1 Sketch of Esher Palace, Surrey, by Luke Sullivan; home of Henry Pelham and birthplace of the *Apology*.

of Chesterfield's own catchphrases, imparted many times to his son as the object of life, and apparently imbibed by Cibber.

What is the relationship between the familiar conversational mode of Cibber's readings to Pelham and the idea that the *Apology* is a sustained pose, perhaps contrived to distract us from the living being who was the author? Unlike many recent critics, Hume finds Cibber's command of facts a more fruitful topic than his alleged posturing. Still, he argues that the *Apology* is 'written to seem as though a chatty and digressive old raconteur were just rambling on to a friend, allowing others to overhear', suggesting that the 'humble, bumbling' result is 'radically at variance with the smart, tough-minded, and highly political administrator we see at work' elsewhere in the *Apology*.[95] Unless the book's dedication lays a false trail, it originated precisely as the intimate recollections of an 'old raconteur'. The introductory chapters (1–3), with their deliberations on method, childhood, and adolescence, may not have featured in Cibber's evenings with Pelham; the latter occasions are described in the dedication as 'lecture[s]', the kind of 'carefully considered history' Hume finds in the finished product.[96] Nev-

95 Hume, 'Aims', 688 and 675.
96 *Apology*, p.4; Hume, 'Aims', 688.

ertheless, it is reasonable to conclude that the bulk of the *Apology* took shape in distinct phases, from a chronologically structured draft, to the live delivery from Cibber to Pelham, to a more considered manuscript (at one point Cibber refers to writing during a stay at Bath), to the first edition, each stage strongly marked with traces of its predecessor(s), the outcome self-consciously poised between talking and writing, between the lived moment and the professional self crafted for posterity.[97]

Since Paul de Man's celebrated essay, 'Autobiography as De-facement', it has been commonplace to argue that 'life writing' does not represent its subject but, via conventions of narrative prose, constructs it, so rendering the concept of a true self somewhat elusive, if not fictional.[98] At least one early reader agreed, protesting that the *Apology* is a calculated performance, a distraction from the acquisitive, self-serving manager, actor, and playwright: 'Colley Cibber is not the character he pretends to be in this book', *The Laureate* protested, 'but a mere charlatan, a persona dramatis, a mountebank, a counterfeit Colley.'[99] That bruising charge has it both ways: if the narrator of the *Apology* is 'a counterfeit Colley', the real 'Colley Cibber' is also 'a mere charlatan' – perhaps a more productive insight than to argue that the book is simply a sustained reprise of Cibber's signature role. He had, certainly, acted Lord Foppington so often that the line between self and role must sometimes have been hard to discern (the two men are undoubtedly linguistic cousins), and it is true that the *Apology* bears witness to a literary culture of impersonation.[100] But it stretches credibility that Foppington could have been thought an ideal vehicle for narrating

---

97 On the draft, *Apology*, pp.3–4; on talking and writing, p.29; on Bath, p.204.
98 Paul de Man, 'Autobiography as De-facement', *Comparative Literature* vol. 94, no. 5 (December 1979), 919–30.
99 *Laureate*, p.15.
100 For Foppington, *Love's Last Shift*, V.iii.469–78, in *The Plays of Colley Cibber*, I.110:

> Why this, sir – You must know, she being still possessed with a brace of implacable devils called revenge and jealousy, dogged me this morning to the chocolate-house, where I was obliged to leave a letter for a young foolish girl, that – (you'll excuse me, sir) which I had no sooner delivered to the maid of the house, but whip! she snatches it out of her hand, flew at her like a dragon, tore off her headcloths, flung down three or four sets of lemonade glasses, dashed my Lord Whiffle's chocolate in his face, cut him over the nose, and had like to have strangled me in my own steinkirk.

> For suggestions that Cibber wrote spoof letters about himself, *Apology*, p.40 ns.46 & 47. *The Egotist* suggests that Cibber had been 'so used to play the fool in comedy' that he became 'quite as easy in the same character in real life', and that the success of the 'coxcomb' Lord Foppington was explained by Cibber himself having 'a good deal of the same stuff' (*Egotist*, pp.35 and 38).

the pressures of theatre management; or, for that matter, that such a performance could have been sustained for the 488 pages of the early editions.

When Cibber refers to the 'part I have acted in real life' and states that it 'shall be all of a piece', he means not a particular role, but the social persona he had cultivated for decades. He will not attempt 'to be wiser than I can be, or by being more affectedly pensive than I need be', or even to assume a 'new character' when the one he has inhabited for so long has served him well.[101] Moreover, 'if vanity be one of my natural features, the portrait would not be like me without it'; this is, he writes, a portrait like most others, painted to cast the sitter in a favourable light, a work of knowing impudence.[102] To the extent that he has engaged in 'honest examination of [his] heart', the result is merely an affirmation of his right to be selective, a picture created not in full daylight but 'chiaroscuro', a conscious mingling of light and dark.[103] The result, he hopes, is consistency, but that of the lifetime performer: a consistent reflection of the part he has always acted in real life, whether on stage or off it.[104] Three years after the *Apology* he maintained the image of a man confessedly self-obsessed, acknowledging Henry Cheere's painted bust with an octavo volume called *The Egotist, or Colley upon Cibber. Being his own face retouched to so plain a likeness that no one now would have the face to own it but himself.*[105] The book takes the form of a dialogue between a sceptical reader of the *Apology* called Frankly, and an 'Author' (Cibber), who is caught surveying the 'parcel of rubbish' that is his literary output.[106]

Cibber's posturing and selective reporting, in other words, do not necessarily make the *Apology* a less authentic representation of Pelham's fireside companion (who presumably gave something of a performance at the time), or of the cajoling, simpering, passive-aggressive manner that probably served him well as a manager in tiptoeing round the interests and egos of his fellow managers. There is therefore merit in Patricia Meyer Spacks's conclusion that Cibber 'recognized an identity between story and self', even if that relationship is fraught with contradictions (as such relationships generally are).[107] The book's origins in oral narrative invite slippage and inconsistency but also serve to bring story and self closer together. To argue that the *Apology* is nothing more than a pose is to risk assuming what

---

101 *Apology*, p.23. 102 *Apology*, p.13. 103 *Ibid.* 104 *Apology*, p.153.
105 While the title may suggest another author, this does appear to be Cibber's work; see DeWitt C. Croissant, 'A Note on the *Egotist, or Colley upon Cibber*', *Philological Quarterly* vol. 3 (1924), 76–7.
106 *Egotist*, p.5.
107 Patricia Meyer Spacks, *Imagining a Self: Autobiography and Novel in Eighteenth-Century England* (Cambridge, MA: Harvard University Press, 1976), p.195.

Cibber and the author of *The Laureate* knew to be false: that somewhere in London there was a pure Colley uncontaminated by his long history of acting and of dodging the bullets that came the way of theatre managers. A habit of studious omission does not make a persona; it may equally characterize a person, not least someone seeking vindication from memory alone. In de Man's terms, the persona may be a construct, but not alone for the purposes of the *Apology*.

Cibber had reason to present his self-portrait in chiaroscuro. The consequences of an actor biography over-indulging on private business were all too familiar. He refers disapprovingly to the biographies of his former colleagues Anne Oldfield, Barton Booth, and Robert Wilks that had been published 'in less time after their deaths than one could suppose it cost to transcribe them'.[108] Benjamin Victor's 1733 biography of Booth contains a stomach-turning account of the actor's post-mortem, while the publishing war that broke out after Wilks's death was alarming.[109] Cibber's co-manager for more than two decades, the recently deceased Wilks, was accused of bigamy in a colourful memoir by a man claiming to be an old schoolmate. A counterblast from the house of Edmund Curll, purporting to represent the views of Wilks's brother-in-law, did nothing to dampen the controversy, adding a suggestion of military desertion to the list of charges.[110] Promoting the status of acting was, as far as Cibber was concerned, continuous with promoting the good name of actors. To be author of his own life – to listen to the prompting of 'something inwardly inciting' – was far preferable to leaving the job to a coffin-chasing hack.[111]

He cannot but have sensed a commercial opportunity honed by years of scheduling plays that tapped more or less successfully into the mood of their times. When actor biographies were emerging into the market, he was uniquely placed to give the public an inside view of the country's most successful theatre. Keen to see his work enjoy an after-life on terms strictly designed to enhance his reputation, the collection of his plays published by subscription in 1721 omitted those that had flopped in the theatre or seemed of lesser merit. *Love's Last Shift*, *The Careless Husband*, and eight others made the cut; those he valued less did not.[112] If the *Apology* is reticent

108 *Apology*, p.12.
109 For commentary on Victor's biography, see Fawcett, p.12.
110 *Apology*, p.13 n.4.   111 *Apology*, p.12.
112 Besides the two titles mentioned, the two-volume quarto *Plays Written by Mr. Cibber* (1721) includes *The Tragical History of Richard III*, *Love Makes a Man*, *She Would and She Would Not*, *The Lady's Last Stake*, *The Rival Fools*, *Ximena*, *The Non-Juror*, and *The Refusal*. It excludes *Woman's Wit* (1697), *Xerxes* (1699), *The Rival Queans* (1703), *Perolla and Izadora* (1705), *Venus and Adonis* (1715), and *Myrtillo* (1715).

when it comes to Cibber's plays, it is because he knew some of them had little value artistically or commercially. The *Apology* itself was another matter. At a time when, in spite of the 1710 Copyright Act (8 Anne c.21), many authors were still handing over rights in their work to booksellers, Cibber elected to claim his life story for himself. The decision would pay off, if not quite as handsomely as his detractors would claim.

Publishing the Apology

He did not have to look far for a publisher who shared his appreciation of the *Apology*'s commercial potential, not to mention the need to present it as though it were a proper object of interest for people of taste. Early in his career, he had worked with a variety of booksellers, some of them undistinguished operators who probably paid him no more than £10 for the copyright to a play.[113] For the *Apology*, however, there was one who for prestige, quality, and trust was the obvious choice.

Born in 1682 and baptized at St Martin-in-the-Fields, John Watts was apprenticed to the bookseller Robert Everingham on 3 October 1698. He became a Freeman of the Stationers' Company on 9 June 1707 and ran a business at Little Queen Street, Lincoln's Inn Fields. Watts began printing under his own name from 1715, sometimes in partnership with Jonas Brown and John Pemberton, but some of his most distinguished work was produced in partnership with Jacob Tonson the Younger, such as the duodecimo editions of Greek classics prepared by Michel Maittaire between 1713 and 1719 (Maittaire, incidentally, was known to Cibber's acquaintance Lord Chesterfield as tutor to his illegitimate son, Philip). Watts published a number of prestigious editions, including *The Architecture of A. Palladio*, 4 vols. (1715–20) and *The Works of Molière, in French and English*, 10 vols. (1739 and 1748). He was also active in publishing plays, including the first seven editions of the runaway success Cibber did not take, *The Beggar's Opera* (1728–54).

Before the *Apology*, Watts had published a number of works by Cibber, often reissues of older plays: *Love in a Riddle* (1719, 1729, and 1736); *Caesar in Egypt* (1725 and 1736); *The Careless Husband* (1725); *The Provoked Husband* (1728 and 1735), Cibber's completion of an unfinished Vanbrugh play; *Damon and Phillida* (1729 and 1737); *An Ode for His Majesty's Birthday* (1731), which was Cibber's inaugural and much-maligned outing as Poet Laureate;

---

113 An exception was his first play, *Love's Last Shift*, which because of its success in the theatre attracted the interest of the better-known partnership of Richard Parker and Samuel Briscoe. For some of his more 'offbrand outlets', see Milhous and Hume, *Publication*, pp.72–3.

She Would and She Would Not (1734); *Love Makes a Man* (1735); *The Refusal* (1735 and 1736); *Ximena* (1735); and *The Tragical History of King Richard III* (1736). Watts's final Cibber project was a 1753 edition of *The Refusal*. If the deal Cibber struck for *The Provoked Husband* is any guide, Watts offered relatively generous terms; it is equally true that the same deal suggests Cibber could be shameless in his appropriation of others' work. Three-quarters of the play had been completed by Vanbrugh under the title *A Journey to London*, before his death in 1726. Cibber completed the piece and on 15 September 1727 received from Watts no less than £105 for the rights.[114] He appears to have regarded that sum as par. In 1724 the Drury Lane prompter, William Rufus Chetwood, had paid Cibber £105 for the rights to *Caesar in Egypt*, a moderate success at Drury Lane that December. Probably as a kindness to Chetwood, Cibber agreed to the immediate onward sale of copyright to Watts for £110.[115]

Watts's most celebrated compositor, between 1724 and 1726, was Benjamin Franklin (1706–90), whose autobiography includes a remarkable account of life in the Watts workshop, where it was usual for employees to drink liberally.[116] It is a matter for speculation whether those habits explain the existence of a curious, perhaps discarded, copy of the second edition of the *Apology* that recently came into the present editor's hands.[117] Instead of sitting between the dedication and Chapter 1, the Contents page may be found nestling by some accident in the middle of Chapter 2. Someone – presumably Cibber himself – could not resist using the purely functional genre of the Contents page as a vehicle for the *Apology*'s characteristic irony: '*The author's distress in being thought a worse actor than a poet*', he records for Chapter 6.

The first edition was published on 7 April 1740, handsomely presented in leather-bound quarto format with a full-page frontispiece engraving of the author, re-presented as the frontispiece to this edition. Unlike the title page, the engraving advertises Cibber's position as Poet Laureate. This quarto first edition is fully the equal in material quality of Watts's editions of Maittaire and Molière, so offering a further source of potential irritation to Cibber's critics. The steep price of 1 guinea (a probability, it must be said, since there is no authoritative record) reflected the exclusive market value Watts placed on the inside story of Drury Lane Theatre. That it was 'Printed by John Watts for the Author' suggests Cibber may have contributed to production costs: an act of vanity publishing in dual respects. The following month, on 14 May,

114 BL Add.MS 38,728, fol.43, in *Document Register* no.3377 (current value c.£23,000).
115 *Document Register* no.3250.
116 *The Private Life of the Late Benjamin Franklin* (London: J. Parsons, 1793), pp.31–2.
117 Thanks to the kindness of Professor David Hopkins, University of Bristol.

a second and much cheaper octavo edition appeared, but not because the first edition had sold well; the respective markets were quite different. Cibber made a number of amendments to the text – some in response to readers who had mocked his occasional errors – and Watts sold it at 5 shillings a copy (still, Hume estimates, equivalent to somewhere between £50 and £75 in current values).[118] Doubtless for economy's sake, the grand frontispiece was dropped. Cibber defended his rights in the work, going to court to block a pirate edition; ten years later, the book retained sufficient market value for him to dispose of the copyright to Robert and John Dodsley for a further 50 guineas.[119] The Dodsleys reissued the book in 1750, 1756, and 1761.

However exquisite the material appearance of the first edition, in other ways it was a jumble. Faced with Cibber's stylistic exuberance and occasionally erratic grasp of sentence structure, the compositor (perhaps partaking liberally of the regime noted by Benjamin Franklin) scattered commas and other punctuation marks with an abandoned disregard for – or possibly bafflement at – the text's meaning, a problem exacerbated in the octavo edition. The consequences for future editions, including this one, are explored in the last section of this Introduction.

On Acting

Defending his own career, Cibber goes to great pains to defend his profession. In the *Apology*, good actors demonstrate 'industry', like careful members of any other profession; they are, besides, required to be 'sober' in every sense of the word. Mindful of those who accused him of social climbing, Cibber argues that for an actor who 'excels on the stage, and is irreproachable in his personal morals and behaviour, his profession is so far from being an impediment that it will be oftener a just reason for his being received among people of condition with favour'.[120] Chapter 7 of the *Apology* concludes with the more drastic assessment that 'the briskest loose liver or intemperate man … can never arrive at the necessary excellencies of a good or useful actor'.[121] As Cibber antagonized some theatrical associates with his defence of the Licensing Act, so he risked being thought to align himself with another canonical enemy of free speech, the Reverend Jeremy Collier, whose 1698

118 Hume, 'Aims', 664.
119 Document of assignment dated 24 March 1750 and quoted by Lowe as being in the possession of his acquaintance, Julian Marshall. For the piracy action, Cibber v Walker in the National Archive, C11/1559/15 (https://discovery.nationalarchives.gov.uk/details/r/ C10512890; accessed 30 July 2021). 50 guineas is equivalent to £13,000 in current values.
120 *Apology*, p.62.   121 *Apology*, p.175.

Short View of the Immorality and Profaneness of the English Stage had led to actors and playwrights facing prosecution for blasphemy.[122] The outrage that characterized Collier's response to the rakish comedy of the Restoration period is echoed in the *Apology*: 'It has often given me amazement', Cibber writes, 'that our best authors of that time could think the wit and spirit of their scenes could be an excuse for making the looseness of them public'; such plays, he maintains, 'are sometimes too gross to be recited'.[123]

When it came to the business of writing about acting, Cibber had scant models to work from. What is now called theatre criticism – that is to say, concerning performance rather than dramaturgy – did not emerge in periodical form until the late eighteenth century. Lewis Theobald's *The Censor*, published between 1715 and 1717, claimed to 'entertain the town with the beauties or defects in writing, as well as the graces or imperfections in action', but went through dozens of editions without so much as mentioning the theatre.[124] The *Universal Spectator* and the *Grub-Street Journal* promised similar fare but frequently descended to character assassination (sometimes of Cibber's).[125] Not until Aaron Hill's *The Prompter*, which ran from 1734 to 1736, did performance criticism start to emerge in a recognizable form. Hill found plenty of other topics to write about, including bad management, bad playwrights, bad proposals for regulating the stage, bad behaviour by audiences, and bad preparation by actors, whom he accused of 'relax[ing] themselves, as soon as any speech in their own part is over, into an absent unattentiveness'.[126] Many of his barbs were directed against Cibber, whose managerial legacy he lamented and in whose Richard III he saw merely 'a succession of comic shruggings' that resembled 'the distorted heavings of an unjointed caterpillar'.[127] Contemplating Hill's own brief and utterly disastrous record of theatre management, Cibber could afford to consign him to the *Apology*'s ranks of the scarcely mentioned.[128] Hill's reflections on Robert Wilks's Hamlet may have encouraged Cibber not just to proclaim the superiority of Thomas Betterton's, but to adopt a language of critical mediation that mirrored the balancing forces of the actor's performance. 'When he grieves, he is never sullen: when he trifles, he is never light', wrote Hill of Wilks's Danish Prince; '[w]hen alone, he is seriously solid; when in company, designedly flexible'.[129] To such summary appreciation

122 *Apology*, pp.182–3.   123 *Apology*, p.178.
124 Cited in C. Harold Gray, *Theatrical Criticism in London to 1795* (New York: Columbia University Press, 1931), p.53.
125 Gray, *Theatrical Criticism*, pp.76–7.
126 Aaron Hill, *The Prompter* (London, 1734–6), no.62, 13 June 1735.
127 Hill, *The Prompter*, no.3, 19 November 1734.   128 *Apology*, p.280.
129 Hill, *The Prompter*, no.100.

Cibber added a fellow professional's eye for individual inflection and impact, so that the performances seem to live in the moment of reading, resisting reduction to Hill's formulaic summaries.

Aware of the pitfalls of writing about acting, Cibber moved between textual quotation and description as though the words of Shakespeare were self-explanatory, when what he strove to do was show how actors inflected them. He was equally conscious of the reviewer's classic pitfall: that 'the common foible of us old fellows' is to show 'a tedious partiality for the pleasures we have formerly tasted'.[130] Yet in reminiscing about the performances of the past, he elevates acting above painting because it is, more than his memorial writing, a full-blown resurrection. Van Dyck may 'make his portraits of great persons seem to think', but an actor such as Betterton 'calls them from the grave to breathe and be themselves again'.[131] Doing so, he proposes a bold reconfiguration of the traditional hierarchy of the arts imparted by classical literature while borrowing the language of painting to describe acting ('master strokes' is one of his favourite idioms).[132] A quality comparable to what is now called 'verse speaking' is one of the facets of the best acting that places it on a par with music, one of the original 'sister arts':

The voice of a singer is not more strictly tied to time and tune than that of an actor in theatrical elocution. The least syllable too long, or too slightly dwelt upon in a period, it depreciates to nothing; which very syllable, if rightly touched, shall, like the heightening stroke of light from a master's pencil, give life and spirit to the whole.[133]

In the very power of presence Cibber finds danger, both emotional and political. Casting an eye towards Fielding's attacks on Walpole's ministry, he asserts that the damage inflicted by satire in the theatre is 'ten times more severe' than anything imparted in print, since '[r]eading is but hearing at the secondhand'.[134] The result risks stirring rebellion: such satire 'may unite and warm a whole body of the malicious or ignorant into a plaudit'.[135] Underwriting such threats is the abiding consciousness of Jacobite opposition to the Crown and government that surfaces in occasional references to James II, who 'lost his crown by too arbitrary a use of his power', a fault Cibber repeatedly attributes to his former manager, Christopher Rich.[136]

At the peak of Cibber's evaluation of acting stands 'Nature', the touchstone prized, among many others at the time, by Pope in his *Essay on*

---

130 *Apology*, p.112.   131 *Apology*, p.79.
132 In Greek mythology (as recorded in Hesiod's *Theogeny*), poetry, music, and dance are the original 'sister arts', with painting and architecture coming after, and acting nowhere. Cibber goes on to claim, partly with Italian opera in mind, that 'a good play is certainly the most rational and the highest entertainment that human invention can produce' (*Apology*, p.124).
133 *Apology*, p.83.   134 *Apology*, p.192.   135 *Apology*, p.195.   136 *Apology*, p.154.

Criticism.[137] Betterton's performance as Hamlet stood out not because it conformed to a theory of acting or gesture, or went out of its way to seek applause, but because it embodied the conflicted reactions of a young man alarmingly reunited with his father, and in so doing provided a model of classical restraint opposed to the rabble-rousing (and implicitly Jacobite) style of lesser actors. When Cibber, to the disgust of his critics, took to task the acting of his erstwhile colleague Barton Booth, he at least did so from a credible critical standpoint.[138] The greatest acting, Cibber argues, takes account of the blend of tragedy and comedy Samuel Johnson so praised in the work of Shakespeare;[139] Booth, it is argued, 'carried his reverence for the buskin too far', flattening Shakespeare's 'familiar strokes ... so highly natural to each particular disposition' into monotonous declamation.[140]

The value Cibber places on 'Nature' is related to his absorption in the ethics of sentimentalism, and indeed that of social ambition. As Henry IV confronting wayward Prince Hal, Edward Kynaston performed 'that sort of grief which only majesty could feel'; his 'paternal concern for the errors of the son made the monarch much more revered and dreaded', even though his reproaches were 'unmixed with anger ... opening as it were the arms of Nature'. So doing, Kynaston expressed 'all the various motions of the heart'.[141] If Kynaston succeeded in realizing the part 'with the same force, dignity and feeling' with which it was written, William Mountfort's gentlemanly ease effected a transformation of libertine comedy similar to the one Cibber achieved with *Love's Last Shift*. As Willmore in Aphra Behn's *The Rover*, 'he seemed to wash off the guilt from vice, and gave it charms and merit' to a degree that 'Queen Mary was pleased to make in favour of [him], notwithstanding her disapprobation of the play'.[142] The instinct for balance Cibber displays in such passages, for preserving the *status quo*, is also a convenient means of self-defence. He objects to satire (so often deployed against him) because it lacks a rounded, established feeling for justice: 'Are defects and disproportions', he asks, 'to be the only laboured features in a portrait?'[143] The simple question sets out to secure Cibber's own position while, in its very naivety, highlighting a fundamental limitation in his opponents' work.

In his *Preface to Shakespeare*, Samuel Johnson would propose that Shakespeare was at his most free in writing comedy, and a forerunner of that view lies in Cibber's argument that actors best express their individuality in comic roles. Where the 'decency ... that must be observed in tragedy'

---

137 See, for example, lines 68–9: 'First follow NATURE, and your judgment frame / By her just standard, which is still the same'; in Pope, *Poems*, p.146.
138 For *The Laureate* on Cibber's critique of Booth, *Apology*, p.91 n.10.
139 In his *Preface to Shakespeare* (London, 1765). See *Apology*, p.92 n.13.
140 *Apology*, p.91.
141 *Apology*, p.93. 142 *Apology*, pp.94–5. 143 *Apology*, p.313.

makes actors conform to a single 'manner of speaking', comedy gives a per-former 'such free, and almost unlimited liberties, to play and wanton with Nature', with the result that 'the voice, look, and gesture of a comedian may be as various as the manners and faces of the whole of mankind'.[144] Here, the epitome of skill was James Nokes, whose 'palpable simplicity of na-ture' made his stage presence indistinguishable from his private manner.[145] Describing Nokes's performance as Dryden's Sir Martin Mar-all, Cibber ventures to conclude that no tragedy or tragedian could exhibit 'such a tu-mult of passions rising at once in one bosom'. Moreover, the effect was achieved without words, only a 'silent eloquence and piteous plight of his features'.[146] In framing a language to describe such moments Cibber again anticipates Sterne, this time not in his chatty digressions and asides, but in his slow-motion, defamiliarizing narration of gesture, movement, and facial expression.[147] It is a method he uses to describe off-stage behaviour too, describing Wilks's imminent outburst at a perceived slight as though scripting stage directions.[148] Evoking Susannah Mountfort as the *précieuse* Melantha in Dryden's *Marriage à la Mode*, he writes,

she is too much a court lady to be under so vulgar a confusion. She reads the letter, therefore, with a careless, dropping lip and an erected brow, humming it hastily over, as if she were impatient to outgo her father's commands by making a com-plete conquest of him at once; and, that the letter might not embarrass her attack, crack! – she crumbles it at once into her palm, and pours upon him her whole artillery of airs, eyes and motion.[149]

Such passages raise an important point about Cibber's command of language, so clearly of interest to critics who thought of it as, like his name, a manifestation of his not-quite-Englishness. His sentences are inclined to run beyond their natural life; his intended witticisms often stay rooted to the page; he has an almost Malapropian liking for polysyllabic words. His trademark spellings of 'manager' as 'menager' and 'contemporaries' as 'co-temporaries' (both corrected in this edition) may have been part-affectation and part-imitation of his father's accent; his struggles with language accen-tuate an air of pomposity driven by his over-riding determination to prove the importance of his profession. Cibber was the first to acknowledge his linguistic struggles: 'I know too that I have too bold a disregard for that

144 *Apology*, p.101. 145 *Ibid* p.102. 146 *Apology*, p.104.
147 See, for example, Sterne, *The Life and Opinions of Tristram Shandy*, ed. Graham Petrie with an Introduction by Christopher Ricks (Harmondsworth: Penguin, 1979), pp.126, 202, *passim*.
148 *Apology*, p.357. 149 *Apology*, p.120.

correctness which others set so just a value upon', he admits.[150] But there is a relationship between his fluid, sometimes improvised grammar and his extraordinary knack of observing and re-creating live performance with such a vivid awareness of the interplay of text, gesture, facial expression, and audience response. The improvised, serpentine quality of his English mimics the fluctuations of the great performances he witnessed.

Where embodying 'Nature' is the prime objective of the actor, it is not surprising that Cibber should see such skill as largely in-born rather than achieved 'from the bare imitation of another's genius'.[151] That does not mean he diminishes the value of meticulous preparation in crafting a performance. Thomas Doggett was in some ways a comedian in the mould of James Nokes, but while 'his manner was his own', he was accomplished 'in dressing a character to the great exactness' so that 'the least article of whatever habit he wore seemed in some degree to speak and mark the different humour he presented'. Such care was exercised in more than costume: 'His greatest success was in characters of lower life, which he improved from the delight he took in his observations of that kind in the real world.'[152] Cibber does not go so far in assessing what qualifies an actor to lead a company, but he is emphatic on the value of a relationship of trust between owners and actor-managers. No one – not even Pope or Fielding – incurred his mistrust as much as his former manager, Christopher Rich: the man he once served, but who is referred to throughout simply as 'the manager' or, more often, 'the patentee', an act of distancing designed, perhaps, to obscure the ways in which Cibber came to resemble him.

When it comes to acting, Cibber makes no attempt to disguise his own strengths and weaknesses. Apparently, he could learn lines very quickly (witness his claim to have mastered the 200 and more lines of Lord Touchwood in Congreve's *The Double Dealer* during an afternoon), while admitting that some writers made the task easier than others. Vanbrugh, he recalls, was so valued 'by all the actors of my time' that 'no author whatsoever gave their memory less trouble'.[153] Still, he concedes that his own facility for remembering parts gave way to Wilks's. Vocally he was, he further admits, very much in the second rank: his 'want of a strong and full voice soon cut short [his] hopes of making any valuable figure in tragedy'.[154] In this he mirrored his modest claims to success as a playwright who sometimes turned out a mere 'bauble'.[155] He wrote for money, to support his family, and was unashamed to admit it.[156]

150 *Apology*, p.42. 151 *Apology*, p.108. 152 *Apology*, pp.312–13. 153 *Apology*, pp.129 and 149.
154 *Apology*, p.150. 155 *Apology*, p.167. 156 *Apology*, p.177.

Reception and Reaction

Watts's second, cheaper edition indicates that he always foresaw a wide and enthusiastic market for the *Apology*. According to Thomas Davies, Swift borrowed a copy from his friend the bookseller George Faulkner and read it in one sitting; Davies adds that Cibber cried when he heard the story.[157] Even Samuel Johnson found the book 'very entertaining'.[158] Their enjoyment seems to have been widely shared, and the commercial success of the *Apology* was, inevitably, as aggravating to Cibber's critics as its alleged looseness of style and vanity. In *The Laureate* a profit is estimated which, if accurate, is up to half what Cibber earned from the sale of his interest in Drury Lane: '[i]ngenious indeed, who from such a pile of indigested incoherent ideas huddled together by the misnomer of a history, could raise a contribution on the town (if fame says true) of fifteen hundred pounds'.[159]

But fame probably did not say true. Hume's analysis of print runs and production costs proposes instead that fame exaggerated wildly. A normal run for a quarto (first edition) did not exceed 500 copies; for an octavo, 1,500 was the upper limit. That would mean gross receipts for the first edition of no more than £435 (assuming the sale price of a guinea is correct), and for the second edition £300. Deduct normal production costs and Cibber may have been left with something like £250 rather than the rumoured £1,500. It is hard to imagine that a gift from the dedicatee, Pelham, could have made up the difference, although a successful play dedicated to royalty might attract a substantial sum.[160] Nevertheless, Hume calculates that Cibber did well enough from the book, his profit yielding the purchasing power of between £50,000 and £75,000 in today's money.[161] It is worth adding that the 50 guineas later gained from selling the copyright to the *Apology* was not as spectacular as it might appear, amounting to only half what he had gained from selling the rights to *The Provoked Husband* and *Caesar in Egypt*.[162]

If it was in his critics' interests to exaggerate Cibber's gains, it was not in Cibber's to correct them. Imaginary profits were, like real ones, good social capital. He had already played along with every other game his critics offered. He foresaw objections to his written style:

---

157 Davies, III.477.   158 Boswell, I.368.
159 *The Laureate*, p.96. The same figure is given in Davies, III.506, but possibly on the authority of *The Laureate*. Cibber earned either £3,000 or 3,000 guineas from his sale to John Highmore in 1733 (*Apology*, p.197 n.73). See also above, p.xxiv n.27.
160 Richard Steele dedicated *The Conscious Lovers* (1722) to George I and was rewarded with £500 (see *Document Register* no.3144); c.£118,000 in current value.
161 Hume, 'Aims', 665–6.   162 See above, p.xliii.

I presume the terms of 'doting trifler', 'old fool', or 'conceited coxcomb' will carry contempt enough for an impartial censor to bestow on me: that my style is unequal, pert and frothy, patched and parti-coloured like the coat of a Harlequin; low and pompous, crammed with epithets, strewed with scraps of secondhand Latin from common quotations, frequently aiming at wit without ever hitting the mark, a mere ragout, tossed up from the offals of other authors.[163]

Repeated comparisons between statecraft and the affairs of the theatre emphasize his role as an instrument of the political establishment, while also suggesting he had no sense of the mock-heroic; he dares us not to take his grandiose comparisons seriously. Implicitly aligning his own long career in leadership with Walpole's (not to mention an impressive array of other leaders from world history), he provoked the wrath of Walpole's many enemies. He did so in the name of an allegedly impartial patriotism that was, of course, deeply partisan: 'you may see what sort of an English subject I am … I still flatter myself that I have kept a simple, honest head above water.'[164] His final chapter begins with the statement that it was all in the name of a project aligned to national politics: to bring 'the government of the stage through such various changes and revolutions to this settled state'.[165] Hume characterizes the *Apology*'s initial appearance of autobiography as 'a diversionary tactic', the equivalent of 'waving red flags at a bull', but that tactic is not limited to the early chapters.[166] Throughout the book, Cibber's defence is a calculated provocation that dares his enemies to disclose their true colours. Typically, he wanted it both ways; his lofty comparisons did not prevent him objecting to the journalist Nathaniel Mist for criticizing him and his fellow managers 'with the same freedom and severity as if we had been so many ministers of state'.[167]

His provocations are key to an attempt to situate his own conception of theatre at the centre of national life and to cast opponents in the light of subversives, both of the theatre and the state: a form of satire that uses self-mockery to draw out the enemy. The first salvoes were not long in coming. In *The Champion* of 6 May 1740, Fielding derided 'our author's comparisons of himself to King James, the Prince of Orange, Alexander the Great, Charles the XIIth, and Harry IV of France', and sought to show that Cibber's political principles were muddled. Angered by thinly veiled references to him in the *Apology*, he had already published a withering assessment of Cibber's English. Objecting to a report 'that whatever language [the *Apology*] was writ in, it certainly could not be English', Fielding quips

---

163 *Apology*, p.38.   164 *Apology*, p.52.   165 *Apology*, p.332.   166 Hume, 'Aims', 685.
167 *Apology*, p.317.

that the only way to determine that it was written in English was its lack of resemblance to any other known language.[168] Three weeks later he composed a mock trial, alleging that,

with a certain weapon called a goosequill, value one farthing, which you in your left hand then held, several very broad wounds (but of no depth at all) on the said English Language did make, and so you, the said Col. Apol., the said English Language did murder.[169]

In July 1740, a writer sometimes thought to be Fielding produced a book purporting to be the work of Cibber's son Theophilus, the doomed actor, playwright, and drunkard who at one stage looked set to inherit the management of Drury Lane.[170] Its very title was an act of mimicry: *An Apology for the Life of Mr T...C..., Comedian. Being a Proper Sequel to the Apology for the Life of Mr Colley Cibber, Comedian. With an Historical View of the Stage to the Present Year. Supposed to Be Written by Himself. In the Style and Manner of the Poet Laureate.* Its attack turned out to be multi-pronged. Beginning as an outright pastiche of the *Apology*, it proceeds to give a more straightforward account of London theatre during the 1730s, offering readers an insight into the many unsavoury episodes Cibber neglects to mention, including the actors' rebellion of 1733 which was led by Theophilus himself.[171] The final cut was its price: 2 shillings compared to the more extravagant sums charged by Watts, and all for the kind of salacious material Cibber declined to touch upon. His father may have been the intended target, but no one could have been more disappointed than Theophilus himself, who had been planning such a book but failed to get it out in time.[172]

Fielding probably did not write *The Laureate*, published on 29 November 1740, but he would certainly have enjoyed a work offering *Explanations, Amendments, and Observations* on the *Apology* in a tone charitably described as 'less genial, less amusing, and less accurate' than Theophilus's supposed memoir.[173] *The Laureate* casts Cibber as a species of religious obscurantist who had risen from nowhere, belying any claim to social

---

168 Henry Fielding, *Contributions to the Champion, and Related Writings*, ed. William B. Coley (Oxford: Clarendon Press, 2003), 29 April 1740. For Fielding on Cibber's politics, *Apology*, p.51 n.28.

169 Fielding, *The Champion*, 17 May 1740.

170 *St James's Evening Post* for 28–31 October 1732 reported that 'Mr Cibber, jun. succeeds his father [at Drury Lane], who has resigned to him.'

171 *Apology*, p.370 n.101.

172 See his 'Life of Booth', in Theophilus Cibber, *The Lives and Characters of the Most Eminent Actors* (London, 1753), p.xiii. Theophilus states that he tried and failed to identify the author of the second *Apology* but only obtained an apology from the publisher.

173 Barker, p.202.

distinction: he is, as an author and a person, 'obscure, unconnected, and wrapped up and concealed in the clinquant tinsel of metaphor', intent on leading 'you continually out of the way, by long, tedious and unnecessary digressions'. Future editors of the *Apology* be warned: to 'unravel the meaning' of such an author is 'not only groping in the dark, but it is an unpleasant and a tedious labour'.[174] When Fielding came to write *Joseph Andrews* (1742) he paid ironic tribute to a man who, 'by insinuating that he escaped being promoted to the highest stations in church and state, teach[es] us a contempt of worldly grandeur' and 'inculcate[s] an absolute submission to our superiors'.[175]

To anger one canonical author is, as far as reputations are concerned, unfortunate; to anger two may prove fatal. Cibber's feud with Alexander Pope went back twenty-three years, to a performance of *The Rehearsal* in 1717 which had mocked Pope's jointly authored farce, *Three Hours after Marriage*.[176] It continued later that year with an attack on the politics and language of *The Non-Juror*, published anonymously as *The Plot Discovered*, but advertised in 1718 as Pope's work. From 1728 onwards Pope's enmity had been channelled into some of his finest poetry: the first version of *The Dunciad*, *The First Satire of the Second Book of Horace*, and the *Epistle to Arbuthnot*. Yet 'feud' is not the right term for an enmity that initially, at any rate, seemed remarkably one-sided. Cibber's attitude to Pope's attacks was, in Barker's words, 'apparently one of complete indifference';[177] when it came to reflecting on the poet in the *Apology* he seems, as we might expect from a champion of sentimentalism, decidedly forgiving (bar, perhaps, a reference to Pope as an 'imitator' rather than a poet, and pointed remarks about the limitations of satire).[178] That is not to deny he had demonstrated considerable pique when attacked by other writers, in particular John Dennis.[179]

In response to the *Apology*, Pope chose to turn up the temperature, doubtless irritated by Cibber's high-minded reflections on satire. The 1743 version of *The Dunciad* has Cibber lying stupefied in the lap of the Goddess Dullness, his name chiming with that of the Cimmerians, dwellers in perpetual night. Having seen a draft, Cibber chose to respond, calling on the capacity for 'jeering and making a jest' which the *Apology* states had

174 *The Laureate*, p.1.
175 Henry Fielding, *Joseph Andrews*, ed. Douglas Brooks-Davis (Oxford: Oxford University Press, 1966), p.16.
176 As described in full by Barker, pp.204–5.
177 Barker, p.207. In *Egotist*, p.31, Cibber maintains his indifference, stating that for all the criticism of his 'egotism', he has 'not yet arrived at the pain of repenting it'.
178 *Apology*, p.25.   179 *Apology*, p.318 n.18. For Pope as 'imitator', p.25.

characterized his behaviour from school onwards.[180] He published his *Letter from Mr Cibber to Mr Pope*: friends, he claims, encouraged him; if he did not respond to Pope, it would be thought 'a plain confession' that he was indeed 'bankrupt in wit'. He added that '[a]fter near twenty years having been libelled by our daily-paper scribblers, I never was so hurt as to give them one single answer'.[181] For the majority of the *Letter*, he sticks to the high ground he had claimed in the *Apology*. Satire, he continues to argue, is a genre for noble rather than spiteful minds, yet even he is forced to admit that some of Pope's attacks on him are authentically witty. But the more he writes, the more Cibber exhibits spite of his own, referencing his rival's physical stature in comparing him to 'a little angry bee', and recounting a scandalous tale of how Pope's 'little-tiny manhood' failed to cope on encountering a generously proportioned prostitute.[182] The minor pamphlet war that followed further skewered Pope as an anti-establishment imp, a freak of nature whose thirst for satire was hypocritical.[183] Worst of all, a series of prints set out in graphic detail what was alleged to have happened that day in, to use Cibber's phrase, 'a house of carnal recreation' (Figure 2).[184] Even so, hearing of Pope's illness in 1744, Cibber is said to have exercised the compassion of the best sentimental hero and asked the author of another anti-Pope pamphlet not to publish, because it would have made his adversary's health worse.[185]

Cibber's treatment at the hands of Pope, in particular, handed him an unfortunate role in narratives of the traditional English literary canon. He became the epitome of the non-canonical: the man so evidently lacking in talent as to prove the validity of the canon, the definitive literary-historical fall guy. The reception of the *Apology* has become an inalienable part of the work itself. Approximately half Cibber's entry in *The Oxford Companion to English Literature* is devoted to the criticism he incurred.[186] 'The vain and blandly ingenuous Cibber', writes Roger Lonsdale in another well-known reference work, 'precisely embodied the process in the *Dunciad* by which

---

180 *Apology*, p.18.   181 Cibber, *Letter*, p.7.   182 Cibber, *Letter*, pp.30 and 46–9.

183 See, for example, the following works, all published in August 1742: Lord John Hervey, *The Difference between Verbal and Practical Virtue, with a Prefatory Epistle from Mr C-b-r to Mr P*; Anon., *Blast upon Blast and Lick for Lick, or a New Lesson for P-pe*; Anon., *Sawney and Colley*; Anon., *A Letter to Mr C-b-r on His Letter to Mr P-*.

184 Alternative versions of the scene, 'The Poetical Tom-Tit perched upon the Mount of Love', and 'An Essay on Woman', are reproduced in McGirr, pp.86–7. Cibber, *Letter*, p.46.

185 Benjamin Victor, *Original Letters, Dramatic Pieces, and Poems*, 3 vols. (London: 1776), I.95. A full account of Cibber's exchanges with Pope following the *Apology* is in Barker, pp.210–20.

186 Margaret Drabble, ed., *The Oxford Companion to English Literature*, 5th ed. (Oxford: Oxford University Press, 1985), pp.198–9.

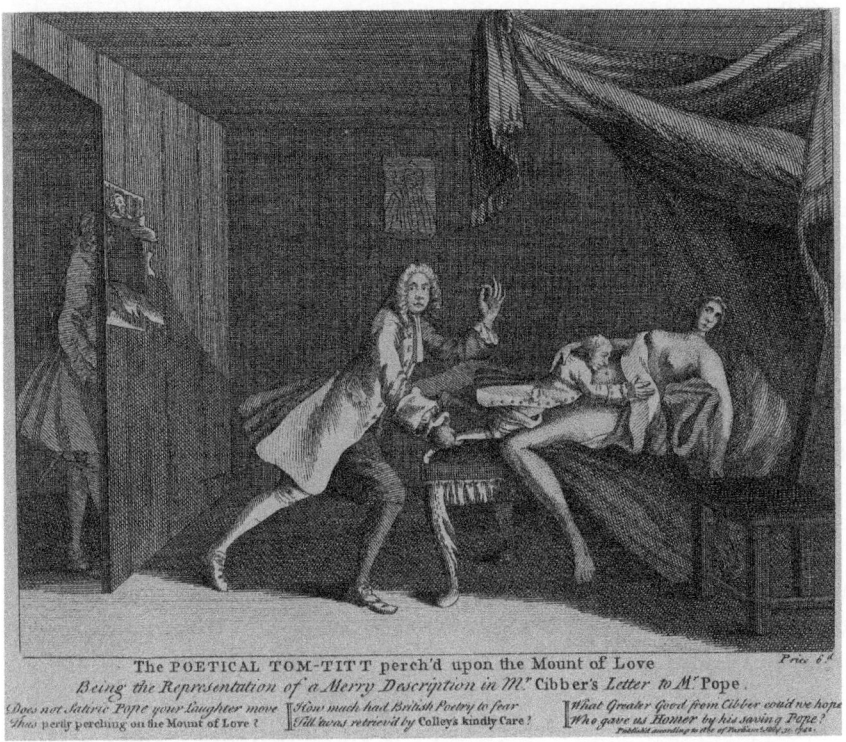

The POETICAL TOM-TITT perch'd upon the Mount of Love
Being the Representation of a Merry Description in Mr Cibber's Letter to Mr Pope.

Does not Satiric Pope your Laughter move | *How much had British Poetry to fear* | *What Greater Good from Cibber could we hope*
Thus pertly perching on the Mount of Love ? | *Till 'twas retriev'd by Colley's kindly Care !* | *Who gave us Homer by his saving Pope ?*

2. The Poetical Tom-Tit: Alexander Pope in a brothel.

Pope believed debased literary taste had spread upwards through a degenerating society.'[187] That was an attractive theme for students of English literature encouraged to find in Pope's satire qualities of what F. R. Leavis called a 'complex harmony', an exercise of 'urbane speech' to set against (or rather, some distance above) the clatter of commercialism, whether heard in the eighteenth century or since.[188] Such judgments may betray a preference for literary over theatre studies; yet in the *Apology*, Cibber goes out of his way to distinguish what is merely commercial from the higher species of entertainment the theatre has to offer. His literary-historical misfortune has been compounded by recent attention to Charlotte Charke's *Narrative*, with its portrayal of an unforgiving patriarch by a marginalized, convention-defying daughter, so that the apologist who set out to secure his good name has constantly been found in need of further apology.

187 Roger Lonsdale, 'Alexander Pope', in *The Sphere History of Literature in the English Language, Volume IV: Dryden to Johnson* (London: Sphere Books, 1971), p.132.

188 F. R. Leavis, *Revaluation: Tradition and Development in English Poetry* (London: Chatto & Windus, 1936), pp.96 and 89.

Themes in Modern Criticism

Cibber scholarship over the last century has approached his rehabilitation from a variety of angles, and with varying attention to the *Apology*. The two major biographies differ markedly in method, focus, and reliability. In Richard Hindry Barker's *Mr Cibber of Drury Lane* (1939), the chapter devoted to the *Apology* is the shortest of fourteen. Barker writes admiringly about Cibber's skill in evoking live performance and praises his occasional 'neat turns of wit'. For a study completed without the benefit of modern research resources, it is a substantial and largely reliable achievement.[189] But Barker is also unduly preoccupied by the 'inflated paragraphs' and 'uncertain style' that drew mockery in 1740, and he takes as read the idea that the *Apology* is fundamentally disorganized.[190] Rather than focusing on structure or themes, Barker highlights characters. As though drafting a treatment for a film, he describes the *Apology* as a 'narrative of prolonged disaster and final triumph', a contest between Cibber and Christopher Rich, the latter standing for 'everything that is undesirable and disorderly in the theatre'.[191] Variants of the word 'master' lend strength to such a reading; in Cibber's lexicon, the 'masterly' performances of great actors are often set against the oppressive ways of their 'masters' (except when the latter are themselves actors, of course). But the *Apology* has other significant antagonists, not least the also unnamed Charles Killigrew, long-serving Master of the Revels, who charged Cibber's company for licensing and sometimes mutilating their plays.[192]

Helene Koon's 1986 biography, *Colley Cibber*, draws upon the wealth of reference and critical material that had appeared since Barker's book. The result is atmospheric, if somewhat hazily so. Koon succeeds in knitting together episodes narrated in the *Apology* with some of those conveniently or diplomatically excluded from it. A transcription of Cibber's will, a partial list of his roles, and an extensive bibliography form useful resources. As a text in its own right, however, the *Apology* blends almost invisibly into the texture of Koon's prose. Discussion of the work is confined to a few pages in the middle of a chapter entitled 'Misfortunes', but the *Apology* resurfaces everywhere else, transformed through Koon's creative way with narrative (witness the first sentence of her 'Prologue': 'Late on a chill January afternoon in 1696, Colley Cibber stood in the wings of the Theatre Royal, Drury Lane, shivering with excitement').[193] In finding Cibber a 'charming, delightful and worthwhile companion', Koon pays tribute to the effect of

---

189 The same may be said of F. Dorothy Senior's *The Life and Times of Colley Cibber* (London: Constable & Co., 1928).
190 Barker, pp.200–1.   191 Barker, p.198.   192 *Apology*, pp.184–5.   193 Koon, p.1.

easy familiarity promised by the dedication to the *Apology*, but leaves aside the question of whether readers should succumb to it.

In a study of the plays published in 1912, DeWitt C. Croissant showed how the effect of Cibber's style was embedded in the ethics and practice of sentimentalism, whose moral purpose is reflected in the *Apology*. The idea of a normative, benevolent masculinity is shown to be key to social and spiritual welfare, and that benevolence entails a proper regard for women. It is no accident that Cibber befriended Samuel Richardson, whose novels feature what John Mullan has described as 'a decorous yet guilelessly tremulous language of feeling'.[194] It is a language that, like the quasi-oral narrative of the *Apology*, creates a vivid sense of the here and now, and Mullan's phrase might describe how Cibber builds a relationship with readers of the *Apology* no less than it does Clarissa Harlowe's own way with words. So often described as the work of a vain man, the *Apology* is distinctive – or, subject to preference, irritating – partly for its constant enquiries after its readers' comfort. 'I must therefore a little make bold with your patience', Cibber declares at the outset, setting the tone for an exchange in which we receive regular reassurance that our feelings are being considered.[195] 'Patience' and its variants embody a core value for Cibber (there are fifty-four occurrences in the *Apology*, about one every six pages), either in his transactions with the reader or his evaluations of others' behaviour. Exhibiting or asking for it is to extend a rational courtesy; 'rational', 'polite', 'agreeable', 'sincere', 'pleasing', and other weapons in the armoury of sentimentalism also feature frequently.

When he encountered it in Richardson, Fielding judged such language the expression of an over-heated effeminacy. In Kristina Straub's influential book, *Sexual Suspects*, it stretches the boundaries of conventional masculinity.[196] According to Straub, the *Apology* is a lengthy reprise of Lord Foppington, who departs from normal standards of masculinity while shadowing them. We are not to understand this fop's sexuality as 'deviant', still less effeminate (contemporary directors of Restoration Comedy take note). In Straub's reading, the rupture of foppishness and manliness occurs in the

---

194 John Mullan, *Sentiment and Sociability: The Language of Feeling in the Eighteenth Century* (Oxford: Clarendon Press, 1988), p.63. For Cibber's friendship with Richardson, see Barker, pp.250–5.

195 *Apology*, p.12.

196 Kristina Straub, *Sexual Suspects: Eighteenth-Century Players and Sexual Ideology* (Princeton, NJ: Princeton University Press, 1992). Straub develops an argument advanced by Lois Potter in 'Colley Cibber: The Fop as Hero', in J. C. Hilson, M. M. B. Jones, and J. R. Watson, eds., *Augustan Worlds: Essays in Honour of A. R. Humphreys* (Leicester: Leicester University Press, 1978).

later eighteenth century; it is worth remembering that another signature
Cibber role, Sir Fopling Flutter in Etherege's *The Man of Mode*, is a threat
to the alpha male hero, Dorimant, rather than his antithesis. Both Fopling
and Sir Novelty are, for all their shows of flamboyant self-confidence, *ar-
rivistes*, men fundamentally uncertain of their place in society. The *Apology*
is certainly rich in foppish features: a narrator eager to talk up his social
standing, to review the way he has made a career of parading himself in
public, careful to keep his family well behind the scenes, and appearing
casually dismissive of the children who survived and the ones who did not;
a narrator nervous of being on the outside whose most treasured memories
of adolescence include nothing more momentous than waiting at table for
a duchess.[197]

As Elaine M. McGirr points out, however, by 1740 Cibber was no
mincing parvenu but a 'middle-aged and corpulent' public figure, 'exuding
the confidence, ease and arrogance earned after forty years of theatrical and
social success'; he did, after all, tender his *Apology* principally as a manager
rather than as an actor, expecting to be held accountable for his 'share of administration in the state of the theatre'.[198] Straub's reading of the *Apology* as
a foppish text, McGirr argues, filters out 'the many masculinities, both marginal and dominant, that Cibber popularized on the stage and the page'.
A survey of the characters he played reveals, after all, 'a dutiful son, a few
successful lovers, some wise men, some devious men, a handful of old men
and many tyrants'; to that list we may add what appear to be a number of
brown-face roles.[199] McGirr's book is as much an apology as the *Apology* itself, and inclined to be no less partial in its familiarity as it reviews Cibber's
performing, managerial, writing, and domestic lives. On the latter, Cibber
himself had least to say, yet lived with accusations that he gambled, treated
his children poorly, and kept a prostitute. Of those sins McGirr seeks to ab-
solve him. Recent interest in the work of his alienated daughter Charlotte
has confirmed a caricature of Cibber as an unfeeling father whose approach
to parenting is summed up in his alleged response to Charlotte's plea for
help: 'I am sorry I am not in a position to assist you further. You have made
your own bed, and thereon you must lie.'[200] Since the bed in question was
almost certainly Henry Fielding's, and since Charlotte had recently mimicked her father in a performance of Fielding's *Pasquin* with Cibber in the

197 *Apology*, p.53.   198 *Apology*, p.13.
199 McGirr, p.38. For brown-face roles, *Apology*, pp.90 n.7 and 91 n.11.
200 The letter is quoted by Koon, p.143. However, as McGirr notes, p.185, its authenticity is
    questionable.

audience, he was entitled to be unimpressed.[201] However, when McGirr refers to 'the unusual warmth' of his marriage and his 'close relations with his real and theatrical families', her defence lapses into sentimentality.[202] Contrary to his own claims, Cibber was as capable as Christopher Rich of working against the financial interests of actors and ancillary workers; and if the *Apology* leaves out plenty of facts that are hardly to Cibber's credit, even the ones it includes demonstrate that the companies he served were rarely harmonious.[203] It is, moreover, possible to have long ceased to be a parvenu without shedding the anxiety that comes with it.

A broad focus on Cibber's life and work, however well intentioned in its desire to correct Cibberian myths, risks underestimating the liminal, experimental nature of the *Apology* itself. Such is the focus of Cheryl Wanko's history of the emergence of theatrical biography.[204] In her account, Cibber attempted to put paid to a prejudice not just against actors, but in particular against actors who had the temerity to write. 'The players have all got the itching leprosy of scribbling, as Ben Jonson calls it; 'twill in time descend to the scene-keepers and candle-snuffers', complained one writer in 1702.[205] The prophecy proved true: six years later, the former Duke's Company prompter, John Downes, published his memoir of the stage, *Roscius Anglicanus*. Wanko shows Cibber seizing the opportunity of print as a project of 'commercial self-fashioning' that is more threatening to established social hierarchies than stage performance. His habit of 'caress[ing] and cajol[ing]' his readers opens their eyes to the possibility that actors are, after all, central to civil society.[206] To do so, he must find a middle ground between those scandalizing, 'low' biographies of Wilks and others, and high-minded treatises on theatrical action that justified their social purpose by proposing that clergymen and barristers might equally profit from them. Cibber's is, Wanko argues, a new kind of authority that derives from close observation of performers and their individual traits. Even as it is conceived, however, that authority withers in the face of two stark facts: the 'monstrous presentations' he complains have begun to fill the stage, sacrificing art to the

---

201 McGirr, p.164. During the performance, Charke spoke lines that made fun of her father's official post: 'Faith, sir, I can't tell well what [odes] are; but I know you may be qualified for the place without being a poet.' In *Egotist*, pp.27–8, Cibber claims to have laughed with the rest of the audience.

202 McGirr, p.19.

203 On Cibber deducting sums from ancillary workers, see *Apology* p.285 n.30; on his agreement effectively to limit actors' salaries, see Judith Milhous and Robert D. Hume, 'The London Theatre Cartel of the 1720s: British Library Additional Charters 9306 and 9308', *Theatre Survey* vol. 26 (1985), 21–37.

204 Wanko, esp. pp.120–35. 205 *Comparison*, p.16. 206 Wanko, p.113.

counting of bums on seats; and the stark truth that all the actors Cibber held up as role models were either retired or dead (a poignant fact of timing is that the book was published just before the emergence of David Garrick, who did not especially impress Cibber).[207] The *Apology*'s place in a long-running print controversy underlines the fragility of its authority: a definitive word on the functioning of a theatre that merely sparked new kinds of antagonism and partiality. Nevertheless, Wanko concludes, it is manifestly a landmark text, deserving more attention in its own right than it tends to be given. Part of a moment in the specialization of historical knowledge, it offers proof of its own concept that actors might write their own lives and, less loftily, encouragement for 'a type of textual paparazzi who attempt to create a celebrity aura for themselves'.[208]

The place of the *Apology* in a literary market increasingly inclined towards celebrity persuades Brian Glover that Cibber set out to graft a pseudo-aristocratic persona onto the more mundane reality of his humbler, industrious self, part of a Habermasian project to understand private selves in the context of the public domain.[209] Noelle Gallagher goes further: the *Apology* was Cibber's bid to be remembered as a great man alongside the global worthies he cites.[210] In Julia Fawcett's 2016 study, *Spectacular Disappearances*, the book's 'overexpression' of gender invites and proceeds to disrupt the public gaze, as does Charlotte Charke's *Narrative* (in her case, by mimicking her father in his vast Foppington wig). Emphasizing the 'illusion of interiority', Fawcett offers a riposte to those who lament the absence of an authentic self in the *Apology*; such absences are, she argues, endemic to the literature of celebrity.[211] It is hard to resist finding a parallel here with the disappointment felt by J. Paul Hunter;[212] since it is not clear why anyone should expect to find an abundance of 'interiority' in the *Apology*, celebrating its absence is arguably beside the point. Where there is celebrity in recent criticism, anxiety invariably follows, but whether Cibber's book discloses 'anxieties about publicity' remains debatable, so overwhelming is the *Apology*'s many-sided confidence:[213] a quality born of the approval of its

---

207 Davies, III.470: in 1742, seeing Garrick as Bayes in *The Rehearsal*, Cibber thought him 'well enough, but ... not superior to my boy Theophilus'. He modified his opinion slightly following Garrick's play, *Miss in her Teens* (1747), in which the author played Fribble. For further discussion see Barker, pp.235–6.
208 Wanko, p.134.
209 Brian Glover, 'Nobility, Visibility, and Publicity in Colley Cibber's *Apology*', *Studies in English Literature* vol. 42 (2002), 523–39.
210 Noelle Gallagher, *Historical Literatures: Writing about the Past in England, 1660–1740* (Manchester: Manchester University Press, 2012), p.34.
211 Fawcett, pp.3 and 6. 212 See above, p.xxx. 213 Fawcett, p.10.

patron and manifested in its familiar tone, its pre-empting of criticism, and in the certainty of the eye-witness observation that shaped its unique inside history of the early eighteenth-century London stage.

Editions of the Apology

Thanks to the labours of four editors over a period of two centuries – not to mention the creation of extraordinary resources such as *The London Stage*, *A Biographical Dictionary of Actors*, and *A Register of Theatrical Documents* – the idea that to 'unravel the meaning' of a text such as the *Apology* is 'not only groping in the dark, but … an unpleasant and a tedious labour' is less intimidating than it once was.[214] Yet the warning issued in *The Laureate* is still pertinent. The task of editing and annotating the *Apology* may be less arduous than it has ever been and the debt to previous scholars greater, but it remains far from straightforward.

In 1822 the first annotated version appeared from the house of Simpkin and Marshall. It was the work of Edmund Bellchambers, who at the time was amassing material for five substantial titles published between 1834 and 1837, including *A General Biographical Dictionary* (1835), *The Scripture Cabinet, comprehending the principal events of the Old and New Testaments* (1837), and *The British Tourist* (1834). Bellchambers's preface begins with the optimistic assessment that the *Apology* is 'very clearly explained'[215] (that is, self-explanatory) but ends with an admission that '[i]t was thought necessary by the booksellers that some notes should be attached to the present edition'.[216] It is characteristic of Bellchambers's approach that the blame for that necessity is placed squarely at Cibber's door: the notes would be 'for the purpose of elucidating various points that Cibber has not thoroughly handled'.[217] Not quite: at frequent intervals, Bellchambers intervenes not to elucidate Cibber's 'various points' but to dispute them. To Cibber's assertion that acting requires 'as ample endowments of Nature as any one profession', Bellchambers retorts, 'And what value is intrinsically attached to the most "ample endowments of nature"? … if [acting's] highest excellence lie beyond the grasp of science … we may pronounce it to be a profession which no being can embrace with any solid claims to intellectual consideration.'[218]

Bellchambers's preface sets the tone for his intermittently truculent footnotes, some of which are essays in themselves. From the outset he gives a strong impression of having fallen under the sway of Fielding and Pope.

214 *The Laureate*, p.1.   215 Bellchambers, p.iv.
216 Bellchambers, p.xv.   217 *Ibid*.   218 Bellchambers, p.60.

'The frivolity of Cibber was highly contemptible', he writes; 'inordinate vanity alone', he adds, 'induced him to apologize for a life over which neither his notions nor his talents allowed him to affect the slightest superiority'.[219] Yet he applauds Cibber's defence of the theatre as both 'dignified and useful' and finds in the *Apology* the 'frank and cordial vivacity' that reflects the book's origins as a series of fireside lectures in a country house.[220]

When Robert W. Lowe set to work on his edition of 1889, he aimed to correct errors and misapprehensions in Bellchambers and to make the *Apology* newly navigable. With often extensive footnotes listing (for example) entire casts, a supplementary chapter by the editor himself, occasional digressions on Victorian theatre, biographies of the major actors discussed by Cibber, and a valuable reprint of Anthony Aston's *A Brief Supplement*, Lowe's edition stretches to two fat volumes and stands as a kind of variorum *Apology*, often cited by scholars in preference to those that have appeared since. In its approach it recalls the Dodsley editions, which reprinted James Wright's 1699 *Historia Histrionica* as a way of covering the period before Cibber joined the United Company. Lowe's actor biographies testify to the difficulty of finding a convenient format for all Cibber's references to his contemporaries, and they clear space for lengthy quotations from those infuriated by the *Apology*. The result is an edition as much about the reception of Cibber's work as its origins and design. Lowe can be robust with both Cibber and Bellchambers: on the reference to Addison's *Cato*, 'which was first acted in 1712', Lowe comments, 'This is a blunder, which, by the way, Bellchambers does not correct.'[221] His severity is turned up a notch seventy pages on. To Cibber's dating his legal case against Richard Steele at 1726, Lowe remarks, 'This is one of Cibber's bad blunders. The case was heard in 1728.'[222] In general, Lowe's annotation is inconsistent by modern standards: sometimes encyclopaedic, if not always for clear reasons, but frequently passing over allusions for which readers plainly need a gloss.

B. R. S. Fone's edition of 1968 has the advantage of being contained in a single volume with an attractively presented text, reproduced almost as it appears in the first edition, and a textual collation that lists a good proportion of variants among the imprints of 1740 (two), 1750, and 1756. Fone provides a pithy introduction and a brief list of changes in the regulatory environment of the theatre from 1660, but – puzzlingly – only as far as 1715. He also glosses the summaries that appear at the head of each chapter, anchoring their loose descriptions in firm dates. His lightness of touch

219 Bellchambers, pp.vii and ix.   220 Bellchambers, p.xiv.   221 Lowe, II.120.
222 Lowe, II.198.

with annotation, frustrating in itself, skews understanding of the *Apology*'s distinctiveness. With blunt statements of contradiction that echo Lowe's reproving manner, Fone exaggerates the fallibility of Cibber's memory, whereas a more extensive enquiry into the *Apology*'s field of reference suggests that he was indeed, as Hume argues, 'remarkably accurate'.[223] Fone's edition also underestimates the problems caused by Cibber's evidently high opinion of his readers' memories. The *Apology* is awash with cross-references and – whatever view is taken of its organization – its style can be hypnotic. Lowe recognized that readers are entitled to extra help with navigating Cibber's back-and-forth style, but Fone is reluctant to give it (the price both in this new edition and in Lowe's is, inevitably, an element of see-sawing between notes). Fone also recycles errors made by Bellchambers and Lowe, and, like them, he identifies few of the people indirectly associated with theatre who crossed Cibber's line of vision.

In his 'Critical Edition' of 1987, John Maurice Evans provides a step up in annotation from his predecessors, drawing amply on *The London Stage*. He takes a cautious view of the status of the second edition of the *Apology*, arguing that in all but four cases the changes were carried out by one of Watts's compositors rather than Cibber himself. The result is a version based on the first edition. Which passages to annotate can, Evans notes, 'be debated', and it is undeniably true that 'how much expansion and background are required' for this text 'can be argued indefinitely'.[224] Every one of Cibber's sentences might be annotated with ten more; one has to stop somewhere. Drawing a distinction between 'historical' and 'illustrative' annotation, Evans is generally thorough and accurate when it comes to the theatre, but less so in charting Cibber's references to the world beyond. Perhaps for reasons of series protocols, the presentation of his edition severely compromises the experience of reading it. With an austere typewriter font for Cibber's text and facing pages of notes that sometimes stray backwards onto otherwise blank paper, Evans's is not, therefore, an edition designed to carry the *Apology* to anything more than a highly restricted audience.

The current edition is annotated more consistently and fully than its predecessors, with previously untraced allusions explained for the first time. Notes generally focus on the topics Cibber wrote about rather than documenting in detail the controversy he provoked; the latter has been described in this Introduction. However, in some cases I have followed Lowe and Evans in citing material that sheds light on responses to the

223 Hume, 'Aims', 662. 224 Evans, p.vii.

Apology. The introductory timeline is an attempt to anchor the reader in an undeviatingly linear history and to indicate landmarks in historical and cultural context. Full use has been made of *A Register of Theatrical Documents* and *The London Stage* with a view to indicating the accuracy or otherwise of Cibber's recollections, and the extent to which his observations were made first hand. In the case of *The London Stage*, references are given to the print editions, with the proviso that page numbers for the period 1700–11 generally refer to Milhous and Hume's ongoing revision of Part 2 (here marked as LS2a). There is a caveat. Indispensable though it is, *The London Stage* captures only a small fraction of all the performances that took place in Cibber's lifetime, and for some of those the *Apology* is a key source.

The text presented here is based on the second edition of 1740. Approximately one hundred alterations were made to the text of the first edition; where those were made in error, the first edition has been followed. Cibber was evidently responsible for some of the changes, and the reasons were various. Sometimes he addressed errors pointed by his critics; on other occasions he wondered if he had been a little harsh on particular actors, or too grandiose in claims about his own actions, or had implied through choice of the wrong tense the breakdown of a relationship. He also considered whether he had been historically accurate, either in reviewing whether 'agreement' was the right term to express the arrangement whereby the Duke's and King's Companies avoided each other's repertoire, or misdating the award of titles to the Duke of Devonshire. The fact that those corrections were published within weeks of the first edition shows Cibber's eagerness to get as many of his facts right as he could, as well as to mollify particular readers. The corrections also justify the choice of the second edition as the basis for this new undertaking. Lowe provides a composite of both 1740 texts, while Fone prefers the first: 'It is the first, not the second, edition which is ... historically important', he argues, but on the questionable premiss that Cibber's corrections were, unlike the redrafting he undertook for the 1721 edition of his plays, 'not rewritings', but merely 'corrections and grammatical changes'.[225] Each text, surely, is 'historically important', but the second represents a degree of reflection and accommodation to the interests of readers and subjects.

The current edition differs from its predecessors in no respect more significantly than in its modernization of spelling and punctuation, an editorial principle that also applies to quotations by other authors in the

225 Fone, p.xxvii.

footnotes and in this Introduction, as well as to the titles of plays. The latter decision may be seen as controversial, but play titles of the period were spelled in different ways (*City Politiques, City Politicks*, etc.), and there seems no reason to invoke authorial authority in an otherwise modernized edition. Colloquial abbreviations (*t'other, 'em*), and those designed to preserve verse metre, are exceptions to the general rule. In a small handful of instances, a word or letter has been inserted in square brackets where Cibber's meaning would be unclear without it, or where the second edition is clearly wrong; in one instance the order of two words has been reversed for the same reasons.[226] The early editions make occasional use of italics where a particular emphasis was sought; those have largely been retained in the interest of retaining the appearance of a speaking voice. Decisions have had to be made in instances where it is not clear whether Cibber is referring to the title of a play or its eponymous hero (like most of his contemporaries, he would write of being 'in' rather than 'as' a particular character).

For an example of the difficulty of reading the *Apology* as originally set by Watts's compositors, take this single 198-word sentence from the second edition of 1740:

Now, whether we might certainly have acted without any License at all, I shall not pretend to determine; but this I have, of my own Knowledge, to say, That in Queen *Anne's* Reign, the Stage was in such Confusion, and its Affairs in such Distress, that Sir *John Vanbrugh,* and Mr. *Congreve,* after they had held it about one Year, threw up the Menagement of it, as an unprofitable Post, after which, a License for Acting was not thought worth any Gentleman's asking for, and almost seem'd to go a begging, 'till some time after, by the Care, Application, and Industry of three Actors, it became so prosperous, and the Profits so considerable, that it created a new Place, and a *Sine-cure* of a Thousand Pounds a Year, which the Labour of those Actors constantly paid, to such Persons as had from time to time, Merit or Interest enough, to get their Names inserted as Fourth Menagers in a License with them, for acting Plays, *&c.* a Preferment, that many a Sir *Francis Wronghead* would have jump'd at.[227]

Such presentation, much as is found in existing editions, guarantees that a landmark text for both biography and theatre studies will be read only by the most determined specialist. The work of modernizing involves difficult choices. In 1740 punctuation was still in transition from the rhetorical to the grammatical tradition: from a representation of speech patterns to an exercise in parsing that was frequently undertaken by printers rather than

226 *Apology*, p.95: the early editions have 'he had not been an entire master', whereas the sense clearly indicates 'had he not been an entire master'.

227 *Apology*, p.188–9, where the sentence is annotated.

authors.[228] An influential printer's manual of the period, John Smith's *A Printer's Grammar* (1755), complains about 'high-pointing gentlemen' who 'propose to increase the number of points [i.e. punctuation marks] now in use', and suggests that printers should mount a resistance.[229] Smith also observed that 'most authors expect the printer to spell, point and digest their copy, that it may be intelligible and significant to the reader'.[230]

Might the busily punctuated 1740 editions of the *Apology* indicate that Cibber was one those high-pointing gentlemen, an author who – unusually for the time, according to John Smith – took responsibility for punctuating his own text? In other aspects of the project he showed a marked diligence: by holding onto his copyright until he could extract maximum value from it, and by making changes during the short space of time between the first and second editions. Then there is the matter of his having read aloud the manuscript to Pelham, presumably with the aid of markings to signal moments where it was necessary to draw breath, point a contrast, or create an emphasis. It is hard to believe the manuscript version of the 198-word sentence cited above did not give him some help. In its unwieldy expanse, the sentence is a typically Cibberian (or, perhaps, Foppingtonian) performance: an exercise in floor-holding that celebrates his own success with a show of false modesty (he was, of course, one of those three actors who showed such care, application, and industry).

But it is hard to reconcile the presentation of that and many other passages in the *Apology* either with the rhetorical or the grammatical tradition: too many of those commas make little sense either as breathing points or indices of grammatical relationships. Faced with the task of taming to intelligibility the beast that was Cibber's manuscript, Watts's compositors appear simply to have littered it with punctuation in the hope that some of their 'points' would stick. In doing so, they no doubt (albeit intermittently) retained a feeling of Cibber's voice, so helping create precisely the effect described by Hume, of 'a chatty and digressive old raconteur ... just rambling on to a friend'; but they equally drew a veil between reader and text.[231]

Since the *Apology* is a landmark in the history of life writing as well as theatre studies, and since it deserves a wider audience, Cibber's extraordinary 'theatrical character' is more likely to emerge for a modern reader

228 See M. B. Parkes, *Pause and Effect: An Introduction to Punctuation in the West* (Aldershot: Scolar Press, 1992), and David Crystal, *Making a Point: The Pernickety Story of English Punctuation* (London: Profile Books, 2015).
229 Cited in Crystal, *Making a Point*, p.71.   230 Cited in Crystal, *Making a Point*, p.70.
231 Hume, 'Aims', 688.

if his meaning is consistently clear. There are many passages in editions going back to 1740 where busy punctuation places an unnecessary obstacle in the way of understanding, let alone enjoyment. It may even be argued that the fussy markings of the early editions were partly responsible for the work's hostile reception among those who took issue with Cibber's command of English. Measured use has been made here of features that appear in the two editions of 1740: parentheses, initial use of 'And', semi-colons, and other devices help bring under control sentences whose meaning might otherwise prove too hard won. The effect, it is intended, is to clarify many of Cibber's lines of thought while exposing others, doubtless, to yet harsher criticism. To use his own analogy, this new edition seeks to restore a painting done in chiaroscuro: sharpening the colours and the distinction between light and dark, it helps readers appreciate what this landmark text reveals of its author and his times, and what it hides.

TIMELINE

This is a selection of key events in Cibber's life and times. It includes some of his own plays, roles he played in them, and other roles in which he achieved renown; where they are referred to in the *Apology*, a page reference is given in square brackets. Contextual information is given in the right-hand column.

Key to theatres: DL = Drury Lane; CG = Covent Garden; LIF = Lincoln's Inn Fields; QH = Queen's Theatre, Haymarket; GF = Goodman's Fields

Year	Event in Colley Cibber's Life	Public/Literary/Theatrical Events
1660		Accession of Charles II and establishment of King's and Duke's theatre companies under Thomas Killigrew and Sir William Davenant [66]; Sir Henry Herbert reappointed as Master of the Revels under Edward Montagu, Earl of Manchester
1671	Born in Southampton Row, Bloomsbury; first son of Caius Gabriel Cibber of Flensborg and second wife, Jane Colley of Rutland, m. 1670 [14]	Duke's Company opens Dorset Garden Theatre
1673	Caius Gabriel summoned for unpaid debts while in Marshalsea prison	Thomas Killigrew becomes Master of the Revels
1674	Caius Gabriel working on the monument to the Great Fire [15]	Opening of Theatre Royal, Drury Lane
1677	Caius Gabriel serves further term in Marshalsea prison	Charles Killigrew appointed Master of the Revels under Lord Chamberlain Arlington, and Master of the King's Company
1681	Caius Gabriel working for Wren at Cambridge following completion of statues at Bedlam [47]	Height of Popish Plot fever; Dryden, *Absalom and Achitophel*

Year	Event in Colley Cibber's Life	Public/Literary/Theatrical Events
1682	Enrolled at Free School in Grantham [16]	Union of Duke's and King's theatre companies [72]
1685		Death of Charles II [29]; accession of James II; Earl of Mulgrave appointed Lord Chamberlain
1687	Fails exam for Winchester College; goes to London [45]	Thomas Skipwith acquires a share in the United Company
1688	Travels to Chatsworth to be with Caius Gabriel; fails to obtain army commission [54]	James II flees the country; accession of William III and Mary II [54]
1689		Earl of Dorset appointed Lord Chamberlain
1690	Joins United Company: plays Servant to Sir Gentle in Thomas Southerne's *Sir Anthony Love* (DL) [74]	William III defeats James II's forces at the Battle of the Boyne [159]
1691		Christopher Rich and Thomas Skipwith gain full control of the United Company; death of George Etherege
1692	Plays the Chaplain in Thomas Otway's *The Orphan* (DL) [127]	Purcell, *The Fairy Queen* (DG); French victory at the Battle of Steenkirk
1693	Marries Katherine Shore, who joins the United Company [128]; Caius Gabriel appointed Sculptor in Ordinary to William III	French victory at the Battle of Landen
1694	Plays Lord Touchwood in Congreve's *The Double Dealer* (DL) in place of Kynaston [129]; birth and death of first daughter, Veronica	Death of Mary II [134]
1695	Publishes elegiac ode on death of Mary II; plays Fondlewife in Congreve's *The Old Batchelor* (DL) [141]; birth and death of second daughter, Mary; birth of third daughter, Catherine	Betterton's breakaway company starts performing (LIF); opens with Congreve, *Love for Love* [136]

Year	Event in Colley Cibber's Life	Public/Literary/Theatrical Events
1696	Plays Sir Novelty Fashion in his own *Love's Last Shift* (DL) [144]; agrees new contract with Christopher Rich for *Woman's Wit* etc. and plays Longville (DL); plays Lord Foppington in Sir John Vanbrugh's *The Relapse* (DL) [147] and title role in Vanbrugh's *Aesop* (DL) [148]	Failed Jacobite assassination plot against William III [258]
1697	Plays title role in Part 2 of Vanbrugh's *Aesop* (DL); briefly imprisoned for alleged assault on Jane Lucas; birth and death of first son, Colley; younger brother, Lewis, admitted to Winchester College [46], where Caius Gabriel has created a statue of the founder; death of Jane Colley	Earl of Sunderland appointed Lord Chamberlain; Congreve, *The Mourning Bride* [137]
1698	Birth and death of second son, Lewis	Jeremy Collier, *A Short View of the Immorality and Profaneness of the English Stage* [182]
1699	Own play *Xerxes* performed (LIF); birth of fourth daughter, Anne	Earl of Shrewsbury appointed Lord Chamberlain
1700	Plays Richard in own adaptation of *Richard III* (DL) [101] and Clodio in own play *Love Makes a Man; or, The Fop's Fortune* (DL); death of Caius Gabriel Cibber	Earl of Jersey appointed Lord Chamberlain; Congreve, *The Way of the World* [137]; death of Dryden
1701	Birth of fifth daughter, Elizabeth	Death of James II, his son recognized as rightful king by Louis XIV; Steele, *The Funeral* [176]
1702	Own play, *The School-Boy; or, The Comical Rival* completed but not performed until 1703 (DL); acquitted of profanity in performances; plays Don Manuel in his own *She Would and She Would Not* (DL); birth and death of third son, William	Death of William III and accession of Anne; Defoe, *The Shortest Way with the Dissenters*

Year	Event in Colley Cibber's Life	Public/Literary/Theatrical Events
1703	Plays title role in Crowne's *Sir Courtly Nice* (DL); attacked in 'Religio Poetae: or, a Satire on the Poets'; birth of fourth son, Theophilus	The Great Storm ravages southern England
1704	Agrees new part-managerial contract with Christopher Rich; plays Lord Foppington in own play, *The Careless Husband* (DL)	Earl of Kent appointed Lord Chamberlain; Vanbrugh's licence for QH [210]; Marlborough's victory at Blenheim [353]
1705	Plays Pacuvius in own play *Perolla and Izadora* (DL)	Christopher Rich acquires lease to LIF [277]; opening of QH under Sir John Vanbrugh [210]
1706	Defects from Rich to join Haymarket Company [263]; plays Sir Fopling Flutter in Etherege's *The Man of Mode* (QH); birth of fifth son, James; plays Atall in own play, *The Double Gallant* (QH) and Sir George Brilliant in own play, *The Lady's Last Stake* (QH); birth and death of sixth son, a second Colley	Marlborough's victory at the Battle of Ramillies
1707		Union with Scotland ratified [197]
1708	Drury Lane and Queen's Haymarket Theatres merge under a single company following an order of December 1707, with QH largely reserved for opera [249]; in the augural show, plays Osric to Wilks's Hamlet; Henry Brett acquires patent and appoints Cibber, Robert Wilks, and Richard Estcourt as managers [240]; plays Gloucester in Tate's *King Lear*, to Betterton's Lear (DL)	Marlborough's victory at the Battle of Oudenarde; capture of Menorca; topping out of Wren's St Paul's Cathedral; John Downes, *Roscius Anglicanus*
1709	Plays Samuel Simple in own play, *The Rival Fools* (DL); Brett returns patent [256]; Owen Swiney makes	Pope, *An Essay on Criticism*; Theatre Royal Drury Lane closed [263]; Nicholas Rowe's six-volume edition of

Year	Event in Colley Cibber's Life	Public/Literary/Theatrical Events
	new agreement with Cibber and co-managers Wilks and Doggett [261]; plays Iago to Betterton's Othello (DL); sued by Christopher Rich, counter-sues; critiques of Cibber in *The Female Tatler* and other publications	Shakespeare; Steele begins *The Tatler*; William Collier takes over DL [273]
1710	Order for Rich's arrest after Cibber's counter-suit; Cibber, Wilks, Thomas Doggett, and Owen Swiney receive new licence; dispute with Swiney over non-payment of dividends	Earl of Shrewsbury reappointed as Lord Chamberlain; death of Thomas Betterton [88]; trial of Henry Sacheverell [274]; passage of the Copyright Act; Charles Shadwell, *The Fair Quaker of Deal* [275]
1711	Swiney sues, alleging misappropriation of funds by Cibber and co-managers	Addison and Steele begin *The Spectator*
1712	Articles between Cibber, co-managers, and Swiney cancelled; William Collier becomes a sleeping partner in Swiney's place, with Cibber, Doggett, and Wilks as managers [279]; Cibber plays Don Alvarez in own play, *Ximena* (DL); Barton Booth asserts right to DL share [302]	Swiney licensed to produce opera at the QH; Pope, *The Rape of the Lock*; Ambrose Philips, *The Distressed Mother* [317]
1713	Booth joins DL management [307]; Cibber plays Syphax in Addison's *Cato*, in London and Oxford [294]; birth of sixth daughter, Charlotte (later Charke)	Owen Swiney escapes to Europe; Addison's opera, *Rosamond*
1714	Cibber and Wilks lodge complaint against Doggett for lack of engagement [305]; Collier's salary cancelled; Doggett's share stopped; Cibber seeks Lord Chamberlain's protection against legal action; Doggett sues over profit share; death of Cibber's fifth son, James, aged 8	Death of Queen Anne and accession of George I; reopening of LIF by Christopher Rich's sons, John and Christopher Mosyer [267]; desertion of eight DL actors to LIF [318]; death of Christopher Rich [267]

Year	Event in Colley Cibber's Life	Public/Literary/Theatrical Events
1715	Dispute with Vanbrugh over opera stock from QH; Cibber's *Venus and Adonis* and *Myrtillo* performed (DL). Patent awarded to Steele with Cibber as co-manager [315]; Cibber defies the Master of the Revels' demands for licensing fees [186]	Duke of Bolton appointed Lord Chamberlain; Charles Killigrew petitions for his rights as Master of the Revels; licensing arrangements lapse; first Jacobite rebellion [327]; deaths of Louis XIV and William Wycherley
1716	Sues John and Christopher Mosyer Rich	Executions of Jacobite leaders
1717	Doggett case settled in Cibber and Wilks's favour [307]; Cibber satirized in Breval's farce, *The Confederates*; plays Dr Wolf in own play, *The Non-Juror* (DL) [328]	Duke of Newcastle appointed Lord Chamberlain; Pope, Gay, and Arbuthnot, *Three Hours after Marriage*; birth of David Garrick
1718	Presents a copy of *The Non-Juror* to George I at court, for £200; withdraws a play by John Breval and puts on *Cato* with a junior cast – riot follows; suit against Rich's heirs dismissed	The Holy Roman Empire joins Britain in the Quadruple Alliance
1719	Wilks stages *The Masquerade* (DL) against Cibber's wishes; John Dennis attacks DL repertory, addressing Cibber as 'Judas Iscariot'; Lord Chamberlain demands DL financial statements amid accusations of fraud and failure to submit scripts for licensing; Cibber forbidden to act or manage	Jacobite landing in Scotland; Defoe, *Robinson Crusoe*
1720	Licence of Cibber and fellow managers temporarily revoked; Steele debarred	Completion of the Little Haymarket Theatre [189]; Pope completes translation of *The Iliad*; South Sea Bubble crisis
1721	Publication of two-volume *Plays Written by Mr Cibber* [177]; plays Witling in own play, *The Refusal* (DL); dispute with Steele over his non-engagement, pay, and retirement [331]; ordered to pay Steele by Lord Chamberlain	Robert Walpole becomes Lord Treasurer and de facto First Minister

Year	Event in Colley Cibber's Life	Public/Literary/Theatrical Events
1722	Continuing attacks on Cibber ('Keyber') in the *Weekly Journal*, *Saturday's Post*, etc.; Theatre Royal surveyed following malicious rumours about its safety [323]	Defoe, *Moll Flanders* and *A Journal of the Plague Year*; Steele, *The Conscious Lovers* [339]
1724	Attack on Cibber and co-managers in *The Tea-Table*; dispute with Steele temporarily resolved; DL company ordered to stay near London for visit of King of Prussia; plays Achoreus in own *Caesar in Egypt* and sells rights to Chetwood for £105; urges Steele to re-engage [337]	Duke of Grafton appointed Lord Chamberlain; *Bishop Burnet's History of his own time*, Volume I [342]
1725	Cibber and co-managers sued by Steele for withholding payments	Death of Charles Killigrew, succeeded as Master of the Revels by Francis Henry Lee
1726	Counter-sues Steele; sued for non-payment of licensing fees by Master of Revels Francis Lee	Death of Sir John Vanbrugh; Swift, *Gulliver's Travels*
1727	Sells publication rights to *The Provoked Husband* (completion of Vanbrugh's *A Journey to London*) to John Watts for £105	Death of George I and accession of George II
1728	Plays Sir Francis Wronghead in *The Provoked Husband* (DL) [330]; numerous attacks on Cibber in *The Daily Journal*, *Mist's Weekly Journal* [330], *Fog's Weekly Journal*, etc.; dispute with Steele comes to court [333]; visits France	First version of Alexander Pope's *The Dunciad* published; John Gay's *The Beggar's Opera* performed (LIF) [164]
1729	Plays Philautus in own play, *Love in a Riddle* (DL) [165], imitating *The Beggar's Opera*; own play, *Damon and Phillida* performed, recycling material from *Love in a Riddle* (DL)	Thomas Odell granted patent for new theatre in GF; deaths of Congreve and Steele; Gay's *Polly* suppressed [166]
1730	Appointed Poet Laureate in succession to Laurence Eusden [39]; sued by actor Josias Miller	Death of Anne Oldfield [369]

Year	Event in Colley Cibber's Life	Public/Literary/Theatrical Events
1731	First Birthday Ode to the monarch published; 21-year extension of DL patent drafted for Cibber, Wilks, and Booth; DL actors to perform at Hampton Court [340]	Henry Fielding, *Tom Thumb*; George Lillo, *The London Merchant*
1732	Booth sells half his share to John Highmore; Cibber rents his share to his son Theophilus and becomes a salaried actor; death of Wilks [369]	John Rich opens new theatre in CG
1733	Sells entire share to John Highmore [369]; son Theophilus leads DL actors' rebellion and they are locked out of the theatre; death of Booth [369]	Alexander Pope, *Essay on Man* and *First Satire of Second Book of Horace Imitated* [25]
1734	Death of Cibber's wife, Katherine; Charles Fleetwood buys out the DL management; daughter Charlotte occupies the Little Haymarket Theatre	Death of John Dennis; Engraving Copyright Act; *Bishop Burnet's History of his own time*, Volume II
1736	Sued by James Calthorpe for non-payment of dividends	Henry Fielding, *Pasquin*
1737		Passage of the Licensing Act, reinforcing the monarch's monopoly over granting of licences to perform [191]
1740	Publication by John Watts of the first (quarto) and second (octavo) editions of the *Apology*	Samuel Richardson, *Pamela*
1741		Henry Fielding, *Shamela Andrews*; Edward Young, *Poetical Works*; Garrick's debut as Richard III (GF)
1742		Alexander Pope, revised version of *The Dunciad*
1742	*A Letter from Mr Cibber to Mr Pope* published	Fall of Walpole as First Minister
1743	*A Second Letter from Mr Cibber to Mr Pope* published; *The Egotist* published	Pope, further version of *The Dunciad*; Garrick's first Hamlet

Year	Event in Colley Cibber's Life	Public/Literary/Theatrical Events
1744	*Another Occasional Letter from Mr Cibber to Mr Pope* published	Death of Pope
1745	Plays Cardinal Pandulph in own play, *Papal Tyranny in the Reign of King John* (CG)	Second Jacobite rebellion; death of Walpole
1747	*The Character and Conduct of Cicero* published	Samuel Richardson, *Clarissa*; Garrick and Lacy take over DL patent
1748	*The Ladies Lecture. A Theatrical Dialogue* published	Death of Anne Bracegirdle; Liverpool established as main slave trading port
1750	Sells copyright of the *Apology* to Robert Dodsley for 50 guineas	Johnson begins *The Rambler*
1755	Daughter Charlotte publishes *A Narrative of the Life of Mrs Charlotte Charke*	Johnson's *Dictionary*; conflict with France in Canada
1756	Dodsley's second edition of the *Apology* published	Start of the Seven Years' War with France
1757	Dies at home in Berkeley Square, succeeded as Poet Laureate by William Whitehead	Robert Clive's victory at Plassey in India; defeat of British at Fort William Henry in Canada
1758	Death of fourth son, Theophilus	Johnson begins *The Idler*
1760	Death of third daughter, Catherine	Death of George II and succession of George III
1761	Death of sixth daughter, Charlotte; Dodsley's third edition of the *Apology* published	George III acquires Buckingham Palace; Matthew Boulton's manufactory opens

AN

APOLOGY

for the LIFE of

Mr COLLEY CIBBER,

COMEDIAN and Late PATENTEE of the

THEATRE ROYAL

With an Historical View of the STAGE *during his* OWN TIME.

WRITTEN BY HIMSELF.

Hoc est

Vivere bis, vitâ posse priore frui.　　　　　　　　Mart. lib. 2.[1]

When years no more of active life retain,
'Tis youth renew'd, to laugh 'em o'er again.　　　　Anonym.

LONDON:

Printed by JOHN WATTS[2] for the AUTHOR.
MDCCXL.

---

1 From Marcus Valerius Martialis ('Martial', AD 40–104), *Epigrams*, Book 10 no.23 (c. AD 87): 'this is to live twice, to be able to enjoy your earlier life'; Cibber repeats the quotation below, p.287. *The Laureate* questioned his knowledge of Latin: Cibber 'had humour and a kind of wit, but not conducted by any judgment or reflection, nor seasoned with any tincture of letters. He affected to know much; and as it must often happen to those who would be thought knowing when they are ignorant, he frequently got out of his depth and exposed himself to ridicule and contempt' (p.106).
2 For Watts and his other projects for Cibber, see Introduction, pp.xlii–xliii.

TO A
CERTAIN GENTLEMAN.[1]

SIR,

Because I know it would give you less concern to find your name in an impertinent satire than before the daintiest dedication of a modern author, I conceal it.

Let me talk never so idly to you this way, you are at least under no necessity of taking it to yourself.[2] Nor, when I boast of your favours, need you blush to have bestowed them, or I may now give you all the attributes that raise a wise and good-natured man to esteem and happiness, and not be censured as a flatterer by my own or your enemies (I place my own first because as they are the greater number; I am afraid of not paying the greater respect to them).[3] Yours, if such there are, I imagine are too well-bred to declare themselves, but as there is no hazard or visible terror in an attack upon my defenceless station, my censurers have generally been persons of an intrepid sincerity.[4] Having therefore shut the door against them while I am thus privately addressing you, I have little to apprehend from either of them.

Under this shelter, then, I may safely tell you that the greatest encouragement I have had to publish this work has risen from the several hours of patience you have lent me at the reading it. It is true, I took the advantage of your leisure in the country, where moderate matters serve for amusement;[5] and there, indeed, how far your good nature for an old acquaintance

---

1 Since Thomas Davies's *Memoirs of the Life of David Garrick*, 2 vols. (1780), II.359, the consensus has been that Cibber's dedicatee was Henry Pelham (1695–1754), MP for Sussex, loyal supporter of Sir Robert Walpole's Whig government, and younger brother of the Duke of Newcastle, Thomas Pelham-Holles (1693–1768). In 1740 Pelham held the office of Paymaster of the Forces and in 1743 became Chancellor of the Exchequer. During the 1719–21 dispute about the Drury Lane patent, a serious threat to Cibber's position, the Duke of Newcastle had been the Lord Chamberlain and Pelham his Secretary; Pelham received a number of representations from Steele about his (then) lost patent (*Document Register* nos.3016, 3017, and 3058). Here, withholding Pelham's name further helped gloss over an unpleasant episode not mentioned in the *Apology*.
2 i.e. Pelham is not obliged to accept any of Cibber's compliments since he has not been named.
3 Cibber's claim to have more enemies is, notwithstanding Pelham's position, plausible: according to the entry in *DNB*, Pelham was 'a timid and peace-loving politician' with a conciliatory manner and tolerant opinions (XV.691).
4 i.e. because no one has anything to lose from attacking a retired theatre manager as opposed to a politician, they can afford to be as direct as they like.
5 In 1729 Pelham had bought Esher Place in Surrey and employed William Kent (1695–1748) to improve the estate (Figure 1). Alexander Pope (1688–1744) saluted Kent's work and the power of Pelham's patronage; he wrote of 'Esher's peaceful grove / Where Kent and Nature vie for Pelham's love', in 'Epilogue to the Satires' (Pope, *Poems*, p.697, lines 66–7).

(or your reluctance to put the vanity of an author out of countenance) may have carried you, I cannot be sure – and yet appearances give me stronger hopes. For was not the complaisance of a whole evening's attention as much as an author of more importance ought to have expected? Why then was I desired the next day to give you a second lecture? Or why was I kept a third day with you, to tell you more of the same story? If these circumstances have made me vain, shall I say, sir, you are accountable for them? No, sir: I will rather so far flatter myself as to suppose it possible that your having been a lover of the stage (and one of those few good judges who know the use and value of it under a right regulation) might incline you to think so copious an account of it a less tedious amusement than it may naturally be to others of different good sense, who may have less concern or taste for it. But be all this as it may; the brat is now born, and rather than see it starve upon the bare parish provision,[6] I choose thus clandestinely to drop it at your door, that it may exercise one of your many virtues – your charity – in supporting it.

If the world were to know into whose hands I have thrown it, their regard to its patron might incline them to treat it as one of his family; but in the consciousness of what *I* am, I choose not, sir, to say who *you* are. If your equal in rank were to do public justice to your character, then indeed the concealment of your name might be an unnecessary diffidence. But am I, sir, of consequence enough in any guise to do honour to Mr—? Were I to set him in the most laudable lights that truth and good sense could give him, or his own likeness would require, my officious mite[7] would be lost in that general esteem and regard which people of the first consequence, even of different parties, have a pleasure in paying him. Encomiums to superiors from authors of lower life, as they are naturally liable to suspicion, can add very little lustre to what before was visible to the public eye. Such offerings (to use the style they are generally dressed in), like pagan incense, evaporate on the altar and rather gratify the priest than the deity.[8]

But you, sir, are to be approached in terms within the reach of common sense. The honest oblation[9] of a cheerful heart is as much as you desire or I am able to bring you – a heart that has just sense enough to mix respect with intimacy, and is never more delighted than when your rural hours of leisure admit me with all my laughing spirits to be my idle self, and

6 i.e. relief as specified under the Poor Relief Act of 1662 (14 Car. 2 c. 12).
7 Metaphorical: a small amount of money (*OED* 2).
8 An analogy often used to discredit Catholics and the conventions of the Roman Church.
9 i.e. presentation of a gift, often to God, sealing for Cibber the distinction between Protestant sincerity and allegedly empty Catholic rituals.

in the whole day's possession of you! Then, indeed, I have reason to be vain; I am then distinguished by a pleasure too great to be concealed, and could almost pity the man of graver merit that dares not receive it with the same unguarded transport! This nakedness of temper the world may place in what rank of folly or weakness they please; but till wisdom can give me something that will make me more heartily happy, I am content to be gazed at as I am, without lessening my respect for those whose passions may be more soberly covered.

Yet, sir, will I not deceive you. 'Tis not the lustre of your public merit, the affluence of your fortune, your high figure in life, nor those honourable distinctions which you had rather deserve than be told of, that have so many years made my plain heart hang after you. These are but incidental ornaments that, 'tis true, may be of service to you in the world's opinion; and though, as one among the crowd, I may rejoice that Providence has so deservedly bestowed them, yet my particular attachment has risen from a mere natural and more engaging charm – the agreeable companion! Nor is my vanity half so much gratified in the *honour* as my sense is in the *delight* of your society! When I see you lay aside the advantages of superiority and, by your own cheerfulness of spirits, call out all that Nature has given me to meet them, then 'tis I taste you! Then, life runs high! I desire! I possess you!

Yet, sir, in this distinguished happiness, I give not up my farther share of that pleasure, or of that right I have to look upon you with the public eye, and to join in the general regard so unanimously paid to that uncommon virtue, your integrity! This, sir, the world allows so conspicuous a part of your character that, however invidious the merit, neither the rude licence of detraction nor the prejudice of party has ever once thrown on it the least impeachment or reproach.[10] This is that commanding power that in public speaking makes you heard with such attention! This it is that discourages and keeps silent the insinuations of prejudice and suspicion, and almost renders your eloquence an unnecessary aid to your assertions. Even your opponents, conscious of your integrity, hear you rather as a witness than an orator.[11] But this, sir, is drawing you too near the light; integrity is too particular a virtue to be covered with a general application. Let me therefore only talk to you as at Tusculum[12] (for so I will call that sweet retreat which

10 Cibber's flattery contains some truth. Pelham had voted against his own party's government in 1737, when he supported an opposition motion to convert the national debt.
11 According to *DNB*, Pelham was 'not a brilliant orator [but] an able debater and an excellent parliamentary tactician' (XV.691).
12 Ancient Roman resort, 15 miles south-east of the capital, favoured by the Roman aristocracy; Esher is, similarly, 18 miles from central London.

your own hands have raised), where, like the famed orator of old, when public cares permit, you pass so many rational, unbending hours. There, and at such times, to have been admitted, still plays in my memory more like a fictitious than a real enjoyment! How many golden evenings, in that theatrical paradise of watered lawns and hanging groves, have I walked and prated down the sun in social happiness! Whether the retreat of Cicero[15] in cost, magnificence, or curious luxury of antiquities, might not out-blaze the *simplex munditiis*,[16] the modest ornaments of your villa, is not within my reading to determine; but that the united power of Nature, Art, or elegance of taste could have thrown so many varied objects into a more delightful harmony is beyond my conception.

When I consider you in this view, and as the gentleman of eminence surrounded with the general benevolence of mankind, I rejoice, sir, for you and for myself: to see you in this particular light of merit, and myself sometimes admitted to my more than equal share of you.

If this *Apology* for my past life discourages you not from holding me in your usual favour, let me quit this greater stage the world whenever I may, I shall think this the best acted part of any I have undertaken since you first condescended to laugh with,

> *SIR,*
> *Your most obedient,*
> *most obliged, and*
> *most humble servant,*

COLLEY CIBBER.

Novemb. 6.
1739.[17]

---

15 Marcus Tullius Cicero (b. 106 BC), celebrated orator, kept a country villa at Tusculum.
16 i.e. a simple or natural elegance, from Horace, *Odes*, Book 1 no.5, line 5.
17 The date of Cibber's sixty-eighth birthday.

CONTENTS

CHAPTER 1

The introduction. The author's birth. Various fortune at school. Not liked by those he loved there. Why. A digression upon raillery. The use and abuse of it. The comforts of folly. Vanity of greatness. Laughing no bad philosophy.

CHAPTER 2

He that writes of himself not easily tired. Boys may give men lessons. The author's preferment at school attended with misfortunes. The danger of merit among equals. Of satirists and backbiters. What effect they have had upon the author. Stanzas published by himself against himself.

CHAPTER 3

The author's several chances for the church, the court, and the army. Going to the University. Met the Revolution at Nottingham. Took arms on that side. What he saw of it. A few political thoughts. Fortune willing to do for him. His neglect of her. The stage preferred to all her favours. The profession of an actor considered. The misfortunes and advantages of it.

CHAPTER 4

A short view of the stage from the Year 1660 to the Revolution. The King's and Duke's Company united composed the best set of English actors yet known. Their several theatrical characters.

CHAPTER 5

The theatrical characters of the principal actors in the Year 1690 continued. A few words to critical auditors.

CHAPTER 6

The author's first step upon the stage. His discouragements. The best actors in Europe ill used. A revolution in their favour. King William grants them a licence

CHAPTER 12

A short view of the opera when first divided from the comedy. Plays recover their credit. The old patentee uneasy at their success. Why. The occasion of Colonel Brett's throwing up his share in the patent. The consequences of it. Anecdotes of Goodman the actor. The rate of favourite actors in his time. The patentees, by endeavouring to reduce their price, lose them all a second time. The principal comedians return to the Haymarket in shares with Swiney. They alter that theatre. The original and present form of the theatre in Drury Lane compared. Operas fall off. The occasion of it. Farther observations upon them. The patentee dispossessed of Drury Lane Theatre. Mr Collier, with a new licence, heads the remains of that company.

CHAPTER 13

The patentee having now no actors, rebuilds the new theatre in Lincoln's Inn Fields. A guess at his reasons for it. More changes in the state of the stage. The beginning of its better days under the triumvirate of actors. A sketch of their governing characters.

CHAPTER 14

The stage in its highest prosperity. The managers not without errors. Of what kind. Cato first acted. What brought it to the stage. The company go to Oxford. Their success, and different auditors there. Booth made a sharer. Doggett objects to him. Quits the stage upon his admittance. That not his true reason. What was. Doggett's theatrical character.

CHAPTER 15

Sir Richard Steele succeeds Collier in the Theatre Royal. Lincoln's Inn Fields House rebuilt. The patent restored. Eight actors at once desert from the King's Company. Why. A new patent obtained by Sir Richard Steele and assigned in shares to the managing actors of Drury Lane. Of modern pantomimes. The rise of them. Vanity invincible and ashamed. The Non-Juror *acted. The author not forgiven, and rewarded for it.*

CHAPTER 16

The author steps out of his way. Pleads his theatrical cause in Chancery. Carries it. Plays acted at Hampton Court. Theatrical anecdotes in former reigns. Ministers and managers always censured. The difficulty of supplying the stage with good actors considered. Courtiers and comedians governed by the same passions. Examples of both. The author quits the stage. Why.

AN APOLOGY FOR THE LIFE OF
MR COLLEY CIBBER, &c.

CHAPTER I

The introduction. The author's birth. Various fortune at school. Not liked by those he loved there. Why. A digression upon raillery. The use and abuse of it. The comforts of folly. Vanity of greatness. Laughing no bad philosophy.

You know, sir, I have often told you that one time or other I should give the public some memoirs of my own life, at which you have never failed to laugh like a friend, without saying a word to dissuade me from it; concluding, I suppose, that such a wild thought could not possibly require a serious answer. But you see I was in earnest. And now you will say the world will find me, under my own hand, a weaker man than perhaps I may have passed for even among my enemies. With all my heart! My enemies will then read me with pleasure and you, perhaps, with envy, when you find that follies, without the reproach of guilt upon them, are not inconsistent with happiness. But why make my follies public? Why not? I have passed my time very pleasantly with them, and I don't recollect that they have ever been hurtful to any other man living. Even admitting they were injudiciously chosen, would it not be vanity in me to take shame to myself for not being found a wise man? Really, sir, my appetites were in too much haste to be happy, to throw away my time in pursuit of a name I was sure I could never arrive at.

Now, the follies (I frankly confess) I look upon as in some measure discharged, while those I conceal are still keeping the account open between me and my conscience. To me, the fatigue of being upon a continual guard to hide them is more than the reputation of being without them can repay. If this be weakness, *defendit numerus;*[1] I have such comfortable numbers

---

[1] i.e. 'there is safety in numbers', from Juvenal, Satire 2 line 46. Cibber repeated the quotation and the line of argument in his 1742 *Letter to Pope*, in answer to the line from the 'Epistle to Dr Arbuthnot', 'And has not Colley still his lord and whore?' (Pope, *Poems*, p.601, line 97). Cibber objected that

> without some particular circumstances to aggravate the vice, is the flattest piece of satire that ever fell from the formidable pen of Mr Pope, because (*defendit numerus*), take the first ten thousand men you meet, and I believe you would be no loser if you betted ten to one that every single sinner of them, one with another, had been guilty of the same frailty (p.6).

on my side that were all men to blush that are not wise, I am afraid in ten, nine parts of the world ought to be out of countenance. But since that sort of modesty is what they don't care to come into, why should I be afraid of being stared at for not being particular? Or if the particularity lies in owning my weakness, will my wisest reader be so inhuman as not to pardon it? But if there should be such a one, let me at least beg him to show me that strange man who is perfect! Is anyone more unhappy, more ridiculous, than he who is always labouring to be thought so, or that is impatient when he is not thought so? Having brought myself to be easy under whatever the world may say of my undertaking, you may still ask me why I give myself all this trouble. Is it for fame or profit to myself, or use or delight to others?[2] For all these considerations I have neither fondness nor indifference. If I obtain none of them, the amusement (at worst) will be a reward that must constantly go along with the labour. But behind all this there is something inwardly inciting which I cannot express in few words. I must therefore a little make bold with your patience.

A man who has passed above forty years of his life upon a theatre where he has never appeared to be himself, may have naturally excited the curiosity of his spectators to know what he really was when in nobody's shape but his own; and whether he, who by his profession had so long been ridiculing his benefactors, might not, when the coat of his profession was off, deserve to be laughed at himself; or, from his being often seen in the most flagrant and immoral characters, whether he might not see as great a rogue when he looked into the glass himself as when he held it to others.

It was doubtless from a supposition that this sort of curiosity would compensate their labours, that so many hasty writers have been encouraged to publish the lives of the late Mrs Oldfield, Mr Wilks and Mr Booth in less time after their deaths than one could suppose it cost to transcribe them.[3]

Now sir, when my time comes, lest they should think it worthwhile to handle my memory with the same freedom, I am willing to prevent its

2 In fact, the *Apology* brought Cibber significant financial advantage. See Introduction, p. 1.
3 Cibber highlights the cases of former Drury Lane colleagues whose biographies appeared within weeks of their deaths: Anon., *Authentic Memoirs of the Life of that Celebrated Actress, Mrs Anne Oldfield* (London, 1730); Daniel O'Bryan, *Authentic Memoirs, or the life and character of that most celebrated comedian Mr Robert Wilks* (London, 1732); and Benjamin Victor, *Memoirs of the Life of Mr Barton Booth, Esq; with his character* (London, 1733). Victor's book was published by John Watts, Cibber's own publisher for the *Apology*. In each case, further biographies followed quickly, among them William Egerton, *Faithful Memoirs of the Life, Amours and Performances of that justly celebrated, and most eminent actress of her time, Mrs Anne Oldfield* (London, 1731); Edmund Curll, *The Life of that Eminent Comedian Robert Wilks, Esq.* (London, 1733); Anon., *The Life of that excellent tragedian Barton Booth, Esq* (London, 1733). The trend had begun earlier,

being so oddly besmeared (or at best but flatly whitewashed) by taking upon me to give the public this, as true a picture of myself as natural vanity will permit me to draw.[4] For to promise you that I shall never be vain were a promise that, like a looking-glass too large, might break itself in the making. Nor am I sure I ought wholly to avoid that imputation, because if vanity be one of my natural features, the portrait would not be like me without it. In a word, I may palliate and soften as much as I please; but upon an honest examination of my heart, I am afraid the same vanity which makes even homely people employ painters to preserve a flattering record of their persons has seduced me to print off this *chiaroscuro* of my mind.[5]

And when I have done it, you may reasonably ask me of what importance can the history of my private life be to the public. To this, indeed, I can only make you a ludicrous answer, which is that the public very well knows my life has not been a private one; that I have been employed in their service ever since many of their grandfathers were young men; and though I have voluntarily laid down my post,[6] they have a sort of right to enquire into my conduct (for which they have so well paid me) and to call for the account of it during my share of administration in the state of the theatre. This work, therefore, which I hope they will not expect a man of hasty head should confine to any regular method (for I shall make no scruple of leaving my history when I think a digression may make it lighter for my reader's digestion) – this work, I say, shall not only contain the various impressions of my mind (as in Louis the Fourteenth his cabinet you have seen the growing medals of his person from infancy to old age)[7] but shall likewise include with them

---

with such works as the anonymous *Account of the Life … of the Famously Notorious Matt Coppinger* (1695), Tobyas Thomas, *The Life of the Late Famous Comedian, Jo Haynes* (1701), and Charles Gildon's *The Life of Mr Thomas Betterton, the late eminent tragedian* (1710), all appearing in the year of their subjects' deaths. For discussion, see Wanko pp.22–50 and 90–109. For images of Betterton, Oldfield, Wilks, and Booth, see Figures 5, 9, 13, and 14.

4   Cibber doubtless had in mind the furore surrounding the first biographies of his former co-manager, Robert Wilks; see Introduction, p.xli.

5   An Italian term for the painting technique that produces strong contrasts of light and dark, most famously practised by Caravaggio (1573–1610).

6   Cibber sold his interest in Drury Lane to John Highmore in 1733; *The Daily Post* reported the event on 27 March (*Document Register* no.3695).

7   A reference to the cabinet of medals installed in Louis XIV's private apartments at Versailles, containing his collection of ancient coins and more recent medals carrying his image, now housed in the Bibliothèque Nationale. Cibber visited France in 1728 (see below, p.366 n.88), but his knowledge of the cabinet may have derived from Le Sieur Combes, *An historical explication of what there is most remarkable in that wonder of the world, the French King's royal house at Versailles, and in that of Monsieur, at St. Cloud. Written in the French tongue by the Sieur Combes, and now faithfully done into English* (London: Matthew Turner, 1684).

the *Theatrical History of my Own Time*, from my first appearance on the stage to my last exit.[8]

If, then, what I shall advance on that head may any ways contribute to the prosperity or improvement of the stage in being, the public must of consequence have a share in its utility.

This, sir, is the best apology I can make for being my own biographer. Give me leave, therefore, to open the first scene of my life from the very day I came into it; and though (considering my profession) I have no reason to be ashamed of my original, yet I am afraid a plain, dry account of it will scarce admit of a better excuse than what my brother Bayes makes for Prince Prettyman in *The Rehearsal*, *viz.*, I only do it for fear I should be thought to be nobody's son at all;[9] for if I have led a worthless life, the weight of my pedigree will not add an ounce to my intrinsic value. But be the inference what it will, the simple truth is this.

I was born in London on the 6th of November 1671[10] in Southampton Street, facing Southampton House.[11] My father, Caius Gabriel Cibber, was a native of Holstein who came into England some time before the Restoration of King Charles II to follow his profession, which was that of a statuary, etc.[12] The *basso relievo* on the pedestal of the great column in the

---

8 An allusion to *Bishop Burnet's History of His Own Time*, 2 vols. (1724); see Introduction, p. xxxii Cibber's first role was in 1690; his last known performance was not until February 1745, when he appeared as Cardinal Pandulph in his own Shakespeare adaptation, *Papal Tyranny in the Reign of King John*.

9 In *The Rehearsal* (1671) by George Villiers, Duke of Buckingham, Bayes is an incompetent playwright. Challenged by the wit Smith to explain why the character Prettyman 'is so mightily troubled to find he is not a fisherman's son', Bayes replies, 'Phoo! That is not because he has a mind to be his son, but for fear he should be thought to be nobody's son at all'; Buckingham vol. I, III.iv.57–60. *The Rehearsal*, a satire on Restoration heroic tragedy, remained popular throughout the eighteenth century. Cibber played Volscius in the Drury Lane production at least from 18 January 1709 (LS2a 463) with Richard Estcourt as Bayes, later a signature role for Cibber.

10 Cibber's christening is recorded in the Baptismal Register of the Church of St Giles-in-the-Fields as follows:
   November 1671
   Christenings 20
   Colly, son of Caius Gabriell Sibber and Jane ux ('ux' = 'uxor' or wife).

11 Not the Southampton Street that links The Strand to Covent Garden, but Southampton Row, running just to the north of Bloomsbury Square. Southampton House was built c. 1657 for Thomas Wriothesley, 4th Earl of Southampton, on the north side of the square. Cibber uses the name he recalled from childhood: from 1734 the building was known as Bedford House, following inheritance by family of the Duke of Bedford.

12 Cibber's father, the sculptor Caius Gabriel Cibber (1630–1700), was born in Flensborg, in Schleswig rather than Holstein. Since there are no Danish names resembling 'Cibber' but many German and Dutch ones (Siewerts, Sievert, etc.), it is likely that the family's roots lay outside Denmark. Raised as a Lutheran, Caius Gabriel was the son of a

City, and the two figures of the lunatics (the Raving and the Melancholy) over the gates of Bethlehem Hospital, are no ill monuments of his fame as an artist.[13] My mother was the daughter of William Colley Esq, of a very ancient family of Glaiston in Rutlandshire, where she was born.[14] My mother's brother, Edward Colley Esq (who gave me my Christian name) being the last heir male of it, the family is now extinct.[15] I shall only add

cabinet-maker, himself a migrant employed by the Danish court. The name Cibber was adopted, probably following a trip to Italy, in imitation of Cibo, a family whose coat of arms Caius Gabriel incorporated into his own. There is no reason to doubt Cibber's statement that his father arrived in England during the Commonwealth period. See Faber, pp.3–4.

13 Cibber refers to Christopher Wren's **Monument** to the Great Fire of London on Fish Street Hill. Wren frequently gave work to Caius Gabriel, who carved the relief on the west side of the pedestal. It shows the rebuilding of London. The left background shows the city burning; the right, its reconstruction. In the left foreground, a languishing female represents London, but being lifted by Time; encouraged by a female figure representing manual arts, and pointing upwards to Peace and Plenty sitting on a cloud. Behind, citizens deplore their ill luck. To the right, Charles II in Roman garb orders three attendants to help London: they are Science (with a statue of fecundity), Architecture (drawing and square), and Liberty (with a broad-brimmed hat). 'Liberty' has a particular meaning, since there was from 1667 a space of seven years when 'foreigners' were allowed to work in London (or as long as it took) to add to the numbers of freemen of the branches of the building trade – a cause for personal celebration on Caius Gabriel's part. Behind Charles II may be either the Duke of York or Victory; then Justice and Fortitude, with a lion. At the bottom of the stone arch where Charles II stands is Envy, or possibly Religious Malice (referencing the popular notion that the Fire had been started by Catholics). Caius Gabriel was paid £600 for the work. See Faber, pp.26–7. The two **figures of the lunatics** known as 'The Madnesses' sat on the pillars of the iron gates of the Bethlehem lunatic asylum. One is raving, the other stupefied (see Figure 3). Their design was influenced by figures in Michaelangelo's Medici Chapel, which Caius Gabriel had seen on his trip to Italy. One figure was allegedly based on a servant of Oliver Cromwell. They have been described as 'the earliest indications of the appearance of a distinct and natural spirit in sculpture, and stand first in conception and only second in execution among all the productions of the island' (Allan Cunningham, *The Lives of British Painters, Sculptors and Architects* (1830), p.26). Pope refers to them in *The Dunciad* (1742 version) as 'Great Cibber's brazen, brainless brothers' (Pope, *Poems*, p.722, line 32); for Cibber disputing Pope's terminology, see Barker, p.216. In this passage Cibber might also have mentioned his father's work at Hampton Court, St Paul's Cathedral, and (not least) the Danish Church in Wellclose Square, where his father and mother were buried, and where he himself would be interred in 1757.

14 Jane Colley (1646–97) was Caius Gabriel's second wife. She was the daughter of William Colley of Glaston, Rutland, and his wife Jane, daughter of John Wirly of Dortford, Northamptonshire.

15 Edward's death made Caius Gabriel party to a family dispute which may have affected Cibber's chances at Winchester (see below, pp.45–6). Edward left his estate to his wife, Anne. She then remarried, and her second husband, Thomas Woodhall, disputed the will with Caius Gabriel. The case was referred to the Court of Chancery in November 1699. For details, see Faber, pp.17–18. Abolished in 1875, the Court of Chancery heard cases of disputed wills and trusts.

BETHLEMII ad portas fe tollit dupla columna.
Εἰκόνα τῶν ἐντὸς καὶ λόγος ἐκτὸς ἔχει.
Hic calvum ad dextram triti caput ore reclinat.
Vix illum ad levam ferrea vincla tenent.
Diffimilis furor eſt Statuis, fed utrumque laborem.
Et genium artificis laudat uterque furor.

3. Engraving by C. Warren, after Caius Gabriel Cibber, *Raving and Melancholy.*

that in Wright's *History of Rutlandshire*, published in 1684, the Colleys are recorded as Sheriffs and Members of Parliament from the reign of Henry VII to the latter end of Charles I, in whose cause chiefly Sir Anthony Colley, my mother's grandfather, sunk his estate from three thousand to about three hundred per annum.[16]

In the year 1682, at little more than ten years of age, I was sent to the free school of Grantham, in Lincolnshire, where I stayed till I got through it from the lowest form to the uppermost.[17] And such learning as that school could give me is the most I pretend to (which, though I have not

16 James Wright's *History and Antiquities of Rutlandshire* was published in 1687. Wright records that it was 'in the 13th year of H. 8. that John Colley, deceased, held the manor and advowson of Glaiston of Edward, Duke of Buckingham, as of his Castle of Okeham by knight's service' (p.64). He continues, 'In the 26. *Car.* I. (1640) Sir Anthony Colley, Knight, then Lord of this Manor, joined with his son and heir apparent, William Colley Esquire, in a conveyance of diverse parcels of land in Glaiston, together with the advowson of the church there, to Edward Andrews of Bisbroke in this County, Esquire; which advowson is since conveyed over to Peterhouse in Cambridge' (p.65).

17 Now known as The King's School; founded in 1329 and re-endowed in 1528; see Figure 4. Isaac Newton was a scholar there between 1655 and 1660. The curriculum consisted

4. 'I was sent to the free school at Grantham'; now the King's School, Grantham.

utterly forgot, I cannot say I have much improved by study), but even there I remember I was the same inconsistent creature I have been ever since! Always in full spirits, in some small capacity to do right, but in a more frequent alacrity to do wrong, and consequently often under a worse character than I wholly deserved. A giddy negligence always possessed me; and so much, that I remember I was once whipped for my theme, though my master told me at the same time what was good of it was better than any boy's in the form.[18] And (whatever shame it may be to own it) I have observed the same odd fate has frequently attended the course of my later conduct in life. The unskilful openness or, in plain terms, the indiscretion I have always acted with from my youth, has drawn more ill will towards me than men of worse morals and more wit might have met with. My ignorance and want of jealousy of mankind has been so strong, that it is with reluctance I even

principally of Greek, Latin, and divinity. Passing over the first ten years of his life, Cibber does not mention his father's repeated detention for debt in the Marshalsea Prison, Southwark, between 1673 and 1678 (see Faber, pp.17–21). During that time the Marshalsea also served as a county jail for Surrey; riots and starvation were common. A petition of 1722 described it as 'the worst prison in the nation'; cited in Jerry White, *Mansions of Misery: A Biography of the Marshalsea Debtors' Prison* (London: Vintage, 2016), p.52.

18 By 'theme' Cibber means 'an essay or exercise in translation' (*OED* 3).

yet believe any person I am acquainted with can be capable of envy, malice, or ingratitude.[19] And to show you what a mortification it was to me in my very boyish days to find myself mistaken, give me leave to tell you a school story.

A great boy near the head taller than myself, in some wrangle at play had insulted me, upon which I was foolhardy enough to give him a box on the ear; the blow was soon returned with another that brought me under him and at his mercy. Another lad, whom I really loved and thought a good-natured one, cried out with some warmth to my antagonist while I was down, 'Beat him, beat him soundly!' This so amazed me that I lost all my spirits to resist, and burst into tears! When the fray was over, I took my friend aside and asked him how he came to be so earnestly against me; to which, with some glouting confusion,[20] he replied, 'Because you are always jeering and making a jest of me to every boy in the school'. Many a mischief have I brought upon myself by the same folly in riper life. Whatever reason I had to reproach my companion's declaring against me, I had none to wonder at it while I was so often hurting him. Thus, I deserved his enmity by my not having sense enough to know I had hurt him; and he hated me, because he had not sense enough to know that I never intended to hurt him.

As this is the first remarkable error of my life I can recollect, I cannot pass it by without throwing out some farther reflections upon it – whether flat or spirited, new or common, false or true, right or wrong, they will be still my own, and consequently like me.

I will therefore boldly go on, for I am only obliged to give you my *own*, and not a *good* picture: to show as well the weakness as the strength of my understanding. It is not on what I write, but on my reader's curiosity I rely to be read through. At worst, though the impartial may be tired, the ill natured (no small number) I know will see the bottom of me.

What I observed then, upon my having undesignedly provoked my school friend into an enemy, is a common case in society. Errors of this kind often sour the blood of acquaintance into an inconceivable aversion where it is little suspected. It is not enough to say of your raillery that you intended no offence; if the person you offer it to has either a wrong head, or wants a capacity to make that distinction, it may have the same effect as the intention of the grossest injury. And in reality, if you know

19 Lowe cites Henry Fielding's *Joseph Andrews* (1742), in which Parson Abraham Adams's innocence is compared to Cibber's: 'Simplicity was his characteristic: he did, no more than Mr Colley Cibber, apprehend any such passions as malice and envy to exist in mankind'; in the edition by Douglas Brooks-Davies (Oxford, 1966), p.19.
20 To 'glout' was to scowl or frown (*OED* 2).

his parts are too slow to return it in kind, it is a vain and idle inhumanity, and sometimes draws the aggressor into difficulties not easily got out of.[21] Or, to give the case more scope, suppose your friend may have a passive indulgence for your mirth: if you find him silent at it, though you were as intrepid as Caesar, there can be no excuse for your not leaving it off. When you are conscious that your antagonist can give as well as take, then indeed the smarter the hit, the more agreeable the party. A man of cheerful sense among friends will never be grave upon an attack of this kind, but rather thank you that you have given him a right to be even with you. There are few men (though they may be masters of both) that on such occasions had not rather show their parts than their courage, and the preference is just; a bulldog may have one, and only a man can have the other. Thus it happens that in the coarse merriment of common people, when the jest begins to swell into earnest, for want of this election[22] you may observe he that has least wit generally gives the first blow. Now, as among the better sort a readiness of wit is not always a sign of intrinsic merit, so the want of that readiness is no reproach to a man of plain sense and civility – who therefore (methinks) should never have these lengths of liberty taken with him. Wit there becomes absurd, if not insolent;[23] ill natured I am sure it is, which imputation a generous spirit will always avoid for the same reason that a man of real honour will never send a challenge to a cripple. The inward wounds that are given by the inconsiderate insults of wit to those that want it, are as dangerous as those given by oppression to inferiors: as long in healing, and perhaps never forgiven. There is besides (and little worse than this) a mutual grossness in raillery that sometimes is more painful to the hearers that are not concerned in it than to the persons engaged. I have seen a couple of these clumsy combatants drub one another with as little manners or mercy as if they had two flails in their hands; children at play with case knives could not give you more apprehension of their doing one another a mischief.[24] And yet, when the contest has been over, the boobies have looked round them for approbation, and upon being told they were admirably well matched, have sat down (bedaubed as they were) contented at making it a drawn battle. After all that I have said, there is no clearer way of giving rules for raillery than by example.

---

21 *parts*: intellectual ability (*OED* n.15).   22 *election*: choice (*OED* 2).
23 In his opposition to malicious wit, Cibber deploys the mainstream values of sentimental comedy against his critics; see, for example, Frank H. Ellis, *Sentimental Comedy: Theory and Practice* (Cambridge: Cambridge University Press, 1991), pp.25–42. For Cibber on his own lack of true wit, see below, p.150 n.88.
24 A *flail* is a sharp instrument for threshing corn; a *case knife* is a large kitchen knife.

There are two persons now living who, though very different in their manner, are as far as my judgment reaches complete masters of it:[25] one of a more polite and extensive imagination, the other of a knowledge more closely useful to the business of life. The one gives you perpetual pleasure and seems always to be taking it; the other seems to take none till his business is over, and then gives you as much as if pleasure were his only business. The one enjoys his fortune; the other thinks it first necessary to make it, though that he will enjoy it then I cannot be positive, because when a man has once picked up more than he wants, he is apt to think it a weakness to suppose he has enough. But as I don't remember ever to have seen these gentlemen in the same company, you must give me leave to take them separately.

The first of them, then, has a title and – no matter what. I am not to speak of the great but the happy part of his character, and in this one single light: not of his being an illustrious, but a delightful companion.

In conversation he is seldom silent but when he is attentive, nor ever speaks without exciting the attention of others; and though no man might with less displeasure to his hearers engross the talk of the company, he has a patience in his vivacity that chooses to divide it, and rather gives more freedom than he takes, his sharpest replies having a mixture of politeness that few have the command of. His expression is easy, short, and clear;[26] a stiff

25 Bellchambers identifies these two men as Philip Dormer Stanhope, 4th Earl of Chesterfield (1694–1773), politician, diplomat, and letter-writer, and George Bubb Dodington, 1st Baron Melcombe (1691–1762), but Melcombe's circumstances bear little relationship to those described by Cibber. Lowe cites *The Laureate*, which states that the portraits were 'L — d C— d and Mr. E — e' (p.18); Lowe adds that this was 'probably Erskine', but Cibber's description does not fit any known bearers of that name. Evans follows an anonymous *Notes and Queries* article from 1911 (11th series, vol. IV), pp.382 and 475 in preferring Giles Earle (1678–1758), MP for Malmesbury, notable wit, and so favoured by Walpole as to be regarded as his successor. Chesterfield had opposed Walpole's anti-theatrical Licensing Act (1737) and, for all his own high standards of conversation, appears to have enjoyed Cibber's company. According to *The Laureate*, 'the gentlemen who condescended to be his companions were contented to be diverted with him as he could divert them. They would delight to hear him squeak in an eunuch's treble, or mimic Roscius, or rehearse the little histories of his scenic amours, or invent new oaths at play' (p.106). But compare that with a letter written by Chesterfield to his son in 1749: 'Horse-play, romping, frequent and loud fits of laughter, jokes, waggery, and indiscriminate familiarity, will sink both merit and knowledge into a degree of contempt. They compose at most a merry fellow; and a merry fellow was never yet a respectable man' (10 August 1749). See *Lord Chesterfield: Letters*, ed. David Roberts (Oxford: Oxford University Press, 1992), p.140.

26 By contrast, Lord Hervey observed of Chesterfield's manner in Parliament that 'he never made any figure in a reply, nor was his manner of speaking like debating, but declaiming'. See Hervey, *Memoirs of George II*, ed. J. W. Croker, 2 vols. (1848), II.341.

or studied word never comes from him; it is in a simplicity of style that he gives the highest surprise, and his ideas are always adapted to the capacity and taste of the person he speaks to. Perhaps you will understand me better if I give you a particular instance of it. A person at the University, who from being a man of wit easily became his acquaintance there, from that acquaintance found no difficulty in being made one of his chaplains. This person afterwards leading a life that did no great honour to his cloth, obliged his patron to take some gentle notice of it; but as his patron knew the patient was squeamish, he was induced to sweeten the medicine to his taste, and therefore with a smile of good humour told him that if to the many vices he had already he would give himself the trouble to add one more, he did not doubt but his reputation might still be set up again. Sir Crape,[27] who could have no aversion to so pleasant a dose, desiring to know what it might be, was answered, 'Hypocrisy, Doctor, only a little hypocrisy!' This plain reply can need no comment; but *ex pede Herculem*,[28] he is everywhere proportionable. I think I have heard him since say the doctor thought hypocrisy so detestable a sin that he died without committing it.[29] In a word, this gentleman gives spirit to society the moment he comes into it; and whenever he leaves it, they who have business have then leisure to go about it.

Having often had the honour to be myself the butt of his raillery, I must own I have received more pleasure from his lively manner of raising the laugh against me than I could have felt from the smoothest flattery of a serious civility. Though wit flows from him with as much ease as common sense from another, he is so little elated with the advantage he may have over you that whenever your good fortune gives it against him, he seems more pleased with it on your side than his own. The only advantage he makes of his superiority of rank is that by always waiving it himself, his inferior finds he is under the greater obligation not to forget it.

When the conduct of social wit is under such regulations, how delightful must those *convivia*, those meals of conversation be, where such a member presides who can with so much ease (as Shakespeare phrases it) 'set

27 According to a source cited by *OED* 1b, 'In the 18th cent., a sort of thin worsted stuff, of which the dress of the clergy is sometimes made ... hence, sometimes put for those who are dressed in crape, the clergy, a clergyman.' This particular chaplain has not been identified; Cibber's description does not fit Chesterfield's best-known holder of that office, Richard Chenevix (1698–1779), later Bishop of Waterford.

28 Literally, to judge the size of Hercules from his foot; the whole from the part.

29 When Chesterfield's letters were published in 1774, they would attract a storm of criticism for the very quality Chesterfield recommended (ironically) to his chaplain. See *Lord Chesterfield: Letters*, pp.x–xi.

the table in a roar'.[30] I am in no pain that these imperfect outlines will be applied to the person I mean, because everyone who has the happiness to know him must know how much more in this particular attitude is wanting to be like him.

The other gentleman, whose bare interjections of laughter have humour in them, is so far from having a title that he has lost his real name, which some years ago he suffered his friends to rally him out of; in lieu of which they have equipped him with one they thought had a better sound in good company. He is the first man of so sociable a spirit that I ever knew capable of quitting the allurements of wit and pleasure for a strong application to business. In his youth (for there was a time when he was young) he set out in all the heyday expenses of a modish man of fortune; but finding himself over-weighted with appetites he grew restive, kicked up in the middle of the course, and turned his back upon his frolics abroad to think of improving his estate at home. In order to which, he clapped collars upon his coach horses and, that their mettle might not run over other people, he tied a plough to their tails; which, though it might give them a more slovenly air, would enable him to keep them fatter in a foot pace with a whistling peasant beside them, than in a full trot with a hot-headed coachman behind them. In these unpolite amusements he has laughed like a rake and looked about him like a farmer for many years. As his rank and station often find him in the best company, his easy humour, whenever he is called to it, can still make himself the fiddle of it.[31]

And though some say he looks upon the follies of the world like too severe a philosopher, yet he rather chooses to laugh than to grieve at them. To pass his time therefore more easily in it, he often endeavours to conceal himself by assuming the air and taste of a man in fashion, so that his only uneasiness seems to be that he cannot quite prevail with his friends to think him a worse manager than he really is; for they carry their raillery to such a height that it sometimes rises to a charge of downright avarice against him. Upon which head, it is no easy matter to be more merry upon him than he will be upon himself. Thus, while he sets that infirmity in a pleasant light, he so disarms your prejudice that if he has it not, you can't find in your heart to wish he were without it. Whenever he is attacked where he seems to lie so open, if his wit happens not to be ready for you, he receives you with an assenting laugh till he has gained time enough to whet it sharp enough for

---

30 From Shakespeare, *Hamlet*, V.i.182. Hamlet is describing the late clown, Yorick; the comparison with Lord Chesterfield seems not entirely apt.
31 i.e. the player who allows others to dance (*OED* 1b).

a reply, which seldom turns out to his disadvantage. If you are too strong for him (which may possibly happen from his being obliged to defend the weak side of the question), his last resource is to join in the laugh till he has got himself off by an ironical applause of your superiority.

If I were capable of envy, what I have observed of this gentleman would certainly incline me to it. For sure, to get through the necessary cares of life with a train of pleasures at our heels in vain calling after us; to give a constant preference to the business of the day and yet be able to laugh while we are about it; to make even society the subservient reward of it, is a state of happiness which the gravest precepts of moral wisdom will not easily teach us to exceed. When I speak of happiness, I go no higher than that which is contained in the world we now tread upon; and when I speak of laughter, I don't simply mean that which every oaf is capable of, but that which has its sensible motive and proper season, which is not more limited than recommended by that indulgent philosophy,

Cum ratione insanire.[32]

When I look into my present self and afterwards cast my eye round all my hopes, I don't see any one pursuit of them that should so reasonably rouse me out of a nod in my great chair as a call to those agreeable parties I have sometimes the happiness to mix with, where I always assert the equal liberty of leaving them when my spirits have done their best with them.

Now sir, as I have been making my way for above forty years through a crowd of cares (all which, by the favour of Providence, I have honestly got rid of), is it a time of day for me to leave off these fooleries and to set up a new character? Can it be worth my while to waste my spirits, to bake my blood, with serious contemplations and perhaps impair my health in the fruitless study of advancing myself into the better opinion of those very, very few wise men that are as old as I am? No – the part I have acted in real life shall be all of a piece:

Servetur ad imum,
Qualis ab incepto processerit.[33]   Hor.

I will not go out of my character by straining to be wiser than I can be, or by being more affectedly pensive than I need be. Whatever I am, men of

---

32 From Terence, *Eunuchus*, I.i.18: to be mad by method. Cibber reinflects 'cum ratione insanias'.
33 From Horace, *The Art of Poetry*, lines 126–7; Horace writes of the importance of maintaining a character 'to the end as it began and be true to itself'.

sense will know me to be, put on what disguise I will. I can no more put off my follies than my skin; I have often tried, but they stick too close to me. Nor am I sure my friends are displeased with them, for besides that in this light I afford them frequent matter of mirth, they may possibly be less uneasy at their own foibles when they have so old a precedent to keep them in countenance. Nay, there are some frank enough to confess they envy what they laugh at; and when I have seen others whose rank and fortune have laid a sort of restraint upon their liberty of pleasing their company by pleasing themselves, I have said softly to myself, 'Well, there is some advantage in having neither rank nor fortune!' Not but there are among them a third sort who have the particular happiness of unbending into the very wantonness of good humour without depreciating their dignity; he that is not master of that freedom, let his condition be never so exalted, must still want something to come up to the happiness of his inferiors who enjoy it.[34] If Socrates could take pleasure in playing at even or odd with his children, or Agesilaus divert himself in riding the hobbyhorse with them, am I obliged to be as eminent as either of them before I am as frolicsome?[35] If the Emperor Adrian, near his death, could play with his very soul, his *animula* etc, and regret that it could be no longer companionable;[36] if greatness at the same time was not the delight he was so loath to part with, sure then these cheerful amusements I am contending for must have no inconsiderable share in our happiness. He that does not choose to live his own way suffers others to choose for him. Give me the joy I always took in the end of an old song:

My mind, my mind is a kingdom to me![37]

---

34 Perhaps a reflection on the manner of Lord Chesterfield, as described above, pp.20–21.

35 Socrates (469–399 BC), philosopher, teacher, and, like Cibber, the son of a sculptor. *Even or odd* refers to a game of chance where players have to guess whether opponents will show an even or an odd number of fingers, coins, or other objects; the Greeks called it *artiazein* and the Romans, *par impar*. Agesilaus (444–360 BC) was King of Sparta from 399 BC; his fondness for children's games is referred to in Plutarch's *Life of Agesilaus*. In his *Satires*, Book 2 no.3, line 248, Horace refers to both games. Evans argues that since early commentators glossed the line with the anecdote about Socrates, Cibber 'confused text and commentary'. He was not the only one: the games played by Agesilaus and Socrates are referred to in the same sentence in Pierre Bayle, *A General Dictionary, Historical and Critical* (London, 1735), p.327.

36 Publius Aelius Hadrian (AD 76–138), Roman Emperor from AD 117, and said to have died reciting a valedictory poem to his soul, imitated by Pope as 'Ah fleeting spirit!' in 'Adaptations of the Emperor Hadrian'; Pope, *Poems*, p.116.

37 Cf. Sir Edward Dyer (1543–1607), from William Byrd's *Psalms, Sonnets, & songs of sadness and piety* (London, 1588): 'My mind to me a kingdom is' begins Dyer's lyric rather than, as Cibber states, ending it.

If I can please myself with my own follies, have not I a plentiful provision for life? If the world thinks me a trifler, I don't desire to break in upon their wisdom; let them call me any fool but an uncheerful one! I live as I write; while my way amuses me, it's as well as I wish it. When another writes better, I can like him too, though he should not like me. Not our great imitator of Horace himself can have more pleasure in writing his verses than I have in reading them, though I sometimes find myself there (as Shakespeare terms it) 'dispraisingly' spoken of.[38] If he is a little free with me, I am generally in good company; he is as blunt with my betters, so that even here I might laugh in my turn. My superiors, perhaps, may be mended by him; but for my part I own myself incorrigible. I look upon my follies as the best part of my fortune, and am more concerned to be a good husband of them than of that; nor do I believe I shall ever be rhymed out of them. And if I don't mistake, I am supported in my way of thinking by Horace himself, who in excuse of a loose writer says,

> Praetulerim scriptor delirus, inersque videri,
> Dum mea delectent, mala me, aut denique fallant,
> Quam sapere, et ringi —[39]

which, to speak of myself as a loose philosopher, I have thus ventured to imitate:

> Me, while my laughing follies can deceive,
> Blest in the dear delirium let me live,
> Rather than wisely know my wants, and grieve.[40]

We had once a merry monarch of our own, who thought cheerfulness so valuable a blessing that he would have quitted one of his kingdoms where he could not enjoy it; where, among many other conditions they had tied

---

38 Shakespeare, *Othello*, III.iii.73. The 'great imitator of Horace' is Pope, whose eleven poems in imitation of the Roman poet were published between 1733 and 1738. In 'The First Epistle of the Second Book of Horace Imitated', Pope chastised Cibber as 'idle' (Pope, *Poems*, p.645, line 292). For Cibber's enmity with Pope, see Introduction, pp.liii–liv, and Barker, pp.204–20.

39 Horace, *Epistles*, Book 2 no.2, lines 126–8: literally translated as 'if my failings give people pleasure, or I remain blind to them, I'd rather be thought a foolish and clumsy writer than be wise and miserable'.

40 Comparison of Cibber's version with Pope's is not to Cibber's advantage: 'If such the plague and pains to write by rule, / Better (say I) be pleas'd, and play the fool; / Call, if you will, bad rhyming a disease, / It gives men happiness, or leaves them ease' ('The Second Epistle of the Second Book of Horace', in Pope, *Poems*, p.654, lines 180–3).

him to, his sober subjects would not suffer him to laugh on a Sunday.[41] And though this might not be the avowed cause of his elopement, I am not sure, had he had no other, that this alone might not have served his turn; at least, he has my hearty approbation either way, for had I been under the same restriction, though my staying were to have made me his successor I should rather have chosen to follow him.

How far his subjects might be in the right is not my affair to determine; perhaps they were wiser than the frogs in the fable, and rather chose to have a log than a stork for their king; yet I hope it will be no offence to say that King Log himself must have made but a very simple figure in history.[42]

The man who chooses never to laugh, or whose becalmed passions know no motion, seems to me only in the quiet state of a green tree; he vegetates, 'tis true, but shall we say he lives? Now, sir, for amusement – reader, take heed, for I find a strong impulse to talk impertinently! If, therefore, you are not as fond of seeing as I am of showing myself in all my lights, you may turn over two leaves together, and leave what follows to those who have more curiosity and less to do with their time than you have. As I was saying then, let us for amusement advance this, or any other prince, to the most glorious throne; mark out his empire in what clime you please; fix him on the highest pinnacle of unbounded power, and in that state let us enquire into his degree of happiness; make him at once the terror and the envy of his neighbours; send his ambition out to war and gratify it with extended fame and victories; bring him in triumph home, with great unhappy captives behind him, through the acclamations of his people to repossess his realms in peace – well, when the dust has been brushed from his purple,[43]

---

41 Six days after the execution of his father on 30 January 1649, Charles II was declared king by the Covenanter Parliament of Scotland, but was permitted to enter the country only on condition that he implement the Presbyterian Church across his kingdom. He agreed, arriving in Scotland on 23 June 1650. However, he later fell out with the Covenanters, tiring of their political manoeuvring and moralistic reflections on his conduct and that of his family. Bishop Gilbert Burnet's *History* may have been Cibber's source; for a modern account, see Ronald Hutton, *Charles II: King of England, Scotland and Ireland* (Oxford: Oxford University Press, 1989). Cibber's comparison between his situation and that of the Stuart family is at odds with the anti-Jacobite position he adopted elsewhere.

42 The reference is to the forty-fourth of Aesop's *Fables*; Cibber played Aesop in Vanbrugh's two plays featuring the character (see below, p.148), and doubtless read the *Fables* at school. A group of frogs calls out to Zeus for a king; he throws down a log, which terrifies them at first until they begin to stand on and mock it. The fable has attracted numerous political interpretations.

43 Indicating the cloak of an emperor.

what will he do next? Why, this envied monarch (who we will allow to have a more exalted mind than to be delighted with the trifling flatteries of a congratulating circle) will choose to retire, I presume, to enjoy in private the contemplation of his glory: an amusement, you will say, that well becomes his station! But there, in that pleasing rumination, when he has made up his new account of happiness, how much, pray, will be added to the balance more than as it stood before his last expedition? From what one article will the improvement of it appear? Will it arise from the conscious pride of having done his weaker enemy an injury? Are his eyes so dazzled with false glory that he thinks it a less crime in him to break into the palace of his princely neighbour because he gave him time to defend it, than for a subject feloniously to plunder the house of a private man? Or is the outrage of hunger and necessity more enormous than the ravage of ambition? Let us even suppose the wicked usage of the world, as to that point, may keep his conscience quiet; still, what is he to do with the infinite spoil that his imperial rapine has brought home? Is he to sit down and vainly deck himself with the jewels which he has plundered from the crown of another, whom self-defence had compelled to oppose him? No – let us not debase his glory into so low a weakness. What appetite, then, are these shining treasures food for? Is their vast value in seeing his vulgar subjects stare at them, wise men smile at them, or his children play with them? Or can the new extent of his dominions add a cubit to his happiness?[44] Was not his empire wide enough before to do good in? And can it add to his delight that now no monarch has such room to do mischief in? But farther: if even the great Augustus, to whose reign such praises are given, could not enjoy his days of peace free from the terrors of repeated conspiracies which lost him more quiet to suppress than his ambition cost him to provoke them, what human eminence is secure?[45] In what private cabinet, then, must this wondrous monarch lock up his happiness that common eyes are never to behold it? Is it like his person, a prisoner to its own superiority? Or does he at last poorly place it in the triumph of his injurious devastations? One moment's search into himself will plainly show him that real and reasonable happiness can have no existence without innocence and liberty. What a mockery is greatness without them? How lonesome must be the life of that monarch who, while he governs only by being feared, is restrained from letting down his grandeur sometimes to forget himself and to humanise him into the benevolence and joy of society? To throw off his cumbersome robe

44 *Cubit*: an ancient measure of length, approximately equal to an adult's forearm.
45 Caius Octavius Augustus (63 BC – AD 14), Roman emperor and patron of the arts.

of majesty, to be a man without disguise, to have a sensible taste of life in its simplicity till he confess from the sweet experience that *dulce est desipere in loco,* was no fool's philosophy.[46] Or, if the gaudy charms of pre-eminence are so strong that they leave him no sense of a less pompous (though a more rational) enjoyment, none sure can envy him but those who are the dupes of an equally fantastic ambition.

My imagination is quite heated and fatigued in dressing up this phantom of felicity; but I hope it has not made me so far misunderstood as not to have allowed that in all the dispensations of Providence, the exercise of a great and virtuous mind is the most elevated state of happiness. No, sir: I am not for setting up gaiety against wisdom nor for preferring the man of pleasure to the philosopher, but for showing that the wisest or greatest man is very near an unhappy man if the unbending amusements I am contending for are not sometimes admitted to relieve him.

How far I may have over-rated these amusements, let graver casuists decide. Whether they affirm or reject what I have asserted hurts not my purpose, which is not to give laws to others but to show by what laws I govern myself. If I am misguided, 'tis Nature's fault, and I follow her from this persuasion: that as Nature has distinguished our species from the mute creation by our risibility, her design must have been, by that faculty, as evidently to raise our happiness as, by our *os sublime*[47] (our erected faces), to lift the dignity of our form above them.

Notwithstanding all I have said, I am afraid there is an absolute power in what is simply called our constitution, that will never admit of other rules for happiness than her own, from which (be we never so wise or weak) without divine assistance we only can receive it – so that all this, my parade and grimace of philosophy, has been only making a mighty merit of following my own inclination (a very natural vanity, though it is some sort of satisfaction to know it does not impose upon me). Vanity again! However, think it what you will that has drawn me into this copious digression, 'tis now high time to drop it. I shall therefore in my next chapter return to my school, from whence, I fear, I have too long been truant.

---

46 Horace, *Odes*, Book 4 no.12, line 28: 'it is pleasant to play the fool occasionally'.
47 Ovid, *Metamorphoses*, Book 1 line 85: 'Os homini sublime dedit.' The whole passage is translated as 'To man the Creator gave a noble visage and urged him to look up to the sky, and gaze upon the stars.' Cibber conflates two explanations of the superiority of humans over animals: that we alone are able to laugh, and that laughter causes us to lift our heads, if not in the way imagined by Ovid.

CHAPTER 2

He that writes of himself not easily tired. Boys may give men lessons. The author's preferment at school attended with misfortunes. The danger of merit among equals. Of satirists and backbiters. What effect they have had upon the author. Stanzas published by himself against himself.

It often makes me smile to think how contentedly I have sat myself down to write my own life – nay, and with less concern for what may be said of it than I should feel were I to do the same for a deceased acquaintance. This you will easily account for when you consider that nothing gives a coxcomb more delight than when you suffer him to talk of himself, which sweet liberty I here enjoy for a whole volume together: a privilege which neither could be allowed me, nor would become me to take, in the company I am generally admitted to.[1] But here, when I have all the talk to myself and have nobody to interrupt or contradict me, sure to say, whatever I have a mind other people should know of me is a pleasure which none but authors as vain as myself can conceive. But to my history.

However little worth notice the life of a schoolboy may be supposed to contain, yet as the passions of men and children have much the same motives and differ very little in their effects (unless where the elder experience may be able to conceal them) – as therefore what arises from the boy may possibly be a lesson to the man, I shall venture to relate a fact or two that happened while I was still at school.

In February 1684/5 died King Charles II,[2] who being the only king I had ever seen, I remember (young as I was) his death made a strong impression upon me, as it drew tears from the eyes of multitudes who looked no farther into him than I did. But it was then a sort of school doctrine to regard our monarch as a deity, as in the former reign it was to insist he was accountable

---

1 Lowe notes that 'Cibber is pardonably vain throughout [the *Apology*] at the society he moved in' and claims his 'greatest social distinction' was his membership of White's Club in St James's Street, founded as a chocolate-house in 1693 but soon notorious for gambling. Sir Robert Walpole was a member; in *The Dunciad* (1743 version), Pope sourly imagines a future where he will 'chaired at White's amidst the doctors sit, / Teach oaths to gamesters, and to nobles wit' (Pope, *Poems*, p.730, lines 203–4). From 1730, Cibber's position as Poet Laureate gave him access to circles that might otherwise have excluded him.
2 Charles II died on 6 February 1685 (new style).

to this world as well as to that above him.[3] But what, perhaps, gave King Charles II this peculiar possession of so many hearts was his affable and easy manner in conversing,[4] which is a quality that goes farther with the greater part of mankind than many higher virtues which, in a prince, might more immediately regard the public prosperity. Even his indolent amusement of playing with his dogs and feeding his ducks in St James's Park (which I have seen him do) made the common people adore him,[5] and consequently overlook in him what in a prince of a different temper they might have been out of humour at.

I cannot help remembering one more particular in those times, though it be quite foreign to what will follow. I was carried by my father to the chapel in Whitehall, where I saw the King and his royal brother the then Duke of York with him in the closet, and present during the whole divine service. Such dispensation, it seems, for his interest had that unhappy prince from his real religion, to assist at another to which his heart was so utterly averse.[6] I now proceed to the facts I promised to speak of.

King Charles his death was judged by our schoolmaster a proper subject to lead the form I was in into a higher kind of exercise; he therefore enjoined us severally to make his funeral oration. This sort of task, so entirely new to us all, the boys received with astonishment as a work above their capacity; and though the master persisted in his command, they one and all, except myself, resolved to decline it. But I, sir, who was ever giddily forward and thoughtless of consequences, set myself roundly to work, and got through it as well as I could. I remember to this hour, that single topic of his affability (which made me mention it before) was the chief motive that warmed me into the undertaking; and to show how very childish a notion I had of his character at that time, I raised his humanity and love of those who served him to such height that I imputed his death to the shock he received from the Lord Arlington's being at the point of death about a week before him.[7] This oration, such as it was, I produced the next morning.

---

3 A reference to Charles I's belief that it was not in the power of Parliament to challenge a monarch appointed by God and to Parliament's contrary view.

4 John Evelyn described the King as 'debonnair, easy of access' and with 'a particular talent in telling a story' (*Diary*, 4 February 1685).

5 Charles II's walks in St James's Park are recorded by Pepys (6 March 1668, 14 January 1669, etc.), who was not always impressed by the King's frivolous way with conversation (2 January 1668, 2 December 1668, 28 May 1669).

6 James, Duke of York (1633–1701), the future King James II, became a Catholic in 1668 but attended Anglican services until 1676; Cibber is therefore writing about events that took place before he turned 5 years old. Charles II converted to Catholicism on his deathbed.

7 Henry Bennet, Earl of Arlington (1618–85), had been a member of Charles's inner cabinet or 'Cabal'. He survived the king by six months after suffering a long illness.

All the other boys pleaded their inability, which the master taking rather as a mark of their modesty than their idleness, only seemed to punish by setting me at the head of the form – a preferment dearly bought! Much happier had I been to have sunk my performance in the general modesty of declining it. A most uncomfortable life I led among them for many a day after! I was so jeered, laughed at and hated as a pragmatical[8] bastard (schoolboys' language) who had betrayed the whole form, that scarce any of 'em would keep me company; and though it so far advanced me into the master's favour that he would often take me from the school to give me an airing with him on horseback while they were left to their lessons, you may be sure such envied happiness did not increase their good will to me; notwithstanding which, my stupidity could take no warning from their treatment. An accident of the same nature happened soon after that might have frightened a boy of a meek spirit from attempting anything above the lowest capacity. On the 23rd of April following, being the coronation day of the new King,[9] the school petitioned the master for leave to play; to which he agreed, provided any of the boys would produce an English ode upon that occasion. The very word 'ode', I know, makes you smile already and so it does me, not only because it still makes so many poor devils turn wits upon it, but from a more agreeable motive: from a reflection of how little I then thought that, half a century afterwards, I should be called upon twice a year, by my post,[10] to make the same kind of oblations[11] to an 'unexceptionable' prince,[12] the serene happiness of whose reign my halting rhymes are still so unequal to. This, I own, is vanity without disguise; but *hæc olim meminisse juvat.*[13] The remembrance of the miserable prospect we had then before us (and have since escaped by a revolution) is now a pleasure which, without that remembrance, I could not so heartily have enjoyed.[14] The ode I was

---

Evans states that 'Cibber's memory betrays him', but the reference is Arlington's being so ill as to be merely at 'the point of death' rather than actually dead.

8   i.e. conceited, pompous (*OED* 3a).

9   The date is correct. Evelyn recorded that 'the King begins his reign with great expectations, and hopes of much reformation as to the late vices and profaneness both of court and country' (*Diary*, 23 April 1685).

10 Cibber became Poet Laureate on 3 December 1730 following the death of Laurence Eusden. He had not published an ode since his first known publication, 'A Poem on the Death of Our Late Sovereign Lady Queen Mary' (London, 1695). See also below, p.39 n.45.

11 i.e. the act of offering or presenting a gift.

12 i.e. King George II (1683–1760), who assumed the throne on 11 June 1727.

13 From Virgil, *Aeneid*, I.207: 'Forsan et haec olim meminisse juvabit', or 'Perhaps one day you will come to rejoice even at this' (Aeneas is attempting to cheer up his weary crew).

14 A reference to the Glorious Revolution of 1688, which saw the defeat of the Catholic James II.

speaking of fell to my lot, which in about half an hour I produced. I cannot say it was much above the merry style of 'Sing! Sing the day, and sing the song', in the farce.[15] Yet, bad as it was, it served to get the school a play day and to make me not a little vain upon it; which last effect so disgusted my playfellows that they left me out of the party I had most a mind to be of in that day's recreation. But their ingratitude served only to increase my vanity; for I considered them as so many beaten tits, that had just had the mortification of seeing my hack of a Pegasus come in before them.[16] This low passion is so rooted in our nature that sometimes riper heads cannot govern it. I have met with much the same silly sort of coldness even from my contemporaries of the theatre, from having the superfluous capacity of writing myself the characters I have acted.[17]

Here, perhaps, I may again seem to be vain; but if all these facts are true (as true they are), how can I help it? Why am I obliged to conceal them? The merit of the best of them is not so extraordinary as to have warned me to be nice upon it; and the praise due to them is so small a fish, it was scarce worthwhile to throw my line into the water for it. If I confess my vanity while a boy, can it be vanity when a man to remember it? And if I have a tolerable feature, will not that as much belong to my picture as an imperfection? In a word, from what I have mentioned, I would observe only this: that when we are conscious of the least comparative merit in ourselves, we should take as much care to conceal the value we set upon it as if it were a real defect. To be elated or vain upon it, is showing your money before people in want; ten to one but some who may think you to

---

15 Cibber recalls Act 1 Scene 1 of Henry Fielding's play *The Historical Register, for the Year 1736* (1737), which contains the lines, 'Then sing the day, / And sing the song / And thus be merry / All day long' (Fielding, *Plays*, III.471), themselves a parody of one of Cibber's own odes as Poet Laureate. In *Egotist* Cibber claims that 'none but dunces' would regard celebratory odes as serious subjects for criticism (p.49).

16 'Tit' refers to an undergrown horse (*OED* n.4) and 'hack' to a worn-out horse for hire (*OED* n.2). Pegasus is the winged horse of Greek myth – the analogy that may justify Congreve's observation below (p.150) that Cibber's writing contained many things that were like wit, but were not witty.

17 By 'superfluous' Cibber means 'indulgent' (*OED* 3a). He acted in most of his own plays: *Love's Last Shift* (1696, Sir Novelty Fashion); *Woman's Wit* (1697, Longville); *The Tragical History of King Richard III* (1700, Richard); *Love Makes a Man* (1700, Clodio); *She Would and She Would Not* (1702, Don Manuel); *The Careless Husband* (1704, Lord Foppington); *Perolla and Izadora* (1705, Pacuvius); an adaptation of Dryden's *Marriage à la Mode* (1707, Celadon); *The Double Gallant* (1707, Atall); *The Lady's Last Stake* (1707, Sir George Brilliant); *The Rival Fools* (1709, Samuel Simple); *Ximena* (1712, Don Alvarez); *The Non-Juror* (1717, Dr Wolf); *The Refusal* (1721, Witling); *Caesar in Egypt* (1724, Achoreus); *The Provoked Husband* (1728, Wronghead); *Love in a Riddle* (1729, Philautus); and, after the *Apology* had been published, *Papal Tyranny in the Reign of King John* (1745, Cardinal Pandulph). Not all those roles were particularly significant or demanding.

have too much may borrow, or pick your pocket, before you get home. He who assumes praise to himself, the world will think overpays himself. Even the suspicion of being vain ought as much to be dreaded as the guilt itself. Caesar was of the same opinion in regard to his wife's chastity.[18] Praise, though it may be our due, is not like a bank bill, to be paid upon demand; to be valuable it must be voluntary. When we are dunned[19] for it, we have a right and privilege to refuse it. If compulsion insists upon it, it can only be paid as persecution in points of faith is: in a counterfeit coin. And whoever believed occasional conformity to be sincere? Nero, the most vain coxcomb of a tyrant that ever breathed, could not raise an unfeigned applause of his harp by military execution.[20] Even where praise is deserved, ill nature and self-conceit (passions that poll[21] a majority of mankind) will with less reluctance part with their money than their approbation. Men of the greatest merit are forced to stay till they die, before the world will fairly make up their account. Then, indeed, you have a chance for your full due, because it is less grudged when you are incapable of enjoying it. Then, perhaps, even malice shall heap praises upon your memory; though not for your sake, but that your surviving competitors may suffer by a comparison.[22] 'Tis from the same principle that satire shall have a thousand readers where panegyric has one. When I therefore find my name at length in the satirical works of our most celebrated living author,[23] I never look upon those lines as malice meant to me (for he knows I never provoked it) but profit to himself. One of his points must be to have many readers. He considers that my face and name are more known than those of many thousands of more consequence in the kingdom; that therefore, right or wrong, a lick at the Laureate[24] will

18 In Suetonius's 'Life of Julius Caesar', Caesar is asked why he divorced his wife Pompeia on the mere suspicion of adultery: 'Because I cannot have members of my household accused or even suspected', he replies. See Suetonius, *The Twelve Caesars*, trans. Robert Graves (Harmondsworth: Penguin, 1957), p.45.

19 i.e. approached for repayment of a debt.

20 Suetonius's 'Life of Nero' relates how the emperor ordered troops to applaud his singing and playing on the lyre. See *The Twelve Caesars*, pp.222–3.

21 i.e. cheat or spoil (*OED* v.5a).

22 Lowe comments, 'Curiously enough, Cibber's praise of his deceased companion-actors has been attributed to something of this motive.'

23 i.e. Alexander Pope.

24 'Lick' in this context refers to a smart blow (*OED* 4a). Editors dispute the reference. Bellchambers contends that it refers to the title of a pamphlet; Lowe points out that none of that title was published before the *Apology*. Fone speculates that Cibber may have been referring to *A Lash for the Laureate* (London, 1718) and notes that in 1742 there appeared a pamphlet called *A Blast Upon Bays: or, a New Lick at the Laureate* (its title possibly inspired by the *Apology*) but without suggesting that the word 'New' implies the existence of a previous publication. However, Cibber may simply be coining a phrase, without reference to any other work, as suggested in *Egotist*, p.21.

always be a sure bait, *ad captandum vulgus*,[25] to catch him little readers; and that to gratify the unlearned by now and then interspersing those merry sacrifices of an old acquaintance to their taste is a piece of quite right poetical craft.[26]

But as a little bad poetry is the greatest crime he lays to my charge, I am willing to subscribe to his opinion of it.[27] That this sort of wit is one of the easiest ways too of pleasing the generality of readers is evident from the comfortable subsistence which our weekly retailers of politics have been known to pick up, merely by making bold with a government that had unfortunately neglected to find their genius a better employment.[28]

Hence too arises all that flat poverty of censure and invective that so often has a run in our public papers upon the success of a new author; when, God knows, there is seldom above one writer among hundreds in being at the same time whose satire a man of common sense ought to be moved at. When a master in the art is angry, then indeed we ought to be alarmed! How terrible a weapon is satire in the hand of a great genius! Yet even there, how liable is prejudice to misuse it? How far, when general, it may reform our morals, or what cruelties it may inflict by being angrily particular, is perhaps above my reach to determine.[29] I shall therefore only beg leave to interpose what I feel for others whom it may personally have fallen upon. When I read those mortifying lines of our most eminent author in his character of Atticus[30] (Atticus, whose genius in verse and whose morality in prose has been so justly admired), though I am charmed with the poetry, my imagination is hurt at the severity of it; and though I allow the satirist to have had personal provocation, yet methinks for that

---

25 i.e. to please the crowd; an expression widely used in classical rhetoric to encourage or deplore demagogues.

26 For Pope's attacks on Cibber, see Introduction, pp.liii–iv, and Barker, pp.204–20.

27 For other adverse contemporary judgments of Cibber's verse, see Barker, pp.154–64.

28 As Evans notes, probably a reference to *The Craftsman*, edited by Nicholas Amhurst from 1726 under the protection of the leading Tory, Henry St John, Viscount Bolingbroke (1678–1751) and with anti-government satire by Pope, Gay, and others. There may be a further dig at Pope, who could not be considered for the Poet Laureateship because of his anti-government views and Catholic faith.

29 In *The Champion* (29 April 1740) Fielding lighted on this phrase as typical of Cibber's erratic grammar.

30 Pope's withering description of Joseph Addison (1672–1719) as the patrician critic 'Atticus' is in 'Epistle to Dr Arbuthnot' (e.g. 'Damn with faint praise, assent with civil leer, / And without sneering, teach the rest to sneer; / Willing to wound, and yet afraid to strike, / Just hint a fault, and hesitate dislike'; Pope, *Poems*, p.604, lines 193–214).

very reason he ought not to have troubled the public with it. For, as it is observed in the 242nd *Tatler*, 'In all terms of reproof, when the sentence appears to arise from personal hatred or passion, it is not then made the cause of mankind, but a misunderstanding between two persons'.[31] But if such kind of satire has its incontestable greatness – if its exemplary brightness may not mislead inferior wits into a barbarous imitation of its severity – then I have only admired the verses, and exposed myself by bringing them under so scrupulous a reflection. But the pain which the acrimony of those verses gave me is in some measure allayed in finding that this inimitable writer, as he advances in years, has since had candour enough to celebrate the same person for his visible merit.[32] Happy genius, whose verse, like the eye of beauty, can heal the deepest wounds with the least glance of favour!

Since I am got so far into this subject, you must give me leave to go through all I have a mind to say upon it, because I am not sure that in a more proper place my memory may be so full of it. I cannot find, therefore, from what reason satire is allowed more licence than comedy; or why either of them, to be admired, ought not to be limited by decency and justice.[33] Let Juvenal and Aristophanes have taken what liberties they please, if the learned have nothing more than their antiquity to justify their laying about them at that enormous rate, I shall wish they had a better excuse for them![34] The personal ridicule and scurrility thrown upon Socrates (which Plutarch too condemns), and the boldness of Juvenal in writing real names over

31 From Richard Steele, *The Tatler*, no.242, 24–6 October 1710. Steele's essay distances true satire, which deals with 'the concern of society in general', from the kind that reveals merely a 'malignity at heart'. In quoting it, Cibber again shows his sentimentalist credentials, with the effect on the reader's imagination and feelings taking precedence over the artfulness of the author.

32 The 'Epistle to Arbuthnot' was published in 1735; Pope later published evidence of his formerly friendly relationship with Addison in his *Letters of Mr Alexander Pope* (1737), nos.lv–lx, and praised the moral purity of Addison's verse in 'The First Epistle of the Second Book of Horace': 'He from the taste obscene reclaims our youth, / And sets the passions on the side of truth' (Pope, *Poems*, p.643, lines 217–18).

33 A reflection of how Cibber's comic style addressed concerns raised by readers of Collier's *A Short View of the Immorality and Profaneness of the English Stage* (1698), of his own former position as a manager, and of his support for the Licensing Act.

34 Decimus Junius Juvenalis (b. AD 60 [?]), author of sixteen satirical poems. Cibber's view of his work appears to differ from Steele's in *The Tatler*, no.242, 24–6 October 1710; Steele found no 'ill-natured expression' in Juvenal, only a desire to attack 'vice as it passes by in triumph, not as it breaks into conversation'. Aristophanes (c. 450–385 BC), the leading comic dramatist of the 'old Attic' style, wrote at least sixteen plays satirizing politicians, poets, philosophers, and others.

guilty characters, I cannot think are to be pleaded in right of our modern liberties of the same kind.[35] *Facit indignatio versum*[36] may be a very spirited expression, and seems to give a reader hopes of a lively entertainment, but I am afraid reproof is in unequal hands when anger is its executioner; and though an outrageous invective may carry some truth in it, yet it will never have that natural, easy credit with us which we give to the laughing ironies of a cool head. The satire that can smile *circum praecordia ludit*,[37] and seldom fails to bring the reader quite over to his side whenever ridicule and folly are at variance. But when a person satirised is used with the extremest rigour, he may sometimes meet with compassion instead of contempt, and throw back the odium that was designed for him upon the author. When I would therefore disarm the satirist of this indignation, I mean little more than that I would take from him all private or personal prejudice, and would still leave him as much general vice to scourge as he pleases – and that, with as much fire and spirit as Art and Nature demand to enliven his work and keep his reader awake.

Against all this, it may be objected that these are laws which none but phlegmatic writers will observe, and only men of eminence should give. I grant it, and therefore only submit them to writers of better judgment. I pretend not to restrain others from choosing what I don't like; they are welcome (if they please too) to think I offer these rules more from an incapacity to break them than from a moral humanity. Let it be so! Still, that will not weaken the strength of what I have asserted, if my assertion be true. And though I allow that provocation is not apt to weigh out its resentments by drachms and scruples,[38] I shall still think that no public revenge can be honourable where it is not limited by justice; and, if honour is insatiable in its revenge, it loses what it contends for and sinks itself, if not into cruelty, at least into vainglory.

35 A philosopher thought by some to be Socrates is represented as a corrupt teacher of rhetoric in Aristophanes' *Clouds* (423 BC). Mestrius Plutarchus (c. AD 49–121), philosopher and biographer, wrote a comparison of old and new Attic comedy called *Moralia*, in which he criticized the satirical spirit of Aristophanes. Juvenal identified the subjects of his satire rather than resorting to 'characters', or types of people. Evans detects an allusion to the opposition's regular use of the word 'liberty' in arguing against the 1737 Licensing Act and other measures introduced by Walpole's government.
36 i.e. 'Indignation gives inspiration to my poetry', from Juvenal, Satire 1 line 79.
37 i.e. 'plays with emotions', from Persius, Satire 1 lines 116–17. Persius Flaccus (AD 34–62) was a Stoic thinker and satirist. As elsewhere in the *Apology*, Cibber relies on Latin grammar to make the sentence grammatically correct.
38 'Drachms' means 'a small quantity' (*OED* 3); 'scruple', a small weight or measurement (*OED* n.1).

This so singular concern which I have shown for others may naturally lead you to ask me what I feel for myself, when I am unfavourably treated by the elaborate authors of our daily papers.[39] Shall I be sincere and own my frailty? Its usual effect is to make me vain! For I consider, if I were quite good for nothing, these piddlers[40] in wit would not be concerned to take me to pieces; or (not to be quite so vain), when they moderately charge me with only ignorance or dullness, I see nothing in that which an honest man need be ashamed of. There is many a good soul who, from those sweet slumbers of the brain, are never awakened by the least harmful thought, and I am sometimes tempted to think those retailers of wit may be of the same class: that what they write proceeds not from malice but industry, and that I ought no more to reproach them than I would a lawyer that pleads against me for his fee; that their detraction, like dung thrown upon a meadow, though it may seem at first to deform the prospect, in a little time it will disappear of itself and leave an involuntary crop of praise behind it.

When they confine themselves to a sober criticism upon what I write, if their censure is just, what answer can I make to it? If it is unjust, why should I suppose that a sensible reader will not see it as well as myself? Or, admit I were able to expose them by a laughing reply, will not that reply beget a rejoinder? And though they might be gainers by having the worst on it in a paper war, that is no temptation for me to come into it. Or (to make both sides less considerable), would not my bearing ill language from a chimney sweeper do me less harm than it would be to box with him, though I were sure to beat him? Nor, indeed, is the little reputation I have as an author worth the trouble of a defence. Then, as no criticism can possibly make me worse than I really am, so nothing I can say of myself can possibly make me better. When therefore a determined critic comes armed with wit and outrage to take from me that small pittance I have, I would no more dispute with him than I would resist a gentleman of the road[41] to save a little pocket money. Men that are in want themselves seldom make a conscience of taking it from others. Whoever thinks I have too much is welcome to what share of it he pleases. Nay, to make him more merciful (as I partly guess the worst he can say of what I now write), I will prevent even the imputation of his doing me injustice, and honestly say it myself, *viz.*, that of all the assurances I was ever guilty of, this – of writing my own life – is the most hardy. I beg his pardon! 'Impudent' is what I should have said: that

39 A reference to the writings of Nathaniel Mist (see below, p.317 n.16).
40 i.e. dilettantes (*OED* 1).   41 i.e. highwayman.

through every page there runs a vein of vanity and impertinence which no French ensign's memoirs[42] ever came up to. But as this is a common error, I presume the terms of 'doting trifler', 'old fool', or 'conceited coxcomb' will carry contempt enough for an impartial censor to bestow on me: that my style is unequal, pert and frothy, patched and parti-coloured like the coat of a Harlequin; low and pompous, crammed with epithets, strewed with scraps of secondhand Latin from common quotations, frequently aiming at wit without ever hitting the mark, a mere ragout,[43] tossed up from the offals of other authors; my subject below all pens but my own, which, whenever I keep to [it], is flatly daubed by one eternal egotism – that I want nothing but wit to be as an accomplished a coxcomb here as ever I attempted to expose on the theatre; nay, that this very confession is no more a sign of my modesty than it is a proof of my judgment; that in short, you may roundly tell me that *Cinna* (or *Cibber*) *vult videri pauper, et est pauper.*[44]

> When humble Cinna cries, 'I'm poor and low',
> You may believe him – he is really so.

Well, Sir Critic! And what of all this? Now I have laid myself at your feet, what will you do with me? Expose me? Why, dear sir, does not every man that writes expose himself? Can you make me more ridiculous than Nature has made me? You could not sure suppose that I would lose the pleasure of writing because you might possibly judge me a blockhead, or perhaps might pleasantly tell other people they ought to think me so too. Will not they judge as well from what *I* say, as what *you* say? If then you attack me merely to divert yourself, your excuse for writing will be no better than mine. But perhaps you may want bread. If that be the case, even go to dinner in God's name!

If our best authors, when teased by these triflers, have not been masters of this indifference, I should not wonder if it were disbelieved in me; but when it is considered that I have allowed my never having been disturbed into a reply has proceeded as much from vanity as from philosophy, the matter then may not seem so incredible. And, though I confess

---

42 Possibly a reference to Anthony Hamilton's semi-autobiographical *Memoirs of the Life of Comte de Grammont* (London, 1714); if so, Cibber's disapproval was perhaps politically motivated, because Hamilton had served in the French regiments that supported James II against William III. Alternatively, he may have had in mind Walter Pope's *The Memoirs of Monsieur Du Vall* (London, 1670).
43 i.e. a highly seasoned dish with assorted meat and vegetables.
44 From Martial, Book 8 no.19, which reads 'Pauper videri Cinna vult; et est pauper', i.e. 'Cinna wants to appear poor, and he is poor.'

the complete revenge of making them immortal dunces in immortal verse might be glorious, yet, if you will call it insensibility in me never to have winced at them, even that insensibility has its happiness, and what could glory give me more? For my part, I have always had the comfort to think, whenever they designed me a disfavour, it generally flew back into their own faces, as it happens to children when they squirt at their playfellows against the wind. If a scribbler cannot be easy because he fancies I have too good an opinion of my own productions, let him write on and mortify; I owe him not the charity to be out of temper myself merely to keep him quiet or give him joy. Nor, in reality, can I see why anything misrepresented (though believed of me by persons to whom I am unknown) ought to give me any more concern than what may be thought of me in Lapland. 'Tis with those with whom I am to live only, where my character can affect me; and I will venture to say, he must find out a new way of writing that will make me pass my time there less agreeably.

You see, sir, how hard it is for a man that is talking of himself to know when to give over, but if you are tired, lay me aside till you have a fresh appetite; if not, I'll tell you a story.

In the year 1730 there were many authors whose merit wanted nothing but interest to recommend them to the vacant Laurel, and who took it ill to see it at last conferred upon a comedian, insomuch that they were resolved at least to show specimens of their superior pretensions, and accordingly enlivened the public papers with ingenious epigrams and satirical flirts at the unworthy successor.[45] These papers my friends (with a wicked smile) would often put into my hands and desire me to read them fairly in company. This was a challenge which I never declined and, to do my doughty

---

45 Before Cibber succeeded Laurence Eusden as Poet Laureate, four other names had been considered, all of them (like Cibber) with the right political credentials: Ambrose Phillips (1674–1749), pastoral poet, playwright, and translator; Lewis Theobald (1688–1744), editor of Shakespeare, playwright, and translator; John Dennis (1658–1734), critic, poet, and playwright; and the favourite, Stephen Duck (1705–56), poet and author of *The Thresher's Labour* (1730), which became popular in the year of the succession and reflected Duck's past as an agricultural labourer. With the word 'comedian' Cibber suggests that his rivals saw him as an actor rather than a writer; but three of them had written plays, and as Hume points out ('Aims', p.693), six out of the seven previous Laureates (assuming Ben Jonson was *de facto* the first) were playwrights. Pope satirized the shortlist in the *Grub Street Journal* of 12 November 1730, recommending that the Court 'save the salary and drink the sack' (i.e. the sherry that remains part of the remuneration for the post). Among the many writers who took to the press and stage when Cibber's appointment was announced, Duck is the most likely candidate among the unsuccessful contenders: a parody of Cibber's first poem as Laureate appeared under his name in the *London Evening Post* of 7 January 1731. For an extended account of Cibber's election, see Barker, pp.154–64.

antagonists justice, I always read them with as much impartial spirit as if I had writ them myself. While I was thus beset on all sides, there happened to step forth a poetical knight errant to my assistance, who was hardy enough to publish some compassionate stanzas in my favour.[46] These, you may be sure, the raillery of my friends could do no less than say I had written to myself. To deny it I knew would but have confirmed their pretended suspicion. I therefore told them, since it gave them such joy to believe them my own, I would do my best to make the whole town think so too.[47] As the oddness of this reply was, I knew, what would not be easily comprehended, I desired them to have a day's patience, and I would print an explanation to it. To conclude, in two days after, I sent this letter with some doggerel rhymes at the bottom:

> To the Author of the Whitehall Evening Post.
> SIR,
> THE verses to the Laureate in yours of Saturday last have
> occasioned the following reply which I hope you'll give a place
> in your next, to show that we can be quick as well as smart
> upon a proper occasion; and, as I think it the lowest mark of
> a scoundrel to make bold with any man's character in print
> without subscribing the true name of the author, I therefore
> desire, if the Laureate is concerned enough to ask the question,
> that you will tell him my name and where I live. Till then, I
> beg leave to be known by no other than that of,
> > Your Servant,
> Monday, Jan 11, 1730/1.   FRANCIS FAIRPLAY.

These were the verses:[48]

I.

Ah, ha! Sir Coll, is that thy way,
Thy own dull praise to write?
And would'st thou stand so sure a lay?[49]
No, that's too stale a bite.

---

46 So far unidentified, but in the light of the subsequent passage it is hardly out of the question that it was Cibber himself.

47 William Ayre's *Memoirs of the Life and Writings of Alexander Pope*, 2 vols. (London, 1745) records that Cibber would write spoof critiques of himself 'for the pleasure of sitting in coffee houses and hearing them … praised and called palpable hits' (II.82).

48 According to *The Laureate*, 'The things he calls verses carry the most evident marks of their parent Colley' (p.24).

49 *Lay*: a short lyric (*OED* n.4).

II.

Nature and Art in thee combine,
Thy talents here excel:
All shining brass[50] thou dost outshine,
To play the cheat so well.

III.

Who sees thee in Iago's part,[51]
But thinks thee such a rogue?
And is not glad with all his heart
To hang so sad a dog?

IV.

When Bayes[52] thou play'st, thyself thou art;
For that by nature fit,
No blockhead better suits the part,
Than such a coxcomb wit.

V.

In Wronghead[53] too, thy brains we see,
Who might do well at plough;
As fit for Parliament was he,
As for the Laurel, thou.

VI.

Bring thy protected verse from court,
And try it on the stage;
There it will make much better sport,
And set the town in rage.

VII.

There beaux and wits and cits and smarts,
Where hissing's not uncivil,

---

50 A reference both to Cibber's alleged mercenary qualities and his insensitivity to shame (*OED* n.4a).

51 The first record of Cibber's Iago is a performance of *Othello* at Drury Lane on 24 March 1709, with Thomas Betterton in the title role. This was to have been a benefit performance for Betterton, but the benefit was postponed to 7 April and a performance of Congreve's *Love for Love*. See LS2a 479.

52 The playwright in Buckingham's *The Rehearsal*. See above, p.14 n.9.

53 Sir Francis Wronghead, a character in Cibber's *The Provoked Husband* (1728), his completion of *A Journey to London* by Sir John Vanbrugh (1664–1726). Cibber played the role.

Will show their parts to thy deserts,
And send it to the devil.

VIII.

But, ah! in vain 'gainst thee we write,
In vain thy verse we maul!
Our sharpest satire's thy delight,
For – 'Blood! thou'lt stand it all'.[54]

IX.

Thunder, 'tis said, the Laurel spares;[55]
Nought but thy brows could blast it:
And yet – Oh curst, provoking stars!
Thy comfort is, thou hast it.

This, sir, I offer as a proof that I was seven years ago[56] the same cold candidate for fame which I would still be thought; you will not easily suppose I could have much concern about it while, to gratify the merry pique of my friends, I was capable of seeming to head the poetical cry then against me; and at the same time of never letting the public know till this hour that these verses were written by myself. Nor do I give them you as an entertainment, but merely to show you this particular cast of my temper.

When I have said this, I would not have it thought affectation in me when I grant that no man worthy the name of an author is a more faulty writer than myself; that I am not master of my own language, I too often feel when I am at a loss for expression. I know too that I have too bold a disregard for that correctness which others set so just a value upon.[57] This I ought to be ashamed of when I find that persons perhaps of colder imaginations are allowed to write better than myself. Whenever I speak of anything that highly delights me, I find it very difficult to keep my words within the bounds of common sense. Even when I write too, the same failing will sometimes get the better of me; of which I cannot give you a stronger instance than in that wild expression I made use of in the first edition of my Preface to *The Provoked Husband*, where, speaking of Mrs Oldfield's excellent performance in the part of Lady Townly, my words ran

---

54 From the epilogue to Cibber's *The Non-Juror* (1717): 'These blows I told him / On his play would fall, / But he unmov'd, cried / Blood! We'll stand it all.'

55 In Ovid's *Metamorphoses*, Book 1 lines 450–568, Apollo chases Daphne, who turns into a laurel bush; the plant is then sacred to Apollo.

56 An indication that Cibber began writing the *Apology* in 1737 or 1738. See also below, p.204.

57 For criticism of Cibber's English, see Introduction, pp. li–liii.

thus, *viz*: 'It is not enough to say, that here she outdid her usual outdoing'.[58] A most vile jingle, I grant it! You may well ask me how could I possibly commit such a wantonness to paper? And I owe myself the shame of confessing I have no excuse for it but that, like a lover in the fullness of his content, by endeavouring to be floridly grateful I talked nonsense. Not but it makes me smile to remember how many flat writers have made themselves brisk upon this single expression; wherever the verb 'outdo' could come in, the pleasant accusative, 'outdoing', was sure to follow it. The provident wags knew that *decies repetita placeret*;[59] so delicious a morsel could not be served up too often! After it had held them nine times told for a jest, the public has been pestered with a tenth skull thick enough to repeat it.[60] Nay, the very learned in the law have at last facetiously laid hold of it! Ten years after it first came from me, it served to enliven the eloquence of an eminent pleader before a House of Parliament![61] What author would not envy me so frolicsome a fault that had such public honours paid to it?

After this consciousness of my real defects, you will easily judge, sir, how little I presume that my poetical labours may outlive those of my mortal contemporaries.[62]

At the same time that I am so humble in my pretensions to fame, I would not be thought to undervalue it; Nature will not suffer us to despise it, but she may sometimes make us too fond of it. I have known more than one good writer very near ridiculous from being in too much heat about it. Whoever intrinsically deserves it will always have a proportionable right to it. It can neither be resigned nor taken from you by violence. Truth, which is unalterable, must (however his fame may be contested) give every man his due. What a poem weighs, it will be worth; nor is it in the power of human eloquence, with favour or prejudice, to increase or diminish its value. Prejudice, 'tis true, may a while discolour it; but it will always have its appeal to the equity of good sense, which will never fail in the end to reverse all

---

58 In 1727, the year before *The Provoked Husband*, Pope had mockingly used the same term in *Peri-Bathos; or The Art of Sinking in Poetry*: 'They continue to out-do even their own out-doings.' The expression worried Cibber sufficiently for him to change it in subsequent editions of *The Provoked Husband* to 'She here out-did her usual excellence', so undermining his claim to have taken pleasure in its repetition in Parliament.
59 i.e. 'it will please [even] if you look it over ten times'; from Horace, *The Art of Poetry*, lines 365–6.
60 The trend began with *Mist's Weekly Journal*, 24 February 1728; for an extract, see Barker, p.148.
61 The reference has not been traced, but Cibber did not coin the word: *OED* dates the earliest use of 'outdoing' at 1679, in Robert Hooke's *Philosophical Collections*.
62 The 1740 texts have 'cotemporaries' – possibly a personal affectation; *OED* has no record of such a spelling. See also Introduction, p.xlviii.

false judgment against it. Therefore, when I see an eminent author hurt and impatient at an impotent attack upon his labours, he disturbs my inclination to admire him. I grow doubtful of the favourable judgment I have made of him, and am quite uneasy to see him so tender in a point he cannot but know he ought not himself to be judge of; his concern, indeed, at another's prejudice or disapprobation may be natural, but to own it seems to me a natural weakness.[63] When a work is apparently great, it will go without crutches; all your art and anxiety to heighten the fame of it then becomes low and little. He that will bear no censure must be often robbed of his due praise. Fools have as good a right to be readers as men of sense have, and why not to give their judgements too? Methinks it would be a sort of tyranny in wit for an author to be publicly putting every argument to death that appeared against him; so absolute a demand for approbation puts us upon our right to dispute it. Praise is as much the reader's property as wit is the author's; applause is not a tax paid to him as a prince, but rather a benevolence given to him as a beggar, and we have naturally more charity for the dumb beggar than the sturdy one. The merit of a writer and a fine woman's face are never mended by their talking of them. How amiable is she that seems not to know she is handsome!

To conclude: all I have said upon this subject is much better contained in six lines of a reverend author, which will be an answer to all critical censure for ever.

> Time is the judge; time has nor friend nor foe;
> False fame must wither, and the true will grow:
> Arm'd with this truth, all critics I defy,
> For if I fall, by my own pen I die.
> While snarlers strive with proud but fruitless pain,
> To wound immortals, or to slay the slain.[64]

63 The passage probably refers to Pope.
64 From Edward Young, *Second Epistle to Mr. Pope* (1730). A 'Reverend Author', Young (1683–1765) was a Doctor of Canon Law, a royal chaplain, and vicar of Welwyn, Hertfordshire.

CHAPTER 3

The author's several chances for the church, the court, and the army. Going to the university. Met the Revolution at Nottingham. Took arms on that side. What he saw of it. A few political thoughts. Fortune willing to do for him. His neglect of her. The stage preferred to all her favours. The profession of an actor considered. The misfortunes and advantages of it.

I am now come to that crisis of my life when Fortune seemed to be at a loss what she should do with me. Had she favoured my father's first designation of me, he might then perhaps have had as sanguine hopes of my being a bishop as I afterwards conceived of my being a general, when I first took arms at the Revolution.[1] Nay, after that I had a third chance too, equally as good, of becoming an under-propper of the state.[2] How at last I came to be none of all these, the sequel will inform you.

About the year 1687, I was taken from school to stand at the election of children into Winchester College. My being by my mother's side a descendant of William of Wykeham (the founder), my father, who knew little how the world was to be dealt with, imagined my having that advantage would be security enough for my success, and so sent me simply down thither without the least favourable recommendation or interest but that of my naked merit and a pompous pedigree in my pocket.[3] Had he tacked a

---

1 i.e. the 'Glorious Revolution' of 1688.   2 i.e. a clerk or civil servant.
3 The 'Election' at Winchester College was not a formal examination but a process whereby a group of college staff (the Electors) decided at an annual meeting which boys should be given places and scholarships. Candidates had to demonstrate a basic level of education; two places a year were reserved for the system known as 'Founder's Kin'. Cibber's mother, Jane Colley, was directly descended from Agnes, sister of William of Wykeham (?1320–1404), who founded Winchester College in 1382; Faber, p.18, prints a family tree showing thirteen generations from Agnes to Jane. Jane's elder brother, Edward Colley, had been admitted to Winchester as Scholar and Founder's Kin in 1654, which may have been the source of Caius Gabriel's information. Many of the Electors' decisions were taken on the basis of references before the candidates arrived; from the early nineteenth century at least, there is evidence that Founder's Kin places might be decided years in advance. It is entirely possible, then, that Caius Gabriel had not done the required research and that Cibber's academic prowess, lauded in Grantham, was found wanting at Winchester. See David Roberts and Suzanne Foster, 'Colley Cibber and Winchester College', *Notes and Queries* vol. 67, no.3 (September 2020), 395–6.

direction to my back and sent me by the carrier to the mayor of the town to be chosen Member of Parliament there, I might have had just as much chance to have succeeded in the one as the other. But I must not omit in this place to let you know that the experience which my father then bought at my cost taught him, some years after, to take a more judicious care of my younger brother, Lewis Cibber, whom (with the present of a statue of the founder, of his own making) he recommended to the same college.[4] This statue now stands, I think, over the school door there, and was so well executed that it seemed to speak – for its kinsman.[5] It was no sooner set up than the door of preferment was open to him.

Here, one would think my brother had the advantage of me in the favour of fortune by this, his first laudable step into the world. I own I was so proud of his success that I even valued myself upon it. And yet it is but a melancholy reflection to observe how unequally his profession and mine were provided for when I, who had been the outcast of Fortune, could find means from my income of the theatre (before I was my own master there) to supply, in his highest preferment, his common necessities.[6] I cannot part with his memory without telling you I had as sincere a concern for this brother's wellbeing as my own. He had lively parts and more than ordinary learning, with a good deal of natural wit and humour; but, from too great a disregard to his health, he died a Fellow of New College in Oxford soon after he had been ordained by Dr Compton, then Bishop of London.[7] I now return to the state of my own affair at Winchester.

After the election, the moment I was informed that I was one of the unsuccessful candidates, I blessed myself to think what a happy reprieve I

---

4 The inscription on the statue states that it was donated in 1697; Caius Gabriel is described as 'statuaris regius', reflecting the position he had held since 30 May 1693 as Sculptor in Ordinary to William III; it is noteworthy that Cibber did not make more of his father's royal service. Lewis Cibber studied at Winchester from 1697 to 1700 as both Scholar and Founder's Kin. Like his father, Lewis was often in debt, but also had a drinking problem. Barker, pp.4–5, quotes a story from Joseph Spence's *Anecdotes, Observations, and Characters of Books and Men* (1820), p.377, in which Lewis approaches a Dr Burton for money, saying he had committed every except sin avarice, 'and if the doctor would give him a guinea, he would do his utmost to be guilty of that too'.

5 i.e. for Lewis.

6 The implication is that Lewis needed financial support from his brother between his ordination in 1700 and 1708, when Cibber became his 'own master' in the theatre. During those eight years Cibber also had to support his wife and five children.

7 Henry Compton (1632–1713), Bishop of London from 1675; deprived of the office under James II and restored to it after the Glorious Revolution. A published botanist as well as a theologian, Compton was one of the seven bishops who opposed James II and helped bring in William III, over whose coronation he presided. Cibber drops Compton's name to boost his own political credentials.

had got from the confined life of a schoolboy; and the same day took post back to London, that I might arrive time enough to see a play (then my darling delight) before my mother might demand an account of my travelling charges.[8] When I look back to that time, it almost makes me tremble to think what miseries, in fifty years farther in life, such an unthinking head was liable to! To ask why Providence afterwards took more care of me than I did of myself, might be making too bold an enquiry into its secret will and pleasure.[9] All I can say to that point is that I am thankful and amazed at it!

'Twas about this time I first imbibed an inclination which I durst not reveal: for the stage. For besides that I knew it would disoblige my father, I had no conception of any means practicable to make my way to it. I therefore suppressed the bewitching ideas of so sublime a station, and compounded with my ambition by laying a lower scheme of only getting the nearest way into the immediate life of a gentleman-collegiate. My father being at this time employed at Chatsworth in Derbyshire by the then Earl of Devonshire, who was raising that seat from a Gothic to a Grecian magnificence,[10] I made use of the leisure I then had in London to open to him, by letter, my disinclination to wait another year for an uncertain preferment at Winchester, and to entreat him that he would send me, *per saltum*[11] (by a shorter cut) to the University.[12] My father, who was naturally indulgent to me, seemed to comply with my request, and wrote word that as soon as his affairs would permit, he would carry me with him and settle me in some college, but rather at Cambridge, where (during his late residence at that place in making some statues that now stand upon Trinity College New Library) he had contracted some acquaintance with the heads of houses,

---

8 Coaches travelled at up to 12 miles an hour; Winchester to London is 65 miles; by the late 1680s, plays began from 3pm to 4pm. Cibber must have had a very early start for a journey that would have involved changes of horse, stretching the time to perhaps seven or eight hours.

9 Evans suggests this passage may be 'an instance of Cibber's rumoured impiety' but shows that such rumours derived either from personal enemies or opponents of the theatre.

10 William Cavendish (1640–1707), 4th Earl of Devonshire, created 1st Duke of Devonshire in 1694. Devonshire had begun the transformation of Bess of Hardwick's Elizabethan house in 1686, employing William Talman to design the neo-classical south and east fronts. Thomas Archer took over in 1705. Caius Gabriel worked at Chatsworth from December 1687 to December 1690, earning £320 for making garden statues (Faber, pp.49–51).

11 Literally, 'hopping', or passing over an initial stage.

12 Many of Cibber's contemporaries (Congreve included) entered university at the age of 16. As the subsequent passage makes clear, Cibber initially had Oxford in mind.

who might assist his intentions for me.[13] This I liked better than to go discountenanced to Oxford, to which it would have been a sort of reproach to
me not to have come elected.[14] After some months were elapsed, my father,
not being willing to let me lie too long idling in London, sent for me down
to Chatsworth, to be under his eye till he could be at leisure to carry me to
Cambridge. Before I could set out on my journey thither, the nation fell
in labour of the Revolution, the news being then just brought to London
that the Prince of Orange, at the head of an army, was landed in the west.[15]
When I came to Nottingham I found my father in arms there, among those
forces which the Earl of Devonshire had raised for the redress of our vio-
lated laws and liberties. My father judged this a proper season for a young
stripling to turn himself loose into the bustle of the world; and, being himself too advanced in years to endure the winter fatigue which might possibly follow, entreated that noble lord that he would be pleased to accept
of his son in his room, and that he would give him (my father) leave to
return and finish his works at Chatsworth.[16] This was so well received by his
lordship that he not only admitted of my service, but promised my father
in return that when affairs were settled he would provide for me. Upon this,
my father returned to Derbyshire while I, not a little transported, jumped
into his saddle. Thus, in one day, all my thoughts of the University were
smothered in ambition! A slight commission for a Horse Officer was the
least view I had before me. At this crisis, you cannot but observe that the
fate of King James and of the Prince of Orange – and that of so minute
a being as myself – were all at once upon the anvil. In what shape they
would severally come out (though a good guess might be made) was not
then demonstrable to the deepest foresight; but as my fortune seemed to
be of small importance to the public, Providence thought fit to postpone
it till that of those great rulers of nations was justly perfected. Yet, had my
father's business permitted him to have carried me one month sooner (as he

13 Caius Gabriel had been contracted to make four statues on the outer east wall of
    Christopher Wren's library at Trinity College Cambridge (1676), representing Divinity,
    Physics, Law, and Mathematics. Faber, p.40, records that originally they were to be made
    of plaster (Wren wrote that 'there are Flemish artists that do them cheap'), but Caius
    Gabriel completed them in stone. On 7 May 1681 he was paid £80 for the work; separate
    payments were made to a 'Widow Bats' and 'Mr Martin' for hosting Caius Gabriel and
    his men.
14 The Election process at Winchester also ruled on some places at its partner institution,
    New College Oxford.
15 The future King William III landed at Torbay in Devon on 5 November 1688.
16 Caius Gabriel was 58 at this time.

intended) to the University, who knows but, by this time, that purer fountain might have washed my imperfections into a capacity of writing, instead
of plays and annual odes, sermons and pastoral letters.[17] But whatever care
of the church might so have fallen to my share, as I dare say it may be now
in better hands, I ought not to repine at my being otherwise disposed of.

You must now consider me as one among those desperate thousands
who, after a patience sorely tried, took arms under the banner of necessity –
the natural parent of all human laws and government. I question if, in all
the histories of empire, there is one instance of so bloodless a revolution as
that in England in 1688, wherein Whigs, Tories, princes, prelates, nobles,
clergy, common people and a standing army were unanimous.[18] To have
seen all England of one mind is to have lived at a very particular juncture.
Happy nation, who are never divided among themselves but when they
have least to complain of! Our greatest grievance since that time seems to
have been that we cannot all govern; and till the number of good places are
equal to those who think themselves qualified for them, there must ever
be a cause of contention among us. While great men want great posts, the
nation will never want real or seeming patriots;[19] and while great posts are
filled with persons whose capacities are but human, such persons will never
be allowed to be without errors. Not even the Revolution, with all its advantages, it seems, has been able to furnish us with unexceptionable statesmen!
For from that time, I don't remember any one set of ministers that have not
been heartily railed at – a period long enough, one would think (if all of
them have been as bad as they have been called) to make a people despair
of ever seeing a good one. But as it is possible that envy, prejudice or party
may sometimes have a share in what is generally thrown upon 'em, it is not
easy for a private man to know who is absolutely in the right from what
is said against them, or from what their friends or dependants may say in
their favour; though I can hardly forbear thinking that they who have been

17 Writing odes for the New Year and the monarch's birthday was one of the duties of the
    Poet Laureate. See also above, pp.31–2.
18 A standard claim of Whig propaganda that overlooks subsequent episodes such as
    the extremely bloody Battle of the Boyne in 1690. The word 'revolution', one historian
    comments, 'did not have the significance which it has acquired since 1789 … Rather
    it was employed in the sense of the revolution of a wheel turning round to a former
    state,' in this case 'an ancient constitution of mixed or limited monarchy' (W. A. Speck,
    Reluctant Revolutionaries: Englishmen and the Revolution of 1688 (Oxford: Oxford
    University Press, 1989), p.1.
19 Evans detects a reference to Viscount Bolingbroke and his allies (see above, p.34 n.28).

longest railed at must, from that circumstance, show in some sort a proof of capacity.[20] But to my history.

It were almost incredible to tell you, at the latter end of King James's time (though the rod of arbitrary power was always shaking over us), with what freedom and contempt the common people, in the open streets, talked of his wild measures to make a whole Protestant nation Papists.[21] And yet, in the height of our secure and wanton defiance of him, we of the vulgar had no farther notion of any remedy for this evil than a satisfied presumption that our numbers were too great to be mastered by his mere will and pleasure: that though he might be too hard for our laws, he would never be able to get the better of our nature, and that to drive all England into Popery and slavery, he would find would be teaching an old lion to dance.[22]

But happy was it for the nation that it had then wiser heads in it, who knew how to lead a people so disposed into measures for the public preservation.

Here, I cannot help reflecting on the very different deliverances England met with at this time, and in the very same year of the century before. Then (in 1588), under a glorious princess who had at heart the good and happiness of her people, we scattered and destroyed the most formidable navy of invaders that ever covered the seas.[23] And now (in 1688), under a prince who had alienated the hearts of his people by his absolute measures to oppress them, a foreign power is received with open arms in defence of our laws, liberties and religion, which our native prince had invaded! How widely different were these two monarchs in their sentiments of glory! But, *tantum religio potuit suadere malorum*.[24]

When we consider in what height of the nation's prosperity the successor of Queen Elizabeth came to this throne, it seems amazing that such a pile of English fame and glory which her skilful administration had erected

20 A reference to Sir Robert Walpole (1676–1745), First Lord of the Treasury and in effect Prime Minister from 1721 to 1742, the subject of numerous satires, but also an allusion to Cibber's own long tenure at Drury Lane. *The Laureate* countered that such people 'may have deserved to have been railed at a long time' (p.26).

21 James II's 'wild measures' included a plan to instate Catholics into public office, and the building of an army with the help of Louis XIV of France.

22 In *The Champion*, 6 May 1740, Fielding mocks Cibber's preference for animal similes, adducing evidence from Booth, who alleged he had used a lion simile in a play set 'in some island or country where lions did not grow'. When Booth informed him, he begged to know 'where there is a lion' because he did not want to give up his simile.

23 The story of the Spanish Armada of 1588 is referred to in the titles of thirty-three works published between 1688 and 1700.

24 i.e. 'To such extremes of evil are men driven by religion', from Lucretius (99–55 BC), *De Rerum Natura* (*On the Nature of Things*), Book 1 line 102.

should in every following reign, down to the Revolution, so unhappily moulder away in one continual gradation of political errors; all which must have been avoided if the plain rule which that wise princess left behind her had been observed, *viz.*, 'that the love of her people was the surest support of her throne'.[25] This was the principle by which she so happily governed herself and those she had the care of. In this she found strength to combat and struggle through more difficulties and dangerous conspiracies than ever English monarch had to cope with.[26] At the same time that she professed to *desire* the people's love, she took care that her actions should *deserve* it, without the least abatement of her prerogative; the terror of which she so artfully covered that she sometimes seemed to flatter those she was determined should obey. If the four following princes[27] had exercised their regal authority with so visible a regard to the public welfare, it were hard to know whether the people of England might have ever complained of them, or even felt the want of that liberty they now so happily enjoy. 'Tis true that before her time, our ancestors had many successful contests with their sovereigns for their ancient right and claim to it; yet what did those successes amount to? Little more than a declaration that there was such a right in being; but whoever saw it enjoyed? Did not the actions of almost every succeeding reign show there were still so many doors of oppression left open to the prerogative that, whatever value our most eloquent legislators may have set upon those ancient liberties, I doubt it will be difficult to fix the period of their having a real being before the Revolution? Or if there ever was an elder period of our unmolested enjoying them, I own my poor judgment is at a loss where to place it. I will boldly say then, it is to the Revolution only we owe the full possession of what, till then, we never had more than a perpetually contested right to.[28] And from thence, from the Revolution it is that the Protestant successors of King William have found their paternal care and maintenance of that right [which] has been the surest basis of their glory.

25 Cibber may have recalled the words of Elizabeth I through those of Queen Anne. In her speech to the House of Commons on 30 November 1602, Elizabeth 'account[ed] the glory of my crown, that I have reigned with your love'. In William Cobbett's *The Parliamentary History of England* (1820), p.47, there is a record of Queen Anne's address to the Lords in 1702: 'the love and good affection of my subjects is the surest pledge of their duty and obedience, and the truest and justest support of their throne.'
26 Something of an overstatement, given Charles I's fate.
27 i.e. James I, Charles I, Charles II, and James II.
28 Evans notes that Fielding objected to this statement on the grounds that it compromised the rightfulness of the Glorious Revolution, illustrating Cibber's 'patched and piebald principles' (*The Champion*, 6 May 1740).

These, sir, are a few of my political notions, which I have ventured to expose that you may see what sort of an English subject I am. How wise or weak they may have shown me is not my concern; let the weight of these matters have drawn me never so far out of my depth, I still flatter myself that I have kept a simple, honest head above water. And it is a solid comfort to me to consider that how insignificant soever my life was at the Revolution, it had still the good fortune to make one among the many who brought it about; and that I now, with my coevals as well as with the millions since born, enjoy the happy effects of it.

But I must now let you see how my particular fortune went forward with this change in the government, of which I shall not pretend to give you any farther account than what my simple eyes saw of it.

We had not been many days at Nottingham before we heard that the Prince of Denmark[29] with some other great persons were gone off from the King to the Prince of Orange, and that the Princess Anne, fearing the King her father's resentment might fall upon her for her consort's revolt, had withdrawn herself in the night from London and was then within half a day's journey of Nottingham;[30] on which very morning we were suddenly alarmed with the news that two thousand of the King's dragoons were in close pursuit to bring her back prisoner to London. But this alarm, it seems, was all stratagem, and was but a part of that general terror which was thrown into many other places about the kingdom at the same time, with design to animate and unite the people in their common defence; it being then given out that the Irish were everywhere at our heels, to cut off all the Protestants within the reach of their fury.[31] In this alarm our troops scrambled to arms in as much order as their consternation would admit of, when – having advanced some few miles on the London road – they met the Princess in a coach, attended only by the Lady Churchill (now Duchess Dowager of Marlborough)[32] and the Lady Fitzharding,[33] whom they

29 Prince George of Denmark and Norway, Duke of Cumberland (1653–1708) married Anne, daughter of James II and future queen, in 1683. His loyalty to his father-in-law evaporated on 24 November 1688.

30 Soon after Prince George's change of allegiance, Henry Compton, Bishop of London (see above, p.46 n.7), arranged for Princess Anne to travel to Nottingham. There, Devonshire had assembled his forces and issued a manifesto which denounced James II and called for a free Parliament.

31 A longstanding fear in England, at least since Charles I's attempts to raise an Irish army in 1640. By February 1689 large numbers of Irish Catholics were in arms against William III.

32 Sarah Churchill, Duchess of Marlborough (1660–1744), close companion of Anne.

33 Barbara Berkeley, Viscountess Fizthardinge (1654–1708), lady-in-waiting to Anne, and sometimes believed to be a closet Jacobite. Evans notes the description of this episode in Burnet, I.792.

conducted into Nottingham through the acclamations of the people. The same night, all the noblemen and the other persons of distinction then in arms had the honour to sup at her Royal Highness's table, which was then furnished (as all her necessary accommodations were) by the care and at the charge of the Lord Devonshire. At this entertainment, of which I was a spectator, something very particular surprised me. The noble guests at the table happening to be more in number than attendants out of liveries could be found for, I being well known in the Lord Devonshire's family, was desired by his lordship's *maitre d'hotel* to assist at it. The post assigned me was to observe what the Lady Churchill might call for. Being so near the table, you may naturally ask me what I might have heard to have passed in conversation at it, which I should certainly tell you had I attended to above two words that were uttered there; and those were, 'Some wine and water'. These, I remember, came distinguished and observed to my ear, because they came from the fair guest whom I took such pleasure to wait on. Except at that single sound, all my senses were collected into my eyes, which during the whole entertainment wanted no better amusement than of stealing now and then the delight of gazing on the fair object so near me. If so clear an emanation of beauty, such a commanding grace of aspect, struck me into a regard that had something softer than the most profound respect in it, I cannot see why I may not without offence remember it, since beauty (like the sun) must sometimes lose its power to choose, and shine into equal warmth the peasant and the courtier.[34] Now to give you, sir, a farther proof of how good a taste my first hopeful entrance into manhood set out with, I remember above twenty years after, when the same lady had given the world four of the loveliest daughters[35] that ever were gazed on, even after they were all nobly married and were become the reigning toasts of every party of pleasure, their still lovely mother had at the same time her votaries, and her health very often took the lead in those involuntary triumphs of beauty. However presumptuous or impertinent these thoughts might have appeared at my first entertaining them, why may I not hope that my having kept them decently secret for full fifty years may be now a good round plea

---

34 Fielding lavishes particular criticism on the grammar of this passage in *The Champion*, 29 April 1740.

35 Five of the duchess's seven children survived infancy; Cibber tactfully omits to mention her only son, John, who died aged 12 in 1703. Her four daughters were Henrietta (1681–1733), Anne (1683–1716), Elizabeth (1687–1714), and Mary (1689–1751). As Cibber states, they all married 'nobly': Henrietta to the Honourable Francis Godolphin, later 2nd Earl of Godolphin (Cibber passes over her well-known intimacy with Congreve); Anne to Charles Spencer, 3rd Earl of Sunderland; Elizabeth to Scroop Egerton, 4th Earl of Bridgewater; and Mary to John, 2nd Duke of Montagu.

for their pardon? Were I now qualified to say more of this celebrated lady, I should conclude it thus: that she has lived to all appearance a peculiar favourite of Providence; that few examples can parallel the profusion of blessings which have attended so long a life of felicity. A person so attractive! A husband so memorably great![36] An offspring so beautiful! A fortune so immense! And a title which (when royal favour had no higher to bestow) she only could receive from the author of Nature: a great grandmother without grey hairs! These are such consummate indulgences that we might think heaven has centred them all in one person to let us see how far, with a lively understanding, the full possession of them could contribute to human happiness. I now return to our military affairs.

From Nottingham our troops marched to Oxford; through every town we passed, the people came out in some sort of order with such rural and rusty weapons as they had, to meet us in acclamations of welcome and good wishes. This, I thought, promised a favourable end of our civil war, when the nation seemed so willing to be all of a side! At Oxford the Prince and Princess of Denmark met for the first time after their late separation, and had all possible honours paid them by the University.[37] Here we rested in quiet quarters for several weeks till the flight of King James into France;[38] when, the nation being left to take care of itself, the only security that could be found for it was to advance the Prince and Princess of Orange to the vacant throne. The public tranquillity being now settled, our forces were remanded back to Nottingham. Here, all our officers who had commanded them from their first rising received commissions to confirm them in their several posts; and at the same time, such private men as chose to return to their proper business or habitations were offered their discharges. Among the small number of those who received them, I was one; for not hearing that my name was in any of these new commissions, I thought it time for me to take my leave of ambition, as ambition had before seduced me from the imaginary honours of the gown, and therefore resolved to hunt my fortune in some other field.[39]

---

36 i.e. John Churchill, 1st Duke of Marlborough (1650–1722).

37 Cibber perhaps exaggerates: these 'honours' apparently did not include an honorary degree. The University's Register of Convocation (OUA/NEP/subtus/Reg Bb) has no record of such an honour to Prince George in 1688 or any subsequent year (Anne was ineligible because of her gender).

38 James II eventually fled to France on 23 December 1688. William and Mary acceded to the throne on 12 February 1689. Supporters of James, including Jeremy Collier in *The Desertion Discussed* (1689), maintained he had not abdicated; Cibber's is the standard Whig version of events.

39 Bellchambers construes this as an admission of cowardice on Cibber's part.

From Nottingham I again returned to my father at Chatsworth, where I stayed till my lord came down with the new honours of Lord Steward of His Majesty's Household and Knight of the Garter![40] A noble turn of fortune! And a deep stake he had played for; which calls to my memory a story we had then in the family which, though too light for our graver historians' notice, may be of weight enough for my humble memoirs. This noble lord being in the presence chamber in King James's time, and known to be no friend to the measures of his administration, a certain person in favour there and desirous to be more so, took occasion to tread rudely upon his lordship's foot, which was returned with a sudden blow upon the spot. For this misdemeanour his lordship was fined thirty thousand pounds, but I think had some time allowed him for the payment. In the summer preceding the Revolution, when his lordship was retired to Chatsworth and had been there deeply engaged with other noblemen in the measures which soon after brought it to bear, King James sent a person down to him with offers to mitigate his fine upon conditions of ready payment; to which his lordship replied that if His Majesty pleased to allow him a little longer time, he would rather choose to play double or quit with him. The time of the intended rising being of then so near at hand, the demand, it seems, came too late for a more serious answer.[41]

However low my pretensions to preferment were at this time, my father thought that a little court favour added to them might give him a chance for saving the expense of maintaining me, as he had intended, at the University. He therefore ordered me to draw up a petition to the Duke and, to give it some air of merit, to put it into Latin; the prayer of which was that his Grace would be pleased to do something (I really forget what) for me. However, the Duke upon receiving it was so good as to desire my father would send me to London in the winter, where he would consider of some provision for me. It might indeed well require time to consider it, for I believe it was

---

40 Cavendish acquired his 'new honours' in March 1689. In the first edition Cibber states that he was made a duke at the same time, when in fact that honour was not bestowed until 1694; the error was corrected in the second edition. He overlooked a further, less significant error: the Garter was not bestowed until two months later, in May 1689.

41 A violent quarrel between the Earl of Devonshire and Colonel Thomas Colpepper is recorded in Evelyn, *Diary*, 9 July 1685. Colpepper accused the Earl of favouring James II's exclusion, and they started to fight; Colpepper was imprisoned. A further encounter, on 26 April 1687, is recorded by Luttrell, I.401. This time the Earl challenged Colpepper to step outside and hit him with a cane when he refused; the Earl was fined £30,000 and imprisoned. By October 1687 the quarrel was over: Luttrell, I.418, reports that the Earl 'hath made his peace at court' and 'given his own bond for the fine'. Neither Luttrell nor Evelyn mentions an offer to 'play double or quit'.

then harder to know what I was really fit for, than to have got me anything I was not fit for. However, to London I came, where I entered into my first state of attendance and dependence for about five months, till the February following.[42] But alas! In my intervals of leisure, by frequently seeing plays my wise head was turned to higher views. I saw no joy in any other life than that of an actor, so that (as before, when a candidate at Winchester) I was even afraid of succeeding to the preferment I sought for. 'Twas on the stage alone I had formed a happiness preferable to all that camps or courts could offer me; and there was I determined, let father and mother take it as they pleased, to fix my *non ultra*.[43] Here I think myself obliged, in respect to the honour of that noble lord, to acknowledge that I believe his real intentions to do well for me were prevented by my own inconsiderate folly, so that if my life did not then take a more laudable turn, I have no one but myself to reproach for it; for I was credibly informed by the gentlemen of his house-hold that his Grace had, in their hearing, talked of recommending me to the Lord Shrewsbury, then Secretary of State, for the first proper vacancy in that office.[44] But the distant hope of a reversion was too cold a temptation for a spirit impatient as mine, that wanted immediate possession of what my heart was so differently set upon. The allurements of a theatre are still so strong in my memory that perhaps few, except those who have felt them, can conceive. And I am yet so far willing to excuse my folly that I am convinced, were it possible to take off that disgrace and prejudice which custom has thrown upon the profession of an actor, many a well-born younger brother and beauty of low fortune would gladly have adorned the theatre – who, by their not being able to brook such dishonour to their birth, have passed away their lives decently unheeded and forgotten.[45]

42 i.e. February 1690. Cibber's first intensive experience of watching plays occurred at a time of renewed buoyancy for the stage: of the 1689–90 season, LS1 records that 'More new plays appeared than in previous seasons, and a great many old ones were reprinted (and possibly revived) at this time' (LS1 373).

43 i.e. 'not beyond'. Davies, III.444, reports that Cibber became friends with Jack Verbruggen and that the two pestered the United Company prompter, John Downes, for minor roles.

44 Charles Talbot, 1st Duke of Shrewsbury (1660–1718), had played a key role in deposing James II and became William III's Secretary of State for the Southern Department. He resigned in 1690, pleading ill health, but throughout his career he was accused of having Jacobite sympathies. He served two terms as Lord Chamberlain: 1699–1700 and 1710–15.

45 Evans quotes Steele's *The Theatre* (no.1, 2 January 1720): 'I take leave to say, that the world gives the profession of an actor very unjust discountenance.' For discussion of the complex social status of Restoration actors, see David Roberts, 'Social Status and the Actor: The Case of Thomas Betterton', *Studies in Theatre and Performance* vol. 30, no. 2 (summer 2010), 173–85.

Many years ago, when I was first in the management of the theatre, I remember a strong instance which will show you what degree of ignominy the profession of an actor was then held at. A lady with a real title, whose female indiscretions had occasioned her family to abandon her, being willing in her distress to make an honest penny of what beauty she had left, desired to be admitted as an actress; when, before she could receive our answer, a gentleman (probably by her relations' permission) advised us not to entertain her, for reasons easy to be guessed. You may imagine we could not be so blind to our interest as to make an honourable family our unnecessary enemies by not taking his advice, which the lady too being sensible of, saw the affair had its difficulties and therefore pursued it no farther. Now is it not hard that it should be a doubt whether this lady's condition or ours were the more melancholy? For here, you find her honest endeavour to get bread from the stage was looked upon as an addition of new scandal to her former dishonour; so that I am afraid, according to this way of thinking, had the same lady stooped to have sold patches and pomatum in a band-box[46] from door to door, she might in that occupation have starved with less infamy than had she relieved her necessities by being famous on the theatre. Whether this prejudice may have arisen from the abuses that so often have crept in upon the stage, I am not clear in;[47] though when that is grossly the case, I will allow there ought to be no limits set to the contempt of it. Yet in its lowest condition in my time, methinks there could have been no pretence of preferring the bandbox to the buskin. But this severe opinion, whether merited or not, is not the greatest distress that this profession is liable to.

I shall now give you another anecdote quite the reverse of what I have instanced, wherein you will see an actress as hardly used for an act of modesty (which, without being a prude, a woman even upon the stage may

---

46 'Patches' were small pieces of black material cut into shapes and applied to the face as decoration or to hide blemishes; 'pomatum' was an ointment applied to the skin or hair; a 'band-box' was a flimsy cardboard box usually covered in paper and used for keeping trinkets.

47 The longstanding historical association of actors and vagrancy resurfaced in the 1737 Licensing Act, which addressed the need to reduce 'the laws relating to rogues, vagabonds, sturdy beggars, and vagrants into one Act of Parliament'. For a summary of the 1572 Act for the Punishment of Vagabonds and its implication for actors, see Andrew Gurr, *The Shakespearean Stage 1574–1642* (Cambridge: Cambridge University Press, 1992), pp.27–33. Cibber's reference to 'abuses' may reflect the Collier controversy which beset the theatre when he started to succeed as an actor and playwright during the late 1690s, or his subsequent claims of a general decline in standards of taste since the Restoration period (see below, 182–4 and 236–8).

sometimes think it necessary not to throw off). This too I am forced to premise, that the truth of what I am going to tell you may not be sneered at before it be known. About the year 1717, a young actress of a desirable person, sitting in an upper box at the opera, a military gentleman thought this a proper opportunity to secure a little conversation with her, the particulars of which were probably no more worth repeating than, it seems, the *damoiselle* then thought them worth listening to; for, notwithstanding the fine things he said to her, she rather chose to give the music the preference of her attention. This indifference was so offensive to his high heart that he began to change the tender into the terrible and, in short, proceeded at last to treat her in a style too grossly insulting for the meanest female ear to endure unresented. Upon which, being beaten too far out of her discretion, she turned hastily upon him with an angry look, and a reply which seemed to set his merit in so low a regard that he thought himself obliged in honour to take his time to resent it. This was the full extent of her crime, which his glory delayed no longer to punish than till the next time she was to appear upon the stage. There, in one of her best parts, wherein she drew a favourable regard and approbation from the audience, he (dispensing with the respect which some people think due to a polite assembly) began to interrupt her performance with such loud and various notes of mockery as other young men of honour, in the same place, have sometimes made themselves undauntedly merry with. Thus, deaf to all murmurs or entreaties of those about him, he pursued his point even to throwing near her such trash as no person can be supposed to carry about him, unless to use on so particular an occasion.

A gentleman then behind the scenes, being shocked at his unmanly behaviour, was warm enough to say that no man but a fool or a bully could be capable of insulting an audience or a woman in so monstrous a manner. The former valiant gentleman, to whose ear the words were soon brought by his spies (whom he had placed behind the scenes to observe how the action was taken there), came immediately from the pit in a heat, and demanded to know of the author of those words if he was the person that spoke them; to which he calmly replied that though he had never seen him before, yet since he seemed so earnest to be satisfied, he would do him the favour to own that indeed the words were his, and that they would be the last words he should choose to deny, whoever they might fall upon. To conclude, their dispute was ended the next morning in Hyde Park, where the determined combatant who first asked for satisfaction was obliged afterwards to ask his life too. Whether he mended it or not I have not yet heard; but his antagonist, in a few years after, died in one of the principal posts of the government.[48]

Now, though I have sometimes known these gallant insulters of audiences draw themselves into scrapes which they have less honourably got out of,[49] yet alas, what has that availed? This generous, public-spirited method of silencing a few was but repelling the disease in one part to make it break out in another. All endeavours at protection are new provocations to those who pride themselves in pushing their courage to a defiance of humanity. Even when a royal resentment has shown itself in the behalf of an injured actor, it has been unable to defend him from farther insults, an instance of which happened in the late King James's time. Mr Smith[50] (whose

48 In an entry dated 8 March 1711, Narcissus Luttrell reported a duel between 'James Craggs, Esq … and one Mr Montague upon some differences between them at the playhouse, and the last wounded, but not mortal' (Luttrell, VI.699). According to *The Laureate*, the three parties in this business were Hester Santlow (the actress), Captain Montague (her aggressor), and James Craggs the Younger (1686–1721), who was Santlow's lover (p.28; see also below, p.316 n.12). By 1717 Santlow (?1694–1773) was acquiring a reputation as a dancer as well as an actress. She appeared in John Weaver's *The Loves of Mars and Venus* in March 1717, a 'New Dramatic Entertainment of Dancing' praised by Cibber below, p.324. In *The Incomparable Hester Santlow: A Dancer–Actress on the Georgian Stage* (Aldershot: Ashgate, 2007), p.47, Moira Goff calculates that the 'opera' to which Cibber refers may have been an early performance of Handel's *Rinaldo*, first performed at the Queen's Theatre on 24 February 1711, and that the subsequent play was Etherege's *The Man of Mode*, performed on 1 March 1711 with Santlow as Harriet. Craggs was MP for Tregony and Secretary at War. In 1718 he became Secretary of State for the Southern Department and died of smallpox in February 1721; he was buried in Westminster Abbey at night, the authorities fearing disturbances because of his implication in the South Sea Bubble crisis. Goff, p.47, estimates that he became Hester Santlow's lover by May 1712, which was probably when they conceived a daughter. In 1718 Santlow married her Drury Lane colleague, the actor Barton Booth. Luttrell, VI.68, identifies a Captain Montague in the service of James Stewart, 5th Earl of Galloway, in Spain during July 1706.
49 Evans cites Steele's *The Theatre*, no. 7 (23 January 1720), on Cibber's own history of being abused in this way, allegedly because audiences confused him with the villains he played (see below, pp.151–2); Sir Richard Steele, *The Theatre*, ed. and publ. John Nichols, 2 vols., 1791.
50 William Smith was a long-serving member of the Duke's Company, one of the two patent companies founded after the Restoration. He appears to have joined the company for the 1662–3 season following a brief legal career. His reputation was untarnished by an incident in November 1666 reported by Pepys: '[Mrs Knipp] tells me how Smith, of the Duke's house, hath killed a man upon a quarrel in a play; which makes everybody sorry, he being a good actor, and, they say, a good man, however this happens. The ladies of the Court do much bemoan him, she says' (14 November 1666). Smith became co-manager of the Duke's Company with Thomas Betterton following the withdrawal of Henry Harris in 1676. The Duke therefore had strong motives to protect a loyal servant who had played a significant role in producing and performing pro-Jamesian plays.

character as a gentleman could have been no way impeached had he not degraded it by being a celebrated actor) had the misfortune, in a dispute with a gentleman behind the scenes, to receive a blow from him. The same night, an account of this action was carried to the King, to whom the gentleman was represented so grossly in the wrong that the next day His Majesty sent to forbid him the Court upon it. This indignity, cast upon a gentleman only for having maltreated a player, was looked upon as the concern of every gentleman; and a party was soon formed to assert and vindicate their honour by humbling this favoured actor, whose slight injury had been judged equal to so severe a notice. Accordingly, the next time Smith acted, he was received with a chorus of cat-calls that soon convinced him he should not be suffered to proceed in his part, upon which, without the least discomposure he ordered the curtain to be dropped; and, having a competent fortune of his own, thought the conditions of adding to it by his remaining upon the stage were too dear, and from that day entirely quitted it.[51] I shall make no observation upon the King's resentment or on that of his good subjects; how far either was or was not right is not the point I dispute for. Be that as it may, the unhappy condition of the actor was so far from being relieved by this royal interposition in his favour that it was the worse for it.

While these sort of real distresses on the stage are so unavoidable, it is no wonder that young people of sense (though of low fortune) should be so rarely found to supply a succession of good actors. Why then may we not, in some measure, impute the scarcity of them to the wanton inhumanity of those spectators who have made it so terribly mean to appear there? Were there no ground for this question, where could be the disgrace of entering into a society whose institution, when not abused, is a delightful school of morality, and where to excel requires as ample endowments of Nature as any one profession (that of holy institution excepted) whatsoever? But alas, as Shakespeare says,

> Where's that palace whereinto sometimes
> Foul things intrude not?[52]

51 LS1 327 judges that the performance in question was as Lorenzo in Thomas Southerne's *The Disappointment*, performed by the United Company (of which Smith was co-manager with Betterton) in April 1684. That date is, however, nearly a year before 'the late King James's time'. No performances featuring Smith are recorded between then and 25 April 1687, when he appeared as Armusia in Nahum Tate's adaptation of John Fletcher's *The Island Princess* (see LS1 357). There is evidence that he continued with his managerial duties; in an advertisement of November 1686, he and Betterton sought news of a lost play by Thomas Otway (LS1 354).
52 Iago's question to Othello, III.iii.156–7: 'As where's that palace whereinto foul things / Sometimes intrude not?' For Cibber's Iago, see above, p.41 n.51.

Look into St Peter's at Rome, and see what a profitable farce is made of religion there![53] Why, then, is an actor more blemished than a cardinal? While the excellence of the one arises from his innocently seeming what he is not, and the eminence of the other from the most impious fallacies that can be imposed upon human understanding? If the best things, therefore, are most liable to corruption, the corruption of the theatre is no disproof of its innate and primitive utility.

In this light, therefore, all the abuses of the stage – all the low, loose, or immoral supplements to wit, whether in making virtue ridiculous or vice agreeable, or in the decorated nonsense and absurdities of pantomimical trumpery[54] – I give up to the contempt of every sensible spectator as so much rank theatrical Popery; but cannot still allow these enormities to impeach the profession while they are so palpably owing to the depraved taste of the multitude. While vice and farcical folly are the most profitable commodities, why should we wonder that, time out of mind, the poor comedian, when real wit would bear no price, should deal in what would bring him most ready money? But this, you will say, is making the stage a nursery of vice and folly, or at least keeping an open shop for it. I grant it. But who do you expect should reform it? The actors? Why so? If people are permitted to buy it without blushing, the theatrical merchant seems to have an equal right to the liberty of selling it without reproach. That this evil wants a remedy is not to be contested, nor can it be denied that the theatre is as capable of being preserved by a reformation as matters of more importance; which, for the honour of our national taste, I could wish were attempted. And then if it could not subsist, under decent regulations, by not being permitted to present anything there but what were worthy to be there, it would be time enough to consider whether it were necessary to let it totally fall, or effectually support it.[55]

Notwithstanding all my best endeavours to recommend the profession of an actor to a more general favour, I doubt, while it is liable to such

---

53 The rituals, symbolism, and alleged hypocrisy of the Roman Catholic Church had been a popular subject for drama since the Renaissance, not least because of their theatricality. Cibber's own hostility towards Catholicism was shaped by his Whig politics and found voice in such plays as *The Non-Juror* (see below, pp.327–9) and *Papal Tyranny in the Reign of King John*.

54 John Rich's 'pantomimes' at Lincoln's Inn Fields from c. 1723 had drawn audiences away from Drury Lane (see also below, pp.324–5).

55 Cibber endorses the passing of the 1737 Licensing Act, which had the initial effect of limiting performances to only two licensed playhouses (for further views, see below, pp.191–4). For a commentary on, transcript of, and responses to the Act, see Thomas and Hare, pp.205–20.

corruptions and the actor himself to such unlimited insults as I have already mentioned – I doubt (I say) we must still leave him adrift with his intrinsic merit, to ride out the storm as well as he is able.

However, let us now turn to the other side of this account, and see what advantages stand there to balance the misfortunes I have laid before you. There we shall still find some valuable articles of credit that sometimes overpay his incidental disgraces.

First, if he has sense, he will consider that as these indignities are seldom or never offered him by people that are remarkable for any one good quality, he ought not to lay them too close to his heart. He will know too that when malice, envy, or a brutal nature can securely hide or fence themselves in a multitude, virtue, merit, innocence, and even sovereign superiority have been (and must be) equally liable to their insults; that therefore, when they fall upon him in the same manner, his intrinsic value cannot be diminished by them. On the contrary, if with a decent and unruffled temper he lets them pass, the disgrace will return upon his aggressor and perhaps warm the generous spectator into a partiality in his favour.

That while he is conscious that as an actor he must be always in the hands of injustice, it does him at least this involuntary good: that it keeps him in a settled resolution to avoid all occasions of provoking it, or of even offending the lowest enemy who, at the expense of a shilling, may publicly revenge it.

That if he excels on the stage and is irreproachable in his personal morals and behaviour, his profession is so far from being an impediment that it will be oftener a just reason for his being received among people of condition with favour; and sometimes with a more social distinction than the best (though more profitable) trade he might have followed could have recommended him to.

That this is a happiness to which several actors within my memory – as Betterton, Smith, Mountfort, Captain Griffin, and Mrs Bracegirdle (yet living) – have arrived at, to which I may add the late, celebrated Mrs Oldfield.[56] Now let us suppose these persons (the men, for example) to

---

56 The virtuous actors referred to are Thomas **Betterton** (1635–1710), the leading actor of the period and manager of successive companies. He counted lords, MPs, and archbishops among his acquaintance, and amassed a library and picture collection worthy of any gentleman. For a modern biography, see David Roberts, *Thomas Betterton: The Greatest Actor of the Restoration Stage* (Cambridge: Cambridge University Press, 2010); for his collection, Jacob Hooke, *Pinacotheca Bettertonaeana*, ed. David Roberts (London: The Society for Theatre Research, 2013); for further appreciation by Cibber, see below, pp.76–83. See also Figure 5. For William **Smith**, see p.59 n.50 above. William

5. 'Without competitors': Thomas Betterton; engraving after the
portrait by Godfrey Kneller

Mountfort (c. 1660–92), also a playwright, made his first known appearance for the
Duke's Company in 1678 and was murdered for defending Anne Bracegirdle from
kidnappers; for details, see LS1 416 and Albert S. Borgman, *The Life and Death of William
Mountfort* (Cambridge, MA: Harvard University Press, 1935); Cibber's praise for his
acting is below, pp.94–6. Philip **Griffin** was a member of the King's Company from 1672
and became a member of the United Company, playing middling roles. There is a gap
of six years in his acting career from 1692 to 1698; on 2 June 1698 he played Manly in
Wycherley's *The Plain Dealer* at a Drury Lane charity performance, when *The Post Boy*
described him as 'formerly a famous actor, and lately Captain of a company of foot in
His Majesty's service, through the wars in Ireland' (see LS1 497); his role as manager of
the company goes unmentioned (for his appointment, 1695–9, by Christopher Rich, see
Document Register no.1692). For an anecdote about him, see below, p.259. He is not to be
confused with Edward Griffin, a court official who appeared in an amateur production of
Katherine Philips's *Horace* in February 1668 and was Treasurer of the Chamber by 1679

have been all eminent mercers, and the women as famous milliners: can we imagine that merely as such, though endowed with the same natural understanding, they could have been called into the same honourable parties of conversation?[57] People of sense and condition could not but know it was impossible they could have had such various excellencies on the stage without having something naturally valuable in them. And I will take upon me to affirm, who knew them all living, that there was not one of the number who were not capable of supporting a variety of spirited conversation, though the stage were never to have been the subject of it.

That to have trod the stage has not always been thought a disqualification from more honourable employments. Several have had military commissions. Carlisle[58] and Wiltshire[59] were both killed captains: one in King William's reduction of Ireland and the other in his first war, in Flanders; and the famous Ben Jonson, though an unsuccessful actor, was afterwards made Poet Laureate.[60]

(see LS1 128 and 275). Anne **Bracegirdle** (c. 1671–1748) was believed to be the adopted daughter of Thomas and Mary Betterton and may have made her first stage appearance at the age of 5 (LS1 245); a specialist in comic roles, she created many of Congreve's heroines and was included in his will. She retired from acting no later than 1709. Like Betterton, she acquired a reputation for probity that was countered by gossip; for further discussion, see below, pp.108–10. Anne **Oldfield** (1683–1730) joined Christopher Rich's company in 1699; for her emergence as a future star and successor to Bracegirdle, see below, pp.201–5. For an early biography, see above, p.12 n.3. See also Figure 9.

57 A mercer deals in textiles. In fact, many actors in the Duke's Company came from a trade background; Betterton himself began his career working for a bookseller.

58 James Carlisle is first mentioned as an actor in the United Company in the 1682–3 season; his first recorded role was Aumale in Dryden and Lee's *The Duke of Guise* in November 1682. According to *Biographia Dramatica* he was killed at the Battle of Aughrim on 11 July 1691 (I.87). His last recorded performance was as Brunetto in Nahum Tate's *A Duke and No Duke*, August 1684 (LS1 328), but he was the author of a play, *The Fortune Hunters*, staged at Drury Lane in March 1689 (LS1 370).

59 John Wiltshire joined the King's Company for the 1674–5 season but moved to the rival Duke's Company in 1679, i.e. before the merger. He played a variety of middle-ranking roles, including Kent in Tate's *The History of King Lear* (March 1681). Like Carlisle, his last recorded performance was in *A Duke and No Duke* in August 1684. Cibber's reference to William III's 'first war, in Flanders' is probably to the unsuccessful campaign of 1692, contrasting with the brutally successful 'reduction of Ireland' in 1690–1.

60 Ben Jonson (1573–1637) began his theatrical career as an actor and is believed to have played at least one leading role, Hieronimo in Thomas Kyd's *The Spanish Tragedy*. He turned to playwriting after serving a prison sentence for his role in Nashe's politically controversial *The Isle of Dogs* (15 97). Cibber's characterization of him as an 'unsuccessful actor' may have been motivated by a wish to draw a contrast with his own career. The post of Poet Laureate did not formally exist until after the Restoration, but James I's award of a pension to Jonson in 1617 gave the role substance. In his list of soldier-actors, Cibber omitted to mention the early stalwarts of the King's Company, Michael Mohun and Charles Hart, who had fought in the royalist army during the English Civil War.

To these laudable distinctions let me add one more: that of public applause, which, when truly merited, is perhaps one of the most agreeable gratifications that venial vanity can feel. A happiness almost peculiar to the actor – insomuch that the best tragic writer, however numerous his separate admirers may be, yet to unite them into one general act of praise, to receive at once those thundering peals of approbation which a crowded theatre throws out, he must still call in the assistance of the skilful actor to raise and partake of them.[61]

In a word, 'twas in this flattering light only (though not perhaps so thoroughly considered) I looked upon the life of an actor when but eighteen years of age; nor can you wonder if the temptations were too strong for so warm a vanity as mine to resist. But whether excusable or not, to the stage at length I came; and it is from thence, chiefly, your curiosity (if you have any left) is to expect a farther account of me.

61 However, compare this passage with the account of Betterton below, p.82, which gives a different view of the value of 'thundering peals of approbation'.

CHAPTER 4

A short view of the stage from the year 1660 to the Revolution. The King's and Duke's Company united composed the best set of English actors yet known. Their several theatrical characters.

Though I have only promised you an account of all the material occurrences of the theatre during my own time, yet there was one which happened not above seven years before my admission to it which may be as well worth notice as the first great revolution of it in which (among numbers) I was involved.[1] And as the one will lead you into a clearer view of the other, it may therefore be previously necessary to let you know that King Charles II at his Restoration granted two patents: one to Sir William Davenant and the other to Henry Killigrew Esq, and their several heirs and assigns forever, for the forming of two distinct companies of comedians.[2] The first were called the King's Servants and acted at the Theatre Royal in Drury Lane;[3] and the other, the Duke's Company, who acted at the Duke's Theatre in Dorset Garden.[4] About ten of the King's Company were on the Royal

1 The 'first great revolution' in which Cibber was 'involved' was the breakaway of a group of actors led by Betterton in 1695; the 'one which happened seven years before' he became an actor was in 1682, and therefore eight years before Cibber joined the United Company in 1690.
2 Sir William Davenant (1606–68), playwright, poet, and theatre manager, had been issued with a theatre patent by Charles I, whom he served as Poet Laureate from 1637; during the Commonwealth he staged operatic entertainments at Rutland House and is credited with bringing movable scenery to the London stage. Thomas Killigrew (1612–83), the other patentee, is not to be confused with his clergyman and playwright brother Henry (1613–1700); Cibber did not correct the error in the second edition. Thomas Killigrew was a prominent playwright in the 1630s and had attended Charles II in exile. Davenant and Killigrew's duopoly was agreed on 21 August 1660 (BL Add. MS 19,256, fol.47; *Document Register* no.19) and formally granted to Killigrew for the King's Company on 25 April 1662 (PRO C66/3013, no.20; *Document Register* no.131), and to Davenant for the Duke's on 15 January 1663 (PRO C66/3009, no.3; *Document Register* no.186).
3 In fact, the King's Company began acting at the old Red Bull playhouse in November 1660 before moving to Vere Street and then Bridges Street; the Theatre Royal in Drury Lane opened in 1674. Earlier performances involving actors from both companies had taken place at the Cockpit Theatre.
4 The Duke's Company opened in February 1661 at Salisbury Court, moving to Lincoln's Inn Fields in June of the same year; their Dorset Garden Theatre opened in 1671.

Household establishment, having each ten yards of scarlet cloth, with a proper quantity of lace allowed them for liveries; and in their warrants from the Lord Chamberlain were styled 'Gentlemen of the Great Chamber'.[5] Whether the like appointments were extended to the Duke's Company I am not certain;[6] but they were both in high estimation with the public, and so much the delight and concern of the Court that they were not only supported by its being frequently present at their public presentations, but by its taking cognizance even of their private government, insomuch that their particular differences, pretensions or complaints were generally ended by the King or Duke's personal command or decision.[7] Besides their being thorough masters of their art, these actors set forwards with two critical advantages which perhaps may never happen again in many ages. The one was their immediate opening after the so long interdiction of plays during the Civil War and the anarchy that followed it.[8] What eager appetites, from so long a fast, must the guests of those times have had to that high and fresh variety of entertainments which Shakespeare had left prepared for them! Never was a stage so provided! A hundred years are wasted and another silent century well advanced, and yet what unborn age shall say Shakespeare has his equal? How many shining actors have the warm scenes of his genius given to posterity, without being himself, in his action, equal to his writing – strong proof that actors, like poets, must be born such! Eloquence and elocution are quite different talents: Shakespeare could write *Hamlet*, but tradition tells us that the Ghost in the same play was one of his

<hr>

5   According to an order dated 6 October 1660, thirteen King's Company actors were sworn in as 'Grooms of the Chamber in Ordinary' (LC 3/25, pp.157 and 161; *Document Register* no.30). A further actor was struck off the list; several others were added during the 1660s. Warrants for royal livery were issued from 29 July 1661 (LC 5/12, p.207; *Document Register* no.83), including one dated 4 November 1662 for '4 yards of bastard scarlet for a cloak and a quarter yard of crimson velvet for a cape' for sixteen King's Company actors (LC 5/137, p.173; *Document Register* no.171).

6   A document dated 24 September 1662 simply notes that five of Davenant's troupe were 'sworn to attend his Royal Highness the Duke of York' (LC 3/25, p.162; *Document Register* no.155).

7   A conspicuous example of such 'differences' in the early years of the companies was the attempt by Henry Harris of the Duke's to secure a transfer to the King's for better pay, as reported by Pepys on 22 July 1663. By 24 October of the same year the dispute was settled because the King had prohibited the transfer and the Duke had pressured Davenant into giving Harris a pay rise. Cibber's 'public presentations' were the many visits paid by the Court to the theatres.

8   Modern scholarship has challenged the longstanding idea that playwriting, at least, was moribund during the Interregnum. See, for example, Dale B. J. Randall, *Winter Fruit: English Drama 1642–1660* (Lexington: University Press of Kentucky, 1995).

best performances as an actor.[9] Nor is it within the reach of rule or precept to complete either of them. Instruction, 'tis true, may guard them equally against faults or absurdities, but there it stops. Nature must do the rest. To excel in either art is a self-born happiness which something more than good sense must be the mother of.

The other advantage I was speaking of is that before the Restoration, no actresses had ever been seen upon the English stage.[10] The characters of women on former theatres were performed by boys, or young men of the most effeminate aspect. And what grace or masterstrokes of action can we conceive such ungain hoydens to have been capable of?[11] This defect was so well considered by Shakespeare that in few of his plays he has any greater dependence upon the ladies than in the innocence and simplicity of a Desdemona, an Ophelia, or in the short specimen of a fond and virtuous Portia.[12] The additional objects, then, of real, beautiful women could not but draw a proportion of new admirers to the theatre. We may imagine too that these actresses were not ill chosen, when it is well known that more than one of them had charms sufficient at their leisure hours to calm and mollify the cares of empire.[13] Besides these peculiar advantages, they

9 This 'tradition' was first recorded by Nicholas Rowe in his six-volume 1709 edition of Shakespeare's works: 'though I have inquired, I could never meet with any further account of him this way [i.e. as an actor], than that the top of his performance was the Ghost in his own *Hamlet*' (I.xii–xiii). Cibber may have derived the idea directly from Rowe, who wrote the prologue for *The Non-Juror*.

10 True only of the professional or public stage: Davenant had employed a Mrs Coleman for his shows at Rutland House in 1656, while many women had acted in court performances earlier in the seventeenth century. The first recorded use of the word 'actress' appears to date from 1626, following a performance by Queen Henrietta Maria. The current consensus is that Anne Marshall was the first woman to appear on the Restoration Stage, in a performance of *Othello* on 8 December 1660. See Howe, p.24.

11 A judgment contradicted by a letter of 1610 following an Oxford performance of *Othello* by the King's Men, which uses female pronouns to describe a boy actor playing Desdemona and emphasizes his emotional impact; as cited by Geoffrey Tillotson in *The Times Literary Supplement*, 20 July 1933, 494. 'Ungain' is an early form of 'ungainly'; *OED* dates the first use at 1400. 'Hoyden': a rude, or ill-bred girl (*OED*).

12 Cibber's summary is not surprising, given the unpopularity of Shakespeare's comedies during his lifetime, the prevailing preference for Dryden's *All for Love* over Shakespeare's *Antony and Cleopatra*, and the omission of Margaret from his own adaptation of *Richard III*. The 'few' exceptions he refers to presumably included *Macbeth* and *King Lear*, regularly performed during his career. His reference to Portia is to the character in *Julius Caesar* rather than *The Merchant of Venice*, although the latter was performed in Cibber's lifetime, in both its adapted and original form (see, for example, LS3 889 *et al.*).

13 Charles II had affairs with at least three actresses, starting with Elizabeth Farley (later Weaver) in 1660, followed by Nell Gwyn and Mary ('Moll') Davis. On 11 January 1668

had a private rule or argument[14] which both houses were happily tied down to, which was that no play acted at one house should ever be attempted at the other. All the capital plays therefore of Shakespeare, Fletcher, and Ben Jonson were divided between them by the approbation of the Court and their own alternate choice;[15] so that when Hart[16] was famous for Othello, Betterton had no less a reputation for Hamlet.[17] By this order, the stage was supplied with a greater variety of plays than could possibly have been shown had both companies been employed at the same time upon the same play – which liberty too must have occasioned such frequent repetitions of 'em, by their opposite endeavours to forestall and anticipate one another, that the best actors in the world must have grown tedious and tasteless to the spectator.[18] For what pleasure is not languid to satiety? It was therefore one of our greatest happinesses during my time of being in the management[19] of the stage that we had a certain number of select plays which no other company had the good fortune to make a tolerable figure in, and consequently could find little or no account by acting them against us. These plays therefore, for many years, by not being too often seen, never failed to bring us crowded audiences, and it was to this conduct we owed

Pepys heard that Davis had left the Duke's Company to become Charles II's mistress; he observed that there was 'hope for no good to the state from having a prince so devoted to his pleasure'.

14 The first edition reads 'agreement', amended to 'argument' for the second edition, with the change retained in subsequent eighteenth-century editions. Other modern editors prefer 'agreement', but it appears 'argument' was used in the now obsolete sense listed by *OED* 5b of 'a subject of discussion', distinct from the formal agreement which fell into place in December 1660 (see n.15, below).

15 Killigrew appears to have acquired performing rights to the twenty plays listed for the Red Bull actors in August 1660 (LS1 12), by Shakespeare (*Henry IV, The Merry Wives of Windsor*, and *Othello*), Fletcher, Jonson, Chapman, and himself. Contrary to Cibber's suggestion, Davenant was not given rights to any of Jonson's plays when his own grants were issued in December 1660, but – among others and including his own – to *The Tempest, Measure for Measure, Much Ado About Nothing, Romeo and Juliet, Twelfth Night, Henry VIII, King Lear, Macbeth, Hamlet*, and *Pericles* (LC 5/137, pp.343–4; *Document Register* no.50).

16 Charles Hart (1625–83) took over the role of Othello from Nicholas Burt during the 1670s. Following the union of the companies and Hart's retirement in 1682, Betterton probably adopted the role, although there is no record of him playing it until 1691 (LS1 387).

17 For Cibber's appreciation of Betterton's Hamlet, see below, p.77.

18 As Bellchambers points out, there have been many occasions in theatre history when audiences have been attracted to seeing two famous actors playing the same role in different productions.

19 In the editions of 1740 the spelling is 'menagement': apparently an idiosyncrasy of Cibber's; *OED* has no record of it. See Introduction, p.xlviii.

no little share of our prosperity. But when four houses[20] are at once (as very lately they were) all permitted to act the same pieces, let three of them perform never so ill, when plays come to be so harrassed and hackneyed out to the common people (half of which too, perhaps, would as lieve see them at one house as another), the best actors will soon feel that the town has enough of them.

I know it is the common opinion that the more playhouses, the more emulation. I grant it; but what has this emulation ended in? Why, a daily contention which shall soonest surfeit you with the best plays; so that when what *ought* to please can no *longer* please, your appetite is again to be raised by such monstrous presentations as dishonour the taste of a civilized people.[21] If, indeed, to our several theatres we could raise a proportionable number of good authors, to give them all different employment, then perhaps the public might profit from their emulation. But while good writers are so scarce and undaunted critics so plenty, I am afraid a good play and a blazing star will be equal rarities. This voluptuous expedient, therefore, of indulging the taste with several theatres, will amount to much the same variety as that of a certain economist who, to enlarge his hospitality, would have two puddings and two legs of mutton for the same dinner.[22] But to resume the thread of my history.

These two excellent companies were both prosperous for some few years till their variety of plays began to be exhausted. Then, of course, the better actors (which the King's seem to have been allowed) could not fail of drawing the greater audiences.[23] Sir William Davenant, therefore (master

20 Immediately before the 1737 Licensing Act there were four spoken-word theatres operating in London, two with royal patents (Drury Lane and Covent Garden) and two without (Little Haymarket and subsequently Lincoln's Inn Fields). According to LS3 cxlvii, audiences grew as a result, contrary to Cibber's assertion. The 1737 Act enforced the exclusive rights of patentees.

21 A reference either to the 'newfangled foppery' discussed below, p.324, or to a succession of farces by Fielding during the 1730s that satirized the pretensions of the patent theatres (see below, p.191 n.53).

22 This appears to be a reference to 'An Essay on Eating' which appears in the *Universal Spectator*, 14 and 21 August 1736, under the name Will Lovemeal, but whose real author is believed to be Henry Fielding. Fielding would in turn mock Cibber's use of the simile in *The Champion*, 6 May 1740, suggesting he was 'too much inclined to write on a full stomach'.

23 Killigrew's actors were more experienced from the outset, but Davenant's were more disciplined; Pepys was emphatic in his praise of the Duke's Company's Thomas Betterton, describing him as 'the best actor in the world' (4 November 1661). As early as 4 July 1661 Pepys reported that the King's Theatre at Vere Street had been virtually empty since the opening of Davenant's *The Siege of Rhodes* at 'the opera', or Lincoln's Inn

of the Duke's Company), to make head against their success was forced to add spectacle and music to action, and to introduce a new species of plays since called dramatic operas; of which kind were *The Tempest, Psyche, Circe,* and others, all set off with the most expensive decorations of scenes and habits, with the best voices and dancers.[24]

This sensual supply of sight and sound coming in to the assistance of the weaker party, it was no wonder they should grow too hard for sense and simple nature when it is considered how many more people there are that can see and hear, than think and judge. So wanton a change of the public taste, therefore, began to fall as heavy upon the King's Company as their greater excellence in action had, before, fallen upon their competitors; of which encroachment upon wit several good prologues in those days frequently complained.[25]

But alas! What can truth avail when its dependence is much more upon the ignorant than the sensible auditor? A poor satisfaction, that the due praise given to it must at last sink into the cold comfort of *laudatur & alget*.[26] Unprofitable praise can hardly give it a *soupe maigre*.[27] Taste and fashion, with us, have always had wings and fly from one public spectacle to another so wantonly that I have been informed by those who remember it that a famous puppet show in Salisbury Change (then standing where Cecil Street now is) so far distressed these two celebrated companies that

---

Fields. *The Siege of Rhodes* featured some of the 'spectacle and music' that characterized the shows mentioned by Cibber in the subsequent passage, and Killigrew sought to follow suit in his fit-out of the Theatre Royal on Bridges Street in 1663 (BL Add.MS 27,962, fols.320–1, *Document Register* no.206; and Pepys, 12 February 1667) and in plans to hire 'two Italians and Mrs Yates, who ... is come to sing the Italian manner as well as ever he heard any' (Pepys, 9 September 1667).

24 It was in fact Killigrew who first mounted a production of Thomas Heywood's *Psyche* with 'a well-arranged ballet, regulated by the sound of various instruments' and praised by the King for its 'novelty and ingenuity' (*The Travels of Cosmo III*, 24 May 1669, cited in LS1 162); Thomas Shadwell's *Psyche* was staged by the Duke's Company in February 1675, seven years after Davenant's death in 1668. Davenant's adaptation (with Dryden) of *The Tempest* opened in 1667; for an account of its music, see Pepys, 7 November 1667. *Circe*, by Davenant's son, Charles, was performed by the Duke's Company in 1677, with music by John Banister (LS1 256).

25 The foremost example is Dryden's 'Prologue Spoken at the Opening of the New House', 26 March 1674, written to mark the opening of the Theatre Royal Drury Lane. Dryden took aim at the Duke's Company's lavish Dorset Garden Theatre, opened three years before; he accused audiences there of preferring the draughtsman's 'pencil' to the playwright's 'pen' (Dryden, p.313, line 37).

26 i.e. 'honesty is praised but ignored', from Juvenal, Satire 1 line 74.

27 i.e. a soup with simple ingredients and minimal seasoning, comparable to praising what is not valued.

they were reduced to petition the King for relief against it.[28] Nor ought we perhaps to think this strange when, if I mistake not, Terence himself reproaches the Roman auditors of his time with the like fondness for the *funambuli*, the rope dancers.[29] Not to dwell too long therefore upon that part of my history which I have only collected from oral tradition, I shall content myself with telling you that Mohun[30] and Hart now growing old (for, above thirty years before this time, they had severally born the King's commission of Major and Captain in the Civil Wars), and the younger act-ors – as Goodman,[31] Clark,[32] and others – being impatient to get into their parts and growing intractable, the audiences too of both houses then falling off, the patentees of each, by the King's advice (which perhaps amounted to a command), united their interests and both companies into one, exclusive

28 Puppet shows were a source of contention throughout the period Cibber discusses. Here, he may be referring to a petition by residents of Lincoln's Inn Fields thought to date from January 1664, appealing against Thomas Newton's 'puppet plays, dancing on the ropes, mountebanks, and other like uses, whereby multitudes of loose and disorderly people are daily drawn together' (SP 29/91, no.94; *Document Register* no.264); Newton's licence expired on 19 April 1664 (LC 5/185, fol.148; *Document Register* no.280). In January 1672 the puppeteer Anthony Devoto complained of 'several proceedings against him in the Crown Office' (SP 44/37, p.16; *Document Register* no.663). Bridges Street and Cecil Street are close by on opposite sides of The Strand, so it is possible that Cibber has in mind an action of the King's Company against Devoto.

29 In his prologue to the Second Production of *Hecyra* (*The Mother-in-Law*), Terence complained that the play 'could neither be seen nor heard through the stupid whim of the public whose interest was taken up by a tight-rope walker' (*Plays*, ed. Radice, p.292).

30 Michael Mohun (c. 1616–84) was one of the early leading actors of the King's Company. His last known performance was in 1682 as Mardonius in Beaumont and Fletcher's *A King and No King* (LS1 314). In December 1667 he fell out so badly with Charles Hart that the Theatre Royal had to be closed (Pepys, 7 December 1667).

31 Cardell Goodman (c. 1649–99), dismissed as Charles II's page, joined the King's Company in 1673. His last known performance was as Alexander in Lee's *The Rival Queens* for the United Company in October 1686; it had been one of Hart's signature roles in the King's Company. In 1678 he left London to act in Edinburgh along with Thomas Clark (see n.32, below), but returned the following season. He left the United Company in 1688 and supported the Jacobite cause. For his acting and turbulent life, see below, pp.257–8.

32 Thomas Clark was sworn in as a member of the King's Company for the 1673–4 season. His first recorded role was Drusillus in Lee's *The Tragedy of Nero* (May 1674, LS1 216); his last, Gayland in Settle's *The Heir of Morocco* (March 1682, LS1 307). Although he is listed by LS1 313 as a member of the United Company for 1682–3, there is no record of him performing for them; he may have been a casualty of Betterton's rationalization of staff following the union (see Milhous, *Management*, p.41).

of all others, in the year 1684.[33] This union was, however, so much in favour of the Duke's Company that Hart left the stage upon it, and Mohun survived not long after.[34]

One only theatre[35] being now in possession of the whole town, the united patentees imposed their own terms upon the actors; for the profits of acting were then divided into twenty shares, ten of which went to the proprietors, and the other moiety to the principal actors in such sub-divisions as their different merit might pretend to.[36] These shares of the patentees were promiscuously sold out to money making persons called adventurers,[37] who, though utterly ignorant of theatrical affairs, were still admitted to a proportionate vote in the management of them; all particular encouragements to actors were by them, of consequence, looked upon as so many sums deducted from their private dividends. While, therefore, the theatrical hive had so many drones in it, the labouring actors sure were

33 The correct date is 1682, with the articles of union signed in May that year (BL Add. MS 20,726, fols.10–13; *Document Register* no. 1151). Events leading up to the union were not quite as Cibber describes them. The King's Company as a whole was in disarray; in March 1682 'there happened a difference between the senior and young men … which grew to such a height that they all drew their swords which occasioned the wounding of several' (MS letter in *Document Register*, no.1147). However, audiences for the Duke's Company were better, which put them in a strong position when it came to negotiating the merger. There is no evidence that the King promoted the move; rather, Charles Hart and Edward Kynaston came to a secret agreement with Betterton, Smith, and Charles Davenant, promising to withdraw their labour from the King's Company and hand over properties and scripts (see Gildon, *The Life of Mr Thomas Betterton*, pp.8–9).

34 Cibber implies that Hart was unhappy with the deal; in fact, Hart had used the negotiations to secure a pension. Mohun was cut out and had to petition the King to be allowed the same terms (LC 5/191, fol.102; *Document Register* no.1169); an order of 23 November 1682 ruled in his favour (LC 5/191, fol.103; *Document Register* no.1170).

35 i.e. company; the United Company continued to use both the Drury Lane and Dorset Garden Theatres.

36 Cibber's account broadly captures the 1682 Articles of Union, except that Charles Killigrew, manager of the King's Company and Master of the Revels since 1677, was allowed three of the twenty shares (BL Add.MS 20,726, fols.10–13; *Document Register* no.1151).

37 A reference to the sale of shares in the United Company to business people rather than actors; here, for example, Alexander Davenant agreeing to sell out to Thomas Skipwith on 12 September 1687 (BL Add.Charter 9299; *Document Register* no.1309). Cibber does not mention (or did not know) that 'adventurers' had had a stake in the theatre for much longer; when Christopher Rich acquired his first share on 22 March 1688, it was one of the original Duke's Company shares, as granted to Sir William Russell by Sir William Davenant, who had died in 1668 (BL Add.Charter 9301; *Document Register*, no.1320).

under the highest discouragement, if not a direct state of oppression.[38] Their hardship will at least appear in a much stronger light when compared to our later situation, who with scarce half their merit succeeded to be sharers under a patent upon five times easier conditions. For as they had but half the profits divided among ten or more of them, we had three fourths of the whole profits divided only among three of us. And as they might be said to have ten taskmasters over them, we never had but one assistant manager (not an actor) joined with us; who, by the Crown's indulgence, was sometimes too of our own choosing.[39] Under this heavy establishment, then, groaned this United Company when I was first admitted into the lowest rank of it.[40] How they came to be relieved by King William's licence in 1695, how they were again dispersed early in Queen Anne's reign and from what accidents fortune took better care of us, their unequal successors, will be told in its place.[41] But, to prepare you for the opening so large a scene of their history, methinks I ought (in justice to their memory too) to give you such particular characters of their theatrical merit as in my plain judgment they seemed to deserve. Presuming, then, that this attempt may not be disagreeable to the curious or the true lovers of the theatre, take it without farther preface.

In the year 1690, when I first came into this company, the principal actors then at the head of it were,

38 In the November 1694 'Petition of the Players' (LC 7/3, fols.2–4; *Document Register* no.1483), Betterton and others submitted nine principal grievances against Rich's management, including the cancellation or alteration of retirement and performance benefits, misappropriation of fines, engrossing of profits, pressure to reduce salaries, and sidelining senior actors to make room for 'ignorant insufficient fellows'. The petition is reproduced in full as Appendix A of Milhous, *Management*, pp.225–9. Cibber worked closely with Rich following the breakaway of Betterton's company in 1695, signing a playwriting contract with him on 29 October 1696 (LC 7/3, fols.76–7; *Document Register* no.1540) and declining to join his fellow actors in a petition against him in April 1700 (LC 7/3, fols.173–4; *Document Register* no.1628). Koon, p.43, describes Cibber as 'Rich's right-hand man' at Drury Lane; neither Rich nor his heirs are explicitly named in the *Apology*.

39 A reference to the actor-manager 'triumvirate' of Cibber, Robert Wilks, and Barton Booth (the latter replacing Thomas Doggett, who in turn replaced Richard Estcourt) at Drury Lane; Owen Swiney, William Collier, and Sir Richard Steele played at various times the non-actor 'assistant manager' (see, for example, licence of 18 October 1714 in *Document Register* no.2435). See also below, p.126 n.1.

40 Cibber's earliest recorded role in the United Company's 1690–1 season was as a servant to Sir Gentle Golding in Thomas Southerne's *Sir Anthony Love*, which LS1 388 dates as late September 1690. He had approximately twenty lines to learn across two brief scenes in Act III.

41 For an account and notes, see below, pp.133–4 ('relieved') and pp.211–12 ('dispersed').

Of men: Of women:

Mr Betterton   Mrs Betterton

Mr Mountfort   Mrs Barry

Mr Kynaston   Mrs Leigh

Mr Sandford   Mrs Butler

Mr Nokes   Mrs Mountfort and

Mr Underhill and   Mrs Bracegirdle.[42]

Mr Leigh.[43]

These actors whom I have selected from their contemporaries were all original masters in their different style: not mere auricular imitators of one another, which commonly is the highest merit of the middle rank, but self-judges of Nature, from whose various lights they only took their true

---

42 Mary **Betterton**, née Saunderson (1637–1712) married Betterton in 1662 or 1663; a
   founding member of the Duke's Company, she played Lady Macbeth and Florinda
   in Behn's *The Rover*, and ran the Company's actors' nursery as her roles thinned.
   Elizabeth **Barry** (1658–1713) joined the Duke's Company in 1673 and was renowned
   for tragic roles including all the heroines of Thomas Otway, who became obsessed
   with her. Elinor **Leigh** (née Dixon?) joined the Duke's Company in 1669 and acted in
   companies led by Betterton until 1707, but with an extended break between 1685 and
   1688. Charlotte **Butler**, who also sang and danced, joined the Duke's Company in 1673;
   her last recorded role for the United Company was La Pupsey in Thomas Durfey's
   The Marriage-Hater Matched (January 1692). Susanna **Mountfort** (c. 1667–1703, née
   Percival) joined the King's Company in its final season (1681–2) and acted for the
   United Company, but was not part of Betterton's 1695 breakaway; after Mountfort's
   murder, she married the actor Jack Verbruggen in 1694. For **Bracegirdle**, see above, p.62
   n.55.
43 For Thomas Betterton and William Mountfort, see above, p.62 n.55. Edward
   Kynaston (c. 1640–1706) was still performing women's roles in the early Restoration
   period; a longstanding middle-rank performer in the King's Company, he joined the
   United Company in 1682 but broke away with Betterton in 1695. Samuel **Sandford**
   was a member of the Duke's Company from 1661, renowned for playing villains
   including Iago, Richard III, and even Hecate in Davenant's version of *Macbeth*; he is
   last heard of in a list of Betterton's 'sworn comedians' that may date from July 1700
   (LC 3/4, pp.32–3; *Document Register* no.1647). James **Nokes** (c. 1642–96) was a comic
   actor who had also played older women's roles, including the Nurse in *Romeo and
   Juliet*. A founding actor-shareholder of the Duke's Company, his last known role for
   the United Company was as Puny in Cowley's *The Cutter of Coleman of Street*, which
   LS1 399 calculates was revived in the 1691–2 season; on his death, *The Protestant
   Mercury* (7–9 September 1696) reported that he had 'left a considerable estate, though
   he has not frequented the playhouse constantly for some years' (LS1 468). Cave
   Underhill (1634–1710?) was also a founding actor-shareholder of the Duke's Company
   who followed Betterton into the United Company and then broke away in 1695; he
   was a specialist in (literally) heavyweight comic roles. Anthony **Leigh** (d. 1692) joined
   the Duke's Company in 1671 and then the United Company; a key comic actor, his
   death from illness in December 1692 came days after Mountfort's murder (Luttrell,
   II.647).

instruction.[44] If, in the following account of them, I may be obliged to hint at the faults of others, I never mean such observations should extend to those who are now in possession of the stage; for as I design not my memoirs shall come down to their time, I would not lie under the imputation of speaking in their disfavour to the public, whose approbation they must depend upon for support.[45] But to my purpose.

Betterton was an actor as Shakespeare was an author: both without competitors, formed for the mutual assistance and illustration of each other's genius! How Shakespeare wrote, all men who have a taste for Nature may read and know[46] – but with what higher rapture would he still be read, could they conceive how Betterton played him! Then might they know, the one was born alone to speak what the other only knew to write! Pity it is that the momentary beauties flowing from an harmonious elocution cannot, like those of poetry, be their own record! That the animated graces of the player can live no longer than the instant breath and motion that presents them; or, at best, can but faintly glimmer through the memory or imperfect attestation of a few surviving spectators. Could *how* Betterton spoke be as easily known as *what* he spoke, then might you see the muse of Shakespeare in her triumph, with all her beauties in their best array, rising into real life and charming her beholders. But alas, since all this is so far out of the reach of description, how shall I show you Betterton? Should I therefore tell you that all the Othellos, Hamlets, Hotspurs, Macbeths, and Brutuses whom you may have seen since his time have fallen far short of him,[47] this still would give you no idea of his particular excellence. Let us

44 A judgment complicated by other evidence. Downes (p.52) wrote that Davenant 'taught Mr Betterton in every particle' of the role of Hamlet, having seen a production by the King's Men, while Davies (III.271–2) reported that Betterton had asked for 'Hart's key' in delivering a line from Lee's *The Rival Queens*. As usual, Cibber insists that the best actors had their own ideas about how to play particular roles; see below, pp.201 and 312.

45 Lowe notes: 'The only one of Cibber's contemporaries of any note who was alive when the *Apology* was published, was Benjamin Johnson. This admirable comedian died in August, 1742, in his seventy-seventh year, having played as late as the end of May of that year.'

46 The status of Shakespeare as 'the poet of Nature' as opposed to classical correctness had been commonplace since Ben Jonson's tribute in the First Folio of 1623: 'Nature herself was proud of his designs.'

47 Records of Betterton's performances of these roles are as follows: Othello, from 1691; Hamlet, 1661–1709; Hotspur, no other record exists; Macbeth, from 1664; Brutus, from 1684. Cibber refers to his early visits to the theatre above, p.47: on that basis Betterton would have been about 52 when Cibber first saw him in the roles cited. More importantly, he acted with him: as Iago to Betterton's Othello (see above, p.41 n.51) and Osric to his Hamlet; *1 Henry IV*, *Julius Caesar*, and *Macbeth* were all performed during the period when Cibber and Betterton were in the same company, although the casts are not recorded.

see then what a particular comparison may do – whether that may yet draw
him nearer to you.

You have seen a Hamlet, perhaps, who on the first appearance of his
father's spirit has thrown himself into all the straining vociferation requisite to express rage and fury, and the house has thundered with applause,
though the misguided actor was all the while (as Shakespeare terms it)
tearing a passion into rags.[48] I am the more bold to offer you this particular instance because the late Mr Addison, while I sat by him to see
this scene acted, made the same observation, asking me with some surprise if I thought Hamlet should be in so violent a passion with the Ghost,
which though it might have astonished, it had not provoked him. For you
may observe that in this beautiful speech the passion never rises beyond an
almost breathless astonishment, or an impatience limited by filial reverence,
to enquire into the suspected wrongs that may have raised him from his
peaceful tomb! And a desire to know what a spirit so seemingly distressed
might wish or enjoin a sorrowful son to execute towards his future quiet in
the grave! This was the light into which Betterton threw this scene, which
he opened with a pause of mute amazement! Then, rising slowly to a solemn, trembling voice, he made the Ghost equally terrible to the spectator as
to himself![49] And in the descriptive part of the natural emotions which the
ghastly vision gave him, the boldness of his expostulation was still governed
by decency: manly but not braving, his voice never rising into that seeming
outrage or wild defiance of what he naturally revered. But alas! To preserve
this medium between mouthing and meaning too little, to keep the attention more pleasingly awake by a tempered spirit than by mere vehemence
of voice, is of all the masterstrokes of an actor the most difficult to reach.
In this, none yet have equalled Betterton. But I am unwilling to show his
superiority only by recounting the errors of those who now cannot answer
to them; let their farther failings therefore be forgotten! Or rather, shall I
in some measure excuse them? For I am not yet sure that they might not
be as much owing to the false judgment of the spectator as the actor. While
the million are so apt to be transported when the drum of their ear is so

48 *An Apology for the Life of Mr T...C...* (1740), the satire written in response to Cibber's
   Apology, identifies this actor as Robert Wilks. Davies, III.32, reports a protest by Barton
   Booth, who played the Ghost: 'last night', he is said to have told Wilks, 'you wanted to
   play at fisty-cuffs with me: you bullied that which you ought to have revered.' However,
   comments elsewhere in the *Apology* suggest George Powell (c. 1668–1714) may also be a
   candidate. For Powell's career, see below, p.113 n.83. For Shakespeare, *Hamlet*, III.ii.7: 'tear
   a passion to tatters, to very rags'.
49 Davies, III.32, reports Barton Booth as saying that 'When I acted the Ghost with
   Betterton, instead of my awing him, he terrified me. But divinity hung round that man!'

roundly rattled – while they take the life of elocution to lie in the strength of the lungs – it is no wonder the actor whose end is applause should be also tempted at this easy rate to excite it. Shall I go a little farther, and allow that this extreme is more pardonable than its opposite error? I mean that dangerous affectation of the monotone, or solemn sameness of pronunciation, which to my ear is insupportable; for of all faults that so frequently pass upon the vulgar, that of flatness will have the fewest admirers. That this is an error of ancient standing seems evident by what Hamlet says in his instructions to the players, *viz.*:

> Be not too tame, neither, *etc.*[50]

The actor, doubtless, is as strongly tied down to the rules of Horace as the writer:

> *Si vis me flere, dolendum est*
> *Primum ipsi tibi* – [51]

He that feels not himself the passion he would raise will talk to a sleeping audience. But this never was the fault of Betterton, and it has often amazed me to see those who soon came after him throw out, in some parts of a character, a just and graceful spirit which Betterton himself could not but have applauded; and yet, in the equally shining passages of the same character, have heavily dragged the sentiment along like a dead weight, with a long-toned voice and absent eye, as if they had fairly forgot what they were about.[52] If you have never made this observation, I am contented you should not know where to apply it.

A farther excellence in Betterton was that he could vary his spirit to the different characters he acted. Those wild impatient starts, that fierce and flashing fire which he threw into Hotspur never came from the unruffled temper of his Brutus (for I have more than once seen a Brutus as warm as Hotspur); when the Betterton Brutus was provoked in his dispute with Cassius, his spirit flew only to his eye. His steady look alone supplied that terror which he disdained an intemperance in his voice should rise to. Thus, with a settled dignity of contempt, like an unheeding rock, he repelled upon

---

50 *Hamlet*, III.ii.12.

51 Horace, *The Art of Poetry*, lines 102–3: 'If you want me to cry, mourn first yourself; *then* your misfortunes will hurt me.' The dictum was widely quoted in the eighteenth century, not least by Cibber's prized acquaintance, Lord Chesterfield; see *Lord Chesterfield: Letters*, p.263.

52 A reference to Cibber's fellow actor-manager, Barton Booth; cf. below, p.90. *The Laureate* found this passage 'not quite so tender a one as it ought to have been on a deceased brother' (pp.30–1).

himself the foam of Cassius. Perhaps the very words of Shakespeare will better let you into my meaning:

> Must I give way and room to your rash choler?
> Shall I be frighted when a madman stares?[53]

And a little after,

> There is no terror, Cassius, in your looks! *etc.*[54]

Not but in some part of this scene where he reproaches Cassius, his temper is not under this suppression, but opens into that warmth which becomes a man of virtue; yet this is that hasty spark of anger which Brutus himself endeavours to excuse.[55]

But with whatever strength of Nature we see the poet show at once the philosopher and the hero, yet the image of the actor's excellence will be still imperfect to you unless language could put colours in our words to paint the voice with.

Et, si vis similem pingere, pinge sonum[56] is enjoining an impossibility. The most that a Van Dyck can arrive at is to make his portraits of great persons seem to think;[57] a Shakespeare goes farther yet and tells you what his pictures thought; a Betterton steps beyond 'em both and calls them from the grave to breathe and be themselves again, in feature, speech and motion. When the skilful actor shows you all these powers at once united and gratifies at once your eye, your ear, your understanding, to conceive the pleasure rising from such harmony you must have been present at it! 'Tis not to be told you!

There cannot be a stronger proof of the charms of harmonious elocution than the many (even unnatural) scenes and flights of the false sublime it has lifted into applause. In what raptures have I seen an audience at the furious fustian and turgid rants in Nat Lee's *Alexander the Great*![58] For though I can allow this play a few great beauties, yet it is not without its extravagant blemishes. Every play of the same author has more or less of

---

53 *Julius Caesar*, IV.iii.39–40.
54 *Julius Caesar*, IV.iii.66: 'There is no terror, Cassius, in your threats.'
55 'Hasty spark' is from *Julius Caesar*, IV.iii.111.
56 i.e. 'if you would paint my likeness, paint sound'; from Decimus Magnus Ausonius (d. 395), Epigram 11 in *Ausonius: Epigrams*, edited and translated by N. M. Kay (London: Bloomsbury, 2001).
57 Anthony Van Dyck (1599–1641), Flemish painter of Charles I and others of his Court.
58 *The Rival Queens; or, The Death of Alexander the Great* by Nathaniel Lee (c. 1652–93) opened in March 1677 and remained in repertory throughout the first half of the eighteenth century. Charles Hart created the role of Alexander; Cardell Goodman and then William Mountfort took it over, then Betterton.

them. Let me give you a sample from this. Alexander, in a full crowd of courtiers, without being occasionally called or provoked to it, falls into this rhapsody of vainglory:

> Can none remember? Yes, I know all must!

And therefore they shall know it again.

> When glory, like the dazzling eagle, stood
> Perched on my beaver, in the granic flood,
> When Fortune's self my standard trembling bore,
> And the pale Fates stood frighted on the shore,
> When the immortals on the billows rode,
> And I myself appeared the leading god.[59]

When these flowing numbers came from the mouth of a Betterton, the multitude no more desired sense to them than our musical connoisseurs think it essential in the celebrate[d] airs of an Italian opera. Does not this prove that there is very near as much enchantment in the well-governed voice of an actor as in the sweet pipe of an eunuch?[60] If I tell you there was no one tragedy for many years more in favour with the town than *Alexander*, to what must we impute this its command of public admiration?[61] Not to its intrinsic merit, surely, if it swarms with passages like this I have shown you! If this passage has merit, let us see what figure it would make upon canvas – what sort of picture would rise from it. If Le Brun, who was famous

---

59 From Act II of Lee, *The Rival Queens* (London: James Magnes and Richard Bentley, 1677), p.18 ; 'beaver' refers to the face-guard on a helmet.

60 Two celebrated castrati were rivals on the London stage: Carlo Broschi, known as Farinelli (1705–82), male soprano in the opera company led by Nicola Porpora at the King's Theatre, Lincoln's Inn Fields, 1733–6 (the so-called Opera of the Nobility); and Francesco Bernardi, known as Sinesino (1686–1758), who sang for Handel at the Royal Academy of Music. By the time Cibber began to write the *Apology*, Handel had turned his attention away from Italian opera and towards English-language oratorios. Cibber's views on Italian opera are close to those expressed by Addison in *The Spectator* no.18 (21 March 1711): 'If the Italians have a genius for music above the English, the English have a genius for other performances of a much higher nature.'

61 Judging by performance records in *The London Stage*, and excluding Shakespearean tragedies, Cibber is accurate. John Banks's *The Unhappy Favourite* (1681) had more performances than *The Rival Queens* in the first four decades of the eighteenth century, but Lee's play helped generate a fervid atmosphere of female celebrity, on which see Felicity Nussbaum, *Rival Queens: Actresses, Performance, and the Eighteenth-Century British Theater* (Philadelphia: Philadelphia University Press, 2010). Cibber's parody, *The Rival Queans*, was probably staged in 1699 and eventually published in Dublin in 1729; in 1710 he had appeared in it as a mock-Alexander (see Cheryl Wanko, 'Colley Cibber's *The Rival Queans*: A New Consideration', *Restoration and Eighteenth-Century Theatre Research*, 2nd series, vol. 3, no.2 (1988), 38–52.

for painting the battles of this hero, had seen this lofty description, what one image could he have possibly taken from it?[62] In what colours would he have shown us 'glory perched upon a beaver'? How would he have drawn fortune 'trembling'? Or, indeed, what use could he have made of 'pale Fates', or 'immortals riding upon billows', with this blustering god of his own making at the 'head' of them?[63] Where, then, must have lain the charm that once made the public so partial to this tragedy? Why plainly, in the grace and harmony of the actor's utterance. For the actor himself is not accountable for the false poetry of his author – *that*, the hearer is to judge of. If it passes upon him, the actor can have no quarrel to it, who (if the periods given him are round, smooth, spirited, and high-sounding) even in a false passion must throw out the same fire and grace as may be required in one justly rising from Nature, where those his excellencies will then be only more pleasing in proportion to the taste of his hearer. And I am of opinion that to the extraordinary success of this very play we may impute the corruption of so many actors and tragic writers as were immediately misled by it. The unskilful actor, who imagined all the merit of delivering those blazing rants lay only in the strength and strained exertion of the voice, began to tear his lungs upon every false or slight occasion to arrive at the same applause. And it is from hence I date our having seen the same reason prevalent for above fifty years. Thus equally misguided too, many a barren-brained author has streamed into a frothy, flowing style, pompously rolling into sounding periods, signifying – roundly nothing;[64] of which number, in some of my former labours, I am something more than suspicious that I may myself have made one.[65] But to keep a little closer to Betterton.

62 Charles Le Brun (1619–90), responsible for the decoration of Versailles and Vaux-le-Vicomte, created a series of paintings from 1662 onwards depicting the life and battles of Alexander the Great, increasingly comparing him to Louis XIV, who duly described Le Brun as the greatest French artist of all time.
63 This passage is the subject of a dispute between previous editors. Bellchambers's note reads,

> The criticisms of Cibber upon a literary subject are hardly worth the trouble of confuting, and yet it may be mentioned that Bishop Warburton adduced these lines as containing not only the most sublime, but the most judicious imagery that poetry can conceive. If Le Brun, or any other artist, could not succeed in portraying the terrors of fortune, it conveys, perhaps, the highest possible compliment to the powers of Lee, to admit that he has mastered a difficulty beyond the most daring aspirations of an accomplished painter.

To which Lowe responds, 'With all respect to Warburton and Bellchambers, I cannot help remarking that this last sentence seems to me perilously like nonsense.'
64 Quoting *Macbeth*, V.v.28.
65 Cibber had made a number of attempts at tragedy, of which only *Ximena* enjoyed a good run: *Xerxes* (1699), *Perolla and Izadora* (1705, publ. 1706), *Ximena, or the Heroick Daughter* (1712, publ. 1719), and *Caesar in Egypt* (1724).

When this favourite play I am speaking of, from its being too frequently acted was worn out and came to be deserted by the town, upon the sudden death of Mountfort (who had played Alexander with success for several years) the part was given to Betterton; which, under this great disadvantage of the satiety it had given, he immediately revived with so new a lustre that for three days together it filled the house.[66] And had his then declining strength been equal to the fatigue the action gave him, it probably might have doubled its success – an uncommon instance of the power and intrinsic merit of an actor. This I mention, not only to prove what irresistible pleasure may arise from a judicious elocution with scarce sense to assist it, but to show you too that though Betterton never wanted fire and force when his character demanded it, yet where it was not demanded, he never prostituted his power to the low ambition of a false applause. And farther, that when from a too advanced age he resigned that toilsome part of Alexander, the play for many years after never was able to impose upon the public;[67] and I look upon his so particularly supporting the false fire and extravagancies of that character to be a more surprising proof of his skill than his being eminent in those of Shakespeare; because there, Truth and Nature coming to his assistance, he had not the same difficulties to combat, and consequently we must be less amazed at his success where we are more able to account for it.

Notwithstanding the extraordinary power he showed in blowing Alexander once more into a blaze of admiration, Betterton had so just a sense of what was true or false applause that I have heard him say he never thought any kind of it equal to an attentive silence: that there were many ways of deceiving an audience into a loud one, but to keep them hushed and quiet was an applause which only truth and merit could arrive at – of which art there never was an equal master to himself. From these various excellencies, he had so full a possession of the esteem and regard of his auditors, that upon his entrance into every scene he seemed to seize upon the eyes and

66 A 1694 reprint of *The Rival Queens* suggests a possible revival in that year, but there is no other evidence of a three-day run, unless Cibber misremembered dates and is referring to a later revival witnessed by Peter the Great during his visit to London in February 1698 (see LS1 492); for Betterton learning the role of Alexander, see above, p.76 n.44.
67 Robert Wilks played the part for Rich's company at Drury Lane in 1704 (LS2a 170), while Jack Verbruggen took over from Betterton at the Queen's Theatre, Haymarket, in 1706 (LS2a 331). From 1704 the play was often accompanied by 'new entertainments of vocal and instrumental music' as well as dancing (LS2a 170). According to Aston, George Powell also played Alexander, but 'maintained not the dignity of a king but out-heroded Herod, and in his poisoned mad scene out-raved all probability; while Betterton kept his passion under and showed it most' (II.301).

ears of the giddy and inadvertent! To have talked, or looked another way, would then have been thought insensibility or ignorance.[68] In all his soliloquies of moment, the strong intelligence of his attitude and aspect drew you into such an impatient gaze and eager expectation that you almost imbibed the sentiment with your eye before the ear could reach it.

As Betterton is the centre to which all my observations upon action tend, you will give me leave, under his character, to enlarge upon that head. In the just delivery of poetical numbers, particularly where the sentiments are pathetic, it is scarce credible upon how minute an article of sound depends their greatest beauty or inaffection. The voice of a singer is not more strictly tied to time and tune than that of an actor in theatrical elocution.[69] The least syllable too long, or too slightly dwelt upon in a period, depreciates it to nothing; which very syllable if rightly touched shall, like the heightening stroke of light from a master's pencil, give life and spirit to the whole. I never heard a line in tragedy come from Betterton wherein my judgment, my ear, and my imagination were not fully satisfied; which, since his time, I cannot equally say of any one actor whatsoever – not but it is possible to be much his inferior with great excellencies, which I shall observe in another place. Had it been practicable to have tied down the clattering hands of all the ill judges who were commonly the majority of an audience, to what amazing perfection might the English Theatre have arrived with so just an actor as Betterton at the head of it![70] If what was truth only could have been applauded, how many noisy actors had shook their plumes

---

68 Aston, II.300, writes that Betterton 'enforced universal attention even from the fops and orange-girls'.

69 Cibber's views on what today might be called 'verse speaking' deserve examination. In the earlier passage on Hamlet and the Ghost, he had described a naturalistic engagement enhanced by musical shaping, while, in what may be Betterton's own preface to *The Fairy Queen* (1692), it is argued that 'he must be a very ignorant player who knows not there is a musical cadence in speaking; and that a man may as well speak out of tune as sing out of tune', sentiments endorsed by the sections of Gildon's *Life of Mr Thomas Betterton* which purport to record the actor's views on his craft. Decrying the habits of the so-called oratorical school, Aaron Hill lamented the pursuit of sound for its own sake (see *The Prompter*, nos.64 and 66, 20 and 27 June 1735, and his dedication of *The Fatal Vision* (1716), where he writes of the 'affected, vicious, and unnatural tone of voice, so common on the stage'). Aston, however, points to the less metrical style of Elizabeth Barry and suggests it was typical of her contemporaries: she 'had a manner of drawing out her words, which became her … Neither she, nor any of the actors of those times had any tone [i.e. intoned delivery] in their speaking, (too much, lately, in use)' (II.303).

70 *An Apology for the Life of Mr T…C…* argues there was no reason for Betterton's supremacy other than nostalgia: 'they who remember Betterton shake their heads at Booth; they that are in full memory of Booth, with pitiful scorn see some modern performers' (p.42).

with shame who, from the injudicious approbation of the multitude, have bawled and strutted in the place of merit?[71] If therefore the bare speaking voice has such allurements in it, how much less ought we to wonder (however we may lament) that the sweeter notes of vocal music should so have captivated even the politer world into an apostasy from sense to an idolatry of sound?[72] Let us enquire from whence this enchantment rises. I am afraid it may be too naturally accounted for: for when we complain that the finest music, purchased at such vast expense, is so often thrown away upon the most miserable poetry, we seem not to consider that when the movement of the air and tone of the voice are exquisitely harmonious, though we regard not one word of what we hear, yet the power of the melody is so busy in the heart that we naturally annex ideas to it of our own creation and, in some sort, become ourselves the poet to the composer; and what poet is so dull as not to be charmed with the child of his own fancy? So that there is even a kind of language in agreeable sounds which, like the aspect of beauty without words, speaks and plays with the imagination. While this taste therefore is so naturally prevalent, I doubt to propose remedies for it were but giving laws to the winds or advice to inamoratos.[73] And however gravely we may assert that profit ought always to be inseparable from the delight of the theatre (nay, admitting that the pleasure would be heightened by the uniting them), yet, while instruction is so little the concern of the auditor, how can we hope that so choice a commodity will come to a market where there is so seldom a demand for it?

It is not to the actor, therefore, but to the vitiated and low taste of the spectator that the corruptions of the stage (of what kind soever) have been owing. If the public, by whom they must live, had spirit enough to discountenance and declare against all the trash and fopperies they have been so frequently fond of, both the actors and the authors, to the best of their power, must naturally have served their daily table with sound and wholesome diet.[74] But I have not yet done with my article of elocution.

---

71 Actors who played heroes often wore plumed headdresses. In *The Spectator* no.42 (18 April 1711), Addison writes that they were 'so very high, that there is often a greater length from his chin to the top of his head, than to the sole of his foot'.

72 Again, Cibber deploys terms that are laden in a politico-religious sense: the craving for Italian opera is represented as Catholic deviance or 'idolatry'.

73 i.e lovers, unlikely to listen to rational advice.

74 In his *Discourse Upon Comedy* (1702), George Farquhar had argued that the audience, rather than a small group of classically educated connoisseurs, should be the arbiter of taste in the theatre (Farquhar, *Works*, II.380). Cibber deplores the consequences of that argument and instead attempts to reconcile pleasure with instruction, so charting a middle course in his response to the Collier controversy.

As we have sometimes great composers of music who cannot sing, we have as frequently great writers that cannot read; and though, without the nicest ear, no man can be master of poetical numbers, yet the best ear in the world will not always enable him to pronounce them. Of this truth Dryden, our first great master of verse and harmony, was a strong instance.[75] When he brought his play of Amphitryon to the stage, I heard him give it his first reading to the actors; in which, though it is true he delivered the plain sense of every period, yet the whole was in so cold, so flat and unaffecting a manner that I am afraid of not being believed when I affirm it.[76]

On the contrary, Lee (far his inferior in poetry) was so pathetic a reader of his own scenes[77] that I have been informed by an actor who was present, that while Lee was reading to Major Mohun at a rehearsal, Mohun, in the warmth of his admiration, threw down his part and said, 'Unless I were able to play it as well as you read it, to what purpose should I undertake it?'[78] And yet this very author, whose elocution raised such admiration in so capital an actor, when he attempted to be an actor himself soon quitted the stage in an honest despair of ever making any profitable figure there.[79] From all this I would infer that let our conception of what we are to speak be ever so just, and the ear ever so true, yet when we are to deliver it to an audience (I will leave fear out of the question) there must go along with the whole a natural freedom and becoming grace, which is easier to conceive than to describe. For without this inexpressible somewhat, the performance will come out oddly disguised, or somewhere defectively unsurprising to

75 Although earlier poets such as John Denham and John Suckling had been credited with regularizing English metre, the consensus was that Dryden had, as Samuel Johnson put it, found the English language brick and left it marble; Johnson, *Lives*, II.155.

76 It was common practice for playwrights to read their scripts out to the cast; see Stern, pp.169–76. Dryden's *Amphitryon; or, The Two Sosias* opened at Drury Lane in October 1690 (LS1 389), with Betterton as Jupiter and Barry as Alcmena. Cibber is not listed as a performer, but the play would have been read to the actors a matter of weeks or even days after he joined the United Company. According to Boswell, Samuel Johnson consulted Cibber while writing his 'Life of Dryden', but Cibber only 'remembered [Dryden] a decent old man, arbiter of critical disputes at Will's' (Boswell, II.271). In *The Champion*, 29 April 1740, Fielding mischievously accused Cibber of suggesting that Dryden, a great writer, could not read. Cibber's 'period' refers to a sentence.

77 i.e. arousing passion, sadness, or sympathy (*OED* adj.1).

78 Mohun played leading roles in five plays by Lee: Britannicus in *The Tragedy of Nero* (1674, publ. 1675); Hannibal in *Sophonisba* (1675, publ. 1676); Augustus in *Gloriana* (1676); Clytus in *The Rival Queens* (1677); and the title role in *Mithridates* (1678). His temper is evident from a quarrel with Charles Hart (see above, p.72 n.30).

79 Downes, pp.72–3, identifies the role as Duncan in *Macbeth*, for which Lee is credited in the 1673 and 1674 editions of the play. It was an unusual choice for an actor still in his twenties, and, in Downes's words, it 'ruined him for an actor'. Lee is also credited as an actor in Henry Nevil Payne's *The Fatal Jealousie*, performed around August 1672.

the hearer. Of this defect too I will give you yet a stranger instance, which you will allow fear could not be the occasion of. If you remember Estcourt,[80] you must have known that he was long enough upon the stage not to be under the least restraint from fear in his performance. This man was so amazing and extraordinary a mimic that no man or woman, from the coquette to the Privy Counsellor, ever moved or spoke before him but he could carry their voice, look, mien and motion instantly into another company. I have heard him make long harangues and form various arguments, even in the manner of thinking of an eminent pleader at the Bar, with every the least article and singularity of his utterance so perfectly imitated that he was the very *alter ipse*,[81] scarce to be distinguished from his original. Yet more: I have seen, upon the margin of the written part of Falstaff which he acted, his own notes and observations upon almost every speech of it, describing the true spirit of the humour, and with what tone of voice, look and gesture, each of them ought to be delivered.[82] Yet in his execution upon the stage, he seemed to have lost all those just ideas he had formed of it, and almost through the character laboured under a heavy load of flatness.[83] In a word, with all his skill in mimicry and knowledge of what ought to be done, he never upon the stage could bring it truly into practice, but was upon the whole a languid, unaffecting actor.[84] After I have shown you so many necessary qualifications, not one of which can be spared in true theatrical elocution, and have at the same time proved that with the assistance of them all united, the whole may still come forth defective, what talents shall we say will infallibly form an actor? This, I confess, is one of Nature's secrets, too deep for me to dive into; let us content ourselves therefore with affirming that genius, which Nature only gives, only can complete him. This genius then was so strong in Betterton that it shone out in every speech and motion of him. Yet voice and person are such necessary supports to it that, by the multitude, they have been preferred to genius itself, or at least often mistaken for it. Betterton had a voice of that kind which gave more spirit

---

80 Richard Estcourt (1668–1712) began his career in Dublin and joined the company at Drury Lane in 1704, becoming co-manager in 1708. He created the role of Sergeant Kite in Farquhar's *The Recruiting Officer* (1706). Downes, p.107, described him as 'a superlative mimic'.

81 Second self; in the Latin proverb, referring to a good friend.

82 Actors were given individual written parts rather than a whole script; see Stern, pp.148–52.

83 For 'through' read 'throughout'.

84 Cibber's view was not shared by Downes, p.107, who praised Estcourt's 'easy, free, unaffected mode of elocution'. The first date Estcourt is known to have played Falstaff is 25 November 1704 (LS2a 195). Davies, III.312 attributes Cibber's assessment to professional rivalry.

to terror than to the softer passions – of more strength than melody.[85] The rage and jealousy of Othello became him better than the sighs and tenderness of Castalio.[86] For though in Castalio he only excelled others, in Othello he excelled himself; which you will easily believe when you consider that, in spite of his complexion, Othello has more natural beauties than the best actor can find in all the magazine of poetry to animate his power and delight his judgment with.[87]

The person of this excellent actor was suitable to his voice. More manly than sweet, not exceeding the middle stature; inclining to the corpulent; of a serious and penetrating aspect; his limbs nearer the athletic than the delicate proportion: yet, however formed, there arose from the harmony of the whole a commanding mien of majesty which the fairer faced or (as Shakespeare calls 'em) the curlèd darlings of his time ever wanted something to be equal masters of.[88] There was, some years ago, to be had almost in every print shop a *metzotinto* from Kneller, extremely like him.[89]

In all I have said of Betterton, I confine myself to the time of his strength and highest power in action, that you may make allowances from what he was able to execute at fifty, to what you might have seen of him at past seventy. For though to the last he was without his equal, he might not then be equal to his former self; yet so far was he from being ever overtaken that for many years after his decease, I seldom saw any of his parts in Shakespeare supplied by others but it drew from me the lamentation of Ophelia upon Hamlet's being unlike what she had seen him.

---

85 Aston gave a complementary assessment: 'His voice was low and grumbling; yet he could tune it by an artful climax' (II.300).

86 In Thomas Otway's *The Orphan* (1680), Castalio is a twin who falls for the same woman as his brother. A sentimental tragedy, the play features lines that would tax any performer. Asked 'where's they pain?', Castalio replies ''Tis here! 'Tis in my head; 'tis in my heart, / 'Tis everywhere; it rages like a madness' (IV.i.108–9); in J. C. Ghosh, ed., *The Works of Thomas Otway*, 2 vols. (Oxford: Clarendon Press, 1932), II.55.

87 By 'magazine' Cibber means a storehouse or repository (*OED* n.1). His reflections on the relationship between Othello's colour and the quality of his poetry indicate how theatrical black-face performance, in its very exceptionalism, reinforced racial stereotypes of the period.

88 In *Othello*, Brabantio says that Desdemona has declined marriage to 'the wealthy curlèd darlings of our nation' (I.ii.81). By 'fairer faced' Cibber means 'more handsome actors' while continuing the racial reflection on Othello's 'complexion' and 'natural beauties'. Aston's description of Betterton's physique is less charitable: he 'laboured under [an] ill figure, being clumsily made, having a great head, a short thick neck stooped in the shoulders, and had fat short arms' (II.299).

89 A mezzotint is a print made from a copper or steel engraving, in this case, a reproduction of the portrait by Godfrey Kneller, thought to date from 1695, and now in the Garrick Club, London (Figure 5).

Ah, woe is me!
To have seen what I have seen, see what I see![90]

The last part this great master of his profession acted was Melantius in
The Maid's Tragedy, for his own benefit;[91] when, being suddenly seized by
the gout, he submitted by extraordinary applications to have his foot so
far relieved that he might be able to walk on the stage in a slipper, rather
than wholly disappoint his auditors. He was observed that day to have
exerted a more than ordinary spirit, and met with suitable applause; but
the unhappy consequence of tampering with his distemper was that it flew
into his head and killed him in three days, I think in the seventy-fourth
year of his age.[92]

I once thought to have filled up my work with a select dissertation
upon theatrical action;[93] but I find, by the digressions I have been tempted
to make in this account of Betterton, that all I can say upon that head will
naturally fall in (and possibly be less tedious) if dispersed among the various characters of the particular actors I have promised to treat of. I shall,
therefore, make use of those several vehicles which you will find waiting
in the next chapter to carry you through the rest of the journey, at your
leisure.

90 *Hamlet*, III.i.158–9.
91 The performance was on 13 April 1710 at the Queen's Theatre Haymarket (LS2a 561).
    Betterton was 74 and Elizabeth Barry as the heroine, Evadne, was 52. A notice for the
    evening advertised 'Three designs, representing the three principal actions of the play,
    in imitation of so many great pieces of history painting.' Beaumont and Fletcher's *The
    Maid's Tragedy* (1619) had been assigned to the King's Company (Nicoll, *Restoration*,
    p.316), when Michael Mohun played Melantius; Betterton probably took over the role
    when the United Company was formed in 1682.
92 In fact, Betterton died on 28 April, two weeks after the benefit performance. Steele's *The
    Tatler*, no.167, 4 May 1710, dates his funeral as 2 May 1710.
93 Lowe speculates that Cibber may have been prompted by Gildon's *The Life of Mr Thomas
    Betterton*, the majority of which is a treatise on acting that bears a strong resemblance to
    Michel Le Faucheur's *The Art of the Orator* (1657).

CHAPTER 5

The theatrical characters of the principal actors in the year 1690 continued. A few words to critical auditors.

Though, as I have before observed, women were not admitted to the stage till the return of King Charles, yet it could not be so suddenly supplied with them but that there was still a necessity for some time to put the handsomest young men into petticoats, which Kynaston was then said to have worn with success – particularly in the part of Evadne in *The Maid's Tragedy* (which I have heard him speak of),[1] and which calls to my mind a ridiculous distress that arose from these sort of shifts which the stage was then put to.[2] The King coming a little before his usual time to a tragedy, found the actors not ready to begin, when His Majesty (not choosing to have as much patience as his good subjects) sent to them to know the meaning of it; upon which the master of the company came to the box and, rightly judging that the best excuse for their default would be the true one, fairly told His Majesty that the Queen was not shaved yet.[3] The King, whose good humour loved to laugh at a jest as well as to make one, accepted the excuse, which served to divert him till the male Queen could

1 Cibber's 'some time' meant, in reality, four or five months. On 3 January 1661, Pepys saw Fletcher and Massinger's *The Beggar's Bush* (1622) performed by Killigrew's troupe at the Theatre Royal, Vere Street, remarking that it was 'the first time that ever I saw women come upon the stage'. He had seen the play performed by Killigrew's male actors at the former Gibbons's Tennis Court on 20 November 1660; on 18 August he had seen Edward Kynaston in Fletcher's *The Loyal Subject*, describing him as 'the loveliest lady that ever I saw in my life, only her voice not very good'. A prologue dated 8 December 1660 by Thomas Jordan was written 'to introduce the first woman that came to act on the stage', at the Theatre Royal, Vere Street. On 7 January 1661 Pepys saw Jonson's *Epicoene, or The Silent Woman* (1609), with Kynaston in a title role with 'three shapes: first, as a poor woman … then in fine clothes, as a gallant, and in them was clearly the prettiest woman in the whole house, and lastly, as a man; and then likewise did appear the handsomest man in the house'. There is no other record of Kynaston playing Evadne in *The Maid's Tragedy*, but the play was performed by Killigrew's company at least from 17 November 1660. Cibber does not mention that men continued to play some older women's roles into the 1670s (e.g. LS2 48 and 203).

2 Cibber's pun on 'shifts' (both 'woman's undergarment' and 'expediency') is probably deliberate.

3 The play that best fits this description (i.e. a tragedy featuring a queen in the period before actresses began to appear) is not *The Maid's Tragedy* but Beaumont and Fletcher's *A King and No King* (1611), performed by Killigrew's company at Vere Street by 3 December 1660 (see LS1 22). Downes, p.16, gives a cast list for the period 1663 onwards.

be effeminated. In a word, Kynaston at that time was so beautiful a youth that the ladies of quality prided themselves in taking him with them in their coaches to Hyde Park, in his theatrical habit after the play; which in those days they might have sufficient time to do, because plays then were used to begin at four o'clock,[4] the hour that people of the same rank are now going to dinner. Of this truth I had the curiosity to enquire, and had it confirmed from his own mouth in his advanced age. And indeed, to the last of him, his handsomeness was very little abated; even at past sixty his teeth were all sound, white and even as one would wish to see in a reigning toast of twenty.[5] He had something of a formal gravity in his mien, which was attributed to the stately step he had been so early confined to in a female decency. But even that, in characters of superiority, had its proper graces; it misbecame him not in the part of Leon in Fletcher's *Rule a Wife, etc*,[6] which he executed with a determined manliness and honest authority well worth the best actor's imitation. He had a piercing eye and, in characters of heroic life, a quick, imperious vivacity in his tone of voice that painted the tyrant truly terrible. There were two plays of Dryden in which he shone with uncommon lustre. In *Aurenge-Zebe* he played Morat and in *Don Sebastian*, Muley Moloch;[7] in both these parts he had a fierce, lion-like majesty in his port and utterance that gave the spectator a kind of trembling admiration!

Here I cannot help observing upon a modest mistake which I thought the late Mr Booth committed in his acting the part of Morat.[8] There are in this fierce character so many sentiments of avowed barbarity, insolence, and vainglory that they blaze even to a ludicrous lustre, and doubtless the poet

4 In the early part of the Restoration period, probably more like 3pm or 3.30 (LS1 lxix).
5 i.e. a young lady famed for beauty who had her health drunk by admirers. Kynaston was approximately 66 when he died.
6 Fletcher's *Rule a Wife and Have a Wife* (1624) belonged to the King's Company but was assigned to the Duke's for two months only by a grant dated 12 December 1660 (LC 5/137, pp.343–4; *Document Register* no.50). However, Pepys saw a performance by them at Salisbury Court on 1 April 1661 and was unimpressed: 'I never saw [the play] before, but do not like it.' On 2 February 1662 the play was performed by the King's Company; Pepys saw it at Vere Street and found it 'very well done'. In the play, Leon is a jealous, scheming soldier.
7 The first known performance of Dryden's *Aureng-Zebe* was on 17 November 1675, by the King's Company at Drury Lane; Morat is the brother of the eponymous Mughal emperor. The play is in rhyming couplets, and it seems likely that Kynaston 'browned up' for his role. The first known performance of Dryden's *Don Sebastian* was on 4 December 1689, by the United Company at Drury Lane. Kynaston's was another brown-face role, Muley-Moluch, Emperor of Barbary (i.e. Morocco).
8 Barton Booth may have taken over the role in November 1705 (LS2a 253).

intended those to make his spectators laugh while they admired them;[9] but Booth thought it depreciated the dignity of tragedy to raise a smile in any part of it, and therefore covered these kind of sentiments with a scrupulous coldness and unmoved delivery, as if he had feared the audience might take too familiar a notice of them.[10] In Mr Addison's *Cato*, Syphax has some sentiments of near the same nature which I ventured to speak as I imagined Kynaston would have done, had he been then living to have stood in the same character.[11] Mr Addison, who had something of Mr Booth's diffidence at the rehearsal of his play, after it was acted came into my opinion and owned that even tragedy, on such particular occasions, might admit of a 'laugh of approbation'.[12] In Shakespeare instances of them are frequent, as in Macbeth, Hotspur, Richard the Third, and Harry the Eighth; all which characters, though of a tragical cast, have sometimes familiar strokes in them so highly natural to each particular disposition, that it is impossible

9 See, for example, this speech: 'My fancy is too exquisite, / And tortures me with their imagined bliss. / Some earthquake should have risen and rent the ground, / Have swallowed him, and left the longing bride / In agony of unaccomplished love. [*Walks disorderly*]'; Dryden, *Don Sebastian, King of Portugal* (London, Joseph Hindmarsh, 1690), p.44. Cibber may implicitly be claiming that it is not the words but the brown-face performance that audiences found funny.

10 Lowe quotes *The Laureate*: 'I am of opinion Booth was not wrong in this. There are many of the sentiments in this character where Nature and common sense are outraged; and an actor who should give the full comic utterance to them in his delivery would raise what they call a "horse-laugh", and turn it into burlesque' (p.33). For a contrasting view, Lowe then quotes Cibber's son, Theophilus: 'The remark is just — Mr. Booth would sometimes slur over such bold sentiments so flightily delivered by the poet. As he was good-natured — and would "hear each man's censure, yet reserve his judgment," I once took the liberty of observing that he had neglected (as I thought) giving that kind of spirited turn in the afore-mentioned character. He told me I was mistaken; it was not negligence, but design made him so slightly pass them over; for though, added he, in these places one might raise a laugh of approbation in a few, yet there is nothing more unsafe than exciting the laugh of simpletons who never know when or where to stop; and, as the majority are not always the wisest part of an audience, I don't choose to run the hazard'; Theophilus Cibber, from *The Lives and Characters of the Most Eminent actors and actresses of Great Britain and Ireland* (London: R. Griffiths, 1753), p.72.

11 Cibber's reflections on Joseph Addison's *Cato* (1713) are below, pp.237–9. The play opened on 14 April 1713 and played for twenty performances between then and 9 May. Cibber created the role of Syphax, an ageing Numidian general; since Numidia included parts of Algeria and Tunisia, it is likely this was another brown-face role.

12 Lowe cites *The Laureate*: 'I have seen the original Syphax in *Cato* use many ridiculous distortions, crack in his voice, and writhe his muscles and his limbs, which created not a smile of approbation but a loud laugh of contempt and ridicule on the actor … In my opinion, the part of Syphax as it was originally played was the only part in *Cato* not tolerably executed' (pp.33–4).

not to be transported into an honest laughter at them.[13] And these are those happy liberties which, though few authors are qualified to take, yet when justly taken may challenge a place among their greatest beauties. Now, whether Dryden in his Morat, *feliciter audet*[14] – or may be allowed the happiness of having hit this mark – seems not necessary to be determined by the actor, whose business, sure, is to make the best of his author's intention, as in this part Kynaston did, doubtless not without Dryden's approbation. For these reasons, then, I thought my good friend Mr Booth (who certainly had many excellencies) carried his reverence for the buskin too far in not following the bold flights of the author with that wantonness of spirit which the nature of those sentiments demanded. For example, Morat having a criminal passion for Indamora, promises at her request for one day to spare the life of her lover Aurenge-Zebe. But, not choosing to make known the real motive of his mercy when Nourmahal says to him,

'Twill not be safe to let him live an hour,

Morat silences her with this heroical rhodomontade:

I'll do't, to show my arbitrary power.[15]

Risum teneatis?[16] It was impossible not to laugh, and reasonably too, when this line came out of the mouth of Kynaston with the stern and haughty

---

13 While *The Laureate* (p.35) mocked the comedy of Cibber's Richard III as unintentional, Cibber's reflections on the role anticipate Samuel Johnson's *Preface to Shakespeare* (1765): 'Shakespeare's plays are not in the rigorous and critical sense either tragedies or comedies, but compositions of a distinct kind; exhibiting the real state of sublunary nature, which partakes of good and evil, joy and sorrow, mingled with endless variety of proportion and innumerable modes of combination.' Lowe rejects Bellchambers's use of the word 'venom' to describe Cibber's critique of Booth, again citing Theophilus Cibber's *Lives*, p.75:

> Mr Booth [as Henry VIII], though he gave full scope to the humour, never dropped the dignity of the character. You laughed at Henry, but lost not your respect for him. When he appeared most familiar, he was by no means vulgar. The people most about him felt the ease they enjoyed was owing to his condescension. He maintained the monarch ... When angry, his eye spoke majestic terror; the noblest and the bravest of his courtiers were awe-struck. He gave you the full idea of that arbitrary prince who thought himself born to be obeyed; the boldest dared not to dispute his commands. He appeared to claim a right divine to exert the power he imperiously assumed.

Booth probably first played Henry VIII from November 1716 (LS2 422).

14 From Horace, 'Letter to Augustus', line 166: 'The spirit was tragic enough, the innovations daring and felicitous.'

15 Dryden, *Aurenge-Zebe* (London: Henry Herringman, 1676), p.41. A 'rhodomontade' is a bombastic, meaningless utterance.

16 i.e. can you help laughing? From Horace, *Art of Poetry*, line 114.

look that attended it. But above this tyrannical, tumid superiority of character, there is a grave and rational majesty in Shakespeare's Harry the Fourth
which, though not so glaring to the vulgar eye, requires thrice the skill and
grace to become and support. Of this real majesty Kynaston was entirely
master.[17] Here, every sentiment came from him as if it had been his own, as
if he had himself that instant conceived it: as if he had lost the player, and
were the real king he personated! A perfection so rarely found that very
often, in actors of good repute, a certain vacancy of look, inanity of voice,
or superfluous gesture, shall unmask the man to the judicious spectator;
who, from the least of those errors, plainly sees the whole but a lesson given
him to be got by heart from some great author whose sense is deeper than
the repeater's understanding. This true majesty Kynaston had so entire a
command of, that when he whispered the following plain line to Hotspur,

Send us your prisoners, or you'll hear of it,[18]

he conveyed a more terrible menace in it than the loudest intemperance of
voice could swell to. But let the bold imitator beware; for without the look
and just elocution that waited on it, an attempt of the same nature may fall
to nothing.

But the dignity of this character appeared in Kynaston still more
shining in the private scene between the King and Prince, his son.[19] There
you saw majesty in that sort of grief which only majesty could feel! There
the paternal concern for the errors of the son made the monarch more
revered and dreaded: his reproaches so just, yet so unmixed with anger (and
therefore the more piercing), opening as it were the arms of Nature with
a secret wish that filial duty, and penitence awaked, might fall into them
with grace and honour. In this affecting scene, I thought Kynaston showed
his most masterly strokes of Nature: expressing all the various motions of
the heart with the same force, dignity and feeling they are written; adding
to the whole that peculiar and becoming grace which the best writer cannot inspire into any actor that is not born with it. What made the merit
of this actor and that of Betterton more surprising was that though they
both observed the rules of Truth and Nature, they were each as different in
their manner of acting as in their personal form and features. But Kynaston

17 *1 Henry IV* was performed by the King's Company from 1660 and, in Betterton's
   adapted version, by Betterton's Lincoln's Inn Fields company from January 1700; there
   is no record other than Cibber's of Kynaston playing the title role. According to Koon,
   pp.190–1, Cibber played Worcester at least from 1704, and Glendower from 1709.
18 *1 Henry IV*, I.iii.124. The King speaks this line in an aside to Hotspur, having just
   addressed the latter's father, Northumberland.
19 i.e. *1 Henry IV*, III.ii.

stayed too long upon the stage, till his memory and spirit began to fail him. I shall not therefore say anything of his imperfections, which at that time were visibly not his own, but the effects of decaying Nature.[20]

Mountfort, a younger man by twenty years and at this time in his highest reputation, was an actor of a very different style. Of person he was tall, well made, fair, and of an agreeable aspect; his voice clear, full and melodious. In tragedy he was the most affecting lover within my memory. His addresses had a resistless recommendation from the very tone of his voice, which gave his words such softness that, as Dryden says,

> Like flakes of feathered snow,
> They melted as they fell![21]

All this he particularly verified in that scene of Alexander where the hero throws himself at the feet of Statira for pardon of his past infidelities.[22] There we saw the great, the tender, the penitent, the despairing, the transported and the amiable in the highest perfection. In comedy, he gave the truest life to what we call the 'fine gentleman'; his spirit shone the brighter for being polished with decency. In scenes of gaiety, he never broke into the regard that was due to the presence of equal or superior characters, though inferior actors played them; he filled the stage not by elbowing and crossing it before others, or disconcerting their action, but by surpassing them in true, masterly touches of Nature. He never laughed at his own jest, unless the point of his raillery upon another required it. He had a particular talent in giving life to *bon mots* and repartees. The wit of the poet seemed always to come from him *extempore*, and sharpened into more wit from his brillant manner of delivering it; he had himself a good share of it or (what is equal to it) so lively a pleasantness of humour, that when either of these fell into his hands upon the stage, he wantoned with them to the highest delight of his auditors. The *agreeable* was so natural to him that even in that dissolute character of the Rover he seemed to wash off the guilt from vice, and gave it charms and merit.[23] For, though it may be a reproach to the poet to

---

20 Kynaston's last known performance was as the Earl of Warwick in Mary Pix's *Queen Catharine* (1698). He does not appear in the list of actors for Betterton's company in the 1699–1700 season (LS1 514).

21 Dryden, *The Spanish Friar, or the Double Discovery* (London: Richard and Jacob Tonson, 1680), p.15. The lines are spoken by Leonora, Queen of Aragon, in admiration of Torrismond. Neither Mountfort nor Cibber appears to have had a role.

22 i.e. in Act III of Lee's *The Rival Queens* (1677 edition), pp.33–4.

23 The rakish Willmore in Aphra Behn's *The Rover* (1677) was a role Mountfort had taken over from William Smith by 4 November 1690, when there was a court performance (see LS1 391).

draw such characters not only unpunished but rewarded, the actor may still be allowed his due praise in his excellent performance. And this is a distinction which, when this comedy was acted at Whitehall, King William's Queen Mary was pleased to make in favour of Mountfort, notwithstanding her disapprobation of the play.

He had, besides all this, a variety in his genius which few capital actors have shown, or perhaps have thought it any addition to their merit to arrive at. He could entirely change himself, could at once throw off the man of sense for the brisk, vain, rude, and lively coxcomb, the false, flashy pretender to wit, and the dupe of his own sufficiency. Of this he gave a delightful instance in the character of Sparkish in Wycherley's *Country Wife*.[24] In that of Sir Courtly Nice his excellence was still greater.[25] There, his whole man, voice, mien and gesture was no longer Mountfort but another person. There, the insipid, soft civility, the elegant and formal mien, the drawling delicacy of voice, the stately flatness of his address and the empty eminence of his attitudes were so nicely observed and guarded by him that had he not been an entire master of Nature – had he not kept his judgment, as it were, a sentinel upon himself not to admit the least likeness of what he used to be to enter into any part of his performance – he could not possibly have so completely finished it. If, some years after the death of Mountfort, I myself had any success in either of these characters, I must pay the debt I owe to his memory in confessing the advantages I received from the just idea and strong impression he had given me from his acting them. Had he been remembered when I first attempted them, my defects would have been more easily discovered, and consequently my favourable reception in them must have been very much (and justly) abated. If it could be remembered how much he had the advantage of me in voice and person, I could not here be suspected of an affected modesty, or of over-valuing his excellence. For he sung a clear countertenor, and had a melodious, warbling throat which could not but set off the last scene of *Sir Courtly* with an uncommon happiness;[26] which I, alas, could only struggle through with the faint excuses

24 There is no other record of Mountfort playing this role, but LS1 322 and 368 note the likelihood of revivals of *The Country Wife* in 1683 and 1688, when he was in the United Company. Cibber played Sparkish from 1709 (LS2a 480).

25 John Crowne's comedy, *Sir Courtly Nice* (1685), was scheduled for performance when Charles II died. The first recorded performance was on 9 May 1685 at Drury Lane, with Mountfort in the title role. Cibber played Sir Courtly from 1703 (LS2a 126).

26 In Act V of Crowne's play, Sir Courtly states he has 'above forty [songs] here in a sweet bag', and proceeds to sing one of them: 'As I gazed unaware / On a face so fair'; Crowne, *Sir Courtly Nice; or, It Cannot Be* (London: Richard Bentley and Joseph Hindmarsh, 1685), p.51.

and real confidence of a fine singer, under the imperfection of a feigned and screaming treble (which at best could only show you what I would have done had Nature been more favourable to me).

This excellent actor was cut off by a tragical death in the 33rd year of his age, generally lamented by his friends and all lovers of the theatre. The particular accidents that attended his fall are to be found at large in the trial of the Lord Mohun, printed among those of the state, in folio.[27]

Sandford might properly be termed the Spagnolet of the theatre,[28] an excellent actor in disagreeable characters. For as the chief pieces of that famous painter were of human nature in pain and agony, so Sandford (upon the stage) was generally as flagitious as a Creon, a Maligni, an Iago, or a Machiavel could make him.[29] The painter, 'tis true, from the fire of his genius might think the quiet objects of Nature too tame for his pencil, and therefore chose to indulge it in its full power upon those of violence and horror. But poor Sandford was not the stage villain by choice but from necessity. For, having a low and crooked person, such bodily defects were too strong to be admitted into great or amiable characters; so that whenever, in any new or revived play, there was a hateful or mischievous person, Sandford was sure to have no competitor for it. Nor indeed (as we are not to suppose a villain or traitor can be shown for our imitation, or not for our abhorrence) can it be doubted, but the less comely the actor's person, the fitter he may be to perform them. The spectator too, by not being misled by a tempting form, may be less inclined to excuse the wicked or immoral views or sentiments of them. And, though the hard fate of an Oedipus might naturally give the humanity of an audience thrice the pleasure that could arise from the wilful wickedness of the best acted Creon, yet who could say that Sandford, in such a part, was not master of as true and just action as the best tragedian could be, whose happier person had recom-

---

27 Charles, Lord Mohun was tried for Mountfort's murder but acquitted on 6 February 1693; he joined the House of Lords in 1701, with a second acquittal for murder to his name. Cibber's 'folio' is *The Trial of Charles Lord Mohun before the House of Peers in Parliament, for the Murder of William Mountfort* (London, 1693).

28 José de Ribera (1591–1652), known as El Spagnoletto, was a Spanish painter celebrated for his realistic and often menacing *chiaroscuro* portraits.

29 Sandford played Creon in Dryden and Lee's *Oedipus* from September 1678 (LS1 273). He was still playing the role in October 1692, after Cibber had joined the United Company; in that month he was reported to have accidentally stabbed George Powell during the performance (Luttrell, II.593). He created the role of Maligni in Thomas Porter's *The Villain* in October 1662 (LS1 56–7); the play was probably revived by the United Company in 1693, when Sandford was already playing Iago (LS1 428). William Smith created the role of Machiavel for the Duke's Company in Lee's *Caesar Borgia* in May 1679 (LS1 276–7); there is no other record of Sandford playing it. 'Flagitious' means deeply criminal, wicked (*OED* 1a).

mended him to the virtuous hero, or any other more pleasing favourite of the imagination? In this disadvantageous light, then, stood Sandford as an actor: admired by the judicious, while the crowd only praised him by their prejudice.[30] And so unusual had it been to see Sandford an innocent man in a play, that whenever he was so, the spectators would hardly give him credit in so gross an improbability. Let me give you an odd instance of it, which I heard Mountfort say was a real fact. A new play (the name of it I have forgot) was brought upon the stage, wherein Sandford happened to perform the part of an honest statesman. The pit, after they had sat three or four acts in a quiet expectation that the well-dissembled honesty of Sandford (for such of course they concluded it) would soon be discovered – or at least, from its security, involve the actors in the play in some surprising distress or confusion which might raise and animate the scenes to come – when, at last, finding no such matter, but that the catastrophe had taken quite another turn, and that Sandford was really an honest man to the end of the play, they fairly damned it, as if the author had imposed upon them the most frontless or incredible absurdity.[31]

It is not improbable but that from Sandford's so masterly personating characters of guilt, the inferior actors might think his success chiefly owing to the defects of his person; and from thence might take occasion, whenever they appeared as bravos or murderers, to make themselves as frightful and as inhuman figures as possible. In King Charles's time, this low skill was carried to such an extravagance that the King himself, who was black-browed and of a swarthy complexion, passed a pleasant remark upon his observing the grim looks of the murderers in *Macbeth*; when, turning to his people in the box about him, 'Pray, what is the meaning', said he, 'that we never see a rogue in a play but Godsfish, they always clap him on a black periwig, when it is well known one of the greatest rogues in England always wears a fair

30 Lowe cites *The Tatler*, no. 134, 16 February 1710: 'I must own there is something very horrid in the public executions of an English tragedy. Stabbing and poisoning, which are performed behind the scenes in other nations, must be done openly among us to gratify the audience. When poor Sandford was upon the stage, I have seen him groaning upon a wheel, stuck with daggers, impaled alive, calling his executioners, with a dying voice, cruel dogs and villains! And all this to please his judicious spectators, who were wonderfully delighted with seeing a man in torment so well acted.'

31 Lowe speculates that the play, which has not been identified beyond doubt, may never have been printed because of its failure in the theatre, but Behn's *The Widow Ranter* (1689, publ. 1690) is a plausible candidate; Sandford played the honourable Daring, while Mountfort (from whom Cibber heard the story) was in the company, but not in this play. As Bellchambers notes, Sandford also played a number of comic roles, so the audience was used to seeing him as something other than a scheming villain. Evans notes a resemblance between this passage and Steele's account of Cibber in dignified roles, in *The Theatre*, no. 7 (23 January 1720).

one?' Now whether or no Dr Oates at that time wore his own hair, I cannot be positive;[32] or, if His Majesty pointed at some greater man then out of power, I leave those to guess at him who may yet remember the changing complexion of his ministers.[33] This story I had from Betterton, who was a man of veracity; and I confess I should have thought the King's observation a very just one, though he himself had been fair as Adonis. Nor can I, in this question, help voting with the Court; for were it not too gross a weakness to employ in wicked purposes men whose very suspected looks might be enough to betray them? Or are we to suppose it unnatural that a murder should be thoroughly committed out of an old red coat and a black periwig?

For my own part, I profess myself to have been an admirer of Sandford, and have often lamented that his masterly performance could not be rewarded with that applause which I saw much inferior actors met with, merely because they stood in more laudable characters. For though it may be a merit in an audience to applaud sentiments of virtue and honour, yet there seems to be an equal justice that no distinction should be made as to the excellence of an actor, whether in a good or evil character, since neither the vice nor the virtue of it is his own, but given him by the poet. Therefore, why is not the actor who shines in either equally commendable? No sir; this may be reason, but that is not always a rule with us. The spectator will tell you that when virtue is applauded he gives part of it to himself, because his applause, at the same time, lets others about him see that he himself admires it. But when a wicked action is going forward – when an Iago is meditating revenge and mischief – though Art and Nature may be equally strong in the actor, the spectator is shy of his applause lest he should in some sort be looked upon as an aider or an abettor of the wickedness in view; and therefore rather chooses to rob the actor of the praise he may merit, than give it him in a character which he would have you see his silence modestly discourages. From the same fond principle, many actors have made it a point to be seen in parts sometimes (even flatly written) only because they stood in the favourable light of honour and virtue.[34]

32 Titus Oates (1649–1705) achieved celebrity by claiming there was a Catholic plot to assassinate Charles II, who regarded him with suspicion. Oates claimed to have a doctorate from the University of Salamanca. See J. P. Kenyon, *The Popish Plot* (Harmondsworth: Penguin, 1979).

33 Perhaps a reference to Oates's sponsor, Anthony Ashley Cooper, Earl of Shaftesbury (1621–83), leader of the Whig opposition to the succession of James II, but formerly Chancellor of the Exchequer, 1661–72. He was imprisoned during 1677–8 and arrested for high treason in 1681; *Macbeth* was in the Duke's Company repertory throughout that period.

34 Plausibly a reflection of actors' anxieties in the wake of Jeremy Collier's *Short View*, which had resulted in some performers being prosecuted for indecency; see below, pp.182–3.

I have formerly known an actress carry this theatrical prudery to such a height that she was very near keeping herself chaste by it. Her fondness for virtue on the stage, she began to think, might persuade the world that it had made an impression on her private life; and the appearances of it actually went so far that, in an epilogue to an obscure play (the profits of which were given to her, and wherein she acted a part of impregnable chastity) she bespoke the favour of the ladies by a protestation that, in honour of their goodness and virtue, she would dedicate her unblemished life to their example. Part of this vestal vow, I remember, was contained in the following verse:

Study to live the character I play.[35]

But alas, how weak are the strongest works of art when Nature besieges it! For though this good creature so far held out her distaste to mankind that they could never reduce her to marry any one of 'em, yet we must own she grew (like Caesar) greater by her fall! Her first heroic motive to a surrender was to save the life of a lover who, in his despair, had vowed to destroy himself; with which act of mercy (in a jealous dispute once, in my hearing) she was provoked to reproach him in these very words: 'Villain! Did not I save your life?' The generous lover, in return to that first tender obligation, gave life to her first-born, and that pious offspring has since raised to her memory several innocent grandchildren.[36]

So that, as we see, it is not the hood that makes the monk, nor the veil the vestal;[37] I am apt to think that if the personal morals of an actor were to be weighed by his appearance on the stage, the advantage and favour (if any were due to either side) might rather incline to the traitor than the hero: to the Sempronius than the Cato, or to the Syphax

---

35 From the anonymous *The Triumphs of Virtue* (London: Abel Roper and Richard Wellington, 1697), p.4, acted by Rich's Company at Drury Lane in February 1697. Cibber played Antonio and the actress was Jane Rogers, believed to have been the lover of the married Robert Wilks and to have borne their child. According to *Comparison*, the piece was 'no ill play, yet 'twas damned' (p.18).

36 According to Chetwood, Rogers and Wilks's girl would marry the actor Christopher Bullock. Wilks's private life was the subject of controversy after his death in 1732 (see above, pp.12–13, ns.3–4); Cibber hints that he is on the side of O'Bryan's scandal-mongering *Authentic Memoirs*, whose account was hotly disputed by Curll's *The Life of That Eminent Comedian Robert Wilks Esq*. See also Introduction, p.xli.

37 Cibber translates the Latin proverb, *cucullus non facit monachum*, quoted by Shakespeare in *Twelfth Night*, I.v.41; see also Tilley, H586.

than the Juba,[38] because no man can naturally desire to cover his honesty with a wicked appearance (but an ill man might possibly incline to cover his guilt with the appearance of virtue, which was the case of the frail fair one now mentioned). But be this question decided as it may, Sandford always appeared to me the honester man in proportion to the spirit wherewith he exposed the wicked and immoral characters he acted. For had his heart been unsound or tainted with the least guilt of them, his conscience must in spite of him, in any too near a resemblance of himself, have been a check upon the vivacity of his action. Sandford, therefore, might be said to have contributed his equal share with the foremost actors to the true and laudable use of the stage. And in this light too, of being so frequently the object of common distaste, we may honestly style him a theatrical martyr to poetical justice. For in making vice odious or virtue amiable, where does the merit differ? To hate the one or love the other are but leading steps to the same temple of fame, though at different portals.

This actor, in his manner of speaking, varied very much from those I have already mentioned. His voice had an acute and piercing tone which struck every syllable of his words distinctly upon the ear. He had likewise a peculiar skill in his look, of marking out to an audience whatever he judged worth their more than ordinary notice. When he delivered a command, he would sometimes give it more force by seeming to slight the ornament of harmony. In Dryden's plays of rhyme, he as little as possible glutted the ear with the jingle of it, rather choosing (when the sense would permit him) to lose it than to value it.[39]

Had Sandford lived in Shakespeare's time, I am confident his judgment must have chose him above all other actors to have played his Richard the Third. I leave his person out of the question, which, though naturally made for it, yet that would have been the least part of his recommendation. Sandford had stronger claims to it: he had sometimes an uncouth stateliness in his motion, a harsh and sullen pride of speech, a meditating brow, a stern aspect occasionally changing into an almost ludicrous triumph over all goodness and virtue; from thence, falling into the most assuasive

---

38 Imagining what it would be like if actors' private morality was more important to an audience than the morality of the characters they played, Cibber reflects on his fellow managers: the virtuous John Mills had played Sempronius in Addison's *Cato* and Barton Booth the title role; Robert Wilks had played Juba, the Prince of Numidia, to Cibber's own Syphax.

39 However, none of the five plays by Dryden in which Sandford is known for certain to have appeared (*Don Sebastian, Oedipus, The Duke of Guise, Cleomenes, Amphitryon*) is written in rhyme.

gentleness, and soothing candour of a designing heart. These, I say, must have preferred him to it; these would have been colours so essentially shining in that character, that it will be no dispraise to that great author to say Sandford must have shown as many masterly strokes in it (had he ever acted it) as are visible in the writing it.[40]

When I first brought *Richard the Third* (with such alterations as I thought not improper) to the stage, Sandford was engaged in the company then acting under King William's licence in Lincoln's Inn Fields;[41] otherwise you cannot but suppose my interest must have offered him that part.[42] What encouraged me, therefore, to attempt it myself at the Theatre Royal was that I imagined I knew how Sandford would have spoken every line of it. If, therefore, in any part of it I succeeded, let the merit be given to him; and how far I succeeded in that light, those only can be judges who remember him. In order, therefore, to give you a nearer idea of Sandford, you must give me leave (compelled as I am to be vain) to tell you that the late Sir John Vanbrugh, who was an admirer of Sandford, after he had seen me act it assured me that he never knew any one actor so particularly profit by another as I had done by Sandford in Richard the Third. 'You have', said he, 'his very look, gesture, gait, speech, and every motion of him, and have borrowed them all only to serve you in that character'. If, therefore, Sir John Vanbrugh's observation was just, they who remember me in Richard the

40 Unless the reference is to Cibber's own version of *Richard III*, he appears to drift from arguing that Sandford could have played Richard III for Shakespeare (but clearly did not) to implying that he did not play the role at all; however, according to LS1 400, Sandford was probably playing the role for the United Company when Cibber joined in 1690, having first played it during the Duke's Company's 1671–2 season (LS1 188). Annotating this passage, Lowe writes that 'It is a very common mistake to state that Cibber founded his playing of Richard III on that of Sandford. He merely says that he tried to act the part as he knew Sandford *would* have played it.'

41 i.e. as a member of Betterton's breakaway company, under licence as of 25 March 1695 (LC 7/3, fol.7; *Document Register* no.1499).

42 Cibber's adaptation, *The Tragical History of King Richard III*, opened at Drury Lane early in 1700; it opens up the 'back story' of the play by imagining Henry VI's death in the Tower at Richard's hands – a scene censored for the first performance (see below, pp.184–5) – along with other significant alterations, criticism of which did not prevent the adaptation from holding the stage for nearly 200 years. Lowe quotes Genest (II.195–219): 'One has no wish to disturb Cibber's own tragedies in their tranquil graves, but while our indignation continues to be excited by the frequent representation of Richard the 3rd in so disgraceful a state, there can be no peace between the friends of unsophisticated Shakespeare and Cibber.' In the 1699–1700 season, Sandford continued to play for Betterton's company at Lincoln's Inn Fields. Cibber would need to have shown great generosity to offer the part to Sandford, since the author himself had not yet played a title role.

Third may have a nearer conception of Sandford than from all the critical account I can give of him.[43]

I come now to those other men actors who at this time were equally famous in the lower life of comedy. But I find myself more at a loss to give you them in their true and proper light than those I have already set before you. Why the tragedian warms us into joy or admiration, or sets our eyes on flow with pity, we can easily explain to another's apprehension. But it may sometimes puzzle the gravest spectator to account for that familiar violence of laughter that shall seize him at some particular strokes of a true comedian. How, then, shall I describe what a better judge might not be able to express? The rules to please the fancy cannot so easily be laid down as those that ought to govern the judgment. The decency, too, that must be observed in tragedy reduces, by the manner of speaking it, one actor to be much more like another than they can or need be supposed to be in comedy. There, the laws of action give them such free and almost unlimited liberties to play and wanton with Nature, that the voice, look, and gesture of a comedian may be as various as the manners and faces of the whole mankind are different from one another. These are the difficulties I lie under. Where I want words, therefore, to describe what I may commend, I can only hope you will give credit to my opinion. And this credit I shall most stand in need of when I tell you that Nokes was an actor of a quite different genius from any I have ever read, heard of, or seen, since or before his time;[44] and yet his general excellence may be comprehended in one article, *viz.*, a plain and palpable simplicity of nature which was so utterly his own that he was often as unaccountably diverting in his common speech as on the stage. I saw him once giving an account of some table talk[45] to another actor behind

---

43 Lowe quotes the blistering assessment of Cibber's performance in *The Laureate,*which accuses him of confusing Richard III with Lord Foppington:

> This same mender of Shakespeare chose the principal part, *viz.* the King, for himself; and accordingly being invested with the purple robe, he screamed through four acts without dignity or decency. The audience, ill pleased with the farce, accompanied him with a smile of contempt, but in the fifth act he degenerated all at once into Sir Novelty; and when, in the heat of the battle at Bosworth Field, the king is dismounted, our comic-tragedian came on the stage, really breathless and in a seeming panic, screaming out this line thus: 'A harse, a harse, my kingdom for a harse'. This highly delighted some, and disgusted others of his auditors (p.35).

44 James Nokes (see above, p.75 n.43) was a leading comic actor in the Duke's Company from its formation, noted for playing dimwits. His last known performance was as Puny in the United Company's revival of Cowley's *The Cutter of Coleman Street* during the 1691–2 season, at least a year after Cibber had joined (see LS1 399). He is not to be confused (as Bellchambers does) with his brother, Robert Nokes, also a founding member of the Duke's Company, believed to have died in the Great Plague of 1665.

the scenes; which a man of quality accidentally listening to, was so deceived by his manner that he asked him if that was a new play he was rehearsing. It seems almost amazing that this simplicity, so easy to Nokes, should never be caught by any one of his successors. Leigh and Underhill have been well copied, though not equalled, by others.[46] But not all the mimical skill of Estcourt (famed as he was for it), though he had often seen Nokes, could scarce give us an idea of him.[47] After this, perhaps it will be saying less of him when I own that though I have still the sound of every line he spoke in my ear (which used not to be thought a bad one), yet I have often tried by myself – but in vain – to reach the least distant likeness of the *vis comica* of Nokes.[48] Though this may seem little to his praise, it may be negatively saying a good deal to it, because I have never seen any one actor except himself whom I could not, at least, so far imitate as to give you a more than tolerable notion of his manner. But Nokes was so singular a species, and was so formed by Nature for the stage that I question if (beyond the trouble of getting words by heart) it ever cost him an hour's labour to arrive at that high reputation he had, and deserved.

The characters he particularly shone in were Sir Martin Mar-all, Gomez in *The Spanish Friar*, Sir Nicolas Cully in *Love in a Tub*, Barnaby Brittle in *The Wanton Wife*, Sir Davy Dunce in *The Soldier's Fortune*, Sosia in *Amphitryon*,[49] etc etc etc. To tell you how he acted them is beyond the reach of criticism; but to tell you what effect his action had upon the spectator is not impossible. This, then, is all you will expect from me, and from hence I must leave you to guess at him.

45 i.e. informal conversation, often by celebrities.
46 For Anthony Leigh and Cave Underhill, see above, p.75 n.43.
47 For Richard Estcourt, see above, p.86 n.80.
48 i.e. comic force. *OED* 2f records other uses from the eighteenth to the twentieth centuries.
49 James Nokes played Sir Martin in Dryden's *Sir Martin Mar-all; or, the Feigned Innocence*, which opened at Lincoln's Inn Fields in August 1667; it may have been revived in 1691 and again in 1697, after Nokes's death (LS1 111, 388, 466). Dryden's *The Spanish Friar* opened at Dorset Garden in November 1680; Cibber may have seen Nokes as Gomez in a revival in 1689 or 1693 (LS1 375, 427). Etherege's *The Comical Revenge; or, Love in a Tub* opened in March 1664; Cibber could have seen Nokes's Sir Nicholas in a 1690 revival (LS1 76, 374). Thomas Betterton's *The Amorous Widow; or, The Wanton Wife* is believed to have opened in November 1670 at Lincoln's Inn Fields; there are no known performances during Cibber's stint with the United Company, although the play was revived after Nokes's death (LS1 176, 521). Thomas Otway's *The Soldier's Fortune* opened at Dorset Garden in June 1680 and may have been revived in the 1694–5 season, just before Nokes's death (LS1 287, 441). Dryden's *Amphitryon; or, The Two Sosias* opened at Drury Lane in October 1690, just after the start of Cibber's first season with the United Company (see above, p.85 n.76).

He scarce ever made his first entrance in a play but he was received with an involuntary applause – not of hands only, for those may be (and have often been) partially prostituted and bespoken – but by a general laughter which the very sight of him provoked and Nature could not resist. Yet the louder the laugh, the graver was his look upon it; and sure, the ridiculous solemnity of his features were enough to have set a whole bench of bishops into a titter, could he have been honoured (may it be no offence to suppose it) with such grave and right reverend auditors. In the ludicrous distresses which, by the laws of comedy, folly is often involved in, he sunk into such a mixture of piteous pusillanimity and a consternation so ruefully ridiculous and inconsolable, that when he had shook you to a fatigue of laughter it became a moot point whether you ought not to have pitied him. When he debated any matter by himself he would shut up his mouth with a dumb, studious pout, and roll his full eye into such a vacant amazement, such a palpable ignorance of what to think of it, that his silent perplexity (which would sometimes hold him several minutes) gave your imagination as full content as the most absurd thing he could say upon it. In the character of Sir Martin Mar-all (who is always committing blunders to the prejudice of his own interest), when he had brought himself to a dilemma in his affairs by vainly proceeding upon his own head and was afterwards afraid to look his governing servant and counsellor in the face,[50] what a copious and dis-tressful harangue have I seen him make with his looks (while the house has been in one continued roar for several minutes) before he could prevail with his courage to speak a word to him! Then might you have, at once, read in his face vexation (that his own measures, which he had piqued himself upon, had failed), envy (of his servant's superior wit), distress (to retrieve the occasion he had lost), shame (to confess his folly), and yet a sullen desire to be reconciled, and better advised for the future! What tragedy ever showed us such a tumult of passions, rising at once in one bosom! Or what buskined hero, standing under the load of them, could have more effectu-ally moved his spectators by the most pathetic speech than poor miserable Nokes did by this silent eloquence and piteous plight of his features?

His person was of the middle size; his voice clear and audible; his nat-ural countenance grave and sober; but the moment he spoke, the settled seriousness of his features was utterly discharged, and a dry, drolling or laughing levity took such full possession of him that I can only refer the idea of him to your imagination. In some of his low characters that became

50 During the play Sir Martin has a series of disagreements with his servant, Warner. Cibber's description best fits their rapid-fire dialogue that concludes Act II; Dryden, *Sir Martin Mar-all* (London: Henry Herringman, 1668), pp.21–2.

it, he had a shuffling shamble in his gait, with so contented an ignorance in his aspect and an awkward absurdity in his gesture that had you not known him, you could not have believed that naturally he could have had a grain of common sense. In a word, I am tempted to sum up the character of Nokes as a comedian in a parody of what Shakespeare's Mark Antony says of Brutus as a hero:

> His life was laughter, and the ludicrous
> So mixed in him that Nature might stand up
> And say to all the world, 'This was an actor'.[51]

Leigh was of the mercurial kind, and though not so strict an observer of Nature, yet never so wanton in his performance as to be wholly out of her sight. In humour, he loved to take a full career,[52] but was careful enough to stop short when just upon the precipice. He had great variety in his manner, and was famous in very different characters. In the canting, grave hypocrisy of the Spanish Friar,[53] he stretched the veil of piety so thinly over him that in every look, word and motion you saw a palpable, wicked slyness shine through it. Here, he kept his vivacity demurely confined till the pretended duty of his function demanded it; and then he exerted it with a choleric, sacerdotal insolence. But the Friar is a character of such glaring vice, and so strongly drawn, that a very indifferent actor cannot but hit upon the broad jests that are remarkable in every scene of it. Though I have never yet seen anyone that has filled them with half the truth and spirit of Leigh,[54] Leigh raised the character as much above the poet's imagination as the character has sometimes raised other actors above themselves! And I do not doubt but the poet's knowledge of Leigh's genius helped him to many a pleasant stroke of Nature which, without that knowledge, never might have entered into his conception. Leigh was so eminent in this character that the late Earl of Dorset (who was equally an admirer and a judge of theatrical merit) had a whole length of him, in the Friar's habit, drawn by Kneller.[55] The

---

51 *Julius Caesar*, V.v.78–80: 'His life was gentle, and the elements / So mixed in him that Nature might stand up / And say to all the world, "This was a man!"' Cibber is typically (and perhaps unjustifiably) proud of his Shakespearean adaptation.

52 i.e. he went full tilt at a role, playing with great energy.

53 Leigh created the role of Father Dominic in Dryden's *The Spanish Friar*, which opened at Dorset Garden in November 1680. There may have been a revival in Cibber's first season with the United Company (see LS1 375) before Leigh's death in 1692.

54 The role was subsequently played by Richard Estcourt and William Bullock.

55 Charles Sackville, 6th Earl of Dorset (1643–1706), patron of the arts and Lord Chamberlain from 1689 to 1697, was instrumental in securing the freedom of Betterton's company in 1695. Godfrey Kneller's portrait in oils of Leigh as Father Dominic was completed in 1689 and hangs in the National Portrait Gallery, London.

whole portrait is highly painted, and extremely like him. But no wonder Leigh arrived to such fame in what was so completely written for him, when characters that would made the reader yawn in the closet have, by the strength of his action, been lifted into the loudest laughter on the stage. Of this kind was the Scrivener's great boobily son in *The Villain*,[56] Ralph (a stupid, staring under-servant) in *Sir Salomon Single*;[57] quite opposite to those were Sir Jolly Jumble in *The Soldier's Fortune*[58] and his Old Belfond in *The Squire of Alsatia*.[59] In Sir Jolly he was all life and laughing humour; and when Nokes acted with him in the same play, they returned the ball so dexterously upon one another that every scene between them seemed but one continued rest[60] of excellence. But alas, when those actors were gone, that comedy and many others (for the same reason) were rarely known to stand upon their own legs; by seeing no more of Leigh or Nokes in them, the characters were quite sunk and altered.[61] In his Sir William Belfond, Leigh showed a more spirited variety than ever I saw any actor, in any one character, come up to. The poet, 'tis true, had here exactly chalked for him the outlines of Nature; but the high colouring, the strong lights and shades of humour, that enlivened the whole and struck our admiration with surprise and delight, were wholly owing to the actor. The easy reader might, perhaps, have been pleased with the author without discomposing a feature; but the

---

56 In the dramatis personae of Thomas Porter's *The Villain* (1662, publ. 1663), Coligni is described as 'an impertinent young scrivener', and son of Cortaux. The role was created by Joseph Price, praised by Downes as an 'inimitable sprightly actor' (p.54). The play was reprinted in 1694, possibly indicating a revival that year (LS1 428).

57 John Caryll's *Sir Salomon Single* (1670, publ. 1671), adapted from Molière's *L'École des femmes (The School for Wives)* and *L'École des maris (The School for Husbands)*; Ralph is Sir Salomon's hapless servant. The play was reprinted in 1691, indicating a possible revival that year.

58 In Thomas Otway's *The Soldier's Fortune* (1680, publ. 1681), Sir Jolly Jumble is an 'old goat'; the role anticipates the perverted senator, Antonio, in *Venice Preserved* (1682), also played by Leigh. *The Soldier's Fortune* may have been revived in the 1694–5 season (LS1 441).

59 Thomas Shadwell's *The Squire of Alsatia* opened in May 1688; editions of 1692, 1693, and 1699 may point to revivals. In the dramatis personae, Sir William Belfond is described as 'A gentleman of above £3000 per annum, who in his youth had been a spark of the town; but married and retired into the country, where he turned to the other extreme – rigid, morose, most sordidly covetous, clownish, obstinate, positive and forward.'

60 James Nokes played Sir Davy Dunce in *The Soldier's Fortune*. In Act III Sir Davy and Sir Jolly have an extended quickfire exchange which Cibber compares to a rally ('rest') in tennis. Lowe points to a parallel in Cibber's *The Careless Husband*, IV.i: 'No, faith, that's odds at tennis, my lord: not but if your ladyship pleases, I'll endeavour to keep your backhand a little; though upon my soul you may safely set me up at the line: for, knock me down, if ever I saw a rest of wit better played, than that last, in my life.'

61 In the revival on 9 March 1708, Sir Jolly was played by William Bullock and Sir David by Benjamin Johnson (LS2a 421).

spectator must have heartily held his sides, or the actor would have heartily made them ache for it.

Now, though I observed before that Nokes never was tolerably touched by any of his successors, yet in this character, I must own, I have seen Leigh extremely well imitated by my late facetious friend Penketh-man; who, though far short of what was inimitable in the original, yet as to the general resemblance was a very valuable copy of him.[62] And, as I know Penkethman cannot yet be out of your memory, I have chosen to mention him here to give you the nearest idea I can of the excellence of Leigh in that particular light. For Leigh had many masterly variations which the other could not, nor ever pretended to reach: particularly in the dotage and follies of extreme old age, in the characters of Fumble in *The Fond Husband*[63] and the toothless lawyer in the *City Politics*,[64] both which plays lived only by the extraordinary performance of Nokes and Leigh.[65]

There were two other characters of the farcical kind – Geta in *The Prophetess* and Crack in *Sir Courtly Nice* – which, as they are less con-fined to Nature, the imitation of them was less difficult to Penkethman,[66]

62 William Penkethman or Pinkethman (c. 1660–1725) had appeared in many of Cibber's plays, beginning with the role of Snap, Loveless's servant in *Love's Last Shift* (1696). An entrepreneurial performer, he went on to set up a booth at Bartholomew Fair (C7/229/34; *Document Register* no.1987), planned a theatre in Richmond (Report in the *Weekly Journal* of 31 May 1718; Document *Register* no.2883), and formed a company at Greenwich (*The Tatler*, no.4, 16–19 April 1709), amid other problem-ridden projects. His relationship with Cibber may not always have been harmonious: in April 1700, when the Drury Lane actors complained to the Lord Chamberlain about their manager, Christopher Rich (LC 7/3, fols.173–4; *Document Register* no.1628), Penkethman's name was on the petition, but that of Cibber, Rich's right-hand man, was not.

63 In the dramatis personae of Thomas Durfey's *A Fond Husband* (1677), Old Fumble is described as 'a superannuated alderman that dotes on black women: he's very deaf and almost blind; and, seeking to cover his imperfection of not hearing what is said to him, answers quite contrary'.

64 In John Crowne's *City Politics* (1683), Bartoline is 'An old corrupt lawyer'. The play is a Whig satire of the Popish Plot and those who believed in it.

65 *A Fond Husband* was still being performed in 1716, with Knap as Old Fumble (LS2 385); *City Politics* was performed as late as July 1717, with William Bullock as Bartoline (LS2 456). James Nokes had played Peregrine Bubble in *A Fond Husband*; it is not certain which role he took in *City Politics*, but it was probably Paulo Camillo, 'A factious, proud, busy, credulous, foolish, rich citizen, chosen chief magistrate or Lord Podesta of Naples'.

66 John Fletcher and Philip Massinger's *The Prophetess* (1622, publ. 1647) was adapted by Thomas Betterton and performed at Dorset Garden in June 1690 (LS1 382). The play was reprinted from 1716, perhaps indicating revivals during the eighteenth century; Penkethman played Leigh's role of Geta, Dioclesian's servant. Crowne's *Sir Courtly Nice* opened in May 1685 (LS1 336). Crack is a 'young, subtle, intriguing fellow', who pretends to be the fictitious Sir Nicholas Callico, the name given to the role in Downes, p.84.

who to say the truth delighted more in the whimsical than the natural. Therefore, when I say he sometimes resembled Leigh, I reserve this distinction on his master's side: that the pleasant extravagancies of Leigh were all the flowers of his own fancy, while the less fertile brain of my friend was contented to make use of the stock his predecessor had left him. What I have said, therefore, is not to detract from honest Pinky's merit, but to do justice to his predecessor. And though 'tis true we as seldom see a good actor as a great poet arise from the bare imitation of another's genius,[67] yet if this be a general rule, Penkethman was the nearest to an exception from it; for, with those who never knew Leigh, he might very well have passed for a more than common original. Yet again, as my partiality for Penkethman ought not to lead me from truth, I must beg leave (though out of its place) to tell you fairly what was the best of him, that the superiority of Leigh may stand in its due light. Penkethman had certainly, from Nature, a great deal of comic power about him, but his judgment was by no means equal to it, for he would make frequent deviations into the whimsies of a Harlequin.[68] By the way (let me digress a little farther), whatever allowances are made for the licence of that character (I mean of a Harlequin) – whatever pretences may be urged from the practice of the ancient comedy for its being played in a mask resembling no part of the human species – I am apt to think the best excuse a modern actor can plead for his continuing it, is that the low, senseless, and monstrous things he says and does in it, no theatrical assurance could get through with a bare face. Let me give you an instance of even Penkethman's being out of countenance for want of it. When he first played Harlequin in *The Emperor of the Moon*,[69] several gentlemen (who inadvertently judged by the rules of Nature) fancied that a great deal of the drollery and spirit of his grimace was

---

67 As Evans notes, probably a swipe at Pope for his imitations of Horace.
68 Harlequin plays (including dances, burlesque tragedies, histories, and pastorals) were popular on the early eighteenth-century stage (see LS2 cx–cxix), not least in the plays of Cibber's antagonist, Fielding. Penkethman's habit of improvising was notorious; *Comparison*, p.106, claimed he 'spoils many a part with his own stuff'. See below, p.110 n.72.
69 Aphra Behn's *The Emperor of the Moon* opened at Dorset Garden in March 1687, with Thomas Jevon (1652–88) as Harlequin. Penkethman may have assumed the role for a possible revival in 1699 (LS1 514). For the mask-free performance at Drury Lane, see *The Daily Courant*, 18 September 1702: 'At the desire of some persons of quality ... will be presented a comedy called *The Emperor of the Moon*, wherein Mr Penkethman acts the part of Harlequin without a mask, for the entertainment of an African Prince lately arrived here.'

lost by his wearing that useless, unmeaning mask of a black cat, and therefore insisted that the next time of his acting that part he should play without it. Their desire was accordingly complied with – but, alas, in vain. Penkethman could not take to himself the shame of the character without being concealed: he was no more Harlequin; his humour was quite disconcerted! His conscience could not with the same effrontery declare against Nature without the cover of that unchanging face, which he was sure would never blush for it! No! It was quite another case! Without that armour, his courage could not come up to the bold strokes that were necessary to get the better of common sense. Now, if this circumstance will justify the modesty of Penkethman, it cannot but throw a wholesome contempt on the low merit of a Harlequin. But how farther necessary the mask is to that fool's coat, we have lately had a stronger proof: in the favour that the *Harlequin Sauvage* met with at Paris, and the ill fate that followed the same *Sauvage* when he pulled off his mask in London.[70] So that it seems what was wit from a Harlequin was something too extravagant from a human creature. If, therefore, Penkethman, in characters drawn from Nature, might sometimes launch out into a few gamesome liberties which would not have been excused from a more correct comedian, yet in his manner of taking them he always seemed to me (in a kind of consciousness of the hazard he was running) as if he fairly confessed that what he did was only as well as he could do: that he was willing to take his chance for success, but if he did not meet with it, a rebuke should break no squares.[71] He would mend it another time and would take whatever pleased his judges to think of him in good part; and I have often thought that a good deal of the favour he met with was owing to this seeming humble way of waiving all pretences to merit but what the town would please to allow him. What confirms me in this opinion is that when it has been his ill fortune to meet with a *disgraccia,* I have known him say apart to himself, yet loud enough to be heard, 'Odso! I believe I am a little wrong here!' – which

70 As Lowe notes, a reference to James Miller's *Art and Nature,* which opened at Drury Lane on 16 February 1738. Cibber played Julio; LS3 703 records only one performance of a play which, according to Miller's Preface, was 'destroyed with so much art'.
   Cibber also refers to Louis-François De L'Isle de la Drevetière's *Arlequin Sauvage* (Paris, 1731), whose central character Theophilus Cibber introduced into Miller's play. See Figure 6.
71 i.e. rules or standards (*OED* 2a).

6. Harlequin in Paris: Drevetière's *Arlequin Sauvage.*

once was so well received by the audience that they turned their reproof
into applause.[72]

Now, the judgment of Leigh always guarded the happier sallies of his
fancy from the least hazard of disapprobation: he seemed not to court but
to attack your applause, and always came off victorious. Nor did his highest

---

72 Lowe cites Davies, III.89:
> In the play of *The Recruiting Officer,* Wilks was the Captain Plume, and Penketh-
> man one of the recruits. The Captain, when he enlisted him, asked his name: in-
> stead of answering as he ought, Pinkey replied, 'Why! Don't you know my name,
> Bob? I thought every fool had known that!' Wilks, in rage, whispered to him
> the name of the recruit – Thomas Appletree. The other retorted aloud, '*Thomas
> Appletree?* Thomas Devil! My name is Will Pinkethman': and, immediately ad-
> dressing an inhabitant of the upper regions, he said 'Hark you, friend; don't you
> know my name?' 'Yes, Master Pinkey', said a respondent, 'we know it very well'.
> The playhouse was now in an uproar: the audience, at first, enjoyed the petulant
> folly of Penkethman and the distress of Wilks; but, in the progress of the joke,
> it grew tiresome, and Pinkey met with his deserts, a very severe reprimand in a
> hiss; and this mark of displeasure he changed into applause by crying out, with
> a countenance as melancholy as he could make it, in a loud and nasal twang,
> 'Odso! I fear I am wrong'.

assurance amount to any more than that just confidence without which the commendable spirit of every good actor must be abated; and of this spirit, Leigh was a most perfect master. He was much admired by King Charles, who used to distinguish him when spoke of by the title of *his* actor;[73] which, however, makes me imagine that in his exile that prince might have received his first impression of good actors from the French stage,[74] for Leigh had more of that farcical vivacity than Nokes. But Nokes was never languid by his more strict adherence to Nature; and (as far as my judgment is worth taking) if their intrinsic merit could be justly weighed, Nokes must have had the better in the balance. Upon the unfortunate death of Mountfort, Leigh fell ill of a fever and died in a week after him, in December 1692.[75]

Underhill was a correct and natural comedian. His particular excellence was in characters that may be called still life: I mean the stiff, the heavy, and the stupid. To these he gave the exactest and most expressive colours, and in some of them looked as if it were not in the power of human passions to alter a feature of him. In the solemn formality of Obadiah in *The Committee*[76] and in the boobily heaviness of Lolpoop in *The Squire of Alsatia*,[77] he seemed the immoveable log he stood for! A countenance of wood could not be more fixed than his when the blockhead of a character required it. His face was full and long; from his crown to the end of his nose was the shorter half of it, so that the disproportion of his lower features, when soberly composed with an unwandering eye hanging over them, threw him into the most lumpish, moping mortal that ever made beholders merry! Not but at other times he could be wakened into spirit equally ridiculous: in the coarse, rustic humour of Justice Clodpate in *Epsom Wells*[78] he was a

---

73 Charles II may have seen Leigh for the first time as Ralph in *Sir Salomon Single*, which was performed at Court in November 1671 (LC 5/141, p.2, reprinted in Nicoll, *Restoration*, p.309).

74 Charles lived in exile in France between 1646 and 1648.

75 Luttrell, II.647, gives the date as 21 December 1692; Mountfort had been murdered on 9 December (see above, p.63 n.56).

76 Sir Robert Howard's *The Committee*, a satire on the Sequestration Committee set up by Cromwell to redistribute royalist estates, had been first performed by the King's Company in November 1662. Underhill, a Duke's Company actor, presumably created the role of Obadiah, solemn clerk to the eponymous committee. The play was revived by the United Company in December 1685 (LS1 345), then by Rich's company in October 1697 (LS1 487) with another actor, probably Benjamin Johnson, as Obadiah. For Anthony Leigh as Teague in an Oxford performance, see below, pp.298–9

77 In the dramatis personae to Shadwell's *The Squire of Alsatia*, Lolpoop is described as 'A North Country fellow, servant to Belfond Senior, much displeased at his master's proceedings'. A 1692 reprint may indicate a revival that year (LS1 400).

78 Underhill created the role of Justice Clodpate in Shadwell's *Epsom Wells*, first performed at Dorset Garden in December 1672. A 1693 reprint may indicate a revival that year (LS1 412).

delightful brute; and in the blunt vivacity of Sir Sampson in *Love for Love* he showed all that true perverse spirit that is commonly seen in much wit and ill nature.[79] This character is one of those few so well written, with so much wit and humour, that an actor must be the grossest dunce that does not appear with an unusual life in it; but it will still show as great a proportion of skill to come near Underhill in the acting it which (not to undervalue those who soon came after him) I have not yet seen. He was particularly admired, too, for the Gravedigger in *Hamlet*.[80] The author of *The Tatler* recommends him to the favour of the town upon that play's being acted for his benefit; wherein, after his age had some years obliged him to leave the stage, he came on again for that day to perform his old part[81] – but alas, so worn and disabled, as if himself was to have lain in the grave he was digging! When he could no more excite laughter, his infirmities were dismissed with pity. He died soon after, a superannuated pensioner in the list of those who were supported by the joint sharers, under the first patent granted to Sir Richard Steele.[82]

The deep impressions of these excellent actors which I received in my youth, I am afraid may have drawn me into the common foible of us old fellows, which is a fondness and perhaps a tedious partiality for the pleasures we have formerly tasted, and think are now fallen off because we can no longer enjoy them. If therefore I lie under that suspicion, though I have related nothing incredible or out of the reach of a good judge's conception, I must appeal to those few who are about my own age for the truth and likeness of these theatrical portraits.

79 Underhill created the role of Sir Sampson Legend in Congreve's *Love for Love*, the first play to be performed by Betterton's company at the Lincoln's Inn Fields theatre in April 1695 (LS1 445). The reference to 'much wit and ill nature' may be another of Cibber's swipes at Pope.

80 Underhill's first known performance of the role was on 24 August 1661 (LS1 32); revivals continued during the 1690s.

81 *The Tatler*, no.20, 26 May 1709, advertised Underhill's benefit appearance in *Hamlet* as follows: 'Mr Cave Underhill, the famous comedian in the Reigns of K. Charles II, K. James II, K. William and Q. Mary, and her present Majesty Q. Anne, but now not able to perform so often as heretofore in the playhouse, and having had losses to the value of near £2,500, is to have the tragedy of *Hamlet* acted for his benefit on Friday the third of June next, at the Theatre Royal in Drury Lane, in which he is to perform his original part, the Gravemaker. Tickets may be had at the Mitre Tavern in Fleet Street.'

82 In fact, Underhill did not die 'soon after' his benefit performance in *Hamlet*: he played the Gravedigger again on 23 February 1710. He had begun to scale back his performances from the beginning of 1707. On 11 May 1710 *The Daily Courant* announced he would receive a further benefit performance the following day, as Trincalo in the Dryden–Davenant version of *The Tempest*. Steele's patent, allowing him to operate a theatre for the duration of his life plus three years for his grantees, was issued on 19 January 1715 (C66/3501, no.13; *Document Register* no.2498).

There were, at this time, several others in some degree of favour with the public: Powell, Verbruggen, Williams, *etc.*[83] But as I cannot think their best improvements made them in any wise equal to those I have spoke of, I ought not to range them in the same class. Neither were Wilks or Doggett yet come to the stage;[84] nor was Booth initiated till about six years after them, or Mrs Oldfield known till the year 1700.[85] I must therefore reserve the four last for their proper period, and proceed to the actresses that were famous with Betterton at the latter end of the last century.

Mrs Barry was then in possession of almost all the chief parts in tragedy. With what skill she gave life to them, you will judge from the words of Dryden in his Preface to *Cleomenes*, where he says,

Mrs Barry, always excellent, has in this tragedy excelled herself, and gained a reputation beyond any woman I have ever seen on the theatre.[86]

83 By 'at this time' Cibber means the 1690s. George **Powell** (c. 1668–1714) probably joined the United Company in 1686. He stayed with Rich's company after Betterton broke away; significant roles included Buckingham in Cibber's version of *Richard III*. Reporting his death, the *Weekly Packet* stated that 'none came nearer to the perfections of Hart and Betterton' (11–18 December 1714, in *Document Register* no.2479). For Cibber's further accounts of him, see below, pp.171–4. John or Jack **Verbruggen** (d. 1708) joined the United Company in 1687; his first recorded performance was as Termagant in Shadwell's *The Squire of Alsatia* (May 1688). He remained with Rich's company after the 1695 breakaway, appearing in the leading role of Loveless both in Cibber's *Love's Last Shift* and in Vanbrugh's sequel, *The Relapse* (1697). Moving to Betterton's company in 1697, he was the first Mirabell in Congreve's *The Way of the World* (1700). Lowe cites a defence of Verbruggen in *The Laureate*: 'I wonder, considering our author's particularity of memory, that he hardly ever mentions Mr Verbruggen, who was in many characters an excellent actor ... I cannot conceive why Verbruggen is left out of the number of his excellent actors; whether some latent grudge has robbed him of his immortality in this work' (p.58). That is perhaps unfair to Cibber, who valued classical restraint over the more instinctive, impulsive style of both Powell and Verbruggen. Joseph **Williams** joined the Duke's Company in 1670 and played numerous middle-ranking roles. In spite of his long association with the company, he was not invited to join Betterton's breakaway troupe in 1695; see also below, pp.137–8.

84 In fact, Robert Wilks had re-joined Rich's company in 1698 and enjoyed huge success as Sir Harry Wildair in Farquhar's *The Constant Couple* from November 1699 (LS1 517); while Thomas Doggett (c. 1670–1721) had joined the United Company in the same year as Cibber (1690), playing significant character roles, such as Sir Paul Plyant in Congreve's *The Double Dealer* (1693).

85 Barton Booth had acted in Dublin for two years before joining Betterton's company for the 1700–1 season (LS2a 6), while Anne Oldfield's first known role for Rich's company was as Candiope in Dryden's *Secret Love*, believed to have been revived early in 1700 (LS1 515).

86 Dryden's *Cleomenes, The Spartan Hero* opened at Drury Lane in April 1692, following censorship for its perceived criticism of the government. Elizabeth Barry played Cassandra (LS1 407). In the preface, Dryden wrote 'beyond any women whom I have seen'.

I very perfectly remember her acting that part; and, however unnecessary it may seem to give my judgment after Dryden's, I cannot help saying I do not only close with his opinion but will venture to add that (though Dryden has been dead these thirty-eight years)[87] the same compliment, to this hour, may be due to her excellence. And though she was then not a little past her youth, she was not till that time fully arrived to her maturity of power and judgment;[88] from whence, I would observe that the short life of beauty is not long enough to form a complete actress. In men, the delicacy of person is not so absolutely necessary, nor the decline of it so soon taken notice of. The fame Mrs Barry arrived to is a particular proof of the difficulty there is in judging with certainty from their first trials whether young people will ever make any great figure on a theatre. There was, it seems, so little hope of Mrs Barry at her first setting out that she was, at the end of the first year, discharged the company, among others that were thought to be a useless expense to it.[89] I take it for granted that the objection to Mrs Barry at that time must have been a defective ear, or some unskilful dissonance in her manner of pronouncing. But where there is a proper voice and person with the addition of a good understanding, experience tells us that such defect is not always invincible; of which not only Mrs Barry but the late Mrs Oldfield are eminent instances. Mrs Oldfield had been a year in the Theatre Royal before she was observed to give any tolerable hope of her being an actress, so unlike to all manner of propriety was her speaking![90] How unaccountably, then, does a genius for the stage make its way towards perfection! For, notwithstanding these equal disadvantages, both these actresses (though of different excellence) made themselves complete mistresses of their art by the prevalence of their understanding. If this observation may be of any use to the masters of future theatres, I shall not then have made it to no purpose.

Mrs Barry, in characters of greatness, had a presence of elevated dignity: her mien and motion superb and gracefully majestic; her voice full,

---

87 Dryden died in 1700; Cibber began writing the *Apology* in 1737.

88 Barry was 33 or 34 when *Cleomenes* opened.

89 According to Downes, p.74, Barry joined the Duke's Company during the 1673–4 season, but there is no firm record of a performance until her Draxilla in Otway's *Alcibiades* in September 1675. The 1741 *History of the English Stage*, purporting to be Betterton's posthumous work, claims that Rochester coached her for the role of Isabella in Orrery's *Mustapha* in the previous season, following her initial failure (LS1 221).

90 For a further account of Anne Oldfield, including her late emergence, see below, pp.201–4. She was befriended by Farquhar, who is believed to have addressed to her some of the letters collected in his *Love and Business* (1701). In 1702, *Comparison* described her as 'rubbish that ought to be swept off the stage' (p.200). For a modern biography, see Joanne Lafler, *The Celebrated Mrs Oldfield: The Life and Art of an Augustan Actress* (Carbondale and Edwardsville: Southern Illinois University Press, 1989). See also Figure 9.

clear, and strong, so that no violence of passion could be too much for her; and when distress or tenderness possessed her, she subsided into the most affecting melody and softness. In the art of exciting pity she had a power beyond all the actresses I have yet seen, or what your imagination can conceive. Of the former of these two great excellencies she gave the most delightful proofs in almost all the heroic plays of Dryden and Lee; and of the latter, in the softer passions of Otway's Monimia and Belvidera.[91] In scenes of anger, defiance or resentment, while she was impetuous and terrible she poured out the sentiment with an enchanting harmony; and it was this particular excellence for which Dryden made her the above-recited compliment upon her acting Cassandra in his *Cleomenes*. But here, I am apt to think his partiality for that character may have tempted his judgment to let it pass for her masterpiece, when he could not but know there were several other characters in which her action might have given her a fairer pretence to the praise he has bestowed on her for Cassandra; for in no part of that is there the least ground for compassion, as in Monimia, nor equal cause for admiration as in the nobler love of Cleopatra, or the tempestuous jealousy of Roxana.[92] 'Twas in these lights I thought Mrs Barry shone with a much brighter excellence than in Cassandra. She was the first person whose merit was distinguished by the indulgence of having an annual benefit play; which was granted to her alone, if I mistake not, first in King James's time, and which became not common to others till the division of this company after the death of King William's Queen Mary.[93] This great actress died of a fever towards the latter end of Queen

91 Barry's known roles in 'heroic' plays by **Dryden** were Almeyda in *Don Sebastian* (1689), Cassandra in *Cleomenes* (1692), and Victoria in *Love Triumphant* (1694); she was Marmoutier in **Dryden and Lee's** *The Duke of Guise* (1682). In plays by **Lee** she was Athenais in *Theodosius* (1680), Fausta in *Constantine the Great* (1683), Roxana in *The Rival Queens* (took on the role in 1690), and Marguerite in *The Massacre of Paris* (1689). In **Otway's** *The Orphan* (1680) and *Venice Preserved* (1682) she played Monimia and Belvidera respectively.

92 There is no other evidence of Barry playing Cleopatra; Elizabeth Boutell had created the role in Dryden's *All for Love* (1677). However, a 1692 reprint may indicate a revival that season, when Barry was the obvious choice for the role. For Roxana, see above, n.91.

93 Cibber refers to contractually guaranteed annual and individual benefit performances rather than the one-off collective benefit performances that existed for actresses and younger performers from the 1660s onwards (see LS1 lxxix–lxxx), or the one-off performances for senior actors such as referred to in the agreement dated 14 October 1681 of Charles Hart and Edward Kynaston with the Duke's Company Management (lost manuscript; *Document Register* no.1134). In the 1694 'Petition of the Players' (PRO LC 7/3, in Milhous, *Management*, p.227), it is noted that 'Mrs Barry made an agreement [with previous management] for 50s per week and the profit of a play every year.' That was a gamble; the guarantee of an annual benefit performance meant a lower salary.

Anne; the year I have forgot, but perhaps you will recollect it by an expression that fell from her in blank verse in her last hours, when she was delirious, *viz.*,

<blockquote>Ha, ha! And so they make us lords by dozens![94]</blockquote>

Mrs Betterton, though far advanced in years, was so great a mistress of Nature that even Mrs Barry, who acted the Lady Macbeth after her, could not in that part – with all her superior strength and melody of voice – throw out those quick and careless strokes of terror from the disorder of a guilty mind, which the other gave us with a facility in her manner that rendered them at once tremendous and delightful.[95] Time could not impair her skill, though he had brought her person to decay. She was, to the last, the admiration of all true judges of Nature and lovers of Shakespeare, in whose plays she chiefly excelled, and without a rival. When she quitted the stage, several good actresses were the better for her instruction.[96] She was a woman of an unblemished and sober life, and had the honour to teach Queen Anne (when Princess) the part of Semandra in *Mithridates*, which she acted at court in King Charles's time.[97] After the death of Mr Betterton her husband, that princess (when Queen) ordered her a pension for life, but she lived not to receive more than the first half year of it.[98]

Mrs Leigh, the wife of Leigh already mentioned, had a very droll way of dressing the pretty foibles of superannuated beauties.[99] She had in herself a good deal of humour, and knew how to infuse it into the affected mothers, aunts and modest, stale maids that had missed their market; of this sort were the modish mother in *The Chances*, affecting to be politely

---

94 In the winter of 1711–12 First Minister Robert Harley pressurized Queen Anne into creating twelve new Tory peers in order to stabilize the government, a move that caused widespread concern and derision among the Whig opposition. Elizabeth Barry died in 1713. As Evans notes, Cibber uses Mrs Barry to voice party allegiance.

95 The first record of Mary Betterton playing Lady Macbeth is in November 1664. She probably surrendered the role to Barry in the early 1680s.

96 Mary Betterton seems to have been responsible for coaching junior performers for the Duke's Company since the 1670s. Her last known Shakespearean role was as the Duchess of York in *Richard III*, during the 1691–2 season (LS1 400).

97 However, LS1 267 refers to Benjamin Bathurst's *Letters of Two Queens* (London, 1924), p.61, which reprints correspondence indicating that Princess Anne played Ziphares in the performance of Lee's *Mithridates, King of Pontus* that took place either at St James's Palace or Apsley House, St James's Square, between January 1678 and August 1679. Frances Apsley played Semandra. Mary and Thomas Betterton coached the Princesses Mary and Anne for the court performance of Crowne's *Calisto* in February 1675.

98 Thomas Betterton died in April 1710, and Mary in 1712. Applying for a royal pension could be a lengthy process, and it was not unusual for payments to be delayed.

99 For Elinor Leigh (née Dixon?) see above, p.75 n.42.

commode for her own daughter;[100] the coquette prude of an aunt in *Sir Courtly Nice*, who prides herself in being chaste and cruel at fifty;[101] and the languishing Lady Wishfort in *The Way of the World*.[102] In all these, with many others, she was extremely entertaining and painted in a lively manner the blind side of Nature.[103]

Mrs Butler, who had her christian name of Charlotte given her by King Charles, was the daughter of a decayed knight, and had the honour of that prince's recommendation to the theatre[104] – a provident restitution, giving to the stage in kind what he had sometimes taken from it.[105] The public, at least, was obliged by it, for she proved not only a good actress but was allowed in those days to sing and dance to great perfection.[106] In the dramatic operas of *Dioclesian* and that of *King Arthur* she was a capital and admired performer.[107] In speaking, too, she had a sweet-toned voice which, with her naturally genteel air and sensible pronunciation, rendered her wholly mistress of the amiable in many serious characters. In parts of humour, too, she had

---

100 A reference to the adaptation of John Fletcher's *The Chances* (c. 1617) by George Villiers, Duke of Buckingham. LS1 102 gives the King's Company premiere as February 1667; see Buckingham, I.16–19 for a date of spring/summer 1664. LS2 398 notes a possible revival in 1692. Cibber refers to the role of Don John's Landlady.

101 The 1685 edition of Crowne's *Sir Courtly Nice* does not give a cast, while Downes's cast (p.84) excludes Leigh's role of the Aunt, 'Leonora's governess – an old, amorous, envious maid'.

102 Congreve's play opened at Lincoln's Inn Fields in March 1700. Leigh had played the comparable role of Lady Plyant in the same author's *The Double Dealer* in 1693.

103 i.e. the unguarded or weak side of a person's nature.

104 Charlotte Butler (see above, p.75 n.42) is believed to have joined the Duke's Company in 1673.

105 A reference to Moll Davis and Nell Gwyn, who stopped performing after affairs with Charles II. Downes, p.55, records that after performing the song 'My lodging it is on the cold ground' in William Davenant's *The Rivals* (plausibly on 19 November 1667), Davis was 'raised … from her bed on the cold ground, to a bed royal'. Gwyn became Charles's mistress in 1669 and wound down her acting commitments until her eventual retirement in 1671 (Howe, p.74).

106 William Mountfort's *The Successful Strangers* (1690) featured a special showcase, with the end of Act III marked by 'Mrs Butler's Dance' (LS1 379). Her singing was a feature of such plays as George Powell's *Alphonso King of Naples* (1690), Thomas Southerne's *The Wives Excuse* (1691), and Dryden's *Cleomenes* (1692). In this context 'allowed to' means 'considered to'.

107 For Betterton's adaptation, *The Prophetess; or the History of Dioclesian*, see above, p.107 n.66. The music was by Henry Purcell and the choreography by Josias Priest; the concluding set piece is an elaborate masque of Cupid and shepherds in which Butler probably sang Cupid. Dryden's *King Arthur* was the following year's Dorset Garden spectacular, again with music by Purcell and dances by Priest. Butler played Philidel and sang Cupid in the Act III masque, for an appreciation of which, see John Wilson, ed., *Roger North on Music* (London, 1959), pp.217–18: her singing was 'beyond anything I ever heard upon the English Stage'.

a manner of blending her assuasive softness even with the gay, the lively and the alluring. Of this she gave an agreeable instance in her action of the (Villiers) Duke of Buckingham's second Constantia in *The Chances*;[108] in which, if I should say I have never seen her exceeded, I might still do no wrong to the late Mrs Oldfield's lively performance of the same character.[109] Mrs Oldfield's fame may spare Mrs Butler's action this compliment without the least diminution or dispute of her superiority in characters of more moment.

Here I cannot help observing, when there was but one theatre in London, at what unequal salaries (compared to those of later days) the hired actors were then held by the absolute authority of their frugal masters, the patentees;[110] for Mrs Butler had then but forty shillings a week, and could she have obtained an addition of ten shillings more (which was refused her) would never have left their service; but, being offered her own conditions to go with Mr Ashbury to Dublin (who was then raising a company of actors for that theatre, where there had been none since the Revolution), her discontent here prevailed with her to accept of his offer, and he found his account in her value.[111] Were not those patentees most sagacious economists, that could lay hold on so notable an expedient to lessen their charge? How gladly, in my time of being a sharer, would we have given four times her income to an actress of equal merit?

Mrs Mountfort, whose second marriage gave her the name of Verbruggen, was mistress of more variety of humour than I ever knew in any one woman actress.[112] This variety, too, was attended with an equal vivacity, which made her excellent in characters extremely different. As she was

---

108   For Buckingham's adaptation of Fletcher, see above, p.117 n.100. The play hinges on a confusion of identities between a famous beauty called Constantia and a second Constantia who is Petrucchio's wronged sister; Butler probably played the latter role in 1692 (LS1 398).

109   Anne Oldfield played the Second Constantia at Drury Lane from 1708 (LS2 167).

110   A reference to the last days of the United Company under the patentees Thomas Skipwith and Christopher Rich.

111   Joseph Ashbury (1638–1720) was born in London and became a leading figure in Irish theatre. Deputy Master of the Revels in Ireland from 1662, he became Master of the Revels in Dublin. He staged a series of semi-professional performances at the Smock Alley Theatre and nurtured the early careers of Robert Wilks, Barton Booth, James Quin, and George Farquhar. He also had a track record of attracting established London actors to Dublin. Charlotte Butler is known to have played there in the 1695–6 season with Richard Estcourt, among others. Her name is not recorded for any of the London companies after the 1691–2 season.

112   Susannah Mountfort (see above, p.75 n.42) married John Verbruggen after the murder of her first husband, William (see above, p.63 n.56). She joined the King's Company as a teenager and, declining Betterton's offer, stayed with Rich's company in 1695. The versatility Cibber praises is evident from her taking on breeches roles such as Southerne's *Sir Anthony Love* (1690) and roles originally written for men (Bayes in *The*

naturally a pleasant mimic, she had the skill to make that talent useful on
the stage – a talent which may be surprising in a conversation and yet be
lost when brought to the theatre, which was the case of Estcourt already
mentioned. But where the elocution is round, distinct, voluble and various
as Mrs Mountfort's was, the mimic *there* is a great assistant to the actor.
Nothing, though ever so barren – if within the bounds of Nature – could
be flat in her hands. She gave many heightening touches to characters but
coldly written, and often made an author vain of his work that in itself had
but little merit. She was so fond of humour in what low part soever to be
found, that she would make no scruple of defacing her fair form to come
heartily into it. For when she was eminent in several desirable characters of
wit and humour in higher life, she would be in as much fancy when des-
cending into the antiquated Abigail of Fletcher as when triumphing in all
the airs and vain graces of a fine lady[113] – a merit that few actresses care for.
In a play of Durfey's now forgotten, called *The Western Lass* (which part she
acted), she transformed her whole being, body, shape, voice, language, look
and features into almost another animal, with a strong Devonshire dialect,
a broad laughing voice, a poking head, round shoulders, an unconceiving
eye, and the most bedizzening, dowdy dress that ever covered the untrained
limbs of a Joan Trott.[114] To have seen her here, you would have thought it
impossible the same creature could ever have been recovered to what was
as easy to her: the gay, the lively and the desirable. Nor was her humour
limited to her sex; for while her shape permitted, she was a more adroit
pretty fellow than is usually seen upon the stage, her easy air, action, mien
and gesture quite changed from the quoif to the cocked hat, and cavalier
in fashion.[115] People were so fond of seeing her a man that when the part of
Bayes in *The Rehearsal* had for some time lain dormant, she was desired to
take it up; which I have seen her act with all the true, coxcombly spirit and
humour that the sufficiency of the character required.[116]

Rehearsal, possibly from January 1687; LS1 354) alongside more conventional roles in
tragedy and comedy.

113 The reference is to Beaumont and Fletcher's *The Scornful Lady* (1616), a 1691 reprint of
which may indicate a revival that year.

114 Thomas Durfey's *The Bath; or, The Western Lass* opened at Drury Lane in late May 1701,
with Susannah Verbruggen as Gillian; Cibber spoke the prologue and played Crab.
'Joan' is a generic name for a country woman, while 'Trott' refers to an older woman;
for her counterpart, John, see below, p.239. To 'bedizzen' was to dress in a vulgar or
gaudy fashion (*OED* 1).

115 Aston, by contrast, states that she was reluctant to take on men's roles because of her
'thick legs and thighs' and 'corpulent and large posteriors' (II.313).

116 *The Rehearsal* was reprinted in 1692, indicating a revival that year (LS1 399); the most
recent recorded performance was in April 1689 (LS1 370).

But what found most employment for her whole various excellence at once was the part of Melantha in *Marriage à la Mode*.[117] Melantha is as finished an impertinent as ever fluttered in a drawing room, and seems to contain the most complete system of female foppery that could possibly be crowded into the tortured form of a fine lady. Her language, dress, motion, manners, soul and body are in a continual hurry to be something more than is necessary or commendable. And though I doubt it will be a vain labour to offer you a just likeness of Mrs Mountfort's action, yet the fantastic impression is still so strong in my memory that I cannot help saying something (though fantastically) about it. The first ridiculous airs that break from her are upon a gallant never seen before, who delivers her a letter from her father, recommending him to her good graces as an honourable lover.[118] Here, now, one would think she might naturally show a little of the sex's decent reserve, though never so slightly covered! No, sir. Not a tittle of it. Modesty is the virtue of a poor-souled country gentlewoman; she is too much a court lady to be under so vulgar a confusion. She reads the letter, therefore, with a careless, dropping lip and an erected brow, humming it hastily over, as if she were impatient to outgo her father's commands by making a complete conquest of him at once; and, that the letter might not embarrass her attack, crack! – she crumbles it at once into her palm, and pours upon him her whole artillery of airs, eyes and motion. Down goes her dainty, diving body to the ground, as if she were sinking under the conscious load of her own attractions; then launches into a flood of fine language and compliment, still playing her chest forward in fifty falls and risings, like a swan upon waving water; and, to complete her impertinence, she is so rapidly fond of her own wit that she will not give her lover leave to praise it. Silent, assenting bows and vain endeavours to speak are all the share of the conversation he is admitted to; which at last he is relieved from by her engagement to half a score visits, which she *swims* from him to make, with a promise to return in a twinkling.[119]

117 Dryden's *Marriage à la Mode* opened at Lincoln's Inn Fields in November 1671, when the King's Company had been burned out of their Bridges Street Theatre; Elizabeth Boutell played the 'affected lady', Melantha. A reprint of 1691 may indicate a revival that year (LS1 387), although the dramatis personae does not list actors' names. Aston, II.314, states that 'Melantha was [Verbruggen's] masterpiece'. She played similar *précieuse* roles such as Lady Froth in Congreve's *The Double Dealer* (1693) and Marsillia in the anonymous *The Female Wits* (1696).

118 In Act II, Melantha breaks off from reading the letter to exclaim, 'O Venus, a new servant sent me! And let me die but he has the air of a gallant *homme*'; Dryden, *Marriage à la Mode* (London: Henry Herringman, 1673), p.14.

119 See *Marriage à la Mode*, p.15: 'I'll make haste to kiss hands, and then make half a score visits more, and be with you again in a twinkling.'

If this sketch has colour enough to give you any near conception of her, I then need only tell you that throughout the whole character, her variety of humour was every way proportionable; as, indeed, in most parts that she thought worth her care (or that had the least matter for her fancy to work upon) I may justly say that no actress, from her own conception, could have heightened them with more lively strokes of Nature.

I come now to the last (and only living) person of all those whose theatrical characters I have promised you: Mrs Bracegirdle, who I know would rather pass her remaining days forgotten as an actress, than to have her youth recollected in the most favourable light I am able to place it. Yet as she is essentially necessary to my theatrical history, and as I only bring her back to the company of those with whom she passed the spring and summer of her life, I hope it will excuse the liberty I take in commemorating the delight which the public received from her appearance while she was an ornament to the theatre.

Mrs Bracegirdle was now but just blooming to her maturity,[120] her reputation as an actress gradually rising with that of her person. Never any woman was in such general favour of her spectators, which to the last scene of her dramatic life she maintained by not being unguarded in her private character.[121] This discretion contributed not a little to make her the *cara*, the darling of the theatre. For it will be no extravagant thing to say, scarce an audience saw her that were less than half of them lovers, without a suspected favourite among them; and though she might be said to have been the universal passion, and under the highest temptations, her constancy in resisting them served but to increase the number of her admirers. And this, perhaps, you will more easily believe when I extend not my encomiums on her person beyond a sincerity that can be suspected; for she had no greater claim to beauty than what the most desirable brunette might pretend to. But her youth and lively aspect threw out such a glow of health and cheerfulness, that on the stage few spectators that were not past it could behold her without desire. It was even a fashion among the gay and young to have a taste or *tendre* for Mrs. Bracegirdle. She inspired the best authors to write for her, and two of them, when they gave her a lover in a play, seemed palpably to plead their own passions and make their private court to her in

---

120   i.e. when Cibber joined the United Company in 1690; Bracegirdle was only 17 but already playing significant roles.

121   In what Lowe describes as 'a most uncharitable note', Bellchambers disputes Cibber's assessment of Bracegirdle's 'private character' on the basis of her alleged affairs with William Mountfort and William Congreve, who remembered her and her sister in his will. Bellchambers's evidence is in Tom Brown, *A Continuation or second part of the Letters from the Dead to the Living* (London: Benjamin Bragg, 1707), p.186.

fictitious characters.[122] In all the chief parts she acted, the desirable was so predominant that no judge could be cold enough to consider from what other particular excellence she became delightful. To speak critically of an actress that was extremely good were as hazardous as to be positive in one's opinion of the best opera singer. People often judge by comparison where there is no similitude in the performance: so that, in this case, we have only taste to appeal to, and of taste there can be no disputing. I shall therefore only say of Mrs Bracegirdle that the most eminent authors always chose her for their favourite character, and shall leave that uncontestable proof of her merit to its own value. Yet let me say there were two very different characters in which she acquitted herself with uncommon applause. If anything could excuse that desperate extravagance of love, that almost frantic passion, of Lee's Alexander the Great, it must have been when Mrs Bracegirdle was his Statira.[123] As when she acted Millamant, all the faults, follies and affectations of that agreeable tyrant were venially melted down into so many charms and attractions of a conscious beauty.[124] In other characters, where singing was a necessary part of them, her voice and action gave a pleasure which good sense, in those days, was not ashamed to give praise to.[125]

She retired from the stage in the height of her favour from the public (when most of her contemporaries whom she had been bred up with were declining) in the year 1710;[126] nor could she be persuaded to return to it under new masters, upon the most advantageous terms that were offered her, excepting one day about a year after, to assist her good friend Mr Betterton, when she played Angelica in *Love for Love* for his benefit.[127] She has

---

122   Bracegirdle played the hero's object of desire in all Congreve's major comedies, from Cynthia in *The Double Dealer* (1693) to Angelica in *Love for Love* (1695) and Millamant in *The Way of the World* (1700). Fone and Evans follow Lowe in stating that the other author Cibber had in mind was Nicholas Rowe (1674–1718), but the plays of Thomas Southerne (1660–1746) contain more Bracegirdle roles that fit Cibber's description.

123   Bracegirdle's earliest performance in this role (in Lee's *The Rival Queens*) was in January 1690, with revivals during the following two years (LS1 380 and 400).

124   Cibber echoes the words of Millamant's lover, Mirabell, who likes her 'with all her faults, nay ... for her faults' (*The Way of the World*, I.iii.21–2, in Congreve, *Works*, II.110).

125   However, in *The Way of the World*, III.xii.5–23 (Congreve, *Works*, II.162–3), Congreve assigns a song to an offstage performer rather than have Millamant (Bracegirdle) sing it.

126   In fact, as Lowe notes, Bracegirdle's name appeared for the last time in a playbill of 20 February 1707. *The Laureate* (p.36) alleged that Bracegirdle had retired because Cibber himself was giving her roles to Anne Oldfield; as Lowe observes, it is not clear that Cibber would have had responsibility for casting at that point.

127   Betterton's benefit, as reported by Steele in *The Tatler*, no.1, 12 April 1709, took place on 7 April 1709. Steele reported that 'Those excellent players Mrs Barry, Mrs Bracegirdle and Mr Doggett, though not at present concerned in the house, acted on that occasion.' Stage seating was provided to cope with demand for tickets.

still the happiness to retain her usual cheerfulness and to be, without the transitory charm of youth, agreeable.

If, in my account of these memorable actors, I have not deviated from truth (which in the least article I am not conscious of), may we not venture to say they had not their equals at any one time, upon any theatre in Europe? Or, if we confine the comparison to that of France alone, I believe no other stage can be much disparaged by being left out of the question, which cannot properly be decided by the single merit of any one actor. Whether their Baron[128] or our Betterton might be the superior (take which side you please), that point reaches either way but to a thirteenth part of what I contend for, *viz.*, that no stage, at any one period, could show thirteen actors standing all in equal lights of excellence in their profession. And I am the bolder in this challenge to any other nation, because no theatre having so extended a variety of natural characters as the English can have a demand for actors of such various capacities.[129] Why, then, where they could not be equally wanted, should we suppose them at any one time to have existed?

How imperfect soever this copious account of them may be, I am not without hope at least it may in some degree show what talents are requisite to make actors valuable. And if that may any ways inform or assist the judgment of future spectators, it may as often be of service to their public entertainments. For as their hearers are, so will actors be: worse or better, as the false or true taste applauds or discommends them. Hence only can our theatres improve, or must degenerate.

There is another point, relating to the hard condition of those who write for the stage, which I would recommend to the consideration of their hearers; which is that the extreme severity with which they damn a bad play seems too terrible a warning to those whose untried genius might hereafter give them a good one. Whereas it might be a temptation to a latent author to make the experiment, could he be sure that though not approved, his muse might at least be dismissed with decency. But the vivacity of our modern critics is of late grown so riotous that an unsuccessful author has no more mercy shown him than a notorious cheat in a pillory; every fool, the lowest member of the mob, becomes a wit and will have a fling at him. They come now to a new play like hounds to a carcass, and are all in a full cry sometimes for an hour together before the curtain rises to throw it amongst

---

128   Michel Baron (1653–1729) joined Molière's troupe in the 1660s and went on to be a founder member of the Comédie Française, creating leading roles in plays by Corneille and Racine.

129   A sentiment similar to one expressed by Farquhar in his *Discourse Upon Comedy*: 'As we are a mixture of many nations, so we have the most unaccountable medley of humours among us of any people upon earth' (Farquhar, *Works*, II.378–9).

them. Sure, those gentlemen cannot but allow that a play condemned after a fair hearing falls with thrice the ignominy as when it is refused that common justice.

But when their critical interruptions grow so loud and of so long a continuance that the attention of quiet people (though not so complete critics) is terrified, and the skill of the actors quite disconcerted by the tumult, the play then seems rather to fall by assassins than by a lawful sentence.[130] Is it possible that such auditors can receive delight, or think it any praise to them, to prosecute so injurious, so unmanly a treatment? And though, perhaps, the compassionate on the other side (who know they have as good a right to clap and support as others have to catcall, damn and destroy) may oppose this oppression, their good nature, alas, contributes little to the redress. For in this sort of civil war, the unhappy author, like a good prince, while his subjects are at mortal variance, is sure to be a loser by a victory on either side; for still the commonwealth (his play) is, during the conflict, torn to pieces. While this is the case, while the theatre is so turbulent a sea and so infested with pirates, what poetical merchant of any substance will venture to trade in it? If these valiant gentlemen pretend to be lovers of plays, why will they deter gentlemen from giving them such as are fit for gentlemen to see? In a word, this new race of critics seem to me like the lion whelps in the Tower, who are so boisterously gamesome at their meals that they dash down the bowls of milk brought for their own breakfast.[131]

As a good play is certainly the most rational and the highest entertainment that human invention can produce, let that be my apology (if I need any) for having thus freely delivered my mind in behalf of those gentlemen who, under such calamitous hazards, may hereafter be reduced to write for the stage; whose case I shall compassionate from the same motive that prevailed on Dido to assist the Trojans in distress.

Non ignara mali miseris succurrere disco. Virg.[132]

Or, as Dryden has it,

I learn to pity woes so like my own.

130   Cibber revisits sentiments he had set out in his preface to *Ximena* (publ. 1719), which in turn reflected on the riotous reception of his earlier play, *The Non-Juror* (1717): 'There is in human nature a certain low, latent malice to all laudable undertakings, which never dares break out upon anything with so much licence as on the fame of a dramatic writer ... [I]f he succeeds in a first play, let him look well to the rest, for then he is entered the herd as a common enemy.'

131   For approximately 600 years, until 1835, the Tower of London maintained a menagerie of wild animals. On Cibber's fondness for lion similes, see above, p.50 n.22.

132   Virgil, *Aeneid*, I.630. Dryden's translation was published in 1697.

If those particular gentlemen have sometimes made me the humbled object of their wit and humour, their triumph at least has done me this involuntary service: that it has driven me a year or two sooner into a quiet life, than otherwise my own want of judgment might have led me to.[133] I left the stage before my strength left me; and though I came to it again for some few days a year or two after, my reception there not only turned to my account, but seemed a fair invitation that I would make my visits more frequent. But, to give over a winner can be no very imprudent resolution.[134]

133 Cibber may be conflating his diminishing activity as a playwright from the late 1720s with the sale of his interest in Drury Lane to John Highmore in 1733 (see above, p.13 n.6) and his increasingly infrequent appearances as an actor (his official farewell performance at Drury Lane, as Richard III on 31 January 1739, took place while he was writing the *Apology*).

134 Cibber made a comeback from 1734 to 1736, playing such favourite roles as Bayes in *The Rehearsal*, Lord Foppington in *The Relapse*, Sir John Brute in *The Provoked Wife*, Sir Courtly Nice in Crowne's play of that name, and Sir Fopling in *The Man of Mode*. According to *Biographia Dramatica* he charged 50 guineas (c.£12,600 in current value) for each performance (cited in Barker, p.175). By 'give over' Cibber means 'give up' (i.e. he quit when he was ahead).

CHAPTER 6

The author's first step upon the stage. His discouragements. The best actors in Europe ill used. A revolution in their favour. King William grants them a licence to act in Lincoln's Inn Fields. The author's distress in being thought a worse actor than a poet. Reduced to write a part for himself. His success. More remarks upon theatrical action. Some upon himself.

Having given you the state of the theatre at my first admission to it, I am now drawing towards the several revolutions it suffered in my own time. But as you find by the setting out of my history that I always intended myself the hero of it, it may be necessary to let you know me in my obscurity as well as in my higher light, when I became one of the theatrical triumvirate.[1]

The patentees,[2] who were now masters of this united and only company of comedians, seemed to make it a rule that no young persons desirous to be actors should be admitted into pay under at least half a year's probation, wisely knowing that how early soever they might be approved of, there could be no great fear of losing them while they had then no other market to go to. But alas, pay was the least of my concern! The joy and privilege of every day seeing plays for nothing, I thought, was a sufficient consideration for the best of my services, so that it was no pain to my patience that I waited full three quarters of a year before I was taken into a salary of ten shillings per week;[3] which, with the assistance of food and raiment at my

---

1   On 31 March 1708 Henry Brett appointed Cibber, Estcourt, and Wilks as co-managers of Drury Lane (manuscript in *Document Register* no.1971); Doggett and then Booth replaced Estcourt.
2   Cibber joined the United Company at the start of the 1690–1 season; transfer of ownership to Christopher Rich and Thomas Skipwith was underway but not yet formalized, since it was only in March 1691 that Alexander Davenant assigned his shares to Rich and agreed to manage for him (BL Add.Charter 9298 and 9302; *Document Register* nos.1392 and 1393).
3   If true, it is odd that Cibber does not recount Davies's story (via Richard Cross, former Drury Lane prompter) of how he came to be salaried, unless he was ashamed to do so: '[Cibber] was known only, for some years, by the name of Master Colley. After waiting impatiently a long time for the prompter's notice, by good fortune he obtained the honour of carrying a message on the stage, in some play, to Betterton. Whatever was the cause, Master Colley was so terrified that the scene was disconcerted by him. Betterton asked, in some anger, who the young fellow was that had committed the blunder.

father's house,[4] I then thought a most plentiful accession and myself the happiest of mortals.

The first thing that enters into the head of a young actor is that of being a hero. In this ambition I was soon snubbed by the insufficiency of my voice, to which might be added an uninformed,[5] meagre person (though then not ill made) with a dismal, pale complexion.[6] Under these disadvantages I had but a melancholy prospect of ever playing a lover with Mrs Bracegirdle, which I had flattered my hopes that my youth might one day have recommended me to. What was most promising in me then was the aptness of my ear, for I was soon allowed to speak justly, though what was grave and serious did not equally become me. The first part, therefore, in which I appeared with any glimpse of success, was the Chaplain in *The Orphan* of Otway.[7] There is in this character (of one scene only) a decent pleasantry, and sense enough to show an audience whether the actor has any himself.[8] Here was the first applause I ever received, which you may be sure made my heart leap with a higher joy than may be necessary to describe; and yet my transport was not then half so high as at what Goodman (who had now left the stage) said of me the next day, in my hearing.[9] Goodman often came to a rehearsal for amusement and, having sat out *The Orphan* the day before, in a conversation with some of the principal actors enquired what new young fellow that was whom he had seen in the Chaplain; upon which, Mountfort

Downes replied, "Master Colley." — "Master Colley! Then forfeit him." — "Why, sir," said the prompter, "he has no salary." — "No?" said the old man; "why then put him down ten shillings a week, and forfeit him 5ˢ" (Davies, III. 444).

4 At this time Caius Gabriel Cibber was working on the Danish Church in Wellclose Square, at the eastern end of Smithfield (Faber, p.61).

5 *OED* 3: 'not animated, enlivened, or inspired'.

6 The implication is that while young actresses used stage make-up, sometimes in abundance (see Pepys on Nell Gwyn, 5 October 1667), young actors in romantic roles did not, but were expected to rely on their natural colour at a time when the stage was lit by candles. *The Laureate* (p. 103) is predictably harsh on the subject of the young Cibber's appearance:

He was in stature of the middle size, his complexion fair, inclinable to the sandy, his legs somewhat of the thickest, his shape a little clumsy, not irregular, and his voice rather shrill than loud or articulate, and cracked extremely when he endeavoured to raise it. He was in his younger days so lean as to be known by the name of Hatchet Face.

7 Cibber's anecdote corroborates the claim in LS1 387 that a 1691 reprint of *The Orphan* (1680) indicates a performance in the 1690–1 season.

8 A reference to the scene between Chamont and the Chaplain in III.i.171–3 of Otway's *The Orphan* (ed. J. C. Ghosh), in which the Chaplain explains his unclerical approach to life: 'I meddle with no man's business but my own; / I rise in a morning early, study moderately, / Eat and drink cheerfully'.

9 For Goodman, see above, p.72 n.31, and below, pp.257–8.

replied, 'That's he, behind you'. Goodman then turning about, looked earnestly at me and after some pause, clapping me on the shoulder, rejoined, 'If he does not make a good actor, I'll be damned!' The surprise of being commended by one who had been himself so eminent on the stage, and in so positive a manner, was more than I could support; in a word, it almost took away my breath and (laugh if you please) fairly drew tears from my eyes! And though it may be as ridiculous as incredible to tell you what a full vanity and content at that time possessed me, I will still make it a question whether Alexander himself or Charles the Twelfth of Sweden,[10] when at the head of their first victorious armies, could feel a greater transport in their bosoms than I did then in mine, when but in the rear of this troop of comedians. You see to what low particulars I am forced to descend, to give you a true resemblance of the early and lively follies of my mind. Let me give you another instance of my discretion, more desperate than that of preferring the stage to any other views of life. One might think that the madness of breaking from the advice and care of parents to turn player could not easily be exceeded. But what think you, sir, of – matrimony?[11] Which, before I was two-and-twenty, I actually committed when I had but twenty pounds a year which my father had assured to me, and twenty shillings a week from my theatrical labours, to maintain (as I then thought) the happiest young couple that ever took a leap in the dark![12] If after this, to complete my fortune I turned poet too, this last folly indeed had something a better excuse: necessity. Had it never been my lot to have come to the stage, 'tis probable I might never have been inclined (or reduced) to have wrote for it. But having once exposed my person there, I thought it could be no additional dishonour to let my parts, whatever they were, take their fortune along with it. But to return to the progress I made as an actor.

10 Charles XII was King of Sweden from 1696 until his death in 1718. At the Battle of Narva in 1700 his army defeated larger Russian forces, compelling Peter the Great to sue for peace, which Charles declined.

11 Perhaps an echo of Webster's *The Duchess of Malfi*, I.ii.311 in the edition by Elizabeth M. Brennan (London: A & C Black, 1983); the play was intermittently performed on the Restoration stage (see LS1, 345).

12 Cibber married Katherine Shore on 6 May 1693; she was four years his senior. The couple may have been introduced by Katherine's brother, John, who played the trumpet at Drury Lane. Matthias Shore, Katherine and John's father, held the court post of Royal Sergeant Trumpeter; according to the *Biographia Dramatica*, I.117, he disapproved of Katherine's marriage and withheld her dowry, which helps explain why she joined the United Company for the 1693–4 season. An accomplished singer, her first recorded acting role was Aglaura in the anonymous *The Rape of Europa by Jupiter*, performed at Dorset Garden (LS1 427). She went on to create the roles of Hillaria and Olivia in her husband's *Love's Last Shift* (1696) and *Woman's Wit* (1697).

Queen Mary having commanded *The Double Dealer* to be acted, Kynaston happened to be so ill that he could not hope to be able next day to perform his part of the Lord Touchwood.[13] In this exigence the author, Mr Congreve, advised that it might be given to me, if at so short a warning I would undertake it. The flattery of being thus distinguished by so celebrated an author, and the honour to act before a queen, you may be sure made me blind to whatever difficulties might attend it. I accepted the part and was ready in it before I slept.[14] Next day, the Queen was present at the play and was received with a new prologue from the author, spoken by Mrs Barry, humbly acknowledging the great honour done to the stage, and to his play in particular. Two lines of it, which though I have not since read, I still remember:

> But never were in Rome nor Athens seen,
> So fair a circle, or so bright a Queen.[15]

After the play, Mr Congreve made me the compliment of saying that I had not only answered but had exceeded his expectations, and that he would show me he was sincere by his saying more of me to the masters. He was as good as his word, and the next payday I found my salary of fifteen was then advanced to twenty shillings a week.[16] But alas, this favourable opinion of Mr Congreve made no farther impression upon the judgment of my good masters; it only served to heighten my own vanity, but could not recommend me to any new trials of my capacity. Not a step farther could I get till the company was again divided: when the desertion of the best actors left a clear stage for younger champions to mount, and show their best preten-

13 Congreve's *The Double Dealer* opened at Drury Lane in October 1693. Cibber's debut as Lord Touchwood may have been on 13 January 1694. Nicoll, *Restoration*, p.314, reproduces a warrant (LC 5/151, p.369) for a performance of the play on that day which specifies a box for the Queen and another for the maids of honour, at the cost of £15. Giving the role of an ageing cuckold to the 22–year-old Cibber was a tribute to his powers of mimicry as much as memory; Kynaston, who had created the role, was 53.
14 The part of Lord Touchwood runs to a little over 200 lines.
15 Cibber quotes from Congreve's 'Prologue to Queen Mary, Upon Her Majesty's coming to see *The Old Batchelor*, after having seen *The Double Dealer*', in Congreve, *Works*, II.351. McKenzie (Congreve, *Works*, II.644) dates the Queen's second visit at the week 9–16 April 1694, notes an order of 16 April 1694 to pay Elizabeth Barry £25, and gives the publication date of the new prologue as June/July 1694 (as part of *The Annual Miscellany*), so indicating that Cibber conflated two separate events.
16 Cf. Cibber's statement on p.128 that he had 20 shillings a week when he was first married.

sions to favour.[17] But it is now time to enter upon those facts that immediately preceded this remarkable revolution of the theatre.

You have seen how complete a set of actors were under the government of the united patents in 1690;[18] if their gains were not extraordinary, what shall we impute it to but some extraordinary ill management? I was then too young to be in their secrets and therefore can only observe upon what I saw, and have since thought visibly wrong.

Though the success of *The Prophetess* and *King Arthur* (two dramatic operas in which the patentees had embarked all their hopes) was in appearance very great, yet their whole receipts did not so far balance their expense[19] as to keep them out of a large debt, which it was publicly known was about this time contracted, and which found work for the Court of Chancery for about twenty years following, till one side of the cause grew weary.[20] But this was not all that was wrong; every branch of the theatrical trade had been sacrificed to the necessary fitting out those tall ships of burthen that were to bring home the Indies.[21] Plays of course were neglected, actors held cheap and slightly dressed, while singers and dancers were better paid and embroidered. These measures, of course, created murmurings on one side, and ill humour and contempt on the other. When it became necessary therefore to lessen the charge, a resolution was taken to begin with the sal-

17 i.e. from 1695, when Betterton's troupe broke away. The subsequent passage about *Love for Love* (below, p.136) suggests Congreve had no intention of writing a part for Cibber in his next play.
18 Technically the patent was owned by the heirs of Sir William Davenant and Thomas Killigrew: Charles Davenant and Charles Killigrew respectively. For a dispute between the families leading up to the ownership by Christopher Rich and Thomas Skipwith in 1691, see *Document Register* no.1389.
19 According Luttrell, II.435, 'the clothes, scenes, and music [for *The Prophetess*] cost £3000', or approximately three-quarters of the annual production budget. Downes, p.89, wrote that it 'gratified the expectation of court and city'. Contrary to Cibber's claim about Dryden and Purcell's *King Arthur* (premiered at Dorset Garden in May 1691; LS1 395), Downes recalled that that show was 'very gainful to the company' (p.89). For *The Prophetess* see above, p.107 n.66.
20 A reference to the disagreement eventually brought to court in 1704 by Sir Edward Smith, married to Bridget, widow of the former Duke's Company lawyer, Richard Bayly. By that connection the Smiths owned half of the investors' shares in Dorset Garden but discovered no dividends had been paid for nine years; the defendants claimed that insufficient profit had been made. They also made a number of false accusations. The case was settled or dropped in 1708 (hence Cibber's 'about twenty years': i.e. from the premiere of *The Prophetess* in 1690). For details, see Milhous, *Management*, pp.152–9; for relevant documents, *Document Register* nos. 1616, 1748, 1749, 1772, 1777, 1795, 1810, 1824, 1832, 1847, and 1997.
21 i.e. lavish shows like *The Prophetess*, which consumed such a high proportion of annual production budgets.

aries of the actors; and what seemed to make this resolution more necessary at this time was the loss of Nokes, Mountfort and Leigh, who all died about the same year.[22] No wonder, then, if when these great pillars were at once removed, the building grew weaker and the audiences very much abated. Now in this distress, what more natural remedy could be found than to incite and encourage (though with some hazard) the industry of the surviving actors? But the patentees, it seems, thought the surer way was to bring down their pay in proportion to the fall of their audiences. To make this project more feasible, they proposed to begin at the head of 'em, rightly judging that if the principals acquiesced, their inferiors would murmur in vain. To bring this about with a better grace, they (under pretence of bringing younger actors forward) ordered several of Betterton's and Mrs Barry's chief parts to be given to young Powell and Mrs Bracegirdle.[23] In this they committed two palpable errors. For while the best actors are in health and still on the stage, the public is always apt to be out of humour when those of a lower class pretend to stand in their places; or, admitting at this time they might have been accepted, this project might very probably have lessened but could not possibly mend an audience, and was a sure loss of that time in studying which might have been better employed in giving the auditor variety, the only temptation to a palled appetite – and variety is only to be given by industry, but industry will always be lame when the actor has reason to be discontented. This the patentees did not consider, or pretended not to value while they thought their power secure and uncontrollable. But farther their first project did not succeed; for though the giddy head of Powell accepted the parts of Betterton, Mrs Bracegirdle had a different way of thinking, and desired to be excused from those of Mrs Barry. Her good sense was not to be misled by the insidious favour of the patentees. She knew the stage was wide enough for her success without entering into any such rash and invidious competition with Mrs Barry, and therefore wholly refused acting any part that properly belonged to her.[24] But this proceeding, however, was warning enough to make Betterton be upon his guard, and to alarm others with apprehensions of their own safety from the design that was laid against him. Betterton, upon this, drew into his party most of the valuable actors; who, to secure their unity, entered with him into a sort of

---

22 Mountfort and Leigh died in December 1692, but Nokes in 1696.
23 A complaint made in the 1694 'Petition of the Players' (see above, p.74 n.38). Cibber has now moved on to the period of Rich's management, leading to the 1695 breakaway.
24 'Belonging' was a literal matter, since actors were custodians of the manuscripts of their individual roles; see Stern, pp.148–52.

association to stand or fall together.²⁵ All this the patentees for some time slighted; but when matters drew towards a crisis, they found it advisable to take the same measures and accordingly opened an association on their part, both which were severally signed as the interest or inclination of either side led them.²⁶

During these contentions, which the impolitic patentees had raised against themselves (not only by this I have mentioned, but by many other grievances which my memory retains not), the actors offered a treaty of peace; but their masters, imagining no consequence could shake the right of their authority, refused all terms of accommodation.²⁷ In the meantime, this dissention was so prejudicial to their daily affairs that I remember it was allowed by both parties that before Christmas the patent had lost the getting of at least a thousand pounds by it.²⁸

My having been a witness of this unnecessary rupture was of great use to me when, many years after, I came to be a manager myself. I laid it down as a settled maxim that no company could flourish while the chief actors and the undertakers²⁹ were at variance. I therefore made it a point, while it was possible upon tolerable terms, to keep the valuable actors in humour with their station. And though I was as jealous of their encroachments as

25 Fifteen actors signed the 'Petition of the Players' in late November 1694: Thomas Betterton, Cave Underhill, Edward Kynaston, William Bowen, Joseph Williams, Thomas Doggett, George Bright, Samuel Sandford, Elizabeth Barry, Anne Bracegirdle, Susannah Verbruggen, Elizabeth Bowman, Mary Betterton, Elinor Leigh, and John Bowman. Of those, only seven were signatories to the sharing agreement for the new company drafted in late March 1695 (LC 7/1, pp.44–6; *Document Register* no.1500): Betterton, Barry, Bracegirdle, Bowman, Underhill, Bright, and Leigh, with Jack Verbruggen latterly forming an eighth.

26 Christopher Rich and Thomas Skipwith wrote a lengthy rebuttal of the petition on 10 December 1694 (LC 7/3, fols.8–20; *Document Register* no.1486, reprinted in Milhous, *Management*, Appendix B, pp.230–45).

27 However, it appears from a letter from Skipwith, Rich, and Charles Killigrew to Lord Chamberlain Dorset dated 11 February 1695 that they had sought a meeting with Betterton and his allies but been refused (manuscript listed in *Document Register* no.1495). On 19 March 1695, moreover, Dorset proposed a settlement to which the patentees agreed and Betterton did not; on 22 March the patentees asked Dorset to assert his authority and submit their grievances to two proposed arbitrators, the former Duke's Company actors Henry Harris and William Smith (LC 7/3, fols.62–3; *Document Register* no.1498). On 25 March the new company's licence was issued (LC 7/3, fol.7; *Document Register* no.1499). The 'other grievances' consisted of cost savings and the loss of an annual new wig for Betterton (see Milhous, *Management*, Appendix A, pp.225–9).

28 The record of performances between September and December 1694 is extremely thin; LS1 442 lists a handful of music concerts and other events.

29 i.e. business investors or entrepreneurs (*OED* 6b).

any of my co-partners could be, I always guarded against the least warmth in my expostulations with them; not but at the same time they might see I was perhaps more determined in the question than those that gave a loose to their resentment, and when they were cool, were as apt to recede.[30] I do not remember that ever I made a promise to any that I did not keep, and therefore was cautious how I made them. This coldness, though it might not please, at least left them nothing to reproach me with; and if temper and fair words could prevent a disobligation, I was sure never to give offence or receive it. But as I was but one of three, I could not oblige others to observe the same conduct. However, by this means I kept many an unreasonable discontent from breaking out, and both sides found their account in it.[31]

How a contemptuous and overbearing manner of treating actors had like to have ruined us in our early prosperity shall be shown in its place.[32] If future managers should chance to think my way right, I suppose they will follow it; if not, when they find what happened to the patentees who chose to disagree with their people, perhaps they may think better of it.

The patentees then, who by their united powers had made a monopoly of the stage, and consequently presumed they might impose what conditions they pleased upon their people, did not consider that they were all this while endeavouring to enslave a set of actors whom the public (more arbitrary[33] than themselves) were inclined to support; nor did they reflect that the spectator naturally wished that the actor who gave him delight might enjoy the profits arising from his labour, without regard of what pretended damage or injustice might fall upon his owners, whose personal merit the public was not so well acquainted with. From this consideration, then, several persons of the highest distinction espoused their cause and sometimes, in the circle, entertained the King

---

30 Cibber appears to criticize his fellow manager, Robert Wilks, whose 'unsociable temper' he recalls below, p.358. The idea is inflected to Cibber's disadvantage by *The Laureate*: '[Cibber] was always against raising, or rewarding, or by any means encouraging merit of any kind ... [and had] many disputes with Wilks on this account, who was impatient, when justice required it, to reward the meritorious' (p.39).

31 Cibber's assessment of his relationship with performers may be a little rosy, given his dispute with Nicolini in 1710 (HTC Coke no.67; *Document Register* no.2083), his alleged assault on Jane Lucas (see below, p.157 n.15), and litigation against him and his fellow managers by the actor Josias Miller in 1730 (C11/83/17; *Document Register* no.3525).

32 The reference is to the desertion of eight actors from Drury Lane, as noted in the *Weekly Packet* of 11–18 December 1714 (LS2 334; *Document Register* no.2478). Some of the group played at a revival of (ironically) *The Recruiting Officer* at Lincoln's Inn Fields (LS2 334) but were 'ordered to return to their colours'. For Cibber's account, see below, pp.318–19.

33 i.e. more in the business of, and qualified in, judging the actors.

with the state of the theatre.³⁴ At length their grievances were laid before
the Earl of Dorset, then Lord Chamberlain, who took the most effectual
method for their relief.³⁵ The learned of the law were advised with, and
they gave their opinion that no patent for acting plays *etc* could tie up the
hands of a succeeding prince from granting the like authority, where it
might be thought proper to trust it. But while this affair was in agitation,
Queen Mary died, which of course occasioned a cessation of all public
diversions.³⁶ In this melancholy interim, Betterton and his adherents had
more leisure to solicit their redress, and the patentees now finding that
the party against them was gathering strength, were reduced to make
sure of as good a company as the leavings of Betterton's interest could
form; and these, you may be sure, would not lose this occasion of setting
a price upon their merit equal to their own opinion of it, which was but
just double to what they had before. Powell and Verbruggen, who had
then but forty shillings a week, were now raised each of them to four
pounds, and others in proportion. As for myself, I was then too insignificant to be taken into their councils, and consequently stood among
those of little importance like cattle in a market, to be sold to the first
bidder. But the patentees, seeming in the greater distress for actors, condescended to purchase me. Thus, without any farther merit than that
of being a scarce commodity, I was advanced to thirty shillings a week.
Yet our company was so far from being full that our commanders were
forced to beat up for volunteers in several distant counties;³⁷ it was this
occasion that first brought Johnson and Bullock to the service of the
Theatre Royal.³⁸

34 Betterton and his fellow performers were on good terms with a number of aristocratic
   patrons. A letter from the actor to the agent of Lord Weymouth even shows him sharing
   details of his art collection; see Roberts, *Thomas Betterton*, pp.176–7. By 'circle' Cibber
   means the assembly of advisers and others around the king (*OED* n.20).

35 For Dorset, see above, p.105 n.55.

36 Queen Mary died on 28 December 1694; theatres were closed until after Easter 1695.
   Cibber marked the occasion with *A Poem on the Death of Our Late Sovereign Lady Queen
   Mary* (London: John Whitlock, 1695).

37 Lowe cites *Comparison*, p.7: ''twas almost impossible in Drury Lane to muster up a
   sufficient number to take in all the parts of any play'.

38 Benjamin **Johnson** (c. 1665–1742) is listed in Rich's Company from the 1694–5 season
   (LS1 440), but his earliest recorded role was Sir Simon Barter in Thomas Scott's *The
   Mock-Marriage* (September 1695; LS1 452); originally a scene painter, he graduated to
   acting in the provinces before joining Drury Lane. William **Bullock** (c. 1657–c. 1740)
   also joined Rich's Company in the 1694–5 (LS1 440), and his first recorded role was also
   in *The Mock Marriage*, as the Landlady. He appeared as Sly in Cibber's *Love's Last Shift*
   (1696). His physique made him the natural choice for such roles as Sir Tunbelly Clumsy
   in Vanbrugh's *The Relapse* (1696, publ. 1697).

Forces being thus raised and the war declared on both sides, Betterton and his chiefs had the honour of an audience of the King, who considered them as the only subjects whom he had not yet delivered from arbitrary power, and graciously dismissed them with an assurance of relief and support. Accordingly, a select number of them were empowered by his royal licence to act in a separate theatre for themselves.[39] This great point being obtained, many people of quality came into a voluntary subscription of twenty (and some of forty) guineas a-piece for erecting a theatre within the walls of the tennis court in Lincoln's Inn Fields.[40] But as it required time to fit it up, it gave the patentees more leisure to muster their forces, who notwithstanding were not able to take the field till the Easter Monday in April following.[41] Their first attempt was a revived play called *Abdelazar, or the Moor's Revenge*, poorly written by Mrs Behn.[42] The house was very full, but whether it was the play or the actors that were not approved, the next day's audience sunk to nothing. However, we were assured that let the audiences be never so low, our masters would make good all deficiencies; and so indeed they did till towards the end of the season, when dues to balance came too thick upon 'em. But, that I may go gradually on with my own fortune, I must take this occasion to let you know by the following circumstance how very low my capacity as an actor was then rated. It was thought necessary at our opening that the town should be addressed in a new prologue; but to our great distress, among several that were offered, not one was judged fit to be spoken. This I thought a favourable occasion to do myself some remarkable service, if I should have the good fortune to

---

39 Issued on 25 March 1695 (LC 7/3, fol.7; *Document Register* no.1499). The 'select number' of eleven was not quite the same group as the eventual shareholders (as above, p.132 n.25). Authority to operate was given to Betterton, Barry, Bracegirdle, Bowman, Underhill, Leigh, and Bright, with the addition of Thomas Doggett, William Bowen, Joseph Williams, and Susannah Verbruggen. For the fate of the latter two, see below, pp. 137–8.

40 The theatre in Lincoln's Inn Fields opened by Davenent in 1661 had been converted back to its original function as a tennis court since its fall into disuse following the opening of the Dorset Garden and Drury Lane theatres in the early 1670s. The new sharing agreement between Betterton and his partners notes the 'extraordinary charge & expense' of the work. Lowe cites *Comparison*, p.12: 'We know what importuning and dunning the noblemen there was, what flattering, and what promising there was, till at length, the encouragement they received by liberal contributions set 'em in a condition to go on.'

41 As noted in LS1 443–4, Cibber's dates are slightly out: the first Monday following Easter in 1695 was 25 March. LS1 dates the performance of Behn's play at 1 April.

42 First performed in July 1676, with Betterton in the title role (LS1 245–6); for the 1695 revival, LS1 443–4. The choice of play may be explained by Powell's wish to outdo Betterton, or to show off the superior scenic resources of Dorset Garden for the play's sumptuous palace scenes.

produce one that might be accepted. The next, memorable day, my muse brought forth her first fruit that was ever made public.[43] How good or bad, imports not: my prologue was accepted and resolved on to be spoken. This point being gained, I began to stand upon terms (you will say) not unreasonable; which were that if I might speak it myself, I would expect no farther reward for my labour. This was judged as bad as having no prologue at all! You may imagine how hard I thought it that they durst not trust my poor poetical brat to my own care. But since I found it was to be given into other hands, I insisted that two guineas should be the price of my parting with it; which with a sigh I received, and Powell spoke the prologue. But every line that was applauded went sorely to my heart, when I reflected that the same praise might have been given to my own speaking it; nor could the success of the author compensate the distress of the actor. However, in the end it served in some sort to mend our people's opinion of me; and whatever the critics might think of it, one of the patentees (who, it is true, knew no difference between Dryden and Durfey) said upon the success of it that in sooth I was an ingenious young man.[44] This sober compliment, though I could have no reason to be vain upon it, I thought was a fair promise to my being in favour. But to matters of more moment. Now let us reconnoitre the enemy.

After we had stolen some few days' march upon them, the forces of Betterton came up with us in terrible order. In about three weeks following,[45] the new theatre was opened against us with a veteran company and a new train of artillery; or, in plainer English, the old actors in Lincoln's Inn Fields began with a new comedy of Mr Congreve's called *Love for Love*, which ran on with such extraordinary success that they had seldom occasion to act any other play till the end of the season.[46] This valuable play had a narrow escape from falling into the hands of the patentees, for before the division of the company it had been read and accepted of at the Theatre Royal. But while the articles of agreement for it were preparing, the rupture in the theatrical state was so far advanced that the author took time to pause before he signed them; when, finding that all hopes of

43 In fact, Cibber had already published a poem on the death of Queen Mary (as above, p.134 n.36).
44 Given his reputation as a philistine, this patentee was probably Christopher Rich.
45 In fact, the breakaway company gave their first performance on 30 April 1695 (LS1 445).
46 LS1 445–7 records thirteen performances of *Love for Love* from 30 April to 14 May 1695, with *Hamlet*, Congreve's *The Old Batchelor* (his first play, and a success in March 1693; see LS1 418–19), and Charles Hopkins's *Pyrrhus, King of Epirus* as the only other recorded plays by the breakaway company until the end of the season (LS1 446–7). *Love for Love* was dedicated to the Earl of Dorset, who had facilitated the breakaway.

accommodation were impracticable, he thought it advisable to let it take its fortune with those actors for whom he had first intended the parts.

Mr Congreve was then in such high reputation as an author that besides his profits from this play, they offered him a whole share with them, which he accepted;[47] in consideration of which he obliged himself, if his health permitted, to give them one new play every year. Dryden, in King Charles's time, had the same share with the King's Company, but he bound himself to give them two plays every season.[48] This, you may imagine, he could not hold long, and I am apt to think he might have served them better with one in a year, not so hastily written. Mr Congreve (whatever impediment he met with) was three years before, in pursuance to his agreement, he produced *The Mourning Bride*, and if I mistake not, the interval had been much the same when he gave them *The Way of the World*.[49] But it came out the stronger for the time it cost him, and to their better support when they sorely wanted it. For though they went on with success for a year or two and, even when their affairs were declining, stood in much higher estimation of the public than their opponents, yet in the end both sides were great sufferers by their separation – the natural consequence of two houses, which I have already mentioned in a former chapter.

The first error this new colony of actors fell into was their inconsiderately parting with Williams and Mrs Mountfort[50] upon a too nice (not to say severe) punctilio in not allowing them to be equal sharers with the rest; which, before they had acted one play, occasioned their return to the service of the patentees. As I have called this an error, I ought to give my reasons

---

47 Congreve is not listed among the shareholders in the company (see above, p.135 n.39), contrary to a statement by Downes (p.91) which Cibber may have consulted. If such an offer was made, and on the condition Cibber subsequently mentions, it seems likely Congreve would have declined it; as the prologue to *The Way of the World* indicates (Congreve, *Works*, II.101), he knew he was a slow writer. See also below, p.211.

48 John Dryden (1631–1700) is listed among King's Company shareholders in a licence to use the Drury Lane Theatre dated 17 December 1673 (BL Add.MS 20,726, fols.8–9; *Document Register* no.817). Between 1663 and 1677 he had thirteen plays performed by the company, with *Sir Martin Mar-all* (putatively co-authored with the Duke of Newcastle) performed by the Duke's. Evans notes a 1668 agreement for Dryden to write three plays a year in return for one and a quarter shares in the company.

49 Congreve's *The Mourning Bride* opened in February 1697 (LS1 474), less than two years after *Love for Love*; *The Way of the World* opened three years later, in March 1700. Cibber's subsequent claim reflects accurately the success of *The Mourning Bride*, which ran for at least thirteen performances in March and April 1697 (LS1 474–6), but not of *The Way of the World*, whose five performances in March 1700 (LS1 525–6) were in comparison mildly disappointing.

50 i.e. Joseph Williams and Susannah Verbruggen (formerly Mountfort), whose names appear in the initial swearing in of comedians for the new company on 22 February 1695 (LC 3/31, p.108; *Document Register* no.1496).

for it. Though the industry of Williams was not equal to his capacity (for he loved his bottle better than his business), and though Mrs Mountfort was only excellent in comedy, yet their merit was too great, almost on any scruples, to be added to the enemy; and, at worst, they were certainly much more above those they would have ranked them with, than they could possibly be under those they were not admitted to be equal to. Of this fact there is a poetical record in the prologue to *Love for Love*, where the author, speaking of the then happy state of the stage, observes that if in paradise, when two only were there, they both fell, the surprise was less if from so numerous a body as theirs, there had been any deserters:

> Abate the wonder, and the fault forgive,
> If, in our larger family, we grieve
> One falling Adam, and one tempted Eve.[51]

These lines alluded to the revolt of the persons above mentioned.

Notwithstanding the acquisition of these two actors, who were of more importance than any of those to whose assistance they came, the affairs of the patentees were still in a very creeping condition.[52] They were now, too late, convinced of their error in having provoked their people to this civil war of the theatre! Quite changed and dismal now was the prospect before them! Their houses thin, and the town crowding into a new one! Actors at double salaries and not half the usual audiences to pay them! And all this brought upon them by those whom their full security had contemned, and who were now in a fair way of making their fortunes upon the ruined interest of their oppressors.

Here, though at this time my fortune depended on the success of the patentees, I cannot help (in regard to truth) remembering the rude and riotous havoc we made of all the late dramatic honours of the theatre! All became at once the spoil of ignorance and self-conceit! Shakespeare was defaced and tortured in every signal character. Hamlet and Othello lost in one hour all their good sense, their dignity and fame. Brutus and Cassius

---

51 Congreve's prologue reads, 'And to our world such plenty you afford, / It seems like Eden, fruitful of its own accord. / But since in paradise frail flesh gave way, / And when but two were made, both went astray; / Forbear your wonder, and the fault forgive, / If in our larger family we grieve / One falling Adam, and one tempted Eve' (lines 16–22 in Congreve, *Works*, I.251).

52 Lowe cites Cibber's preface to his *Woman's Wit* (1697): 'But however a fort is in a very poor condition, that (in a time of general war) has but a handful of raw young fellows to maintain it.' For commentary on the state of Rich's company in the aftermath of the breakaway, and Powell's attempts to lead it in the face of a drinking problem and withholding of payment by Rich, see Milhous, *Management*, pp.88–91.

became noisy blusterers, with bold unmeaning eyes, mistaken sentiments, and turgid elocution![53] Nothing, sure, could more painfully regret[54] a judicious spectator than to see, at our first setting out, with what rude confidence those habits which actors of real merit had left behind them were worn by giddy pretenders that so vulgarly disgraced them! Not young lawyers in hired robes and plumes at a masquerade could be less what they would seem, or more awkwardly personate the characters they belonged to. If, in all these acts of wanton waste, these insults upon injured Nature, you observe I have not yet charged one of them upon myself, it is not from an imaginary vanity that I could have avoided them, but that I was rather safe by being too low, at that time, to be admitted even to my chance of falling into the same eminent errors – so that, as none of those great parts ever fell to my share, I could not be accountable for the execution of them. Nor indeed could I get one good part of any kind till many months after, unless it were of that sort which nobody else cared for or would venture to expose themselves in. The first unintended favour, therefore, of a part of any value, necessity threw upon me on the following occasion.

As it has been always judged their natural interest, where there are two theatres, to do one another as much mischief as they can, you may imagine it could not be long before this hostile policy showed itself in action. It happened upon our having information on a Saturday morning that the Tuesday after, *Hamlet* was intended to be acted at the other house, where it had not yet been seen. Our merry managing actors (for they were now in a manner left to govern themselves) resolved, at any rate, to steal a march upon the enemy, and take possession of the same play the day before them. Accordingly, *Hamlet* was given out that night to be acted with us on Monday. The notice of this sudden enterprise soon reached the other house, who in my opinion too much regarded it, for they shortened their first orders and resolved that *Hamlet* should to *Hamlet* be opposed on the same day; whereas, had they given notice in their bills that the same play would have been acted by them the day after, the town would have been in no doubt

---

53 No other records exist of revivals of these plays by Rich's company in the period in question. It is likely that George Powell took Betterton's former roles; here as elsewhere, Cibber barely disguises his contempt for Powell's acting. Evans notes the list of Drury Lane plays attended by Lady Morley between 1696 and 1701: *Timon of Athens, The Tempest,* and *King Lear* are the only Shakespeare plays (but adapted), as reprinted in Hotson, pp.377–8.

54 Bellchambers notes that 'Mr Cibber's usage of the verb "regret" here, may be said to confirm the censure of Fielding, who urged, in reviewing some other of his inadvertencies, that it was "needless for a great writer to understand his grammar".' The reference is to Fielding's *The Champion*, 29 April 1740.

which house they should have reserved themselves for. Ours must certainly have been empty and theirs, with more honour, have been crowded. Experience, many years after in like cases, has convinced me that this would have been the more laudable conduct. But be that as it may: when, in their Monday's bills, it was seen that *Hamlet* was up against us, our consternation was terrible to find that so hopeful a project was frustrated. In this distress Powell, who was our commanding officer, and whose enterprising head wanted nothing but skill to carry him through the most desperate attempts (for, like others of his cast, he had murdered many a hero only to get into his clothes) – this Powell, I say, immediately called a council of war, where the question was whether he should fairly face the enemy, or make a retreat to some other play of more probable safety. It was soon resolved that to act *Hamlet* against *Hamlet* would be certainly throwing away the play, and disgracing themselves to little or no audience. To conclude, Powell (who was vain enough to envy Betterton as his rival) proposed to change plays with them; and that, as they had given out *The Old Batchelor* and had changed it for *Hamlet* against us, we should give up our *Hamlet* and turn *The Old Batchelor* upon them. This motion was agreed to, *nemine contradicente*,[55] but upon enquiry it was found that there were not two persons among them who had ever acted in that play.[56] But that objection, it seems (though all the parts were to be studied in six hours), was soon got over. Powell had an equivalent, *in petto*,[57] that would balance any deficiency on that score, which was that he would play the Old Batchelor himself and mimic Betterton throughout the whole part.[58] This happy thought was approved with delight and applause, as whatever can be supposed to ridicule merit generally gives joy to those that want it. Accordingly, the bills were changed and at the bottom inserted,

The part of the Old Batchelor to be performed in imitation of the original.

Printed books of the play were sent for in haste[59] and every actor had one, to pick out of it the part he had chosen. Thus, while they were each of them chewing the morsel they had most mind to, someone happening to cast his eye over the dramatis personae found that the main matter was still

---

55 i.e. 'without contradiction', now shortened to 'nem con'.
56 When Congreve's *The Old Batchelor* was first performed in March 1693, the cast actually included three actors who were now senior members of Rich's company: Jack Verbruggen (Sharper), Joseph Williams (Vainlove), and George Powell himself (Bellmour).
57 i.e. privately, in reserve (literally, 'in the chest').
58 i.e. Heartwell, the eponymous hero.
59 The play was published by Peter Buck at the Temple, Fleet Street, easily accessible from Drury Lane. If the company bought new copies, they would have cost 1 shilling each.

forgot: that nobody had yet been thought of for the part of Alderman Fondlewife.[60] Here we were all aground again! Nor was it to be conceived who could make the least tolerable shift with it. This character had been so admirably acted by Doggett[61] that though it is only seen in the fourth act, it may be no dispraise to the play to say it probably owed the greatest part of its success to his performance. But, as the case was now desperate, any resource was better than none. Somebody must swallow the bitter pill or the play must die. At last it was recollected that I had been heard to say, in my wild way of talking, what a vast mind I had to play Nykin, by which name the character was more frequently called.[62] Notwithstanding they were thus distressed about the disposal of this part, most of 'em shook their heads at my being mentioned for it;[63] yet Powell, who was resolved at all hazards to fall upon Betterton, and having no concern for what might become of anyone that served his ends or purpose, ordered me to be sent for; and, as he naturally loved to set other people wrong, honestly said before I came, 'If the fool has a mind to blow himself up at once, let us even give him a clear stage for it'. Accordingly, the part was put into my hands between eleven and twelve that morning, which I durst not refuse, because others were as much straitened in time for study as myself. But I had this casual advantage of most of them: that having so constantly observed Doggett's performance, I wanted but little trouble to make me perfect in the words; so that when it came to my turn to rehearse, while others read their parts from their books, I had put mine in my pocket and went through the first scene without it. And though I was more abashed to rehearse so remarkable a part before the actors (which is natural to most young people) than to act before an audience, yet some of the better natured encouraged me so far as to say they did not think I should make an ill figure in it. To conclude, the curiosity to see Betterton mimicked drew us a pretty good audience, and Powell (as far as applause is a proof of it) was allowed to have burlesqued him very well.[64] As I have questioned the certain value of applause, I hope I may venture with less vanity to say how

60 Fondlewife is an ageing banker with a young wife, Laetitia.
61 Doggett created the role; however, the 1710 collected edition of Congreve's works lists
   Joseph Haines in the role, with Doggett as the pimp, Setter.
62 After the exchanges between Fondlewife and Laetitia, for example IV.iv.44–6ff: 'See you
   have made me weep – made poor Nykin weep – Nay come kiss, buss poor Nykin – and I
   won't leave – I'll lose all first' (Congreve, *Works*, I.74). Congreve may have had in mind the
   scenes between Antonio and Aquilina ('Nicky-Nacky') in Otway's *Venice Preserved* (1682).
63 Cibber's previous success as another ageing cuckold, Lord Touchwood in *The Double
   Dealer*, had perhaps been forgotten. See above, p.129.
64 Lowe quotes Chetwood, p.155, on Powell's parallel impersonation of Betterton's Falstaff:
   an imitation not just of an acting style but of 'the infirmities of distemper, old age, and
   the afflicting pains of the gout, which that great man was often seized with'.

particular a share I had of it in the same play. At my first appearance, one might have imagined by the various murmurs of the audience that they were in doubt whether Doggett himself were not returned, or that they could not conceive what strange face it could be that so nearly resembled him; for I had laid the tint of forty years more than my real age upon my features and, to the most minute placing of an hair, was dressed exactly like him. When I spoke, the surprise was still greater, as if I had not only borrowed his clothes, but his voice too. But though that was the least difficult part of him to be imitated, they seemed to allow I had so much of him in every other requisite that my applause was, perhaps, more than proportionable. For whether I had done so much where so little was expected, or that the generosity of my hearers were more than usually zealous upon so unexpected an occasion, or from what other motive such favour might be poured upon me, I cannot say; but in plain and honest truth, upon my going off from the first scene, a much better actor might have been proud of the applause that followed me. After one loud plaudit was ended and sunk into a general whisper that seemed still to continue their private approbation, it revived to a second, and again to a third still louder than the former. If, to all this, I add that Doggett himself was in the pit at the same time, it would be too rank affectation if I should not confess that to see him there a witness of my reception was, to me, as consummate a triumph as the heart of vanity could be indulged with. But, whatever vanity I might set upon myself from this unexpected success, I found that was no rule to other people's judgment of me. There were few or no parts of the same kind to be had; nor could they conceive, from what I had done in this, what other sort of characters I could be fit for. If I solicited for anything of a different nature, I was answered, 'that was not in my way'. And what *was* in my way, it seems, was not as yet resolved upon.[65] And though I replied that I thought 'anything naturally written ought to be in everyone's way that pretended to be an actor', this was looked upon as a vain, impracticable conceit of my own. Yet it is a conceit that in forty years' farther experience I have not yet given up. I still think that a painter who can draw but one sort of object, or an actor that shines but in one light, can neither of them boast of that ample genius which is necessary to form a thorough master of his art. For though genius may have a particular inclination, yet a good history painter or a good actor will, without being at a loss, give you upon demand a proper likeness of whatever nature produces. If he cannot

65 As above, p.141 n.63, a curious conclusion, given the resemblances between the roles of Lord Touchwood and Fondlewife. Evans cites Davies, II.469–71, on Cibber exposing himself 'to severe censure, and sometimes the highest ridicule' by writing and performing in tragedies.

do this, he is only an actor as the shoemaker was allowed a limited judge of Apelles's painting; but *not beyond his last.*[66] Now, though to do any one thing well may have more merit than we often meet with, and may be enough to procure a man the name of a good actor from the public, yet in my opinion it is but still the name without the substance. If his talent is in such narrow bounds that he dares not step out of them to look upon the singularities of mankind, and cannot catch them in whatever form they present them-selves; if he is not master of the *quicquid agunt homines*[67] etc in any shape that human nature is fit to be seen in; if he cannot change himself into several distinct persons so as to vary his whole tone of voice, his motion, his look and gesture, whether in high or lower life, and at the same time keep close to those variations, without leaving the character they singly belong to; if his best skill falls short of this capacity, what pretence have we to call him a complete master of his art? And though I do not insist that he ought always to show himself in these various lights, yet before we compliment him with that title he ought, at least, by some few proofs to let us see that he has them all in his power. If I am asked who ever arrived at this imaginary excellence, I confess the instances are very few; but I will venture to name Mountfort as one of them, whose theatrical character I have given in my last chapter.[68] For in his youth he had acted low humour with great success, even down to Tallboy in the *Jovial Crew*;[69] and when he was in great esteem as a tragedian, he was in comedy the most complete gentleman that I ever saw upon the stage. Let me add too that Betterton in his declining age was as eminent in Sir John Falstaff as, in the vigour of it, in his Othello.[70]

66 Apelles, the greatest painter of the Ancient Greek world, was active from c. 340 BC to c. 330. According to legend, he liked to conceal himself behind a panel while people viewed his work. One day he overheard a cobbler criticize the way he had painted a slipper; when he corrected it, the emboldened cobbler criticized his painting of the leg. See Michael Bryan, *Dictionary of Painters and Engravers*, ed. Robert Edmund Graves (London: George Bell & Sons, 1886), pp.45–6.

67 From Juvenal, Satire 1 line 85: 'Quicquid agunt homines, votum, timor, ira, voluptas, / Gaudia, discursus, nostri est farrago libelli'; i.e. 'whatever men get up to – a promise, fear, anger, pleasure, joy, rambling around – forms part of the medley of my book'.

68 See above, pp.94–6.

69 Richard Brome's *A Jovial Crew* (1641) had been in the King's Company repertory and is listed by Downes, pp.82–3, as one of the 'several old and modern plays' that transferred to the United Company. Master Talboy [sic] is in love with Amie, niece to the Justice, Master Clack. An immature lover, he is prone to tears: 'I scorn it again', he declares at the start of Act IV, 'and any man that says I cry, or I will cry again'; Brome, *A Jovial Crew: or, the Merry Beggars* (London: J.Y., 1652), np.

70 Betterton first played Falstaff at the age of 64 in his own edited version, *King Henry the Fourth: with the Humours of Sir John Falstaff*, in January 1700 (LS1 522). For his Othello, see above, p.87.

While I thus measure the value of an actor by the variety of shapes he is able to throw himself into, you may naturally suspect that I am all this while leading my own theatrical character into your favour. Why really – to speak as an honest man, I cannot wholly deny it. But in this I shall endeavour to be no farther partial to myself than known facts will make me, from the good or bad evidence of which, your better judgment will condemn or acquit me. And to show you that I will conceal no truth that is against me, I frankly own that had I been always left to my own choice of characters, I am doubtful whether I might ever have deserved an equal share of that estimation which the public seemed to have held me in. Nor am I sure that it was not vanity in me often to have suspected that I was kept out of the parts I had most mind to by the jealousy or prejudice of my contemporaries, some instances of which I could give you were they not too slight to be remembered. In the meantime, be pleased to observe how slowly, in my younger days, my good fortune came forward.

My early success in *The Old Batchelor* (of which I have given so full an account) having opened no farther way to my advancement was enough, perhaps, to have made a young fellow of more modesty despair; but being of a temper not easily disheartened, I resolved to leave nothing unattempted that might show me in some new rank of distinction. Having then no other resource, I was at last reduced to write a character for myself; but as that was not finished till about a year after, I could not in the interim procure any one part that gave me the least inclination to act it; and consequently, such as I got, I performed with a proportionable negligence. But this misfortune (if it were one) you are not to wonder at, for the same fate attended me, more or less, to the last days of my remaining on the stage. What defect in me this may have been owing to, I have not yet had sense enough to find out, but I soon found out as good a thing, which was never to be mortified at it; though I am afraid this seeming philosophy was rather owing to my inclination to pleasure than business. But to my point. The next year I produced the comedy of *Love's Last Shift*; yet the difficulty of getting it to the stage was not easily surmounted, for at that time as little was expected from me as an author as had been from my pretensions to be an actor. However, Mr Southerne (the author of *Oroonoko*) having had the patience to hear me read it to him, happened to like it so well that he immediately recommended it to the patentees, and it was accordingly acted in January 1695.[71] In this play I gave myself the part of Sir Novelty,

---

71 Cibber gives the Old Style date. *Love's Last Shift* opened in January 1696. Thomas Southerne (1660–1746) was by this time the author of seven plays, including such

7. 'Foppery then in fashion': Cibber as Lord
Foppington, by John Simon after Giovanni Grisoni.

which was thought a good portrait of the foppery then in fashion. Here
too Mr Southerne, though he had approved my play, came into the common diffidence of me as an actor. For when, on the first day of it, I was
standing myself to prompt the prologue, he took me by the hand and said,
'Young man! I pronounce thy play a good one; I will answer for its success,
if thou dost not spoil it by thy own action'.[72] Though this might be a fair
salvo for his favourable judgment of the play, yet if it were his real opinion

successes as *Sir Anthony Love* (1690, publ. 1691), *The Fatal Marriage* (1694), and, only a
few weeks before *Love's Last Shift* opened, *Oroonoko* (1695, publ. 1696). For Cibber as
Foppington, see Figure 7.
72 Dedicating the play to Richard Norton, the MP for Southwick who hosted
performances in his constituency home and subsequently wrote a play (see below, p.147
n.78), Cibber overlooked the sting in Southerne's tail he reports in the *Apology*: 'Mr
Southerne's good nature (whose own works best recommend his judgment) engaged
his reputation for the success; which its reception, and your approbation, sir, has since
redeemed.'

of me as an actor, I had the good fortune to deceive him. I succeeded so well in both, that people seemed at a loss which they should give the preference to.[73] But now let me show a little more vanity, and my apology for it shall come after: the compliment which my Lord Dorset (then Lord Chamberlain)[74] made me upon it is, I own, what I had rather not suppress, *viz.*, 'That it was the best first play that any author in his memory had produced, and that for a young fellow to show himself such an actor and such a writer in one day was something extraordinary'.[75] But as this noble lord has been celebrated for his good nature, I am contented that as much of this compliment should be supposed to exceed my deserts as may be imagined to have been heightened by his generous inclination to encourage a young beginner. If this excuse cannot soften the vanity of telling a truth so much in my own favour, I must lie at the mercy of my reader. But there was a still higher compliment passed upon me which I may publish without vanity, because it was not a designed one, and apparently came from my enemies, *viz.*, that to their certain knowledge *it was not my own*. This report is taken notice of in my dedication to the play.[76] If they spoke truth – if they knew what other person it really belonged to – I will at least

73 On the popularity of the play, and the contribution made by Cibber's acting, see *Comparison*, p.25: '*Ramble*: Ay, marry, that play was the philosopher's stone; I think it did wonders. *Sullen*: It did so, and very deservedly, there being few comedies that came up to it for purity of plot, manners and moral. It's often acted nowadays, and by the help of the author's own good action, it pleases to this day.' Davies, III.436–9, described it as 'the first comedy acted since the Restoration in which were preserved purity of manners and decency of language', noting that the reconciliation scene between Loveless and Amanda prompted 'uncommon rapture and pleasure in the audience'.

74 See above, p.105 n.55. Dorset was the dedicatee of sixteen plays between 1664 and 1695.

75 Among the actors Cibber has so far mentioned, Betterton, Powell, and Mountfort all wrote plays, but none as successful as *Love's Last Shift*.

76 In the dedication, Cibber states that 'the fable is entirely my own; nor is there a line or thought throughout the whole for which I am willingly obliged either to the dead or living'; nevertheless, the modern critical consensus is that the play is what Hume, *Development* (p.412), calls a 'potpourri' of familiar material. Lowe quotes Davies, III.437:

> So little was hoped from the genius of Cibber, that the critics reproached him with stealing his play. To his censurers he makes a serious defence of himself in his dedication to Richard Norton, Esq., of Southwick, a gentleman who was so fond of stage plays and players that he has been accused of turning his chapel into a theatre. The furious John Dennis, who hated Cibber for obstructing, as he imagined, the progress of his tragedy called *The Invader of his Country*, in very passionate terms denies his claim to this comedy: 'When *The Fool in Fashion* was first acted (says the critic) Cibber was hardly twenty years of age — how could he, at the age of twenty, write a comedy with a just design, distinguished characters, and a proper dialogue, who now, at forty, treats us with Hibernian sense and Hibernian English?'

allow them true to their trust, for above forty years have since passed and they have not yet revealed the secret.[77]

The new light in which the character of Sir Novelty had shown me, one might have thought were enough to have dissipated the doubts of what I might now be possibly good for. But to whatever chance my ill fortune was due – whether I had still but little merit, or that the managers, if I had any, were not competent judges of it, or whether I was not generally elbowed by other actors (which I am most inclined to think the true cause) when any fresh parts were to be disposed of – not one part of any consequence was I preferred to till the year following.[78] Then indeed, from Sir John Vanbrugh's favourable opinion of me, I began with others to have a better of myself. For he not only did me honour as an author by writing his *Relapse* as a sequel or second part to *Love's Last Shift*; but as an actor too, by preferring me to the chief character in his own play, which from Sir Novelty he had ennobled by the style of Baron of Foppington. This play (*The Relapse*), from its new and easy turn of wit, had great success and gave me, as a comedian, a second flight of reputation along with it.[79]

As the matter I write must be very flat or impertinent to those who have no taste or concern for the stage (and may to those who delight in it, too, be equally tedious when I talk of nobody but myself), I shall endeavour to relieve your patience by a word or two more of this gentleman, so far as he lent his pen to the support of the theatre.

Though *The Relapse* was the first play this agreeable author produced, yet it was not, it seems, the first he had written, for he had at that time by him more than all the scenes that were acted of *The Provoked Wife*;[80] but being then doubtful whether he should ever trust them to the stage, he thought no more of it. But after the success of *The Relapse* he was more

---

77 Cibber's fondness for adaptation aroused suspicion about the authenticity of his work, notably from John Dennis, who as noted above cast doubt on his authorship of *Love's Last Shift*; Dennis, *Original Letters*, 2 vols. (London, 1720), I.138–43. As Lowe points out, Cibber found an unexpected ally in Samuel Johnson, as reported in Boswell, II.340: 'There was no reason to believe that *The Careless Husband* was not written by himself.'

78 Records exist for only three Cibber roles between January and early November 1696: Smyrna in Mary Manley's *The Lost Lover* (March 1696; LS1 459), Artabazus in Richard Norton's *Pausanius* (April 1690; LS1 461), and Praiseall in *The Female Wits* (September 1696; LS1 467). Cibber's dislike of George Powell may explain the relatively fallow period: just as there was no part in *Love's Last Shift* for Powell, so there was nothing for Cibber in Powell's *The Cornish Comedy* (June 1696; LS1 463).

79 Vanbrugh's *The Relapse* opened at Drury Lane on 21 November 1696 and ran for the following week (LS1 470–1). *Comparison*, p.32, describes it as one of the 'masterpieces [that] subsisted Drury Lane House the first two or three years'.

80 Performed by the breakaway company at Lincoln's Inn Fields in April 1697 (LS1 477), with Betterton and Barry in the leading roles. See also below, pp.356–7.

strongly importuned than able to refuse it to the public. Why the last written play was first acted, and for what reason they were given to different stages, what follows will explain.

In his first step into public life (when he was but an ensign and had a heart above his income) he happened, somewhere at his winter quarters, upon a very slender acquaintance with Sir Thomas Skipwith, to receive a particular obligation from him which he had not forgot at the time I am speaking of.[81] When Sir Thomas's interest in the theatrical patent (for he had a large share in it, though he little concerned himself in the conduct of it)[82] was rising but very slowly, he thought that to give it a lift by a new comedy – if it succeeded – might be the handsomest return he could make to those his former favours; and having observed that in *Love's Last Shift* most of the actors had acquitted themselves beyond what was expected of them, he took a sudden hint from what he liked in that play and in less than three months, in the beginning of April following, brought us *The Relapse,* finished. But the season being then too far advanced, it was not acted till the succeeding winter.[83] Upon the success of *The Relapse,* the late Lord Halifax[84] (who was a great favourer of Betterton's company), having formerly by way of family amusement heard *The Provoked Wife* read to him in its looser sheets, engaged Sir John Vanbrugh to revise it, and gave it to the theatre in Lincoln's Inn Fields. This was a request not to be refused to so eminent a patron of the muses as the Lord Halifax, who was equally a friend and admirer of Sir John himself; nor was Sir Thomas Skipwith in the least disobliged by so reasonable a compliance. After which, Sir John was again at liberty to repeat his civilities to his friend, Sir Thomas; and about the same time or not long after gave us the comedy of *Aesop,*[85] for his inclination always led him to serve Sir Thomas. Besides,

81 Vanbrugh's army career began with a commission in the Earl of Huntington's regiment dated 30 January 1686. 'Ensign' was the lowest commissioned rank. The 'obligation' Cibber refers to probably took place between then and the early part of 1690; from the summer of 1690 to November 1692 Vanbrugh was detained in French prisons as a pawn in a prisoner-exchange dispute. During this time, it is believed he drafted scenes that later became *The Provoked Wife.* On 31 January 1696, soon after *Love's Last Shift* opened, he received a commission as captain in Lord Berkeley's Marine Regiment.

82 Skipwith resigned his share in the patent to Henry Brett on 6 October 1707 (manuscript listed in *Document Register* no.1904). See also below, pp.241–3.

83 i.e. in November 1696; see above, p.147 n.79.

84 i.e. Charles Montagu, 1st Earl of Halifax (1661–1715), Whig politician and poet, whose patronage of writers was satirized by Pope in 'Epistle to Dr Arbuthnot' ('full-blown Bufo, puffed by every quill'; Pope, *Poems,* p.605, line 232).

85 Vanbrugh's *Aesop* opened at Drury Lane in December 1696 (LS1 471), a month after *The Relapse,* with Cibber in the title role. A brief sequel followed in March 1697, again with Cibber in the title role (LS1 475).

our company about this time began to be looked upon in another light; the late contempt we had lain under was now wearing off, and from the success of two or three new plays, our actors (by being originals in a few good parts where they had not the disadvantage of comparison against them) sometimes found new favour in those old plays where others had exceeded them.[86]

Of this good fortune, perhaps, I had more than my share from the two very different chief characters I had succeeded in; for I was equally approved in Aesop as the Lord Foppington, allowing the difference to be no less than as wisdom in a person deformed may be less entertaining to the general taste than folly and foppery finely dressed.[87] For the character that delivers precepts of wisdom is in some sort severe upon the auditor, by showing him one wiser than himself. But when folly is his object, he applauds himself for being wiser than the coxcomb he laughs at. And who is not more pleased with an occasion to commend than accuse himself?

Though to write much in a little time is no excuse for writing ill, yet Sir John Vanbrugh's pen is not to be a little admired for its spirit, ease and readiness in producing plays so fast upon the neck of one another; for notwithstanding this quick dispatch, there is a clear and lively simplicity in his wit that neither wants the ornament of learning nor has the least smell of the lamp in it. As the face of a fine woman with only her locks loose about her may be then in its greatest beauty, such were his productions, only adorned by Nature. There is something so catching to the ear, so easy to the memory in all he writ, that it has been observed by all the actors of my time that the style of no author whatsoever gave their memory less trouble than that of Sir John Vanbrugh; which I myself, who have been charged with several of his strongest characters, can confirm by a pleasing experience. And, indeed, his wit and humour was so little laboured that his most entertaining scenes seemed to be no more than his common conversation committed to paper. Here, I confess my judgment at a loss whether, in this, I give him more or less than his due praise. For may it not be more laudable to raise an estate (whether in wealth or fame) by pains and honest industry than to be born to it? Yet if his scenes really were (as to me they always seemed) delightful, are they not, thus expeditiously written, the

---

86 Lowe cites *Comparison*, p.12: 'In the meantime the mushrooms in Drury Lane shoot up from such a desolate fortune into a considerable name, and not only grappled with their rivals, but almost eclipsed 'em.' See also below, pp.207–8.

87 Evans argues that Cibber confuses Aesop's 'aphoristic mode of speech' with true wisdom; however, the play shows the eponymous hero emerging from cynicism to create a generous reconciliation, after the pattern of Cibber's own *Love's Last Shift*.

more surprising? Let the wit and merit of them, then, be weighed by wiser critics than I pretend to be. But no wonder, while his conceptions were so full of life and humour, his muse should be sometimes too warm to wait the slow pace of judgment, or to endure the drudgery of forming a regular fable to them. Yet we see *The Relapse*, however imperfect in the conduct, by the mere force of its agreeable wit ran away with the hearts of its hearers; while *Love's Last Shift*, which (as Mr Congreve justly said of it) had only in it a great many things that were like wit, that in reality were not wit,[88] and what is still less pardonable (as I say of it myself), has a great deal of puerility and frothy stage language in it – yet, by the mere moral delight received from its fable, it has been with the other in a continued and equal possession of the stage for more than forty years.[89]

As I have already promised you to refer your judgment of me as an actor rather to known facts than my own opinion (which I could not be sure would keep clear of self-partiality), I must a little farther risk my being tedious, to be as good as my word. I have elsewhere allowed that my want of a strong and full voice soon cut short my hopes of making any valuable figure in tragedy; and I have been many years since convinced that whatever opinion I might have of my own judgment or capacity to amend the palpable errors that I saw our tragedians most in favour commit, yet the auditors who would have been sensible of any such amendments (could I have made them) were so very few that my best endeavour would have been but an unavailing labour – or, what is yet worse, might have appeared both to our actors and to many auditors the vain mistake of my own self-conceit. For so strong – so very near indispensable – is that one article of voice in the forming a good tragedian, that an actor may want any other qualification whatsoever, and yet have a better chance for applause than he will ever have with all the skill in the world if his voice is not equal to it. Mistake me not: I say for *applause* only, but applause does not always stay for, nor always follow, intrinsic merit. Applause will frequently open like a young hound upon a wrong scent; and the majority of auditors, you know, are generally composed of babblers that are profuse of their voices before there

---

88 In *The Way of the World*, Witwoud's similes are Cibber-like, funny only to himself: the sign of 'a wit, which at the same time that it is affected, is also false' (from Congreve's dedication of the play to Ralph, Earl of Mountague, in Congreve, *Works*, II.97). See Introduction, p.xxiii.

89 Both *The Relapse* and *Love's Last Shift* were among the staples of the eighteenth-century stage identified by Shirley Strum Kenny in 'Perennial Favourites: Congreve, Vanbrugh, Cibber, Farquhar and Steele', *Modern Philology* 73 (1976), 4–11. On the basis of records in *The London Stage*, Cibber's plays were more often performed than Vanbrugh's and every other playwright's except Shakespeare.

is anything on foot that calls for them. Not but, I grant, to lead or mislead the many will always stand in some rank of a necessary merit; yet when I say a good tragedian, I mean one in opinion of whose real merit the best judges would agree.

Having so far given up my pretensions to the buskin, I ought now to account for my having been, notwithstanding, so often seen in some particular characters in tragedy as Iago, Wolsey, Syphax, Richard the Third, *etc.*[90] If in any of this kind I have succeeded, perhaps it has been a merit dearly purchased; for from the delight I seemed to take in my performing them, half my auditors have been persuaded that a great share of the wickedness of them must have been in my own nature. If this is true, as true I fear (I had almost said 'hope') it is, I look upon it rather as a praise than censure of my performance. Aversion there, is an involuntary commendation where we are only hated for being like the thing we ought to be like – a sort of praise, however, which few actors besides myself could endure. Had it been equal to the usual praise given to virtue, my contemporaries would have thought themselves injured if I had pretended to any share of it. So that you see it has been as much the dislike others had to them as choice that has thrown me sometimes into these characters. But it may be farther observed that in the characters I have named, where there is so much close-meditated mischief, deceit, pride, insolence or cruelty, they cannot have the least cast or proffer of the amiable in them; consequently, there can be no great demand for that harmonious sound or pleasing, round melody of voice which in the softer sentiments of love, the wailings of distressful virtue, or in the throws and swellings of honour and ambition, may be needful to recommend them to our pity or admiration – so that, again, my

---

90 For Cibber's first known Iago, see above p.41 n.51; he took over the role from John Verbruggen and passed it to John Mills during the 1720s. On 15 February 1707 Cibber is recorded as playing Surrey in *Henry VIII* (LS2a 343); on 26 January 1709 he played Cranmer (LS2a 464–5); he may have graduated to Wolsey for the performance attended by the Prince of Wales on 19 November 1716 (LS2 422), but his reference here is probably to the role of Wolsey in a revival of John Banks's 1682 *Virtue Betrayed; or Anna Bullen* (see, for example, LS2 349 on a performance of Banks's play on 28 March 1715). He played Syphax in Addison's *Cato* from its opening on 14 April 1713, and Richard III in his own adapation from January 1700. Lowe cites Davies, III.469: 'The truth is, Cibber was endured in ... tragic parts, on account of his general merit in comedy.' He also cites the even less charitable view of *The Laureate*: 'I have often heard him blamed as a trifler ... [H]e was rarely perfect, and, abating for the badness of his voice and the insignificancy and meanness of his action, he did not seem to understand either what he said or what he was about' (p.41). Neither of those commentaries (nor even Cibber himself) mentions the comedic aspects of the roles of Iago and Richard in particular as justification for his casting.

want of that requisite voice might less disqualify me for the vicious than the virtuous character. This too may have been a more favourable reason for my having been chosen for them. A yet farther consideration that inclined me to them was that they are generally better written, thicker sown with sensible reflections, and come by so much nearer to common life and Nature than characters of admiration, as vice is more the practice of mankind than virtue. Nor could I sometimes help smiling at those dainty actors that were too squeamish to swallow them, as if they were one jot the better men for acting a good man well, or another man the worse, for doing equal justice to a bad one! 'Tis not, sure, *what* we act but *how* we act what is allotted us that speaks our intrinsic value, as in real life the wise man or the fool (be he prince or peasant) will in either state be equally the fool or the wise man! But alas, in personated life this is no rule to the vulgar! They are apt to think all before them real, and rate the actor according to his borrowed vice or virtue.

If, then, I had always too careless a concern for false or vulgar applause, I ought not to complain if I have had less of it than others of my time, or not less of it than I desired. Yet I will venture to say that from the common, weak appetite of false applause, many actors have run into more errors and absurdities than their greatest ignorance could otherwise have committed.[91] If this charge is true, it will lie chiefly upon the better judgment of the spectator to reform it.

But, not to make too great a merit of my avoiding this common road to applause, perhaps I was vain enough to think I had more ways than one to come at it: that in the variety of characters I acted, the chances to win it were the stronger on my side; that if the multitude were not in a roar to see me in Cardinal Wolsey, I could be sure of them in Alderman Fondlewife.[92] If they hated me in Iago, in Sir Fopling they took me for a fine gentleman;[93] if they were silent at Syphax, no Italian eunuch was more applauded than when I sung in Sir Courtly.[94] If the morals of Aesop were too grave for them, Justice Shallow was as simple and as merry an old rake as the wisest of our young ones could wish me.[95] And though the terror and detestation

---

91 Lowe cites *The Laureate*: 'Whatever the actors appeared upon the stage, they were most of them barbarians off on't, few of them having had the education, or whose fortunes could admit them to the conversation of gentlemen' (p.44).
92 See above, pp.141–2.   93 See above, p.125 n.134.   94 See above, p.95
95 Lowe cites Davies, I.306, on Cibber's Shallow:

> Whether he was a copy or an original in Shallow, it is certain no audience was ever more fixed in deep attention at his first appearance, or more shaken with laughter in the progress of the scene than at Colley Cibber's exhibition of this ridiculous Justice of Peace. Some years after he had left the stage he acted

raised by King Richard might be too severe a delight for them, yet the more gentle and modern vanities of a poet Bayes,[96] or the well-bred vices of a Lord Foppington, were not at all more than their merry hearts or nicer morals could bear.

These few instances (out of fifty more I could give you) may serve to explain what sort of merit I at most pretended to; which was, that I supplied with variety whatever I might want of that particular skill wherein others went before me. How this variety was executed (for by that only is its value to be rated), you who have so often been my spectator are the proper judge. If you pronounce my performance to have been defective, I am condemned by my own evidence; if you acquit me, these outlines may serve for a sketch of my theatrical character.

Shallow for his son's benefit, I believe in 1737, when Quin was the Falstaff, and Milward the king. Whether it was owing to the pleasure the spectators felt on seeing their old friend return to them again, *though for that night only* after an absence of some years, I know not; but, surely, no actor or audience were better pleased with each other. His manner was so perfectly simple, his look so vacant, when he questioned his cousin Silence about the price of ewes and lamented in the same breath, with silly surprise, the death of Old Double, that it will be impossible for any surviving spectator not to smile at the remembrance of it. The want of ideas occasions Shallow to repeat almost every thing he says. Cibber's transition from asking the price of bullocks, to trite but grave reflections on mortality, was so natural and attended with such an unmeaning roll of his small pigs-eyes, accompanied with an important utterance of tick! tick! tick! not much louder than the balance of a watch, that I question if any actor was ever superior in the conception or expression of such solemn insignificancy.

96 See above, p.14 n.9.

CHAPTER 7

The state of the stage continued. The occasion of Wilks's commencing actor. His success. Facts relating to his theatrical talent. Actors more or less esteemed from their private characters.

The Lincoln's Inn Fields company were now, in 1693, a commonwealth like that of Holland, divided from the tyranny of Spain.[1] But the similitude goes very little farther. Short was the duration of the theatrical power; for though success poured in so fast upon them at their first opening that everything seemed to support itself, yet experience in a year or two showed them that they had never been worse governed than when they governed themselves![2] Many of them began to make their particular interest more their point than that of the general; and though some deference might be had to the measures and advice of Betterton, several of them wanted to govern in their turn, and were often out of humour that their opinion was not equally regarded.[3] But have we not seen the same infirmity in senates? The tragedians seemed to think their rank as much above the comedians as in the characters they severally acted; when the first were in their finery, the latter were impatient at the expense and looked upon it as rather laid out upon the real than the fictitious person of the actor. Nay, I have known in our own company this ridiculous sort of regret carried so far that the tragedian has thought himself injured when the comedian pretended to

1 1695 is the true date; the error was not corrected in the second edition. 'Commonwealth' indicates freedom from the management of Christopher Rich and the distribution of shares among members of the new company; the comparison is with the rebellion of the Dutch against Spanish rule in 1572–3, a tribute to William III's dynasty and Whig politics.
2 However, Milhous, *Management*, p.107, concludes that for the 1696–7 season 'the score card adds up even more in favor of the rebels than the last; they had more successes and fewer failures than the Patent Company'. It is during the 1697–8 season that Milhous detects the 'dangerous inclination toward stasis' that contributed to internal dissent in the new company.
3 Milhous, *Management*, pp.114–15, dates this collapse of authority to the period 1698–1700. David Craufurd's preface to his 1700 play, *Courtship à la Mode*, describes a chaotic and ultimately aborted rehearsal process at Lincoln's Inn Fields that led him to transfer the play to Rich's Company. On 11 November 1700 Lord Chamberlain Jersey published an order that Betterton should 'take upon him ye sole management' of the company to suppress its 'frequent disorders' (LC 5/153, p.23; *Document Register* no.1655), so recommending an end to what Cibber describes as the 'commonwealth' of the original licence.

wear a fine coat! I remember Powell, upon surveying my first dress in *The Relapse*, was out of all temper and reproached our master in very rude terms that he had not so good a suit to play Caesar Borgia in,[4] though he knew at the same time, my Lord Foppington filled the house when his bouncing Borgia would do little more than pay fiddles and candles to it.[5] And though a character of vanity might be supposed more expensive in dress than possibly one of ambition, yet the high heart of this heroical actor could not bear that a comedian should ever pretend to be as well dressed as himself. Thus again, on the contrary, when Betterton proposed to set off a tragedy, the comedians were sure to murmur at the charge of it,[6] and the late reputation which Doggett had acquired from acting his Ben in *Love for Love* made him a more declared malcontent on such occasions. He over-valued comedy for its being nearer to Nature than tragedy, which is allowed to say many fine things that Nature never spoke in the same words; and supposing his opinion were just, yet he should have considered that the public had a taste as well as himself, which in policy he ought to have complied with. Doggett, however, could not with patience look upon the costly trains and plumes of tragedy, in which (knowing himself to be useless) he thought were all a vain extravagance. And when he found his singularity could no longer oppose that expense, he so obstinately adhered to his own opinion that he left the society of his old friends and came over to us at the Theatre Royal;[7] and yet this actor always set up for a theatrical patriot.[8] This happened in the winter following the first division of the

4 Lee's *Caesar Borgia* had been premiered by the Duke's Company in May 1679 with Betterton in the title role (LS1 276). A 1696 reprint indicates a possible revival that year following Betterton's defection (LS1 450), with Powell taking over the role and, presumably, the costume.

5 i.e. the cost of music and lighting, but here meant figuratively. *Document Register* nos.2444–5 show bills for sconces and candles at Drury Lane in 1714 of £3 10s and 3s 9d respectively. Music scores typically cost a little over £1 (see, for example, *Document Register* no.2746), plus the cost of the players.

6 Cibber uses the term 'tragedy' loosely. The loss of Dorset Garden and its scenic potential, not to mention its stock of costumes, did not dent Betterton's belief in the appeal of musical extravaganzas. In November 1698 his company staged John Dennis's *Rinaldo and Armida*, a production which, according to *Comparison*, p.22, 'surprised not only Drury Lane, but indeed all the town, nobody ever dreaming of an opera there'. A letter from Elizabeth Barry to Lady Lisburne dated 5 January 1699 (LS1 507) named the show as the company's only success that winter.

7 On 26 October 1696, Lord Chamberlain Dorset accused both companies of trying to poach each other's actors and renewed the prohibition on transfers, while allowing Doggett to join Rich's company and John Verbruggen to move the other way (LC 7/1, p.47; *Document Register* no.1539). This was therefore the second winter after the breakaway rather than the first, as Cibber states below.

8 For Cibber's later difficulties with Doggett, see below, pp.284–6 and 304–8.

(only) company. He came time enough to the Theatre Royal, to act the part of Lory in *The Relapse*: an arch valet, quite after the French cast – pert and familiar.[9] But it suited so ill with Doggett's dry and closely natural manner of acting that upon the second day he desired it might be disposed of to another; which the author complying with, gave it to Penkethman, who though in other lights much his inferior, yet this part he seemed better to become. Doggett was so immovable in his opinion of whatever he thought was right or wrong that he could never be easy under any kind of theatrical government, and was generally so warm in pursuit of his interest that he often outran it. I remember him three times, for some years, unemployed in any theatre, from his not being able to bear in common with others the disagreeable accidents that in such societies are unavoidable.[10] But whatever pretences he had formed for this first deserting from Lincoln's Inn Fields, I always thought his best reason for it was that he looked upon it as a sinking ship; not only from the melancholy abatement of their profits, but likewise from the neglect and disorder in their government. He plainly saw that their extraordinary success at first had made them too confident of its duration, and from thence had slackened their industry – by which he observed at the same time the old house, where there was scarce any other merit than industry, began to flourish.[11] And indeed they seemed not enough to consider that the appetite of the public, like that of a fine gentleman, could only be kept warm by variety: that let their merit be never so high, yet the taste of a town was not always constant nor infallible; that it was dangerous to hold their rivals in too much contempt,[12] for they found

9 Lory is Young Fashion's servant in the play. His 'pert' repartee includes an objection to moral scruples because they are 'strong symptoms of death'; in Vanbrugh, *Four Comedies*, ed. Michael Cordner (Harmondsworth: Penguin Books, 1989), p.66 (I.iii.298).

10 Thomas Doggett's numerous petitions and run-ins with authority are recorded in *Document Register* nos. 1742, 2263, 2422, 2441, 2477, *passim*. Lowe gives the three periods of absence Cibber refers to as 1698–1700, 1706–8, and 1708–9. However, Doggett certainly performed in Betterton's *The Amorous Widow* in the 1699–1700 season (LS1 521). His intermittent attempts to run his own company led to appearances at Norwich (October 1697 and January 1700; letter and newspaper report in *Document Register* nos.1565 and 1624); at his booth in Bartholomew Fair (23 August 1699, LS1 512); and at Cambridge, where the Vice-Chancellor had him jailed for performing without permission (Defoe, *Review*, in *Document Register* no.1858).

11 Milhous, *Management*, p.109, cites the 1699–1700 season as the one that marked the Patent Company's 'ascendancy', i.e. three years after Doggett quit the breakaway company and soon after he rejoined it.

12 Lowe cites Dryden's reflections on the breakaway company in his Address to George Granville on the latter's *Heroic Love* (1698): 'Their setting sun still shoots a glimmering ray, / Like ancient Rome, majestic in decay.' See Dryden, p.509.

that a young, industrious company were soon a match for the best actors when too securely negligent. And negligent they certainly were, and fondly fancied that had each of their different schemes been followed, their audiences would not so suddenly have fallen off.[13]

But alas! The vanity of applauded actors, when they are not crowded to as they may have been, makes them naturally impute the change to any cause rather than the true one – satiety. They are mighty loath to think a town once so fond of them could ever be tired; and yet, at one time or other, more or less thin houses have been the certain fate of the most prosperous actors, ever since I remember the stage! But against this evil, the provident patentees had found out a relief which the new house were not yet masters of, *viz.*, never to pay their people when the money did not come in; nor then neither, but in such proportions as suited their conveniency.[14] I myself was one of the many who, for six acting weeks together, never received one day's pay and, for some years after, seldom had above half our nominal salaries. But to the best of my memory, the finances of the other house held it not above one season more before they were reduced to the same expedient of making the like scanty payments.[15]

---

13 Lowe cites *Comparison*, p.13: 'But this [the success of *Love for Love*], like other things of that kind, being only nine days' wonder, and the audiences being in a little time sated with the novelty of the new house, return in shoals to the old.' As noted above, p.154 n.2, Milhous places the decline of the breakaway company at least eighteen months after *Love for Love*.

14 Milhous, *Management*, p.109, adds that Rich also failed to pay shareholder dividends or the rent on Dorset Garden between 1695 and 1704.

15 Cibber does not mention two significant episodes that occurred during this period. Jane Lucas, who had played Amanda's maid in *Love's Last Shift*, alleged in April 1697 that Cibber had assaulted her, for which he was imprisoned (LC 7/3, fol.158; *Document Register* no.1553). Although he was ordered to appear before the Westminster magistrates, the case appears to have been dropped; Lucas carried on acting at Drury Lane until 1702 (Koon, p.34). The second episode required discretion for other reasons. In the preface to *Woman's Wit*, which opened at Drury Lane in January 1697 (LS1 472), Cibber reveals that 'during the time of [his] writing the first two acts, [he] was entertained at the new theatre', intending to write parts for 'the two most experienced' actors, presumably Betterton and Barry. Halfway through the third act, however, 'not liking [his] station there', he returned to the Patent Company. Lowe interprets this as meaning that Cibber had briefly joined the breakaway company, but since the episode probably took place during the summer break between seasons in 1696 it may be better understood as an instance of 'tapping up', as prohibited in Lord Chamberlain Dorset's order of 26 October that year (LC 7/1, p.47; *Document Register* no.1539). Cibber may have been angling for a better deal with Rich: the two signed a new contract for Cibber's plays on 29 October (LC 7/3, fols.76–7; *Document Register* no.1540).

Such was the distress and fortune of both these companies since their division from the Theatre Royal: either working at half wages or, by alternate successes, intercepting the bread from one another's mouths;[16] irreconcilable enemies, yet without hope of relief from a victory on either side; sometimes both parties reduced, and yet each supporting their spirits by seeing the other under the same calamity.

During this state of the stage it was that the lowest expedient was made use of to ingratiate our company in the public favour. Our master, who had sometime practised the law[17] and therefore loved a storm better than fair weather (for it was his own conduct, chiefly, that had brought the patent into these dangers), took nothing so much to heart as that partiality wherewith he imagined the people of quality had preferred the actors of the other house to those of his own. To balance this misfortune, he was resolved at least to be well with their domestics, and therefore cunningly opened the upper gallery to them *gratis*; for before this time no footman was ever admitted (or had presumed to come into it) till after the fourth act was ended. This additional privilege (the greatest plague that ever playhouse had to complain of) he conceived would not only incline them to give us a good word in the respective families they belonged to, but would naturally incite them to come all hands aloft in the crack of our applauses. And indeed it so far succeeded that it often thundered from the full gallery above while our thin pit and boxes below were in the utmost serenity. This riotous privilege, so craftily given, and which from custom was at last ripened into right, became the most disgraceful nuisance that ever depreciated the theatre.[18] How often have the most polite audiences, in the most affecting scenes of the best plays, been disturbed and insulted by the noise and clamour of these savage spectators? From the same narrow way of thinking, too, were so many ordinary people and unlicked cubs of condition admitted

16 Lowe cites *Comparison*, p.14: 'The town ... changed their inclinations for the two houses, as they found 'emselves inclined to comedy or tragedy: if they desired a tragedy they went to Lincoln's Inn Fields; if to comedy, they flocked to Drury Lane.' The known repertory of the companies at this time does not consistently show they played to those alleged strengths.

17 On Christopher Rich, Lowe cites *Comparison*, p.15: 'In the other house there's an old snarling lawyer master and sovereign; a waspish, ignorant, pettifogger in law and poetry; one who understands poetry no more than algebra; he would sooner have the grace of God than do everybody justice.'

18 During March 1737 there were several disturbances at Drury Lane involving what the *Grub-street Journal* of 17 March 1737 described as 'frequent disputes ... between the gentlemen and the footmen about good breeding'. On 26 March, *Fog's Weekly Journal* reported that a fifty-strong guard had been posted to the theatre, and on 23 April the *London Magazine* recorded the sentencing to hard labour of two footmen for inciting a riot. Lowe dates the granting of the privilege Cibber mentions to 1697–8.

behind our scenes for money, and sometimes without it; the plagues and inconveniences of which custom we found so intolerable when we afterwards had the stage in our hands, that at the hazard of our lives we were forced to get rid of them, and our only expedient was by refusing money from all persons, without distinction, at the stage door. By this means we preserved to ourselves the right and liberty of choosing our own company there,[19] and by a strict observance of this order we brought what had been before debased into all the licences of a lobby, into the decencies of a drawing room.

About the distressful time I was speaking of, in the year 1696[20] Wilks, who now had been five years in great esteem on the Dublin Theatre, returned to that of Drury Lane, in which last he had first set out and had continued to act some small parts for one winter only. The considerable figure which he so lately made upon the stage in London makes me imagine that a particular account of his first commencing actor may not be unacceptable to the curious. I shall therefore give it them as I had it from his own mouth.[21]

In King James's reign he had been some time employed in the Secretary's office in Ireland (his native country) and remained in it till after the Battle of the Boyne, which completed the Revolution.[22] Upon that happy and unexpected deliverance, the people of Dublin, among the various expressions of their joy, had a mind to have a play; but the actors being dispersed during the war, some private persons agreed (in the best manner they were able) to give one to the public *gratis*, at the theatre. The play was *Othello*, in which Wilks acted the Moor, and the applause he received in it

19 Cibber implies that this was a recent phenomenon, yet orders exist from 1665 against 'hindrance of the actors and interruption of the scenes' by members of the public going backstage (SP 44/22, pp.31–2; *Document Register* nos.306–7). Further such orders were issued in 1668 (*Document Register* no.447), 1670 (*Document Register* no.567), and 1677 (*Document Register* no.990), and were repeated in 1708 (*Document Register* no. 1959) and 1711 (*Document Register* no.2160).

20 Following his initial and unsuccessful period in London, Wilks returned in 1698, eventually triumphing in November as Sir Harry Wildair in his friend Farquhar's *The Constant Couple* (LS1 517). It is sometimes asserted that he appeared in Pierre Motteux's *The Island Princess* in November 1698; however, his name does not appear in the cast list.

21 Cibber insists on the authenticity of the account because of the controversy surrounding Wilks's past sparked by O'Bryan's *Authentic Memoirs* (see above, p.12 n.3); elsewhere he appears doubtful on Wilks's private conduct (above, p.99).

22 According to the testimony of Wilks's brother-in-law, Alexander Knapton, Wilks joined the office of Sir Robert Southwell, Secretary of State for Ireland, in 1683, aged 18; as recorded in Edmund Curll's *The Life of that Eminent Comedian Robert Wilks, Esq.* (London, 1733). Cibber's statement that Wilks 'remained' a clerk until after the Battle of the Boyne (11 July 1690 NS) is qualified by Alexander Knapton's recollection that he was drafted into the army but by special pleading was allowed to continue in his former role. The Battle of the Boyne 'completed' the victory of William III over the exiled James II.

warmed him to so strong an inclination for the stage that he immediately preferred it to all his other views in life; for he quitted his post, and with the first fair occasion came over to try his fortune in the (then) only company of actors in London. The person who supplied his post in Dublin, he told me, raised to himself from thence a fortune of fifty thousand pounds. Here you have a much stronger instance of an extravagant passion for the stage than that which I have elsewhere shown in myself. I only quitted my hopes of being preferred to the like post for it; but Wilks quitted his actual possession for the imaginary happiness which the life of an actor presented to him. And though possibly we might both have bettered our fortunes in a more honourable station, yet whether better fortunes might have equally gratified our vanity (the universal passion of mankind) may admit of a question.

Upon his being formerly received into the Theatre Royal (which was in the winter after I had been initiated), his station there was much upon the same class with my own;[23] our parts were generally of an equal insignificancy, not of consequence enough to give either a preference. But Wilks being more impatient of his low condition than I was (and indeed, the company was then so well stocked with good actors that there was very little hope of getting forward), laid hold of a more expeditious way for his advancement, and returned again to Dublin with Mr Ashbury, the patentee of that theatre, to act in his new company there.[24] There went with him at the same time Mrs Butler, whose character I have already given, and Estcourt, who had not appeared on any stage and was yet only known as an excellent mimic.[25] Wilks, having no competitor in Dublin, was immediately preferred to whatever parts his inclination led him, and his early reputation on that stage as soon raised in him an ambition to show himself on a better. And I have heard him say (in raillery of the vanity which young actors are liable to) that when the news of Mountfort's death came to Ireland, he from that time thought his fortune was made, and took a resolution to return a second time to England with the first opportunity;[26] but, as his engagements to the stage where he was were too strong to be suddenly broke from, he returned not to the Theatre Royal till the year 1696.[27]

23 Curll, *Life*, p.6, states that Wilks was offered 15 shillings a week, with 2s 6d deducted for dancing lessons; he married Elizabeth Knapton in 1691.

24 Curll, *Life*, p.7, dates Wilks's conversation with Joseph Ashbury at 1693 and describes the offer as £50 a year plus a benefit performance: not a huge increase, but attractive for its promise of better roles. For Ashbury, see above, p.118 n.111.

25 See above, p.75 n.42 (Butler) and p.86 n.80 (Estcourt).

26 In Alexander Knapton's chronology for Curll, Wilks was still in London when Mountfort died in December 1692.

27 Actually 1698: see above, p.159 n.20.

Upon his first arrival, Powell (who was now in possession of all the chief parts of Mountfort, and the only actor that stood in Wilks's way), in seeming civility offered him his choice of whatever he thought fit to make his first appearance in, though in reality the favour was intended to hurt him. But Wilks rightly judged it more modest to accept only of a part of Powell's, and which Mountfort had never acted: that of Palamede in Dryden's *Marriage à la Mode*.[28] Here too he had the advantage of having the ball played into his hand by the inimitable Mrs Mountfort, who was then his Melantha in the same play. Whatever fame Wilks had brought with him from Ireland, he as yet appeared but a very raw actor to what he was afterwards allowed to be. His faults however, I shall rather leave to the judgments of those who then may remember him than to take upon me the disagreeable office of being particular upon them, farther than by saying that in this part of Palamede he was short of Powell, and missed a good deal of the loose humour of the character which the other more happily hit.[29] But however – he was young, erect, of a pleasing aspect and, in the whole, gave the town and the stage sufficient hopes of him. I ought to make some allowances, too, for the restraint he must naturally have been under from his first appearance upon a new stage. But from that he soon recovered, and grew daily more in favour not only of the town but likewise of the patentee, whom Powell (before Wilks's arrival) had treated in almost what manner he pleased.[30]

Upon this visible success of Wilks, the pretended contempt which Powell had held him in began to sour into an open jealousy; he now plainly saw he was a formidable rival, and (which more hurt him) saw too that other people saw it, and therefore found it high time to oppose and be troublesome to him. But Wilks happening to be as jealous of his fame as the other, you may imagine such clashing candidates could not be long without a rupture. In short, a challenge, I very well remember, came from Powell when he was hot headed; but the next morning he was cool enough to let it end in favour of Wilks. Yet, how-

28 In the preface to the anonymous *The Fatal Discovery*, which opened in February 1698 (LS1 491), George Powell writes that *Marriage à la Mode* had recently been revived by the company.

29 Lowe cites *The Laureate*, which disagreed with Cibber's assessment: 'Wilks, in this part of Palamede, behaved with a modest diffidence and yet maintained the spirit of his part, [whereas Powell's] conversation, his manners, his dress, neither on nor off the stage bore any similitude to that character' (p.44).

30 George Powell was notoriously ill-disciplined. On 1 May 1698 he was the subject of an arrest warrant for assaulting Thomas Davenant, and threatening one Colonel Stanhope who had stepped in (SP 44/349, p.70; *Document Register* no.1580); two days later the company was silenced because it had not punished Powell (LC 5/152, p.80; *Document Register* no.1581); on 19 May the company was ordered to suspend him until further notice (LC 5/152, p.89; *Document Register* no.1590).

ever the magnanimity on either part might subside, the animosity was as deep in the heart as ever, though it was not afterwards so openly avowed. For when Powell found that intimidating would not carry his point but that Wilks, when provoked, would really give battle,[31] he (Powell) grew so out of humour that he cocked his hat, and in his passion walked off to the service of the company in Lincoln's Inn Fields. But there, finding more competitors, and that he made a worse figure among them than in the company he came from, he stayed but one winter with them before he returned to his old quarters in Drury Lane; where, after these unsuccessful pushes of his ambition, he at last became a martyr to negligence and quietly submitted to the advantages and superiority which, during his late desertion, Wilks had more easily got over him.[32]

However trifling these theatrical anecdotes may seem to a sensible reader, yet, as the different conduct of these rival actors may be of use to others of the same profession and from thence may contribute to the pleasure of the public, let that be my excuse for pursuing them. I must therefore let it be known that though in voice and ear, Nature had been more kind to Powell, yet he so often lost the value of them by an unheedful confidence that the constant, wakeful care and decency of Wilks left the other far behind in the public esteem and approbation. Nor was his memory less tenacious than that of Wilks, but Powell put too much trust in it and idly deferred the studying of his parts (as schoolboys do their exercise) to the last day,[33] which commonly brings them out proportionably defective. But Wilks never lost an hour of precious time and was, in all his parts, perfect to such an exactitude that I question if, in forty years, he ever five times changed or misplaced an article in any one of them. To be master of this uncommon diligence is

31 Lowe cites *The Laureate*, p.44: 'I believe he (Wilks) was obliged to fight the heroic George Powell, as well as one or two others who were piqued at his being so highly encouraged by the town, and their rival, before he could be quiet.'

32 Powell probably joined the breakaway company for the 1702–3 and 1703–4 seasons, and part of the subsequent one; he is listed in LS2a 41 as a member of the breakaway company in the 1701–2 season, but a document dated 23 February 1702 puts him first among 'Comedians in Ordinary to King William' (i.e. of Rich's Patent Company – LC 5/153, p.160; *Document Register* no.1682). At some point before or during his time with the breakaway company he petitioned Lord Chamberlain Jersey for official release from Rich's company on the grounds that his salary had not been paid; this was allowed on condition that he pay his debts to the company (*Document Register* no.1695). After the breakaway company had moved to the Queen's Theatre, Haymarket, Powell's 'great insolence' in refusing to act led to orders in November 1705 to arrest him and prevent him from rejoining Drury Lane (LC 5/154, pp.119 and 124; *Document Register* nos.1825 and 1826). Cibber's commentary on that episode is below, pp.232–3.

33 Companies relied on actors undertaking private study before any group rehearsal, which might only take place on 'the last day' before (or even on the morning of) performance. See Stern, pp.167–8.

adding to the gift of Nature all that is in an actor's power; and this duty of studying perfect, whatever actor is remiss in, he will proportionably find that Nature may have been kind to him in vain.[34] For though Powell had an assurance that covered this neglect much better than a man of more modesty might have done, yet with all his intrepidity, very often the diffidence and concern for what he was to *say* made him lose the look of what he was to *be*. While, therefore, Powell presided, his idle example made this fault so common to others that I cannot but confess, in the general infection, I had my share of it. Nor was my too critical excuse for it a good one, *viz.* that scarce one part in five that fell to my lot was worth the labour. But to show respect to an audience is worth the best actor's labour and, his business considered, he must be a very impudent one that comes before them with a conscious negligence of what he is about.[35] But Wilks was never known to make any of these venial distinctions; nor, however barren his part might be, could bear even the self-reproach of favouring his memory. And I have been astonished to see him swallow a volume of froth and insipidity in a new play that we were sure could not live above three days, though favoured and recommended to the stage by some good person of quality. Upon such occasions, in compassion to his fruitless toil and labour, I have sometimes cried out with Cato, 'Painful pre-eminence!',[36] so insupportable (in my sense) was the task when the bare praise of not having been negligent was sure to be the only reward of it. But so indefatigable was the diligence of Wilks that he seemed to love it as a good man does virtue, for its own sake, of which the following instance will give you an extraordinary proof.

In some new comedy, he happened to complain of a crabbed speech in his part which, he said, gave him more trouble to study than all the rest of it

---

34 i.e. any actor who neglects his duty to learn his lines perfectly will find that his natural talents do not compensate.

35 Lowe observes that 'Cibber is here somewhat in the position of Satan reproving sin', citing Davies, III.480: 'This attention to the gaming table would not, we may be assured, render him [i.e. Cibber] fitter for his business of the stage. After many an unlucky run at Tom's coffee house, he has arrived at the playhouse in great tranquillity and then, humming over an opera-tune, he has walked on the stage not well prepared in the part he was to act. Cibber should not have reprehended Powell so severely for neglect and imperfect representation. I have seen him at fault where it was least expected, in parts which he had acted a hundred times, and particularly in Sir Courtly Nice, but Colley dexterously supplied the deficiency of his memory by prolonging his ceremonious bow to the lady and drawling out "Your humble servant, madam" to an extraordinary length; then, taking a pinch of snuff and strutting deliberately across the stage, he has gravely asked the prompter what is next.' McGirr, pp.156–7, questions the evidence behind Davies's account.

36 From Addison's *Cato*, III.i, in which the eponymous hero exclaims to his followers, 'Am I distinguished from you but by toils, / Superior toils, and heavier weight of cares? / Painful pre-eminence!' For Cibber's role in the play, see above, p.91 n.11.

had done; upon which, he applied to the author either to soften or shorten it. The author, that he might make the matter quite easy to him, fairly cut it all out. But when he got home from the rehearsal, Wilks thought it such an indignity to his memory that anything should be thought too hard for it, that he actually made himself perfect in that speech, though he knew it was never to be made use of. From this singular act of supererogation, you may judge how indefatigable the labour of his memory must have been when his profit and honour were more concerned to make use of it.[37]

But besides this indispensable quality of diligence, Wilks had the advantage of a sober character in private life, which Powell not having the least regard to, laboured under the unhappy disfavour (not to say contempt) of the public, to whom his licentious courses were no secret.[38] Even when he did well, that natural prejudice pursued him: neither the hero nor the gentleman, the young Ammon[39] nor the Dorimant,[40] could conceal from the conscious spectator the true George Powell. And this sort of disesteem (or favour) every actor will feel and more or less have his share of, as he has or has not a due regard to his private life and reputation. Nay, even false reports shall affect him and become the cause, or pretence at least, of undervaluing or treating him injuriously. Let me give a known instance of it and, at the same time, a justification of myself from an imputation that was laid upon me not many years before I quitted the theatre, of which you will see the consequence.

After the vast success of that new species of dramatic poetry, *The Beggar's Opera*,[41] the year following I was so stupid as to attempt something of the same kind upon a quite different foundation: that of recommending virtue and innocence, which I ignorantly thought might not have a less

---

37 Lowe cites *The Laureate*: 'I have known [Wilks] lay a wager and win it, that he would repeat the part of Truewit in *The Silent Woman*, which consists of thirty lengths of paper, as they call 'em (that is, one quarter of a sheet on both sides to a length), without misplacing a single word or missing an "and" or an "or"' (p.45).

38 Whether Wilks's private life in Ireland had been 'sober' was disputed by early biographers (see Introduction, p.xli); Cibber's reference to Jane Rogers betrays his own doubts (above, p.99 n.35). Amid Powell's other offences, his dismissal for beating Aaron Hill in a riot of 2 June 1710 stands out (LC 5/155, fol.24; *Document Register* no.2091).

39 i.e. Alexander the Great in Lee's *The Rival Queens*; Alexander venerated the god Ammon. No other evidence survives of Powell in the role.

40 In Etherege's *The Man of the Mode*. No other evidence survives of Powell playing the role.

41 John Gay's masterpiece opened at Lincoln's Inn Fields on 29 January 1728. It was first offered to Drury Lane but Cibber turned it down. As Koon puts it (p.118), 'Given his loyalty to the King and his personal friendship with Walpole, [Cibber] could not have found humour in the picture of England's Prime Minister as a highwayman and his ministry as a den of thieves.' The piece had an unprecedented initial run of thirty-two performances and received a further thirty before the end of the season. See Figure 8.

THE BEGGARS OPERA

Brittons attend — view this harmonious Stage
And listen to those notes which charm the age
Thus shall your tastes in Sounds & Sense be shonn
And Beggars Opras ever be your own Printed for John Bowles at the Black Horse in Cornhill.

8. Caricature of *The Beggar's Opera* and of Lincoln's Inn Fields theatre.

pretence to favour than setting greatness and authority in a contemptible (and the most vulgar vice and wickedness in an amiable) light. But behold how fondly I was mistaken! *Love in a Riddle* (for so my newfangled performance was called) was as vilely damned and hooted at as so vain a presumption in the idle cause of virtue could deserve.[42] Yet this is not what I

42 Cibber's pastoral romance, *Love in a Riddle*, opened at Drury Lane on 7 January 1729. It is set in Arcadia, and its characters are drawn from the world of Sidneyan romance. As in *The Beggar's Opera*, popular tunes punctuate the action, but with new lyrics. Cibber himself played Philatus, 'a conceited Corinthian courtier'. Lowe quotes Chetwood, p.128:
> I remember the first night of *Love in a Riddle* (which was murdered in the same year), a pastoral opera wrote by the Laureate, which the hydra-headed multitude resolved to worry without hearing (a custom with authors of merit), when Miss Rafter came on in the part of Phillida, the monstrous roar subsided. A person in the stage-box, next to my post, called out to his companion in the following elegant style, 'Zounds Tom! Take care, or this charming little devil will save all!'
Rafter was the maiden name of Catherine (Kitty) Clive (1711–85), later a celebrated singer and actress.

complain of; I will allow my poetry to be as much below the other as taste or criticism can sink it. I will grant, likewise, that the applauded author of *The Beggar's Opera* (whom I knew to be an honest, good natured man and who, when he had descended to write more like one in the cause of virtue, had been as unfortunate as others of that class) – I will grant, I say, that in his *Beggar's Opera* he had more skilfully gratified the public taste than all the brightest authors that ever writ before him; and I have sometimes thought, from the modesty of his motto, *nos' hæc novimus esse nihil*,[43] that he gave them that performance as a satire upon the depravity of their judgment (as Ben Jonson, of old, was said to have given his *Bartholomew Fair* in ridicule of the vulgar taste which had disliked his *Sejanus*),[44] and that by artfully seducing them to be the champions of the immoralities he himself detested, he should be amply revenged on their former severity and ignorance. This were indeed a triumph which even the author of *Cato* might have envied! *Cato*, 'tis true, succeeded, but reached not by full forty days the progress and applauses of *The Beggar's Opera*. Will it, however, admit of a question which of the two compositions a good writer would rather wish to have been the author of? Yet on the other side, must we not allow that to have taken a whole nation, high and low, into a general applause, has shown a power in poetry which, though often attempted in the same kind, none but this one author could ever yet arrive at? By what rule, then, are we to judge of our true national taste? But to keep a little closer to my point.

The same author the next year had, according to the laws of the land, transported his hero to the West Indies in a second part to *The Beggar's Opera*;[45] but so it happened, to the surprise of the public, this second part was forbid to come upon the stage! Various were the speculations upon this act of power. Some thought that the author, others that the town was hardly dealt with; a third sort, who perhaps had envied him the success of his first part, affirmed when it was printed that whatever the intention might be, the fact was in his favour that he had been a greater gainer by subscriptions to his copy than he could have been by a bare theatrical presentation. Whether any part of these opinions were true, I am not

43 i.e. 'we know these things are worthless', from Martial, *Epigrams*, Book 13 no. 2. The epigram appears on the title page of early editions of *The Beggar's Opera*, prepared by Cibber's own publisher, John Watts.
44 Cibber probably means Jonson's *Catiline*, whose address 'To the Reader in Ordinary' includes reflections on the play's poor reception.
45 Gay's *Polly* was banned on 12 December 1728, but published via private subscription the following year by Thomas Astley (Watts, who had published *The Beggar's Opera*, stayed clear of it). The piece eventually made it to the stage in 1777.

concerned to determine or consider. But how they affected me, I am going to tell you. Soon after this prohibition, my performance was to come upon the stage at a time when many people were out of humour at the late disappointment, and seemed willing to lay hold of any pretence of making a reprisal. Great umbrage was taken that I was permitted to have the whole town to myself, by this absolute forbiddance of what they had more mind to have been entertained with. And, some few days before my bauble was acted, I was informed that a strong party would be made against it. This report I slighted, as not conceiving why it should be true; and when I was afterwards told what was the pretended provocation of this party, I slighted it still more, as having less reason to suppose any persons could believe me capable (had I had the power) of giving such a provocation. The report, it seems, that had run against me was this: that to make way for the success of my own play I had privately found means, or made interest, that the second part of *The Beggar's Opera* might be suppressed. What an involuntary compliment did the reporters of this falsehood make me, to suppose me of consideration enough to influence a great officer of state! To gratify the spleen or envy of a comedian so far as to rob the public of an innocent diversion (if it were such) that none but that cunning comedian might be suffered to give it them![46] This is so very gross a supposition that it needs only its own senseless face to confound it; let that alone, then, be my defence against it. But against blind malice and staring inhumanity, whatever is upon the stage has no defence! There, they knew I stood helpless and exposed to whatever they might please to load or asperse me with. I had not considered, poor devil, that from the security of a full pit, dunces might be critics, cowards valiant, and 'prentices gentlemen! Whether any such were concerned in the murder of my play I am not certain, for I never endeavoured to discover any one of its assassins (I cannot afford them a milder name, from their unmanly manner of destroying it). Had it been heard, they might have left me nothing to say to them. 'Tis true, it faintly held up its wounded head a second day and would have spoke for mercy, but was not suffered. Not even the presence of a royal heir apparent could protect it.[47] But then I was reduced to be serious with them; their clamour

46 The 'great officer of state' over whom Cibber was thought to have influence was Charles Fitzroy, 2nd Duke of Grafton (1683–1757), Lord Chamberlain from 1724 until his death. *The Craftsman* offered the sarcastic reflection that 'It is hoped from this circumstance that the celebrated Mr Cibber's opera (which we are assured is perfectly inoffensive) will now be acted with great success' (14 December 1728; *Document Register* no.3437).

47 i.e. Frederick, son of George II and Caroline of Ansbach, created Prince of Wales on 8 January 1729; his visit to the second performance of *Love in a Riddle* was evidently intended as a celebration.

then became an insolence which I thought it my duty, by the sacrifice of any interest of my own, to put an end to. I therefore quitted the actor for the author and, stepping forward to the pit, told them that since I found they were not inclined that this play should go forward, I gave them my word that after this night it should never be acted again; but that in the meantime I hoped they would consider in whose presence they were and for that reason, at least, would suspend what farther marks of their displeasure they might imagine I had deserved. At this there was a dead silence; and, after some little pause, a few civilised hands signified their approbation.[48] When the play went on, I observed, about a dozen persons of no extraordinary appearance sullenly walked out of the pit; after which, every scene of it, while uninterrupted, met with more applause than my best hopes had expected. But it came too late: peace to its *manes*![49] I had given my word it should fall, and I kept it by giving out another play for the next day, though I knew the boxes were all let for the same again. Such then was the treatment I met with. How much of it the errors of the play might deserve, I refer to the judgment of those who may have curiosity and idle time enough to read it.[50] But if I had no occasion to complain of the reception it met with from its *quieted* audience, sure it can be no great vanity to impute its disgraces chiefly to that severe resentment which a groundless report of me had inflamed. Yet those disgraces have left me something to boast of: an honour preferable, even, to the applause of my enemies. A noble lord came behind the scenes and told me, from the box where he was in waiting, that 'what I said to quiet the audience was extremely well taken there and that I had been commended for it in a very obliging manner'. Now, though this was the only tumult that I have known to have been so effectually appeased these fifty years by anything that could be said to an audience, in the same humour I will not take any great merit to myself upon it; because when, like me, you will but humbly submit to their doing you all the mischief they can, they will at any time be satisfied.

I have mentioned this particular fact to enforce what I before observed: that the private character of an actor will always more or less affect his pub-lic performance. And if I suffered so much from the bare suspicion of my

48 The *Universal Spectator*, 11 January 1729, carries a report of this incident.
49 Shades of the dead.
50 The play was published approximately three months after the premiere. Cibber felt so little urge to make a case for it that the printed edition includes no dedication or preface. He promptly recycled some material from it in a further 'Ballad Opera' of 1729, *Damon and Phillida*, which opened at the Haymarket Theatre on 16 August 1729.

having been guilty of a base action, what should not an actor expect that is hardy enough to think his whole private character of no consequence? I could offer many more, though less severe, instances of the same nature. I have seen the most tender sentiment of love in tragedy create laughter instead of compassion, when it has been applicable to the real engagements of the person that uttered it. I have known good parts thrown up from an humble consciousness that something in them might put an audience in mind of – what was rather wished might be forgotten. Those remarkable words of Evadne in *The Maid's Tragedy* – 'A maidenhead, Amintor, at my years?' – have sometimes been a much stronger jest for being a true one.[51] But these are reproaches which in all nations the theatre must have been used to, unless we could suppose actors something more than human creatures, void of faults or frailties. 'Tis a misfortune, at least, not limited to the English stage. I have seen the better bred audience in Paris made merry even with a modest expression, when it has come from the mouth of an actress whose private character it seemed not to belong to. The apprehension of these kind of fleers from the witlings of a pit has been carried so far in our own country, that a late valuable actress (who was conscious her beauty was not her greatest merit) desired the warmth of some lines might be abated when they have made her too remarkably handsome.[52] But in this discretion she was alone; few others were afraid of undeserving the finest things that could be said to them. But to consider this matter seriously, I cannot but think, at a play a sensible auditor would contribute all he could to his being well deceived, and not suffer his imagination so far to wander from the well acted character before him as to gratify a frivolous spleen by mocks or personal sneers on the performer, at the expense of his better entertainment. But I must now take up Wilks and Powell again where I left them.

51 Beaumont and Fletcher's *The Maid's Tragedy* (1611, publ. 1619): '*Amintor*: If you have sworn to any of the virgins / That were your old companions to preserve / Your maidenhead a night, it may be done / Without this means. *Evadne*: A maidenhead, Amintor, / At my years!'; in *Five Stuart Tragedies*, ed. A. K. McIlwraith (Oxford: Oxford University Press, 1972), p.127 (II.i.195–9). LS1 399 indicates a revival in the 1691–2 season, Cibber's second in the company. The cast is not known, but Elizabeth Barry, in her mid-thirties at the time, is the most likely contender. Rich's company revived the play on 3 February 1704 (LS2a 144); Wilks, the beneficiary, was Amintor, and Evadne probably Anne Oldfield.
52 Probably also a reference to Elizabeth Barry. Lowe disputes Bellchambers's speculation that Cibber was referring to Anne Oldfield on the grounds that Oldfield was not shy about her physical appearance; she was, after all, cast as Helen of Troy in Elkanah Settle's *The Virgin Prophetess*, which opened at Drury Lane in May 1701 (LS2a 28). See also Cibber's reference to her 'natural attractions' below, p.204.

Though the contention for superiority between them seemed about this time to end in favour of the former, yet the distress of the patentee in having his servant his master (as Powell had lately been) was not much relieved by the victory;[53] he had only changed the man, but not the malady. For Wilks, by being in possession of so many good parts, fell into the common error of most actors: that of over-rating their merit or never thinking it is so thoroughly considered as it ought to be, which generally makes them proportionably troublesome to the master who, they might consider, only pays them to profit by them. The patentee, therefore, found it as difficult to satisfy the continual demands of Wilks as it was dangerous to refuse them; very few were made that were not granted, and as few were granted as were not grudged him. Not but our good master was as sly a tyrant as ever was at the head of a theatre, for he gave the actors more liberty and fewer days' pay than any of his predecessors. He would laugh with them over a bottle and bite them in their bargains.[54] He kept them poor that they might not be able to rebel, and sometimes merry that they might not think of it. All their articles of agreement had a clause in them that he was sure to creep out at, viz., their respective salaries were to be paid in such manner and proportion as others of the same company were paid, which in effect made them all (when he pleased) but limited sharers of loss and himself sole proprietor of profits; and this loss or profit they only had such verbal accounts of as he thought proper to give them. 'Tis true, he would sometimes advance them money (but not more than he knew at most could be due to them) upon their bonds; upon which, whenever they were mutinous, he would threaten to sue them. This was the net we danced in for several years, but no wonder we were dupes while our master was a lawyer. This grievance, however, Wilks was resolved (for himself, at least) to remedy at any rate, and grew daily more intractable for every day his redress was delayed. Here, our master found himself under a difficulty he knew not well how to get out of; for as he was a close, subtle man, he seldom made use of a confidant in his schemes of government.[55] But here the old expedient of delay would stand him in no longer stead; Wilks must instantly be complied with, or Powell come again into power! In a word, he was pushed so home that he was

53 Cibber's reference to 'about this time' is characteristically broad, indicating the period 1702–4, at the end of which Rich and Wilks came to the agreement noted below, p.172 n.58.
54 i.e. 'deceive, over-reach, take in' (OED v.15). Cibber denounces Christopher Rich, describing the period when he worked closely with him.
55 Cibber is careful to distance himself from the close working relationship with Rich he describes below.

reduced even to take my opinion into his assistance. For he knew I was a rival to neither of them; perhaps, too, he had fancied that from the success of my first play I might know as much of the stage, and what made an actor valuable, as either of them. He saw too that though they had each of them five good parts to my one, yet the applause which in my few I had met with was given me by better judges than as yet had approved of the best they had done. They generally measured the goodness of a part by the quantity or length of it. I thought none bad for being short that were closely natural, nor any the better for being long without that valuable quality. But in this I doubt, as to their interest, they judged better than myself; for I have generally observed that those who do a great deal not ill have been preferred to those who do but little, though never so masterly. And therefore I allow that while there were so few good parts, and as few good judges of them, it ought to have been no wonder to me that as an actor I was less valued by the master, or the common people, than either of them. All the advantage I had of them was that by not being troublesome, I had more of our master's personal inclination than any actor of the male sex; and so much of it, that I was almost the only one whom, at that time, he used to take into his parties of pleasure, very often *tête à tête*, and sometimes in a *partie quarrèe*.[56] These then were the qualifications, however good or bad, to which may be imputed our master's having made choice of me to assist him in the difficulty under which he now laboured. He was himself sometimes inclined to set up Powell again as a check upon the overbearing temper of Wilks; though to say truth, he liked neither of them, but was still under a necessity that one of them should preside, though he scarce knew which of the two evils to choose. This question, when I happened to be alone with him, was often debated in our evening conversation; nor, indeed, did I find it an easy matter to know which party I ought to recommend to his election. I knew they were neither of them wellwishers to me, as in common they were enemies to most actors in proportion to the merit that seemed to be rising in them. But as I had the prosperity of the stage more at heart than any other consideration, I could not be long undetermined in my opinion, and therefore gave it to our master at once, in favour of Wilks. I, with all the force I could muster, insisted that 'if Powell were preferred, the ill example of his negligence and abandoned character (whatever his merit on the stage might be) would reduce our company to contempt and beggary'; observing,

56 i.e. a foursome. *Comparison*, p.16, hints at Rich's private life: 'He is monarch of the stage, though he knows not how to govern one province in his dominion but that of signing, sealing, and something else that shall be nameless.' Rich may have been attracted to the stage partly because of his sexual inclinations.

at the same time, in how much better order our affairs went forward since
Wilks came among us, of which I recounted several instances that are not
so necessary to tire my reader with. All this, though he allowed to be true,
yet Powell (he said) was a better actor than Wilks when he minded his business (that is to say when he was what he seldom was – sober). But Powell,
it seems, had a still greater merit to him, which was (as he observed) that
when affairs were in his hands, he had kept the actors quiet without one
day's pay for six weeks together, and it was not everybody could do that; for
you see, said he, 'Wilks will never be easy unless I give him his whole pay
when others have it not, and what an injustice would that be to the rest if I
were to comply with him? How do I know, but then they may be all in a
mutiny, and *mayhap* (that was his expression) with Powell at the head of
'em?'[57] By this specimen of our debate, it may be judged under how particular and merry a government the theatre then laboured. To conclude, this
matter ended in a resolution to sign a new agreement with Wilks, which
entitled him to his full pay of four pounds a week without any conditional
deductions.[58] How far soever my advice might have contributed to our master's settling his affairs upon this foot, I never durst make the least merit of
it to Wilks, well knowing that his great heart would have taken it as a mortal affront had I (though never so distantly) hinted that his demands had
needed any assistance but the justice of them. From this time, then, Wilks
became First Minister, or Bustle-Master-General of the company.[59] He
now seemed to take new delight in keeping the actors close to their business, and got every play revived with care in which he had acted the chief
part in Dublin.[60] 'Tis true this might be done with a particular view of set-

57 Cibber draws attention to Rich's country idiom (he was from Somerset) but then uses
   the same term below, p.240.
58 An agreement dated 9 October 1704 between Rich and Wilks is referred to in Wilks's
   suit against Rich of 8 November 1707 (C9/464/126; *Document Register* no.1908). The 1704
   agreement specified a five-year term at £4 a week. (c.£950 in current values)
59 The term is not complimentary. Connoting frantic activity or confusion, it recalls a line
   from *Richard III* which Cibber retained in his adaptation: 'And leave the world for me
   to bustle in' (I.ii.359 in Cibber's *The Tragical History of King Richard III*). Lowe cites *The
   Laureate*: 'If Minister Wilks was now alive to hear thee prate thus, Mr Bayes, I would
   not give one halfpenny for thy ears; but if he were alive, thou durst not for thy ears rattle
   on in this affected Machiavellian style' (p.48).
60 If Cibber is referring to the period after Wilks gained his new agreement in October
   1704, this shift towards repertory performed in Dublin may have been partly prompted
   by the arrival of Richard Estcourt, described in the *Diverting-post* of 28 October 1704
   as 'the famous comedian of Ireland'. He was followed in December by Letitia Cross,
   who was returning from a season in Dublin. Milhous, *Management*, pp.171–83, notes
   increasing variety in bills during this period and decreasing competition between Drury
   Lane and Lincoln's Inn Fields.

ting off himself to advantage; but if, at the same time, it served the company, he ought not to want our commendation. Now, though my own conduct neither had the appearance of his merit nor the reward that followed his industry, I cannot help observing that it showed me, to the best of my power, a more cordial commonwealth's man. His first views, in serving himself, made his service to the whole but an incidental merit; whereas, by my prosecuting the means to make him easy in his pay (unknown to him, or without asking any favour for myself at the same time) I gave a more unquestionable proof of my preferring the public to my private interest. From the same principle, I never murmured at whatever little parts fell to my share; and though I knew it would not recommend me to the favour of the common people, I often submitted to play wicked characters, rather than they should be worse done by weaker actors than myself.[61] But perhaps, in all this patience under my situation, I supported my spirits by a conscious vanity; for I fancied I had more reason to value myself upon being sometimes the confidant and companion of our master than Wilks had, in all the more public favours he had extorted from him. I imagined, too, there was sometimes as much skill to be shown in a short part as in the most voluminous, which he generally made choice of: that even the coxcombly follies of a Sir John Daw might as well distinguish the capacity of an actor as all the dry enterprises and busy conduct of a Truewit.[62] Nor could I have any reason to repine at the superiority he enjoyed when I considered at how dear a rate it was purchased: at the continual expense of a restless jealousy and fretful impatience. These were the passions that, in the height of his successes, kept him lean to his last hour, while what I wanted in rank or glory was amply made up to me in ease and cheerfulness. But let not this observation either lessen his merit or lift up my own, since our different tempers were not in our choice but equally natural to both of us. To be employed on the stage was the delight of his life; to be justly excused from

61 Koon's list of new parts for this period (esp. p.190) does not necessarily bear out Cibber's point, while 'little parts' such as Osric exploited his reputation for playing fops; during this period he also played Sir Courtly Nice, Lord Foppington in his own *The Careless Husband* (1704), Sir Fopling Flutter in *The Man of Mode* (1706), and Captain Brazen in Farquhar's *The Recruiting Officer* (1706).

62 In Jonson's *Epicoene*, John Daw is an affected classical pedant given to displaying his knowledge of ancient languages, while Truewit (a much larger role) is a witty if somewhat unpleasant satirist. The point illustrates the tendency of Cibber's critics to attribute to him the characteristics of the roles he played. LS2 records ten performances during the period in question. No casts are available; however, LS2 gives performances from 20 January 1718 showing Cibber as Daw and Wilks as Truewit. Koon (p.190) dates Cibber's first John Daw at 1700. Wilks was a natural for Truewit, as Cibber hints by associating Truewit's 'busy conduct' with Wilks's role as 'Bustle-Master-General' of the company.

it was the joy of mine. I loved ease and he pre-eminence. In that, he might
be more commendable. Though he often disturbed me, he seldom could do
it without more disordering himself. In our disputes, his warmth could less
bear truth than I could support manifest injuries.[63] He would hazard our
undoing to gratify his passions, though otherwise an honest man, and I
rather chose to give up my reason, or not see my wrong, than ruin our community by an equal rashness. By this opposite conduct, our accounts at the
end of our labours stood thus. While he lived, he was the elder man; when
he died, he was not so old as I am. He never left the stage till he left the
world; I never so well enjoyed the world as when I left the stage. He died in
possession of his wishes; and I, by having had a less choleric ambition, am
still tasting mine in health and liberty. But as he, in a great measure, wore
out the organs of life in his incessant labours to gratify the public, the many
whom he gave pleasure to will always owe his memory a favourable report.
Some facts that will vouch for the truth of this account will be found in the
sequel of these memoirs.[64] If I have spoke with more freedom of his quondam competitor Powell, let my good intentions to future actors, in showing
what will so much concern them to avoid, be my excuse for it. For though
Powell had from Nature much more than Wilks (in voice and ear, in elocution in tragedy and humour in comedy, greatly the advantage of him), yet,
as I have observed, from the neglect and abuse of those valuable gifts, he
suffered Wilks to be of thrice the service to our society. Let me give another
instance of the reward and favour which, in a theatre, diligence and sobriety
seldom fail of. Mills the elder grew into the friendship of Wilks, with not a
great deal more than those useful qualities to recommend him.[65] He was an
honest, quiet, careful man, of as few faults as excellencies, and Wilks rather
chose him for his second in many plays than an actor of perhaps greater
skill that was not so laboriously diligent.[66] And from this constant assiduity
Mills, with making to himself a friend in Wilks, was advanced to a larger

63 At a time when theatre people took to the law regularly, there is no indication that
   Cibber's 'disputes' with Wilks were ever formal. Lowe cites *The Laureate*: 'Did you not, by
   your general misbehaviour towards authors and actors, bring an odium on your brother
   managers as well as yourself; and were not these, with many others, the reasons that
   sometimes gave occasion to Wilks to chastise you with his tongue only?' (p.49).
64 Apparently a reference to Chapter 16 (esp. pp.352–5), where his industry is treated
   ironically.
65 i.e. the actor John Mills (d. 1736), married to Margaret, an actress; parents of William
   Mills (d. 1750), also an actor.
66 Performances in which Wilks and Mills are known to have appeared together during the
   period under discussion are Catherine Trotter's *Love at a Loss* (November 1700, Mills as
   Phillamine to Wilks's Beaumine); Cibber's *Love Makes a Man* (December 1700, Mills
   as Don Duart to Wilks's Carlos); Catherine Trotter's *The Unhappy Penitent* (February

salary than any man-actor had enjoyed during my time on the stage.[67] I have yet to offer a more happy recommendation of temperance which a late, celebrated actor was warned into by the misconduct of Powell. About the year that Wilks returned from Dublin, Booth (who had commenced actor upon that theatre) came over to the company in Lincoln's Inn Fields.[68] He was then but an undergraduate of the buskin and, as he told me himself, had been for some time too frank a lover of the bottle; but having had the happiness to observe into what contempt and distresses Powell had plunged himself by the same vice, he was so struck with the terror of his example that he fixed a resolution (which from that time to the end of his days he strictly observed) of utterly reforming it – an uncommon act of philosophy in a young man, of which in his fame and fortune he afterwards enjoyed the reward and benefit. These observations I have not merely thrown together as a moralist, but to prove that the briskest loose liver, or intemperate man (though morality were out of the question) can never arrive at the necessary excellencies of a good or useful actor.

1701, Mills as Charles VIII to Wilks's Duke of Lorrain); George Farquhar's *Sir Harry Wildair* (April 1701, Mills as Colonel Standard to Wilks's Sir Harry); Richard Steele's *The Funeral* (December 1701, Mills as Trusty to Wilks's Campley); Bevil Higgons's *The Generous Conqueror* (December 1701, Mills as Rodomond to Wilks's Almerick); Farquhar's *The Inconstant* (February 1702, Mills as Dugard to Wilks's Young Mirabel); Francis Manning's *All for the Better* (November 1702, Mills as Johnson to Wilks's Woodvil); Charles Gildon's *The Patriot* (?December 1702, Mills as Cosmo de Medici to Wilks's Julio); Farquhar's *The Twin-Rivals* (December 1702, Mills as Trueman to Wilks's Elder Wouldbe); Thomas Baker's *Tunbridge Walks* (January 1703, Mills as Loveworth to Wilks's Reynard); Thomas Durfey's *The Old Mode and the New* (March 1703, Mills as Queenlove to Wilks's Frederick); Susanna Centlivre's *Love's Contrivance* (June 1703, Mills as Octavio to Wilks's Bellmie); Steele's *The Lying Lover* (December 1703, Mills as Lovemore to Wilks's Young Bookwit); 'G.B.', *Love the Leveller* (January 1704, Mills as Semorin to Wilks's Andramont); William Taverner's *The Faithful Bride of Granada* (May 1704, Mills as Abdolin to Wilks's Abinomin); Pierre Motteux's *Farewell Folly* (January 1705, Mills as Townly to Wilks's Young Holdfast); Steele's *The Tender Husband* (April 1705, Mills as Clerimont Senior to Wilks's Captain Clerimont), and Beaumont and Fletcher, rev. Henry Norris, *The Royal Merchant; or Beggar's Bush* (June 1705, Mills as Hubert to Wilks's Merchant). The list largely bears out Cibber's report that Mills tended to play the straight man or friend to Wilks's hero.

67 In the licence papers for the Haymarket company, Mills was promised £60 p.a., compared with £150 each for Betterton, Verbruggen, Powell, and Wilks (Cibber himself was promised £100, as was Barton Booth; see Nicoll, *History*, p.276); on 30 March 1709, Mills's £60 was raised to £100, with a benefit every March (LC 7/3, fols.105–6; *Document Register* no.2004). It is unlikely that would have taken him above Betterton's earnings from acting. A pamphlet issued by Rich's treasurer Zachary Baggs in July 1709 sought to influence public opinion by citing Mills's salary as '£4 a week for himself, and £1 a week for his wife, for little or nothing' (*Document Register* no.2031); see also below, p.266 n.42.

68 Booth joined the Lincoln's Inn Fields Company in 1700, two years after Wilks's return to London.

CHAPTER 8

The patentee of Drury Lane wiser than his actors. His particular management. The author continues to write plays. Why. The best dramatic poets censured by J. Collier in his Short View of the Stage. *It has a good effect. The Master of the Revels from that time cautious in his licensing new plays. A complaint against him. His authority founded upon custom only. The late law for fixing that authority in a proper person considered.*

Though the master of our theatre[1] had no conception himself of theatrical merit either in authors or actors, yet his judgment was governed by a saving rule in both: he looked into his receipts for the value of a play, and from common fame he judged of his actors. But by whatever rule he was governed, while he had prudently reserved to himself a power of not paying them more than their merit could get, he could not be much deceived by their being over or under-valued. In a word, he had with great skill inverted the constitution of the stage, and quite changed the channel of profits arising from it. Formerly, when there was but one company, the proprietors punctually paid the actors their appointed salaries and took to themselves only the clear profits; but our wiser proprietor took first, out of every day's receipts, two shillings in the pound to himself, and left their salaries to be paid only as the less or greater deficiencies of acting (according to his own accounts) would permit. What seemed most extraordinary in these measures was that at the same time he had persuaded us to be contented with our condition, upon his assuring us that as fast as money would come in, we should all be paid our arrears. And – that we might not have it always in our power to say he had never intended to keep his word – I remember, in a few years after this time, he once paid us nine days in one week; this happened when *The Funeral, or Grief à la Mode* was first acted with more than expected success.[2] Whether this well-timed bounty was only allowed us to save appearances, I will not say; but if that was his real motive for it, it was too costly a frolic to be repeated and was, at least, the only grimace of

---

1 i.e. Christopher Rich.
2 Steele's comedy concerns a family quarrel over an inheritance. It opened at Drury Lane in December 1701 (LS2a 46) and remained popular during Cibber's lifetime. Cibber played Lord Hardy, impoverished son to Lord Brumpton.

its kind he vouchsafed us, we never having received one day more of those arrears in above fifteen years' service.[3]

While the actors were in this condition, I think I may very well be excused in my presuming to write plays, which I was forced to do for the support of my increasing family; my precarious income as an actor being then too scanty to supply it with even the necessaries of life.[4]

It may be observable too that my muse and my spouse were equally prolific: that the one was seldom the mother of a child but, in the same year, the other made me the father of a play. I think we had a dozen of each sort between us, of both which kinds some died in their infancy, and near an equal number of each were alive when I quitted the theatre.[5] But it is no wonder, when a muse is only called upon by family duty, she should not always rejoice in the fruit of her labour. To this necessity of writing, then, I attribute the defects of my second play, which, coming out too hastily the year after my first, turned to very little account.[6] But having got as much by my first as I ought to have expected from the success of them both, I had no great reason to complain. Not but (I confess) so bad was my second that I do not choose to tell you the name of it; and, that it might be peaceably forgotten, I have not given it a place in the two volumes of those I published

3 i.e. in fact from 1690, when Cibber joined the United Company, to 1706, when he defected to join Swiney.

4 At this point Cibber and his wife, Katherine, had three daughters: Catherine (b. 1696), Anne (b. 1699), and Elizabeth (b. 1701). A son, William, was born in 1702 but did not survive infancy (see Koon, p.201). A second son, Theophilus, was born in 1703.

5 At the time Cibber describes, Katherine and he had lost four children in infancy: Veronica (1694), Mary (1695), Colley Jr (1697), and Lewis (1698) (baptismal register of St Martin-in-the-Fields, cited in Koon, pp.197–9). It was not uncommon for authors of prologues, epilogues, and prefaces to describe theatrical failures as still-births, but Cibber's blithe reflection on his own and Katherine's history is in questionable taste. His arithmetic is disputed by McGirr, p.153, who counts '13 surviving works' and suggests Cibber is merely being modest about his output. If the criterion is regular performances, however, Cibber's reckoning is valid. Five of his plays were still receiving regular performances when he 'quitted' in 1733: The Careless Husband (1704); The Double Gallant (1707); Love Makes a Man (1700); Love's Last Shift (1696); and She Would and She Would Not (1702). Five of his children – Catherine, Anne, Elizabeth, Theophilus, and Charlotte – were still alive in 1733.

6 Cibber jumps back in time to discuss Woman's Wit, which opened at Drury Lane in January 1697 following Cibber's agreement with Rich the previous October. Cibber played Longville, a young lover; Penkethman, Powell, and Doggett also had significant roles. No subsequent performance is recorded in The London Stage. In the preface, Cibber 'lay[s] down some excuses' for the play's failure: haste of composition; 'too nice observation of regularity'; and his failed negotiation with the breakaway company the previous summer (see above, p.157 n.15).

in quarto in the year 1721.[7] And whenever I took upon me to make some dormant play of an old author (to the best of my judgment) fitter for the stage, it was honestly not to be idle that set me to work, as a good housewife will mend old linen when she has not better employment. But when I was more warmly engaged by a subject entirely new, I only thought it a good subject when it seemed worthy of an abler pen than my own, and might prove as useful to the hearer as profitable to myself. Therefore, whatever any of my productions might want of skill, learning, wit or humour – or however unqualified I might be to instruct others who so ill governed myself – yet such plays (entirely my own) were not wanting, at least, in what our most admired writers seemed to neglect, and without which I cannot allow the most taking play to be intrinsically good, or to be a work upon which a man of sense and probity should value himself: I mean, when they do not as well *prodesse* as *delectare* – give profit with delight![8] The *utile dulci* was of old equally the point,[9] and has always been my aim, however wide of the mark I may have shot my arrow. It has often given me amazement that our best authors of that time could think the wit and spirit of their scenes could be an excuse for making the looseness of them public. The many instances of their talents so abused are too glaring to need a closer comment, and are sometimes too gross to be recited. If, then, to have avoided this imputation (or rather to have had the interest and honour of virtue always in view) can give merit to a play, I am contented that my readers should think such merit the all that mine have to boast of. Libertines of mere wit and pleasure may laugh at these grave laws that would limit a lively genius; but every sensible honest man, conscious of their truth and use, will give these ralliers smile for smile, and show a due contempt for their merriment.[10]

---

7 The two-volume *Plays Written by Mr Cibber* was issued by subscription in 1721 by the two most powerful publishers in London: Jacob Tonson and Bernard Lintott, in partnership with William Mears and William Chetwood. Tonson had published the fourth and fifth editions of *The Careless Husband* in 1714 and 1718; Lintott had published nine of Cibber's previous works. The choice of a quarto format reduced costs, since it replicated that of existing editions; compare this with the more lavish 1710 and 1719 Tonson editions of Congreve's plays, which translated the texts into double-column folio format (albeit in the smaller octavo size) with French-style scene divisions and ornamental engravings.

8 From Horace, *The Art of Poetry*, line 333: 'Poets aim either to do good or to give pleasure' ('Aut prodesse volunt aut delectare poetae').

9 Horace, *The Art of Poetry*, line 344: 'utility joined to pleasure' ('Omne tulit punctum qui miscuit utile dulci').

10 Cibber's views of what is now called 'Libertine Comedy' contrast with those of (e.g.) John Dennis and Richard Steele, the latter of whom defended Wycherley's *The Country Wife* for being 'a good representation of the age in which that comedy was written' and a 'very pleasant and instructive satire' (*The Tatler*, no.3, 14–16 April 1709). Yet in the same

But while our authors took these extraordinary liberties with their wit, I remember the ladies were then observed to be decently afraid of venturing bare-faced to a new comedy till they had been assured they might do it without the risk of an insult to their modesty; or, if their curiosity were too strong for their patience, they took care at least to save appearances, and rarely came upon the first days of acting but in masks (then daily worn, and admitted, in the pit, the side-boxes and gallery); which custom, however, had so many ill consequences attending it that it has been abolished these many years.[11]

These immoralities of the stage had, by an avowed indulgence, been creeping into it ever since King Charles his time. Nothing that was loose could then be too low for it. *The London Cuckolds*, the most rank play that ever succeeded, was then in the highest court favour.[12] In this almost general corruption, Dryden (whose plays were more famed for their wit than their chastity) led the way, which he fairly confesses and endeavours to excuse in his epilogue to *The Pilgrim*, revived in 1700 for his benefit, in his declining age and fortune.[13] The following lines of it will make good my observation:

essay Steele obliquely refers to Cibber as one of his 'friends and fellow labourers, the reformers of manners, in their severity towards plays'.

11 The start of this trend can be traced to the early 1660s. Lowe cites Pepys, 12 June 1663, on Lady Mary Cromwell: 'when the house began to fill, [she] put on her vizard, and so kept it on all the play; which of late is become a great fashion among the ladies, which hides their whole face'. By 1700, a fictional lady such as Congreve's Millamant might be outraged by the mere suggestion that she might wear a mask at the theatre (*The Way of the World*, IV.i.214, in Congreve, *Works*, II.185) because of its association with prostitution, as underlined by Wycherley's dedication of *The Plain Dealer* (publ. 1677): 'by that mask of modesty which women wear promiscuously in public, they are all alike, and you can no more know a kept wench from a woman of honour by her looks than by her dress'; edition by James L. Smith (London: Ernest Benn, 1979), pp.5–6. A proclamation by Queen Anne reported in the *London Gazette*, 17–20 January 1704, prohibited the wearing of masks at the theatres.

12 Edward Ravenscroft's *The London Cuckolds* was premiered by the Duke's Company at Dorset Garden in November 1681 (LS1 303). Its popularity with the Court is vouched for by warrants presented to Lord Chamberlain Arlington for visits by royalty and their entourage on 22 November 1681, 25 November 1682, and 14 December 1682 (LC 5/145, p.120, in Nicoll, *Restoration*, p.311). LS2 and LS3 record numerous performances up to and beyond the publication of the *Apology*, many of them marking the regular November Lord Mayor's Day. There is no record of Cibber acting in it. Steele agreed with his verdict, calling the play 'a heap of vice and absurdity' (*The Tatler*, no.8, 28 April 1709). Lowe cites Genest (I.365) for a different view: 'If it be the province of comedy not to retail morality to a yawning pit but to make the audience laugh, and to keep them in good humour, this play must be allowed to be one of the best comedies in the English Language.'

13 *The Pilgrim* is an adaptation of Fletcher's play by Vanbrugh. It was premiered by Rich's company at Drury Lane, probably on 29 April 1700, with Dryden's *The Secular Masque* as an afterpiece (LS1 527). For Dryden's illness and straitened finances, and his death two days after *The Secular Masque*, see Winn, pp.508–12.

Perhaps the parson stretch'd a point too far,
When with our theatres he wag'd a war.[14]
He tells you that this very moral age
Receiv'd the first infection from the stage.
But sure, a banish'd court, with lewdness fraught,
The seeds of open vice returning brought.[15]
Thus lodg'd (as vice by great example thrives)
It first debauch'd the daughters and the wives.
London, a fruitful soil, yet never bore
So plentiful a crop of horns before.
The poets, who must live by courts or starve,
Were proud so good a government to serve;
And mixing with buffoons, and pimps profane,
Tainted the stage for some small snip of gain:
For they, like harlots under bawds profess'd,
Took all th' ungodly pains, and got the least.
Thus did the thriving malady prevail,
The Court its head, the poets but the tail.
The sin was of our native growth, 'tis true,
The scandal of the sin was wholly new.
Misses there were but modestly conceal'd;
Whitehall the naked Venus first reveal'd.[16]
Who standing, as at Cyprus, in her shrine,
The strumpet was ador'd with rites divine, *etc.*[17]

This epilogue, and the prologue to the same play written by Dryden, I
spoke myself; which, not being usually done by the same person, I have a
mind (while I think of it) to let you know on what occasion they both fell
to my share, and how other actors were affected by it.

14 i.e. the Reverend Jeremy Collier. Dryden had been a particular target for Collier, who
    combed his plays for alleged instances of blasphemy, mistranslation, and abuse of the
    clergy. For Dryden's measured response, see Winn, pp.497–500.
15 A reference to Charles II's exile in France, widely reputed as a source of veneral disease.
16 A reference to one of two paintings by Peter Lely (1618–80): either his nude portrait of
    Barbara Villiers, Duchess of Cleveland, as Venus; or another nude thought to be Nell
    Gwyn in the same guise and believed to have been placed behind a panel in Charles II's
    bedroom in Whitehall Palace.
17 The epilogue continues with a denunciation of Puritans who could accept the
    killing of a king but bridled at sexual misconduct: 'Nothing but open lewdness was a
    crime. / A monarch's blood was venial to the nation, / Compared with one foul act of
    fornication.' Cibber quotes the passage accurately; see Dryden, pp.833–4.

Sir John Vanbrugh, who had given some light touches of his pen to *The Pilgrim* to assist the benefit day of Dryden, had the disposal of the parts; and I being then, as an actor, in some favour with him, he read the play first with me alone, and was pleased to offer me my choice of what I might like best for myself in it. But as the chief characters were not (according to my taste) the most shining, it was no great self-denial in me that I desired he would first take care of those who were more difficult to be pleased. I therefore only chose for myself two short incidental parts, that of the Stuttering Cook and the Mad Englishman,[18] in which homely characters I saw more matter for delight than those that might have a better pretence to the amiable. And when the play came to be acted, I was not deceived in my choice. Sir John,[19] upon my being contented with so little a share in the entertainment, gave me the epilogue to make up my mess, which being written so much above the strain of common authors, I confess I was not a little pleased with. And Dryden, upon his hearing me repeat it to him, made me a farther compliment of trusting me with the prologue. This so particular distinction was looked upon by the actors as something too extraordinary.[20] But no one was so impatiently ruffled at it as Wilks, who seldom chose soft words when he spoke of anything he did not like. The most gentle thing he said of it was that he did not understand such treatment; that for his part, he looked upon it as an affront to all the rest of the company that there should be but one out of the whole judged fit to speak either a prologue or an epilogue. To quiet him, I offered to decline either in his favour or both, if it were equally easy to the author. But he was too much concerned to accept of an offer that had been made to another in preference to himself, and which he seemed to think his best way of resenting was to contemn. But from that time, however, he was resolved to the best of his power never to let the first offer of a prologue escape him, which little ambition sometimes made him pay too dear for his success. The flatness of the many miserable prologues that, by this means, fell to his lot seemed woefully unequal to the few good ones he might have reason to triumph in.

---

18 The play also features a mad Welshman and a mad parson, played by the comedian Joseph Haines, presumably as a dig at Collier (for Cibber on Collier, see below, pp.182–3; for Haines, below, p.183 n.24). The dramatis personae lists only 'servants'; a servant with a stammer appears in Act II of the adaptation, but not in Fletcher's original.
19 Cibber pays respect to Vanbrugh's memory: Vanbrugh was not knighted until 1714.
20 Conventionally prologues and epilogues were not only spoken by different performers, but were also the preserve of acknowledged leaders in the company. In 1700 Cibber had yet to acquire that status. By 'mess', Cibber means, metaphorically, a serving of food (*OED* 1).

I have given you this fact only as a sample of those frequent rubs and impediments I met with when any step was made to my being distinguished as an actor; and from this incident, too, you may partly see what occasioned so many prologues, after the death of Betterton, to fall into the hands of one speaker.[21] But it is not every successor to a vacant post that brings into it the talents equal to those of a predecessor. To speak a good prologue well is, in my opinion, one of the hardest parts and strongest proofs of sound elocution; of which, I confess, I never thought that any of the several who attempted it showed themselves by far equal masters to Betterton. Betterton, in the delivery of a good prologue, had a natural gravity that gave strength to good sense, a tempered spirit that gave life to wit, and a dry reserve in his smile that threw ridicule into its brightest colours. Of these qualities in the speaking of a prologue, Booth only had the first, but attained not to the other two. Wilks had spirit, but gave too loose a rein to it, and it was seldom he could speak a grave and weighty verse harmoniously. His accents were frequently too sharp and violent, which sometimes occasioned his eagerly cutting off half the sound of syllables that ought to have been gently melted into the melody of metre. In verses of humour too, he would sometimes carry the mimicry farther than the hint would bear, even to a trifling light, as if himself were pleased to see it so glittering. In the truth of this criticism, I have been confirmed by those whose judgment I dare more confidently rely on than my own. Wilks had many excellencies, but if we leave prologue-speaking out of the number, he will still have enough to have made him a valuable actor. And I only make this exception from them to caution others from imitating, what, in his time, they might have too implicitly admired. But I have a word or two more to say concerning the immoralities of the stage. Our theatrical writers were not only accused of immorality, but profaneness, many flagrant instances of which were collected and published by a non-juring clergyman, Jeremy Collier, in his *View of the Stage* etc, about the year 1697.[22] However just his charge against the authors that then wrote for it might be, I cannot but think his sentence against the stage itself is unequal; reformation he thinks too mild

21 i.e. Wilks or Booth.

22 The correct date is 1698. Collier was a 'non-juror' because he declined to take the Oath of Allegiance to William III. His defences of James II included *The Desertion discussed in a letter to a country gentleman* (1689), a work that saw him committed to Newgate prison. Cibber's play of 1717, *The Non-Juror*, alluded to Collier and his supporters through the lens of Molière's *Tartuffe*. See also below, pp.327–8.

a treatment for it, and is therefore for laying his axe to the root of it.[23] If this were to be a rule of judgment for offences of the same nature, what might become of the pulpit, where many a seditious and corrupted teacher has been known to cover the most pernicious doctrine with the mask of religion? This puts me in mind of what the noted Joe Haines the comedian (a fellow of a wicked wit) said upon this occasion;[24] who, being asked what could transport Mr Collier into so blind a zeal for a general suppression of the stage when only some particular authors had abused it, whereas the stage (he could not but know) was generally allowed, when rightly conducted, to be a delightful method of mending our morals – 'for that reason', replied Haines. 'Collier is, by profession, a moral-mender himself; and two of trade, you know, can never agree'.

The authors of *The Old Batchelor* and of *The Relapse* were those whom Collier most laboured to convict of immorality, to which they severally published their reply. The first seemed too much hurt to be able to defend himself, and the other felt him so little that his wit only laughed at his lashes.[25]

23 While Collier advocated the suppression of theatres in London, he also praised Ancient Greek drama and held up Jonson, Corneille, and Beaumont and Fletcher as examples of modern playwrights who did not resort to profanity. His work did, however, encourage informers to mount legal action against actors and authors, for example in the King's Bench indictment of 20 November 1701 against the breakaway company for *The Provoked Wife* (Luttrell, V.iii); the following February, Cibber was among the Drury Lane actors acquitted for the same offence of speaking 'immoral expressions' (*The Post Boy*, 24–6 February 1702).

24 Joseph Haines (d. 1701) is first recorded as a member of the King's Company during the 1667–8 season (LSi 116). He moved between companies during the 1670s; Downes, p.69, reports that he was fired from the King's Company for insulting the actor Charles Hart. For all his wit, he specialized in playing fools such as Sparkish in Wycherley's *The Country Wife* (1675). It is believed he pretended to convert to Catholicism during James II's reign. Lowe cites an anecdote from Davies, III.284, regarding Haines's claim that the Virgin Mary had appeared to him:

> Lord Sunderland sent for Joe, and asked him about the truth of his conversion, and whether he had really seen the Virgin? — Yes, my Lord, I assure you it is a fact. — How was it, pray? — Why, as I was lying in my bed, the Virgin appeared to me, and said, 'Arise, Joe' — You lie, you rogue, said the Earl; for, if it had really been the Virgin herself, she would have said Joseph, if it had been only out of respect to her husband.

25 i.e. Congreve, *Amendments of Mr. Collier's false and imperfect Citations, &c* (1698), which indignantly accuses Collier of 'malicious and strained interpretations' and 'sophistry and vast assurance' (Congreve, *Works*, III.75). Vanbrugh's *A Short Vindication of The Relapse and The Provoked Wife, from Immorality and Profaneness* (1698) pursues a similar line but in a more aloof, ironic tone. Lowe cites Davies, III.401: 'Congreve's pride was hurt by Collier's attack on plays which all the world had admired and commended; and no hypocrite showed more rancour and resentment when unmasked than this author, so greatly celebrated for sweetness of temper and elegance of manners.'

My first play of *The Fool in Fashion*[26] too being then in a course of success, perhaps for that reason only this severe author thought himself obliged to attack it; in which, I hope, he has shown more zeal than justice.[27] His greatest charge against it is that it sometimes uses the word 'faith' as an oath, in the dialogue. But if 'faith' may as well signify our given word or credit as our religious belief, why might not his charity have taken it in the less criminal sense? Nevertheless, Mr Collier's book was, upon the whole, thought so laudable a work that King William, soon after it was published, granted him a *nolo prosequi* when he stood answerable to the law for his having absolved two criminals just before they were executed for high treason.[28] And it must be farther granted that his calling our dramatic writers to this strict account had a very wholesome effect upon those who writ after this time. They were now a great deal more upon their guard: indecencies were no longer wit, and by degrees the fair sex came again to fill the boxes on the first day of a new comedy, without fear or censure.[29] But the Master of the Revels, who then licensed all plays for the stage, assisted this reformation with a more zealous severity than ever.[30] He would strike out whole scenes of a vicious or immoral character, though it were visibly shown to be reformed or punished. A severe instance of this kind falling upon myself may be an excuse for my relating it. When *Richard the Third* (as I altered it from Shakespeare) came from his hands to the stage, he expunged the whole first act without sparing a

26 The subtitle of *Love's Last Shift*, a reference to the character Sir Novelty Fashion.

27 Collier's most significant criticism of Cibber's play is in *A Defence of the Short View of the Profaneness and Immorality of the English Stage* (1699), his response to Congreve and Vanbrugh's critiques. Calling *Love's Last Shift* by its subtitle, he claimed to find the Acts 1–4 of the play 'scandalously smutty and profane' ('To the Reader', np.).

28 In 1696 Collier and two other non-juring clergymen officiated at the execution of Sir William Perkins, who had been complicit in plotting to assassinate William III. Collier caused a furore by absolving Perkins and his associate, Sir John Friend; subsequently he published *A Defence of the Absolution given to Sir William Perkins* (1696).

29 Among many examples of playwrights conforming to the new mood: Dryden's preface to *Fables Ancient and Modern* (1700), where he admits that Collier had 'in many things taxed [him] justly'; the prologue to Farquhar's *The Constant Couple* (1699) states that 'The ladies safe may smile: for here's no slander, / No smut, no lewd-tongued beau, no *double entendre*' (ll.13–14, in Farquhar, *Works*, I.151).

30 At this time Charles Killigrew (1655–1725), who succeeded his father Thomas as Master of the Revels in 1677, thereby owning the right to license 'plays, shows, motions, or strange sights' (*London Gazette*, 1–5 February 1677). Killigrew was under pressure to correct 'all obscenities & other scandalous matters' before the Collier controversy; see an order to him from Lord Chamberlain Dorset dated 24 January 1696 (LC 7/1, p.43; *Document Register* no.1523). He was not entirely at fault; the same order also required the theatre companies to submit their scripts to the Office of the Revels.

line of it.[31] This extraordinary stroke of a *sic volo*[32] occasioned my applying to him for the small indulgence of a speech or two, that the other four acts might limp on with a little less absurdity. No – he had not leisure to consider what might be separately inoffensive. He had an objection to the whole act, and the reason he gave for it was that the distresses of King Henry the Sixth, who is killed by Richard in the first act, would put weak people too much in mind of King James, then living in France – a notable proof of his zeal for the government! Those who have read either the play or the history I dare say will think he strained hard for the parallel.[33] In a word, we were forced for some few years to let the play take its fate with only four acts divided into five; by the loss of so considerable a limb, may one not modestly suppose it was robbed of at least a fifth part of that favour it afterwards met with? For though this first act was at last recovered and made the play whole again, yet the relief came too late to repay me for the pains I had taken in it.[34] Nor did I ever hear that this zealous severity of the Master of the Revels was afterwards thought justifiable. But my good fortune, in process of time, gave me an opportunity to talk with my oppressor in my turn.

The patent granted by His Majesty King George the First to Sir Richard Steele and his assigns, of which I was one, made us sole judges of what plays might be proper for the stage, without submitting them to the approbation or licence of any other particular person;[35] notwithstanding which, the Master of the Revels demanded his fee of forty shillings upon our acting a new one, though we had spared him the trouble of perusing it. This occasioned my being deputed to him to enquire into the right of his

---

31 For details of Cibber's adaptation, see above, p.101 n.42.

32 From Juvenal, Satire 6 line 223: 'sic volo, sic jubeo' ('I wish it so; I command it so').

33 In the preface to the play, Cibber claims that he had taken precautions against such an interpretation by showing the piece to 'several persons of the first rank and integrity', some of whom were willing to vouch for its freedom 'from any bold parallel, or ill-mannered reflection'. He goes on to complain that the only reason given by 'him, who had the relentless power of licensing' was that 'Henry the Sixth being a character unfortunate and pitied, would put the audience in mind of the late King James'.

34 The full text was played again on 4 April 1704 in a benefit performance for Cibber, which slightly qualifies his complaint about 'relief' coming too late (LS2a 160). The play was advertised as 'not acted these three years'. Koon, p.47, argues that Cibber was responding to a change of mood in the censor's office when Henry, Earl of Kent, replaced the stricter Earl of Jersey as Lord Chamberlain; however, Kent was not sworn in until 24 April 1704 (LC 5/166, p.164; *Document Register* no.1767).

35 The 18 October 1714 licence to direct the Drury Lane Theatre was issued to Steele, Wilks, Doggett, Booth, and Cibber (LC 5/156, p.31; *Document Register* no.2435); the subsequent patent of 19 January 1715 was solely in Steele's name (C66/3501, no.13; *Document Register* no.2498).

demand, and to make an amicable end of our dispute.[36] I confess I did not dislike the office and told him, according to my instructions, that I came not to defend even our own right in prejudice to his: that if our patent had inadvertently superseded the grant of any former power or warrant whereon he might ground his pretensions, we would not insist upon our broad seal but would readily answer his demands upon sight of such his warrant, anything in our patent to the contrary notwithstanding. This I had reason to think he could not do; and when I found he made no direct reply to my question, I repeated it with greater civilities and offers of compliance, till I was forced in the end to conclude with telling him that as his pretensions were not backed with any visible instrument of right, and as his strongest plea was custom, we could not so far extend our complaisance as to continue his fees upon so slender a claim to them.[37] And from that time, neither our plays or his fees gave either of us any farther trouble. In this negotiation, I am the bolder to think justice was on our side, because the law lately passed (by which the power of licensing plays etc is given to a proper person) is a strong presumption that no law had ever given that power to any such person before.[38]

36 Charles Killigrew was still Master of the Revels in 1715. As Henry Herbert had in 1660 (see CP 40/2753, rot.1190 in *Document Register*, no.122; and BL Add.MS 19,256, fol.66 in *Document Register* no.139), he petitioned the King (now George I) for protection of his rights when the new patent was issued, but unsuccessfully. The new play Cibber refers to is thought to be Charles Johnson's *The Country Lasses*, which opened on 4 February 1715 (LS2 341). Cibber was not an obvious choice of intermediary, given his public criticism of Charles Killigrew following the censorship of *The Tragical History of King Richard III*, but he appears to have forced the Master of the Revels to back down (see below, p.332 n.2), so achieving what Thomas Killigrew and Sir William Davenant had failed to do in the early 1660s. For Charles Killigrew's petition, see Judith Milhous and Robert D. Hume, 'Charles Killigrew's Petition about the Master of the Revels' Power as Censor', *Theatre Notebook* vol. 41 (1987), 74–9.

37 In 1662 Henry Herbert, Master of the Revels, had argued successfully that his office and associated privileges were 'by grant under the great seal' (BL Add.MS 19,256, fol.72; *Document Register* no.133).

38 i.e. the Licensing Act, passed on 6 June 1737 (10 Geo. 2 c. xxviii) by Sir Robert Walpole's government, which restricted the number of licensed theatres and stipulated that any new entertainment, including 'any part or parts therein', be submitted for the Lord Chamberlain's approval fourteen days before performance on pain of a £50 fine and a withdrawal of permission to perform. For a transcript of the Act, see Thomas and Hare, pp.207–10. Bellchambers and Lowe cite at length an undated letter by Jean-Bernard, l'Abbé Le Blanc (1707–81), describing the angry reaction of audiences. The many critiques and defences of the Act between its first reading and implementation are listed in *Document Register* nos.4121–59. Cibber is correct in saying that the authority of the Lord Chamberlain to license plays had not previously been enshrined in statute, only by conventions of office. However, his claim that licensing fees ceased to be an issue from 1715 skates over his later dispute with Lord Chamberlain Newcastle (see below, p.332 n.2).

My having mentioned this law, which so immediately affected the stage, inclines me to throw out a few observations upon it. But I must first lead you gradually through the facts and natural causes that made such a law necessary.

Although it had been taken for granted, from time immemorial, that no company of comedians could act plays *etc* without the royal licence or protection of some legal authority, a theatre was notwithstanding erected in Goodman's Fields about seven years ago, where plays without any such licence were acted for some time, unmolested and with impunity.[39] After a year or two, this playhouse was thought a nuisance too near the city, upon which the Lord Mayor and Aldermen petitioned the Crown to suppress it. What steps were taken in favour of that petition I know not, but common fame seemed to allow (from what had or had not been done in it) that acting plays in the said theatre was not evidently unlawful. However, this question of acting without a licence, a little time after came to a nearer decision in Westminster Hall. The occasion of bringing it thither was this. It happened that the purchasers of the patent, to whom Mr Booth and myself had sold our shares,[40] were at variance with the comedians that were then left to their government; and the variance ended in the chief of those comedians deserting and setting up for themselves in the little house in the Haymarket in 1733, by which desertion the patentees were very much distressed, and considerable losers.[41] Their affairs being in this desperate

39 The *Coffee-House Morning Post* of 24 September 1729 (*Document Register* no.3466) carried news of a patent granted to Thomas Odell to establish a theatre along Ayliffe Street on the north side of Goodman's Fields (i.e. just north of the Tower of London). Objections were lodged by justices of the peace, which Odell countered with offers to provide street lighting and security, and to distribute money to the neighbourhood (*Document Register* nos.3467–9). No licence was granted, but Odell went ahead anyway. On 28 April 1730 an order from Lord Chamberlain Grafton silenced the theatre (LC 5/160, p.130; *Document Register* no.3503). The following year Odell's manager, Henry Giffard, presented proposals for a new theatre in Goodman's Fields; a letter in the *London Daily Post* of 31 March 1735 (*Document Register* no.3872) defended Giffard's record of 'decorum and decency' and charted the economic benefits of having a theatre in the district.

40 *The Daily Post* of 27 March 1733 reported that Cibber had sold 'his entire share of the clothes, scenes and patent to John Highmore, Esq' (*Document Register* no.3695); according to *The Daily Courant* of 13 July 1732, Highmore had already bought half of Barton Booth's share (*Document Register* no.3639). The remaining half was purchased from Booth's widow by Henry Giffard, as reported by the *London Evening Post*, 18–20 September 1733 (*Document Register* no.3744). Cibber skates over the dire implications for his son Theophilus; but see below, p.370 n.101.

41 In May 1733 the Drury Lane actors (Theophilus included) rebelled against the new management, accusing them of amateurism, and were locked out. *The Daily Post* of 29 May 1733 reported 'there will be no more plays acted this season at the Theatre Royal in Drury Lane' (*Document Register* no.3709).

condition, they were advised to put the Act of the twelfth of Queen Anne (against vagabonds) in force against these deserters, then acting in the Haymarket without licence.[42] Accordingly, one of their chief performers was taken from the stage by a Justice of Peace his warrant, and committed to Bridewell as one within the penalty of the said Act.[43] When the legality of this commitment was disputed in Westminster Hall, by all I could observe from the learned pleadings on both sides (for I had the curiosity to hear them) it did not appear to me that the comedian so committed was within the description of the said Act, he being a house keeper and having a vote for the Westminster Members of Parliament.[44] He was discharged accordingly, and conducted through the hall with the congratulations of the crowds that attended, and wished well to his cause.

The issue of this trial threw me at that time into a very odd reflection, *viz.*, that if acting plays without licence did not make the performers vagabonds (unless they wandered from their habitations so to do), how particular was the case of us three late managing actors at the Theatre Royal, who in twenty years before had paid, upon an average, at least twenty thousand pounds to be protected (as actors) from a law that has not since appeared to be against us.[45] Now, whether we might certainly have acted without any licence at all I shall not pretend to determine, but this I have of my own knowledge to say: that in Queen Anne's reign the stage was in such confusion, and its affairs in such distress, that Sir John Vanbrugh and Mr Congreve, after they had held it about one year, threw up the management of it as an unprofitable post,[46] after which a licence for acting was not

---

42 The 1714 Vagrancy Act (13 Anne c. 26) consolidated previous legislation and widened the definition of vagrancy.

43 In the *Gentleman's Magazine*, November 1733 (*Document Register* no.3765), it is reported that 'Mr [John] Harper, one of the comedians in the Haymarket Company, who had been committed to Bridewell by Sir Thomas Clarges, upon the Act made against common strollers, was brought by *habeas corpus* to the Court of King's Bench, where it was agreed he should be discharged out of Bridewell upon his own recognizance.' On 29 November 1733 *The Daily Courant* reported that Harper had been acquitted (*Document Register* no.3786). Lowe cites Thomas Davies, *Memoirs of the Life of David Garrick, Esq*, I.36: 'The reason of the patentees fixing on Harper was in consequence of his natural timidity.' Contrary to Cibber's statement, Harper does not seem to have been one of the company's 'chief performers' but a minor actor of comic roles.

44 The Harper case generated a significant amount of contrasting legal opinion, as listed in *Document Register* no.3787 and explored in Hume, *Fielding*, pp.175–9. By 'house keeper' Cibber means a man with a settled residence of his own.

45 i.e. the cost to Wilks, Cibber, and Booth of maintaining their patent.

46 A licence to operate the new Queen's Theatre, Haymarket, was issued to Vanbrugh and Congreve on 14 December 1704; according to Downes, p.99, the theatre opened on 9 April 1705. On 15 December of the same year, Congreve wrote to Joseph Keally that he

thought worth any gentleman's asking for and almost seemed to go a begging; till some time after, by the care, application and industry of three actors, it became so prosperous and the profits so considerable that it created a new place and a sinecure of a thousand pounds a year, which the labour of those actors constantly paid to such persons as had, from time to time, merit or interest enough to get their names inserted as fourth managers in a licence with them for acting plays *etc* – a preferment that many a Sir Francis Wronghead would have jumped at.[47] But to go on with my story. This endeavour of the patentees to suppress the comedians acting in the Haymarket proving ineffectual, and no hopes of a reunion then appearing, the remains of the company left in Drury Lane were reduced to a very low condition. At this time a third purchaser, Charles Fleetwood Esq, stepped in;[48] who, judging the best time to buy was when the stock was at the lowest price, struck up a bargain at once for five parts in six of the patent, and at the same time gave the revolted comedians their own terms to return and come under his government in Drury Lane, where they now continue to act at very ample salaries, as I am informed in 1738. But (as I have observed) the late cause of the prosecuted comedian having gone so strongly in his

had 'quitted the affair of the Haymarket', quoting Terence to the effect that he had got out as cheaply as possible; see Congreve, *Letters*, p.38. On 10 September 1706 Congreve wrote to Keally that Vanbrugh had 'resign[ed] his authority' to Owen Swiney (Congreve, *Letters*, p.43); in a letter of 11 May 1708 to the Earl of Manchester, following attempts to reduce his personal liability, Vanbrugh reports that he has 'parted with' his financial interest in the company to Swiney (*Document Register* no.1979).

47 i.e. Sir Francis Wronghead in the Vanbrugh/Cibber *The Provoked Husband* (1728). Sir Francis is a country squire who harbours ambitions at court. Lowe cites the episode in Act IV where Sir Francis recalls a conversation with a nobleman:

Sir Francis, says my lord, pray what sort of a place may you have turned your thoughts upon? My lord, says I, beggars must not be choosers; but any place, says I, about a thousand a year, will be well enough to be doing with till something better falls in — for I thought it would not look well to stand haggling with him at first.

Cibber's 'three actors' were in the first instance himself, Wilks, and Estcourt, the latter succeeded by Doggett and then Booth; according to the partnership agreement with Owen Swiney, leaseholder of the Queen's Theatre, Haymarket, Swiney was to be paid half the profits (his 'sinecure') with the three actors sharing the rest equally (C7/668/31; *Document Register* no.2002). A similar agreement was reached with William Collier in 1712 (LC 5/155, fol.97; *Document Register* no.2183, and below, p.262 n.32).

48 Charles Fleetwood of Staffordshire reportedly had an estate worth more than £8,000 a year (c.£2m in current values). *The Daily Journal* of 1 February 1734 reported that he had bought five-sixths of the Drury Lane shares, with Henry Giffard retaining his one-sixth. *The Daily Courant* of 2 February 1734 reported Fleetwood's intention to 'either keep [the shares] himself, or dispose of them to such persons (actors only) as shall be approved of by the players themselves; on which conditions, we hear that the company from the theatre in the Haymarket are about to return to their old house' (*Document Register* nos.3798–9).

favour – and the house in Goodman's Fields, too, continuing to act with as little authority, unmolested – these so tolerated companies gave encouragement to a broken wit to collect a fourth company, who for some time acted plays in the Haymarket, which house the united Drury Lane comedians had lately quitted.[49] This enterprising person, I say (whom I do not choose to name unless it could be to his advantage, or that it were of importance), had sense enough to know that the best plays with bad actors would turn but to a very poor account, and therefore found it necessary to give the public some pieces of an extraordinary kind, the poetry of which he conceived ought to be so strong that the greatest dunce of an actor could not spoil it.[50] He knew too that as he was in haste to get money, it would take up less time to be intrepidly abusive than decently entertaining: that to draw the mob after him, he must rake the channel[51] and pelt their superiors; that to show himself somebody, he must come up to Juvenal's advice and stand the consequence:-

> *Aude aliquid brevibus Gyaris, & carcere dignum*
> *Si vis esse aliquis–*   Juv. Sat. I.[52]

Such, then, was the mettlesome modesty he set out with; upon this principle he produced several frank and free farces that seemed to knock all distinctions of mankind on the head. Religion, laws, government, priests, judges and

---

49 The **broken wit** is Henry Fielding (1707–54). The longstanding enmity between him and Cibber probably dates to Cibber's refusal to stage Fielding's plays during the winter of 1729–30; see also Introduction, p.xxxvi n.84. Fielding responded the following spring with a satire of the Drury Lane management in *The Author's Farce* (1730). For an account, see Hume, *Fielding*, pp.44–6. Fielding's attacks on Cibber continued in *The Champion*, following publication of the *Apology*; see also Introduction, pp.li–liii, and Barker, pp.221–32. By 'the Haymarket' Cibber means not the Haymarket Opera but the non-patent Little Haymarket Theatre, built by the Drury Lane carpenter John Potter in 1720–1 at an alleged cost of £1,000, and from 1733 home to a group of rebellious ex-Drury Lane actors led by Cibber's son, Theophilus. Fielding rented this theatre early in 1736. Cibber is strictly correct in identifying four theatre companies, since the (as of 1714) King's Theatre Haymarket was at this time devoted to opera, as he points out below, p.191.

50 Hume, *Fielding*, p.206, describes the initial company as 'even more a scratch group than scholars have realized', with twenty-two fringe performers, three junior players from the patent companies, and seventeen complete novices. However, Fielding soon acquired the services of a more established Drury Lane performer in the shape of Cibber's own daughter, Charlotte Charke, who had recently satirized Charles Fleetwood in *The Art of Management* (1735).

51 i.e. gutter. *OED* 3a quotes from a legal text of 1689: 'If any person ... sweep any dung, ordure, rubbish, rushes, seacoal-dust, or any other thing annoyant, down into the channel of any street or lane...'.

52 Juvenal, Satire 1 line 73: 'if you want to be somebody, do something bold that puts you at risk of exile or imprisonment – virtue is praised but left out in the cold.'

ministers were all laid flat at the feet of this Herculean satirist,[53] this Draw-cansir in wit, that spared neither friend nor foe;[54] who, to make his poetical fame immortal, like another Erostratus set fire to his stage by writing up to an Act of Parliament to demolish it.[55] I shall not give the particular strokes of his ingenuity a chance to be remembered by reciting them;[56] it may be enough to say, in general terms, they were so openly flagrant that the wisdom of the legislature thought it high time to take a proper notice of them.

Having now shown by what means there came to be four theatres (besides a fifth for operas) in London, all open at the same time – and that while they were so numerous, it was evident some of them must have starved unless they fed upon the trash and filth of buffoonery and licen-tiousness[57] – I now come, as I promised, to speak of that necessary law which has reduced their number, and prevents the repetition of such abuses in those that remain open for the public recreation.

While this law was in debate, a lively spirit and uncommon elo-quence was employed against it.[58] It was urged that one of the greatest goods we can enjoy is liberty; this we may grant to be an incontestable

53 The 'several farces' were all produced in 1736: *Pasquin, Tumble-Down Dick, The Historical Register*, and *Eurydice Hissed.* They are all 'rehearsal' plays, satirizing the theatre as well as public life.

54 Drawcansir is an absurd mock-heroic boaster in Buckingham's *The Rehearsal*, a play well known to Cibber (see above, p.14 n.9). In IV.i.213–14 he declares 'I drink, I huff, I strut, look big and stare; / And all this I can do, because I dare.' Cibber pointedly refers to Fielding's short stature, his fondness for alcohol, and his liking for rehearsal plays.

55 Measures to introduce the Licensing Act began in 1735, the year before Fielding's season of farces (see Hume, *Fielding*, p.249); Cibber's version of events was, however, common at the time. The *Daily Gazeteer* of 4 June 1737 states that Fielding 'paved the way for the subversion of the stage by introducing on it matters quite foreign to its true object'. For discussion of Fielding's possible role in writing the play believed to have triggered the formal introduction of the Licensing Act, *The Golden Rump*, see Hume, *Fielding*, pp.250–3. **Erostratus** or Herostratus was an Ephesian who, on the night Alexander the Great was born (356 BC), set light to the Temple of Artemis; his name was widely used as a byword for someone who seeks fame via crime.

56 Fielding's response to this passage is in *The Champion*, 22 April 1740, drawing a comparison between Cibber's failure to mention his children and his reluctance to have any part of *Pasquin* remembered.

57 The four theatres at this time were Drury Lane, Goodman's Fields, Covent Garden, and the Little Haymarket; the Haymarket was 'the fifth for operas'.

58 A reference to Cibber's acquaintance, Lord Chesterfield (see above, p.20 n.25). Chesterfield's speech against the Licensing Act is reproduced in full in the 1779 edition of his *Miscellaneous Works*, and in part in Thomas and Hare, pp.211–14. Chesterfield argued that current laws were 'sufficient for deterring all players from acting anything that may have the least tendency towards giving a reasonable offence' and feared the new Act would be an 'encroachment upon liberty' likely to extend beyond the theatre.

truth without its being the least objection to this law. It was said too that to bring the stage under the restraint of a licensor was leading the way to an attack upon the liberty of the press.[59] This amounts but to a jealousy at best, which I hope and believe all honest Englishmen have as much reason to think a groundless as to fear it is a just jealousy; for the stage and the press, I shall endeavour to show, are very different weapons to wound with. If a great man could be no more injured by being personally ridiculed or made contemptible in a play, than by the same matter only printed and read against him in a pamphlet or the strongest verse, then indeed the stage and the press might pretend to be upon an equal foot of liberty. But when the wide difference between these two liberties comes to be explained and considered, I dare say we shall find the injuries from one, capable of being ten times more severe and formidable than from the other. Let us see, at least, if the case will not be vastly altered. Read what Mr Collier, in his *Defence* of his *Short View of the Stage etc*, page 25, says to this point;[60] he sets this difference in a clear light. These are his words:

'The satire of a comedian and another poet have a different effect upon reputation. A character of disadvantage upon the stage makes a stronger impression than elsewhere. Reading is but hearing at the secondhand; now hearing, at best, is a more languid conveyance than sight. For, as Horace observes,

Segnius irritant animum, demissa per aurem,
Quam quæ sunt oculis subjecta fidelibus.[61]

The eye is much more affecting, and strikes deeper into the memory, than the ear; besides, upon the stage, both the senses are in conjunction. The life of the actor[62] fortifies the object and awakens the mind to take hold of it. Thus a dramatic abuse is rivetted in the audience, a jest is improved into an argument, and rallying grows up into reason. Thus a character of scandal becomes almost indelible; a man goes for a blockhead upon content, and he that is made a fool in a play is often made one for his life.[63] 'Tis true, he

---

59 As Evans notes, this passage may be a response to the attack on the Licensing Act by James Thomson in his preface to the 1738 edition of Milton's *Areopagitica*.
60 The passage appears on pp.25–6 of Collier's *A Defence of the Short View*; in early editions of the *Apology* it is repunctuated. Minor mistranscriptions are recorded in the notes below.
61 From Horace, *The Art of Poetry*, lines 180–2: 'What comes in through the ear is less effective in stirring the mind than what is put before our faithful eyes.' Cibber alters Collier's 'animios' to 'animum'.
62 Collier has 'action'.   63 Collier has 'for his lifetime'.

passes for such only among the prejudiced and unthinking, but these are no inconsiderable division of mankind. For these reasons, I humbly conceive, the stage stands in need of a great deal of discipline and restraint. To give them an unlimited range is, in effect, to make them masters of all moral distinctions, and to lay honour and religion at their mercy. To show greatness ridiculous is the way to lose the use and abate the value of the quality. Things made little in jest will soon be so in earnest, for laughing and esteem are seldom bestowed on the same object.'

If this was truth and reason (as sure it was) forty years ago, will it not carry the same conviction with it to these days, when there came to be a much stronger call for a reformation of the stage than when this author wrote against it, or perhaps than was ever known since the English stage had a being? And now let us ask another question. Does not the general opinion of mankind suppose that the honour and reputation of a minister is, or ought to be, as dear to him as his life? Yet when the law, in Queen Anne's time, had made even an unsuccessful attempt upon the life of a minister *capital*, could any reason be found that the fame and honour of his character should not be under equal protection?[64] Was the wound that Guiscard gave to the late Lord Oxford when a minister, a greater injury than the theatrical insult which was offered to a later minister in a more valuable part: his character?[65] Was it not as high time, then, to take this dangerous weapon of mimical insolence and defamation out of the hands of a mad poet, as to wrest the knife from the lifted hand of a murderer? And is not that law of a milder nature which *prevents* a crime, than that which *punishes* it after it is committed? May not one think it amazing that the liberty of defaming lawful power and dignity should have been so eloquently contended for? Or, especially, that this liberty ought to triumph in a theatre, where the most able, the most innocent and most upright person must himself be, while the wound is given, defenceless? How long must a man so injured lie bleeding, before the pain and anguish of his fame (if it suffers wrongfully) can be dispelled? Or, say he had deserved reproof and public accusation, yet the weight and greatness of his office never can deserve it from a public stage where the lowest malice, by saucy parallels

64 A reference to the Treason Act of 1708 (7 Ann c. 21).
65 Antoine de Guiscard (1658–1711) was a French double agent who infiltrated the British government. On 8 March 1711, during a meeting of the Privy Council in which he was charged with treason, he stabbed Robert Harley (1661–1724), then Chancellor of the Exchequer, with a penknife. Harley was made Earl of Oxford in 1711. The 'later minister' is Walpole, satirized by Fielding and others.

and abusive innuendos, may do everything but name him.[66] But alas, liberty is so tender, so chaste a virgin that, it seems, not to suffer her to do irreparable injuries with impunity is a violation of her! It cannot sure be a principle of liberty that would turn the stage into a court of inquiry, that would let the partial applauses of a vulgar audience give sentence upon the conduct of authority and put impeachments into the mouth of a Harlequin.[67] Will not every impartial man think that malice, envy, faction and misrule might have too much advantage over lawful power, if the range of such a stage-liberty were unlimited and insisted on to be enrolled among the glorious rights of an English subject?

I remember much such another ancient liberty which many of the good people of England were once extremely fond of – I mean that of throwing squibs and crackers at all spectators, without distinction, upon a Lord Mayor's Day. But about forty years ago a certain nobleman happening to have one of his eyes burned out by this mischievous merriment, it occasioned a penal law to prevent those sorts of jests from being laughed at for the future.[68] Yet I have never heard that the most zealous patriot ever thought such a law was the least restraint upon our liberty.

If I am asked why I am so voluntary a champion for the honour of this law that has limited the number of playhouses, and which now can no longer concern me as a professor of the stage,[69] I reply that it being a law

---

66 The tone of this passage suggests Cibber was as concerned for his own reputation as anyone else's.

67 Both *Pasquin* and *Tumble-Down Dick* feature the character of Harlequin. Theatres might be a topic for his satire as well as government, as in *Pasquin*, V.i, where Harlequin, as 'ambassador from the two theatres', greets the Queen of Ignorance (Fielding, *Plays*, III.304).

68 Luttrell, III.297, reports an order of 26 October 1697 by the new Lord Mayor of London, Sir Humphrey Edwin, banning the making, selling, or throwing of squibs, with a 10-shilling reward for anyone providing information. On 30 October 1697, Luttrell reported a number of arrests in connection with 'Lord Jermyn having [a squib] thrown in his face [which] put his eye out, and will endanger the other, if not his life, being in a fever' (Luttrell, III.299). The unfortunate victim was Thomas, 2nd Baron Jermyn, Governor of Jersey, who in 1684 had succeeded to his title on the death of his uncle, Henry Jermyn, 1st Earl of St Albans. The legislation referred to is 9 Gul. 3 P.1.n.7, a law banning the manufacture, sale, and use of fireworks which was passed on 25 March 1698 and carried the sanction of a 20-shilling fine or hard labour for non-payment.

69 Cibber underplays the fact that the Licensing Act benefited the company he had led (a fact he admits below, p.197), and that he himself continued to receive benefit performances at Drury Lane after the Act came into force. His views of the Act were, however, widely shared. *The Daily Gazeteer* published a series of articles in favour of it between 6 June and 9 July 1737, in opposition to others published by *The Craftsman* and *Fog's Weekly Journal*.

so nearly relating to the theatre, it seems not at all foreign to my history to have taken notice of it; and as I have farther promised to give the public a true portrait of my mind, I ought fairly to let them see how far I am or am not a blockhead when I pretend to talk of serious matters that may be judged so far above my capacity. Nor will it in the least discompose me, whether my observations are contemned or applauded. A blockhead is not always an unhappy fellow, and if the world will not flatter us, we can flatter ourselves; perhaps, too, it will be as difficult to convince us we are in the wrong as that you wiser gentlemen are one tittle the better for your knowledge. It is yet a question with me whether we weak heads have not as much pleasure, too, in giving our shallow reason a little exercise as those clearer brains have that are allowed to dive into the deepest doubts and mysteries; to reflect, or form a judgment upon remarkable things past is as delightful to me as it is to the gravest politician to penetrate into what is present, or to enter into speculations upon what is or is not likely to come. Why are histories written, if all men are not to judge of them? Therefore, if my reader has no more to do than I have, I have a chance for his being as willing to have a little more upon the same subject as I am to give it him.

When direct arguments against this bill were found too weak, recourse was had to dissuasive ones. It was said that this restraint upon the stage would not remedy the evil complained of: that a play refused to be licensed would still be printed with double advantage when it should be insinuated that it was refused for some strokes of wit *etc*, and would be more likely, then, to have its effect among the people.[70] However natural this consequence may seem, I doubt it will be very difficult to give a printed satire or libel half the force or credit of an acted one. The most artful or notorious lie or strained allusion that ever slandered a great man may be read by some people with a smile of contempt or, at worst, it can impose but on one person at once. But when the words of the same plausible stuff shall be repeated on a theatre, the wit of it among a crowd of hearers is liable to be over-valued, and may unite and warm a whole body of the malicious or ignorant into a plaudit. Nay, the partial claps of only twenty illminded persons among several hundreds of silent hearers shall, and often

70 In his speech to the House of Lords opposing the introduction of the Licensing Act, Lord Chesterfield said:

> By this bill you prevent a play's being acted but you do not prevent its being printed: therefore, if a licence should be refused for its being acted, we may depend upon it the play will be printed. It will be printed and published, my Lords, with the refusal in capital letters upon the title page. People are always fond of what is forbidden. (In Thomas and Hare, p.212)

have been, mistaken for a general approbation, and frequently draw into their party the indifferent or inapprehensive – who, rather than be thought not to understand the conceit, will laugh with the laughers and join in the triumph! But alas, the quiet reader of the same ingenious matter can only like for himself, and the poison has a much slower operation upon the body of a people when it is so retailed out than when sold to a full audience by wholesale. The single reader too may happen to be a sensible or unprejudiced person, and then the merry dose meeting with the antidote of a sound judgment perhaps may have no operation at all. With such a one, the wit of the most ingenious satire will only, by its intrinsic truth or value, gain upon his approbation; or, if it be worth an answer, a printed falsehood may possibly be confounded by printed proofs against it. But against contempt and scandal, heightened and coloured by the skill of an actor ludicrously infusing it into a multitude, there is no immediate defence to be made or equal reparation to be had for it; for it would be but a poor satisfaction, at last, after lying long patient under the injury, that time only is to show (which would probably be the case) that the author of it was a desperate indigent that did it for bread. How much less dangerous or offensive, then, is the written than the acted scandal?[71] The impression the comedian gives to it is a kind of double stamp upon the poet's paper that raises it to ten times the intrinsic value. Might we not strengthen this argument, too, even by the eloquence that seemed to have opposed this law? I will say for myself, at least, that when I came to read the printed arguments against it, I could scarce believe they were the same that had amazed and raised such admiration in me when they had the advantage of a lively elocution, and of that grace and spirit which gave strength and lustre to them in the delivery!

Upon the whole, if the stage ought ever to have been reformed – if to place a power *somewhere* of restraining its immoralities was not inconsistent with the liberties of a civilized people (neither of which, sure, any moral man of sense can dispute) – might it not have shown a spirit too poorly prejudiced to have rejected so rational a law only because the honour and office of a minister might happen, in some small measure, to be protected by it?

But, however little weight there may be in the observations I have made upon it, I shall for my own part always think them just, unless I should live to see (which I do not expect) some future set of upright ministers use their utmost endeavours to repeal it.

---

71 Cibber may be characterizing his own enemies as 'desperate' while claiming their writing does him no harm.

And now we have seen the consequence of what many people are apt to contend for: variety of playhouses! How was it possible so many could honestly subsist on what was fit to be seen?[72] Their extraordinary number of course reduced them to live upon the gratification of such hearers as they knew would be best pleased with public offence, and public offence of what kind soever will always be a good reason for making laws to restrain it.

To conclude, let us now consider this law in a quite different light; let us leave the political part of it quite out of the question. What advantage could either the spectators of plays or the masters of playhouses have gained by its having never been made? How could the same stock of plays supply four theatres which (without such additional entertainments as a nation of common sense ought to be ashamed of) could not well support two? Satiety must have been the natural consequence of the same plays being twice as often repeated as now they need be, and satiety puts an end to all tastes that the mind of man can delight in. Had, therefore, this law been made seven years ago, I should not have parted with my share in the patent under a thousand pounds more than I received for it[73] – so that, as far as I am able to judge, both the public as spectators and the patentees as undertakers are, or might be, in a way of being better entertained and more considerable gainers by it.

I now return to the state of the stage where I left it: about the year 1697, from whence this pursuit of its immoralities has led me farther than I first designed to have followed it.

---

72 Theatre historians have reached the opposite conclusion: in fact, the Licensing Act restricted the number of new plays and ushered in a period described by Hume, *Fielding*, as 'stodgy' (p.260).

73 Hume, *Fielding*, p.157, cites different accounts of how much Cibber received from John Highmore for his share: Benjamin Victor has 3,000 guineas (i.e. £3,150), while *The Daily Post* and *The Craftsman* imply it was £3,500. (c.£890,000 in current values).

CHAPTER 9

A small apology for writing on. The different state of the two companies. Wilks invited over from Dublin. Estcourt from the same stage the winter following. Mrs Oldfield's first admission to the Theatre Royal. Her character. The great theatre in the Haymarket built for Betterton's company. It answers not their expectation. Some observations upon it. A theatrical state secret.

I now begin to doubt that the *gaieté du coeur* in which I first undertook this work may have drawn me into a more laborious amusement than I shall know how to away with. For though I cannot say I have yet jaded my vanity, it is not impossible but, by this time, the most candid of my readers may want a little breath; especially when they consider that all this load I have heaped upon their patience contains but seven years of the forty-three I passed upon the stage, the history of which period I have enjoined myself to transmit to the judgment (or oblivion) of posterity.[1] However, even my dullness will find somebody to do it right;[2] if my reader is an ill natured one, he will be as much pleased to find me a dunce in my old age as, possibly, he may have been to prove me a brisk blockhead in my youth. But if he has no gall to gratify, and would for his simple amusement as well know how the playhouses went on forty years ago as how they do now, I will honestly tell him the rest of my story as well as I can. Lest, therefore, the frequent digressions that have broke in upon it may have entangled his memory, I must beg leave just to throw together the heads of what I have already given him, that he may again recover the clue of my discourse.

Let him then remember, from the year 1660 to 1684,[3] the various fortune of the (then) King's and Duke's, two famous companies: their being reduced to one united; the distinct characters I have given of thirteen actors, which in the year 1690 were the most famous then remaining of

---

1 Lowe cites the response of *The Laureate*: 'Indeed, Laureate, notwithstanding what thou mayst dream of the immortality of this work of thine and bestowing the same on thy favourites by recording them here, thou mayst, old as thou art, live to see thy precious labours become the vile wrappers of pastry-grocers and chandlery wares' (p.72). The *Apology* is now more often read (or at least consulted) than *The Laureate*.
2 The word 'dullness' may recall Pope's inclusion of Cibber among those with 'Less human genius than God gives an ape' in his 1729 *Dunciad Variorum*, I.236–40 (Pope, *Poems*, p.368).
3 The King's Company collapsed in 1682 and was absorbed by the Duke's.

them; the cause of their being again divided in 1695, and the consequences of that division till 1697;[4] from whence I shall lead them to our second union in – hold! Let me see – ay, it was in that memorable year when the two kingdoms of England and Scotland were made one.[5] And I remember a particular that confirms me I am right in my chronology; for the play of *Hamlet* being acted soon after, Estcourt (who then took upon him to say anything) added a fourth line to Shakespeare's prologue to the play in that play, which originally consisted but of three, but Estcourt made it run thus:

> For us and for our tragedy,
> Thus stooping to your clemency,
> (This being a year of unity,)
> We beg your hearing patiently.[6]

This new chronological line, coming unexpectedly upon the audience, was received with applause, though several grave faces looked a little out of humour at it. However, by this fact it is plain our theatrical union happened in 1707.[7] But to speak of it in its place, I must go a little back again.

From 1697 to this union, both companies went on without any memorable change in their affairs, unless it were that Betterton's people (however good in their kind) were most of them too far advanced in years to mend; and though we in Drury Lane were too young to be excellent, we were not too old to be better.[8] But what will not satiety depreciate? For though I must own and avow that in our highest prosperity I always thought we

4 1698 was the year of Collier's *A Short View*, and Cibber has given substantive portraits of fourteen actors.

5 The Act Ratifying and Approving the Treaty of Union of the Two Kingdoms of Scotland and England (1707 c. 7) came into effect on 1 May 1707. The Lord Chamberlain's Order of Union between the Haymarket and Drury Lane companies is dated 31 December 1707 (LC 5/154, pp.299–300; *Document Register* no.1927); for an extract, see Thomas and Hare, pp.23–4.

6 LS2a 406 records a Drury Lane performance of *Hamlet* 'By her Majesty's United Company of Comedians' on 15 January 1708, believed to be the company's inaugural show. Cibber played Osric to Wilks's Hamlet. Richard Estcourt is listed as the First Gravedigger, so presumably he doubled as one of the Players. The quotation is from *Hamlet*, III.ii.122–4.

7 In the first edition Cibber had given the date as 1708 but changed it to 1707. Since the Lord Chamberlain's order was dated 31 December 1707 (see above, n.5), and old styles dates for January–March were often given as (e.g.) 1707/8, his confusion is understandable.

8 By contrast Milhous, *Management*, pp.80–181, charts four distinct periods amounting to significant change: the initial success of the breakaway company (1695–8); intense competition (1698–1702); years of uncertainty (1702–5); and the Queen's Haymarket years leading to the union (1705–8).

were greatly their inferiors, yet by our good fortune of being seen in quite
new lights which several new-written plays had shown us in, we now began
to make a considerable stand against them. One good new play to a rising
company is of inconceivable value. In *Oroonoko*[9] and (why may I not name
another, though it be my own?) in *Love's Last Shift*, and in the sequel of
it, *The Relapse*,[10] several of our people showed themselves in a new style of
acting, in which Nature had not as yet been seen.[11] I cannot here forget a
misfortune that befell our society about this time by the loss of a young
actor, Hildebrand Horden, who was killed at the bar of the Rose Tavern
in a frivolous, rash, accidental quarrel, for which a late Resident at Venice,
Colonel Burgess, and several other persons of distinction took their trials
and were acquitted.[12] This young man had almost every natural gift that
could promise an excellent actor; he had, besides, a good deal of table-
wit and humour, with a handsome person, and was every day rising into
public favour.[13] Before he was buried it was observable that two or three

---

9 Thomas Southerne's *Oroonoko*, adapting the novella by Aphra Behn, opened at Drury
   Lane in November 1695 (LS1 454). Cibber's name does not appear in the dramatis
   personae. Verbruggen played the title role, and the anonymous prologue refers to 'war'
   between the two companies. According to *Comparison*, p.19, the play was 'the favourite of
   the ladies' and an 'uncommon success'.
10 For details, see above, p.147 n.79.
11 Cibber's previous comments about the company's acting (above, p.138) may suggest
   this passage laments the loss of 'Nature' as prized by Betterton and Barry. However, the
   context suggests that the new plays encouraged a new kind of naturalism. *Comparison*,
   p.19, praised Southerne's 'style and agreeable manner' and found he had 'drawn the
   passions very well': 'very few exceed him in the dialogue; his gallantry is natural, and
   after the real manner of the town'.
12 Hildebrand **Horden** (1674–96) joined the United Company for its last season in 1694–5
   and remained with Rich's Company after the breakaway. He played Stanmore in
   Oroonoko and Young Worthy in *Love's Last Shift*, among other middling roles. Reports of
   his death following a quarrel at the Rose Tavern are carried in *The London News-Letter*,
   20 May 1696; *The Protestant Mercury*, 18–20 May 1696; and Luttrell, IV.81. The **Rose
   Tavern** was the local for Theatre Royal actors and audiences. Pepys dined there on 18
   May 1668 during a trip to the Theatre Royal; *Comparison*, p.140, describes it as 'the very
   camp of sin', while Farquhar's epilogue to *The Constant Couple* (1699) suggests it was the
   natural place for couples to continue their day's entertainment after a play (Farquhar,
   Works, I.226). Elizeus or Ellis **Burgess** (c. 1670–1736) was a brigadier in the Duke of
   Ormond's Horseguards from 1693 (*CSPD* William and Mary, IV.63) and had previously
   been jailed for killing a Mr Fane in April 1696. He escaped thanks to his connections.
   An Old Bailey report dated 14 October 1696 names 'Elizeus Burgis' as Horden's killer,
   and one of the accomplices as John Pitts. Pitts was acquitted; Burgess received a royal
   pardon on 30 November 1697. He was made a lieutenant-colonel in 1711 and served two
   terms as Resident in Venice: the first from 1719 to 1721 (*PSGB*, XXXIV.505) and the
   second from 1727 until his death in 1736 (*PSGB*, LII.541).
13 Lowe cites Davies, III.443: '[Horden] was bred a scholar: he complimented George
   Powell, in a Latin encomium on his [play, *The*] *Treacherous Brothers*.' Horden wrote and

days together, several of the fair sex, well-dressed, came in masks (then frequently worn) and some in their own coaches to visit this theatrical hero in his shroud. He was the elder son of Dr Horden, minister of Twickenham in Middlesex.[14] But this misfortune was soon repaired by the return of Wilks from Dublin, who upon this young man's death was sent for over, and lived long enough among us to enjoy that approbation from which the other was so unhappily cut off. The winter following, Estcourt (the famous mimic of whom I have already spoken) had the same invitation from Ireland, where he had commenced actor.[15] His first part here, at the Theatre Royal, was the Spanish Friar, in which, though he had remembered every look and motion of the late Tony Leigh so far as to put the spectator very much in mind of him,[16] yet it was visible through the whole, notwithstanding his exactness in the outlines, the true spirit that was to fill up the figure was not the same, but unskilfully daubed on like a child's painting upon the face of a *metzotinto*.[17] It was too plain to the judicious that the conception was not his own but imprinted in his memory by another, of whom he only presented a dead likeness.[18] But these were defects not so obvious to common spectators; no wonder, therefore, if by his being much sought after in private companies, he met with a sort of indulgence, not to say partiality, for what he sometimes did upon the stage.

In the year 1699 Mrs Oldfield was first taken into the house, where she remained about a twelvemonth almost a mute and unheeded till Sir John Vanbrugh, who first recommended her, gave her the part of Alinda in *The Pilgrim* revised.[19] This gentle character happily became that want of confidence which is inseparable from young beginners, who without it seldom

---

delivered the prologue to the anonymous play, *Neglected Virtue*, performed at Drury Lane in February 1696 (LS1 459).

14 Dr John Horden was Rector of St Michael Queenhithe, where Hildebrand was baptized on 19 January 1674. When he drew up his will on 6 March 1690, Dr Horden left 5 shillings to each of his children, including Hildebrand.

15 Horden died in 1696, but Wilks did not return to London until 1698, while Estcourt joined Rich's company in 1704.

16 For Leigh's performance of the role, see above, p.105. Estcourt's first performance in *The Spanish Friar* was not until 18 October 1704 (LS2a 188–9), nearly twelve years after Leigh's death.

17 See above, p.87 n.89.

18 Downes's statement, pp.51–2, that Betterton was taught 'every particle' of the role of Hamlet as performed in the original King's Company performance has led some to believe that actors at this time merely imitated their predecessors. This is one of a number of passages in the *Apology* that suggests the best or most experienced actors developed their own 'conception' of a role.

19 For Oldfield's early career and limited roles, see above, p.114 n.90. For *The Pilgrim* (1700), see above, p.179 n.13.

arrive to any excellence. Notwithstanding, I own I was then so far deceived in my opinion of her that I thought she had little more than her person that appeared necessary to the forming a good actress; for she set out with so extraordinary a diffidence that it kept her too despondingly down to a formal, plain, not to say flat manner of speaking. Nor could the silver tone of her voice, till after some time, incline my ear to any hope in her favour.[20] But public approbation is the warm weather of a theatrical plant, which will soon bring it forward to whatever perfection Nature has designed it. However, Mrs Oldfield (perhaps for want of fresh parts) seemed to come but slowly forward till the year 1703.[21] Our company, that summer, acted at the Bath during the residence of Queen Anne at that place. At that time it happened that Mrs Verbruggen, by reason of her last sickness (of which she some few months after died) was left in London;[22] and though most of her parts were of course to be disposed of, yet so earnest was the female scramble for them that only one of them fell to the share of Mrs Oldfield – that of Leonora in *Sir Courtly Nice*, a character of good plain sense, but not over elegantly written. It was in this part Mrs Oldfield surprised me into an opinion of her having all the innate powers of a good actress, though they were yet but in the bloom of what they promised. Before she had acted this part, I had so cold an expectation from her abilities that she could scarce prevail with me to rehearse with her the scenes she was chiefly concerned in with Sir Courtly, which I then acted. However, we ran them over with a mutual inadvertancy of one another. I seemed careless, as concluding that any assistance I could give her would be to little or no purpose, and she muttered out her words in a sort of mifty manner[23] at my low opinion of her. But when the play came to be acted, she had a just occasion to triumph over the error of my judgment by the almost amazement that her unexpected performance awaked me to. So forward and sudden a step into Nature I had never seen; and what made her performance more valuable was that I knew it all proceeded from her own understanding, untaught and unassisted by any one more experienced actor. Perhaps it may not be unacceptable if I enlarge a little more upon the theatrical character of so memorable an actress.

20 Probably a reference to Oldfield's singing rather than speaking voice, as exhibited in John Oldmixon and Daniel Purcell's Drury Lane opera of February 1700, *The Grove*, in which she played Sylvia (LS1 524).

21 For a harsh estimation of Oldfield's talent the year before, see above, p.114 n.90.

22 For Susannah Mountfort-Verbruggen's career, see above, pp.118–20. According to Davies, III.421, she died giving birth.

23 i.e. miffed, put out. *OED* records only one other use, from *A New Dictionary of the Canting Crew* (1698).

Though this part of Leonora in itself was of so little value that when
she got more into esteem it was one of the several she gave away to inferior actresses,[24] yet it was the first (as I have observed) that corrected my
judgment of her, and confirmed me in a strong belief that she could not
fail, in very little time, of being what she was afterwards allowed to be – the
foremost ornament of our theatre. Upon this unexpected sally, then, of the
power and disposition of so unforeseen an actress, it was that I again took
up the two first acts of *The Careless Husband*, which I had written the summer before and had thrown aside, in despair of having justice done to the
character of Lady Betty Modish by any one woman then among us,[25] Mrs
Verbruggen being now in a very declining state of health, and Mrs Bracegirdle out of my reach and engaged in another company.[26] But, as I have
said, Mrs Oldfield having thrown out such new proffers of a genius, I was
no longer at a loss for support; my doubts were dispelled, and I had now a
new call to finish it. Accordingly, *The Careless Husband* took its fate upon
the stage the winter following, in 1704.[27] Whatever favourable reception
this comedy has met with from the public, it would be unjust in me not to
place a large share of it to the account of Mrs Oldfield – not only from the
uncommon excellence of her action, but even from her personal manner
of conversing. There are many sentiments in the character of Lady Betty
Modish that I may almost say were originally her own, or only dressed with
a little more care than when they negligently fell from her lively humour.
Had her birth placed her in a higher rank of life, she had certainly appeared
in reality what in this play she only excellently acted: an agreeably gay

24 Oldfield was still playing the role in a performance on 21 December 1709 (LS2a 533);
by June 1710 (LS2a 581) Leonora was being played by Mary Kent, a seasoned performer
who had joined the United Company in 1692 (LS1 411). By October 1717 (LS2 463) it
was being played by Mary Porter, who had been recruited to the Lincoln's Inn Fields
company in 1697 and was not generally thought of as 'inferior'. Cibber may have revised
his original 'grew more into esteem' to 'got more into esteem' to avoid the suggestion that
he was reflecting on Oldfield's figure.
25 Lady Betty is a high comic role: an affected woman obsessed with her personal
appearance, like a female version of Lord Foppington.
26 Cibber perhaps had in mind the comic types exploited by Susannah Verbruggen as Lady
Froth in Congreve's *The Double Dealer* (1694) and Marsillia in *The Female Wits* (1696),
and by Anne Bracegirdle as Millamant in *The Way of the World* (1700).
27 Cibber's *The Careless Husband* opened at Drury Lane on 7 December 1704. Powell
played Lord Morelove and Wilks Sir Charles Easy; Cibber wrote another Lord
Foppington role for himself. The play was a commercial success; LS2a 199–202 records
ten further performances over the subsequent month. Cibber reflects on the play's
success in the dedication of the first edition (1705). Even Pope recognized the merits of
the play: see 'The First Epistle of the Second Book of Horace Imitated' (Pope, *Poems*,
p. 639, line 92).

9. 'Proffers of a genius': Anne Oldfield; engraving by Henry
Meyer after Jonathan Richardson.

woman of quality, a little too conscious of her natural attractions. I have
often seen her in private societies where women of the best rank might
have borrowed some part of her behaviour without the least diminution
of their sense or dignity. And this very morning, where I am now writing
at the Bath, November 11, 1738, the same words were said of her by a lady
of condition, whose better judgment of her personal merit in that light
has emboldened me to repeat them.[28] After her success in this character of
higher life, all that Nature had given her of the actress seemed to have risen
to its full perfection. But the variety of her power could not be known till
she was seen in variety of characters, which, as fast as they fell to her, she
equally excelled in. Authors had much more from her performance than

28 Barker, p.238, notes Cibber's fondness for watering places in his retirement: 'from
   Tunbridge to Scarborough, and from Scarborough to Bath'.

they had reason to hope for from what they had written for her; and none had less than another but as their genius in the parts they allotted her was more or less elevated.

In the wearing of her person she was particularly fortunate – her figure was always improving, to her thirty-sixth year[29] – but her excellence in acting was never at a stand. And the last new character she shone in, Lady Townly, was a proof that she was still able to do more, if more could have been done for her.[30] She had one mark of good sense rarely known in any actor of either sex but herself. I have observed several with promising dispositions, very desirous of instruction at their first setting out; but no sooner had they found their least account in it, than they were as desirous of being left to their own capacity, which they then thought would be disgraced by their seeming to want any farther assistance. But this was not Mrs Oldfield's way of thinking; for to the last year of her life, she never undertook any part she liked without being importunately desirous of having all the helps in it that another could possibly give her. By knowing so much herself, she found how much more there was of Nature yet needful to be known. Yet it was a hard matter to give her any hint that she was not able to take or improve. With all this merit she was tractable, and less presuming in her station than several that had not half her pretensions to be troublesome. But she lost nothing by her easy conduct; she had everything she asked, which she took care should be always reasonable, because she hated as much to be grudged as denied a civility. Upon her extraordinary action in *The Provoked Husband*, the

29 i.e. until 1717, when Oldfield began to scale back her acting commitments. In 1712 she had become pregnant by her lover, the Whig politician Arthur Mainwaring, but the baby did not survive. After Mainwaring's death the same year, she had a son by Charles Churchill following a troubled pregnancy from which she did not fully recover. She is believed to have died from cancer of the uterus.

30 Cibber's completion of Vanbrugh's *A Journey to London* opened at Drury Lane on 10 January 1728 with Wilks as Lord Townly and Cibber as Sir Francis Wronghead. As Lowe points out, this was not Oldfield's last new role, but the last one 'she shone in', according to Cibber's perhaps partial estimation. *Mist's Weekly Journal*, 13 January 1728 (cited in LS2 954), was not impressed by the play: 'On Wednesday last a most horrid, barbarous and cruel murder was committed … upon a posthumous child of the late Sir John Vanbrugh by one who, for some time past, has gone by the name of Keyber. It was a fine child born, and would certainly have lived long had it not fallen into such cruel hands.' An article of the day before in *The Daily Journal* had found Vanbrugh's original 'intermixed with obscenity, ribaldry, and nonsense' (cited in *Document Register* no.3394). Lady Townly is another fashionably affected character, swearing that she loves the opera so much that it causes her to expire. On 28 February 1730, eight months before her death, Oldfield played the title role in James Thomson's *Sophonisba* (LS3 40).

managers made her a present of fifty guineas more than her agreement, which never was more than a verbal one;[31] for they knew she was above deserting them to engage upon any other stage, and she was conscious they would never think it their interest to give her cause of complaint. In the last two months of her illness, when she was no longer able to assist them, she declined receiving her salary, though by her agreement she was entitled to it. Upon the whole she was, to the last scene she acted, the delight of her spectators.[32] Why then may we not close her character with the same indulgence with which Horace speaks of a commendable poem?

> *Ubi plura intent – non ego paucis*
> *Offendar maculis –* [33]

> Where in the whole, such various beauties shine,
> 'Twere idle, upon errors to refine.[34]

What more might be said of her as an actress may be found in the preface to *The Provoked Husband*, to which I refer the reader.[35]

---

31 As one of the managers at the time, Cibber may have sought here to emphasize the collective nature of the decision in order to deflect any suggestion that he was rewarding Anne Oldfield for a performance beneficial to him, given the extraordinary success of the play.

32 Lowe gives her last appearance as 28 April 1730 and her death as 23 October of the same year, and quotes from Pope's viciously satirical reminiscence of her as 'Narcissa' (after her role in *Love's Last Shift*) in his first Moral Essay, in Pope, *Poems*, p.558, lines 242–7.

33 From Horace, *The Art of Poetry*, lines 350–2: 'Verum ubi plura nitent in carmine, non ego paucis offendar maculis' ('But when most features of a poem are brilliant, I shan't be offended by a few blemishes').

34 Lowe quotes the riposte of *The Laureate*: 'But I can see no occasion you have to mention any errors. She had fewer as an actress than any; and neither you nor I have any right to enquire into her conduct anywhere else' (p.57).

35 Lowe cites the relevant passage from Cibber's preface to the play:
  But there is no doing right to Mrs Oldfield without putting people in mind of what others of great merit have wanted to come near her. 'Tis not enough to say she here outdid her usual excellence. I might therefore justly leave her to the constant admiration of those spectators who have the pleasure of living while she is an actress. But as this is not the only time she has been the life of what I have given the public, so, perhaps, my saying a little more of so memorable an actress may give this play a chance to be read when the people of this age shall be ancestors. May it therefore give emulation to our successors of the stage to know that, to the ending of the year 1727, a contemporary comedian relates that Mrs Oldfield was then in her highest excellence of action, happy in all the rarely found requisites that meet in one person to complete them for the stage. She was in stature just rising to that height where the graceful can only begin to show itself; of a lively aspect, and a command in her mien that like the principal figure

With the acquisition, then, of so advanced a comedian as Mrs Oldfield, and the addition of one so much in favour as Wilks, and by the visible improvement of our other actors, as Penkethman, Johnson, Bullock, and I think I may venture to name myself in the number (but in what rank I leave to the judgment of those who have been my spectators), the reputation of our company began to get ground.[36] Mrs Oldfield and Mr Wilks, by their frequently playing against one another in our best comedies, very happily supported that humour and vivacity which is so peculiar to our English stage.[37] The French, our only modern competitors, seldom give us their lovers in such various lights. In their comedies (however lively a people they are by nature) their lovers are generally constant, simple sighers, both of a mind and equally distressed about the difficulties of their coming together, which naturally makes their conversation so serious that they are seldom good company to their auditors.[38] And though I allow them many other

in the finest painting, first seizes and longest delights the eye of the spectators. Her voice was sweet, strong, piercing, and melodious; her pronunciation voluble, distinct, and musical; and her emphasis always placed where the spirit of the sense, in her periods, only demanded it. If she delighted more in the higher comic than in the tragic strain, 'twas because the last is too often written in a lofty disregard of Nature. But in characters of modern practised life, she found occasion to add the particular air and manner which distinguished the different humours she presented; whereas, in tragedy, the manner of speaking varies as little as the blank verse it is written in. She had one peculiar happiness from Nature: she looked and maintained the agreeable, at a time when other fine women only raise admirers by their understanding. The spectator was always as much informed by her eyes as her elocution; for the look is the only proof that an actor rightly conceives what he utters, there being scarce an instance, where the eyes do their part, that the elocution is known to be faulty. The qualities she had acquired were the genteel and the elegant; the one in her air, and the other in her dress, never had her equal on the stage; and the ornaments she herself provided (particularly in this play) seemed in all respects the paraphernalia of a woman of quality. And of that sort were the characters she chiefly excelled in; but her natural good sense, and lively turn of conversation, made her way so easy to ladies of the highest rank, that it is a less wonder if, on the stage, she sometimes was what might have become the finest woman in real life to have supported.

36 For Penkethman, see above, p.107 n.62; for Johnson and Bullock, p.134 n.38.
37 Among many examples, Wilks played Mirabell to Oldfield's Millamant in Congreve's *The Way of the World* (14 February 1718; LS2 482) and Dorimant to her Harriet in Etherege's *The Man of Mode* (3 October 1719; LS2 550). Cibber's view of English comedy is endorsed by such studies as John Harrington Smith's *The Gay Couple in Restoration Comedy* (Cambridge, MA: Harvard University Press, 1948).
38 French comedians and adaptations of French plays were almost as regular a presence in London's theatres as editions of French comedies were in its bookshops. John Ozell's 1714 translations of Molière were a landmark in the reception of the dramatist's work in England. Cibber's view of the merits of French romantic comedy accords with the views of French tragedy in Dryden's *Of Dramatic Poesy* (1667).

beauties of which we are too negligent, yet our variety of humour has excellencies that all their valuable observance of rules have never yet attained to.[39] By these advantages, then,[40] we began to have an equal share of the politer sort of spectators, who for several years could not allow our company to stand in any comparison with the other. But theatrical favour, like public commerce, will sometimes deceive the best judgments by an unaccountable change of its channel; the best commodities are not always known to meet with the best markets. To this decline of the old company many accidents might contribute, as the too distant situation of their theatre or their want of a better; for it was not then in the condition it now is, but small and poorly fitted up within the walls of a tennis *quarré* court, which is of the lesser sort.[41] Booth, who was then a young actor among them, has often told me of the difficulties Betterton then laboured under and complained of: how impracticable he found it to keep their body to that common order which was necessary for their support;[42] of their relying too much upon their intrinsic merit; and though but few of them were young, even when they first became their own masters, yet they were all now ten years older, and consequently more liable to fall into an inactive negligence, or were only separately diligent for themselves in the sole regard of their benefit plays, which several of their principals knew, at worst, would raise them contributions that would more than tolerably subsist them for the current year. But as these were too precarious expedients to be always depended upon, and brought in nothing to the general support of the numbers who were at salaries under them, they were reduced to have recourse to foreign novelties. L'Abbé, Balon, and Mademoiselle Subligny, three of the then most famous dancers of the French Opera, were at several times brought over at extraordinary rates to revive that sickly appetite which plain sense

---

39 In his 'Discourse Upon Comedy', part of his *Love and Business*, Farquhar had advanced a similar view (Farquhar, *Works*, II.378–9); in *Of Dramatic Poesy*, Dryden's Neander observes that 'as we, who are a more sullen people, come to be diverted at our plays, so [the French], who are of an airy and gay temper, come thither to make themselves more serious'; in *John Dryden*, The Oxford Authors, ed. Keith Walker (Oxford: Oxford University Press, 1987), pp.104–5.

40 i.e. the development of the actors previously mentioned.

41 Lowe cites Julian Marshall, *The Annals of Tennis* (1878), p.34: 'that which was called *Le Quarré*, or the square; and the other with the *dedans*, which is almost the same as that of the present day'. The *quarré* variety, as at Lincoln's Inn Fields, was smaller; that theatre was about a mile from Covent Garden. After years of decline, the interior fabric was renovated in 1725, with *The Daily Journal* of 27 September 1725 noting 'The gilding, painting, scenes and columns of pier glass, raised for the better illuminating the stage and other parts of the house' (*Document Register* no.3286).

42 As noted above, p.154 n.3.

and Nature had satiated.[43] But alas, there was no recovering to a sound constitution by those mere costly cordials; the novelty of a dance was but of a short duration and perhaps hurtful in its consequence, for it made a play without a dance less endured than it had been before, when such dancing was not to be had. But perhaps their exhibiting these novelties might be owing to the success we had met with in our more barbarous introducing of French mimics and tumblers the year before,[44] of which Mr Rowe thus complains in his prologue to one of his first plays:

> Must Shakespeare, Fletcher, and laborious Ben,
> Be left for Scaramouche and Harlequin?[45]

While the crowd, therefore, so fluctuated from one house to another as their eyes were more or less regaled than their ears, it could not be a question much in debate which had the better actors. The merit of either seemed to be of little moment, and the complaint in the foregoing lines, though it might be just for a time, could not be a just one for ever because the best play that ever was writ may tire by being too often repeated – a misfortune naturally attending the obligation to play every day (not that whenever such satiety commences, it will be any proof of the play's being a bad one, or of its being ill acted). In a word, satiety is seldom enough considered by either critics, spectators or actors, as the true – not to say just – cause of declining audiences to the most rational entertainments. And though I cannot say I

43 Lowe quotes the equally damning assessment of Downes, pp.96–7: 'In the space of ten years past, Mr. Betterton, to gratify the desires and fancies of the nobility and gentry, procured from abroad the best dancers and singers … who, being exhorbitantly expensive, produced small profit to him and his company, but vast gain to themselves.' **Anthony L'Abbé** (c. 1667–c. 1758), dancer at the Paris Opera from 1688, was 'lately come over' when he gave a court performance on 13 May 1698; according to *The Post Boy*, 14–17 May 1698, he was already performing 'at the playhouse'. He returned home in 1705 after a series of contractual disputes. **Claude Balon** (1671–1744) was another Paris Opera dancer; in April 1699 he was hired by Betterton to perform for five weeks at a reported cost of 400 guineas (c.£90,000 in current values). Luttrell's *Brief Relation*, IV.502–3, adds that Lord Cholmley gave him a further 100 guineas; *Comparison*, p.49, notes the 'extravagant' increase in ticket prices that followed and adds, 'there's not a year but some surprising monster lands' (p.67). **Marie-Thérèse de Subligny** (1666–c. 1735) is believed to have appeared in London first with Balon; she returned to Lincoln's Inn Fields for six weeks in December 1701 (LS2a 49).
44 The exact dates Cibber refers to are not clear, but rope dancers and tumblers appeared in and around London during the summer of 1698 (LS1 498–9). *The Post Boy*, 13–15 April 1699, reported that both theatres were employing 'eminent masters in singing and dancing, lately arrived both from France and Italy' (LS1 510).
45 From the epilogue to Nicholas Rowe's *The Ambitious Stepmother*, produced at Lincoln's Inn Fields in December 1700 (LS2a 15). The preceding lines take a swipe at Rich's company: 'Show but a mimic ape, or French buffoon, / You to the other house in shoals are gone, / And leave us here to tune our crowds alone.'

ever saw a good new play not attended with due encouragement, yet to keep
a theatre daily open without sometimes giving the public a bad old one is
more than I doubt the wit of human writers, or excellence of actors, will ever
be able to accomplish. And as both authors and comedians may have often
succeeded where a sound judgment would have condemned them, it might
puzzle the nicest critic living to prove in what sort of excellence the true
value of either consisted. For if their merit were to be measured by the full
houses they may have brought – if the judgment of the crowd were infallible – I am afraid we shall be reduced to allow that *The Beggar's Opera* was
the best-written play and Sir Harry Wildair (as Wilks played it) was the
best-acted part that ever our English Theatre had to boast of.[46] That critic,
indeed, must be rigid to a folly that would deny either of them their due
praise, when they severally drew such numbers after them; all their hearers
could not be mistaken. And yet, if they were all in the right, what sort of
fame will remain to those celebrated authors and actors that had so long and
deservedly been admired before these were in being? The only distinction I
shall make between them is that to write or act like the authors or actors of
the latter end of the last century, I am of opinion, will be found a far better
pretence to success than to imitate these who have been so crowded to in
the beginning of this. All I would infer from this explanation is that though
we had then the better audiences, and might have more of the young world
on our side, yet this was no sure proof that the other company were not, in
the truth of action, greatly our superiors. These elder actors then, besides
the disadvantages I have mentioned, having only the fewer true judges to
admire them, naturally wanted the support of the crowd whose taste was to
be pleased at a cheaper rate, and with coarser fare. To recover them therefore to their due estimation, a new project was formed of building them a
stately theatre in the Haymarket, by Sir John Vanbrugh, for which he raised
a subscription of thirty persons of quality at one hundred pounds each; in
consideration whereof, every subscriber, for his own life, was to be admitted to whatever entertainments should be publicly performed there without
farther payment for his entrance.[47] Of this theatre I saw the first stone laid,

46 For the extraordinary success of *The Beggar's Opera* in 1728 and Cibber's reasons for
    resenting it, see above, p.164 n.41. Cibber also refers to the success of Farquhar's *The
    Constant Couple* from November 1699, rather than to its sequel, *Sir Harry Wildair*, which
    flopped in May 1701 (LS2a 27). In the 'Preface to the Reader' of *The Constant Couple*,
    Farquhar wrote that 'Mr Wilks's performance has set him so far above competition in
    the part of Wildair, that none can pretend to envy the praise due to his merit' (Farquhar,
    Works, I.150).
47 For the opening of the Queen's Theatre, Haymarket in 1705, see above, p.188 n.46.
    A document dated 8 May 1704 describes an agreement between Vanbrugh and the

on which was inscribed 'The Little Whig', in honour to a lady of extraordinary beauty, then the celebrated toast and pride of that party.[48]

In the year 1706, when this house was finished, Betterton and his co-partners dissolved their own agreement and threw themselves under the direction of Sir John Vanbrugh and Mr Congreve,[49] imagining, perhaps, that the conduct of two such eminent authors might give a more prosperous turn to their condition: that the plays it would now be their interest to write for them would soon recover the town to a true taste, and be an advantage that no other company could hope for; that in the interim, till such plays could be written, the grandeur of their house (as it was a new spectacle) might allure the crowd to support them. But if these were their views, we shall see that their dependence upon them was too sanguine. As to their prospect of new plays, I doubt it was not enough considered that good ones were plants of a slow growth, and though Sir John Vanbrugh had a very quick pen, yet Mr Congreve was too judicious a writer to let anything come hastily out of his hands.[50] As to their other dependence – the house – they had not yet discovered that almost every proper quality and convenience of a good theatre had been sacrificed or neglected to show the spectator a vast, triumphal piece of architecture! And that the best play, for the reasons I am going to offer, could not but be under great disadvantages, and be less capable of delighting the auditor here than it could have been in the plain theatre they came from. For what could their vast columns, their gilded cornices, their immoderate high roofs avail, when scarce one word in ten could be distinctly heard in it? Nor had it then the form it now stands in, which necessity two or three years after reduced it to.[51] At the first

Duke of Newcastle, whereby in return for a subscription of 100 guineas the duke was allowed complimentary access to all shows, with the privilege protected in the event of Vanbrugh's selling, renting, or mortgaging the theatre (BL Cavendish Loan 29/237, fol.71; *Document Register* no.1769). The 'thirty persons of quality' were almost all members of the Whig-inclined Kit-Kat Club; see Robert J. Allen, 'The Kit-Kat Club and the Theatre', *The Review of English Studies*, vol. 7 (1931), 56–61.

48 i.e. Anne Spencer (née Churchill), Countess of Sunderland (1683–1716), Lady of the Bedchamber to Queen Anne and daughter of the Duke and Duchess of Marlborough; Lowe notes the alternative story that the cornerstone was laid by Charles, Duke of Somerset, on 18 April 1704.

49 The year was 1705; Vanbrugh and Congreve had obtained their licence for the new company, via Betterton's reassignment, on 14 December 1704 (LC 5/154, p.35; *Document Register* no.1793).

50 In the prologue to his last play for the breakaway company, *The Way of the World*, Congreve admitted he had written 'with toil' (Congreve, *Works*, I.22).

51 A report in a Flemish newspaper dated 1 September 1712 describes improvements to the décor and stage machinery of the theatre (*Document Register* no.2203). Further refurbishment was undertaken eleven years later, as reported in *The British Journal*, 21 September 1723 (*Document Register* no.3198). See also below, pp.267–8.

opening it, the flat ceiling that is now over the orchestra was then a semi-oval arch that sprung fifteen feet higher from above the cornice. The ceiling over the pit, too, was still more raised, being one level line from the highest back part of the upper gallery to the front of the stage. The front boxes were a continued semicircle to the bare walls of the house on each side. This extraordinary and superfluous space occasioned such an undulation from the voice of every actor, that generally what they said sounded like the gabbling of so many people in the lofty aisles in a cathedral. The tone of a trumpet or the swell of an eunuch's holding note, 'tis true, might be sweetened by it; but the articulate sounds of a speaking voice were drowned by the hollow reverberations of one word upon another. To this inconvenience, why may we not add that of its situation? For at that time it had not the advantage of almost a large city which has since been built in its neighbourhood. Those costly spaces of Hanover, Grosvenor, and Cavendish Squares, with the many and great adjacent streets about them, were then all but so many green fields of pasture, from whence they could draw little or no sustenance, unless it were that of a milk diet.[52] The City, the Inns of Court, and the middle part of the town, which were the most constant support of a theatre and chiefly to be relied on, were now too far out of the reach of an easy walk, and coach-hire is often too hard a tax upon the pit and gallery.[53] But from the vast increase of the buildings I have mentioned, the situation of that theatre has since that time received considerable advantages: a new world of people of condition are nearer to it than formerly, and I am of opinion that if the auditory part were a little more reduced to the model of that in Drury Lane, an excellent company of actors would now find a better account in it than in any other house in this populous city.[54] Let me not be mistaken. I say 'an excellent company', and such as might be able to do justice to the best of plays, and throw out those latent beauties in them which only excellent actors can discover and give life to. If such a company were now there, they would meet with a quite different set of auditors than other theatres have lately been used to. Polite hearers would be content with polite entertainments, and I remember the time when plays (without

---

52 The construction of Hanover Square began in 1714; Grosvenor Square in 1725; and Cavendish Square in 1717. See *London Encyclopaedia*, pp.372, 350, and 131.

53 Hire of a hackney coach typically cost 1 shilling, the same price as the cheapest seat in the theatre. To illustrate Cibber's point about convenience, Lowe cites Dryden's epilogue at the opening of the Theatre Royal Drury Lane in 1674, which describes the route to Dorset Garden, at what is now the eastern end of Fleet Street, as 'a cold bleak road, / Where bears in furs dare scarcely look abroad' (Dryden, p.315, lines 29–30).

54 In the event, the theatre came temporarily to be used solely for opera; see below, pp.249–50.

the aid of farce or pantomime) were as decently attended as operas or private assemblies, where a noisy sloven would have passed his time as uneasily in a front box as in a drawing room – when a hat upon a man's head there would have been looked upon as a sure mark of a brute or a booby. But of all this I have seen, too, the reverse: where, in the presence of ladies at a play, common civility has been set at defiance and the privilege of being a rude clown, even to a nuisance, has in a manner been demanded as one of the rights of English liberty. Now, though I grant that liberty is so precious a jewel that we ought not to suffer the least ray of its lustre to be diminished, yet methinks the liberty of seeing a play in quiet has as laudable a claim to protection, as the privilege of not suffering you to do it has to impunity. But since we are so happy as not to have a certain power among us which in another country is called the police, let us rather bear this insult than buy its remedy at too dear a rate;[55] and let it be the punishment of such wrong-headed savages that they never will, or can, know the true value of that liberty which they so stupidly abuse. Such vulgar minds possess their liberty as profligate husbands do fine wives: only to disgrace them. In a word, when liberty boils over, such is the scum of it. But to our new erected theatre.

Not long before this time the Italian opera began first to steal into England, but in as rude a disguise and unlike itself as possible: in a lame, hobbling translation into our own language, with false quantities or metre out of measure to its original notes, sung by our own unskilful voices with graces misapplied to almost every sentiment, and with action lifeless and unmeaning through every character.[56] The first Italian performer that made any distinguished figure in it was Valentini – a true sensible singer at that time, but of a throat too weak to sustain those melodious warblings for which the fairer sex have since idolized his successors.[57] However, this defect

---

55 A reference to the *Maréchaussée*, developed as a central police force by Louis XIV from 1697. The Theatre Royal Drury Lane had seen numerous disturbances during Cibber's career. In January 1722 Cibber had to step forward and ask for silence (*The Daily Journal*, 5 January 1722; *Document Register* no.3092), while in March 1729 there was a full-blown riot 'with a serenade of cat-calls, penny trumpets, clubs ... and volleys of whole oranges' (*Flying-Post*, 1 March 1729; *Document Register* no.3449).

56 A reference to early experiments in English opera staged at Drury Lane, such as John Oldmixon's *The Grove* (February 1700). In his preface, Oldmixon writes of the confusion surrounding the climax of the piece: 'if what he had writ had been spoken, everything would have appeared clear and natural.'

57 Valentino Urbani (fl. 1690–1722), the castrato known as Valentini, probably made his first London appearance at a court performance in February 1706 (BL Add.MS 61,420, fol.31; *Document Register* no. 1983). He sang Eustacio in Handel's *Rinaldo* at the Queen Theatre, Haymarket in February 1711 (LS2a 620). A bill of May 1713 indicates his payment for that year's season as £537 or c.£109,000 in current values (HTC Coke, no.20; *Document Register* no.2222). For 'his successors', see above, p.80 n.60.

was so well supplied by his action that his hearers bore with the absurdity of his singing his first part of Turnus in *Camilla* all in Italian, while every other character was sung and recited to him in English.[58] This I have mentioned to show not only our tramontane taste,[59] but that the crowded audiences which followed it to Drury Lane might be another occasion of their growing thinner in Lincoln's Inn Fields.

To strike in, therefore, with this prevailing novelty, Sir John Vanbrugh and Mr Congreve opened their new Haymarket Theatre with a translated opera, to Italian music, called *The Triumph of Love*; but this not having in it the charms of *Camilla* – either from the inequality of the music or voices – had but a cold reception, being performed but three days, and those not crowded.[60] Immediately upon the failure of this opera, Sir John Vanbrugh produced his comedy called *The Confederacy*, taken (but greatly improved) from the *Bourgeois à la Mode* of Dancour.[61] Though the fate of this play was something better, yet I thought it was not equal to its merit. For it is written with an uncommon vein of wit and humour, which confirms me in my former observation that the difficulty of hearing distinctly in that (then) wide theatre was no small impediment to the

---

58 *Il Trionfo di Camilla* by Antonio Maria Bononcini (1677–1726) was composed in 1696; it opened in an adapted version at Drury Lane on 30 March 1706 (LS2a 289) and remained popular; in a letter of March 1707, Philip Perceval wrote that 'The opera of Camilla has been one of the chief diversions of the town this long time' (LS2 139). The role of Turnus was initially sung by Francis Hughes (d. 1744). For Cibber's confusion of the popularity of this work with that of *Arsinoë, Queen of Cyprus*, see below, n.60. It is disputed whether *Camilla* is really by Antonio's more famous brother Giovanni (1670–1747), who worked for the Royal Academy in London from 1720 but was dismissed in 1722 for 'his most extravagant demands' (letter dated 5 October 1722; *Document Register* no.3122).

59 i.e. pertaining to land beyond the mountains, in this case the Alps.

60 The opera was *Gli Amori D'Ergasto* by Jakob Greber (d. 1731), a German composer whose first name was sometimes given as Giacomo. The performance is noted in LS2a 220. Cibber confuses its title either with Bononcini's *Il Trionfo di Camilla* or the 1712 Haymarket musical medley, *The Triumph of Love* (LS2 288), or both. Downes, p.99, gives the run as five days and refers to 'a new set of singers arrived from Italy (the worst that e'er came from thence)'. However, only four singers were required, and some were already working in London; see Curtis A. Price, 'The Critical Decade for English Music Drama, 1700–1710', *Harvard Library Bulletin* vol. 26 (1978). Cibber implies that the new opera was mounted as a response to Bononcini's, whereas in fact it was Thomas Clayton's *Arsinoë, Queen of Cyprus* that had run successfully at Drury Lane since 16 January 1705 (LS2a 204).

61 Cibber may mean that Vanbrugh only began to write *The Confederacy* when it became clear that Greber's opera would not succeed; the play opened on 30 October 1705 (LS2a 250). It is an adaptation of *Les Bourgeoises à la Mode* by Florent Carton Dancourt (1661–1725). LS2a 250–63 records eight performances in the two months to Boxing Day 1705; the play was a repertory staple long after Cibber published the *Apology*.

applause that might have followed the same actors in it upon every other stage; and indeed, every play acted there before the house was altered seemed to suffer from the same inconvenience. In a word, the prospect of profits from this theatre was so very barren that Mr Congreve, in a few months, gave up his share and interest in the government of it wholly to Sir John Vanbrugh.⁶² But Sir John being sole proprietor of the house was, at all events, obliged to do his utmost to support it. As he had a happier talent of throwing the English spirit into his translation of French plays than any former author who had borrowed from them, he in the same season gave the public three more of that kind, called *The Cuckold in Conceit* (from the *Cocu Imaginaire* of Molière), *Squire Trelooby* (from his *Monsieur de Pourceaugnac*), and *The Mistake*, from the *Dépit Amoureux* of the same author.⁶³ Yet all these, however well executed, came to the ear in the same undistinguished utterance by which almost all their plays had equally suffered. For what few could plainly hear, it was not likely a great many could applaud.

It must farther be considered too that this company were not now what they had been when they first revolted from the patentees in Drury Lane and became their own masters in Lincoln's Inn Fields. Several of them, excellent in their different talents, were now dead, as Smith, Kynaston, Sandford, and Leigh; Mrs Betterton and Underhill being at this time also superannuated pensioners whose places were generally but ill supplied; nor could it be expected that Betterton himself, at past seventy, could retain his former force and spirit, though he was yet far distant from any competitor. Thus, then, were these remains of the best set of actors that I believe were ever known at once in England: by time, death, and the satiety of their hearers, mouldering to decay.

It was now the town-talk that nothing but a union of the two companies could recover the stage to its former reputation, which opinion was

62 For Congreve's resignation, see above, p.188 n.46.

63 Cibber's chronology here is misleading. Vanbrugh's *The Cuckold in Conceit* (now lost) was presented as an afterpiece to a celebratory masque, *The British Enchanters*, on 22 March 1707 (LS2a 351), which featured a new scene with an image of the Vanbrugh-designed Blenheim Palace; Molière's *Sganarelle; ou, Le Cocu Imaginaire* was first performed in Paris in 1660. *Squire Trelooby*, however, had been performed at Lincoln's Inn Fields in March 1704, more than a year before the Haymarket opened (LS2a 158), and was co-authored by Vanbrugh, Congreve, and William Walsh; it was a translation of Molière's 1669 farce, *Monsieur de Pourceaugnac*. Vanbrugh's *The Mistake* was the only play of the three to appear 'in the same season' as *The Confederacy*. A version of Molière's *Le Dépit Amoureux* (1656), it opened in December 1705 (LS2a 263), in the same month as another Molière adaptation Cibber does not mention: *The Cheats of Scapin* (LS2a 258), i.e. the 1676 translation of *Les Fourberies de Scapin* (1671) by Thomas Otway.

certainly true.[64] One would have thought too that the patentee of Drury Lane could not have failed to close with it, he being then on the prosperous side of the question, having no relief to ask for himself, and little more to do in the matter than to consider what he might safely grant. But it seems this was not his way of counting; he had other persons who had great claims to shares in the profits of this stage; which profits, by a union, he foresaw would be too visible to be doubted of, and might raise up a new spirit in those adventurers to revive their suits at law with him. For he had led them a chase in Chancery several years, and when they had driven him into a contempt of that court, he conjured up a spirit in the shape of six and eight pence a day that constantly struck the tipstaff blind whenever he came near him.[65] He knew the intrinsic value of delay, and was resolved to stick to it as the surest way to give the plantiffs enough on it. And by this expedient, our good master had long walked about at his leisure, cool and contented as a fox when the hounds were drawn off and gone home from him. But whether I am right or not in my conjectures, certain it is that this close master of Drury Lane had no inclination to a union, as will appear by the sequel.[66]

Sir John Vanbrugh knew too that to make a union worth his while, he must not seem too hasty for it; he therefore found himself under a necessity in the meantime of letting his whole theatrical farm to some industrious

64 Cibber's 'now' refers to the period 1705–6. Milhous, *Management*, p.201, cites a letter from Sir John Stanley to Christopher Rich dated 21 June 1705 which states Lord Chamberlain Kent's wish to see the two companies joined; an MS newsletter dated 3 September 1706 reports rumours of the Queen's wish that 'all her servants belonging to the several playhouses' should act together (*Document Register* no.1870). Lowe points to earlier rumours such as conveyed by the prologue to Catherine Trotter's *The Unhappy Penitent*, which opened at Drury Lane in February 1701: 'But now the peaceful tattle of the town, / Is how to join both houses into one.'

65 In *The Post-Boy Robbed of his Mail* (1706), Charles Gildon printed a letter from Rich to Vanbrugh dated 25 July 1705 declining the offer of a union (Letter XLII, pp.345–7; *Document Register* no.1815). The letter describes Rich's potential obligations to and legal tussles with 'above forty' former investors and tenants. When he declined Vanbrugh's offer of a union, Rich was named in cases brought principally by Charles Killigrew (C9/317/3; *Document Register* no.1794), Richard Middlemore and Andrew Card (C8/595/71; *Document Register* no.1785) and Sir Edward Smith (C8/599/74; *Document Register*, no.1772). Some time in 1704 Rich had eventually seen off a case concerning share ownership presented by Sir Charles O'Hara in 1700 (C5/284/40; *Document Register* nos.1626 and 1773). Cibber concludes by accusing Rich of bribing the 'tipstaff' (i.e. bailiff or court official) to keep his distance. He does not mention that in July 1705 thirty-three Drury Lane actors also petitioned against the union on the grounds that it could not 'be without great prejudice, if not utter ruin, to them and their numerous families' (*Document Register* no.1814).

66 According to p.218 below, Rich was interested in achieving a union, but on his own terms.

tenant that might put it into better condition.[67] This is that crisis, as I observed in the eighth chapter, when the royal licence for acting plays *etc* was judged of so little value as not to have one suitor for it. At this time then, the master of Drury Lane happened to have a sort of premier agent in his stage affairs that seemed, in appearance, as much to govern the master as the master himself did to govern his actors. But this person was under no stipulation or salary for the service he rendered, but had gradually wrought himself into the master's extraordinary confidence and trust from an habitual intimacy, a cheerful humour, and an indefatigable zeal for his interest. If I should farther say that this person has been well known in almost every metropolis in Europe; that few private men have, with so little reproach, run through more various turns of fortune; that on the wrong side of threescore, he has yet the open spirit of a hale young fellow of five-and-twenty; that though he still chooses to speak what he thinks to his best friends with an undisguised freedom, he is notwithstanding acceptable to many persons of the first rank and condition; that any one of them (provided he likes them) may now send him, for their service, to Constantinople at half a day's warning; that time has not yet been able to make a visible change in any part of him but the colour of his hair, from a fierce coal-black to that of a milder milk-white – when I have taken this liberty with him, methinks it cannot be taking a much greater if I at once should tell you that this person was Mr Owen Swiney,[68] and that it was to him Sir John Vanbrugh, in this exigence of his theatrical affairs, made an offer of his actors under such agreements of salary as might be made with them (and of his house, clothes and scenes, with the Queen's licence) to employ them, upon payment of only the casual rent of five pounds upon every acting day, and not to exceed £700 in the year. Of this proposal Mr Swiney desired a day or two to consider; for however he might like it, he would not meddle in any sort without the consent and approbation of his friend and patron, the master of Drury Lane. Having given the reasons why this patentee was averse to a

67 Vanbrugh agreed to lease the Haymarket Theatre for seven years and £5 per acting day to Owen Swiney on 14 August 1706 (LC 7/2, fol.2; *Document Register* no.1860).
68 Owen Swiney (1676–1754) was born in rural Ireland, graduated from Trinity College Dublin, and joined Rich's company as a general factotum in 1702. The European reputation Cibber refers to was gained from 1713 onwards; Swiney's travels in France, Italy, and the Netherlands saw him working as an agent for opera impresarios, art collectors, and their aristocratic patrons. He returned to London in 1733. Swiney's 'indefatigable zeal' for Rich's 'interest' was exhausted by the time he wrote to Cibber on 5 October 1706, complaining of Rich's conduct (*Document Register* no.1872). Cibber's warm account of Swiney overlooks their legal dispute initiated by Swiney in January 1711, involving allegations of fraud, absence, and other breaches of contract (*Document Register* nos.2120, 2123, etc.).

union, it may now seem less a wonder why he immediately consented that Swiney should take the Haymarket house *etc* and continue that company to act against him; but the real truth was that he had a mind both companies should be clandestinely under one and the same interest, and yet in so loose a manner that he might declare his verbal agreement with Swiney good or null and void, as he might best find his account in either.[69] What flattered him that he had this wholesome project, and Swiney to execute it, both in his power, was that at this time Swiney happened to stand in his books debtor to cash, upwards of two hundred pounds. But here we shall find he over-rated his security. However, Swiney as yet followed his orders; he took the Haymarket Theatre and had, farther, the private consent of the patentee to take such of his actors from Drury Lane as either from inclination or discontent might be willing to come over to him in the Haymarket.[70] The only one he made an exception of was myself. For though he chiefly depended upon his singers and dancers, he said it would be necessary to keep some one tolerable actor with him, that might enable him to set those machines a-going.[71] Under this limitation of not entertaining me, Swiney seemed to acquiesce till after he had opened with the so recruited company, in the Haymarket: the actors that came to him from Drury Lane were Wilks, Estcourt, Mills, Keen, Johnson, Bullock, Mrs Oldfield, Mrs Rogers, and some few others of less note.[72] But I must here let you know that this project was formed and put in execution all in very few days in the summer season, when no theatre was open – to all which I was entirely a stranger,

69 Around the time Vanbrugh came to an agreement with Swiney, he had also petitioned for the removal of Drury Lane's right to stage spoken-word plays; doing so would limit Rich's capacity to cheat his investors (LC 7/3, fols.179–80; *Document Register* no.1856). Contrary to Cibber's account, Rich was reported to be angered by the latest breakaway (letter from William Congreve to Joseph Keally, 10 September 1706 in Congreve, *Letters*, p.43).

70 It was formally Vanbrugh who contracted with a series of Drury Lane actors in the immediate aftermath of his agreement with Swiney: see his agreements with Robert Wilks, Anne Oldfield, Henry Norris, John Mills, William Bullock, and Theophilus Keen, 15–20 August 1706 (*Document Register* nos.1861–6).

71 Rich's company continued to perform spoken-word plays during the 1706–7 season but became proportionally more reliant on shows featuring music and dancing, such as *Il Trionfo di Camilla*, *The Tempest*, *The Island Princess*, and *Arsinoë, Queen of Cyprus*.

72 Richard Estcourt remained with Rich's company and continued in his signature role, Serjeant Kite in Farquhar's *The Recruiting Officer* (1706), which also played in a rival production at the Haymarket. Theophilus Keen (d. 1719) was, according to Chetwood, p.177, a middle-ranking player trained by Joseph Ashbury in Dublin and recruited by Rich to middle-ranking roles. Jane Rogers (d. 1718) joined the United Company in 1692 and remained with Rich after 1695. She created the role of Amanda in *Love's Last Shift* and *The Relapse*. The 'some few others of less note' were Henry Norris, Thomas Kent, and Charles Fairbank.

being at this time at a gentleman's house in Gloucestershire, scribbling (if I mistake not) *The Wife's Resentment*.[73]

The first word I heard of this transaction was by a letter from Swiney inviting me to make one in the Haymarket company, whom he hoped I could not but now think the stronger party.[74] But I confess I was not a little alarmed at this revolution. For I considered that I knew of no visible fund to support these actors but their own industry; that all his recruits from Drury Lane would want new clothing, and that the warmest industry would be always labouring uphill under so necessary an expense, so bad a situation, and so inconvenient a theatre. I was always of opinion too that in changing sides, in most conditions there generally were discovered more unforeseen inconveniencies than visible advantages; and that at worst, there would always some sort of merit remain with fidelity, though unsuccessful. Upon these considerations, I was only thankful for the offers made me from the Haymarket without accepting them, and soon after came to town towards the usual time of their beginning to act, to offer my service to our old master. But I found our company so thinned that it was almost impracticable to bring any one tolerable play upon the stage.[75] When I asked him where were his actors, and in what manner he intended to proceed, he replied, 'Don't you trouble yourself; come along, and I'll show you'. He then led me about all the by-places in the house, and showed me fifty little back doors, dark closets and narrow passages, in alterations and contrivances of which kind he had busied his head most part of the vacation; for he was scarce ever without some notable joiner or a bricklayer extraordinary in pay, for twenty years. And there are so many odd obscure places about a theatre, that his genius in nook-building was never out of employment; nor could the most vain-headed author be more deaf to an interruption in reciting his works

73 Cibber's *The Lady's Last Stake, or the Wife's Resentment* opened at the Queen's Theatre, Haymarket on 13 December 1707 (LS2a 395). Lord and Lady Wronglove were played by Wilks and Barry, with Cibber himself as Sir George Brilliant. The 'gentleman' who offered Cibber hospitality was probably Colonel Henry Brett (d. 1724) of Cowley, Gloucestershire. Briefly MP for Bishop's Castle, Brett was the dedicatee of Farquhar's *The Twin-Rivals* (1702) and in 1707 acquired Thomas Skipwith's share in Rich's company (*Document Register* no.1904); see also below, pp.240–2.

74 As above, p.217 n.68 (letter from Swiney to Cibber dated 5 October 1706).

75 LS2a 314 lists only thirteen actors in Rich's company for the 1706–7 season, eight male and five female; chief among them were Richard Estcourt, William Penkethman, Susannah Mountfort-Verbruggen, and George Powell. Rich retained a much stronger group of dancers and singers. Cibber exaggerates the impact on the quality (if not the quantity) of drama available to Rich's company. In the autumn of 1706 there were performances at either Drury Lane or Dorset Garden of *The Recruiting Officer*, *The Relapse*, Behn's *The Emperor of the Moon*, Shadwell's *The Libertine*, and Buckingham's *The Rehearsal*, as well as two of Cibber's own plays, *Love's Last Shift* and *Love Makes a Man* (LS2a 320–30).

than our wise master was while entertaining me with the improvements he had made in his invisible architecture – all which, without thinking any one part of it necessary (though I seemed to approve), I could not help now and then breaking in upon his delight with the impertinent question of, 'But master, where are your actors?' But it seems I had taken a wrong time for this sort of enquiry; his head was full of matters of more moment and, as you find, I was to come another time for an answer. A very hopeful condition I found myself in, under the conduct of so profound a virtuoso and so considerate a master![76] But to speak of him seriously, and to account for this disregard to his actors, his notion was that singing and dancing, or any sort of exotic entertainments, would make an ordinary company of actors too hard for the best set, who had only plain plays to subsist on. Now, though I am afraid too much might be said in favour of this opinion, yet I thought he laid more stress upon that sort of merit than it would bear; as I therefore found myself of so little value with him, I could not help setting a little more upon myself, and was resolved to come to a short explanation with him. I told him I came to serve him at a time when many of his best actors had deserted him; that he might now have the refusal of me, but I could not afford to carry the compliment so far as to lessen my income by it; that I therefore expected either my casual pay to be advanced, or the payment of my former salary made certain for as many days as we had acted the year before. No – he was not willing to alter his former method, but I might choose whatever parts I had a mind to act, of theirs who had left him. When I found him, as I thought, so insensible or impregnable, I looked gravely in his face and told him he knew upon what terms I was willing to serve him, and took my leave. By this time the Haymarket company had begun acting to audiences something better than usual and were all paid their full salaries, a blessing they had not felt in some years in either house before.[77] Upon this success, Swiney pressed the patentee to execute the articles they had as yet only verbally agreed on, which were in substance that Swiney should take the Haymarket house in his own name and have what actors he thought necessary from Drury Lane, and (after all payments punctually made) the profits should be equally divided between these two undertakers. But soft, and fair! Rashness was a fault that had never yet been

76 'Virtuoso' is intended ironically, in the sense identified by *OED* 2: a connoisseur or dabbler in the fine arts.

77 LS2 130–1 records that the Haymarket company performed fourteen different plays during the first month (October 1706) of their new season. Conceivably at Rich's instigation, twenty-four of the company's actors were indicted for 'immorality and profaneness' on 31 October (Luttrell, VI.102); the case was dismissed as 'frivolous' a week later (MS newsletter in *Document Register* no.1876).

imputed to the patentee; certain payments were methods he had not of a long, long time been used to. That point still wanted time for consideration. But Swiney was as hasty as the other was slow, and was resolved to know what he had to trust to before they parted; and to keep him the closer to his bargain, he stood upon his right of having me added to that company, if I was willing to come into it. But this was a point as absolutely refused on one side as insisted on on the other. In this contest, high words were exchanged on both sides till in the end this, their last private meeting, came to an open rupture; but before it was publicly known, Swiney, by fairly letting me into the whole transaction, took effectual means to secure me in his interest. When the mystery of the patentee's indifference to me was unfolded, and that his slighting me was owing to the security he relied on – of Swiney's not daring to engage me – I could have no farther debate with myself which side of the question I should adhere to. To conclude, I agreed in two words to act with Swiney;[78] and from this time, every change that happened in the theatrical government was a nearer step to that twenty years of prosperity which actors under the management of actors not long afterwards enjoyed. What was the immediate consequence of this last desertion from Drury Lane shall be the subject of another chapter.

78 Cibber's first appearance for the Haymarket company was probably as Lord Foppington in *The Relapse* on 2 November 1706 (LS2a 320), followed by the same role on 7 November in his own *The Careless Husband* (LS2a 321); by the end of the month he had also played Sir Fopling in *The Man of Mode*, Brazen in *The Recruiting Officer*, the title role in *Sir Courtly Nice*, and a new role, Sharper, in Susannah Centlivre's *The Platonick Lady* (LS2a 321–5).

CHAPTER 10

The recruited actors in the Haymarket encouraged by a subscription. Drury Lane under a particular management. The power of a Lord Chamberlain over the theatres considered. How it had been formerly exercised. A digression to tragic authors.

Having shown the particular conduct of the patentee in refusing so fair an opportunity of securing to himself both companies under his sole power and interest, I shall now lead the reader (after a short view of what passed in this new establishment of the Haymarket Theatre) to the accidents that the year following compelled the same patentee to receive both companies, united, into the Drury Lane Theatre, notwithstanding his disinclination to it.[1]

It may now be imagined that such a detachment of actors from Drury Lane could not but give a new spirit to those in the Haymarket: not only by enabling them to act each other's plays to better advantage, but by an emulous industry which had lain too long inactive among them, and without which they plainly saw they could not be sure of subsistence. Plays, by this means, began to recover a good share of their former esteem and favour; and the profits of them, in about a month, enabled our new manager to discharge his debt of something more than two hundred pounds to his old friend the patentee, who had now left him and his troop in trust to fight their own battles. The greatest inconvenience they still laboured under was the immoderate wideness of their house, in which (as I have observed) the difficulty of hearing may be said to have buried half the auditors' entertainment. This defect seemed evident from the much better reception several new plays, first acted there, met with when they afterwards came to be played by the same actors in Drury Lane. Of this number were *The Stratagem* and *The Wife's Resentment*,[2] to which I may add *The Double Gallant*. This last was a play made up

---

1 As discussed below, pp.247–9.
2 In each of these cases Cibber refers to longer-term success following the Haymarket actors' performances at Drury Lane. Farquhar's *The Beaux' Stratagem* opened at the Haymarket Theatre on 8 March 1707 (LS2a 348), with Wilks and Mills as Archer and Aimwell, Oldfield as Mrs Sullen, and Cibber as Gibbet; there were more recorded performances there during the remainder of the 1706–7 season than in the company's first half-season at Drury Lane, where it was first performed on 28 January 1708 (LS2a 409). The same appears to be true of Cibber's *The Lady's Last Stake; or, the Wife's*

of what little was tolerable in two or three others that had no success, and were laid aside as so much poetical lumber; but by collecting and adapting the best parts of them all into one play, *The Double Gallant* has had a place every winter amongst the public entertainments, these thirty years.[3] As I was only the compiler of this piece, I did not publish it in my own name,[4] but as my having but a hand in it could not be long a secret, I have been often treated as a plagiary on that account.[5] Not that I think I have any right to complain of whatever would detract from the merit of that sort of labour; yet a cobbler may be allowed to be useful though he is not famous, and I hope a man is not blameable for doing a little good, though he cannot do as much as another. But so it is – twopenny critics must live, as well as eighteenpenny authors![6]

While the stage was thus recovering its former strength, a more hon-ourable mark of favour was shown to it than it was ever known before or since to have received. The then Lord Halifax was not only the patron of the men of genius of this time, but had likewise a generous concern for the reputation and prosperity of the theatre, from whence the most elegant dramatic labours of the learned, he knew, had often shone in their brightest lustre.[7] A proposal therefore was drawn up and addressed to that noble lord for his approbation and assistance, to raise a public subscription for reviv-ing three plays of the best authors, with the full strength of the company: every subscriber to have three tickets for the first day of each play, for his single payment of three guineas.[8] This subscription his lordship so zealously

---

Resentment, which enjoyed a good initial run at the Haymarket from 13 December 1707 (LS2a 395) and then received only a single recorded performance at Drury Lane in the remainder of the season (LS2a 419). Evans notes Swiney's initial resolve to focus on the core ingredients of drama: Dryden's *The Spanish Friar* was advertised as being 'without singing or dancing', while Rich's revival the following week of Farquhar's *The Recruiting Officer* promised precisely those ingredients (LS2 130).

3   Cibber's *The Double Gallant* opened at the Haymarket Theatre on 1 November 1707 (LS2a 384). The play draws on Susannah Centlivre's *Love at a Venture* (publ. 1706, no performance recorded in LS2a but performed in Bath), William Burnaby's *The Ladies' Visiting Day* (1701, first performed at Lincoln's Inn Fields; LS2a 18), and the same author's *The Reformed Wife* (1700; LS1 525). Rich staged *The Reformed Wife* at Drury Lane on 31 October and 3 November 1707 (LS2a 383–4), probably to embarrass Cibber.

4   As Fone points out, the play was published in November 1708 with Cibber's name on the title page.

5   For accusations of plagiarism against Cibber, see above, p.146 n.76.

6   *The Double Gallant* was written at a time when the cost of a play quarto was rising from 1 shilling to 18 pence; see Milhous and Hume, *Publication*, p.98. Two pence might be paid for a critical pamphlet.

7   For Halifax, see above, p.148 n.84.

8   *Document Register* no.1885 prints an anecdote referring to 'a subscription of four hundred guineas for the encouragement of good comedies', 'all in Lord Halifax's hand'. Halifax is also named as a patron of the opera in a letter dated 27 May 1707 (*Document Register* no.1894).

encouraged that, from his recommendation chiefly, in a very little time it was completed. The plays were *Julius Cæsar* of Shakespeare, the *King and no King* of Fletcher, and the comic scenes of Dryden's *Marriage à la Mode* and of his *Maiden Queen* put together – for it was judged that as these comic episodes were utterly independent of the serious scenes they were originally written to, they might on this occasion be as well episodes either to the other, and so make up five livelier acts between them; at least the project so well succeeded that those comic parts have never since been replaced, but were continued to be jointly acted as one play several years after.[9]

By the aid of this subscription, which happened in 1707, and by the additional strength and industry of this company, not only the actors (several of which were handsomely advanced in their salaries) were duly paid, but the manager himself too, at the foot of his account stood a considerable gainer.

At the same time, the patentee of Drury Lane went on in his usual method of paying extraordinary prices to singers, dancers and other exotic performers, which were as constantly deducted out of the sinking salaries of his actors.[10] 'Tis true his actors perhaps might not deserve much more than he gave them, yet by what I have related it is plain he chose not to be troubled with such as visibly had deserved more. For it seems he had not purchased his share of the patent to mend the stage, but to make money of it; and to say truth, his sense of everything to be shown there was much upon a level with the taste of the multitude, whose opinion (and whose money) weighed with him full as much as that of the best judges. His point was to please the majority, who could more easily comprehend anything

9 *Julius Caesar* was acted at the Haymarket on 14 January 1707 (LS2a 334); the advertisement read, 'For the encouragement of the comedians acting in the Haymarket, and to enable them to keep the diversion of plays under a separate interest from the opera'. Betterton played Brutus and Wilks Mark Antony; according to Koon, p.191, Cibber played one of the Plebeians. The most recent recorded performance had taken place on 14 March 1706. The subscription performance of Beaumont and Fletcher's *A King and No King* took place on 21 January 1707 (LS2a 336); no cast is listed, but previous performances suggest Wilks played the leading role of Arbaces. The most recent recorded performance had taken place on 28 March 1706 (LS2a 289). Cibber's *The Comical Lovers*, a mash-up of Dryden's *Marriage à la Mode* (1671) and *Secret Love, or The Maiden Queen* (1667), was performed on 4 February 1707 (LS2a 341) with Cibber, Wilks, Booth, Bracegirdle, and Oldfield all in significant roles; unlike *Julius Caesar* and *A King and No King*, it enjoyed a brief run. Cibber reported afterwards that he had assembled the piece in six days and 'found the town very favourable to it' (preface to *The Double Gallant*, 1708).
10 This did not stop Rich falling out with his 'exotic performers': in November 1707, for example, the singers Margarita de L'Épine and Catherine Tofts refused to perform because of unpaid expenses (*The Post-Boy*, 13–15 November 1707; *Document Register* no.1909).

they *saw* than the daintiest things that could be *said* to them. But in this notion he kept no medium; for in my memory, he carried it so far that he was (some few years before this time) actually dealing for an extraordinary large elephant at a certain sum, for every day he might think fit to show the tractable genius of that vast quiet creature in any play or farce in the theatre then standing in Dorset Garden.[11] But, from the jealousy which so formidable a rival had raised in his dancers (and by his bricklayer's assuring him that if the walls were to be opened wide enough for its entrance, it might endanger the fall of the house), he gave up his project, and with it so hopeful a prospect of making the receipts of the stage run higher than all the wit and force of the best writers had ever yet raised them to.

About the same time of his being under this disappointment, he put in practice another project of as new (though not of so bold) a nature, which was his introducing a set of rope-dancers into the same theatre, for the first day of whose performance he had given out some play in which I had a material part.[12] But I was hardy enough to go into the pit and acquaint the spectators near me that I hoped they would not think it a mark of my disrespect to them, if I declined acting upon any stage that was brought to so low a disgrace as ours was like to be by that day's entertainment. My excuse was so well taken that I never after found any ill consequences, or heard of the least disapprobation of it; and the whole body of actors, too, protesting against such an abuse of their profession, our cautious master was too much alarmed and intimidated to repeat it.

After what I have said, it will be no wonder that all due regards to the original use and institution of the stage should be utterly lost or neglected.

---

11 Dorset Garden fell into disuse during the early 1700s and was reserved largely for concerts, and circus-type and musical shows; LS2 records no performance there after November 1706. It was demolished in 1709. Animal acts were not uncommon: the Drury Lane prop bills for January and May 1714 included hire of a monkey (Folger W.b. 111, fol.48; *Document Register* no.2258), while the epilogue to D'Urfey's *Don Quixote Part One* (1694) had been spoken by Joseph Haines astride a donkey. An elephant had been exhibited as part of an unlicensed show in September 1685 (LC 5/17, p.7; *Document Register* no.1263); at the May Fair in 1704 William Penkethman rode an elephant 'between nine and ten foot high, arrived from Guinea, led upon the stage by six blacks' (LS2a 166).

12 As noted above (p.209 n.44), rope-dancing was not quite the novelty Cibber suggests: on 12 September 1699 Thomas Brown complained in a letter to his friend George Moult that the theatres were lowering themselves to the level of the fairs by showing 'dancing upon the high ropes' and other circus-type attractions (quoted in LS1 515–16). '[T]he most famous rope dancers of Europe' are advertised on a bill for Widow Barnes's booth at Bartholomew Fair on 23 August 1705 (LS2a 238). The subsequent passage indicates that Cibber is writing about the period before he left Rich's company in October 1706; the performance he mentions has not been identified, but dances were advertised for Drury Lane plays throughout the autumn of 1705.

Nor was the conduct of this manager easily to be altered while he had found the secret of making money out of disorder and confusion. For however strange it may seem, I have often observed him inclined to be cheerful in the distresses of his theatrical affairs, and equally reserved and pensive when they went smoothly forward with a visible profit. Upon a run of good audiences, he was more frighted to be thought a gainer (which might make him accountable to others) than he was dejected with bad houses (which, at worst, he knew would make others accountable to him). And as, upon a moderate computation, it cannot be supposed that the contested accounts of a twenty years' wear and tear in a playhouse could be fairly adjusted by a Master in Chancery under four-score years more, it will be no surprise that by the neglect (or rather the discretion) of other proprietors in not throwing away good money after bad, this hero of a manager, who alone supported the war, should in time so fortify himself by delay, and so tire his enemies that he became sole monarch of his theatrical empire, and left the quiet possession of it to his successors.[13]

If these facts seem too trivial for the attention of a sensible reader, let it be considered that they are not chosen fictions to entertain, but truths necessary to inform him under what low shifts and disgraces, what disorders and revolutions, the stage laboured before it could recover that strength and reputation wherewith it began to flourish towards the latter end of Queen Anne's reign, and which it continued to enjoy for a course of twenty years following. But let us resume our account of the new settlement in the Haymarket.

It may be a natural question why the actors whom Swiney brought over to his undertaking in the Haymarket would tie themselves down to limited salaries.[14] For though he, as their manager, was obliged to make them certain payments, it was not certain that the receipts would enable him to do it; and since their own industry was the only visible fund they had to depend upon, why would they not, for that reason, insist upon their being sharers as well of possible profits as losses? How far in this point they acted right or wrong will appear from the following state of their case.

It must first be considered that this scheme of their desertion was all concerted and put in execution in a week's time,[15] which short warning might make them overlook that circumstance; and the sudden prospect of

13 Rich died on 4 November 1714, having almost finished rebuilding Lincoln's Inn Fields Theatre. He left three-quarters of his theatrical concerns to his eldest son, John Rich, and the remainder to his younger son, Christopher Mosyer Rich (PROB 11/543, fols.144–5; *Document Register* no.2442). For protracted and other cases brought against Rich, see above, p.216 n.65.
14 For the agreements with actors, see above, p.218 n.70.   15 As above, pp.218–19.

being delivered from having seldom more than half their pay was a con-
tentment that had bounded all their farther views. Besides, as there could
be no room to doubt of their receiving their full pay previous to any profits
that might be reaped by their labour, and as they had no great reason to
apprehend those profits could exceed their respective salaries so far as to
make them repine at them, they might think it but reasonable to let the
chance of any extraordinary gain be on the side of their leader and director.
But farther, as this scheme had the approbation of the Court, these actors
in reality had it not in their power to alter any part of it. And what induced
the Court to encourage it was that by having the theatre and its manager
more immediately dependent on the power of the Lord Chamberlain,[16] it
was not doubted but the stage would be recovered into such a reputation
as might now do honour to that absolute command which the Court or its
officers seemed always fond of having over it.

Here, to set the constitution of the stage in a clearer light, it may not
be amiss to look back a little on the power of a Lord Chamberlain, which
(as may have been observed) in all changes of the theatrical government has
been the main spring without which no scheme, of what kind soever, could
be set in motion. My intent is not to enquire how far, by law, this power has
been limited or extended, but merely as an historian to relate facts to gratify
the curious, and then leave them to their own reflections. This, too, I am the
more inclined to because there is no one circumstance which has affected
the stage wherein so many spectators, from those of the highest rank to the
vulgar, have seemed more positively knowing or less informed in.

Though in all the letters patent for acting plays *etc* since King Charles
the First's time there has been no mention of the Lord Chamberlain or of
any subordination to his command or authority, yet it was still taken for
granted that no letters patent, by the bare omission of such a great officer's
name, could have superseded or taken out of his hands that power which,
time out of mind, he always had exercised over the theatre.[17] The common
opinions then abroad were that if the profession of actors was unlawful, it

16 At this time, Henry Grey, 1st Earl of Kent (1671–1740), who held the office from 1704
   to 1710; he was Marquess of Kent from 1706, created Duke of Kent in 1710, and became
   Marquess Grey shortly before his death. Cibber reflects indirectly on the strengthening
   of the Lord Chamberlain's role encoded in the 1737 Licensing Act.

17 None of the patents issued during the period covered by the *Apology* refers to the Lord
   Chamberlain; only with the 1737 Licensing Act were his powers enshrined in written
   law. Between the appointment of Edward Montagu, Earl of Manchester, in June 1660
   (LC 3/25; *Document Register* no.4) and that of the Earl of Kent in 1704, there had been
   eight holders of the office, as well as a period of eighteen months (1697–9) when duties
   were covered by a deputy, Peregrine Bertie. Appointees are listed in the Timeline of this
   edition (pp.lxx–lxxvii).

was not in the power of the Crown to license it; and if it were not unlawful, it ought to be free and independent, as other professions, and that a patent to exercise it was only an honorary favour from the Crown, to give it a better grace of recommendation to the public. But as the truth of this question seemed to be wrapped in a great deal of obscurity in the old laws made in former reigns relating to players *etc*, it may be no wonder that the best companies of actors should be desirous of taking shelter under the visible power of a Lord Chamberlain, who they knew had, at his pleasure, favoured and protected or born hard upon them. But be all this as it may, a Lord Chamberlain (from whencesoever his power might be derived) had, till of later years, had always an implicit obedience paid to it. I shall now give some few instances in what manner it was exercised.

What appeared to be most reasonably under his cognizance was the licensing or refusing new plays, or striking out what might be thought offensive in them; which province had been for many years assigned to his inferior officer, the Master of the Revels.[18] Yet was not this licence irrevocable; for several plays, though acted by that permission, had been silenced afterwards. The first instance of this kind that common fame has delivered down to us is that of *The Maid's Tragedy* of Beaumont and Fletcher, which was forbid in King Charles the Second's time by an order from the Lord Chamberlain. For what reason this interdiction was laid upon it, the politics of those days have only left us to guess. Some said that the killing of the King in that play, while the tragical death of King Charles the First was then so fresh in people's memory, was an object too horribly impious for a public entertainment.[19] What makes this conjecture seem to have

18 On the longstanding controversy surrounding the role of the Master of the Revels, see above, p.186 n.36.

19 Here, 'common fame' was not reliable. John Wilson's *The Cheats* (1663) and Edward Howard's *The Change of Crowns* (1667) were both licensed by Master of the Revels Sir Henry Herbert but suppressed following performance. *The Maid's Tragedy* is listed among plays performed by actors at the Red Bull Theatre in August 1660 (LS1 12) and was a King's Company favourite during the 1660s, although on 16 May 1661 Pepys found it 'too sad and melancholy'. Gerard Langbaine's *Account of the English Dramatic Poets* (London, 1691), p.212, reports that Charles II banned it 'for some particular reasons', possibly (as Cibber speculates below) to do with the scene (V.ii) in which the king is killed in his bed by his unwilling mistress, Evadne; 9 May 1668 saw the last recorded performance in Charles II's lifetime. The tragi-comic adaptation by Edmund Waller was published in 1690 in *The Second Part of Mr. Waller's Poems*; Langbaine, *Account*, p.146, refers to a revival that year. For a full account, including a view that the ban may have been imposed during the Popish Plot crisis of the late 1670s, see Robert D. Hume, '*The Maid's Tragedy* and Censorship in the Restoration Theatre', *Philological Quarterly* vol. 61, no. 4 (1982), 484–9. For a comprehensive account of Herbert's activities as Master of the Revels, see N. W. Bawcutt, ed., *The Control and Censorship of*

some foundation is that the celebrated Waller, in compliment to that court, altered the last act of this play (which is printed at the end of his works) and gave it a new catastrophe, wherein the life of the King is loyally saved and the lady's matter made up with a less terrible reparation. Others have given out that a repenting mistress, in a romantic revenge of her dishonour, killing the King in the very bed he expected her to come into, was showing a too dangerous example to other Evadnes then shining at court in the same rank of royal distinction[20] – who, if ever their consciences should have run equally mad, might have had frequent opportunities of putting the expiation of their frailty into the like execution. But this, I doubt, is too deep a speculation or too ludicrous a reason to be relied on, it being well known that the ladies then in favour were not so nice in their notions as to think their preferment their dishonour, or their lover a tyrant. Besides, that easy monarch loved his roses without thorns; nor do we hear that he much chose to be himself the first gatherer of them.

The *Lucius Junius Brutus* of Nat Lee was in the same reign silenced after the third day of acting it, it being objected that the plan and sentiments of it had too boldly vindicated (and might enflame) republican principles.[21]

A prologue by Dryden to *The Prophetess* was forbid by the Lord Dorset after the first day of its being spoken.[22] This happened when King William was prosecuting the war in Ireland. It must be confessed that this prologue had some familiar metaphorical sneers at the Revolution itself and, as the poetry of it was good, the offence of it was less pardonable.

The Tragedy of Mary Queen of Scotland had been offered to the stage twenty years before it was acted. But from the profound penetration of the

---

Caroline Drama: The Records of Sir Henry Herbert, Master of the Revels 1623–73 (Oxford: Clarendon Press, 1996); for a survey of Restoration theatre censorship, Matthew J. Kinservik, 'Theatrical Regulation during the Restoration Period', in Susan J. Owen, ed., *A Companion to Restoration Drama* (Oxford: Blackwell, 2001), pp.36–52.

20 In 1668 Charles II was involved with Lady Castlemaine, Moll Davis, and Nell Gwyn.

21 LS1 292–3 gives the likely first performance of Lee's play (at Dorset Garden) as 8 December 1680. Lord Chamberlain Arlington's banning order of 11 December 1680 (LC 5/144, p.28; *Document Register* no.1117) refers to 'scandalous expressions and reflections upon the government', while the preface to Charles Gildon's adaptation of the play as *The Patriot* (publ. 1703) states that the original was suppressed after the third performance for its 'anti-monarchical' quality.

22 For details of Betterton's adaptation, premiered in June 1690, see above, p.107 n.66. LS1 382 cites *The Muses Mercury* of January 1707, which reported that Thomas Shadwell was responsible for informing the Secretary of State of a 'double meaning' critical of William III's accession. Lowe argues that particular offence was caused by the lines, 'Never content with what you had before, / But true to change, and Englishmen all o'er', but with its ironic references to 'sweeping tax' and the 'bogland captive[s]' of William's Irish war (Dryden, p.440), the entire prologue is susceptible to Jacobite interpretation.

Master of the Revels (who saw political spectres in it that never appeared in the presentation) it had lain so long upon the hands of the author, who had at last the good fortune to prevail with a nobleman to favour his petition to Queen Anne for permission to have it acted. The Queen had the goodness to refer the merit of his play to the opinion of that noble person, although he was not Her Majesty's Lord Chamberlain; upon whose report of its being every way an innocent piece, it was soon after acted with success.[23]

Reader – by your leave, I will but just speak a word or two to any author that has not yet writ one line of his next play, and then I will come to my point again. What I would say to him is this: sir, before you set pen to paper, think well, and principally of your design or chief action, towards which every line you write ought to be drawn as to its centre. If we can say of your finest sentiments, 'This or that might be left out without maiming the story you would tell us', depend upon it, that fine thing is said in a wrong place; and though you may urge that a bright thought is not to be resisted, you will not be able to deny that those very fine lines would be much finer if you could find a proper occasion for them. Otherwise you will be thought to take less advice from Aristotle or Horace than from poet Bayes in *The Rehearsal*, who very smartly says, 'What the devil is the plot good for, but to bring in fine things?'[24] Compliment the taste of your hearers as much as you please with them, provided they belong to your subject; but don't, like a dainty preacher who has his eye more upon this world than the next, leave your text for them. When your fable is good, every part of it will cost you much less labour to keep your narration alive than you will be forced to bestow upon those elegant discourses that are not absolutely conducive to your catastrophe or main purpose. Scenes of that kind show but (at best)

---

23 John Banks's *The Island Queens; or, the Death of Mary, Queen of Scotland* was published in 1684, 'in defiance … occasioned by its being prohibited the stage'. The story of a Protestant monarch threatened by a Catholic successor was thought too potent in the last year of Charles II's life. It was finally acted at Drury Lane on 6 March 1704 under the title *The Albion Queens* (LS2a 153). On 22 February 1704 *The Daily Courant* carried a report of its being 'revised and amended' and 'acted, by Her Majesty's permission, at the Theatre Royal' (*Document Register* no.1761). The identity of Banks's friendly nobleman is not known; all the dedicatees of his plays were aristocratic women, with the exception of *The Innocent Usurper* (1694), also suppressed by what Banks refers to as the 'civil powers of the stage'; the dedicatee was the publisher Richard Bentley. *The Island Queens* was dedicated to Mary, Duchess of Norfolk, a Catholic. The Master of the Revels at this time was Charles Killigrew, holder of the office from 1677 to 1725; for Cibber's quarrel with him over objections to *Richard III*, see above, pp.184–6.

24 Bayes's exact line, responding to Smith's objection that his 'plot stands still', is 'why, what a devil is the plot good for, but to bring in fine things?' Buckingham, vol. I, III.i.62–3).

the unprofitable or injudicious spirit of a genius. It is but a melancholy commendation of a fine thought to say, when we have heard it, 'Well! but what's all this to the purpose?' Take therefore, in some part, example by the author last mentioned! There are three plays of his – *The Earl of Essex*, *Anna Bullen*, and *Mary Queen of Scots* – which, though they are all written in the most barren, barbarous style that was ever able to keep possession of the stage, have all interested the hearts of his auditors.[25] To what then could this success be owing, but to the intrinsic and naked value of the well-conducted tales he has simply told us? There is something so happy in the disposition of all his fables: all his chief characters are thrown into such natural circumstances of distress that their misery or affliction wants very little assistance from the ornaments of style or words to speak them. When a skilful actor is so situated, his bare plaintive tone of voice, the cast of sorrow from his eye, his slowly graceful gesture, his humble sighs of resignation under his calamities – all these, I say, are sometimes, without a tongue, equal to the strongest eloquence. At such a time, the attentive auditor supplies from his own heart whatever the poet's language may fall short of in expression, and melts himself into every pang of humanity which the like misfortunes in real life could have inspired.

After what I have observed, whenever I see a tragedy defective in its fable, let there be never so many fine lines in it, I hope I shall be forgiven if I impute that defect to the idleness, the weak judgment, or barren invention of the author.

If I should be asked why I have not always myself followed the rules I would impose upon others, I can only answer that whenever I have not, I lie equally open to the same critical censure. But having often observed a better than ordinary style thrown away upon the loose and wandering scenes of an ill-chosen story, I imagined these observations might convince some future author of how great advantage a fable well planned must be to a man of any tolerable genius.

All this, I own, is leading my reader out of the way; but if he has as much time upon his hands as I have (provided we are neither of us tired), it may be equally to the purpose what he reads, or what I write of. But, as I have no objection to method when it is not troublesome, I return to my subject.

---

25 i.e. John Banks's *The Unhappy Favourite; or, The Earl of Essex*, premiered at Drury Lane by the King's Company in 1681 and revived by the United Company from 1685 (LS1 295 and 332); *Virtue Betrayed; or, Anna Bullen*, premiered by the United Company at Dorset Garden in 1682 and revived from 1692 (LS1 308 and 401); and *The Island Queens* (as above, p.230 n.23).

Hitherto we have seen no very unreasonable instance of this absolute power of a Lord Chamberlain, though we were to admit that no one knew of any real law, or construction of law, by which this power was given him. I shall now offer some facts relating to it of a more extraordinary nature, which I leave my reader to give a name to.

About the middle of King William's reign, an order of the Lord Chamberlain was then subsisting that no actor of either company should presume to go from one to the other, without a discharge from their respective managers and the permission of the Lord Chamberlain.[26] Notwithstanding such order, Powell being uneasy at the favour Wilks was then rising into, had without such discharge left the Drury Lane Theatre and engaged himself to that of Lincoln's Inn Fields.[27] But by what follows, it will appear that this order was not so much intended to do both of them good, as to do that which the Court chiefly favoured (Lincoln's Inn Fields) no harm. For when Powell grew dissatisfied at his station there too, he returned to Drury Lane (as he had before gone from it) without a discharge. But halt a little! Here, on this side of the question, the order was to stand in force, and the same offence against it now was not to be equally passed over. He was the next day taken up by a messenger and confined to the Porter's Lodge, where to the best of my remembrance he remained about two days; when the managers of Lincoln's Inn Fields, not thinking an actor of his loose character worth their farther trouble, gave him up (though perhaps he was released for some better reason). Upon this occasion, the next day, behind the scenes at Drury Lane, a person of great quality in my hearing enquiring of Powell into the nature of his offence, after he had heard it told him that if he had had patience or spirit enough to have stayed in his confinement till he had

26 Orders to this effect were routine: issued on 16 April 1695 against the Lincoln's Inn Fields Company (LC 7/3, fol.21; *Document Register* no.1505), then in an expanded version to account for both companies on 25 July 1695 (LC 7/3/, fol.70; *Document Register* no.1514), and reiterated on 27 May 1697 (LC 5/152, p.15; *Document Register* no.1555). Such orders reinforced the provisions of the existing patents and, as Cibber implies below, may have been designed specifically to protect Betterton's breakaway company at Lincoln's Inn Fields; Lord Chamberlain Dorset had effected their secession against the wishes and financial interest of Charles Killigrew, his Master of the Revels (SP44/73, p.20; *Document Register* no.1488).

27 George Powell joined Betterton at Lincoln's Inn Fields for the start of the 1700–1 season and left during 1703–4. Given the subsequent passage, it is possible that Cibber conflates his departure from Lincoln's Inn Fields with the episode in November 1705 when Powell, having deserted Drury Lane for the Haymarket, promptly refused to act for his new company and was arrested (LC 5/154, p.119; *Document Register* no.1825); Rich was warned on 24 November 1705 not to re-employ him at Drury Lane (LC 5/154, p.124; *Document Register* no.1826), following a warning the previous November about offering inducement to Lincoln's Inn Fields actors (LC 7/3, fol.92v; *Document Register* no.1786).

given him notice of it, he would have found him a handsomer way of coming out of it.

Another time the same actor – Powell – was provoked at Will's coffee-house, in a dispute about the playhouse affairs, to strike a gentleman whose family had been sometimes masters of it.[28] A complaint of this insolence was, in the absence of the Lord Chamberlain, immediately made to the Vice-Chamberlain, who so highly resented it that he thought himself bound in honour to carry his power of redressing it as far as it could possibly go. For Powell having a part in the play that was acted the day after, the Vice-Chamberlain sent an order to silence the whole company for having suffered Powell to appear upon the stage before he had made that gentleman satisfaction, although the masters of the theatre had had no notice of Powell's misbehaviour. However, this order was obeyed, and remained in force for two or three days till the same authority was pleased, or advised, to revoke it.[29] From the measures this injured gentleman took for his redress, it may be judged how far it was taken for granted that a Lord Chamberlain had an absolute power over the theatre.

I shall now give an instance of an actor who had the resolution to stand upon the defence of his liberty against the same authority, and was relieved by it.

In the same King's reign, Doggett, who though from a severe exactness in his nature he could be seldom long easy in any theatre where irregularity (not to say injustice) too often prevailed, yet in the private conduct of his affairs he was a prudent, honest man.[30] He therefore took an unusual care, when he returned to act under the patent in Drury Lane, to have his articles drawn firm and binding. But having some reason to think the patentee had not dealt fairly with him, he quitted the stage and would act no more, rather choosing to lose his whatever unsatisfied demands than go

28 Here Cibber switches back in time to Powell's arrest order of 1 May 1698, as described above, p.161 n.30.

29 The order to silence Rich's Company for continuing to allow Powell to perform was issued on 3 May 1698 (LC 5/152, p.80; *Document Register* no.1581); permission to resume acting was issued the following day (LC 5/152, p.80; *Document Register* no.1582). The Lord Chamberlain's 'absence' was caused by the resignation of Robert Spencer, 2nd Earl of Sunderland (1640–1702); the King refused to accept it and did not fill the vacancy, so the Vice-Chamberlain, Peregrine Bertie, stood in. This was not the last time a company suffered on Powell's account. A silencing order dated 5 March 1707 (LC 5/154, p.224; *Document Register* no.1890) was issued against Drury Lane following Powell's defection from there to the Haymarket and back again, without permission (see above, n.27). Powell had been allowed to speak the prologue to 'the subscription opera', i.e. *Rosamond*, by Joseph Addison and Thomas Clayton, which opened at Drury Lane on 4 March 1707 (LS2a 347).

30 For Thomas Doggett and his other brushes with authority, see above, p.156 n.10.

through the chargeable and tedious course of the law to recover it.[31] But
the patentee, who from other people's judgment knew the value of him –
and who wanted too to have him sooner back than the law could possibly
bring him – thought the surer way would be to desire a shorter redress from
the authority of the Lord Chamberlain. Accordingly, upon his complaint a
messenger was immediately dispatched to Norwich, where Doggett then
was, to bring him up in custody. But doughty Doggett, who had money in
his pocket and the cause of liberty at his heart, was not in the least intimidated by this formidable summons.[32] He was observed to obey it with a particular cheerfulness, entertaining his fellow traveller the messenger all the
way in the coach (for he had protested against riding) with as much humour
as a man of his business might be capable of tasting. And as he found his
charges were to be defrayed, he at every inn called for the best dainties the
country could afford or a pretended weak appetite could digest. At this rate
they jollily rolled on, more with the air of a jaunt than a journey, or a party of
pleasure than of a poor devil in durance. Upon his arrival in town he immediately applied to the Lord Chief Justice Holt for his *habeas corpus*.[33] As his
case was something particular, that eminent and learned minister of the
law took a particular notice of it. For Doggett was not only discharged, but
the process of his confinement (according to common fame) had a censure
passed upon it in court, which I doubt I am not lawyer enough to repeat!
To conclude, the officious agents in this affair, finding that in Doggett they

31 Doggett joined Betterton in the 1695 breakaway but returned to Rich's company the
   following year; an agreement dated 3 April 1696 with Thomas Skipwith for £4 every six
   acting days confirms Cibber's reference to 'firm and binding' articles (LC 7/3, fols.71–2;
   Document Register no.1526). In the spring of 1697, Doggett led a petition against Skipwith
   requesting release from their contracts following non-payment of salaries (LC 7/3,
   fol.148; *Document Register* no.1554). Soon afterwards he decided to leave: an order dated
   23 November 1697 demands his arrest for breach of contract (LC 5/152, p.40; *Document
   Register* no.1571).
32 The arrest order was issued on 23 November 1697 (LC 5/152, p.40; *Document Register*
   no.1571), during Sunderland's brief period as Lord Chamberlain. From October 1697,
   Doggett had joined John Power in mounting plays in Norwich under a patent granted
   by the Duke of Norfolk (orders in the Norfolk Record Office of 27 November 1697
   and 12 January 1698; *Document Register* nos.1573 and 1577). He returned there after
   his summons to London; there are further Norwich licences for 24 September and 8
   October 1698 (*Document Register* nos. 1594–5). He was performing at the Angel Inn in
   Norwich on 27 January 1699 when the gallery collapsed, killing one person and injuring
   many others (*Dawks' Newsletter*, 4 February 1699; *Document Register* no.1600). In January
   1700 he announced a production of *The Prophetess* there (*Flying Post*, 20–3 January 1700;
   Document Register no.1624).
33 Sir John Holt (1642–1710) was Lord Chief Justice from 1689 until his death. *Habeas
   corpus* is a writ requiring someone under arrest to be brought before a judge, usually to
   secure the detainee's release unless lawful grounds are shown for their detention.

had mistaken their man, were mollified into milder proceedings, and (as he afterwards told me) whispered something in his ear that took away Doggett's farther uneasiness about it.

By these instances we see how naturally power only founded on custom is apt, where the law is silent, to run into excesses; and while it laudably pretends to govern others, how hard it is to govern itself. But since the law has lately opened its mouth and has said plainly that some part of this power to govern the theatre shall be, and is, placed in a proper person – and as it is evident that the power of that white staff, ever since it has been in the noble hand that now holds it, has been used with the utmost lenity[34] – I would beg leave of the murmuring multitude who frequent the theatre to offer them a simple question or two, *viz.* 'Pray, gentlemen, how came you (or rather your forefathers) never to be mutinous upon any of the occasional facts I have related? And why have you been so often tumultuous upon a law's being made that only confirms a less power than was formerly exercised without any law to support it? You cannot sure, say such discontent is either just or natural, unless you allow it a maxim in your politics that power exercised *without* law is a less grievance than the same power exercised *according* to law!'

Having thus given the clearest view I was able of the usual regard paid to the power of a Lord Chamberlain, the reader will more easily conceive what influence and operation that power must naturally have in all theatrical revolutions; and particularly in the complete reunion of both companies which happened in the year following.

---

34 i.e. Charles Fitzroy, 2nd Duke of Grafton (see above, p.167 n.46); the Lord Chamberlain's symbols of office are a white staff and golden key. In the subsequent passage Cibber returns to his defence of the 1737 Licensing Act. Here, he offers a heavily veiled reflection on his difficulties at the hands of Grafton's predecessor, Newcastle (see below, p.332 n.2).

CHAPTER II

Some chimerical thoughts of making the stage useful; some, to its reputation. The patent unprofitable to all the proprietors but one. A fourth part of it given away to Colonel Brett. A digression to his memory. The two companies of actors reunited by his interest and management. The first direction of operas only, given to Mr Swiney.

From the time that the company of actors in the Haymarket was recruited with those from Drury Lane and came into the hands of their new director, Swiney, the theatre for three or four years following suffered so many convulsions, and was thrown every other winter under such different interests and management before it came to a firm and lasting settlement, that I am doubtful if the most candid reader will have patience to go through a full and fair account of it.[1] And yet I would fain flatter myself that those who are not too wise to frequent the theatre (or have wit enough to distinguish what sort of sights there either do honour or disgrace to it) may think their national diversion no contemptible subject for a more able historian than I pretend to be. If I have any particular qualification for the task more than another, it is that I have been an ocular witness of the several facts that are to fill up the rest of my volume, and am perhaps the only person living (however unworthy) from whom the same materials can be collected. But let them come from whom they may, whether (at best) they will be worth reading, perhaps a judgment may be better formed after a patient perusal of the following digression.

In whatever cold esteem the stage may be among the wise and powerful, it is not so much a reproach to those who contentedly enjoy it in its lowest condition, as that condition of it is to those who (though they cannot but know to how valuable a public use a theatre well established might be raised) yet in so many civilized nations have neglected it. This perhaps will be called thinking my own wiser than all the wise heads in Europe.

---

1   Cibber summarizes the period 1706–10. In this chapter he deals largely with the first half of that period following the acquisition of Thomas Skipwith's share of the patent by Henry Brett; subsequently, Brett returned his share to the Skipwith family. The further 'convulsions' include the reunion of the Haymarket and Theatre Royal, the closure of Drury Lane under Rich and its reopening under William Collier (Chapter 12, one of the least linear in the *Apology*), and the re-separation of the Haymarket and the Theatre Royal (Chapter 13).

But I hope a more humble sense will be given to it; at least, I only mean that if so many governments have their reasons for their disregard of their theatres, those reasons may be deeper than my capacity has yet been able to dive into. If therefore my simple opinion is a wrong one, let the singularity of it expose me. And though I am only building a theatre in the air, it is there, however, at so little expense and in so much better a taste than any I have yet seen, that I cannot help saying of it as a wiser man did (it may be) upon a wiser occasion:

> *Si quid novisti rectius istis,*
> *Candidus imperti; si non –*
>
> Hor.[2]

Give me leave to play with my project in fancy.

I say then, that as I allow nothing is more liable to debase and corrupt the minds of a people than a licentious theatre, so, under a just and proper establishment, it were possible to make it as apparently the school of manners and of virtue. Were I to collect all the arguments that might be given for my opinion, or to enforce it by exemplary proofs, it might swell this short digression to a volume; I shall therefore trust the validity of what I have laid down to a single fact that may be still fresh in the memory of many living spectators. When the tragedy of *Cato* was first acted,[3] let us call to mind the noble spirit of patriotism which that play then infused into the breasts of a free people that crowded to it. With what affecting force was that most elevated of human virtues recommended! Even the false pretenders to it felt an unwilling conviction, and made it a point of honour to be foremost in their approbation; and this, too, at a time when the fermented nation had their different views of government. Yet the sublime sentiments of liberty in that venerable character raised in every sensible hearer such conscious admiration, such compelled assent to the conduct of a suffering virtue, as even *demanded* two almost irreconcilable parties to embrace and join in their equal applauses of it.[4] Now (not to take from the merit of the

---

2 From Horace, Epistles Book 1 no.6, lines 67–8: 'if you can improve on these principles, tell me; if not, [join me in observing them]'.
3 See above, p.91 n.11, and below, pp.294–6, for Cibber's extended account of the opening run.
4 Lowe quotes Johnson's 'Life of Addison' for a more sober view: 'The Whigs applauded every line in which liberty was mentioned as a satire on the Tories, and the Tories echoed every clap to show that the satire was unfelt' (Johnson, *Lives*, III.11). Citing John E. Loftis, *The Politics of Drama in Augustan England* (Oxford: Clarendon Press, 1963), p.56, Evans suggests that for all his Whig credentials, Cibber may have 'performed services for the Tories as a pamphleteer' in 1710.

writer) had that play never come to the stage, how much of this valuable effect of it must have been lost?[5] It then could have had no more immediate weight with the public than our poring upon the many ancient authors through whose works the same sentiments have been, perhaps, less profitably dispersed, though amongst millions of readers; but by bringing such sentiments to the theatre, and into action, what a superior lustre did they shine with? There, Cato breathed again, in life; and though he perished in the cause of liberty, his virtue was victorious, and left the triumph of it in the heart of every melting spectator. If effects like these are laudable, if the representation of such plays can carry conviction with so much pleasure to the understanding, have they not vastly the advantage of any other human helps to eloquence? What equal method can be found to lead or stimulate the mind to a quicker sense of truth and virtue, or warm a people into the love and practice of such principles as might be at once a defence and honour to their country? In what shape could we listen to virtue with equal delight or appetite of instruction? The mind of man is naturally free, and when he is compelled or menaced into any opinion that he does not readily conceive, he is more apt to doubt the truth of it than when his capacity is led by delight into evidence and reason. To preserve a theatre in this strength and purity of morals is, I grant, what the wisest nations have not been able to perpetuate, or to transmit long to their posterity. But this difficulty will rather heighten than take from the honour of the theatre. The greatest empires have decayed for want of proper heads to guide them, and the ruins of them sometimes have been the subject of theatres that could not be themselves exempt from as various revolutions. Yet may not the most natural inference from all this be that the talents requisite to form good actors, great writers, and true judges were (like those of wise and memorable ministers) as well the gifts of Fortune as of Nature, and not always to be found in all climes or ages? Or can there be a stronger modern evidence of the value of dramatic performances than that in many countries where the papal religion prevails, the holy policy (though it allows not to an actor Christian burial)[6] is so conscious of the usefulness of his art that it will frequently take in the assistance of the theatre to give even sacred history, in a tragedy, a recommendation to the more pathetic regard of their people?[7] How can such principles, in the

---

5 For Addison's reluctance to have the play staged, see below, p.294.

6 Cibber perhaps had in mind the burials of Adrienne Lecouvreur, the French actress who had died in 1730 and had to be buried at night in an unmarked grave because she had not renounced her profession; but mostly of Molière himself, buried in a paupers' grave in 1673 for the same reason.

7 Possibly a reference to religious tragedies such as Racine's *Esther* (1689) and *Athalie* (1691) and/or the tradition of drama in Jesuit schools, on which see *The Jesuits and the Arts,*

face of the world, refuse the bones of a wretch the lowest benefit of Christian charity after having admitted his profession (for which they deprive him of that charity) to serve the solemn purposes of religion? How far then is this religious inhumanity short of that famous painter's who, to make his *Crucifix* a masterpiece of Nature, stabbed the innocent hireling from whose body he drew it and, having heightened the holy portrait with his last agonies of life, then sent it to be the consecrated ornament of an altar?[8] Though we have only the authority of common fame for this story, yet be it true or false, the comparison will still be just. Or, let me ask another question more humanly political.

How came the Athenians to lay out an hundred thousand pounds upon the decorations of one single tragedy of Sophocles?[9] Not, sure, as it was merely a spectacle for idleness or vacancy of thought to gape at; but because it was the most rational, most instructive, and delightful composition that human wit had yet arrived at, and consequently the most worthy to be the entertainment of a wise and warlike nation. And it may be still a question whether the Sophocles inspired this public spirit, or this public spirit inspired the Sophocles.[10]

But alas, as the power of giving or receiving such inspirations from either of these causes seems pretty well at an end, now I have shot my bolt I shall descend to talk more like a man of the age I live in. For indeed, what is all this to a common English reader? Why truly, as Shakespeare terms it, 'caviar to the multitude!'[11] Honest John Trott[12] will tell you that if he were to believe what I have said of the Athenians, he is at most but astonished at it; but that if the twentieth part of the sum I have mentioned

---

1540–1773, ed. John W. O'Malley and Gauvin Alexander Bailey (Philadelphia: St Joseph's University Press, 2005).

8 A reference to an apocryphal story about Michelangelo; the alleged crucifix was made for the monastery of San Spirito (see Linda Murray, *Michelangelo*, London: Thames & Hudson, 1980), p.21.

9 The specific source for this claim has not been identified, but John Dennis's riposte to Jeremy Collier, *The Usefulness of the Stage to the happiness of mankind, to government, and to religion* (London: Richard Parker, 1698), reflects on the generous support given the theatre by the Athenian state: 'The Athenians were highly sensible of the advantage which the state received from the theatre, which they maintained at a public prodigious expense, and a revenue appropriated to that peculiar use; and established a law which made the least attempt to alienate the fund capital' (p.60). Cibber's subsequent reference to a 'warlike nation' may suggest the Sophoclean play in question was either *Ajax* or *Philoctetes*.

10 Lowe notes that *The Laureate* accused Cibber of confusing author and play, which he clearly does not.

11 *Hamlet*, II.ii.383–4: 'caviar to the general'.

12 Proverbial for 'ordinary man'; cf. 'Joan Trott', above, p.119 n.114.

were to be applied out of the public money to the setting off the best tragedy the nicest noddle in the nation could produce, it would probably raise
the passions higher in those that did not like it than in those that did. It
might as likely meet with an insurrection as the applause of the people and
so, mayhap, be fitter for the subject of a tragedy than for a public fund to
support it. Truly, Mr Trott, I cannot but own that I am very much of your
opinion. I am only concerned that the theatre has not a better pretence
to the care and farther consideration of those governments where it is
tolerated; but as what I have said will not probably do it any great harm,
I hope I have not put you out of patience by throwing a few good wishes
after an old acquaintance.

To conclude this digression: if, for the support of the stage, what is
generally shown there must be lowered to the taste of common spectators,
or if it is inconsistent with liberty to mend that vulgar taste by making the
multitude less merry there, or by abolishing every low and senseless jollity
in which the understanding can have no share – whenever, I say, such is
the state of the stage, it will be as often liable to unanswerable censure and
manifest disgraces. Yet there was a time, not yet out of many people's memory, when it subsisted upon its own rational labours; when even success
attended an attempt to reduce it to decency; and when actors themselves
were hardy enough to hazard their interest in pursuit of so dangerous a
reformation.[13] And this crisis I am myself as impatient as any tired reader
can be to arrive at. I shall therefore endeavour to lead him the shortest way
to it. But as I am a little jealous of the badness of the road, I must reserve to
myself the liberty of calling upon any matter in my way for a little refresh-
ment, to whatever company may have the curiosity or goodness to go along
with me.

When the sole managing patentee at Drury Lane for several years
could never be persuaded or driven to any account with the adventurers, Sir
Thomas Skipwith (who, if I am rightly informed, had an equal share with
him)[14] grew so weary of the affair that he actually made a present of his
entire interest in it, upon the following occasion.

---

13 One of Cibber's many favourable reflections on his period of management with Wilks
    and Booth.
14 Thomas Skipwith first acquired a financial interest in the United Company on 12
    September 1687, when his investment enabled Alexander Davenant to purchase a
    share of the patent and have Skipwith's shares leased to him (BL Add.Charter 9299;
    Document Register no.1309). Rich acted as Skipwith's counsel for the transaction and
    himself acquired Sir William Davenant's original Duke's Company share the following
    March (BL Add.Charter 9301; *Document Register* no.1320). Lowe cites the description of
    Skipwith in *Biographia Dramatica* (I.487) as 'a weak, vain, conceited coxcomb'.

Sir Thomas happened, in the summer preceding the reunion of the companies, to make a visit to an intimate friend of his, Colonel Brett of Sandywell in Gloucestershire, where the pleasantness of the place and the agreeable manner of passing his time there had raised him to such a gallantry of heart that, in return to the civilities of his friend the Colonel, he made him an offer of his whole right in the patent; but not to overrate the value of his present, told him he himself had made nothing of it these ten years. But the Colonel, he said, being a greater favourite of the people in power and (as he believed) among the actors too than himself was, might think of some scheme to turn it to advantage; and in that light, if he liked it, it was at his service. After a great deal of raillery on both sides of what Sir Thomas had not made of it, and the particular advantages the Colonel was likely to make of it, they came to a laughing resolution that an instrument should be drawn the next morning, of an absolute conveyance of the premises. A gentleman of the law, well known to them both, happening to be a guest there at the same time, the next day produced the deed according to his instructions, in the presence of whom and of others it was signed, sealed and delivered, to the purposes therein contained.[15]

This transaction may be another instance (as I have elsewhere observed) at how low a value the interests in a theatrical licence were then held; though it was visible from the success of Swiney in that very year that, with tolerable management, they could at no time have failed of being a profitable purchase.[16]

The next thing to be considered was what the Colonel should do with his new theatrical commission, which in another's possession had been of so little importance. Here it may be necessary to premise that this gentleman was the first of any consideration, since my coming to the stage, with whom I had contracted a personal intimacy; which might be the reason why, in this debate, my opinion had some weight with him. Of this intimacy, too, I am the more tempted to talk from the natural pleasure of calling back in age the pursuits and happy ardours of youth long past; which, like the ideas

---

15 The transfer took place on 6 October 1707; Brett paid 10 shillings for Skipwith's share (*Document Register* no.1904). Skipwith claimed in February 1709 that the share had been transferred in trust, not as a gift, and sued Brett (C8/481/66; *Document Register* no.1999). The 'gentleman of the law' was identified in Brett's response to Skipwith (reprinted in Hotson, pp.386–96) as Humphrey Brent.

16 Evans follows Barker, p.73, in asserting that the Haymarket company was at this time 'prostrate', with the failure of Cibber's *The Lady's Last Stake* partly responsible, so suggesting that in this passage Cibber is simply skating over his own failure. However, Milhous, *Management*, pp.218–20, shows that Swiney managed his company capably and that the 1708 union was brought about for political rather than economic reasons.

of a delightful spring in a winter's rumination, are sometimes equal to the former enjoyment of them. I shall therefore rather choose in this place to gratify myself than my reader, by setting the fairest side of this gentleman in view, and by indulging a little conscious vanity in showing how early in life I fell into the possession of so agreeable a companion. Whatever failings he might have to others, he had none to me;[17] nor was he, where he had them, without his valuable qualities to balance or soften them. Let, then, what was not to be commended in him rest with his ashes, never to be raked into; but the friendly favours I received from him while living give me still a pleasure in paying this only mite of my acknowledgment in my power to his memory. And if my taking this liberty may find pardon from several of his fair relations still living, for whom I profess the utmost respect, it will give me but little concern, though my critical readers should think it all impertinence.[18]

This gentleman, then (Henry), was the eldest son of Henry Brett Esq of Cowley in Gloucestershire; who, coming early to his estate of about two thousand a year, by the usual negligences of young heirs had, before this his eldest son came of age, sunk it to about half that value, and that not wholly free from encumbrances. Mr Brett whom I am speaking of had his education (and I might say ended it) at the University of Oxford; for though he was settled some time after at the Temple, he so little followed the law there that his neglect of it made the law (like some of his fair and frail admirers) very often follow *him*.[19] As he had an uncommon share of social wit and a handsome person with a sanguine bloom in his complexion, no wonder they persuaded him that he might have a better chance of fortune by throwing such accomplishments into the gayer world than by shutting them up in a study. The first view that fires the head of a young gentleman of this modish ambition, just broke loose from business, is to cut a figure (as they call it) in a side-box at the play, from whence their next step is to the green room behind the scenes, sometimes their *non ultra*.[20] Hither at last, then, in this hopeful quest of his fortune, came this gentleman-errant, not doubting but the fickle dame, while he was thus qualified to receive her, might be tempted to fall into his lap. And though possibly the charms of our theatrical nymphs might have their

---

17 Evans detects a possible allusion to Brett's controversial marriage (see below, p.245 n.25) or to the extra-marital affair alleged by Boswell, I.108–9.

18 Brett's wife and daughter were still alive when the *Apology* was published. His daughter, Anna Margharetta, became mistress to George I, married Sir William Leman, and died in 1743. For mite, see above, p.4 n.9.

19 In his youth Brett lived 'the life of a rake' (see www.historyofparliamentonline.org/volume/1690–1715/member/brett-henry-1675-1724; accessed 4 November 2021). He enrolled as a student at Middle Temple on 5 June 1695; see *Register of Admissions to the Honourable Society of the Middle Temple*, vol. I (London: Butterworth & Co., 1949), p.237.

20 i.e. 'no further'; presumably a hint that some did go further.

share in drawing him thither, yet in my observation the most visible cause of his first coming was a more sincere passion he had conceived for a fair full-bottomed periwig, which I then wore in my first play of *The Fool in Fashion* in the year 1695.[21] For it is to be noted that the beaux of those days were of a quite different cast from the modern stamp, and had more of the stateliness of the peacock in their mien than (which now seems to be their highest emulation) the pert air of a lapwing. Now, whatever contempt philosophers may have for a fine periwig, my friend (who was not to despise the world, but to live in it) knew very well that so material an article of dress upon the head of a man of sense, if it became him, could never fail of drawing to him a more partial regard and benevolence than could possibly be hoped for in an ill-made one.[22] This perhaps may soften the grave censure which so youthful a purchase might otherwise have laid upon him. In a word, he made his attack upon this periwig as your young fellows generally do upon a lady of pleasure: first, by a few familiar praises of her person, and then a civil enquiry into the price of it. But upon his observing me a little surprised at the levity of his question about a fop's periwig, he began to rally himself with so much wit and humour upon the folly of his fondness for it that he struck me with an equal desire of granting anything in my power to oblige so facetious a customer. This singular beginning of our conversation, and the mutual laughs that ensued upon it, ended in an agreement to finish our bargain that night over a bottle.

If it were possible the relation of the happy indiscretions which passed between us that night could give the tenth part of the pleasure I then received from them, I could still repeat them with delight. But, as it may be doubtful whether the patience of a reader may be quite so strong as the vanity of an author, I shall cut it short by only saying that single bottle was the sire of many a jolly dozen that for some years following, like orderly children, whenever they were called for, came into the same company. Nor

21 Cibber gives the old style date and the subtitle; *Love's Last Shift* premiered in January 1696.

22 Lowe cites Davies, III. 84:

> The heads of the English actors were, for a long time, covered with large full-bottomed periwigs, a fashion introduced in the reign of Charles II, which was not entirely disused in public till about the year 1720. Addison, Congreve, and Steele met at Button's coffee house, in large, flowing, flaxen wigs; Booth, Wilks, and Cibber, when full-dressed, wore the same. Till within these twenty-five years, our Tamerlanes and Catos had as much hair on their heads as our judges on the bench ... I have been told, that he [Booth] and Wilks bestowed forty guineas each on the exorbitant thatching of their heads.

For an account of the rise and fall of the wig at court and in fashionable London, see James Laver, *Costume and Fashion: A Concise History* (London: Thames & Hudson, 1969), pp.120–30. Cibber passes over the incident when his daughter Charlotte mocked his own wig during her performance in Fielding's *Pasquin* (see Introduction, pp.xxv and lviii).

indeed did I think from that time, whenever he was to be had, any evening could be agreeably enjoyed without him.[23] But the long continuance of our intimacy, perhaps, may be thus accounted for.

He who can taste wit in another may, in some sort, be said to have it himself. Now, as I always had and (I bless myself for the folly) still have a quick relish of whatever did or can give me delight, this gentleman could not but see the youthful joy I was generally raised to whenever I had the happiness of a *tête-à-tête* with him; and it may be a moot point whether wit is not as often inspired by a proper attention as by the brightest reply to it. Therefore, as he had wit enough for any two people and I had attention enough for any four, there could not well be wanting a sociable delight on either side. And though it may be true that a man of a handsome person is apt to draw a partial ear to everything he says, yet this gentleman seldom said anything that might not have made a man of the plainest person agreeable. Such a continual desire to please, it may be imagined, could not but sometimes lead him into a little venial flattery rather than not succeed in it. And I, perhaps, might be one of those flies that was caught in this honey. As I was then a young, successful author and an actor in some unexpected favour (whether deservedly or not imports not), yet such appearances, at least, were plausible pretences enough for an amicable adulation to enlarge upon, and the sallies of it a less vanity than mine might not have been able to resist. Whatever this weakness on my side might be, I was not alone in it; for I have heard a gentleman of condition say (who knew the world as well as most men that live in it) that let his discretion be ever so much upon its guard, he never fell into Mr Brett's company without being loath to leave it, or carrying away a better opinion of himself from it. If his conversation had this effect among the men, what must we suppose to have been the consequence when he gave it a yet softer turn among the fair sex? Here, now, a French novelist would tell you fifty pretty lies of him; but as I choose to be tender of secrets of that sort, I shall only borrow the good breeding of that language and tell you, in a word, that I knew several instances of his being *un homme à bonne fortune*.[24] But though his frequent successes might generally keep him from the usual disquiets of a lover, he knew this was a life too liquorish to last, and therefore had reflection enough to be governed by the advice of his friends to turn these his advantages of Nature to a better use.

---

23 As Lowe points out, *The Laureate*, p.66, questions whether Brett really considered Cibber to be his friend; Brett once allegedly objected (some time after the period in question here) to Cibber's cursory dismissal of a draft play.

24 A reference to the rakish youth noted above, p.242 n.19, reflecting the proverbial characterization of fortune as female.

Among the many men of condition with whom his conversation had recommended him to an intimacy, Sir Thomas Skipwith had taken a particular inclination to him; and, as he had the advancement of his fortune at heart, introduced him where there was a lady who had enough in her power to disencumber him of the world, and make him every way easy for life.[25]

While he was in pursuit of this affair, which no time was to be lost in (for the lady was to be in town but for three weeks), I one day found him idling behind the scenes before the play was begun. Upon sight of him I took the usual freedom he allowed me to rate him roundly for the madness of not improving, every moment in his power, in what was of such consequence to him. 'Why are you not', said I, 'where you know you only should be? If your design should once get wind in the town, the ill will of your enemies or the sincerity of the lady's friends may soon blow up your hopes, which in your circumstances of life cannot be long supported by the bare appearance of a gentleman'. But it is impossible to proceed without some apology for the very familiar circumstance that is to follow; yet, as it might not be so trivial in its effect as I fear it may be in the narration (and is a mark of that intimacy which is necessary should be known had been between us), I will honestly make bold with my scruples, and let the plain truth of my story take its chance for contempt or approbation.

After twenty excuses to clear himself of the neglect I had so warmly charged him with, he concluded them with telling me he had been out all the morning upon business, and that his linen was too much soiled to be seen in company. 'Oh, ho!' said I, 'is that all? Come along with me, we will soon get over that dainty difficulty'. Upon which, I hauled him by the sleeve into my shifting room, he either staring, laughing, or hanging back all the way. There, when I had locked him in, I began to strip off my upper clothes and bade him do the same. Still he either did not or would not seem to understand me and, continuing his laugh, cried, 'What! Is the puppy mad?' 'No, no, only positive', said I; 'for look you – in short, the play is ready to begin, and the parts that you and I are to act today are

25 Anne Gerard, née Mason, was the divorced former wife of Charles Gerard, 2nd Earl of Macclesfield. Anne had married Gerard in 1683 but separated soon afterwards; she went on to have two children outside marriage, one of whom was rumoured to be the poet Richard Savage. When her divorce from Gerard finally came through in 1698, her dowry was returned to her and she was left with a fortune estimated by Barker, p.15, at between £12,000 and £25,000 a year (up to £4.5m in current values). She married Brett in 1700 and survived him by nearly thirty years, dying in 1753. Boswell, I.174, credits her with having read and commented on a draft of Cibber's *The Careless Husband* (1704).

not of equal consequence. Mine, of Young Reveller (in *Greenwich Park*) is but a rake,[26] but whatever you may be, you are not to appear so; therefore take my shirt and give me yours, for depend upon't, stay here you shall not and so go about your business'. To conclude, we fairly changed linen; nor could his mother have wrapped him up more fortunately, for in about ten days he married the lady. In a year or two after his marriage, he was chosen a Member of that Parliament which was sitting when King William died;[27] and, upon raising of some new regiments, was made Lieutenant Colonel to that of Sir Charles Hotham.[28] But, as his ambition extended not beyond the bounds of a park wall and a pleasant retreat in the corner of it (which, with too much expense, he had just finished), he, within another year, had leave to resign his company to a younger brother.[29]

This was the figure in life he made, when Sir Thomas Skipwith thought him the most proper person to oblige (if it could be an obligation) with the present of his interest in the patent. And from these anecdotes of my intimacy with him, it may be less a surprise, when he came to town invested with this new theatrical power, that I should be the first person to whom he took any notice of it. And notwithstanding he knew I was then engaged in another interest at the Haymarket, he desired we might consider together of the best use he could make of it, assuring me at the same time he should think it of none to himself, unless it could in some shape be turned to my advantage. This friendly declaration, though it might be generous in him to make, was not needful to incline me in whatever might be honestly in my power, whether by interest or negotiation, to serve him. My first advice, therefore, was that he should produce his deed to the other managing patentee of Drury Lane,[30] and demand immediate entrance to a joint possession of all effects and powers to which that deed had given him an equal title. After which, if he met with no opposition to this demand (as upon sight of it he did not), that he should be watchful against any contradiction from

26 William Mountfort's comedy, *Greenwich Park*, was first acted by the United Company between 1689 and 1691; Mountfort himself created the role of Young Reveller. It is plausible that Cibber had taken over the role by the time it was performed by Rich's company on 16 October 1697 (LS1 487).

27 Brett was briefly MP for Bishop's Castle (see above, p.219 n.73). William III died on 8 March 1702.

28 Sir Charles Hotham, 4th Baronet of Scorborough (1663–1723), raised a Yorkshire regiment in 1705 which joined the expeditionary force in Spain the following year.

29 Brett redeveloped Sandywell Park, five miles east of Cheltenham, in 1704, adding Georgian features to the original Jacobean structure.

30 i.e. Christopher Rich.

his colleague in whatever he might propose in carrying on the affair, but to let him see that he was determined in all his measures – yet to heighten that resolution with an ease and temper in his manner, as if he took it for granted there could be no opposition made to whatever he had a mind to. For that this method, added to his natural talent of persuading, would imperceptibly lead his colleague into a reliance on his superior understanding; that however little he cared for business, he should give himself the air, at least, of enquiry into what *had* been done, that what he *intended* to do might be thought more considerable and be the readier complied with. For if he once suffered his colleague to seem wiser than himself, there would be no end of his perplexing him with absurd and dilatory measures – direct and plain dealing being a quality his natural diffidence would never suffer him to be master of (of which, his not complying with his verbal agreement with Swiney, when the Haymarket house was taken for both their uses, was an evidence).[31] And though some people thought it depth and policy in him to keep things often in confusion, it was ever my opinion they over-rated his skill, and that in reality his parts were too weak for his post, in which he had always acted to the best of his knowledge; that his late colleague, Sir Thomas Skipwith, had trusted too much to his capacity for this sort of business and was treated by him accordingly, without ever receiving any profits from it for several years, insomuch that when he found his interest in such desperate hands, he thought the best thing he could do with it was (as he saw) to give it away. Therefore if he (Mr Brett) could once fix himself, as I had advised, upon a different foot with this hitherto untractable manager, the business would soon run through whatever channel he might have a mind to lead it. And though I allowed the greatest difficulty he would meet with would be in getting his consent to a union of the two companies (which was the only scheme that could raise the patent to its former value, and which I knew this close manager would secretly lay all possible rubs in the way to), yet it was visible there was a way of reducing him to compliance. For though it was true his caution would never part with a straw by way of concession, yet to a high hand he would give up anything, provided he were suffered to keep his title to it. If his hat were taken from his head in the street, he would make no farther resistance than to say, 'I am not willing to part with it'. Much less would he have the resolution openly to oppose any just measures when he should find one who, with an equal right to his and with a known interest to bring them about, was resolved to go through with them.

31 As described above, pp.216–18.

Now, though I knew my friend was as thoroughly acquainted with this patentee's temper as myself, yet I thought it not amiss to quicken and support his resolution by confirming to him the little trouble he would meet with in pursuit of the union I had advised him to; for it must be known that on our side, trouble was a sort of physic we did not much care to take. But, as the fatigue of this affair was likely to be lowered by a good deal of entertainment and humour which would naturally engage him in his dealing with so exotic a partner, I knew that this softening the business into a diversion would lessen every difficulty that lay in our way to it.

However copiously I may have indulged myself in this commemoration of a gentleman with whom I had passed so many of my younger days with pleasure, yet the reader may, by this insight into his character and by that of the other patentee, be better able to judge of the secret springs that gave motion to – or obstructed – so considerable an event as that of the reunion of the two companies of actors in 1708.[32] In histories of more weight, for want of such particulars we are often deceived in the true causes of facts that most concern us to be let into; which sometimes makes us ascribe to policy, or false appearances of wisdom, what perhaps in reality was the mere effect of chance or humour.

Immediately after Mr Brett was admitted as a joint patentee, he made use of the intimacy he had with the Vice-Chamberlain to assist his scheme of this intended union,[33] in which he so far prevailed that it was soon after left to the particular care of the same Vice-Chamberlain to give him all the aid and power necessary to the bringing what he desired to perfection. The scheme was, to have but one theatre for plays and another for operas, under separate interests. And this the generality of spectators, as well as the most approved actors, had been some time calling for as the only expedient to recover the credit of the stage and the valuable interests of its managers.[34]

As the condition of the comedians at this time is taken notice of in my dedication of *The Wife's Resentment* to the Marquis (now Duke) of Kent and then Lord Chamberlain (which was published above thirty years ago,[35] when I had no thought of ever troubling the world with this theatrical

---

32 The order was published on 31 December 1707 (LC 5/154, pp.299–300; *Document Register* no.1927). See above, p.199 n.5.

33 The Deputy Lord Chamberlain in question was Thomas Coke (1674–1727).

34 *Muses Mercury* reported in February 1708 that the 'opera has been always crowded since it has been under the present management, and is now in a fairer way to live than ever' (*Document Register* no.1955).

35 *The Lady's Last Stake; or the Wife's Resentment* was published on 30 December 1707 following its premiere on 13 December. For Lord Chamberlain Kent, see above, p.227 n.16.

history), I see no reason why it may not pass as a voucher of the facts I am now speaking of; I shall therefore give them in the very light I then saw them. After some acknowledgment for his Lordship's protection of our Haymarket theatre, it is farther said:

'The stage has for many years, till of late, groaned under the greatest discouragements, which have been very much (if not wholly) owing to the mismanagement of those that have awkwardly governed it. Great sums have been ventured upon empty projects and hopes of immoderate gains, and when those hopes have failed, the loss has been tyrannically deducted out of the actors' salary. And if your lordship had not redeemed them' – this is meant of our being suffered to come over to Swiney – 'they were very near being wholly laid aside or, at least, the use of their labour was to be swallowed up in the pretended merit of singing and dancing.'

What follows relates to the difficulties in dealing with the then impracticable manager, *viz*:

'– And though your lordship's tenderness of oppressing is so very just that you have rather stayed to convince a man of your good intentions to him than to do him even a service against his will, yet since your lordship has so happily begun the establishment of the separate diversions, we live in hope that the same justice and resolution will still persuade you to go as successfully through with it. But while any man is suffered to confound the industry and use of them, by acting publicly in opposition to your lordship's equal intentions under a false and intricate pretence of not being able to comply with them, the town is likely to be more entertained with the private dissensions than the public performance of either; and the actors, in a perpetual fear and necessity of petitioning your lordship every season for new relief.'

Such was the state of the stage immediately preceding the time of Mr Brett's being admitted a joint patentee; who, as he saw with clearer eyes what was its evident interest, left no proper measures unattempted to make this so long despaired of union practicable. The most apparent difficulty to be got over in this affair was what could be done for Swiney, in consideration of his being obliged to give up those actors whom the power and choice of the Lord Chamberlain had, the year before, set him at the head of, and by whose management those actors had found themselves in a prosperous condition.[36] But an accident at this time happily contributed to make that matter easy. The inclination of our people of quality for foreign operas had now reached the ears of Italy, and the credit of their taste had drawn over from thence – without any more particular invitation – one of

36 i.e. in August 1706; see above, pp.218–19.

10. 'One of their capital singers': Nicolini with Lucia Fachinelli, caricature
by Anton Maria Zanetti.

their capital singers, the famous Signior Cavaliero Nicolini;[37] from whose
arrival, and the impatience of the town to hear him, it was concluded that
operas being now so completely provided could not fail of success, and that
by making Swiney sole director of them, the profits must be an ample compensation for his resignation of the actors. This matter being thus adjusted
by Swiney's acceptance of the opera only to be performed at the Haymarket
house, the actors were all ordered to return to Drury Lane, there to remain,
under the patentees, Her Majesty's only company of comedians.[38]

37 Nicolo Grimaldi (1673–1732), known as Nicolini or Nicolino, was a Neapolitan male
   contralto. He made his London debut at the Haymarket in December 1708, as Pyrrhus
   in *Pyrrhus and Demetrius* (LS2a 457), an adaptation by Swiney and Nicola Francesco
   Haym (1678–1729) of Alessandro Scarlatti's 1694 opera, *Pirro e Demetrio*. For a caricature,
   see Figure 10.
38 i.e. the Order of Union dated 31 December 1707 (see above, p.248 n.32), specifying the
   performances of opera solely at the Haymarket, and spoken-word drama only at Drury
   Lane and Dorset Garden. The order was followed up by another that demanded the
   swearing-in of actors (LC 5/154, p.300; *Document Register* no.1930).

CHAPTER 12

A short view of the opera when first divided from the comedy. Plays recover their credit. The old patentee uneasy at their success. Why. The occasion of Colonel Brett's throwing up his share in the patent. The consequences of it. Anecdotes of Goodman the actor. The rate of favourite actors in his time. The patentees, by endeavouring to reduce their price, lose them all a second time. The principal comedians return to the Haymarket in shares with Swiney. They alter that theatre. The original and present form of the theatre in Drury Lane compared. Operas fall off. The occasion of it. Farther observations upon them. The patentee dispossessed of Drury Lane theatre. Mr Collier, with a new licence, heads the remains of that company.

Plays and operas being thus established upon separate interests, they were now left to make the best of their way into favour by their different merit. Although the opera is not a plant of our native growth nor what our plainer appetites are fond of (and is of so delicate a nature that without excessive charge it cannot live long among us, especially while the nicest connoisseurs in music fall into such various heresies in taste, every sect pretending to be the true one), yet as it is called a theatrical entertainment, and by its alliance or neutrality has more or less affected our domestic theatre, a short view of its progress may be allowed a place in our history.

After this new regulation, the first opera that appeared was *Pyrrhus*.[1] Subscriptions at that time were not extended as of late, to the whole season,[2] but were limited to the first six days only of a new opera. The chief performers in this were Nicolini, Valentini, and Mrs Tofts;[3] and for the inferior parts, the best that were then to be found. Whatever praises may have been given to the most famous voices that have been heard since Nicolini, upon the whole I cannot but come into the opinion that still prevails

1 See above, p.250 n.37, but *Pyrrhus and Demetrius* did not open until December 1708; the first opera production following the union was a revival of Christopher Pepusch's *Thomyris, Queen of Scythia* (17 January 1708; LS2a 407), first performed in April 1707 (LS2a 353).
2 From 1721, the Royal Academy instituted a system of annual subscriptions worth 20 guineas to support its opera productions (LS2 lxxv).
3 Catherine Tofts (c. 1695–1756) had sung in *Arsinoë, Queen of Cyprus*; *Il Trionfo di Camilla*; *Rosamond*; and *Thomyris, Queen of Scythia* before Nicolini's arrival for *Pyrrhus and Demetrius*. She continued to sing in English while Nicolini and others sang in Italian, a practice mocked by Addison in *The Spectator* no.18 (21 March 1711). For Valentini see above, p.213 n.57.

among several persons of condition who are able to give a reason for their liking: that no singer since his time has so justly and gracefully acquitted himself in whatever character he appeared, as Nicolini. At most, the difference between him and the greatest favourite of the ladies, Farinelli,[4] amounted but to this: that he might sometimes more exquisitely surprise us. But Nicolini, by pleasing the eye as well as the ear, filled us with a more various and rational delight. Whether in this excellence he has since had any competitor perhaps will be better judged by what the critical censor of Great Britain says of him in his 115th *Tatler*, viz.:

'Nicolini sets off the character he bears in an opera by his action, as much as he does the words of it by his voice; every limb and finger contributes to the part he acts, insomuch that a deaf man might go along with him in the sense of it. There is scarce a beautiful posture in an old statue which he does not plant himself in, as the different circumstances of the story give occasion for it. He performs the most ordinary action in a manner suitable to the greatness of his character, and shows the prince even in the giving of a letter or dispatching of a message' *etc.*[5]

His voice at this first time of being among us (for he made us a second visit when it was impaired) had all that strong, clear sweetness of tone so

---

4 See above, p.80 n.60.
5 From Richard Steele, *The Tatler*, no.155, 3 January 1710. Lowe quotes the passage in full, so showing that Cibber omitted Steele's criticism of 'our best actors':

> I went on Friday last to the opera, and was surprised to find a thin house at so noble an entertainment, till I heard that the tumbler was not to make his appearance that night. For my own part, I was fully satisfied with the sight of an actor who, by the grace and propriety of his action and gesture, does honour to an human figure as much as the other vilifies and degrades it. Everyone will easily imagine I mean Signior Nicolini, who sets off the character he bears in an opera by his action, as much as he does the words of it by his voice. Every limb and every finger contributes to the part he acts, insomuch that a deaf man might go along with him in the sense of it. There is scarce a beautiful posture in an old statue which he does not plant himself in, as the different circumstances of the story give occasion for it. He performs the most ordinary action in a manner suitable to the greatness of his character, and shows the prince even in the giving of a letter, or the dispatching of a message. Our best actors are somewhat at a loss to support themselves with proper gesture as they move from any considerable distance to the front of the stage; but I have seen the person of whom I am now speaking enter alone at the remotest part of it, and advance from it with such greatness of air and mien as seemed to fill the stage, and at the same time commanded the attention of the audience with the majesty of his appearance.

Steele had seen *Pyrrhus and Demetrius* on 30 December 1709 (LS2a 535). In *The Spectator* no.5 (6 March 1711), Addison offered a contrasting view: 'How would the wits of King Charles's time have laughed to have seen Nicoloni exposed to a tempest in robes of ermine, and sailing in an open boat upon a sea of paste-board.' Addison continued in the same vein in no.13 (15 March 1711).

lately admired in Sinesino.[6] A blind man could scarce have distinguished them, but in volubility of throat the former had much the superiority. This so excellent performer's agreement was eight hundred guineas for the year, which is but an eighth part more than half the sum that has since been given to several that could never totally surpass him;[7] the consequence of which is that the losses by operas for several seasons, to the end of the year 1738, have been so great that those gentlemen of quality who last undertook the direction of them found it ridiculous any longer to entertain the public at so extravagant an expense, while no one particular person thought himself obliged by it.[8]

Mrs Tofts, who took her first grounds of music here in her own country before the Italian taste had so highly prevailed, was then not an adept in it.[9] Yet, whatever defect the fashionably skilful might find in her manner, she had (in the general sense of her spectators) charms that few of the most learned singers ever arrive at. The beauty of her fine proportioned figure and exquisitely sweet, silver tone of her voice – with that peculiar, rapid swiftness of her throat – were perfections not to be imitated by art or labour. Valentini I have already mentioned,[10] therefore need only say farther of him that though he was every way inferior to Nicolini, yet, as he had the advantage of giving us our first impression of a good opera singer, he had still his admirers and was of great service in being so skilful a second to his superior.

Three such excellent performers, in the same kind of entertainment at once, England till this time had never seen. Without any farther

---

6 See above, p.80 n.60.
7 Cibber refers to the total amount of money laid out for singers of lesser talent since Nicolini's last London appearance in 1717. The figure of 800 guineas a year for three years is confirmed by a document from April 1709, with the addition of £150 for provision of a new opera score (HTC Coke Papers; *Document Register* no.2005).
8 A letter from Lord Hervey to Henry Fox dated 2 November 1734 cites an estimate by the opera producer John James Heidegger (1666–1749) of the cost of opera at the King's Theatre: the investors 'must receive seventy-six thousand odd hundred pounds to bear their charges, before they become gainers' (*Document Register* no.3834). On 9 March 1737 John Rich reported that three years of losses on Handel's operas had left him unable to pay rent on Covent Garden and other properties (*Document Register* no.4084).
9 The first edition of the *Apology* has 'but an adept', which reverses the meaning of the phrase. Fielding leaped on what may have been a printer's error:
> for surely he must be absolute master of that whose laws he can trample under feet, and which he can use as he pleases. This power he hath exerted, of which I shall give a barbarous instance in the case of the poor word 'adept'... This word our great master hath tortured and wrested to signify a tyro or novice, being directly contrary to the sense in which it hath been hitherto used. (Fielding, *The Champion*, 22 April 1740)
For Tofts' previous experience of opera, see above, p.251 n.3.
10 See above, p.213 n.57.

comparison, then, with the much dearer bought who have succeeded them, their novelty (at least) was a charm that drew vast audiences of the fine world after them. Swiney, their sole director, was prosperous, and in one winter a gainer by them of a moderate younger brother's fortune.[11] But as music, by so profuse a dispensation of her beauties, could not always supply our dainty appetites with equal variety nor for ever please us with the same objects, the opera, after one luxurious season, like the fine wife of a roving husband, began to lose its charms, and every day discovered to our satiety imperfections which our former fondness had been blind to. But of this I shall observe more in its place; in the meantime, let us enquire into the productions of our native theatre.

It may easily be conceived that by this entire reunion of the two companies, plays must generally have been performed to a more than usual advantage and exactness; for now every chief actor, according to his particular capacity, piqued himself upon rectifying those errors which during their divided state were almost unavoidable. Such a choice of actors added a richness to every good play as it was then served up to the public entertainment. The common people crowded to them with a more joyous expectation, and those of the higher taste returned to them as to old acquaintances, with new desires after a long absence.[12] In a word, all parties seemed better pleased but he who, one might imagine, had most reason to be so: the (lately) sole managing patentee. He, indeed, saw his power daily mouldering from his own hands into those of Mr Brett, whose gentlemanly manner of making everyone's business easy to him[13] threw their

11 i.e. the winter of 1708–9. LS2a 457–70 records fifteen performances of *Pyrrhus and Demetrius* from December 1708 to February 1709, with inflated prices of 5 shillings for the pit and half a guinea for the stage boxes (c.£60 and £130 in current values). It ran alongside Nicolini in *Il Trionfo di Camilla*, which ran for eight performances in January and February 1709 with prices at the same level (LS2a 464–8).

12 The *Muses Mercury* report of February 1708 states that new plays were in short supply in the immediate aftermath of the union (*Document Register* no.1955); Cibber's *The Lady's Last Stake* was an exception. In the winter of 1708–9, when Swiney's opera successes were at their height, there was a glut of Restoration and Shakespearean revivals, with plays by Congreve, Dryden, Farquhar, Fletcher, Otway, Shadwell, Shakespeare, and Vanbrugh featuring regularly (see LS2a 453–65).

13 On 31 March 1708 Brett appointed Cibber, Estcourt, and Wilks as co-managers, giving them discretion over hiring, pay, and other responsibilities, but within strict financial rules. No payment in excess of 40 shillings could be made more than once a week without the agreement of all three; benefit performances could only take place after 10 June each season if the recipient deposited £40 with the company treasurer, and a system of deductions from salary was introduced to help pay for the benefit outlay (*Document Register* no.1971). The arrangement instituted after Brett's withdrawal was challenged by Lord Chamberlain Kent on 30 April 1709 (LC 5/154, p.417; *Document Register* no.2015); for the subsequent closure order, see below, p.260 n.25.

old master under a disregard which he had not been used to; nor could, with all his happy change of affairs, support. Although this grave theatrical minister, of whom I have been obliged to make such frequent mention, had acquired the reputation of a most profound politician by being often incomprehensible, yet I am not sure that his conduct at this juncture gave us not an evident proof that he was, like other frail mortals, more a slave to his passions than his interest. For no creature ever seemed more fond of power that so little knew how to use it to his profit and reputation; otherwise he could not possibly have been so discontented, in his secure and prosperous state of the theatre, as to resolve at all hazards to destroy it. We shall now see what infallible measures he took to bring this laudable scheme to perfection.

He plainly saw that as this disagreeable prosperity was chiefly owing to the conduct of Mr Brett, there could be no hope of recovering the stage to its former confusion but by finding some effectual means to make Mr Brett weary of his charge. The most probable he could for the present think of in this distress was to call in the adventurers (whom for many years, by his defence in law, he had kept out) now to take care of their visibly improving interests.[14] This fair appearance of equity being known to be his own proposal, he rightly guessed would incline these adventurers to form a majority of votes on his side in all theatrical questions, and consequently become a check upon the power of Mr Brett, who had so visibly alienated the hearts of his theatrical subjects and now began to govern without him. When the adventurers, therefore, were re-admitted to their old government, after having recommended himself to them by proposing to make some small dividend of the profits (though he did not design that jest should be repeated), he took care that the creditors of the patent – who were then no inconsiderable body – should carry off the every week's clear profits in proportion to their several dues and demands. This conduct, so speciously just, he had hopes would let Mr Brett see that his share in the patent was not so valuable an acquisition as perhaps he might think it, and probably make a man of his turn to pleasure soon weary of the little profit and great plague it gave him.

14 There were apparently eighteen 'adventurers', judging by the number of signatories to the petition presented to Queen Anne in August 1709, claiming a financial interest in the theatre. In addition to Rich himself, the adventurers were Lord Guilford, Lord John Hervey, Dame Alice Brownlow, Mrs Shadwell, Sir Edward Smith, Sir Thomas Skipwith, George Sayer, Charles Killigrew (still Master of the Revels), Charles Davenant, John Metcalfe, Thomas Goodall, Ashburnham Toll, Ashburnham Frowd, William East, Richard Middlemore, Robert Gower, and William Collier (BL Add.MS 20,726, fols.22–3; *Document Register* no.2038).

Now, though these might be all notable expedients, yet I cannot say they would have wholly contributed to Mr Brett's quitting his post had not a matter of much stronger moment – an unexpected dispute between him and Sir Thomas Skipwith – prevailed with him to lay it down. For in the midst of this flourishing state of the patent, Mr Brett was surprised with a subpoena into Chancery from Sir Thomas Skipwith, who alleged in his bill that the conveyance he had made of his interest in the patent to Mr Brett was only intended in trust (whatever the intent might be, the deed itself, which I then read, made no mention of any trust whatever).[15] But whether Mr Brett (as Sir Thomas farther asserted) had previously, or after the deed was signed, given his word of honour that if he should ever make the stage turn to any account or profit, he would certainly restore it – that, indeed, I can say nothing to. But be the deed valid or void, the facts that apparently followed were that though Mr Brett, in his answer to this bill, absolutely denied his receiving this assignment either in trust or upon any limited condition of what kind soever, yet he made no farther defence in the cause.[16] But since he found Sir Thomas had thought fit on any account to sue for the restitution of it (and Mr Brett being himself conscious that as the world knew he had paid no consideration for it, his keeping it might be misconstrued or not favourably spoken of), or perhaps finding, though the profits were great they were constantly swallowed up (as has been observed) by the previous satisfaction of old debts, he grew so tired of the plague and trouble the whole affair had given him and was likely still to engage him in, that in a few weeks after, he withdrew himself from all concern with the theatre and quietly left Sir Thomas to find his better account in it. And thus stood this undecided right till, upon the demise of Sir Thomas, Mr Brett being allowed the charges he had been at in this attendance and prosecution of the union, reconveyed this share of the patent to Sir George Skipwith, the son and heir of Sir Thomas.[17]

---

15 Skipwith's action against Brett was lodged in February 1709 (C8/481/66; *Document Register* no.1999).

16 In fact, Brett continued to counter Skipwith's allegations as late as 29 July 1709, emphasizing the latter's liability in actions taken before Brett's acquisition of his shares (C10/545/39; *Document Register* no.2036).

17 George Brydges Skipwith inherited his father's shares in June 1710; Brett presumably returned them to Sir Thomas between the legal case beginning February 1709 and Lord Chamberlain Kent's intervention in April (as above, p.254 n.13) which resulted in the June closure described below, pp.262–4. Hotson, p.395, cites Brett's testimony that he had 'concerned himself in the management of the affairs' of the theatre and 'been at considerable charge and expense in bringing the same to a better posture'.

Our politician, the old patentee, having thus fortunately got rid of Mr Brett, who had so rashly brought the patent once more to be a profitable tenure, was now again at liberty to choose rather to lose all than not to have it all to himself.

I have elsewhere observed that nothing can so effectually secure the strength or contribute to the prosperity of a good company as the directors of it having always, as near as possible, an amicable understanding with three or four of their best actors, whose good or ill will must naturally make a wide difference in their profitable (or useless) manner of serving them.[18] While the principal are kept reasonably easy, the lower class can never be troublesome without hurting themselves; but when a valuable actor is hardly treated, the master must be a very cunning man that finds his account in it. We shall now see how far experience will verify this observation.

The patentees thinking themselves secure in being restored to their former absolute power over this (now) only company, chose rather to govern it by the reverse of the method I have recommended. For though the daily charge of their united company amounted not, by a good deal, to what either of the two companies now in Drury Lane or Covent Garden singly arises, they notwithstanding fell into their former politics of thinking every shilling taken from a hired actor so much clear gain to the proprietor. Many of their people, therefore, were actually (if not injudiciously) reduced in their pay, and others given to understand the same fate was designed them, of which last number I myself was one – which occurs to my memory by the answer I made to one of the adventurers, who (in justification of their intended proceeding) told me that my salary, though it should be less than it was by ten shillings a week, would still be more than ever Goodman had, who was a better actor than I could pretend to be;[19] to which I replied, 'This may be true but then you know, sir, it is as true that Goodman was forced to go upon the highway for a livelihood'. As this was a known fact of Goodman, my mentioning it on that occasion I believe was of service to me; at least, my salary was not reduced after it. To say a word or two more of Goodman, so celebrated an actor in his time, perhaps may set the conduct of the patentees in a clearer light. Though Goodman had left the stage before I came to it, I had some slight acquaintance with him. About the time of his being expected to be an evidence against Sir

18 Cibber's 'three or four' allows him diplomatic latitude in including Estcourt, Doggett, and/or Booth among the original triumvirate appointed by Brett.
19 i.e. Cardell Goodman (see above, p.72 n.31). As Lowe notes, the episode suggests that Rich allowed investors a direct say in the running of the theatre.

John Fenwick in the assassination plot in 1696,[20] I happened to meet him at dinner at Sir Thomas Skipwith's, who as he was an agreeable companion himself, liked Goodman for the same quality. Here it was that Goodman, without disguise or sparing himself, fell into a laughing account of several loose passages of his younger life, as his being expelled the University of Cambridge for being one of the hot-headed sparks who were concerned in the cutting and defacing the Duke of Monmouth's picture, then Chancellor of that place.[21] But this disgrace, it seems, had not disqualified him for the stage, which, like the sea service, refuses no man for his morals that is able-bodied. There, as an actor, he soon grew into a different reputation; but whatever his merit might be, the pay of a hired hero in those days was so very low that he was forced, it seems, to take the air (as he called it) and borrow what money the first man he met had about him. But this being his first exploit of that kind which the scantiness of his theatrical fortune had reduced him to, King James was prevailed upon to pardon him; which Goodman said was doing him so particular an honour, that no man could wonder if his acknowledgment had carried him a little farther than ordinary into the interest of that prince. But as he had lately been out of luck in backing his old master, he had now no way to get home the life he was out upon his account but by being under the same obligations to King William.

Another anecdote of him (though not quite so dishonourably enterprising) which I had from his own mouth at a different time, will equally show to what low shifts in life the poor provision for good actors under the

20 Lowe quotes from John Doran's *Their Majesties' Servants*, 2nd ed., 2 vols. (1888), I.103, on Goodman's connection with the Jacobite plot to kill William III allegedly hatched by Sir John Fenwick (1645–97):

> King James having saved Cardell's neck, Goodman, out of pure gratitude, perhaps, became a Tory (and something more) when William sat in the seat of his father-in-law. After Queen Mary's death, Scum was in the Fenwick and Charnock plot to kill the king. When the plot was discovered, Scum was ready to peach. As Fenwick's life was thought by his friends to be safe if Goodman could be bought off and got out of the way, the rogue was looked for at The Fleece in Covent Garden, famous for homicides, and at the robbers' and the revellers' den, The Dog in Drury Lane. Fenwick's agent, O'Bryan, erstwhile soldier and highwayman, now a Jacobite agent, found Scum at The Dog, and would then and there have cut his throat, had not Scum consented to the pleasant alternative of accepting £500 a year, and a residence abroad ... Scum suddenly disappeared, and Lord Manchester, our Ambassador in Paris, inquired after him in vain. It is impossible to say whether the rogue died by an avenging hand, or starvation.

The co-conspirator was Robert Charnock (1663–96), Fellow of Magdalen College Oxford and a Catholic priest; both he and Fenwick were executed.

21 James Scott, Duke of Monmouth and Charles II's illegitimate son (1649–85), was Chancellor of the University of Cambridge from 1674 to 1682, when he was deprived of the post by royal injunction. As Evans notes, the destruction of his portrait may, accordingly, have been officially encouraged.

early government of the patent reduced them. In the younger days of their heroism, Captain Griffin and Goodman were confined by their moderate salaries to the economy of lying together in the same bed and having but one whole shirt between them. One of them, being under the obligation of a rendezvous with a fair lady, insisted upon his wearing it out of his turn, which occasioned so high a dispute that the combat was immediately demanded, and accordingly their pretensions to it were decided by a fair tilt upon the spot, in the room where they lay. But whether Clytus or Alexander was obliged to see no company till a worse could be washed for him seems not to be a material point in their history, or to my purpose.[22]

By this rate of Goodman (who, till the time of his quitting the stage, never had more than what is called forty shillings a week) it may be judged how cheap the labour of actors had been formerly; and the patentees thought it a folly to continue the higher price which their divisions had since raised them to, now there was but one market for them. But alas, they had forgot their former fatal mistake of squabbling with their actors in 1695;[23] nor did they make any allowance for the changes and operations of time, or enough consider the interest the actors had in the Lord Chamberlain, on whose protection they might always rely, and whose decrees had been less restrained by precedent than those of a Lord Chancellor.[24]

In this mistaken view of their interest, the patentees, by treating their actors as enemies, really made them so. And when once the masters of a hired company think not their actors' hearts as necessary as their hands, they cannot be said to have agreed for above half the work they are able to do in a day. Or, if an unexpected success should notwithstanding make the profits in any gross disproportion greater than the wages, the wages will always have something worse than a murmur at the head of them, that will not only measure the merit of the actor by the gains of the proprietor, but will never naturally be quiet till every scheme of getting into property has been tried to make the servant his own master. And this (as far as experience can make me judge) will always be, in either of these cases, the state of our English Theatre. What truth there may be in this observation, we are now coming to a proof of.

To enumerate all the particular acts of power in which the patentees daily bore hard upon this (now) only company of actors might be as tedious as unnecessary. I shall therefore come at once to their most material

22 For Griffin, see above, p.63 n.56. Goodman played Alexander in Lee's *The Rival Queens* probably from December 1685 (LS1 344). On Cibber's evidence, Griffin presumably played Clytus, Alexander's Master of Horse, in the same play. Act IV Scene 2 dramatizes the quarrel between them leading to Clytus's death.

23 As described above, pp.130–2.

24 As much, perhaps, because of the high turnover of Lords Chamberlain (an average of one every four years during Cibber's career) as the fragility of previous rulings.

grievance, upon which they grounded their complaint to the Lord Chamberlain, who in the year following (1709) took effectual measures for their relief.[25]

The patentees observing that the benefit plays of the actors towards the latter end of the season brought the most crowded audiences in the year, began to think their own interests too much neglected by these partial favours of the town to their actors; and therefore judged it would not be impolitic in such wholesome annual profits to have a fellow feeling with them. Accordingly, an *indulto*[26] was laid of one third out of the profits of every benefit, for the proper use and behoof of the patent. But, that a clear judgment may be formed of the equity or hardship of this imposition, it will be necessary to show from whence, and from what causes, the actors' claim to benefits originally proceeded.

During the reign of King Charles, an actor's benefit had never been heard of. The first indulgence of this kind was given to Mrs Barry (as has been formerly observed)[27] in King James's time, in consideration of the extraordinary applause that had followed her performance. But there this favour rested to her alone, till after the division of the only company in 1695; at which time the patentees were soon reduced to pay their actors half in good words, and half in ready money. In this precarious condition some particular actors (however binding their agreements might be) were too poor, or too wise, to go to law with a lawyer, and therefore rather chose to compound their arrears, for their being admitted to the chance of having them made up by the profits of a benefit play. This expedient had this consequence: that the patentees, though their daily audiences might and did sometimes mend, still kept the short subsistence of their actors at a stand and grew more steady in their resolution so to keep them, as they found them less apt to mutiny while their hopes of being cleared off by a benefit were depending. In a year or two, these benefits grew so advantageous that they became, at last, the chief article in every actor's agreement.

Now, though the agreements of these united actors I am speaking of (in 1708) were as yet only verbal, yet that made no difference in the honest

25 A reference to Lord Chamberlain Kent's order of 30 April 1709 (LC 5/154, p.417; *Document Register* no.2015), which required Drury Lane management to deduct no more than £40 in costs from actors' benefit earnings; when management failed to comply, the theatre was closed (LC 5/154, p.437; *Document Register* no.2023). Swiney took steps to settle with the investors: on 11 August 1709 he published in *The Daily Courant* a request that anyone with a financial interest in Drury Lane should meet him at Nando's coffee house at 3pm that afternoon. For discussion of the episode, see Judith Milhous and Robert D. Hume, 'The Silencing of Drury Lane in 1709', *Theatre Journal* vol. 32, no.4 (December 1980), 427–47.

26 i.e. the duty levied on imports by the Spanish Crown. Cibber associates Rich's ways with a hostile Catholic power.

27 See above, p.115 n.93.

obligation to keep them. But, as honour at that time happened to have but a loose hold of their consciences, the patentees rather chose to give it the slip and went on with their work without it. No actor, therefore, could have his benefit fixed till he had first signed a paper signifying his voluntary acceptance of it upon the above conditions, any claims from custom to the contrary notwithstanding. Several at first refused to sign this paper, upon which the next in rank were offered, on the same conditions, to come before the refusers. This smart expedient got some few of the fearful the preference to their seniors, who at last – seeing the time was too short for a present remedy and that they must either come into the boat or lose their tide – were forced to comply with what they (as yet silently) resented as the severest injury. In this situation, therefore, they chose to let the principal benefits be over, that their grievances might swell into some bulk before they made any application for redress to the Lord Chamberlain; who, upon hearing their general complaint, ordered the patentees to show cause why their benefits had been diminished one third, contrary to the common usage. The patentees pleaded the signed agreement and the actors' receipts of the other two thirds in full satisfaction. But these were proved to have been exacted from them by the methods already mentioned. They notwithstanding insist[ed] upon them as lawful. But as law and equity do not always agree, they were looked upon as unjust and arbitrary; whereupon the patentees were warned at their peril to refuse the actors full satisfaction.[28] But here it was thought necessary that judgment should be for some time respited, till the actors who had leave so to do could form a body strong enough to make the inclination of the Lord Chamberlain to relieve them practicable.

Accordingly, Swiney (who was then sole director of the opera only) had permission to enter into a private treaty with such of the united actors in Drury Lane as might be thought fit to head a company under their own management, and to be sharers with him in the Haymarket. The actors chosen for this charge were Wilks, Doggett, Mrs Oldfield, and myself.[29] But before I proceed, lest it should seem surprising that neither Betterton, Mrs Barry, Mrs Bracegirdle or Booth were parties in this treaty, it must be observed that Betterton was now seventy-three and rather chose, with the infirmities of age upon him, to rely on such salary as might be appointed him than to involve himself in the cares and hurry that must unavoidably attend the regulation of a new company. As to the two celebrated actresses I have named, this has been my first proper occasion of making it known that they had both quitted the stage the year before this transaction was thought

28 As per p.260 n.25 above.
29 The agreement was dated 10 March 1709 (C7/668/31; *Document Register* no.2002). Anne Oldfield is not named in it, for reasons explained in the subsequent passage.

of.[30] And Booth as yet was scarce out of his minority as an actor, or only in the promise of that reputation which in about four or five years after he happily arrived at. However, at this juncture he was not so far overlooked as not to be offered a valuable addition to his salary; but this he declined, being (while the patentees were under this distress) as much, if not more, in favour with their chief manager as a schematist than as an actor. And indeed, he appeared to my judgment more inclined to risk his fortune in Drury Lane, where he should have no rival in parts or power, than on any terms to embark in the Haymarket, where he was sure to meet with opponents in both.[31] However, this his separation from our interest, when our all was at stake, afterwards kept his advancement to a share with us in our more successful days longer postponed than otherwise it probably might have been.[32]

When Mrs Oldfield was nominated as a joint sharer in our new agreement to be made with Swiney, Doggett – who had no objection to her merit – insisted that our affairs could never be upon a secure foundation if there was more than one sex admitted to the management of them. He therefore hoped that if we offered Mrs Oldfield a *carte blanche* instead of a share, she would not think herself slighted. This was instantly agreed to, and Mrs Oldfield received it rather as a favour than a disobligation. Her demands therefore were two hundred pounds a year certain, and a benefit clear of all charges; which were readily signed to.[33] Her easiness on this occasion, some years after (when our establishment was in prosperity) made us with less reluctancy advance her two hundred pounds to three hundred guineas per annum, with her usual benefit – which upon an average, for several years at least, doubled that sum.[34]

When a sufficient number of actors were engaged under our confederacy with Swiney, it was then judged a proper time for the Lord Chamberlain's power to operate;[35] which, by lying above a month dormant, had so far recovered the patentees from any apprehensions of what might fall upon

---

30 Anne Bracegirdle retired in February 1707 and Elizabeth Barry in June 1708. Barry returned to the Haymarket Company for the 1709–10 season and Bracegirdle for Betterton's benefit performance in Congreve's *Love for Love* on 7 April 1709 (LS2a 479).

31 For the reasons behind Booth's decision, see also below, 350–1.

32 The licensing agreement Booth shared with Cibber, Wilks, Doggett, and William Collier is dated 11 November 1713 (LC 5/155, fol.149; *Document Register* no.2230); for his 'advancement' see below, p.303 n.48. Collier already had a financial interest in the theatre (see above, p.255 n.14).

33 The agreement between Swiney and Oldfield is dated 21 April 1709 and specifies £200 a year for thirteen years, plus a February benefit from which no deductions would be made (LC 7/3, fols.111–12; *Document Register* no.2011).

34 A report in the *Morning Chronicle and London Advertiser* of 22 August 1781 compares salaries then and in earlier times. For 1729, it gives Oldfield's salary as £420 (c.£86,000 in current values), based on 12 guineas a week for acting only until the end of April, with £60 for a 'clear benefit', i.e. without deductions (*Document Register* no.3439).

35 Cibber, Wilks, and Doggett came to their agreement with Swiney on 10 March 1709 (C7/668/31; *Document Register* no.2002), and further agreements followed until 24

them from their late usurpations on the benefits of the actors, that they began to set their marks upon those who had distinguished themselves in the application for redress. Several little disgraces were put upon them, particularly in the disposal of parts in plays to be revived; and as visible a partiality was shown in the promotion of those in their interest, though their endeavours to serve them could be of no extraordinary use. How often does history show us in the same state of courts, the same politics have been practised? All this while the other party were passively silent; till one day, the actor who particularly solicited their cause at the Lord Chamberlain's office being shown there the order signed for absolutely silencing the patentees and ready to be served, flew back with the news to his companions, then at a rehearsal in which he had been wanted;[36] when, being called to his part and something hastily questioned by the patentee for his neglect of business, this actor, I say, with an erected look and a theatrical spirit, at once threw off the mask and roundly told him: 'Sir, I have now no more business here than you have; in half an hour, you will neither have actors to command nor authority to employ them'. The patentee, who though he could not readily comprehend his mysterious manner of speaking, had just a glimpse of terror enough from the words to soften his reproof into a cold formal declaration that if he would not do his work, he should not be paid. But now, to complete the catastrophe of these theatrical commotions, enters the messenger with the order of silence in his hand; whom the same actor officiously introduced, telling the patentee that the gentleman wanted to speak with him, from the Lord Chamberlain. When the messenger had delivered the order, the actor throwing his head over his shoulder towards the patentee, in the manner of Shakespeare's Harry the Eighth to Cardinal Wolsey cried, 'Read o'er that! And now – to breakfast, with what appetite you may'.[37] Though these words might be spoken in too vindictive and insulting a manner to be commended, yet from the fullness of a heart injuriously treated, and now relieved by that instant occasion, why might they not be pardoned?

May with John Mills, William Bullock, Benjamin Johnson, Anne Oldfield, William Penkethman, Benjamin Husband, and Mary Porter (*Document Register* nos.2004, 2006, 2007, 2011, 2016, 2019, and 2022). On 6 June 1709 the silencing order was issued against Rich and Drury Lane (LC 5/154, p.437; *Document Register* no.2023).

36 This actor was doubtless Cibber himself. The date of this episode is presumably 6 June 1709, as per n.35 above. Cibber and Rich were already in dispute; Cibber took legal action on 29 June 1709 (C10/537/22; *Document Register* no.2026). The play scheduled for 7 June was Thomas Shadwell's *Epsom Wells*, in which Cibber played Kick (LS2a 497).

37 *Henry VIII*, III.ii.248–50: 'Read o'er this. / And after, this, and then to breakfast with / What appetite you have.' Cibber played Surrey in the play from 1707; the character is present when the king chastises Wolsey. He took over Wolsey only from 1716; the line he quotes was his cue for the soliloquy beginning, 'What should this mean?'

The authority of the patent now no longer subsisting, all the confederated actors immediately walked out of the house, to which they never returned till they became themselves the tenants and masters of it.

Here again we see an higher instance of the authority of a Lord Chamberlain than any of those I have elsewhere mentioned. From whence that power might be derived, as I have already said, I am not lawyer enough to know; however, it is evident that a lawyer obeyed it, though to his cost, which might incline one to think that the law was not clearly against it. Be that as it may, since the law has lately made it no longer a question, let us drop the enquiry and proceed to the facts which followed this order that silenced the patent.

From this last injudicious disagreement of the patentees with their principal actors, and from what they had suffered on the same occasion in the division of their only company in 1695, might we not imagine there was something of infatuation[38] in their management? For though I allow actors in general, when they are too much indulged or governed by an unsteady head, to be as unruly a multitude as power can be plagued with, yet there is a medium which, if cautiously observed by a candid use of power (making them always know, without feeling their superior, neither suffering their encroachments nor invading their rights, with an immoveable adherence to the accepted laws they are to walk by) – such a regulation, I say, has never failed in my observation to have made them a tractable and profitable society. If the government of a well-established theatre were to be compared to that of a nation, there is no one act of policy or misconduct in the one or the other in which the manager might not in some parallel case (laugh if you please) be equally applauded or condemned with the statesman. Perhaps this will not be found so wild a conceit if you look into the 193rd *Tatler*, vol.4, where the affairs of the state and those of the very stage which I am now treating of are in a letter from Downes the prompter[39] compared and, with

---

38 i.e. extravagant folly, impetuousness (*OED* 1).
39 Lowe quotes the letter in full. John Downes had been made redundant in 1706 and
    devoted the next two years to writing *Roscius Anglicanus*. He continued to observe the
    theatre world until his death in 1712; however, the authorship of the letter is contested.
        Honoured Sir,
                July 1. 1710.
        Finding by diverse of your late papers that you are friend to the profession
        of which I was many years an unworthy member, I the rather make bold to
        crave your advice touching a proposal that has been lately made me of coming
        into business and sub-administration of stage affairs. I have, from my youth,
        been bred up behind the curtain, and been a prompter from the time of the
        Restoration. I have seen many changes, as well of scenes as of actors, and have
        known men within my remembrance arrive to the highest dignities of the theatre

a great deal of wit and humour, set upon an equal foot of policy. The letter is supposed to have been written in the last change of the ministry in Queen Anne's time. I will therefore venture, upon the authority of that author's imagination, to carry the comparison as high as it can possibly go and say that as I remember one of our princes in the last century to have lost his

who made their entrance in the quality of mutes, joint-stools, flowerpots, and tapestry hangings. It cannot be unknown to the nobility and gentry that a gentleman of the Inns of Court, and a deep intriguer, had some time since worked himself into the sole management and direction of the theatre. Nor is it less notorious that his restless ambition and subtle machinations did manifestly tend to the extirpation of the good old British actors and the introduction of foreign pretenders, such as Harlequins, French dancers and Roman singers; which, though they impoverished the proprietors and imposed on the audience, were for some time tolerated by reason of his dexterous insinuations, which prevailed upon a few deluded women, especially the vizard masks, to believe that the stage was in danger. But his schemes were soon exposed, and the great ones that supported him withdrawing their favour, he made his exit and remained for a season in obscurity. During this retreat the Machiavellian was not idle, but secretly fomented divisions, and wrought over to his side some of the inferior actors, reserving a trap door to himself, to which only he had a key. This entrance secured, this cunning person, to complete his company, bethought himself of calling in the most eminent of strollers from all parts of the kingdom. I have seen them all ranged together behind the scenes; but they are many of them persons that never trod the stage before, and so very awkward and ungainly that it is impossible to believe the audience will bear them. He was looking over his catalogue of plays, and indeed picked up a good tolerable set of grave faces for counsellors to appear in the famous scene of *Venice Preserved,* when the danger is over; but they being but mere outsiders, and the actors having a great mind to play *The Tempest,* there is not a man of them when he is to perform anything above dumb show is capable of acting with a good grace so much as the part of Trincalo. However, the master persists in his design, and is fitting up the old storm; but I am afraid he will not be able to procure able sailors or experienced officers for love or money.

Besides all this, when he comes to cast the parts there is so great a confusion amongst them for want of proper actors, that for my part I am wholly discouraged. The play with which they design to open is *The Duke and No Duke;* and they are so put to it, that the master himself is to act the conjurer, and have no one for the General but honest George Powell.

Now, sir, they being so much at a loss for the dramatis personae, *viz.* the persons to enact, and the whole frame of the house being designed to be altered, I desire your opinion whether you think it advisable for me to undertake to prompt 'em. For though I can clash swords when they represent a battle, and have yet lungs enough to huzzah their victories, I question, if I should prompt 'em right whether they would act accordingly. – I am

> *Your Honour's most humble Servant,*
> J.DOWNES.

P.S. Sir, since I writ this, I am credibly informed that they design a new house in Lincoln's Inn Fields, near the Popish chapel, to be ready by Michaelmas next; which indeed is but repairing an old one that has already failed. You know the honest man who kept the office is gone already.

crown by too arbitrary a use of his power (though he knew how fatal the same measures had been to his unhappy father before him),[40] why should we wonder that the same passions taking possession of men in lower life, by an equally impolitic usage of their theatrical subjects, should have involved the patentees in proportionable calamities?

During the vacation which immediately followed the silence of the patent, both parties were at leisure to form their schemes for the winter, for the patentee would still hold out, notwithstanding his being so miserably maimed or over-matched. He had no more regard to blows than a blind cock of the game.[41] He might be beaten, but would never yield; the patent was still in his possession, and the broad seal to it visibly as fresh as ever. Besides, he had yet some actors in his service at a much cheaper rate than those who had left him; the salaries of which last, now they would not work for him he was not obliged to pay.[42] In this way of thinking he still kept together such as had not been invited over to the Haymarket, or had been influenced by Booth to follow his fortune in Drury Lane.

By the patentee's keeping these remains of his broken forces together, it is plain that he imagined this order of silence, like others of the same kind, would be recalled of course after a reasonable time of obedience had been paid to it. But it seems he had relied too much upon former precedents; nor had his politics yet dived into the secret that the Court power, with which the patent had been so long and often at variance, had now a mind to take the public diversions more absolutely into their own hands. Not that I have any stronger reasons for this conjecture than that the patent never, after this order of silence, got leave to play during the Queen's reign. But upon the accession of his late Majesty, power having then a different aspect, the

40 i.e. James II and his father, Charles I.

41 Cockfighting remained a popular sport until it was banned in 1835; cocks were sometimes blinded in advance of the contest. Rich engaged in legal action against individual former actors during the summer (*Document Register* nos.2026, 2027, and 2037) as well as prompting his treasurer, Zachary Baggs, to publish their salaries (see below, n.42).

42 A petition of late July 1709 for the re-opening of Drury Lane was signed by twenty-four actors, among them Barton Booth and George Powell (*Document Register* no.2035). Earlier in the month the Drury Lane treasurer, Zachary Baggs, had published a pamphlet advertising the salaries of the actors who had deserted Rich. Highlights of this *Advertisement Concerning the Poor Actors, who under Pretence of hard Usage from the Patentees, are about to desert their Service* are alleged payments of £259 1s 5d to Wilks, £1,077 3s 8d to Oldfield, and £450 to Betterton for a single benefit performance. This was all in spite of not playing a full season because Prince George's death in the autumn of 1708 caused a two-week suspension (described by Baggs as a seven-week suspension) and the enforced June closure. Cibber's total gain is said to be £162 10s 10d (c.£13,000 in current values), including a benefit profit of £51 with additional gifts of £50 (LS2a 497–8).

patent found no difficulty in being permitted to exercise its former authority for acting plays etc; which, however, from this time of their lying still in 1709, did not happen till 1714, which the old patentee never lived to see. For he died about six weeks before the new-built theatre in Lincoln's Inn Fields was opened, where the first play acted was *The Recruiting Officer*, under the management of his heirs and successors.[43] But of that theatre it is not yet time to give any farther account.[44]

The first point resolved on by the comedians now re-established in the Haymarket[45] was to alter the auditory part of their theatre, the inconveniencies of which have been fully enlarged upon in a former chapter. What embarrassed them most in this design was their want of time to do it in a more complete manner than it now remains in; otherwise they had brought it to the original model of that in Drury Lane, only in a larger proportion, as the wider walls of it would require. As there are not many spectators who may remember what form the Drury Lane Theatre stood in about forty years ago (before the old patentee, to make it hold more money, took it in his head to alter it), it were but justice to lay the original figure which Sir Christopher Wren first gave it,[46] and the alterations of it now standing, in a fair light, that equal spectators may see, if they were at their choice, which of the structures would incline them to a preference. But in this appeal, I only speak to such spectators as allow a good play well acted to be the most valuable entertainment of the stage. Whether such plays (leaving the skill of the dead or living actors equally out of the question) have been more or less recommended in their presentation by either of these different forms of that theatre, is our present matter of enquiry.

It must be observed then, that the area or platform of the old stage projected about four foot forwarder, in a semi-oval figure, parallel to the

43 The new Lincoln's Inn Fields Theatre opened on 18 December 1714 under the management of Rich's sons, John and Christopher Mosyer. According to the former's register of performances, takings for Farquhar's *The Recruiting Officer* were £143 (Folger W.a.32; *Document Register* no.2481). John Rich himself spoke the Prologue, claiming to be 'an orphan of the British Stage' and asking for support in memory of his father (Nottingham MS Pw 2V 133; *Document Register* no.2482).

44 The fortunes of the new theatre are described below, pp.318–19.

45 On 8 July 1709 Lord Chamberlain Kent reaffirmed his Drury Lane closure order of 6 June and gave Owen Swiney permission to recruit its actors to perform spoken-word plays at the Haymarket (LC 5/154, p.446; *Document Register* no.2030).

46 Wren was Surveyor of the King's Works from 24 November 1669 until 1718 and was responsible for preparing the Whitehall Palace theatre for court entertainments (see *Document Register* no.919 etc.). A sketch by him in the library of All Souls College Oxford (Figure 11) bears some relationship to the original Drury Lane theatre described by Cibber.

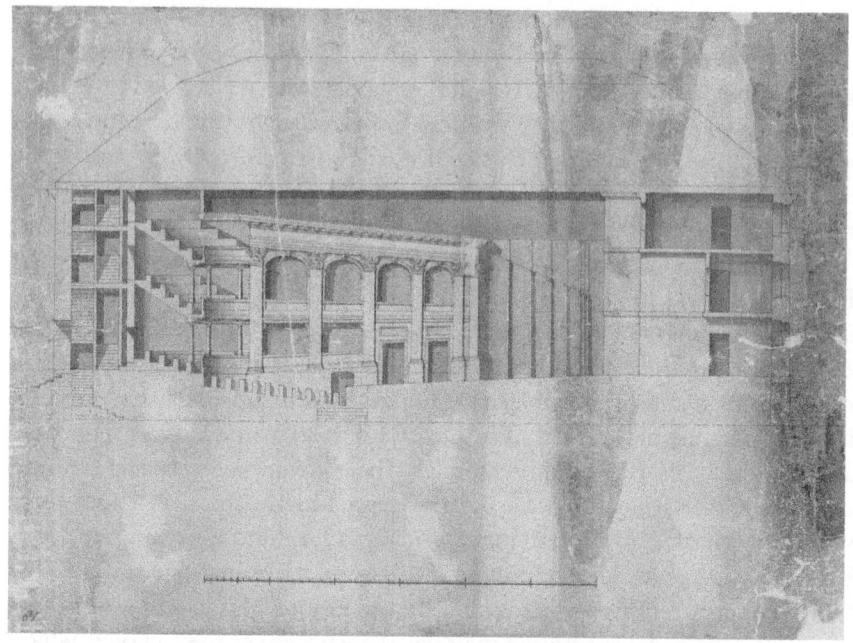

11. Christopher Wren, longitudinal section of a theatre.

benches of the pit, and that the former lower doors of entrance for the actors were brought down between the two foremost (and then only) pilasters; in the place of which doors, now the two stage-boxes are fixed; that where the doors of entrance now are, there formerly stood two additional side-wings in front to a full set of scenes, which had then almost a double effect in their loftiness and magnificence.[47]

By this original form, the usual station of the actors in almost every scene was advanced at least ten foot nearer to the audience than they now can be; because, not only from the stage's being shortened in front, but likewise from the additional interposition of those stage-boxes, the actors (in respect to the spectators that fill them) are kept so much more backward from the main audience than they used to be. But when the actors were in possession of that forwarder space to advance upon, the voice was then more in the centre of the house, so that the most distant ear had scarce the least doubt or difficulty in hearing what fell from the weakest utterance. All objects were thus drawn nearer to the sense; every painted scene was stronger; every grand scene and dance more extended; every rich or fine-coloured habit had a more lively lustre. Nor was the minutest

47 For further illustrations, see Leacroft, pp.90–117.

motion of a feature (properly changing with the passion or humour it suited) ever lost, as they frequently must be in the obscurity of too great a distance; and how valuable an advantage the facility of hearing distinctly is to every well-acted scene, every common spectator is a judge. A voice scarce raised above the tone of a whisper – either in tenderness, resignation, innocent distress or jealousy suppressed – often have as much concern with the heart as the most clamorous passions; and when on any of these occasions such affecting speeches are plainly heard or lost, how wide is the difference from the great or little satisfaction received from them? To all this a master of a company may say, 'I now receive ten pounds more than could have been taken formerly, in every full house!' Not unlikely. But might not his house be oftener full if the auditors were oftener pleased? Might not every bad house, too, by a possibility of being made every day better, add as much to one side of his account as it could take from the other? If what I have said carries any truth in it, why might not the original form of this theatre be restored? But let this digression avail what it may, the actors now returned to the Haymarket, as I have observed, wanting nothing but length of time to have governed their alteration of that theatre by this original model of Drury Lane which I have recommended. As their time therefore was short, they made their best use of it: they did something to it. They contracted its wideness by three ranges of boxes on each side, and brought down its enormous high ceiling within so proportionable a compass that it effectually cured those hollow undulations of the voice formerly complained of. The remedy had its effect; their audiences exceeded their expectation. There was now no other theatre open against them;[48] they had the town to themselves; they were their own masters, and the profits of their industry came into their own pockets.

Yet with all this fair weather, the season of their uninterrupted prosperity was not yet arrived, for the great expense and thinner audiences of the opera (of which they then were equally directors) was a constant drawback upon their gains; yet not so far, but that their income this year was better

---

48 The redeveloped Queen's Theatre Haymarket, reopened on 15 September 1709 with Betterton as Othello. Writing to Elizabeth Stockwell five days later, Sir John Perceval said the play 'drew all the stragglers in town together' (LS2a 512). At some time in November, Swiney learned of plans to reopen Drury Lane and asked Lord Chamberlain Kent to confirm his monopoly (HTC TS992.31D, 37; *Document Register* no.2051). With Aaron Hill as manager, William Collier was then permitted to reopen Drury Lane on 23 November 1709 (LC 7/3, fol.33; *Document Register* no.2057). It did not go to plan; Collier testified that Rich had removed the costumes needed for Dryden's *Aureng-Zebe*. A comedy was probably played instead (LS2a 524). See also below, p.274–5.

than in their late station at Drury Lane.[49] But by the short experience we had then had of operas; by the high reputation they seemed to have been arrived at the year before; by their power of drawing the whole body of nobility (as by enchantment) to their solemnities; by that prodigality of expense at which they were so willing to support them; and from the late extraordinary profits Swiney had made of them – what mountains did we not hope from this molehill? But alas, the fairy vision was vanished: this bridal beauty was grown familiar to the general taste, and satiety began to make excuses for its want of appetite. Or, what is still stranger, its late admirers now as much valued their judgment in being able to find out the faults of the performers as they had before in discovering their excellencies. The truth is that this kind of entertainment being so entirely sensual, it had no possibility of getting the better of our reason but by its novelty, and that novelty could never be supported but by an annual change of the best voices; which, like the finest flowers, bloom but for a season, and when that is over are only dead nosegays. From this natural cause, we have seen within these two years even Farinelli singing to an audience of five-and-thirty pounds; and yet, if common fame may be credited, the same voice, so neglected in one country, has in another had charms sufficient to make that crown sit easy on the head of a monarch which the jealousy of politicians (who had their views in his keeping it) feared, without some such extraordinary amusement, his satiety of empire might tempt him a second time to resign.[50]

There is, too, in the very species of an Italian singer, such an innate, fantastical pride and caprice that the government of them (here at least) is almost impracticable. This distemper, as we were not sufficiently warned or apprised of, threw our musical affairs into perplexities we knew not easily how to get out of.[51] There is scarce a sensible auditor in the kingdom that has not, since that time, had occasion to laugh at the several instances of it. But what is still more ridiculous, these costly canary-birds have sometimes infested the whole body of our dignified lovers of music with the same

49 Between 27 October and 24 November 1709, the Queen's Theatre Haymarket repertory featured numerous performances by Nicolini of past operatic favourites such as *Il Trionfo di Camilla*, *Pyrrhus and Demetrius*, and *Thomyris, Queen of Scythia* (LS2a 518–24). On the evidence of LS2a, however, spoken-word drama predominated, with Cibber's *Love's Last Shift* and *The Careless Husband* prominent.

50 Philip V of Spain (1683–1746) abdicated in 1724, only to reassume the throne later that year when his son died. From August 1737 he was sung to nightly by Farinelli as a cure for depression.

51 In May 1710 Nicolini became embroiled in a bitter dispute about pay and named Cibber as one of those 'trying to get him so disgusted he will cease to support the opera' (HTC Coke, no.67; *Document Register* no.2083).

12. 'Implacable pretensions to superiority': Faustina Bordoni, after
the portrait by Rosalba Carrier.

childish animosities. Ladies have been known to decline their visits upon
account of their being of a different musical party. Caesar and Pompey
made not a warmer division in the Roman republic than those heroines,
their countrywomen the Faustina and Cuzzoni, blew up in our commonwealth of academical music by their implacable pretensions to superiority![52]
And while this greatness of soul is their unalterable virtue, it will never be
practicable to make two capital singers of the same sex do as they should do
in one opera at the same time – no, not though England were to double the

52 Faustina Bordoni (1700–81), an Italian soprano brought to London by Handel in 1726,
and Francesca Cuzzoni (1700–70), initially engaged by John James Heidegger in 1722
but debuting the following year in Handel's *Ottone*. See Figure 12. Cibber's reference
to Caesar and Pompey may be prompted by Cuzzoni's role as Cleopatra in Handel's
Giulio Cesare (1724). The public rivalry between the two singers led to a brawl during a
May 1727 performance of Giovanni Bononcini's *Astynax* (*Astianatte*), with Cuzzoni as
Andromache and Bordoni as Hermione (LS2 924).

sums it has already thrown after them. For even in their own country, where an extraordinary occasion has called a greater number of their best to sing together, the mischief they have made has been proportionable; an instance of which, if I am rightly informed, happened at Parma, where upon the celebration of the marriage of that Duke, a collection was made of the most eminent voices that expense or interest could purchase, to give as complete an opera as the whole vocal power of Italy could form.[53] But when it came to the proof of this musical project, behold what woeful work they made of it! Every performer would be a Caesar or nothing; their several pretensions to preference were not to be limited within the laws of harmony; they would all choose their own songs, but not more to set off themselves than to oppose or deprive another of an occasion to shine. Yet anyone would sing a bad song provided nobody else had a good one, till at last they were thrown together like so many feathered warriors for a battle royal in a cockpit, where every one was obliged to kill another to save himself! What pity it was these forward misses and masters of music had not been engaged to entertain the court of some King of Morocco, that could have known a good opera from a bad one! With how much ease would such a director have brought them to better order? But alas, as it has been said of greater things,

Suis et ipsa Roma viribus ruit.

Hor.[54]

Imperial Rome fell by the too great strength of its own citizens! So fell this mighty opera, ruined by the too great excellency of its singers! For upon the whole it proved to be as barbarously bad as if malice itself had composed it.[55]

Now though something of this kind, equally provoking, has generally embarrassed the state of operas these thirty years, yet it was the misfortune of the managing actors at the Haymarket to have felt the first effects of it.[56] The honour of the singer and the interest of the undertaker were so often at variance that the latter began to have but a bad bargain of it. But not to impute more to the caprice of those performers than was really true,

---

53 Probably a reference to Antonio Farnese (1679–1731), Duke of Parma and Piacenza, known for his extravagant entertainments. He married Enrichetta d'Este of Modena in 1727.

54 i.e. 'Through her own strength, Rome is ruining itself', from Horace, *Epodes* no.14, line 2.

55 Sporadic revivals of *Pyrrhus and Demetrius*, *Thomyris, Queen of Scythia*, and *Almahide* were mounted through the 1709–10 winter season '[a]t the desire of several ladies of quality' (e.g. LS2a 528); otherwise the Queen's Theatre Haymarket began to refocus on comedy and tragedy.

56 i.e. disputes over payment between singers and managers, such as that between Nicolini and Swiney in 1710 (C6/555/27; *Document Register* no.2084).

there were two different accidents that drew numbers from our audiences before the season was ended, which were another company permitted to act in Drury Lane,[57] and the long trial of Doctor Sacheverell in Westminster Hall.[58] By the way, it must be observed that this company was not under the direction of the patent (which continued still silenced) but was set up by a third interest, with a licence from court.[59] The person to whom this new licence was granted was William Collier Esq, a lawyer of an enterprising head and a jovial heart. What sort of favour he was in with the people then in power may be judged from his being often admitted to partake with them those detached hours of life, when business was to give way to pleasure; but this was not all his merit. He was, at the same time, a Member of Parliament for Truro in Cornwall, and we cannot suppose a person so qualified could be refused such a trifle as a licence to head a broken company of actors.[60] This sagacious lawyer, then, who had a lawyer to deal with,[61] observing that his antagonist kept possession of a theatre without making use of it, and for which he was not obliged to pay rent unless he actually did use it, wisely conceived it might be the interest of the joint landlords[62] (since their tenement was in so precarious a condition) to grant a lease to one who had an undisputed authority to be liable, by acting plays in it, to pay the rent of it; especially when he tempted them with an offer of raising it from three to four pounds *per diem*. His project succeeded: the lease was signed, but the means of getting into possession were to be left to his own cost and discretion. This took him up but little time. He immediately laid siege to it with a sufficient number of forces; whether lawless or lawful I

---

57 See above, p.269 n.48.

58 Dr Henry Sacheverell (1674–1724) was tried for his anti-Whig sermon, *The Perils of False Brethren*, given at St Paul's on 5 November 1709. The trial lasted from 27 February to 21 March 1710. Lowe cites Charles Shadwell's preface to *The Fair Quaker of Deal*, which opened on 25 March 1710 (LS2 214): the play did well, wrote Shadwell, 'notwithstanding the trial in Westminster Hall'. See also below, pp.274–5.

59 The authority granted for the new company by Sir John Stanley, Secretary to Lord Chamberlain Kent, stresses that no one with an interest in the patent company is involved (LC 7/3, fol.33; *Document Register* no.2057) – a measure to prevent Christopher Rich from regaining control.

60 William Collier was the second MP for Truro, along with Sir Thomas Hare, but only between 1713 and 1715. Truro was a classic 'rotten borough'. On 13 September 1709 Collier wrote to Barton Booth expressing sympathy for the actors' plight following the silencing of Drury Lane, and suggesting they petition the Queen (BL Add.MS 20,726, fols.33–4; *Document Register* no.2045), no doubt motivated partly by his own financial interest (as above, p.255 n.14).

61 i.e. Christopher Rich.

62 By virtue of a lease dated 29 June 1695, Drury Lane was rented from William Russell, 1st Duke of Bedford, and subsequently his heirs.

forget, but they were such as obliged the old governor to give it up, who notwithstanding had got intelligence of his approaches and design time enough to carry off everything that was worth moving, except a great number of old scenes and new actors that could not easily follow him.[63]

A ludicrous account of this transaction, under fictitious names, may be found in the 99th *Tatler*, vol. 2, which this explanation may now render more intelligible to the readers of that agreeable author.[64]

This other new licence being now in possession of the Drury Lane Theatre, those actors whom the patentee, ever since the order of silence, had retained in a state of inaction, all to a man came over to the service of Collier. Of these, Booth was then the chief.[65] The merit of the rest had as yet made no considerable appearance, and as the patentee had not left a rag of their clothing behind him, they were but poorly equipped for a public review; consequently, at their first opening they were very little able to annoy us. But during the trial of Sacheverell, our audiences were extremely

63 Lowe describes a British Museum copy of the report 'by the Attorney General and Solicitor General, who were ordered by Queen Anne to inquire into this business. Rich declared that Collier broke into the theatre with an armed mob of soldiers, &c., but Collier denied the soldiers, though he admitted the breaking in.' Collier gave as authority his letter from Sir John Stanley (see above, p.273 n.59). For the impact on the opening play, see above, p.269 n.48.

64 Lowe cites the report in full (*The Tatler*, no. 99, 26 November 1709):

> Divito [Rich] was too modest to know when to resign it, till he had the opinion and sentence of the law for his removal … The lawful ruler [of Drury Lane] sets up an attorney to expel an attorney, and chose a name dreadful to the stage [that is, Collier], who only seemed able to beat Divito out of his entrenchments. On the 22nd instant, a night of public rejoicing, the enemies of Divito made a largesse to the people of faggots, tubs and other combustible matter, which was erected into a bonfire before the palace. Plentiful cans were at the same time distributed among the dependences of that principality; and the artful rival of Divito observing them prepared for enterprise, presented the lawful owner of the neighbouring edifice, and showed his deputation under him. War immediately ensued upon the peaceful empire of wit and the muses; the Goths and Vandals sacking Rome did not threaten a more barbarous devastation of arts and sciences. But when they had forced their entrance, the experienced Divito had detached all his subjects and evacuated all his stores. The neighbouring inhabitants report that the refuse of Divito's followers marched off the night before, disguised in magnificence; doorkeepers came out clad like cardinals, and scene-drawers like heathen gods. Divito himself was wrapped up in one of his black clouds, and left to the enemy nothing but an empty stage full of trap-doors known only to himself and his adherents.

65 LS2a 509–10 lists thirty-one actors in the Drury Lane company, including Barton Booth and George Powell, as well as a number of dancers and singers. Twenty-four of them had signed a petition in support of Rich during July 1709 (see above, p.266 n.42), but that was, as Lowe observes, a sign that they would prove awkward under Collier and his manager, Aaron Hill.

weakened by the better rank of people's daily attending it; while at the same time the lower sort, who were not equally admitted to that grand spectacle, as eagerly crowded into Drury Lane to a new comedy called *The Fair Quaker of Deal*. This play, having some low strokes of natural humour in it, was rightly calculated for the capacity of the actors who played it, and to the taste of the multitude who were now more disposed and at leisure to see it.[66] But the most happy incident in its fortune was the charm of the Fair Quaker, which was acted by Miss Santlow (afterwards Mrs Booth), whose person was then in the full bloom of what beauty she might pretend to.[67] Before this, she had only been admired as the most excellent dancer, which perhaps might not a little contribute to the favourable reception she now met with as an actress in this character which so happily suited her figure and capacity. The gentle softness of her voice, the composed innocence of her aspect, the modesty of her dress, the reserved decency of her gesture, and the simplicity of the sentiments that naturally fell from her, made her seem the amiable maid she represented. In a word, not the enthusiastic Maid of Orléans was more serviceable of old to the French Army when the English had distressed them[68] than this fair Quaker was at the head of that dramatic attempt upon which the support of their weak society depended.

But when the trial I have mentioned and the run of this play was over, the tide of the town beginning to turn again in our favour, Collier was reduced to give his theatrical affairs a different scheme,[69] which advanced the stage another step towards that settlement which, in my time, was of the longest duration.

---

66 See above, p.273 n.58. LS2a records sixteen performances of the play during the second half of the 1709–10 season. In his preface, Charles Shadwell reports that he had first shown the play three years earlier to

> a famous comedian belonging to the Haymarket playhouse, who took care to beat down the values of it so much as to offer the author to alter it fit to appear on the stage, on condition he might have half the profits of the third day and the Dedication entire; that is as much as to say, that it may pass for one of his, according to custom.

The 'famous comedian' was almost certainly Cibber. Shadwell's benefit performance took place on 6 March 1710 (LS2a 552).

67 For Hester Santlow, see above, p.59 n.48. She played Dorcas Zeal in Shadwell's play.

68 i.e. Joan of Arc, sent to help lift the Siege of Orléans in 1428.

69 The last known performance of *The Fair Quaker of Deal* in the 1709–10 season was on 24 July 1710 (LS2a 587). Perhaps stung by Shadwell's preface, Cibber omits to mention that the play remained popular in subsequent seasons; indeed, it lasted well beyond the publication of the *Apology* (e.g. LS3 1227, which notes a performance in March 1746).

CHAPTER 13

The patentee having now no actors, rebuilds the new theatre in Lincoln's Inn Fields. A guess at his reasons for it. More changes in the state of the stage. The beginning of its better days under the triumvirate of actors. A sketch of their governing characters.

As coarse mothers may have comely children, so anarchy has been the parent of many a good government, and by a parity of possible consequences we shall find that from the frequent convulsions of the stage arose, at last, its longest settlement and prosperity; which many of my readers (or, if I should happen to have but few of them, many of my spectators, at least who I hope have not yet lived half their time) will be able to remember.

Though the patent had been often under distresses, it had never felt any blow equal to this unrevoked order of silence, which it is not easy to conceive could have fallen upon any other person's conduct than that of the old patentee.[1] For if he was conscious of his being under the subjection of that power which had silenced him, why would he incur the danger of a suspension by his so obstinate and impolitic treatment of his actors? If he thought such power over him illegal, how came he to obey it now more than before, when he slighted a former order that enjoined him to give his actors their benefits on their usual conditions?[2] But to do him justice, the same obstinacy that involved him in these difficulties at last preserved to his heirs the property of the patent in its full force and value;[3] yet to suppose that he foresaw a milder use of power in some future prince's reign might be more favourable to him is begging, at best, but a cold question. But whether he knew that this broken condition of the patent would not make his troublesome friends, the adventurers, fly from it as from a falling house, seems not so difficult a question. However, let the reader form his own judgment of them from the facts that followed. It must therefore be observed that the adventurers seldom came near the house but when there was some visible appearance of a dividend. But I could never hear that upon an ill run of audiences they had ever returned, or brought in a single

---

1 There were other instances of silencing orders during the period covered by the *Apology*, although the duration of this one (effectively June to November 1709) was unusual.
2 For this 'former order', see above, p.260 n.25.
3 For Rich's sons and his their inheritance, see above, p.226 n.13. Cibber, by contrast, did not 'preserve to his heirs' his interest in the patent (see above, p.13 n.6).

shilling to make good the deficiencies of their daily receipts. Therefore, as the patentee in possession had alone for several years supported and stood against this uncertainty of fortune, it may be imagined that his accounts were under so voluminous a perplexity that few of those adventurers would have leisure or capacity enough to unravel them. And as they had formerly thrown away their time and money at law in a fruitless enquiry into them, they now seemed to have entirely given up their right and interest; and (according to my best information) notwithstanding the subsequent gains of the patent have been sometimes extraordinary, the farther demands or claims of right of the adventurers have lain dormant above these five-and-twenty years.[4]

Having shown by what means Collier had dispossessed this patentee not only of the Drury Lane house, but likewise of those few actors which he had kept for some time unemployed in it, we are now led to consider another project of the same patentee which, if we are to judge of it by the event, has shown him more a wise than a weak man; which I confess, at the time he put it in execution, seemed not so clear a point. For notwithstanding he now saw the authority and power of his patent was superseded (or was at best but precarious) and that he had not one actor left in his service, yet, under all these dilemmas and distresses, he resolved upon rebuilding the new theatre in Lincoln's Inn Fields, of which he had taken a lease at a low rent ever since Betterton's company had first left it.[5] This conduct seemed too deep for my comprehension! What are we to think of his taking this lease in the height of his prosperity, when he could have no occasion for it? Was he a prophet? Could he then foresee he should one time or other be turned out of Drury Lane? Or did his mere appetite of architecture urge him to build a house while he could not be sure he should ever have leave to make use of it? But of all this we may think as we please. Whatever was his motive, he at his own expense, in this interval of his having nothing else to do, rebuilt that theatre from the ground as it is

4 The shareholders' fruitless attempt to gain redress over the 1709 silencing of Drury Lane was perhaps responsible for their giving up future claims (BL Add.MS 20,726, fol.24; *Document Register* no.2069). The lack of claims by investors did not prevent Rich's sons from squabbling with each other. On 6 August 1720 they signed a bond with their creditor, John Evans, allowing him to arbitrate in a dispute about how they were to repay him (PRO C107/171; *Document Register* no.3026).

5 Rich had acquired the lease to the Lincoln's Inn Fields in December 1705, but using Penkethman as a front man (*Document Register* no.1828); on 3 September 1714 he signed it over to sixteen investors (including his sons) in thirty-six renters' shares (BL Add.Charter 9303; *Document Register* no.2429). A document of 4 September shows that each share cost £120, or c.£23,000 in current values (BL Add.Charter 9303; *Document Register* no.2430).

now standing.[6] As for the order of silence, he seemed little concerned at it while it gave him so much uninterrupted leisure to supervise a work which he naturally took delight in.

After this defeat of the patentee, the theatrical forces of Collier in Drury Lane, notwithstanding their having drawn the multitude after them for about three weeks during the trial of Sacheverell, had made but an indifferent campaign at the end of the season. Collier, at least, found so little account in it that it obliged him to push his court interest (which, wherever the stage was concerned, was not inconsiderable) to support him in another scheme; which was, that in consideration of his giving up the Drury Lane clothes, scenes and actors to Swiney and his joint sharers in the Haymarket, he (Collier) might be put into an equal possession of the Haymarket Theatre, with all the singers *etc*, and be made sole director of the opera. Accordingly, by permission of the Lord Chamberlain, a treaty was entered into and in a few days ratified by all parties, conformable to the said preliminaries.[7] This was that happy crisis of theatrical liberty which the labouring comedians had long sighed for and which, for above twenty years following, was so memorably fortunate to them.

However, there were two hard articles in this treaty which, though it might be policy in the actors to comply with, yet the imposition of them seemed little less despotic than a tax upon the poor when a government did not want it.

The first of these articles was that whereas the sole licence for acting plays was presumed to be a more profitable authority than that for acting operas only, that therefore two hundred pounds a year should be paid to Collier while master of the opera, by the comedians – to whom a verbal assurance was given by the *plenipos* on the court side that while such payment subsisted, no other company should be permitted to act plays against them within the liberties *etc*.[8] The other article was that on every Wednesday

6 In John Rocque's map of London (1744–6), the theatre is shown on Portugal Street, south of Portugal Row on the south side of Lincoln's Inn Fields. Rocque's map is reproduced as *The A–Z of Georgian London*, ed. Ralph Hyde (London: Harry Margary, 1981). The theatre was abandoned when John Rich moved to Covent Garden in 1732, and converted into a barracks some time in the 1750s (*London Encyclopaedia*, p.473).

7 This scheme may have been Swiney's idea rather than Collier's. In a letter dated 23 September 1710, Swiney offered to pay Collier £500 a year either to swap Drury Lane for Swiney's own Queen's Theatre, Haymarket, or keep out of the business altogether (Coke Papers; *Document Register* no.2101). By then, the Drury Lane actors had rioted in protest against Collier's appointed manager, Aaron Hill (Coke Papers, 5 June 1710; *Document Register* no.2089).

8 i.e. the areas immediately adjoining the old City of London. By *plenipos* Cibber means plenipotentiaries; *OED* records uses by Dryden, Steele, and Fielding.

whereon an opera could be performed, the plays should *toties quoties*[9] be silent at Drury Lane, to give the opera a fairer chance for a full house.[10]

This last article, however partial in the intention, was in its effect of great advantage to the sharing actors, for in all public entertainments a day's abstinence naturally increases the appetite to them. Our every Thursday's audience, therefore, was visibly the better by thus making the day before it a fast.[11] But as this was not a favour designed [by] us, this prohibition of a day methinks deserves a little farther notice, because it evidently took a sixth part of their income from all the hired actors, who were only paid in proportion to the number of acting days. This extraordinary regard to operas was in effect making the day-labouring actors the principal subscribers to them; and the shutting out people from the play every Wednesday many murmured at as an abridgment of their usual liberty. And though I was one of those who profited by that order, it ought not to bribe me into a concealment of what was then said and thought of it.[12] I remember a nobleman of the first rank, then in a high post and not out of court favour, said openly behind the scenes, 'It was shameful to take part of the actors' bread from them to support the silly diversion of people of quality'. But alas, what was all this grievance when weighed against the qualifications of so grave and staunch a senator as Collier? Such visible merit, it seems, was to be made easy, though at the expense of the – I had almost said *honour* of the Court, whose gracious intention for the theatrical commonwealth might have shone with thrice the lustre if such a paltry price had not been paid for it. But as the government of the stage is but that of the world in miniature, we ought not to have wondered that Collier had interest enough to quarter the weakness of the opera upon the strength of the comedy. General good intentions are not always practicable to a perfection. The most necessary law can hardly pass, but a tenderness to some private interest shall often hang such exceptions upon particular clauses, till at last it comes out lame and lifeless with the loss of half its force, purpose and dignity. As,

9 i.e. as often.
10 A representation by Cibber, Doggett, and Wilks to Lord Chamberlain Shrewsbury (for whom see above, p.56 n.44) dated 16 November 1710 accepts the new licence but refers to Saturday rather than Wednesday as the day reserved for Collier's operas (HTC TS 953.10F; *Document Register* no.2106). LS2a 605–21 shows opera performances at the Queen's Theatre on both Wednesdays and Saturdays during the 1710–11 season, with plays performed at Drury Lane on Saturdays.
11 Receipts for the opera suggest that it, too, benefited, with figures of £167 6s 9d for *Pyrrhus and Demetrius* on 9 December 1710 and £153 10s for the same work on 20 December (HTC Coke, nos.62–3; *Document Register* nos.2113–14).
12 As a manager, Cibber took a share of the profits; one acting day fewer meant reduced costs and bigger audiences on the remaining days.

for instance: how many fruitless motions have been made in parliaments to moderate the enormous exactions in the practice of the law? And what sort of justice must that be called which, when a man has not a mind to pay you a debt of ten pounds, it shall cost you fifty before you can get it? How long, too, has the public been labouring for a bridge at Westminster? But the wonder that it was not built a hundred years ago ceases when we are told that the fear of making one end of London as rich as the other has been so long an obstruction to it.[13] And though it might seem a still greater wonder (when a new law for building one had at last got over that apprehension) that it should meet with any farther delay,[14] yet experience has shown us that the structure of this useful ornament to our metropolis has been so clogged by private jobs that were to be picked out of the undertaking, and the progress of the work so disconcerted by a tedious contention of private interests and endeavours to impose upon the public abominable bargains, that a whole year was lost before a single stone could be laid to its foundation. But posterity will owe its praises to the zeal and resolution of a truly noble commissioner, whose distinguished impatience has broke through those narrow artifices – those false and frivolous objections that delayed it – and has already began to raise above the tide that future monument of his public spirit.[15]

How far all this may be allowed applicable to the state of the stage is not of so great importance, nor so much my concern, as that what is observed upon it should always remain a memorable truth to the honour of that nobleman. But now I go on. Collier being thus possessed of his musical government, thought his best way would be to farm it out to a gentleman, Aaron Hill, Esq[16] (who, he had reason to suppose, knew something more of

13 A bridge at Westminster was mooted in 1664 but opposed by the City Corporation and the Thames watermen, who feared loss of trade. Charles II agreed to withdraw the proposal following a loan from the City of £100,000. In 1721 the idea was revived, and in 1722 Colen Campbell appointed as architect. Still no progress was made, and in 1736 Nicholas Hawksmoor drew up an alternative design, which was also rejected. In 1738, during Cibber's drafting of the *Apology*, Charles Labelye was appointed engineer. Compensation of £25,000 was paid to the watermen and £21,025 to the owner of the Horse Ferry, the Archbishop of Canterbury (*London Encyclopaedia*, pp.975–6).

14 The Act for Building a Bridge across the River Thames from the New Palace Yard in the City of Westminster to the opposite Shore in the County Surrey (9 Geo. 2 c. 29) received Royal Assent on 20 May 1736.

15 Henry Herbert, 9th Earl of Pembroke (1693–1750), steered the Act through Parliament, attended meetings of the bridge commissioners, and laid the foundation stone in January 1739. Pembroke supported many other architectural projects, including the design of the Victory Column at Blenheim Palace.

16 There is no record of when exactly Collier appointed Aaron Hill (1685–1750) as manager of Drury Lane; LS2 197 assumes it was from the start of the company's season on 23

theatrical matters than himself) at a rent, if I mistake not, of six hundred pounds per annum; but before the season was ended (upon what occasion, if I could remember, it might not be material to say) took it into his hands again.[17] But all his skill and interest could not raise the direction of the opera to so good a post as he thought due to a person of his consideration. He therefore, the year following, entered upon another high-handed scheme which, till the demise of the Queen,[18] turned to his better account.

After the comedians were in possession of Drury Lane (from whence, during my time upon the stage, they never departed), their swarm of audiences exceeded all that had been seen in thirty years before; which, however, I do not impute so much to the excellence of their acting as to their indefatigable industry and good management. For as I have often said, I never thought, in the general, that we stood in any place of comparison with the eminent actors before us; perhaps, too, by there being now an end of the frequent divisions and disorders that had from time to time broke in upon and frustrated their labours, not a little might be contributed to their success.

Collier then (like a true liquorish courtier) observing the prosperity of a theatre which he, the year before, had parted with for a worse, began to meditate an exchange of theatrical posts with Swiney, who had visibly very fair pretensions to that he was in, by his being first chosen by the Court to regulate and rescue the stage from the disorders it had suffered under its

November 1709. In March 1710 a poem in *British Apollo* (31 March–3 April 1710), which Hill co-edited and often wrote, celebrated the appointment and hailed Hill as a 'mighty genius'. By then Hill had two modestly successful plays to his name: *Elfrid; or The Fair Inconstant*, and its afterpiece, *The Walking Statue; or, The Devil in the Wine Cellar*, both of which were produced at Drury Lane in January 1710 (LS2a 536–8). For an authoritative study, see Christine Gerrard, *Aaron Hill: The Muses' Projector, 1685–1750* (Oxford: Clarendon Press, 2003). As Evans notes, Cibber has reversed the order of the 1709–10 and 1710–11 seasons with his focus on the regulations applied to opera.

17 Collier was presumably motivated to end his arrangement with Hill following the riot of 2 June 1710, when a number of actors beat up their manager after a performance of (ironically enough) *The Fair Quaker of Deal*. Hill described the episode to Collier in a letter dated 5 June (Hyde Collection; *Document Register* no.2089). George Powell was dismissed for his part in the incident while Barton Booth, John Bickerstaff, Theophilus Keen, and Francis Leigh were suspended (LC 5/155, fol.24; *Document Register* no.2091). Legal action followed; Collier accused Hill of not paying bills for two operas, and Hill lodged a counter action dated 9 July 1711 (C10/427/15; *Document Register* no.2151). The episode is discussed in full by Judith Milhous and Robert D. Hume in 'The Haymarket Opera in 1711', *Early Music* vol. 17 (1989), 523–37.

18 Queen Anne died on 1 August 1714. As Evans notes, in the subsequent passage Cibber omits to mention the role he played in excluding Swiney from managerial control. See Swiney's complaints against Cibber, Doggett, and Wilks (*Document Register* nos.2115 and 2120) and their response (C8/621/30; *Document Register* no.2123).

former managers.[19] Yet Collier knew that sort of merit could stand in no competition with his being a Member of Parliament.[20] He therefore had recourse to his court interest (where mere will and pleasure, at that time, was the only law that disposed of all theatrical rights) to oblige Swiney to let him be off from his bad bargain for a better. To this, it may be imagined, Swiney demurred, and as he had reason, strongly remonstrated against it. But as Collier had listed his conscience under the command of interest, he kept it to strict duty and was immoveable; insomuch that Sir John Vanbrugh (who was a friend to Swiney and who, by his intimacy with the people in power, better knew the motive of their actions) advised Swiney rather to accept of the change than, by a non-compliance, to hazard his being excluded from any post or concern in either of the theatres. To conclude, it was not long before Collier had procured a new licence for acting plays *etc* for himself, Wilks, Doggett, and Cibber, exclusive of Swiney, who by this new regulation was reduced to his Hobson's choice of the opera.[21]

Swiney being thus transferred to the opera in the sinking condition Collier had left it, found the receipts of it in the winter following (1711) so far short of the expenses that he was driven to attend his fortune in some more favourable climate, where he remained twenty years an exile from his friends and country;[22] though there has been scarce an English gentleman who, in his tour of France or Italy, has not renewed or created an acquaintance with him. As this is a circumstance that many people may have forgot,

19 i.e. in the 1708–9 season (see above, pp.260–2).
20 As noted above, p.273 n.60, Collier did not become MP for Truro until 1713.
21 Collier's licence for this new acting company jointly names Cibber, Doggett, and Wilks and is dated 17 April 1712 (LC 5/155, fol.97; *Document Register* no.2183). On the same date, Swiney was granted a licence to mount opera and other musical entertainments at the Queen's Theatre, Haymarket (LC 5/155, fol.97v; *Document Register* no.2184). Drury Lane was forbidden to stage musical entertainments or dancing except by their own actors; actor benefits were prohibited on the days of opera performances, while no plays were to be staged on Wednesdays and Fridays during Lent. In addition, the Drury Lane managers were required, with effect from 1 June 1712, to pay Swiney £100 a year in subsidy (LC 5/155, fol.98; *Document Register* nos.2185–6). The phrase 'Hobson's choice' had been in circulation since the legendary meanness of the stable owner Thomas Hobson (1544–1631), who would offer customers the choice of taking the horse nearest the door or none.
22 For Swiney's subsequent career, see above, p.217 n.68. LS2 has no record of a performance at the Queen's Theatre Haymarket in the 1711–12 season until 10 November 1711, when Swiney revived *Almahide*, John James Heidegger's arrangement of music by Giovanni Bononcini and Attilio Ariosti to an Italian libretto developed from Dryden's *The Conquest of Granada*. Subsequent operas played on Wednesdays and Saturdays only and included Mancini's *Hydaspes*, Gasparini's *Antiochus*, Handel's *Rinaldo*, and a *Hercules* with a libretto by Giacomo Rossi and (probably) Heidegger's arrangement of existing music.

I cannot remember it without that regard and concern it deserves from all that know him. Yet it is some mitigation of his misfortune that since his return to England, his grey hairs and cheerful disposition have still found a general welcome among his foreign and former domestic acquaintance.[23]

Collier being now first commissioned manager with the comedians, drove them, too, to the last inch of a hard bargain (the natural consequence of all treaties between power and necessity). He not only demanded six hundred a year neat money (the price at which he had farmed out his opera, and to make the business a sinecure to him), but likewise insisted upon a moiety of the two hundred that had been levied upon us the year before, in aid of the operas – in all, £700.[24] These large and ample conditions, considering in what hands we were, we resolved to swallow without wry faces, rather choosing to run any hazard than contend with a formidable power against which we had no remedy. But so it happened that Fortune took better care of our interest than we ourselves had like to have done. For had Collier accepted of our first offer of an equal share with us, he had got three hundred pounds a year more by complying with it than by the sum he imposed upon us, our shares being never less than a thousand annually to each of us, till the end of the Queen's reign in 1714; after which, Collier's commission was superseded, his theatrical post – upon the accession of his late Majesty – being given to Sir Richard Steele.[25]

From these various revolutions in the government of the theatre – all owing to the patentees' mistaken principle of increasing their profits by too far enslaving their people, and keeping down the price of good actors (and I could almost insist that giving large salaries to bad ones could not have had a worse consequence) – I say, when it is considered that the authority for acting plays *etc* was thought of so little worth that (as has been observed)

23 Cibber repaired his earlier quarrel with Swiney and even appeared in a benefit performance for him, as Fondlewife in Congreve's *The Old Batchelor* (cited in Barker, p.88). Here he overlooks the damaging dispute that began late in 1710, when Cibber and colleagues refused to pay Swiney his share (HTC Coke, no.17; *Document Register* no.2115).

24 On 6 December 1712 Collier agreed with Cibber, Doggett, and Wilks that he should be a sleeping partner at Drury Lane and would take £700 a year (£800 in the event of non-payment of the Haymarket subsidy cited above, n.21) with reductions, should acting be interrupted (LC 7/3, fols.127–8; *Document Register* no.2208). Early in 1714, Cibber told Collier that since Barton Booth had been added to the management team, their previous agreement was void. Collier appealed in vain to Lord Chamberlain Shrewsbury (LC 7/3, fols.127–8; *Document Register* no.2300).

25 The new Drury Lane licence was granted to Steele, Booth, Cibber, Doggett, and Wilks on 18 October 1714 (LC 5/156, p.31; *Document Register* no.2435). George I had acceded to the throne on 1 August 1714. For Charles Killigrew's objections, both as shareholder and Master of the Revels, see above, p.186 n.36.

Sir Thomas Skipwith gave away his share of it, and the adventurers had fled from it, that Mr Congreve at another time had voluntarily resigned it, and Sir John Vanbrugh (merely to get the rent of his new house paid) had by leave of the Court farmed out his licence to Swiney (who not without some hesitation had ventured upon it), let me say, again: out of this low condition of the theatre, was it not owing to the industry of three or four comedians that a new place was now created for the Crown to give away, without any expense attending it, well worth the acceptance of any gentleman whose merit or services had no higher claim to preferment, and which Collier and Sir Richard Steele in the two last reigns successively enjoyed? Though I believe I may have said something like this in a former chapter, I am not unwilling it should be twice taken notice of.[26]

We are now come to that firm establishment of the theatre which, except the admittance of Booth into a share and Doggett's retiring from it, met with no change or alteration for above twenty years after.

Collier (as has been said) having accepted of a certain appointment of seven hundred per annum, Wilks, Doggett and myself were now the only acting managers under the Queen's licence;[27] which, being a grant but during pleasure, obliged us to a conduct that might not undeserve that favour. At this time we were all in the vigour of our capacities as actors, and our prosperity enabled us to pay at least double the salaries to what the same actors had usually received, or could have hoped for, under the government of the patentees. Doggett, who was naturally an economist, kept our expenses and accounts to the best of his power, within regulated bounds and moderation. Wilks, who had a stronger passion for glory than lucre, was a little apt to be lavish in what was not always as necessary for the profit as the honour of the theatre. For example, at the beginning of almost every season he would order two or three suits to be made or refreshed for actors of moderate consequence, that his having constantly a new one for himself might seem less particular, though he had as yet no new part for it.[28] This expeditious care of doing us good, without waiting for our consent to it, Doggett always looked upon with the eye of a man in pain; but I, who hated pain (though I as little liked the favour as Doggett himself) rather chose to laugh at the circumstance than complain of what I knew was not to be

---

26 In Chapter 8, pp.188–9. For the arrangement with Steele and its problems, see below, pp.333–40.

27 This licence is dated 17 April 1712 (LC 5/155, fol.97; *Document Register* no.2183) and follows the terms of its predecessor dated 6 November 1710.

28 The surviving bills for Drury Lane costumes during this period are usually signed by Booth and Cibber as well as Wilks (*Document Register* nos.2448, 2453, 2454, 2458, etc.).

cured but by a remedy worse than the evil. Upon these occasions, therefore, whenever I saw him and his followers so prettily dressed out for an old play, I only commended his fancy or, at most, but whispered him not to give himself so much trouble about others, upon whose performance it would but be thrown away. To which, with a smiling air of triumph over my want of penetration, he has replied, 'Why, now that was what I really did it for! To show others that I love to take care of them as well as of myself'. Thus, whenever he made himself easy he had not the least conception, let the expense be what it would, that we could possibly dislike it. And from the same principle, provided a thinner audience were liberal of their applause, he gave himself little concern about the receipt of it. As in these different tempers of my brother-managers there might be equally something right and wrong, it was equally my business to keep well with them both. And though, of the two, I was rather inclined to Doggett's way of thinking, yet I was always under the disagreeable restraint of not letting Wilks see it.[29] Therefore when, in any material point of management, they were ready to come to a rupture, I found it advisable to think neither of them absolutely in the wrong. But by giving to one as much of the right in his opinion this way as I took from the other in that, their differences were sometimes softened into concessions that I have reason to think prevented many ill consequences in our affairs that otherwise might have attended them. But this was always to be done with a very gentle hand; for as Wilks was apt to be easily hurt by opposition, so, when he felt it, he was as apt to be insupportable. However, there were some points in which we were always unanimous. In the twenty years while we were our own directors, we never had a creditor that had occasion to come twice for his bill;[30] every Monday morning discharged us of all demands before we took a shilling for our own use. And from this time we neither asked any actor, nor were desired by them, to sign any written agreement (to the best of my memory) whatsoever. The rate of their respective salaries were only entered in our daily payroll, which plain record everyone looked upon as good as City security. For where an honest meaning is mutual, the mutual confidence will be bond enough in conscience on both sides. But, that I may not ascribe more

---

29 Nevertheless, Cibber and his fellow managers became embroiled in a two-year legal action against Doggett from 17 December 1714 (C11/6/44; *Document Register* no.2477). Cibber's account of their conflicts is below, pp.303–8.

30 The accumulation of minor bills and associated payments recorded in *Document Register* bears out Cibber's claim, but it also shows that he and his fellow managers sometimes deducted small sums from costume and other invoices (e.g. *Document Register* nos. 2510, 2511, 2521, etc.).

to our conduct than was really its due, I ought to give Fortune her share of the commendation; for had not our success exceeded our expectation, it might not have been in our power so thoroughly to have observed those laudable rules of economy, justice and lenity which so happily supported us. But the severities and oppression we had suffered under our former masters made us incapable of imposing them on others, which gave our whole society the cheerful looks of a rescued people. But notwithstanding this general cause of content, it was not above a year or two before the imperfection of human nature began to show itself in contrary symptoms. The merit of the hazards which the managers had run, and the difficulties they had combated in bringing to perfection that revolution by which they had all so amply profited in the amendment of their general income, began now to be forgotten; their acknowledgments and thankful promises of fidelity were no more repeated, or scarce thought obligatory. Ease and plenty, by an habitual enjoyment, had lost their novelty, and the largeness of their salaries seemed rather lessened than advanced by the extraordinary gains of the undertakers; for that is the scale in which the hired actor will always weigh his performance.[31] But whatever reason there may seem to be in his case, yet (as he is frequently apt to throw a little self-partiality into the balance) that consideration may a good deal alter the justness of it. While the actors, therefore, had this way of thinking, happy was it for the managers that their united interest was so inseparably the same, and that their skill and power in acting stood in a rank so far above the rest that if the whole body of private men had deserted them, it would yet have been an easier matter for the managers to have picked up recruits than for the deserters to have found proper officers to head them. Here, then, in this distinction lay our security: our being actors ourselves was an advantage to our government which all former managers, who were only idle gentlemen, wanted. Nor was our establishment easily to be broken while our health and limbs enabled us to be joint labourers in the work we were masters of.

The only actor who, in the opinion of the public, seemed to have had a pretence of being advanced to a share with us was certainly Booth. But when it is considered how strongly he had opposed the measures that had made us managers by setting himself (as has been observed) at the head of an opposite interest,[32] he could not as yet have much to complain of; beside, if the Court had thought him now an equal object of favour, it could not

---

31 For the actors' desertions, see below, p.319 n.22.
32 A reference to Barton Booth's seniority in Collier's company from its inauguration in 1709 (see above, p.274). For subsequent arguments about his sharing with Cibber, Doggett, and Wilks, see below, pp.303–8.

have been in our power to have opposed his preferment. This I mention, not to take from his merit, but to show from what cause it was not as yet better provided for. Therefore it may be no vanity to say our having, at that time, no visible competitors on the stage was the only interest that raised us to be the managers of it.

But here let me rest a while; and since, at my time of day, our best possessions are but ease and quiet, I must be content, if I will have sallies of pleasure, to take up with those only that are to be found in imagination. When I look back, therefore, on the storms of the stage we had been tossed in; when I consider that various vicissitude of hopes and fears we had for twenty years struggled with, and found ourselves at last thus safely set on shore to enjoy the produce of our own labours, and to have raised those labours by our skill and industry to a much fairer profit than our taskmasters, by all their severe and griping government, had ever reaped from them – a good-natured reader that is not offended at the comparison of great things with small, will allow was a triumph in proportion equal to those that have attended the most heroic enterprises for liberty! What transport could the first Brutus feel, upon his expulsion of the Tarquins, greater than that which now danced in the heart of a poor actor who, from an injured labourer unpaid his hire, had made himself without guilt a legal manager of his own fortune?[33] Let the grave and great contemn or yawn at these low conceits, but let me be happy in the enjoyment of them! To this hour, my memory runs o'er that pleasing prospect of life past with little less delight than when I was first in the real possession of it. This is the natural temper of my mind which my acquaintance are frequently witnesses of; and as this was all the ambition Providence had made my obscure condition capable of, I am thankful that means were given me to enjoy the fruits of it.

> *Hoc est*
> *Vivere bìs, vitâ; posse priore frui.*[34]

Something like the meaning of this, the less learned reader may find in my title page.

---

33 i.e. Lucius Junius Brutus, legendary founder of the Roman Republic in the sixth century BC, victor over the Tarquins, and the subject of a controversial play of 1680 by Nathaniel Lee (see above, p.229 n.21).

34 As Cibber points out, the same quotation from Martial appears on the title page of the *Apology* (see above, p.1 n.1): 'this is to live twice, to be able to enjoy your earlier life.'

The stage in its highest prosperity. The managers not without errors. Of what kind. Cato first acted. What brought it to the stage. The company go to Oxford. Their success, and different auditors there. Booth made a sharer. Doggett objects to him. Quits the stage upon his admittance. That not his true reason. What was. Doggett's theatrical character.

Notwithstanding the managing actors were now in a happier situation than their utmost pretensions could have expected, yet it is not to be supposed but wiser men might have mended it. As we could not all govern ourselves, there were seasons when we were not all fit to govern others. Our passions and our interest drew not always the same way. Self had a great sway in our debates. We had our partialities, our prejudices, our favourites of less merit, and our jealousies of those who came too near us – frailties which societies of higher consideration, while they are composed of men, will not always be free from. To have been constantly capable of unanimity had been a blessing too great for our station. One mind among three people were to have had three masters to one servant; but when that one servant is called three different ways at the same time, whose business is to be done first? For my own part, I was forced almost all my life to give up my share of him. And if I could, by art or persuasion, hinder others from making what I thought a wrong use of their power, it was the all and utmost I desired. Yet whatever might be our personal errors, I shall think I have no right to speak of them farther than where the public entertainment was affected by them. If therefore, among so many, some particular actors were remarkable in any part of their private lives that might sometimes make the world merry without doors, I hope my laughing friends will excuse me if I do not so far comply with their desires or curiosity as to give them a place in my history. I can only recommend such anecdotes to the amusement of a noble person who (in case I conceal them) does me the flattering honour to threaten my work with a supplement.[1] 'Tis enough for me that such actors had their

---

1 The reference to a 'noble person' excepted, this sounds so like a reference to Aston's *Brief Supplement* that it seems possible this passage prompted it. Aston's preface reads,

> Mr Cibber is guilty of omission, that he hath not given us any description of the several personages' beauties or faults – faults (I say) of the several actors etc, for … as the late Duke of Buckingham says of characters, that to show a man not defective 'were to draw / A faultless monster that the world ne'er saw'.

merits to the public; let those recite their imperfections who are themselves without them. It is my misfortune not to have that qualification. Let us see then, whatever was amiss in it, how our administration went forward.

When we were first invested with this power,[2] the joy of our so unexpectedly coming into it kept us, for some time, in amity and good humour with one another; and the pleasure of reforming the many false measures, absurdities and abuses that, like weeds, had sucked up the due nourishment from the fruits of the theatre, gave us as yet no leisure for private dissensions. Our daily receipts exceeded our imagination, and we seldom met as a board to settle our weekly accounts without the satisfaction of joint heirs, just in possession of an unexpected estate that had been distantly entailed upon them.[3] Such a sudden change of our condition, it may be imagined, could not but throw out of us a new spirit in almost every play we appeared in. Nor did we ever sink into that common negligence which is apt to follow good fortune. Industry, we knew, was the life of our business: that it not only concealed faults, but was of equal value to greater talents without it, which the decadence once of Betterton's company in Lincoln's Inn Fields had lately shown us a proof of.

This, then, was that happy period when both actors and managers were in their highest enjoyment of general content and prosperity. Now it was that the politer world too – by their decent attention, their sensible taste, and their generous encouragements to authors[4] and actors – once more saw that the stage, under a due regulation, was capable of being what the wisest ages thought it might be: the most rational scheme that human wit could form to dissipate with innocence the cares of life, to allure even the turbulent or ill disposed from worse meditations, and to give the leisure hours of business and virtue an instructive recreation.

If this grave assertion is less recommended by falling from the pen of a comedian, I must appeal for the truth of it to the tragedy of *Cato*, which was first acted in 1712.[5] I submit to the judgment of those who were then

Aston's work abounds in personal anecdotes and unflattering portraits. Evans notes that Cibber was on particularly friendly terms with three noblemen during the writing of the *Apology* (Chesterfield, Richmond, and Grafton) but adds that *The Laureate*, p.77, doubts the existence of this 'noble person'.

2 i.e. from April 1712 (see above, p.284 n.27).

3 A Drury Lane financial statement for November 1713 to June 1714 shows a clear profit of £1,520 9s, or c.£316,000 in current values (BL Add.MS 38,607, p.13; *Document Register* no.2420).

4 Cibber goes on to cite Addison's *Cato* as an example of the support given to authors, but three other new plays enjoyed long runs during the same 1712–13 season: Charles Johnson's *The Successful Pirate* (premiered 7 November 1712), Cibber's own *Ximena* (premiered 28 November 1712), and Charles Shadwell's *The Humours of the Army* (premiered 29 January 1713); see LS2 287–94.

5 As noted above (p.91 n.11), the actual date was 14 April 1713.

the sensible spectators of it, if the success and merit of that play was not an evidence of every article of that value which I have given to a decent theatre. But as I was observing, it could not be expected the summer days I am speaking of could be the constant weather of the year; we had our clouded hours as well as our sunshine, and were not always in the same good humour with one another. Fire, air and water could not be more vexatiously opposite than the different tempers of the three managers, though they might equally have their useful as well as their destructive qualities. How variously these elements in our several dispositions operated may be judged from the following single instance, as well as a thousand others which, if they were all to be told, might possibly make my reader wish I had forgot them.

Much about this time, then, there came over from the Dublin theatre two uncelebrated actors, to pick up a few pence among us in the winter, as Wilks had a year or two before done on their side the water in the summer.[6] But it was not so clear to Doggett and myself that it was in their power to do us the same service in Drury Lane as Wilks might have done them in Dublin. However, Wilks was so much a man of honour that he scorned to be outdone in the least point of it, let the cost be what it would to his fellow managers, who had no particular accounts of honour open with them. To acquit himself therefore with a better grace, Wilks so ordered it that his Hibernian friends were got upon our stage before any other manager had well heard of their arrival.[7] This so generous dispatch of their affair gave Wilks a very good chance of convincing his friends that himself was sole master of the masters of the company. Here, now, the different elements in our tempers began to work with us. While Wilks was only animated by a grateful hospitality to his friends, Doggett was ruffled into a storm, and looked upon this generosity as so much insult and injustice upon himself and the fraternity. During this disorder I stood by, a seeming quiet passenger; and since talking to the winds I knew could be to no great purpose (whatever weakness it might be called), could not help smiling to observe with what officious ease and delight Wilks was treating his friends at our expense, who were scarce

6 The number of male actors known to have worked at Drury Lane grew substantially between the 1713–14 and 1714–15 seasons, from twenty-two to thirty-four (LS2 308 and 328). *The Laureate* names the two new Irishmen as Thomas Elrington and Thomas Griffith, but Griffith first came to London with Wilks in 1699 and moved between there and the Smock Alley Theatre for the next fifteen years. Elrington and Griffith ran the Smock Alley Theatre in a triumvirate with an actor called Evans, whose name appears at Drury Lane for the first time in the 1714–15 season. For Elrington and his favour with Lord Chamberlain Newcastle, see also below, p.332 n.2.

7 Successive licences for management by groups of actors had specified the need for agreement on the appointment or removal of actors and other company members (e.g. LC 5/155, fol.97; *Document Register* no.2183).

acquainted with them. For it seems all this was to end in their having a benefit play, in the height of the season, for the unprofitable service they had done us without our consent or desire to employ them.⁸ Upon this, Doggett bounced and grew almost as untractable as Wilks himself. Here, again, I was forced to clap my patience to the helm, to weather this difficult point between them. Applying myself, therefore, to the person I imagined was most likely to hear me, I desired Doggett, 'to consider that I must, naturally, be as much hurt by this vain and overbearing behaviour in Wilks as he could be; and that though it was true these actors had no pretence to the favour designed them, yet we could not say they had done us any farther harm than letting the town see the parts they had been shown in had been better done by those to whom they properly belonged; yet as we had greatly profited by the extraordinary labour of Wilks' – who acted long parts almost every day, and at least twice to Doggett's once⁹ – 'and that I granted it might not be so much his consideration of our common interest as his fondness for applause that set him to work; yet even that vanity, if he supposed it such, had its merit to us, and as we had found our account in it, it would be folly upon a punctilio to tempt the rashness of a man who was capable to undo all he had done, by any act of extravagance that might fly into his head; that admitting this benefit might be some little loss to us, yet to break with him upon it could not but be ten times of worse consequence than our overlooking his disagreeable manner of making the demand upon us'.¹⁰

8 Elrington's benefit took place on 21 March 1715; he played the title role in Lee's *Mithridates, King of Pontus* (LS2 348), with Wilks and Booth in secondary roles and Oldfield as Semandra. A benefit for Evans took place on 28 March 1715; he played Henry VIII in Banks's *Virtue Betrayed; or, Anna Bullen* (LS2 349). Cibber played Wolsey. Both performances were '[a]t the desire of several ladies of quality', which may suggest that Elrington and Evans were a greater asset than Cibber supposed.

9 As Lowe points out, Wilks is credited with approximately 150 different roles but Doggett with only around 60.

10 Cibber's account is undermined by the dates of the only known benefit performances for Elrington and Evans (March 1715), because by the early summer of 1714 Doggett had refused to act or participate in the running of Drury Lane. On 14 June 1714 he wrote (it is thought) to Lord Chamberlain Shrewsbury's office asking for a resolution (BL Add.MS 38,607, pp.21–3; *Document Register* no.2418); on 29 June 1714 Cibber and Wilks swore on oath that Doggett had both refused to acknowledge the new licence of November 1713 and declined all duties, while still expecting his quarter-share of the profits (BL Add.MS, 38,607, pp.14–15; *Document Register* no.2419). On advice, Shrewsbury issued a new licence to Steele, Booth, Cibber, Doggett, and Wilks on 18 October 1714 (LC 5/156, p.31; *Document Register* no.2435), but on 3 November 1714 Cibber and Wilks protested that Doggett was still not fulfilling his duties and should be ordered back to the company (LC 7/3, fols.133–4; *Document Register* no.2441). This was the start of a two-year legal dispute. Elrington and Evans may have joined the company earlier than previously thought, but benefits in the spring of 1714 seem unlikely, given the high number of recorded Drury Lane beneficiaries: forty between 1 March and 18 June, including support staff such as the boxkeeper and treasurer (LS2 324–5).

Though I found this had made Doggett drop the severity of his features, yet he endeavoured still to seem uneasy by his starting a new objection, which was that we could not be sure even of the charge they were to pay for it.[11] 'For Wilks', said he, 'you know will go any lengths to make it a good day to them, and may whisper the door-keepers to give them the ready money taken, and return the account in such tickets only as these actors have not themselves disposed of'.[12] To make this easy too, I gave him my word to be answerable for the charge myself. Upon this he acceded, and accordingly they had the benefit play. But so it happened (whether as Doggett had suspected or not, I cannot say) the ready money received fell ten pounds short of the sum they had agreed to pay for it. Upon the Saturday following (the day on which we constantly made up our accounts) I went early to the office, and enquired if the ten pounds had yet been paid in; but not hearing that one shilling of it had found its way thither, I immediately supplied the sum out of my own pocket and directed the treasurer to charge it received from me, in the deficient receipt of the benefit day. Here, now, it might be imagined all this silly matter was accommodated, and that no one could so properly say he was aggrieved as myself. But let us observe what the consequence says – why the effect of my insolent, interposing honesty proved to be this: that the party most obliged was the most offended, and the offence was imputed to me, who had been ten pounds out of pocket, to be able to commit it. For when Wilks found in the account how spitefully the ten pounds had been paid in, he took me aside into the adjacent stone passage, and with some warmth asked me what I meant by pretending to pay in this ten pounds, and that for his part he did not understand such treatment. To which I replied that though I was amazed at his thinking himself ill treated, I would give him a plain, justifiable answer: that I had given my word to Doggett the charge of the benefit should be fully paid, and since his friends had neglected it, I found myself bound to make it good. Upon which he told me I was mistaken if I thought he did not see into the bottom of all this: that Doggett and I were always endeavouring to thwart and make him uneasy, but he was able to stand upon his own legs, and we should find he would not be used so; that he took this payment of the ten

---

11 i.e. the standard deduction of costs from the profit due to the actor-beneficiary.
12 'Ready money' was taken on the door, and for benefit performances actors often sold their own tickets in advance; management costs were deducted from the overall takings. Doggett therefore accused Wilks of withholding money taken on the door from the calculation of the day's earnings as a favour to his Irish colleagues. The agreement between Brett, Cibber, Wilks, and Estcourt dated 31 March 1708 (*Document Register* no.1971) sets out a system of deductions from actor benefits that penalized lower-paid performers.

pounds as an insult upon him and a slight to his friends, but rather than suffer it he would tear the whole business to pieces; that I knew it was in his power to do it; and if he could not do a civil thing to a friend without all this senseless rout about it, he could be received in Ireland upon his own terms and could as easily mend a company there as he had done here; that if he were gone, Doggett and I would not be able to keep the doors open a week, and by God he would not be a drudge for nothing. As I knew all this was but the foam of the high value he had set upon himself, I thought it not amiss to seem a little silently concerned for the helpless condition to which his resentment of the injury I have related was going to reduce us. For I knew I had a friend in his heart that, if I gave him a little time to cool, would soon bring him to reason: the sweet morsel of a thousand pounds a year was not to be met with at every table, and might tempt a nicer palate than his own to swallow it when he was not out of humour. This, I knew, would always be of weight with him when the best arguments I could use would be of none. I therefore gave him no farther provocation than by gravely telling him we all had it in our power to do one another a mischief, but I believed none of us much cared to hurt ourselves; that if he was not of my opinion, it would not be in my power to hinder whatever new scheme he might resolve upon; that London would always have a playhouse and I should have some chance in it, though it might not be so good as it had been; that he might be sure, if I had thought my paying in the ten pounds could have been so ill received, I should have been glad to have saved it. Upon this he seemed to mutter something to himself and walked off, as if he had a mind to be alone. I took the occasion, and returned to Doggett to finish our accounts. In about six minutes Wilks came in to us not in the best humour, it may be imagined, yet not in so ill a one but that he took his share of the ten pounds without showing the least contempt of it; which, had he been proud enough to have refused or to have paid in himself, I might have thought he intended to make good his menaces, and that the injury I had done him would never have been forgiven – but it seems we had different ways of thinking.

Of this kind, more or less delightful, was the life I led with this impatient man for full twenty years. Doggett, as we shall find, could not hold it so long; but as he had more money than I, he had not occasion for so much philosophy. And thus were our theatrical affairs frequently disconcerted by this irascible commander, this Achilles of our confederacy, who I may be bold to say came very little short of the spirit Horace gives to that hero in his –

Impiger, iracundus, inexorabilis, acer.[13]

13 'Active, irascible, implacable and fierce'; from Horace, *The Art of Poetry*, line 121.

This, then, is one of those personal anecdotes of our variances which, as our public performances were affected by it, could not with regard to truth and justice be omitted.

From this time to the year 1712, my memory (from which repository alone every article of what I write is collected) has nothing worth mentioning, till the first acting of the tragedy of *Cato*.[14] As to the play itself, it might be enough to say that the author and the actors had their different hopes of fame and profit amply answered by the performance; but as its success was attended with remarkable consequences, it may not be amiss to trace it from its several years' concealment in the closet to the stage.

In 1703, nine years before it was acted, I had the pleasure of reading the first four acts (which was all of it then written) privately with Sir Richard Steele.[15] It may be needless to say it was impossible to lay them out of my hand till I had gone through them, or to dwell upon the delight his friendship to the author received upon my being so warmly pleased with them. But my satisfaction was as highly disappointed when he told me, whatever spirit Mr Addison had shown in his writing it, he doubted he would never have courage enough to let his *Cato* stand the censure of an English audience; that it had only been the amusement of his leisure hours in Italy and was never intended for the stage. This poetical diffidence Sir Richard himself spoke of with some concern, and in the transport of his imagination could not help saying, 'Good God! What a part would Betterton make of Cato!' But this was seven years before Betterton died, and when Booth (who afterwards made his fortune by acting it) was in his theatrical minority. In the latter end of Queen Anne's reign, when our national politics had changed hands, the friends of Mr Addison then thought it a proper time to animate the public with the sentiments of *Cato*. In a word, their importunities were too warm to be resisted, and it was no sooner finished than hurried to the stage, in April 1712, at a time when three days a week were usually appointed for the benefit plays of particular actors.[16] But a work of that critical importance was to make its way through all private considera-

14 See above, p.91 n.11. Cibber's memory was playing tricks here. *Cato* opened in April 1713; the benefits that caused the argument with Wilks took place more than two years later (as above, p.291 n.8) at a time when Doggett was no longer fulfilling his duties (above, p.291 n.10).

15 Addison began writing *Cato* soon after his election to a fellowship of Magdalen College Oxford in 1698; by 1703, when he returned to England after a continental tour, four acts were complete. Cibber takes his 'nine years' from misdating the year of the premiere as 1712. See Peter Smithers, *The Life of Joseph Addison* (Oxford: Clarendon Press, 1968), pp.250–2.

16 This does not mean members of the wider company missed out as a result of the play's success, or did not benefit from Addison forgoing his own profit (see below, n.18), even though, as Cibber goes on to explain, that money was pre-invested in production costs.

tions; nor could it possibly give place to a custom which the breach of could very little prejudice the benefits that, on so unavoidable an occasion, were in part, though not wholly, postponed. It was therefore (Mondays excepted) acted every day for a month, to constantly crowded houses.[17] As the author had made us a present of whatever profits he might have claimed from it,[18] we thought ourselves obliged to spare no cost in the proper decorations of it. Its coming so late in the season to the stage proved of particular advantage to the sharing actors, because the harvest of our annual gains was generally over before the middle of March, many select audiences being then usually reserved in favour to the benefits of private actors;[19] which fixed engagements naturally abated the receipts of the days before and after them. But this unexpected after-crop of *Cato* largely supplied to us those deficiencies, and was almost equal to two fruitful seasons in the same year; at the close of which, the three managing actors found themselves each a gainer of thirteen hundred and fifty pounds. But to return to the first reception of this play from the public.

Although *Cato* seems plainly written upon what are called Whig principles, yet the Tories of that time had sense enough not to take it as the least reflection upon their administration; but on the contrary, they seemed to brandish and vaunt their approbation of every sentiment in favour of liberty,[20] which by a public act of their generosity was carried so high that

As shown below (n.19), a large number of actor-benefits followed *Cato*'s run; there were many more in the subsequent season (as above, p.291 n.10).

17 i.e. for twenty performances. Of the eighteenth performance, on 7 May 1713, George Berkeley wrote, 'Mr Addison's play has taken wonderfully; they have acted it now almost a month, and would I believe act it a month longer were it not that Mrs Oldfield cannot hold out any longer, having had for several nights past, as I am informed, a midwife behind the scenes' (letter to Sir John Perceval cited in LS2 301).

18 i.e. the profits of every third performance, which by convention went to the author (LS1 lxxxi).

19 The articles of regulation dated 17 April 1712 forbade benefit performances before 1 March in any season. In the run-up to *Cato*, benefits had been scheduled for Barton Booth (Banks's *The Unhappy Favourite*, 23 March 1713; LS2 298), John Mills (*Julius Caesar*, 16 March 1713; LS2 297), and George Powell (Banks's *Virtue Betrayed; or Anna Bullen*, 9 March 1713; LS2 297). The success of *Cato* and the buoyancy of the company are reflected in the number and frequency of further benefit performances in the two months after Addison's play closed. In May alone there were five: Jane Rogers (Steele's *The Funeral*, 11 May 1713; LS2 302), William Bullock (*King Henry the Fourth*, 18 May 1713; LS2 303), Henry Norris (Congreve's *Love for Love*, 25 May 1713; LS2 303), Frances Knight (Etherege's *Love in a Tub*, 27 May 1713; LS2 303), and Susannah Mountfort (Charles Shadwell's *The Fair Quaker of Deal*, 29 May 1713; LS2 303). A further ten followed in June, including one for Richard Castleman, the company treasurer (Vanbrugh's *The Pilgrim*, 1 June 1713; LS2 303).

20 Smithers, *Life of Addison*, p.255, attributes this response to the leadership of Sir Robert Harley, Queen Anne's de facto First Minister, who had recently secured approval for the Treaty of Utrecht, so bringing an end to the War of the Spanish Succession.

one day, while the play was acting, they collected fifty guineas in the boxes and made a present of them to Booth with this compliment: 'for his honest opposition to a perpetual dictator, and his dying so bravely in the cause of liberty'. What was insinuated by any part of these words is not my affair,[21] but so public a reward had the appearance of a laudable spirit which only such a play as *Cato* could have inspired; nor could Booth be blamed if, upon so particular a distinction of his merit, he began himself to set more value upon it. How far he might carry it in making use of the favour he stood in with a certain nobleman then in power at court was not difficult to penetrate,[22] and indeed ought always to have been expected by the managing actors. For which of them (making the case every way his own) could with such advantages have contented himself in the humble station of an hired actor? But let us see how the managers stood severally affected upon this occasion.

Doggett, who expected (though he feared not) the attempt of what after happened, imagined he had thought of an expedient to prevent it. And to cover his design with all the art of a statesman, he insinuated to us (for he was a staunch Whig) that this present of fifty guineas was a sort of a Tory triumph which they had no pretence to; and that for his part, he could not bear that so redoubted a champion for liberty as Cato should be bought off to the cause of a contrary party. He therefore, in the seeming zeal of his heart, proposed that the managers themselves should make the same present to Booth which had been made him from the boxes the day before. This, he said, would recommend the equality and liberal spirit of our management to the town, and might be a means to secure Booth more firmly in our interest, it never having been known that the skill of the best actor had received so round a reward or gratuity in one day before. Wilks, who wanted nothing but abilities to be as cunning as Doggett, was so charmed with the proposal that he longed that moment to make Booth the present with his own hands, and though he knew he

---

21 Lowe detects a reference to continuing support for John Churchill, 1st Duke of Marlborough (1650–1722), who, in spite of his record as a war hero against the 'perpetual dictator', Louis XIV, had been dismissed from all court posts in December 1711 and stood accused of defrauding the Exchequer in the building of Blenheim Palace. The death to which Cibber refers was, of course, Cato's.

22 Lowe quotes Theophilus Cibber's *Lives*, p.6, on the actor's friendship with Henry St John, 1st Viscount Bolingbroke, from 1710 Secretary of State in Harley's government; their relationship was, in Theophilus's words, 'of eminent advantage to Mr Booth, when, on his great success in the part of Cato (of which he was the original actor) my Lord's interest (then Secretary of State) established him as a manager of the theatre'. See also Smithers, *Life of Addison*, p.256. Booth had been soliciting Lord Lansdowne for a managerial share since December 1712 (*Document Register* nos.2210 and 2211).

had no right to do it without my consent, had no patience to ask it; upon which I turned to Doggett, with a cold smile, and told him that if Booth could be purchased at so cheap a rate, it would be one of the best proofs of his economy we had ever been beholden to.[23] I therefore desired we might have a little patience; that our doing it too hastily might be only making sure of an occasion to throw the fifty guineas away, for if we should be obliged to do better for him, we could never expect that Booth would think himself bound in honour to refund them. This seemed so absurd an argument to Wilks that he began, with his usual freedom of speech, to treat it as a pitiful evasion of their intended generosity. But Doggett, who was not so wide of my meaning, clapping his hand upon mine, said (with an air of security), 'Oh, don't trouble yourself! There must be two words to that bargain; let me alone, to manage that matter'. Wilks, upon this dark discourse, grew uneasy, as if there were some secret between us that he was to be left out of. Therefore, to avoid the shock of his intemperance, I was reduced to tell him that it was my opinion that Booth would never be made easy by anything we could do for him till he had a share in the profits and management; and that, as he did not want friends to assist him, whatever his merit might be before, everyone would think (since his acting of Cato) he had now enough to back his pretensions to it. To which Doggett replied that nobody could think his merit was slighted by so handsome a present as fifty guineas; and that for his farther pretensions, whatever the licence might avail, our property of house, scenes, and clothes were our own and not in the power of the Crown to dispose of. To conclude, my objections that the money would be only thrown away, *etc*, were over-ruled, and the same night Booth had the fifty guineas, which he received with a thankfulness that made Wilks and Doggett perfectly easy insomuch that they seemed, for some time, to triumph in their conduct, and often endeavoured to laugh my jealousy out of countenance. But in the following winter the game happened to take a different turn; and then, if it had been a laughing matter, I had as strong an occasion to smile at their former security. But before I make an end of this matter, I cannot pass over the good fortune of the company that followed us to the act at Oxford, which was held in the intervening summer.[24] Perhaps too, a short view of the stage in that different situation may not be unacceptable to the curious.

23 Doggett hoped to buy off Booth's managerial ambitions.
24 i.e. the summer of 1713. An advertisement for *The Tempest* at Drury Lane on 23 June 1713 announces 'This is positively the last time of acting till winter, the company being obliged to go immediately to Oxford' (LS2 305).

After the Restoration of King Charles, before the Cavalier and Round-head parties under their new denomination of Whig and Tory[25] began again to be politically troublesome, public acts at Oxford (as I find by the date of several prologues written by Dryden for Hart on those occasions) had been more frequently held than in later reigns.[26] Whether the same party dis-sensions may have occasioned the discontinuance of them is a speculation not necessary to be entered into. But these academical jubilees have usually been looked upon as a kind of congratulatory compliment to the accession of every new prince to the throne and generally, as such, have attended them. King James,[27] notwithstanding his religion, had the honour of it, at which the players, as usual, assisted. This I have only mentioned to give the reader a theatrical anecdote of a liberty which Tony Leigh the comedian took with the character of the well-known Obadiah Walker, then head of University College, who in that prince's reign had turned Roman Catho-lic.[28] The circumstance is this.

In the latter end of the comedy called *The Committee*, Leigh (who acted the part of Teague)[29] hauling in Obadiah with an halter about his neck, whom according to his written part he was to threaten to hang for no bet-ter reason than his refusing to drink the King's health – but here Leigh, to justify his purpose with a stronger provocation, put himself into a more

25 Terms that arose during the Popish Plot years of 1678–82. Cibber's equation of Whig–Roundhead and Tory–Cavalier is not flippant; there were commonalities on the roles of Church, Crown, and Parliament.

26 Dryden published four Oxford-related prologues and one epilogue in *Miscellany Poems, By the most Eminent Hands* (1684). His 'Prologue, To the University of Oxford' was spoken by Charles Hart before an Oxford performance of Jonson's *Epicoene* in July 1673; Hart spoke a further prologue with the same title before an unnamed play in July 1674, with an epilogue spoken by Rebecca Marshall. Dryden's third Oxford prologue was given in July 1680 and refers to the 'discord and plots which have undone our age'. His fourth and last, given in July 1686, claims that 'Oxford to him a dearer name shall be, / Than his own mother university' (i.e. Cambridge); Dryden, p.311. Oxford visits pre-dated Dryden's prologues: there were several visits by the Duke's Company between July 1661 and 1671. For further details, see Sybil Rosenfeld, 'Some Notes on the Players in Oxford, 1661–1713', *Review of English Studies* vol. 19 (October 1943), 366–75.

27 i.e. James II; the occasion in question was in 1686, as above, n.26. Cibber's explanation for these 'academical jubilees' fits the dates for the accessions of Charles II and James II, but not those of William and Mary, Anne, or George I; the longer summer seasons in London by then made them impractical.

28 Obadiah Walker (1616–99) became Master of University College Oxford in 1676 and declared his conversion to Catholicism following James II's accession in 1685. He fled Oxford in 1688; arrested and tried for treason, he was released in 1690. See also above, p.111 n.76.

29 A crudely stereotypical Irishman; hence the spelling in the quotation that follows. Irish actors Richard Estcourt and Thomas Griffith were sometimes cast in the role (LS2 265 and 273).

than ordinary heat with his captive Obadiah; which, having heightened his master's curiosity to know what Obadiah had done to deserve such usage, Leigh, folding his arms with a ridiculous stare of astonishment, replied, 'Upon my shoul, he has shange his religion!' As the merit of this jest lay chiefly in the auditors' sudden application of it to the Obadiah of Oxford, it was received with all the triumph of applause which the zeal of a different religion could inspire. But Leigh was given to understand that the King was highly displeased at it, in as much as it had shown him that the University was in a temper to make a jest of his proselyte.[30] But to return to the conduct of our own affairs there in 1712.[31]

It had been a custom for the comedians, while at Oxford, to act twice a day; the first play ending every morning before the college hours of dining, and the other never to break into the time of shutting their gates in the evening.[32] This extraordinary labour gave all the hired actors a title to double pay, which at the act in King William's time I had myself accordingly received there.[33] But the present managers considering that by acting only once a day their spirits might be fresher for every single performance, and that by this means they might be able to fill up the term of their residence without the repetition of their best and strongest plays – and, as their theatre was contrived to hold a full third more than the usual form of it had done – one house well filled might answer the profits of two but moderately taken up.[34] Being enabled, too, by their late success at London, to make the journey pleasant and profitable to the rest of their society, they resolved to continue to them their double pay, notwithstanding this new abatement of half their labour. This conduct of the managers more than answered their intention, which was rather to get nothing themselves than not let their fraternity be the better for the expedition. Thus they laid an obligation upon their company, and were themselves considerably (though unexpected) gainers by it. But my chief reason for bringing the reader to

30 Sir Robert Howard's *The Committee* had been a favourite since it was first performed by the King's Company during the 1661–2 season; James II had seen it performed by the United Company as recently as 8 April 1686 (LS1 348). The episode Cibber refers to is in Howard's *Four New Plays* (London: Henry Herringman, 1664), pp.133–4. Teague is asked by Colonel Carless, 'Why dost thou lead Obadiah thus?', to which Teague answers, 'He would not let me make him drunk.' See also above, p.111 n.76.
31 i.e. 1713, as above, p.297 n.24.   32 Typically at midnight.
33 i.e. the visit of July 1693 (Rosenfeld, p.371).
34 Various Oxford venues had been used by visiting companies: the King's Arms (1661), The Guildhall (1669), a new playhouse at Broken Hays, Gloucester Green (1670), the New Tennis Court off St Aldate's (1671), and Robert à Wood's Tennis Court near Merton College (1680); it was probably the latter venue that was expanded as Cibber indicates between 1693 (his own previous visit) and 1713.

Oxford was to show the different taste of plays there from that which prevailed at London. A great deal of that false, flashy wit and forced humour which had been the delight of our metropolitan multitude was only rated there at its bare, intrinsic value. Applause was not to be purchased there but by the true sterling, the *sal atticum* of a genius,[35] unless where the skill of the actor passed it upon them with some extraordinary strokes of Nature. Shakespeare and Jonson had there a sort of classical authority, for whose masterly scenes they seemed to have as implicit a reverence as formerly for the *Ethics* of Aristotle; and were as incapable of allowing moderns to be their competitors as of changing their academical habits for gaudy colours or embroidery.[36] Whatever merit, therefore, some few of our more politely written comedies might pretend to, they had not the same effect upon the imagination there, nor were received with that extraordinary applause they had met with from the people of mode and pleasure in London, whose vain accomplishments did not dislike themselves in the glass that was held to them. The elegant follies of higher life were not, at Oxford, among their acquaintance, and consequently might not be so good company to a learned audience as Nature, in her plain dress and unornamented in her pursuits and inclinations, seemed to be.

The only distinguished merit allowed to any modern writer was to the author of *Cato*, which play being the flower of a plant raised in that learned garden (for there Mr Addison had his education),[37] what favour may we not suppose was due to him from an audience of brethren, who from that local relation to him might naturally have a warmer pleasure in their benevolence

35 i.e. a feeling of well-being, elation. The advantages of playing to a learned audience were a common theme of Dryden's Oxford prologues, as listed above, p.298 n.26. However, a letter from Dryden to the Earl of Rochester, referring to the visit of 1673, tells a different story: 'I have sent Your Lordship a prologue and epilogue which I made for our players when they went down to Oxford. I hear, since, they have succeeded; and by the event your Lordship will judge how easy 'tis to pass anything upon an university, and how gross flattery the learned will endure' (cited in Winn, p.252).

36 Ten plays by Shakespeare and Jonson had been performed in the 1712–13 Drury Lane season, so the company had a rich vein of recent work to draw on: *The Tempest, Macbeth, King Henry the Fourth, Julius Caesar, Othello, Epicoene, Richard III, Bartholomew Fair, Volpone,* and *Hamlet*. The subsequent passage suggests that *Julius Caesar* played with Addison's *Cato*. In writing this section Cibber may have been influenced by the Dryden prologues and epilogues referred to on p.298, above. Dryden's 1673 Oxford epilogue claims that in London 'Fletcher's despised, your Jonson out of fashion', and that Shakespeare is only popular because of the special effects of Davenant's *Macbeth*, 'the Simon Magus of the town'. The 1674 Oxford prologue asks 'That Shakespeare's, Fletcher's and great Jonson's claim / May be renewed from those who gave them fame', and goes on to state that 'None of our living poets dare appear' (Dryden, p.307).

37 Addison matriculated at Queen's College Oxford in 1687 and became a Fellow of Magdalen College in 1698.

to his fame? But not to give more weight to this imaginary circumstance than it may bear, the fact was that on our first day of acting it, our house was in a manner invested; and, entrance demanded by twelve o'clock at noon and before one, it was not wide enough for many who came too late for places. The same crowds continued for three days together (an uncommon curiosity in that place), and the death of Cato triumphed over the injuries of Caesar everywhere. To conclude, our reception at Oxford, whatever our merit might be, exceeded our expectation. At our taking leave, we had the thanks of the Vice-Chancellor for the decency and order observed by our whole society,[38] an honour which had not always been paid upon the same occasions; for at the act in King William's time, I remember some pranks of a different nature had been complained of.[39] Our receipts had not only enabled us (as I have observed) to double the pay of every actor, but to afford out of them, towards the repair of St Mary's Church,[40] the contribution of fifty pounds. Besides which, each of the three managers had to his respective share, clear of all charges, one hundred and fifty more for his one and twenty day's labour;[41] which, being added to his thirteen hundred and fifty shared in the winter preceding, amounted in the whole to fifteen hundred – the greatest sum ever known to have been shared in one year to that time.[42] And to the honour of our auditors here and elsewhere be it spoken: all this was raised without the aid of those barbarous entertainments with which, some few years after (upon the re-establishment of two contending companies), we were forced to disgrace the stage to support it.[43]

This, therefore, is that remarkable period when the stage, during my time upon it, was the least reproachable. And it may be worth the public observation (if anything I have said of it can be so) that *one* stage may, as I have

38 The Vice-Chancellor at this time was Bernard Gardiner (1668–1726), Warden of All Souls College.

39 Presumably the visit of 1693 (see above, p.299 n.33), but complaints about actors' misbehaviour in Oxford went further back. In July 1674 the King's Company actors were 'guilty of such great rudenesses before they left' (Letter from Humphrey Prideaux to John Ellis, 28 July 1674, BL Add.MS 28,929, fol.iv; *Document Register* no.859).

40 i.e. The University Church of St Mary the Virgin, Oxford High Street.

41 Probably a reference to acting days. Since the company began playing in Oxford in the last week of June 1713, this would have taken them into the latter part of July. The London season resumed on 22 September (LS2 308).

42 A report on Drury Lane profits drafted in December 1716 emphasizes the decline since 1713: for the 1713–14 season the managers shared £3,747; two years later that sum had shrunk to £1,288 (C38/335, n.p.; *Document Register* no.2228).

43 A reference to the re-opening of the Lincoln's Inn Fields theatre in December 1714 and of Drury Lane's response (see below, p.302 n.44). Cibber's disparagement of the repertory that resulted is less true of Drury Lane than of Lincoln's Inn Fields, where dancing and farces were common.

proved it has done, very laudably support itself by such spectacles only as are fit to delight a sensible people; but the equal prosperity of *two* stages has always been of a very short duration. If, therefore, the public should ever recover into the true taste of that time and stick to it, the stage must come into it or *starve* as, whenever the general taste is vulgar, the stage must come down to it to *live*. But I ask pardon of the multitude who, in all regulations of the stage, may expect to be a little indulged in what they like. If, therefore, they *will* have a maypole, why the players must *give* them a maypole;[44] but I only speak in case they should keep an old custom of changing their minds, and by their privilege of being in the wrong, should take a fancy (by way of variety) of being in the right. Then, in such a case, what I have said may appear to have been no intended design against their liberty of judging for themselves.

After our return from Oxford, Booth was at full leisure to solicit his admission to a share in the management,[45] in which he succeeded about the beginning of the following winter. Accordingly, a new licence (recalling all former licences) was issued, wherein Booth's name was added to those of the other managers.[46] But still there was a difficulty in his qualification to be adjusted: what consideration he should allow for an equal title to our stock of clothes, scenes, *etc*, without which the licence was of no more use than the stock was without the licence – or at least, if there were any difference, the former managers seemed to have the advantage in it, the stock being entirely theirs and three parts in four of the licence (for Collier, though now but a fifth manager, still insisted on his former appointment of £700 a year, which in equity ought certainly to have been proportionably abated). But court favour was not always measured by that yard. Collier's matter was soon out of the question – his pretensions were too visible to be contested[47] – but the affair of Booth was not so clear a point. The Lord

---

44 Presumably a reference to the dance entertainments mounted by Lincoln's Inn Fields, often punctuating such established plays as Farquhar's *The Recruiting Officer*, Southerne's *Oroonoko*, and even *Macbeth* (February–March 1715; LS2 344, 345, 346).

45 Lowe quotes Theophilus Cibber's *Lives*, p.7, on his father's and Booth's visits to the Court at Windsor 'to push their different interests'. He further quotes Chetwood, p.93, on the schemes the existing patentees forged to frustrate Booth's plans:

> to prevent his soliciting his patrons at court, then at Windsor, [the patentees] gave out plays every night where Mr Booth had a principal part. Notwithstanding this step, he had a chariot and six of a nobleman's waiting for him at the end of every play, that whipped him the twenty miles in three hours, and brought him back to the business of the theatre the next night.

46 The licence for Booth, Cibber, Collier, Doggett, and Wilks is dated 11 November, 1713 (LC 5/155, fol.149; *Document Register* no.2230).

47 However, Collier petitioned Lord Chamberlain Shrewsbury in February 1714 (LC 7/3, fols.127–8; *Document Register* no.2300).

Chamberlain, therefore, only recommended it to be adjusted among ourselves; which, to say the truth, at that time was a greater indulgence than I expected. Let us see, then, how this critical case was handled.

Wilks was of opinion that to set a good round value upon our stock was the only way to come near an equivalent for the diminution of our shares which the admission of Booth must occasion.[48] But Doggett insisted that he had no mind to dispose of any part of his property, and therefore would set no price upon it at all. Though I allowed that both these opinions might be grounded on a good deal of equity, yet I was not sure that either of them was practicable, and therefore told them that when they could both agree which of them could be made so, they might rely on my consent in any shape. In the meantime, I desired they would consider that as our licence subsisted only during pleasure, we could not pretend that the Queen might not recall or alter it, but that to speak out (without mincing the matter on either side), the truth was plainly this: that Booth had a manifest merit as an actor, and as he was not supposed to be a Whig it was as evident that (a good deal for that reason) a Secretary of State had taken him into his protection,[49] which I was afraid the weak pretence of our invaded property would not be able to contend with; that his having signalised himself in the character of Cato (whose principles the Tories had affected to have taken into their own possession) was a very popular pretence of making him free of the stage by advancing him to the profits of it; and, as we had seen, that the stage was frequently treated as if it was not supposed to have any property at all, this favour intended to Booth was thought a right occasion to avow that opinion by disposing of its property at pleasure. But be that as it might, I owned it was not so much my apprehensions of what the Court might do that swayed me into an accommodation with Booth, as what the town (in whose favour he now apparently stood) might think ought to be done: that there might be more danger in contesting their arbitrary will and pleasure than in disputing this less terrible strain of the prerogative; that if Booth were only imposed upon us from his merit to the Court, we were then in the condition of other subjects – then, indeed, law, right and possession might have a tolerable tug for our property. But as the town would

48 On 12 November 1713, the day after Booth was included in the new licence to run Drury Lane, Cibber and Wilks reported the value of the theatre's stock as £5,350, or c.£1.2m in current values (C/11/6/44; *Document Register* no.2231). As Cibber admits while attributing the sleight of hand to Wilks, this was a way of inflating the amount Booth would need to pay for a share (around the double the £600 he eventually paid, as below, p.305). Learning of the new licence, Vanbrugh laid claim to a share of the stock on 20 November 1713 (*Document Register* no.2232).

49 i.e. Henry St John, Viscount Bolingbroke, an arch Tory (see above, p.34 n.28).

always look upon his merit to them in a stronger light and be judges of it themselves, it would be a weak and idle endeavour in us not to sail with the stream, when we might possibly make a merit of our cheerfully admitting him; that though his former opposition to our interest might, between man and man, a good deal justify our not making an earlier friend of him, yet that was a disobligation out of the town's regard, and consequently would be of no weight against so approved an actor's being preferred. But all this notwithstanding, if they could both agree in a different opinion, I would (at the hazard of any consequence) be guided by it.[50]

Here, now, will be shown another instance of our different tempers. Doggett (who, in all matters that concerned our common weal and interest, little regarded our opinion and even to an obstinacy walked by his own) looked only out of humour at what I had said, and without thinking himself obliged to give any reason for it, declared he would maintain his property. Wilks (who upon the same occasions was as remarkably ductile as, when his superiority on the stage was in question, he was assuming and intractable) said, for his part, provided our business of acting was not interrupted, he did not care what we did; but in short, he was for playing on, come what would of it. This last part of his declaration I did not dislike, and therefore I desired we might all enter into an immediate treaty with Booth upon the terms of his admission. Doggett still sullenly replied that he had no occasion to enter into any treaty. Wilks then, to soften him, proposed that if I liked it, Doggett might undertake it himself. I agreed. No! He would not be concerned in it. I then offered the same trust to Wilks, if Doggett approved of it. Wilks said he was not good at making of bargains, but if I was willing, he would rather leave it to me. Doggett, at this, rose up and said we might both do as we pleased, but that nothing but the law should make him part with his property – and so went out of the room, after which he never came among us more, either as an actor or manager.[51]

---

50 Barker, p.93, doubts Cibber's account of this episode, arguing that the price of Booth's share was mandated by Lord Chamberlain Shrewsbury and that Cibber is merely attempting to demonstrate his skill as a negotiator; however, his interpretation relates to the later events of summer 1714 which Cibber describes below, p.306 (and n.55). As for the initial discussion about stock valuation, *Document Register* shows that Booth asked the Lord Chamberlain's office to issue the new licence without waiting for the stock dispute to be settled, that the licence was duly issued only a week later (nos.2229 and 2230), and that Wilks and Cibber presented their stock valuation the following day (as above, p.303 n.48).

51 Doggett's last known appearance for the company that season was on 19 November 1713, as Sir Oliver Cockwood in Etherege's *She Would If She Could* (LS2 311). Wilks played Courtall, but there was no role for Cibber. Cibber and Wilks complained to Lord Chamberlain Shrewsbury's office about Doggett's stance on 16 January 1714 (*Document Register* no.2262), as did William Collier (*Document Register* no.2263).

By his having in this abrupt manner abdicated his post in our government, what he left of it naturally devolved upon Wilks and myself. However, this did not so much distress our affair as I have reason to believe Doggett thought it would. For though, by our indentures tripartite, we could not dispose of his property without his consent, yet those indentures could not oblige us to fast because he had no appetite; and if the mill did not grind, we could have no bread. We therefore determined at any hazard to keep our business still going, and that our safest way would be to make the best bargain we could with Booth, one article of which was to be that Booth should stand equally answerable with us to Doggett for the consequence; to which Booth made no objection, and the rest of his agreement was to allow us six hundred pounds for his share in our property, which was to be paid by such sums as should arise from half his profits of acting, till the whole was discharged. Yet so cautious were we in this affair that this agreement was only verbal on our part, though written and signed by Booth as what entirely contented him. However, bond and judgment could not have made it more secure to him, for he had his share, and was able to discharge the encumbrance upon it by his income of that year only. Let us see what Doggett did in this affair after he had left us.

Might it not be imagined that Wilks and myself, by having made this matter easy to Booth, should have deserved the approbation, at least, if not the favour of the Court that had exerted so much power to prefer him? But shall I be believed when I affirm that Doggett, who had so strongly opposed the Court in his admission to a share, was very near getting the better of us both upon that account, and for some time appeared to have more favour there than either of us? Let me tell out my story, and then think what you please of it.

Doggett, who was equally obliged with us to act upon the stage as to assist in the management of it, though he had refused to do either still demanded of us his whole share of the profits, without considering what part of them Booth might pretend to from our late concessions. After many fruitless endeavours to bring him back to us, Booth joined with us in making him an offer of half a share, if he had a mind totally to quit the stage and make it a sinecure. No! He wanted the whole, and to sit still himself while we (if we pleased) might work for him or let it alone, and none of us all (neither he nor we) be the better for it. What, we imagined, encouraged him to hold us at this short defiance was that he had laid up enough to live upon without the stage (for he was one of those close economists whom prodigals call a miser) and therefore, partly from an inclination as an invincible Whig, to signalise himself in defence of his property[52] (and as much presuming that our necessities would oblige us to come to his own terms), he was determined, even against the opinion of his friends, to make no other peace with us. But not being able, by this inflexible perseverance, to have his wicked will of us, he was resolved to go to the fountain head of his own distress, and try if from thence he could turn the current against us. He appealed to the Vice-Chamberlain,[53] to whose direction the adjusting of all these theatrical difficulties was then committed; but there, I dare say, the reader does not expect he should meet with much favour. However, be that as it may; for whether any regard was had to his having some thousands in his pocket, or that he was considered as a man who would or could make more noise in the matter than courtiers might care for (or what charms, spells or conjurations he might make use of),[54] is all darkness to me. Yet so it was, he one way or other played his part so well that in a few days after we received an order from the Vice-Chamberlain positively commanding us to pay Doggett his whole share, notwithstanding we had complained before of his having withdrawn himself from acting on the stage and from the management of it.[55] This I thought was a dainty distinction indeed: that Doggett's defiance of the commands in favour of Booth should be rewarded with so ample a sinecure and that we, for our obedience, should be condemned to dig in the mine to pay it him! This bitter pill, I confess, was more than I could down with, and therefore soon determined at all events never to take it. But as I had a man in power to deal with, it was not my business to speak out to him or to set forth our treatment in its proper colours. My only doubt was whether I could bring Wilks into the same sentiments (for he never cared to litigate anything that did not affect his figure upon the stage). But I had the good fortune to lay our condition in so precarious and disagreeable a light to him if we submitted to this order, that

---

52 As Evans notes, the importance of 'property' was integral to the Whig ethos of stable government and society, as enshrined in the 1689 Bill of Rights.

53 i.e. Thomas Coke, Vice-Chamberlain as of 3 December 1706 (LC 5/166, p.191; *Document Register* no.1881) and here deputizing for Lord Chamberlain Shrewsbury. On 6 January 1714 Doggett wrote to Coke threatening legal action unless Shrewsbury intervened (Hyde Collection; *Document Register*, no.2243).

54 Cf. *Othello*, I.iii.91–2: 'what drugs, what charms, / What conjuration, and what mighty magic'.

55 During the summer of 1714 Lord Chamberlain Shrewsbury was advised to order Cibber and Wilks to settle with Doggett (HTC Coke no.78; *Document Register* no.2423); following issue of the new Drury Lane licence on 18 October 1714, which included Doggett's name, Cibber and Wilks protested that his role was not a 'sinecure' and asked Shrewsbury to order him back to the company (LC 7/3, fols.133–4; *Document Register* no.2441).

he fired before I could get through half the consequences of it; and I began now to find it more difficult to keep him within bounds than I had before to alarm him. I then proposed to him this expedient: that we should draw up a remonstrance neither seeming to refuse or comply with this order, but to start such objections and perplexing difficulties that should make the whole impracticable; that under such distractions as this would raise in our affairs, we could not be answerable to keep open our doors, which consequently would destroy the fruit of the favour lately granted to Booth as well as of this intended to Doggett himself. To this remonstrance we received an answer in writing, which varied something in the measures to accommodate matters with Doggett. This was all I desired when I found the style of *sic jubeo* was altered;[56] when this formidable power began to parley with us, we knew there could not be much to be feared from it. For I would have remonstrated till I had died, rather than have yielded to the roughest or smoothest persuasion that could intimidate or deceive us. By this conduct we made the affair, at last, too troublesome for the ease of a courtier to go through with; for when it was considered that the principal point – the admission of Booth – was got over, Doggett was fairly left to the law for relief.

Upon this disappointment, Doggett accordingly preferred a bill in Chancery against us.[57] Wilks, who hated all business but that of entertaining the public, left the conduct of our cause to me, in which we had, at our first setting out, this advantage of Doggett: that we had three pockets to support our expense, where he had but one. My first direction to our solicitor was to use all possible delay that the law would admit of (a direction that lawyers seldom neglect). By this means we hung up our plaintiff about two years in Chancery, till we were at full leisure to come to a hearing before the Lord Chancellor Cowper,[58] which did not happen till after the accession of his late Majesty. The issue of it was this. Doggett had about fourteen days allowed him to make his election whether he would return to act as usual, but he declaring by his counsel that he rather chose to quit the stage, he was decreed six hundred pounds for his share in our property, with 15 per cent interest from the date of the last licence; upon the receipt of which, both parties were to sign general releases and severally to pay their

---

56 'I command it so', as above, p.185 n.32.
57 Doggett's action was brought on 17 December 1714 (C11/6/44; *Document Register* no.2477).
58 William Cowper, 1st Earl Cowper (1665–1723), became the first holder of the office of Lord High Chancellor following the Union of 1707. He presided over the Sacheverell trial (see above, p.273 n.58), resigned when the Tory government was elected in 1710, and returned to the role with George I's accession in 1714.

own costs. By this decree, Doggett, when his lawyer's bill was paid, scarce got one year's purchase of what we had offered him without law, which (as he survived but seven years after it) would have been an annuity of five hundred pounds and a sinecure for life.[59]

Though there are many persons living who know every article of these facts to be true, yet it will be found that the strongest of them was not the strongest occasion of Doggett's quitting the stage. If, therefore, the reader should not have curiosity enough to know how the public came to be deprived of so valuable an actor, let him consider that he is not obliged to go through the rest of this chapter, which I fairly tell him beforehand will only be filled up with a few idle anecdotes leading to that discovery.

After our lawsuit was ended, Doggett for some few years could scarce bear the sight of Wilks or myself, though (as shall be shown) for different reasons. Yet it was his misfortune to meet with us almost every day. Button's coffee house, so celebrated in the *Tatlers* for the good company that came there, was at this time in its highest request.[60] Addison, Steele, Pope, and several other gentlemen of different merit then made it their constant rendezvous. Nor could Doggett decline the agreeable conversation there, though he was daily sure to find Wilks or myself in the same place, to sour his share of it. For as Wilks and he were differently proud (the one rejoicing in a captious, overbearing, valiant pride, and the other in a stiff, sullen, purse-pride), it may be easily conceived, when two such tempers met, how agreeable the sight of one was to the other. And as Doggett knew I had been the conductor of our defence against his lawsuit (which had hurt him more for the loss he had sustained in his reputation of understanding business, which he valued himself upon, than his disappointment had of getting so little by it), it was no wonder if I was entirely out of his good graces – which I confess I was inclined upon any reasonable terms to have recovered, he being of all my theatrical brethren the man I most delighted in; for when he was not in a fit of wisdom or not over-concerned about his interest, he had a great deal of entertaining humour. I therefore, notwithstanding his reserve, always left the door open to our former intimacy if he were inclined to come into it. I never failed to give him my hat[61] and 'your servant' wherever I

59 On 6 March 1717 the case was settled in favour of Cibber and Wilks, with an order that Doggett be given the share in Drury Lane that existed before he quit. He was also given fourteen days to return to the company or face a buy-out from the management.
60 Button's coffee house was established in 1712 by Daniel Button, formerly in the service of Addison's wife, Charlotte, Dowager Countess of Warwick. It was billed as a successor to Will's, where Dryden had presided as literary authority in chief.
61 i.e. lifted his hat as a greeting.

met him, neither of which he would ever return for above a year after; but I still persisted in my usual salutation, without observing whether it was civilly received or not. This ridiculous silence between two comedians that had so lately lived in a constant course of raillery with one another was often smiled at by our acquaintance who frequented the same coffee house; and one of them carried his jest upon it so far that when I was at some distance from town, he wrote me a formal account that Doggett was actually dead. After the first surprise his letter gave me was over, I began to consider that this coming from a droll friend to both of us might possibly be written to extract some merriment out of my real belief of it. In this I was not unwilling to gratify him and returned an answer as if I had taken the truth of his news for granted, and was not a little pleased that I had so fair an opportunity of speaking my mind freely of Doggett, which I did in some favour of his character. I excused his faults and was just to his merit. His lawsuit with us I only imputed to his having naturally deceived himself in the justice of his cause. What I most complained of was his irreconcilable disaffection to me upon it, whom he could not reasonably blame for standing in my own defence; that not to endure me after it was a reflection upon his sense, when all our acquaintance had been witnesses of our former intimacy, which my behaviour in his lifetime had plainly shown him I had a mind to renew. But since he was now gone (however great a churl he was to me), I was sorry my correspondent had lost him.

This part of my letter I was sure, if Doggett's eyes were still open, would be shown to him; if not, I had only writ it to no purpose. But about a month after, when I came to town I had some little reason to imagine it had the effect I wished from it. For one day sitting over against him at the same coffee house, where we often mixed at the same table (though we never exchanged a single syllable), he graciously extended his hand for a pinch of my snuff. As this seemed from him a sort of breaking the ice of his temper, I took courage upon it to break silence on my side, and asked him how he liked it. To which, with a slow hesitation, naturally assisted by the action of his taking the snuff, he replied, 'Umm! The best – umm! – I have tasted a great while!' If the reader (who may possibly think all this extremely trifling) will consider that trifles sometimes show characters in as strong a light as facts of more serious importance, I am in hopes he may allow that my matter less needs an excuse than the excuse itself does; if not, I must stand condemned at the end of my story. But let me go on.

After a few days of these coy, ladylike compliances on his side, we grew into a more conversable temper. At last, I took a proper occasion, and desired he would be so frank with me as to let me know what was his real dislike, or motive, that made him throw up so good an income as his share with us annually brought him in. For though, by our admission of Booth, it might not probably amount to so much by a hundred or two a year as formerly, yet the remainder was too considerable to be quarrelled with, and was likely to continue more than the best actors before us had ever got by the stage. And farther to encourage him to be open, I told him, if I had done anything that had particularly disobliged him, I was ready, if he could put me in the way, to make him any amends in my power; if not, I desired he would be so just to himself as to let me know the real truth without reserve. But reserve he could not from his natural temper easily shake off. All he said came from him by half sentences and innuendos, as 'no, he had not taken anything particularly ill – for his part, he was very easy as he was, but where others were to dispose of his property as they pleased – if you had stood it out as I did, Booth might have paid a better price for it – you were too much afraid of the Court – but that's all over – there were other things in the playhouse – no man of spirit – in short, to be always pestered and provoked by a trifling wasp – a – vain – shallow! – A man would sooner beg his bread than bear it' – (here it was easy to understand him; I therefore asked him what he had to bear that I had not my share of) – 'No! It was not the same thing', he said. 'You can play with a bear or let him alone, and do what he would; but I could not let him lay his paws upon me without being hurt; you did not feel him as I did – and for a man to be cutting of throats upon every trifle, at my time of day! – If I had been as covetous as he thought me, may be I might have borne it as well as you – but I would not be a Lord of the Treasury if such a temper as Wilks's were to be at the head of it'. Here, then, the whole secret was out. The rest of our conversation was but explaining upon it. In a word, the painful behaviour of Wilks had hurt him so sorely that the affair of Booth was looked upon as much a relief as a grievance, in giving him so plausible a pretence to get rid of us all with a better grace.

Booth, too, in a little time had his share of the same uneasiness, and often complained of it to me. Yet, as we neither of us could then afford to pay Doggett's price for our remedy, all we could do was to avoid every occasion in our power of inflaming the distemper; so that we both agreed, though Wilks's nature was not to be changed, it was a less evil to live with him than without him.

Though I had often suspected from what I had felt myself that the temper of Wilks was Doggett's real quarrel to the stage, yet I could never thoroughly believe it till I had it from his own mouth. And I then thought the concern he had shown at it was a good deal inconsistent with that

understanding which was generally allowed him. When I give my reasons
for it, perhaps the reader will not have a better opinion of my own. Be
that as it may, I cannot help wondering that he, who was so much more
capable of reflection than Wilks, could sacrifice so valuable an income to
his impatience of another's natural frailty! And though my stoical way of
thinking may be no rule for a wiser man's opinion, yet if it should happen to be right, the reader may make his use of it. Why, then, should we
not always consider that the rashness of abuse is but the false reason of
a weak man? And that offensive terms are only used to supply the want
of strength in argument which, as to the common practice of the sober
world, we do not find every man in business is obliged to resent with
a military sense of honour? Or if he should, would not the conclusion
amount to this: 'because another wants sense and manners, I am obliged
to be a madman'? For such every man is, more or less, while the passion
of anger is in possession of him. And what less can we call that proud
man who would put another out of the world only for putting him out
of humour? If accounts of the tongue were always to be made up with
the sword, all the wise men in the world might be brought in debtors to
blockheads. And when honour pretends to be witness, judge and executioner in its own cause, if honour were a man, would it be an untruth to
say honour is a very impudent fellow? But in Doggett's case, it may be
asked, how was he to behave himself? Were passionate insults to be borne
for years together? To these questions I can only answer with two or three
more. Was he to punish himself because another was in the wrong? How
many sensible husbands endure the teasing tongue of a forward wife only
because she is the weaker vessel? And why should not a weak man have
the same indulgence? Daily experience will tell us that the fretful temper
of a friend, like the personal beauty of a fine lady, by use and cohabitation
may be brought down to give us neither pain nor pleasure. Such, at least,
and no more, was the distress I found myself in upon the same provocations, which I generally returned with humming an air to myself; or if the
storm grew very high, it might perhaps sometimes ruffle me enough to
sing a little out of tune. Thus, too (if I had any ill nature to gratify), I often
saw the unruly passion of the aggressor's mind punish itself by a restless
disorder of the body.

What inclines me, therefore, to think the conduct of Doggett was
as rash as the provocations he complained of, is that in some time after
he had left us he plainly discovered he had repented it. His acquaintance
observed to us that he sent many a long look after his share in the still
prosperous state of the stage; but as his heart was too high to declare (what

we saw too) his shy inclination to return, he made us no direct overtures. Nor, indeed, did we care (though he was a golden actor) to pay too dear for him, for as most of his parts had been pretty well supplied, he could not now be of his former value to us. However, to show the town, at least, that he had not forsworn the stage, he one day condescended to play for the benefit of Mrs Porter, in *The Wanton Wife*, at which he knew his late Majesty was to be present.[62] Now though I speak it not of my own knowledge, yet it was not likely Mrs Porter would have asked that favour of him without some previous hint that it would be granted. His coming among us for that day only had a strong appearance of his laying it in our way to make him proposals; or that he hoped the Court or town might intimate to us their desire of seeing him oftener. But as he acted only to do a particular favour, the managers owed him no compliment for it beyond common civilities. And, as that might not be all he proposed by it, his farther views (if he had any) came to nothing. For after this attempt, he never returned to the stage.[63]

To speak of him as an actor, he was the most an original and the strictest observer of Nature of all his contemporaries.[64] He borrowed from none of them; his manner was his own. He was a pattern to others, whose greatest merit was that they had sometimes tolerably imitated him. In dressing a character to the greatest exactness, he was remarkably skilful; the least article of whatever habit he wore seemed in some degree to speak and mark the different humour he presented – a necessary care in a comedian, in which many have been too remiss or ignorant. He could be extremely ridiculous without stepping into the least impropriety to make him so. His greatest success was in characters of lower life, which he improved from the delight

---

62 *The Wanton Wife* is the subtitle of Betterton's *The Amorous Widow*; this performance on 18 March 1717 was advertised as 'By Their Royal Highnesses' command' (LS2 441). Mary Porter (d. 1765), noted for her variety of roles and envied by Anne Oldfield for her 'tragedy face' (Chetwood, p.201), began her career with the Lincoln's Inn Fields company during the 1697–8 season, moved with Betterton and others to the Queen's Theatre, Haymarket in 1706, but quit in 1707; an order dated 31 December 1707 forbade her employment at Drury Lane (LC 5/154, p.298; *Document Register* no.1926). Illness in 1731 (*Document Register* no.3594) was the prelude to her retirement.

63 LS2 442 and 444 record two further appearances, on 25 March 1717 (Ben in *Love for Love*) and 1 April 1717 (Hob in his own *The Country Wake*), for benefit performances for Hester Santlow and Mary Bicknell respectively.

64 Lowe quotes Downes's description of Doggett (p.108), 'wearing a farce in his face, his thoughts deliberately framing his utterance congruous to his looks'. Downes goes on to cite his signature roles as Ben in *Love for Love*, Solon in Durfey's *The Marriage-Hater Matched*, Fondlewife in *The Old Batchelor*, and the title role in Granville's 1701 Shakespeare adaptation, *The Jew of Venice*.

he took in his observations of that kind in the real world.⁶⁵ In songs (and particular dances too) of humour he had no competitor. Congreve was a great admirer of him, and found his account in the characters he expressly wrote for him. In those of Fondlewife, in his Old Batchelor, and Ben in *Love for Love*, no author and actor could be more obliged to their mutual masterly performances. He was very acceptable to several persons of high rank and taste, though he seldom cared to be the comedian but among his more intimate acquaintance.

And now, let me ask the world a question. When men have any valuable qualities, why are the generality of our modern wits so fond of exposing their failings only, which the wisest of mankind will never wholly be free from? Is it of more use to the public to know their errors than their perfections? Why is the account of life to be so unequally stated? Though a man may be sometimes debtor to sense or morality, is it not doing him wrong not to let the world see, at the same time, how far he may be creditor to both? Are defects and disproportions to be the only laboured features in a portrait? But perhaps such authors may know how to please the world better than I do, and may naturally suppose that what is delightful to themselves may not be disagreeable to others. For my own part, I confess myself a little touched in conscience at what I have just now observed to the disadvantage of my other brother-manager.

If, therefore, in discovering the true cause of the public's losing so valuable an actor as Doggett, I have been obliged to show the temper of Wilks in its natural complexion, ought I not in amends, and balance of his imperfections, to say at the same time of him that if he was not the most correct or judicious, yet (as Hamlet says of the King his father) 'take him for all in all' *etc*,⁶⁶ he was certainly the most diligent, most laborious, and most useful actor that I have seen upon the stage in fifty years?⁶⁷

65 When preparing for the role of Ben in *Love for Love*, Doggett is said to have taken lodgings in Wapping, heart of London's docklands, in order to talk to sailors; see Anon., *An Essay on Acting* (London, 1744), p.10.

66 *Hamlet*, I.ii.188–9: 'He was a man. Take him for all in all. / I shall not look upon his like again.'

67 Lowe cites the sarcastic response of *The Laureate* (p.83): 'Thy partiality is so notorious with relation to Wilks, that everyone sees you never praise him but to rail at him; and only oil your hone, to whet your razor.'

CHAPTER 15

Sir Richard Steele succeeds Collier in the Theatre Royal. Lincoln's Inn Fields house rebuilt. The patent restored. Eight actors at once desert from the King's Company. Why. A new patent obtained by Sir Richard Steele and assigned in shares to the managing actors of Drury Lane. Of modern pantomimes. The rise of them. Vanity invincible and ashamed. The Non-Juror acted. The author not forgiven, and rewarded for it.

Upon the death of the Queen, plays (as they always had been on the like occasions) were silenced for six weeks. But this happening on the first of August (in the long vacation of the theatre), the observance of that ceremony, which at another juncture would have fallen like wet weather upon their harvest, did them now no particular damage.[1] Their licence, however, being of course to be renewed, that vacation gave the managers time to cast about for the better alteration of it. And since they knew the pension of seven hundred a year which had been levied upon them for Collier must still be paid to somebody, they imagined the merit of a Whig might now have as good a chance for getting into it as that of a Tory had for being continued in it.[2] Having no obligations therefore to Collier (who had made the last penny of them), they applied themselves to Sir Richard Steele, who had distinguished himself by his zeal for the House of Hanover and had been expelled the House of Commons for carrying it (as was judged at a certain crisis) into a reproach of the government.[3] This, we knew, was his pretension to that favour in which he now stood at court.[4] We knew too

---

1 Following Queen Anne's death on 1 August 1714, Drury Lane reopened with *The Recruiting Officer* on 21 September (LS2 329); more like seven weeks than Cibber's six, but an opening date similar to previous seasons.

2 For Collier's protest at being deprived of his interest in the patent, see above, p.283 n.24. George I's ministry was largely drawn from the Whig party, following opposition to his accession from some Tories.

3 Steele had been elected MP for Stockbridge in August 1713, but his staunchly Whig pamphlets, *The Importance of Dunkirk Considered* (1713) and *The Crisis* (1714) – the latter a defence of the Hanoverian succession – led to his being denounced in the Tory-controlled House of Commons and expelled for seditious publication. He was knighted after the period Cibber describes, in April 1715.

4 Probably in the spring of 1713, it was reported that Steele had been offered the Drury Lane patent by Lord Lansdowne, Comptroller of the Royal Household (*Document Register* no.2216).

the obligations the stage had to his writings, there being scarce a comedian of merit in our whole company whom his *Tatlers* had not made better by his public recommendation of them.[5] And many days had our house been particularly filled by the influence and credit of his pen.[6] Obligations of this kind, from a gentleman with whom they all had the pleasure of a personal intimacy, the managers thought could not be more justly returned than by showing him some warm instance of their desire to have him at the head of them. We therefore begged him to use his interest for the renewal of our licence, and that he would do us the honour of getting our names to stand with his in the same commission. This, we told him, would put it still farther into his power of supporting the stage in that reputation to which his lucubrations had already so much contributed; and that therefore we thought no man had better pretences to partake of its success.[7]

Though it may be no addition to the favourable part of this gentleman's character to say with what pleasure he received this mark of our inclination to him, yet my vanity longs to tell you that it surprised him into an acknowledgment that people who are shy of obligations are cautious of confessing. His spirits took such a lively turn upon it that had we been all his own sons, no unexpected act of filial duty could have more endeared us to him.

It must be observed, then, that as Collier had no share in any part of our property, no difficulties from that quarter could obstruct this proposal. And the usual time of our beginning to act for the winter season now drawing near, we pressed him not to lose any time in his solicitation of this new licence. Accordingly, Sir Richard applied himself to the Duke of Marlborough (the hero of his heart), who, upon the first mention of it, obtained it

---

5 *The Tatler* contains commendations of many actors, including Thomas Betterton, Mary Bicknell, and Robert Wilks; Wilks subscribed to the collected edition of 1711. Similar sentiments to those above appear in Cibber's dedication of his play *Ximena* (1712, publ. 1719) to Steele and, as Lowe notes, became the subject of acid comment in Mist's *Weekly Journal* (31 October 1719): 'Thus Colley Cibber to his partner Steele, / See here, Sir Knight, how I've outdone Corneille; / See here how I, my patron to inveigle, / Make Addison a wren, and you an eagle. / Safe to the silent shades, we bid defiance; / For living dogs are better than dead lions.' Addison died in 1719.

6 Steele's *The Funeral* and *The Tender Husband* had been Drury Lane staples since their premieres in 1701 and 1705 respectively.

7 Both in *The Tatler* and in his plays, Steele embraced the cause of moral reform while celebrating the drama of the Carolean period (1660–85). It was suspected at court that he was not fully committed to the idea of management; a memo from him thought to date from early October 1714 reports a 'message from the King to know whether I was in earnest in desiring the playhouse or that others thought of it for me', with a promise of further favour (BL Add.MS 61,686, fol.33; *Document Register* no.2434). The new licence was eventually issued to Steele, Cibber, Wilks, Doggett, and Booth on 18 October 1714 (LC 5/156, p.31; *Document Register* no.2435), after the season had begun.

of His Majesty for Sir Richard and the former managers who were actors.[8] Collier we heard no more of.[9]

The Court and town being crowded very early in the winter season upon the critical turn of affairs so much expected from the Hanover succession, the theatre had its particular share of that general blessing by a more than ordinary concourse of spectators.[10]

About this time the patentee, having very near finished his house in Lincoln's Inn Fields, began to think of forming a new company,[11] and in the meantime found it necessary to apply for leave to employ them. By the weak defence he had always made against the several attacks upon his interest and former government of the theatre, it might be a question, if his house had been ready in the Queen's time, whether he would then have had the spirit to ask (or interest enough) to obtain leave to use it. But in the following reign, as it did not appear he had done anything to forfeit the right of his patent, he prevailed with Mr Craggs the younger (afterwards Secretary of State)[12] to lay his case before the King, which he did in so effectual a manner that (as Mr Craggs himself told me) His Majesty was pleased to say upon it, 'That he remembered, when he had been in England before in King Charles his time, there had been two theatres in London; and as the patent seemed to be a lawful grant, he saw no reason why two playhouses might not be continued'.[13]

8 Evans describes the existing good relationship with Marlborough as dating from Steele's tract of 1712, *The Englishman's Thanks to the Duke of Marlborough*, published five days after Marlborough had been deprived of all his state posts.

9 Cibber overlooks a legal dispute begun in March 1715 which continued for more than four years. Collier claimed to have a long lease on the Drury Lane site which Cibber, Wilks, and Booth had been promised in April 1714, but now Collier was refusing to make good his promise, choosing instead to sue for arrears on rent (C11/2674/23; *Document Register* no.2526). A court order of 11 June 1719 (C33/332, fol.347; *Document Register* no.2670) sought to establish what arrears may have been owing, but there is no evidence of further action. Barker, p.102, suggests that Collier dropped the case because of mounting legal expenses.

10 During the first seven weeks of the new Drury Lane season, until the end of October, there was a rapid turnover of revivals. LS2 329–31 lists thirty-three acting days (with one missing for George I's coronation on 20 October 1714) and twenty-eight different plays.

11 Christopher Rich had set up the rental agreement for Lincoln's Inn Fields on 3 September 1714 (as above, p.277 n.5) but died on 4 November. He may have initiated the process of 'forming a new company', but his son and heir John completed it ahead of the opening on 18 December (MS Newsletter; *Document Register* no. 2480).

12 James Craggs the Younger (see above, p.59 n.48) became Secretary of State for the Southern Department in 1718. He had met George I when the King was Elector of Hanover; in 1714 Craggs was MP for Tregony. He had a financial interest in the Lincoln's Inn Fields venture as one of the investors named in Rich's rental agreement of 3 September 1714 (see above, n.11); he subsequently acquired a full share.

13 i.e. the theatre opened under the patent originally granted by Charles II and later acquired by Christopher Rich. As noted above, n.11, Rich died shortly afterwards, leaving his interest in the patent to his sons.

The suspension of the patent being thus taken off, the younger multitude seemed to call aloud for two playhouses! Many desired another from the common notion that two would always create emulation in the actors (an opinion which I have considered in a former chapter).[14] Others, too, were as eager for them from the natural ill will that follows the fortunate or prosperous in any undertaking. Of this low malevolence we had now and then had remarkable instances; we had been forced to dismiss an audience of a hundred and fifty pounds, from a disturbance spirited up by obscure people who never gave any better reason for it than that it was their fancy to support the idle complaint of one rival actress against another in their several pretensions to the chief part in a new tragedy.[15] But as this tumult seemed only to be the wantonness of English liberty, I shall not presume to lay any farther censure upon it.

Now, notwithstanding this public desire of re-establishing two houses – and though I have allowed the former actors greatly our superiors, and the managers I am speaking of not to have been without their private errors – yet, under all these disadvantages, it is certain the stage, for twenty years before this time, had never been in so flourishing a condition. And it was as evident to all sensible spectators that this prosperity could be only owing to that better order and closer industry now daily observed, and which had formerly been neglected by our predecessors. But, that I may not impose upon the reader a merit which was not generally allowed us, I ought honestly to let him know that about this time the public papers, particularly *Mist's Journal*, took upon them very often to censure our management with the same freedom and severity as if we had been so many ministers of state.[16] But so it happened that these unfortunate reformers

14 i.e. Chapter 4, p.70
15 A reference to the premiere of Ambrose Phillips's version of the Andromache story, *The Distressed Mother*, which opened at Drury Lane on 17 March 1712 (LS2 271–2). According to Phillips's preface, Jane Rogers had originally been intended for the leading role, but Phillips and others became convinced that Anne Oldfield would be the better choice. Rogers's supporters caused a commotion which it needed soldiers to suppress. While Cibber laid the blame on 'obscure people', Phillips alleged it was Rogers herself who 'raised a possee of profligates, fond of tumult and riot'.
16 Mist's *Weekly Journal* was published under different titles between 1715 and 1737. It was the brainchild of Nathaniel Mist (d. 1737), a Jacobite who employed a number of distinguished writers, including Daniel Defoe. Mist was often in trouble with the authorities for his political reflections and was jailed in 1721 for publishing a description of George I as a 'cruel, ill-bred, uneducated old tyrant'. His interest in Cibber was sparked by the latter's anti-Jacobite satire of 1717, *The Non-Juror*, which Mist denounced as 'turn[ing] ... to excrement [what] was designed for nourishment' (*The Original Weekly Journal*, 28 December 1717). Barker, pp.125–6, reviews the history of Mist's critiques of Cibber.

of the world, these self-appointed censors,[17] hardly ever hit upon what was really wrong in us, but (taking up facts upon trust or hearsay) piled up many a pompous paragraph that they had ingeniously conceived was sufficient to demolish our administration, or at least to make us very uneasy in it; which, indeed, had so far its effect that my equally injured brethren, Wilks and Booth, often complained to me of these disagreeable aspersions, and proposed that some public answer might be made to them – which I always opposed, by perhaps too secure a contempt of what such writers could do to hurt us. And my reason for it was that I knew but of one way to silence authors of that stamp, which was to grow insignificant and good for nothing, and then we should hear no more of them. But while we continued in the prosperity of pleasing others, and were not conscious of having deserved what they said of us, why should we gratify the little spleen of our enemies by wincing at it, or give them fresh opportunities to dine upon any reply they might make to our publicly taking notice of them?[18] And though silence might in some cases be a sign of guilt, or error confessed, our accusers were so low in their credit and sense that the content we gave the public almost every day from the stage ought to be our only answer to them.

However (as I have observed), we made many blots which these unskilful gamesters never hit; but the fidelity of an historian cannot be excused the omission of any truth which might make for the other side of the question. I shall therefore confess a fact which, if a happy accident had not intervened, had brought our affairs into a very tottering condition. This too is that fact which, in a former chapter, I promised to set forth as a seamark of danger to future managers in their theatrical course of government.[19]

When the new-built theatre in Lincoln's Inn Fields was ready to be opened, seven or eight actors in one day deserted from us to the service of the enemy, which obliged us to postpone many of our best plays for want of some inferior part in them which these deserters had been used

17 Cibber plays on the title of another publication, *The Censor*, the periodical collected in 1717 by Lewis Theobald (1688–1744) that reviewed London theatre and letters. Theobald's partiality is evident from his work with John Rich at Lincoln's Inn Fields.

18 As Lowe points out, Cibber's claim to have turned the other cheek is inconsistent with his response to John Dennis's attacks on his character in the Dedication of his play, *The Invader of His Country* (1720), and the anonymous pamphlet, *The Characters and Conduct of Sir John Edgar* (1719), which denounces Steele, Cibber, Booth, and Wilks. Cibber placed an advertisement in *The Daily Post* offering a £10 reward for anyone who identified the author of the pamphlet (see also Steele, *The Theatre*, II.401).

19 As above, pp.131–3 (Chapter 6), on Rich's conduct towards Betterton and his colleagues.

to fill.²⁰ But the indulgence of the royal family, who then frequently honoured us by their presence, was pleased to accept of whatever could be hastily got ready for their entertainment. And though this critical good fortune prevented in some measure our audiences falling so low as otherwise they might have done, yet it was not sufficient to keep us in our former prosperity; for that year our profits amounted not to above a third part of our usual dividends, though in the following year we entirely recovered them.²¹ The chief of these deserters were Keen, Bullock, Pack, Leigh (son of the famous Tony Leigh), and others of less note.²² 'Tis true, they none of them had more than a negative merit, in being only able to do us more harm by their leaving us without notice than they could do us good by remaining with us. For though the best of them could not support a play, the worst of them, by their absence, could maim it – as the loss of the least pin in a watch may obstruct its motion. But to come to the true cause of their desertion. After my having discovered the long unknown occasion that drove Doggett from the stage before his settled inclination to leave it, it will be less incredible that these actors, upon the first opportunity to relieve themselves, should all in one day have left us from the same cause of uneasiness. For in a little time after, upon not finding their expectations in Lincoln's Inn Fields, some of them (who seemed to answer for the rest) told me the greatest grievance they had in our company was the shocking temper of Wilks – who upon every (almost no) occasion, let loose the unlimited language of passion upon

20 The deserters are listed below, n.22. For the remainder of December, Drury Lane appears to have shown only five plays, with Motteux's *The Island Princess* a favourite (LS2 335–6). What Cibber calls 'the indulgence of the royal family' was exercised on 31 December 1714 and 8, 13, 18, 21, 25, 27, and 29 January 1715, with command performances of *The Beaux' Stratagem*, *The Old Batchelor*, Cibber's own *She Would and She Would Not*, *The Constant Couple*, *Marriage à la Mode*, *Love Makes a Man*, Cibber's *Richard III*, and *Sir Courtly Nice* respectively (LS2 336–40). Lincoln's Inn Fields opened on 18 December 1714 (see above, p.316 n.11).

21 A statement not entirely borne out by reports of surviving financial accounts: see above, p.301 n.42.

22 i.e. Theophilus Keen, William Bullock, George Pack, and Francis Leigh; the others were Christopher Bullock, Frances Knight, and Jane Rogers (LS2 328), but Davies (III.485) adds three more names. Lowe quotes Chetwood, p.210, on George Pack's history, from his singing debut at Lincoln's Inn Fields in 1700, to a benefit performance on 7 May 1724 where a new ballad was advertised with the title *Pack's Invitation to the Town* (see LS2 775), to his retirement and ownership of the Globe Tavern, Charing Cross. The *Weekly Packet* of 11–18 December 1714 reports that 'some' of the deserters had already been ordered to return to Drury Lane, on pain of being banned from acting permanently (*Document Register* no.2478); this perhaps forestalled a petition drafted by Steele to the King later that month (BL Add.MS 61,686, fols.75–6; *Document Register* no.2485).

them in such a manner as their patience was not longer able to support.[23] This, indeed, was what we could not justify! This was a secret that might have made a wholesome paragraph in a critical newspaper! But, as it was our good fortune that it came not to the ears of our enemies, the town was not entertained with their public remarks upon it.

After this new theatre had enjoyed that short run of favour which is apt to follow novelty, their audiences began to flag.[24] But whatever good opinion we had of our own merit, we had not so good a one of the multitude as to depend too much upon the delicacy of their taste. We knew too that this company, being so much nearer to the city than we were, would intercept many an honest customer that might not know a good market from a bad one; and that the thinnest of their audiences must be always taking something from the measure of our profits. All these disadvantages, with many others, we were forced to lay before Sir Richard Steele, and farther to remonstrate to him that as he now stood in Collier's place, his pension of £700 was liable to the same conditions that Collier had received it upon; which were that it should be only payable during our being the only company permitted to act, but in case another should be set up against us, that then this pension was to be liquidated into an equal share with us, and which we now hoped he would be contented with. While we were offering to proceed, Sir Richard stopped us short by assuring us that as he came among us by our own invitation, he should always think himself obliged to come into any measures for our ease and service: that to be a burden to our industry would be more disagreeable to him than it could be to us; and as he had always taken a delight in his endeavours for our prosperity, he should be still ready, on our own terms, to continue them. Everyone who knew Sir Richard Steele in his prosperity (before the effects of his good nature had brought him to distresses)[25] knew that this was his manner of dealing with his friends, in business. Another instance of the same nature will immediately fall in my way.

---

23 Davies (III.485–6) claimed the deserting actors, far from disliking Wilks, merely hoped for better roles and more money, saving their hostility for Cibber himself.

24 LS2 367–8 digests information from John Rich's Register. In contrast to its strong start in 1714–15, with many performances taking more than £100, over the first ten weeks of the 1715–16 season the Lincoln's Inn Fields theatre was losing an average of about £10 per performance (roughly £30 in takings against £40 in cost). A good run of *The Prophetess* in December bucked the trend, but thereafter the average income slumped back to about £33 per performance. During the same period it appears Drury Lane was making only a small average profit.

25 As described below, p.336 n.10. On 8 November 1719 Steele hinted to Lord Chamberlain Newcastle his willingness to surrender the Drury Lane patent (BL Add.MS 32,685, fols.27–8; *Document Register* no.2936); only two months later he protested to the King that Newcastle had taken it from him (SP 35/14, no.39; *Document Register* no.2973).

When we proposed to put this agreement into writing, he desired us not to hurry ourselves, for that he was advised, upon the late desertion of our actors, to get our licence (which only subsisted during pleasure) enlarged into a more ample and durable authority; and which he said he had reason to think would be more easily obtained if we were willing that a patent for the same purpose might be granted to him only, for his life and three years after, which he would then assign over to us. This was a prospect beyond our hopes, and what we had long wished for; for though I cannot say we had ever reason to grieve at the personal severities or behaviour of any one Lord Chamberlain in my time, yet the several officers under them, who had not the hearts of noblemen, often treated us (to use Shakespeare's expression) with all the insolence of office that narrow minds are apt to be elated with; but a patent, we knew, would free us from so abject a state of dependency.[26] Accordingly, we desired Sir Richard to lose no time; he was immediately promised it. In the interim, we sounded the inclination of the actors remaining with us, who had all sense enough to know that the credit and reputation we stood in with the town could not but be a better security for their salaries than the promise of any other stage, put into bonds, could make good to them. In a few days after, Sir Richard told us that His Majesty being apprised that others had a joint power with him in the licence, it was expected we should, under our hands, signify that his petition for a patent was preferred by the consent of us all. Such an acknowledgment was immediately signed, and the patent thereupon passed the Great Seal; for which I remember the Lord Chancellor Cowper, in compliment to Sir Richard, would receive no fee.

We received the patent January 19, 1718,[27] and (Sir Richard being obliged the next morning to set out for Boroughbridge in Yorkshire, where he was soon after elected Member of Parliament)[28] we were forced that very night to draw up in a hurry (till our counsel might more advisably

26 Cibber quotes from *Hamlet*, III.i.74, and skates over the difficulties he experienced in dealing with Lord Chamberlain Newcastle (see below, p.332 n.2). His reference to 'several officers' is unlikely to mean Pelham, Newcastle's secretary and the presumed dedicatee of the *Apology*, but probably includes Charles Killigrew, Master of the Revels (see above, pp.184–6). In *Steele at Drury Lane* (Berkeley: University of California Press, 1952), p.44, John Loftis describes the intervention of the Attorney General and Solicitor General, who were keen to establish that the managers really wanted the patent.

27 The year was 1715 (C66/3501, no.13; *Document Register* no.2498); Cibber overlooked the error in the second, corrected edition. It is possible he confused the date of the original grant with later discussions about Steele's rights to dispose of it (see enquiries by Lord Chamberlain Newcastle dated 25 October 1718, LC5/157, pp.142–4; *Document Register* no.2893).

28 Steele became the second MP, alongside Thomas Wilkinson in 1715. The Duke of Newcastle owned Boroughbridge and secured loyal votes from his leaseholders.

perfect it) his assignment to us of equal shares in the patent, with farther conditions of partnership.[29] But here I ought to take shame to myself, and at the same time to give this second instance of the equity and honour of Sir Richard. For this assignment (which I had myself the hasty penning of) was so worded that it gave Sir Richard as equal a title to our property as it had given us to his authority in the patent. But Sir Richard, notwithstanding, when he returned to town took no advantage of the mistake and consented, in our second agreement, to pay us twelve hundred pounds to be equally entitled to our property, which at his death we were obliged to repay (as we afterwards did) to his executors; and which, in case any of us had died before him, the survivors were equally obliged to have paid to the executors of such deceased person upon the same account.[30] But Sir Richard's moderation with us was rewarded with the reverse of Collier's stiffness. Collier, by insisting on his pension, lost three hundred pounds a year; and Sir Richard, by his accepting a share in lieu of it, was (one year with another) as much a gainer.[31]

The grant of this patent having assured us of a competent term to be relied on, we were now emboldened to lay out larger sums in the decorations of our plays. Upon the revival of Dryden's *All for Love*, the habits of that tragedy amounted to an expense of near six hundred pounds – a sum unheard of for many years before, on the like occasions.[32] But we thought such extraordinary marks of our acknowledgment were due to the favours which the public were now, again, pouring in upon us. About this time we were so much in fashion and followed, that our enemies (who they were it would not be fair to guess, for we never knew them) made their push of a

29 Lowe quotes from Steele in *The Theatre* no.8, p.64: 'The very night I received it, I participated the power and use of it, with relation to the profits that should arise from it, between the gentlemen who invited me into the licence.' In addition, Steele immediately took the opportunity to invite Doggett back into the company; Doggett summarily declined, insisting on his rights and querying Steele's (NYPL Drexel MS 1986, fols.138–40; *Document Register* nos.2499 and 2502).
30 For detailed analysis of the contract, see Loftis, *Steele at Drury Lane*, pp.39–50.
31 i.e. William Collier's stipend had been £700 but that of the sharing managers was now £1,000.
32 Having incorrectly given 1718 as the date of Steele's patent, Cibber lights correctly on the same year for the revival of Dryden's *All for Love* on 3 December 1718. 'All the habits being entirely new. With decoration proper to the play', reads the advertisement (LS2 517), which also stated that the play had not been revived for twelve years – an incorrect claim, since it had played at Drury Lane on 2 May 1709 (LS2a 485). Cibber played Alexas in the 1718 revival, for which Steele's prologue to the play was probably designed (*The Theatre* (2 February 1720)). Cibber may have confused the 'decoration' of *All for Love* with the refurbishment of the theatre itself, as reported in *The Daily Courant* of 6 October 1715. *All for Love* saw the start of Dennis's bitter dislike of Cibber, who had postponed the former's *The Invader of His Country* to make way for Dryden's play (see above, p.146 n.76).

good round lie upon us, to terrify those auditors from our support whom they could not mislead by their private arts or public invectives. A current report that the walls and roof of our house were liable to fall had got such ground in the town that, on a sudden, we found our audiences unusually decreased by it. Wilks was immediately for denouncing war and vengeance on the author of this falsehood, and for offering a reward to whoever could discover him. But it was thought more necessary first to disprove the falsehood, and then to pay what compliments might be thought advisable to the author. Accordingly, an order from the King was obtained to have our tenement surveyed by Sir Thomas Hewett, then the proper officer, whose report of its being in a safe and sound condition, and signed by him, was published in every newspaper.[33] This had so immediate an effect that our spectators, whose apprehensions had lately kept them absent, now made up our losses by returning to us with a fresh inclination and in greater numbers.

When it was first publicly known that the new theatre would be opened against us, I cannot help going a little back to remember the concern that my brother-managers expressed at what might be the consequences of it. They imagined that now, all those who wished ill to us (and particularly a great party who had been disobliged by our shutting them out from behind our scenes, even to the refusal of their money) would now exert themselves in any partial or extravagant measures that might either hurt us or support our competitors.[34] These, too, were some of those farther reasons which had discouraged them from running the hazard of continuing to Sir Richard Steele the same pension which had been paid to Collier. Upon all which, I observed to them that for my own part I had not the same apprehensions, but that I foresaw as many good as bad consequences from two houses: that though the novelty might possibly at first abate a little of our profits, yet if we slackened not our industry, that loss would be amply balanced by an equal increase of our ease and quiet; that those turbulent spirits which were always molesting us would now have other employment; that the questioned merit of our acting would now stand in a clearer light when others

---

33 Sir Thomas Hewett (1656–1726) was a wealthy architect, appointed Surveyor of the King's Works in 1719 in succession to Sir Christopher Wren. Here Cibber skips ahead by four years: Hewett was instructed to survey the Drury Lane Theatre on 18 January 1722 (LC 5/158, p.32; *Document Register* no.3097). On 23 January he reported that the structure was 'sound, and almost as good as when first built' (*The Daily Courant*, 26 January 1722).

34 Presumably in response to complaints from the theatres, a proclamation had been issued on 13 November 1711 forbidding audience members 'of what quality soever' from standing 'behind the scenes' or 'upon the stage' during performances (LC 5/155, fol.81; *Document Register* no.2160). In January 1722, *The Daily Journal* and *The Weekly Journal* carried a series of critical reports about the Drury Lane managers (*Document Register* nos.3092–4).

were faintly compared to us; that though faults might be found with the best actors that ever were, yet the egregious defects that would appear in others would now be the effectual means to make our superiority shine, if we had any pretence to it; and that what some people hoped might ruin us would, in the end, reduce them to give up the dispute and reconcile them to those who could best entertain them.

In every article of this opinion, they afterwards found I had not been deceived; and the truth of it may be so well remembered by many living spectators that it would be too frivolous and needless a boast to give it any farther observation.

But in what I have said, I would not be understood to be an advocate for two playhouses. For we shall soon find that two sets of actors, tolerated in the same place, have constantly ended in the corruption of the theatre; of which the auxiliary entertainments that have so barbarously supplied the defects of weak action have, for some years past, been a flagrant instance. It may not, therefore, be here improper to show how our childish pantomimes first came to take so gross a possession of the stage.

I have upon several occasions already observed that when one company is too hard for another, the lower in reputation has always been forced to exhibit some newfangled foppery, to draw the multitude after them. Of these expedients, singing and dancing had formerly been the most effectual, but at the time I am speaking of, our English music had been so discountenanced since the taste of Italian operas prevailed that it was to no purpose to pretend to it.[35] Dancing, therefore, was now the only weight in the opposite scale, and as the new theatre sometimes found their account in it, it could not be safe for us wholly to neglect it.[36] To give even dancing therefore some improvement, and to make it something more than motion without meaning, the fable of Mars and Venus was formed into a connected presentation of dances in character, wherein the passions were so happily expressed and the whole story so intelligibly told by a mute narration of

35 English music continued to flourish in *entre actes* and songs, sometimes as part of popular larger-scale productions at Lincoln's Inn Fields such as *The Island Princess*. In addition to his reflections above about Italian opera (pp.251–4), Cibber may be referring to performances by French comedians at Lincoln's Inn Fields, and then the newly titled King's Theatre Haymarket, between 12 November 1718 and 19 March 1719 (LS2 514–33).

36 From the 1716–17 season onwards there was an increasing trend for straight plays to conclude with elaborate dancing. Cibber may have been particularly mortified to see some of his own work as writer and actor upstaged in this way. The March 1717 revival of *She Would and She Would Not* ended with dancing 'by Dupré, Boval, Dupré Jr, Mrs Santlow and Mrs Bicknell' (LS2 423), while two of his signature roles, Lord Foppington and Sir Courtly Nice, were rounded off by the same entertainment (LS2 419 and 423).

gesture only, that even thinking spectators allowed it both a pleasing and a rational entertainment;[37] though, at the same time, from our distrust of its reception we durst not venture to decorate it with any extraordinary expense of scenes or habits. But upon the success of this attempt, it was rightly concluded that if a visible expense in both were added to something of the same nature, it could not fail of drawing the town proportionably after it. From this original hint, then (but every way unequal to it), sprung forth that succession of monstrous medleys that have so long infested the stage, and which arose upon one another alternately at both houses, outvying in expense (like contending bribes on both sides at an election) to secure a majority of the multitude.[38] But so it is: Truth may complain and Merit murmur with what justice it may, the few will never be a match for the many unless authority should think fit to interpose and put down these poetical drams, these gin shops of the stage, that intoxicate its auditors and dishonour their understanding with a levity for which I want a name.[39]

If I am asked (after my condemning these fooleries myself) how I came to assent or continue my share of expense to them, I have no better excuse for my error than confessing it. I did it against my conscience, and had not virtue enough to starve by opposing a multitude that would have been too hard for me.[40] Now let me ask an odd question: had Harry the Fourth of France a better excuse for changing his religion?[41] I was still, in my heart (as much as he could be), on the side of truth and sense, but with this

37 John Weaver's *The Loves of Mars and Venus* was first presented as an afterpiece to *The Maid's Tragedy* on 2 March 1717, and then to *Cato* on 5 March (LS2 439), with further performances throughout March. Weaver (1673–1760) was a dancer with the Drury Lane and other companies. *The Loves of Mars and Venus* is often described as the first modern ballet.

38 Cibber may have been particularly unimpressed by the Drury Lane afterpiece to *The Humorous Lieutenant* on 2 April 1717 called *A New Dramatic Entertainment of Dancing in Grotesque Characters* (LS2 444), and by the Lincoln's Inn Fields response on 8 April, which featured a Spanish dance and a piece called *Dutch Skipper* (LS2 445).

39 Cibber began the *Apology* in the wake of new legislation to control the consumption of gin (An Act for Laying a Duty upon the Retailers of Spirituous Liquors, and for Licensing the Retailers thereof; 9 Geo. 2 c. 23), following a virtual doubling of consumption between 1727 and 1735.

40 Lowe cites Pope's *The Dunciad*, III.265–8, and Cibber's response. Pope: 'But lo! to dark encounter in mid air / New wizards rise: I see my Cibber there! / Booth in his cloudy tabernacle shrined, / On grinning dragons thou shalt mount the wind' (Pope, *Poems*, p.761). Cibber (*Letter*, p.37) replied: 'If you, figuratively, mean by this that I was an encourager of those fooleries, you are mistaken, for it is not true; if you intend it literally, that I was dunce enough to mount a machine, there is as little truth in that too.'

41 i.e. Henry IV of France (1553–1610), raised as a Protestant but who converted to Catholicism in 1593; he is alleged to have said, 'Paris vaut bien une messe' (it's worth taking mass to win over Paris).

difference: that I had their leave to quit them when they could not support me. For what equivalent could I have found for my falling a martyr to them? How far the hero or the comedian was in the wrong, let the clergy and the critics decide. Necessity will be as good a plea for the one as the other. But let the question go which way it will, Harry IV has always been allowed a great man; and what I want of his grandeur (you see by the inference), Nature has amply supplied to me in vanity, a pleasure which neither the pertness of wit or the gravity of wisdom will ever persuade me to part with. And why is there not as much honesty in owning as in concealing it? For though to hide it may be wisdom, to be without it is impossible; and where is the merit of keeping a secret which everybody is let into? To say we have no vanity, then, is showing a great deal of it, as to say we have a great deal cannot be showing so much. And though there may be art in a man's accusing himself, even then it will be more pardonable than self-commendation. Do not we find that even good actions have their share of it? That it is as inseparable from our being as our nakedness? And though it may be equally decent to cover it, yet the wisest man can no more be without it than the weakest can believe he was born in his clothes. If then what we say of ourselves be true and not prejudicial to others, to be called vain upon it is no more a reproach than to be called a brown or a fair man. Vanity is of all complexions; 'tis the growth of every clime and capacity. Authors of all ages have had a tincture of it, and yet you read Horace, Montaigne and Sir William Temple with pleasure.[42] Nor am I sure, if it were curable by precept, that mankind would be mended by it! Could vanity be eradicated from our nature, I am afraid that the reward of most human virtues would not be found in this world! And happy is he who has no greater sin to answer for in the next!

But what is all this to the theatrical follies I was talking of? Perhaps not a great deal, but it is to my purpose; for though I am an historian, I do not write to the wise and learned only. I hope to have readers of no more judgment than some of my *quondam* auditors, and I am afraid they will be as hardly contented with dry matters of fact as with a plain play without entertainments. This rhapsody, therefore, has been thrown in as a dance between the acts, to make up for the dullness of what would have been by itself only proper. But I now come to my story again.

Notwithstanding, then, this our compliance with the vulgar taste, we generally made use of these pantomimes but as crutches to our weakest

---

42 Cibber's imputation of vanity appears to rest on Horace's desire to teach precepts from personal experience, on Montaigne's writing about himself, and on Sir William Temple's personal essays, as collected in successive editions of *Miscellanea* (London: Edward Gellibrand, 1680).

plays;[43] nor were we so lost to all sense of what was valuable as to dishonour our best authors in such bad company. We had still a due respect to several select plays that were able to be their own support, and in which we found our constant account, without painting and patching them out like prostitutes, with these follies in fashion. If, therefore, we were not so strictly chaste in the other part of our conduct, let the error of it stand among the silly consequences of two stages. Could the interest of both companies have been united in one only theatre, I had been one of the few that would have used my utmost endeavour of never admitting to the stage any spectacle that ought not to have been seen there (the errors of my own plays, which I could not see, excepted). And, though probably the majority of spectators would not have been so well pleased with a theatre so regulated, yet sense and reason cannot lose their intrinsic value because the giddy and the ignorant are blind and deaf, or numerous; and I cannot help saying it is a reproach to a sensible people to let folly so publicly govern their pleasures.

While I am making this grave declaration of what I *would* have done had one only stage been continued, to obtain an easier belief of my sincerity I ought to put my reader in mind of what I *did* do, even after two companies were again established.

About this time, Jacobitism had lately exerted itself by the most unprovoked rebellion that our histories have handed down to us since the Norman Conquest.[44] I therefore thought that to set the authors and principles of that desperate folly in a fair light – by allowing the mistaken consciences of some their best excuse, and by making the artful pretenders to conscience as ridiculous as they were ungratefully wicked – was a subject fit for the honest satire of comedy, and what might (if it succeeded) do honour to the stage by showing the valuable use of it. And, considering what numbers at that time might come to it as prejudiced spectators, it may be allowed that the undertaking was not less hazardous than laudable.

To give life therefore to this design, I borrowed the *Tartuffe* of Molière, and turned him into a modern non-juror.[45] Upon the hypocrisy of the

43 'Pantomime' is used in the sense of performance through gesture and action only; OED dates the first use of the term in English at 1606. Cibber's claim that such afterpieces were reserved for less significant plays is partly borne out by *The London Stage*, which shows it was rare, for example, for Shakespeare to be followed by an afterpiece.

44 The first Jacobite rising began in the late summer of 1715 under the leadership of the Earl of Mar.

45 Cibber's play opened at Drury Lane on 6 December 1717, with the author in the Tartuffe role of Doctor Wolf. His was not the first consciously political adaptation of the play: from a different ideological standpoint, Matthew Medbourne had turned the eponymous villain into a hypocritical dissenter in his 1670 *Tartuffe; or the French Puritan*.

French character I engrafted a stronger wickedness: that of an English Popish priest, lurking under the doctrine of our own church to raise his fortune upon the ruin of a worthy gentleman, whom his dissembled sanctity had seduced into the treasonable cause of a Roman Catholic outlaw. How this design in the play was executed, I refer to the readers of it; it cannot be mended by any critical remarks I can make in its favour. Let it speak for itself.[46] All the reason I had to think it no bad performance was that it was acted eighteen days running,[47] and that the party that were hurt by it (as I have been told) have not been the smallest number of my back friends ever since.[48] But happy was it for this play that the very subject was its protection; a few smiles of silent contempt were the utmost disgrace that, on the first day of its appearance, it was thought safe to throw upon it. As the satire was chiefly employed on the enemies of the government, they were not so hardy as to own themselves such by any higher disapprobation or resentment. But as it was then probable I might write again, they knew it would not be long before they might with more security give a loose to their spleen, and make up accounts with me. And to do them justice, in every play I afterwards produced, they paid me the balance to a tittle.[49] But to none was I more beholden than that celebrated author Mr Mist, whose *Weekly Journal*, for about fifteen years following, scarce ever failed of passing some of his party compliments upon me.[50] The state and the stage were his frequent parallels, and the minister and *Meinheer Keiber* the manager

46 An anonymous publication of 1718 written in defence of the play, and sometimes attributed to Cibber, spells everything out: *The Comedy called The Non-Juror. Showing the particular scenes wherein that hypocrite is concerned. With remarks, and a key, explaining the characters of that excellent play.* It was written in response to John Breval's hostile *A Complete Key to the Non-Juror*, a pamphlet published early in 1718. For further critiques and defences of *The Non-Juror*, see Koon, pp.87–8, and *Document Register*, nos.2860–77; for 'non-juror', see above p.182 n.22.

47 LS2 472–5 lists sixteen consecutive performances between 6 and 27 December 1717, still the longest initial run since Addison's *Cato* in 1713. George I attended on 19 December 1717 and permitted Cibber to dedicate the printed edition to him (for the presentation, see *Original Weekly Journal*, 28 December 1717 – 4 January 1718). There were author benefit nights on 12 and 21 December, when the *Original Weekly Journal* reported Cibber had 'cleared already by this play near one thousand pounds' (LS2 475). In response, Lincoln's Inn Fields mounted a satirical afterpiece by Christopher Bullock, *The Perjuror*, which according to the same journal did not meet with 'nigh the applause and success' of Cibber's play (LS2 475). In June 1718 the Lincoln's Inn Fields company mounted what appears to be Medbourne's version of *Tartuffe* (LS2 497–8), on which, see above, p.327 n.45.

48 *OED* 1: a secret or unavowed enemy.

49 The hostility was not confined to Cibber's plays. On 22 February 1718, a riot at Drury Lane had been caused by Cibber's alleged pulling of a comedy by one of his *Non-Juror* adversaries, John Breval, in favour of a sub-cast revival of *Cato* (letter in the *Weekly Journal/British Gazetteer*, 1 March 1718; *Document Register* no.2878).

50 See above, p.317 n.16.

were as constantly drolled upon.[51] Now for my own part, though I could never persuade my wit to have an open account with him (for as he had no effects of his own, I did not think myself obliged to answer his bills), notwithstanding, I will be so charitable to his real *manes*,[52] and to the ashes of his paper, as to mention one particular civility he paid to my memory after he thought he had ingeniously killed me. Soon after *The Non-Juror* had received the favour of the town, I read in one of his journals the following short paragraph, *viz.*, 'Yesterday died Mr Colley Cibber, late comedian of the Theatre Royal, notorious for writing *The Non-Juror*.' The compliment in the latter part I confess I did not dislike, because it came from so impartial a judge, and it really so happened that the former part of it was very near being true; for I had that very day just crawled out after having been some weeks laid up by a fever. However, I saw no use in being thought to be thoroughly dead before my time, and therefore had a mind to see whether the town cared to have me alive again. So, the play of *The Orphan* being to be acted that day, I quietly stole myself into the part of the Chaplain, which I had not been seen in for many years before.[53] The surprise of the audience at my unexpected appearance on the very day I had been dead in the news, and the paleness of my looks, seemed to make it a doubt whether I was not the ghost of my real self departed. But when I spoke, their wonder eased itself by an applause, which convinced me they were then satisfied that my friend Mist had told a fib of me. Now, if simply to have shown myself in broad life and about my business (after he had *notoriously* reported me dead) can be called a reply, it was the only one which his paper, while alive, ever drew from me. How far I may be vain, then, in supposing that this play brought me into the disfavour of so many wits and valiant auditors as afterwards appeared against me, let those who may think it worth their notice judge.[54] In the meantime, till I can find a better excuse for their sometimes

51 Cibber's origins became a popular source of satire. In the anonymous *The Theatre Royal Turned into a Mountebank's Stage* (1718) he was denounced as 'a mongrel of Parnassus' who was 'half Dane, half English' (p.7). Mist, an opponent of the Hanoverian court, set out to make Cibber's name sound German.

52 Shades of the departed; Mist died in 1737.

53 Presumably a reference to the performance on 4 February 1718 (LS2 481); contrary to Cibber's claim, he had also appeared in a revival of *The Orphan* as recently as 26 October 1717 (LS2 466). The mock-announcement of his death appears in the *Weekly Journal*, 21–8 January 1718. Mist also printed a claim under the name of Charles Johnson that Cibber had gambled away his earnings from *The Non-Juror* when his children were in need (*Saturday's Post*, 1 March 1718). On the basis of performance listings, Evans suggests Cibber was ill between 1 and 23 March 1717.

54 As Lowe notes, *The Non-Juror* was undoubtedly part-cause of Pope's hatred of Cibber, Pope's father having been a non-juror.

particular treatment of me, I cannot easily give up my suspicion. And if I add a more remarkable fact that afterwards confirmed me in it, perhaps it may incline others to join in my opinion.

On the first day of *The Provoked Husband*, ten years after *The Non-Juror* had appeared,[55] a powerful party (not having the fear of public offence or private injury before their eyes) appeared most impetuously concerned for the demolition of it, in which they so far succeeded that for some time I gave it up for lost; and to follow their blows, in the public papers of the next day it was attacked and triumphed over as a dead and damned piece. A swinging criticism was made upon it in general invective terms, for they disdained to trouble the world with particulars; their sentence, it seems, was proof enough of its deserving the fate it had met with. But this damned play was, notwithstanding, acted twenty-eight nights together, and left off at a receipt of upwards of a hundred and forty pounds, which happened to be more than in fifty years before could be then said of any one play whatsoever.[56]

Now, if such notable behaviour could break out upon so successful a play (which, too, upon the share Sir John Vanbrugh had in it I will venture to call a good one), what shall we impute it to? Why may not I plainly say it was not the play, but me (who had a hand in it) they did not like? And for what reason? If they were not ashamed of it, why did not they publish it? No! The reason had published itself: I was the author of *The Non-Juror*! But perhaps, of all authors, I ought not to make this sort of complaint, because I have reason to think that that particular offence has made me more honourable friends than enemies; the latter of which I am not unwilling should know (however unequal the merit may be to the reward) that part of the bread I now eat was given me for having writ *The Non-Juror*.[57]

And yet I cannot but lament, with many quiet spectators, the helpless misfortune that has so many years attended the stage: that no law has had force enough to give it absolute protection! For till we can civilise its auditors, the authors that write for it will seldom have a greater call to it than necessity; and how unlikely is the imagination of the needy to inform or delight the many in affluence? Or how often does necessity make many unhappy gentlemen turn authors, in spite of Nature?

---

55 Cibber's completion of Vanbrugh's play premiered at Drury Lane on 10 January 1728 (LS2 954). On 13 January, *Mist's Weekly Journal* accused him of murdering Vanbrugh's 'posthumous child' (see above, p.205 n.30).

56 LS2 954–8 records twenty-eight performances from 10 January to 12 February 1728. Lincoln's Inn Fields tried running *The Provoked Wife* against it on 13 January before mounting *The Beggar's Opera* (see above, p.164 n.41).

57 A reference to Cibber's appointment as Poet Laureate for services to the government (see above, pp.39–40).

What a blessing, therefore, is it – what an enjoyed deliverance – after a wretch has been driven by Fortune to stand so many wanton buffets of unmanly fierceness, to find himself at last quietly lifted above the reach of them!

But let not this reflection fall upon my auditors without distinction, for though candour and benevolence are silent virtues, they are as visible as the most vociferous ill nature; and I confess, the public has given me more frequently reason to be thankful than to complain.

CHAPTER 16

The author steps out of his way. Pleads his theatrical cause in Chancery. Carries it. Plays acted at Hampton Court. Theatrical anecdotes in former reigns. Ministers and managers always censured. The difficulty of supplying the stage with good actors considered. Courtiers and comedians governed by the same passions. Examples of both. The author quits the stage. Why.

Having brought the government of the stage through such various changes and revolutions to this settled state (in which it continued to almost the time of my leaving it),[1] it cannot be supposed that a period of so much quiet and so long a train of success, though happy for those who enjoyed it, can afford such matter of surprise or amusement as might arise from times of more distress and disorder. A quiet time in history, like a calm in a voyage, leaves us but in an indolent station. To talk of our affairs when they were no longer ruffled by misfortunes would be a picture without shade – a flat performance at best.[2] As I might, therefore, throw all that tedious time of our tranquillity into one chasm in my history, and cut my way short, at once, to my last exit from the stage, I shall at least fill it up with such matter only as I have a mind should be known, how few soever may have patience to read it. Yet, as I despair not of some readers who may be most awake when they think others have most occasion to sleep – who may be more pleased to find me languid than lively, or in the wrong than in the right – why should I scruple (when it is so easy a matter, too) to gratify

---

1 i.e. in 1733 (as above, p.13 n.6); 'almost' is an admission that the 1732–3 season was hardly 'settled' (see Introduction, p.xxiv).
2 Perhaps prompted by his discussion of *The Provoked Husband*, Cibber deals with the resolution in February 1728 of the longstanding dispute between the Drury Lane management and Sir Richard Steele. So doing, he passes over significant disruption at Drury Lane: his own suspension in December 1719 for persistently declining to submit scripts to the Master of the Revels, using 'forward expressions' (LC 5/157, p.265; *Document Register* no.2957, and *Orphan Revived*; *Document Register* no.2961), and refusing to pay Vanbrugh for use of stock from the opera (LC 7/3, fols. 169–70; *Document Register* no.2501); not to mention the consequent revocation of Steele's licence on 23 January 1720 because of 'the neglect of a due subordination and submission to the authority of our Chamberlain' (LC 5/157, pp.279–80; *Document Register* no.2975). That quarrel went back to the dispute with Master of the Revels Killigrew described above, pp.184–6. Cibber further offended Newcastle with his reluctance to promote the actor Thomas Elrington (see above, p.290 n.6), as described by Barker, p.122.

their particular taste by venturing upon any error that I like, or the weakness of my judgment misleads me to commit? I think too I have a very good chance for my success in this passive ambition, by showing myself in a light I have not been seen in.

By your leave then, gentlemen, let the scene open and at once discover your comedian at the Bar! There you will find him a defendant and pleading his own theatrical cause in a Court of Chancery. But, as I choose to have a chance of pleasing others as well as of indulging you, gentlemen, I must first beg leave to open my case to them; after which, my whole speech on that occasion shall be at your mercy.

In all the transactions of life, there cannot be a more painful circumstance than a dispute at law with a man with whom we have long lived in an agreeable amity.[3] But when Sir Richard Steele, to get himself out of difficulties, was obliged to throw his affairs into the hands of lawyers and trustees, that consideration then could be of no weight. The friend or the gentleman had no more to do in the matter! Thus, while Sir Richard no longer acted from himself, it may be no wonder if a flaw was found in our conduct for the law to make work with. It must be observed then, that about two or three years before this suit was commenced, upon Sir Richard's totally absenting himself from all care and management of the stage (which by our articles of partnership he was equally and jointly obliged with us to attend), we were reduced to let him know that we could not go on at that rate; but that if he expected to make the business a sinecure, we had as much reason to expect a consideration for our extraordinary care of it, and that during his absence we therefore intended to charge ourselves at a salary of £1 13s 4d every acting day (unless he could show us cause to the contrary) for our management.[4] To which, in his composed manner, he only answered that to be sure, we knew what was fitter to be done than he did; that he had always taken a delight in making us easy, and had no reason to doubt of our doing him justice. Now whether, under this easy style of approbation, he concealed any dislike of our resolution, I cannot say. But if I may speak my private opinion, I really believe (from his natural negligence

3 Subsequent testimony suggests the dispute with Steele had been brewing for some years up to the official silencing of Drury Lane in January 1720 that saw his exclusion from the patent (LC 5/157, pp.280–1; *Document Register* no.2977).

4 i.e. £5 split three ways between Cibber, Wilks, and Booth; during a subsequent court action in 1726 Steele denied consenting to the deduction (C11/2416/49; *Document Register* no.3297), but when the case was concluded in 1728 (see below, p.334 n.6) it was deemed justified. Following the restitution of Steele's patent on 2 May 1721, Lord Chamberlain Newcastle ordered all parties to reach agreement about money owing (LC 5/157, pp.415–16; *Document Register* no.3062). As indicated below, the dispute then resumed.

of his affairs) he was glad, at any rate, to be excused an attendance which he was now grown weary of. But whether I am deceived or right in my opinion, the fact was truly this: that he never once, directly nor indirectly, complained or objected to our being paid the above mentioned daily sum in near three years together, and yet still continued to absent himself from us and our affairs.⁵ But notwithstanding he had seen and done all this with his eyes open, his lawyer thought here was still a fair field for a battle in Chancery; in which, though his client might be beaten, he was sure his bill must be paid for it. Accordingly, to work with us he went. But, not to be so long as the lawyers were in bringing this cause to an issue, I shall at once let you know that it came to a hearing before the late Sir Joseph Jekyll, then Master of the Rolls, in the year 1726.⁶ Now, as the chief point in dispute was of what kind or importance the business of a manager was, or in what it principally consisted, it could not be supposed that the most learned counsel could be so well apprised of the nature of it as one who had himself gone through the care and fatigue of it. I was therefore encouraged by our counsel to speak to that particular head myself, which I confess I was glad he suffered me to undertake; but when I tell you that two of the learned counsel against us came afterwards to be successively Lord Chancellors, it sets my presumption in a light that I still tremble to show it in.⁷ But however (not to assume more merit from its success than was really its due), I ought fairly to let you know that I was not so hardy as to deliver my pleading without notes in my hand of the heads I intended to enlarge upon; for though I thought I could conquer my fear, I could not be so sure of my memory. But when it came to the critical moment, the dread and apprehension of what

5   A letter dated 12 December 1724 from Booth, Cibber, and Wilks urged Steele to return to London, since Drury Lane profits were declining against competition from the King's Haymarket and a visiting French troupe (BL Add.MS 5145C, fols.130–1; *Document Register* no.3255); the point was reinforced in their legal action of 11 January 1726 (C11/2416/49; *Document Register* no.3297). Steele's own legal proceedings against Cibber, Wilks, and Booth, alleging financial misdemeanours and contractual breaches, began on 4 September 1725 (C11/300/38; *Document Register* no.3283).

6   The correct date is 1728. The outcome was reported in *St James's Evening Post*, 17–20 February 1728: 'There was an hearing in the Rolls Chapel in a cause between Sir Richard Steele, Mr Cibber, Mr Wilks, and others belonging to Drury Lane theatre, which held five hours – one of which was taken up by a speech of Mr Wilks, which had so good an effect that the cause went against Sir Richard Steele'. The subsequent issue (20–3 February) carried a correction to the effect that it was Cibber, not Wilks, who made the telling speech, as reproduced here. Sir Joseph Jekyll (1663–1738) had been Master of the Rolls since 1717 and a Whig MP since 1697, first for Eye and then Lymington.

7   A reference to Peter, 1st Baron King (1669–1734), Lord Chancellor from 1725 to 1733, and his successor, Charles, 1st Baron Talbot (1685–1737).

I had undertaken so disconcerted my courage, that though I had been used to talk to above fifty thousand different people every winter for upwards of thirty years together, an involuntary and unaffected proof of my confusion fell from my eyes; and, as I found myself quite out of my element, I seemed rather gasping for life than in a condition to cope with the eminent orators against me. But however, I soon found from the favourable attention of my hearers that my diffidence had done me no disservice. And, as the truth I was to speak to needed no ornament of words, I delivered it in the plain manner following, *viz:-*

'In this cause, sir, I humbly conceive there are but two points that admit of any material dispute. The first is whether Sir Richard Steele is as much obliged to do the duty and business of a manager as either Wilks, Booth or Cibber; and the second is whether, by Sir Richard's totally withdrawing himself from the business of a manager, the defendents are justifiable in charging to each of themselves the £1 13s 4d *per diem* for their particular pains and care in carrying on the whole affairs of the stage, without any assistance from Sir Richard Steele.

'As to the first, if I don't mistake the words of the assignment, there is a clause in it that says, "All matters relating to the government or management of the theatre shall be concluded by a majority of voices".[8] Now I presume, sir, there is no room left to allege that Sir Richard was ever refused his voice, though in above three years he never desired to give it. And I believe there will be as little room to say that he could have a voice if he were not a manager. But, sir, his being a manager is so self-evident that it is amazing how he could conceive that he was to take the profits and advantages of a manager without doing the duty of it.[9] And I will be bold to say, sir, that his assignment of the patent to Wilks, Booth and Cibber, in no one part of it, by the severest construction in the world, can be wrested to throw the heavy burden of the management only upon their shoulders. Nor does it appear, sir, that either in his bill or in his answer to our cross-bill, he has offered any hint or glimpse of a reason for his withdrawing from the management at all, or so much as pretend[ed] from the time complained of that he ever took the least part of his share of it. Now, sir, however unaccountable this conduct of Sir Richard may seem, we will

8 Strictly true, whether of the original licence of October 1714 or of the one issued on 27 January 1720 to Cibber, Wilks, and Booth following Steele's exclusion (LC5/157, p.282; *Document Register* no.2979); but see below, n.9.
9 In *The Theatre* no.8 (26 January 1720), Steele set out his belief that he was merely a sleeping partner; see also Loftis, *Steele at Drury Lane*, pp.56–61, and below, p.338 n.13.

still allow that he had some cause for it; but whether or no that cause was a reasonable one, your honour will the better judge if I may be indulged in the liberty of explaining it.

'Sir, the case (in plain truth and reality) stands thus: Sir Richard, though no man alive can write better of economy than himself, yet perhaps he is above the drudgery of practising it.[10] Sir Richard, then, was often in want of money, and while we were in friendship with him we often assisted his occasions. But those compliances had so unfortunate an effect that they only heightened his importunity to borrow more; and the more we lent, the less he minded us or showed any concern for our welfare. Upon this, sir, we stopped our hands at once and peremptorily refused to advance another shilling till, by the balance of our accounts, it became due to him. And this treatment, though we hope not in the least unjustifiable, we have reason to believe so ruffled his temper that he at once was as short with us as we had been with him, for from that day he never more came near us. Nay, sir, he not only continued to neglect what he *should* have done, but actually did what he ought *not* to have done: he made an assignment of his share without our consent, in a manifest breach of our agreement.[11] For, sir, we did not lay that restriction upon ourselves for no reason. We knew beforehand what trouble and inconvenience it would be to unravel and expose our accounts to strangers who, if they were to do us no hurt by divulging our secrets, we were sure could do us no good by keeping them. If Sir Richard had had our common interest at heart, he would have been as warm in it as we were, and as tender of hurting it. But supposing his assigning his share to others may have done us no great injury, it is at least a shrewd proof that he did not care whether it did us any, or no. And if the clause was not strong enough to restrain him from it in law, there was enough in it to have restrained him in honour from breaking it. But take it in its best light, it shows him as remiss a manager in our affairs as he naturally was in his own. Suppose, sir, we had all been as careless as himself (which I can't find he has any more

10 A reference to Steele's various essays on the subject, including 'The Life and Adventures of a Shilling' (*The Tatler*, no.249, 9–11 November 1710) and 'The Industrious Part of Mankind' (*The Spectator* no.552 (3 December 1712)). A document dated 23 April 1724 states that Steele was £4,052 in debt (BL Add.MS 5154C, fols.132–4; *Document Register* no.3235), or c.£855,000 in current values. Steele's financial incompetence was well known, as documented by Loftis, *Steele at Drury Lane*, pp.91–7.

11 The same document that lists Steele's debts (see above, n.10) describes a sequence of mortgages and associated onward sales of the patent going back to 1716, when Steele was said to have assigned his rights in the patent to Edward Minshull as security against debts (C11/1424/35; *Document Register* no.2827). An indenture of 3 June 1724 cites the assignment of a share to David Scurlock, one of Steele's in-laws (*Document Register* no.3240).

right to be than we have), must not our whole affair have fallen to ruin? And may we not, by a parity of reason, suppose that by his neglect a fourth part of it *does* fall to ruin? But, sir, there is a particular reason to believe that from our want of Sir Richard, more than a fourth part *does* suffer by it. His rank and figure in the world, while he gave us the assistance of them, were of extraordinary service to us; he had an easier access and a more regarded audience at court than our low station of life could pretend to, when our interest wanted (as it often did) a particular solicitation there. But since we have been deprived of him, the very end – the very consideration of his share in our profits – is not performed on his part. And will Sir Richard, then, make us no compensation for so valuable a loss in our interests, and so palpable an addition to our labour? I am afraid, sir, if we were all to be as indolent in the managing part as Sir Richard presumes he has a right to be, our patent would soon run us as many hundreds in debt as he had (and still seems willing to have) his share of, for doing of nothing.

'Sir, our next point in question is whether Wilks, Booth and Cibber are justifiable in charging the £1 13s 4d *per diem* for their extraordinary management in the absence of Sir Richard Steele. I doubt, sir, it will be hard to come to the solution of this point, unless we may be a little indulged in setting forth what is the daily and necessary business and duty of a manager. But, sir, we will endeavour to be as short as the circumstances will admit of.

'Sir, by our books it is apparent that the managers have under their care no less than one hundred and forty persons in constant, daily pay. And among such numbers, it will be no wonder if a great many of them are unskilful, idle and sometimes untractable; all which tempers are to be led or driven, watched and restrained, by the continual skill, care and patience of the managers. Every manager is obliged, in his turn, to attend two or three hours every morning at the rehearsal of plays and other entertainments for the stage, or else every rehearsal would be but a rude meeting of mirth and jollity. The same attendance is as necessary at every play during the time of its public action, in which one or more of us have constantly been punctual, whether we have had any part in the play then acted or not. A manager ought to be at the reading of every new play when it is first offered to the stage, though there are seldom one of those plays in twenty which, upon hearing, proves to be fit for it;[12] and upon such occasions the attendance must be allowed to

---

12 On the first-stage 'judgmental reading' and the further stage of reading to the acting company, see Stern, pp.207–11. James Miller's *The Coffee-House* (1737) depicts a first-stage reading in a coffee house, with a distracted Cibber more interested in gossip than the play. See below, p.352 n.54, for a further satirical view.

be as painfully tedious as the getting rid of the authors of such plays must be disagreeable and difficult. Besides this, sir, a manager is to order all new clothes, to assist in the fancy and propriety of them, to limit the expense, and to withstand the unreasonable importunities of some that are apt to think themselves injured if they are not finer than their fellows. A manager is to direct and oversee the painters, machinists, musicians, singers and dancers; to have an eye upon the door-keepers, under-servants and officers, that without such care are too often apt to defraud us or neglect their duty.

'And all this, sir, and more (much more) which we hope will be needless to trouble you with, have we done every day without the least assistance from Sir Richard, even at times when the concern and labour of our parts upon the stage have made it very difficult and irksome to go through with it.[13]

'In this place, sir, it may be worth observing that Sir Richard, in his answer to our cross-bill, seems to value himself upon Cibber's confessing, in the Dedication of a play which he made to Sir Richard, that he (Sir Richard) had done the stage very considerable service by leading the town to our plays and filling our houses by the force and influence of his *Tatlers*.[14] But Sir Richard forgets that those *Tatlers* were written in the late Queen's reign, long before he was admitted to a share in the playhouse. And in truth, sir, it was our real sense of those obligations – and Sir Richard's assuring us they should be continued – that first and chiefly inclined us to invite him to share the profits of our labours, upon such farther conditions as in his assignment of the patent to us are specified. And, sir, as Cibber's public acknowledgment of those favours is at the same time an equal proof of Sir Richard's power to continue them, so, sir, we hope it carries an equal probability that without his promise to use that power, he would never have been thought on, much less have been invited by us, into a joint management of the stage and into a share of the profits. And indeed, what pretence could he have formed for asking a patent from the Crown, had he been possessed of no eminent qualities but in common with other men? But, sir, all these advantages, all these hopes – nay, certainties – of greater profits from those great qualities, have we been utterly deprived of by the wilful and unexpected neglect of Sir Richard. But we find, sir, it is a common thing in the practice of mankind to justify one error by committing another. For Sir Richard has not only refused us the extraordinary assistance which he is able and bound to give us; but, on the contrary (to our great expense

13 In his action of 4 September 1725 (see above, p.334 n.5), Steele denied ever having consented to such duties.
14 As noted above, p.315 n.5, the play was Cibber's *Ximena; or the Heroic Daughter* (1712, publ. 1719).

and loss of time) now calls us to account in this honourable court for the wrong we have done him in not doing his business of a manager for nothing. But, sir, Sir Richard has not met with such treatment from us. He has not writ plays for us for *nothing*; we paid him very well, and in an extraordinary manner, for his late comedy of *The Conscious Lovers*.[15] And though, in writing that play, he had more assistance from one of the managers[16] than becomes me to enlarge upon (of which evidence has been given upon oath by several of our actors), yet, sir, he was allowed the full and particular profits of that play as an author, which amounted to three hundred pounds, besides about three hundred more which he received as a joint sharer of the general profits that arose from it.[17] Now, sir, though the managers are not all of them able to write plays, yet they have all of them been able to do, I won't say as good, but at least as profitable a thing: they have invented and adorned a spectacle that for forty days together has brought more money to the house than the best play that ever was writ. The spectacle I mean, sir, is that of the coronation ceremony of *Anna Bullen*.[18] And though we allow a good play to be the more laudable performance, yet, sir, in the profitable part of it there is no comparison. If, therefore, our spectacle brought in as much (or more) money than Sir Richard's comedy, what is there on his side but usage that entitles him to be paid for one, more than we are for t'other? But then, sir, if he is so profitably distinguished for his play – if we yield him up the preference and pay him for his extraordinary composition, and take nothing for our own, though it turned out more to our common profit – sure, sir, while we do such extraordinary duty as managers, and while he neglects his share of that duty, he cannot grudge us the moderate demand we make for our separate labour.

15 Steele's *The Conscious Lovers* enjoyed twenty-two performances between its premiere on 7 November 1722 and the New Year (LS2 694–702); its success may also have prompted a revival of Steele's earlier *The Funeral* on 17 December 1702 (LS2 700). Cibber played Tom in *The Conscious Lovers*.
16 i.e. Cibber himself; Steele acknowledged this in the Preface to the first edition but later denied receiving any help (C11/2416/49; *Document Register* no.3297). In his *Lives and Characters of the Most Eminent Actors and Actresses*, p.120, Theophilus Cibber states that his father had proposed the subplot, which Steele later criticized.
17 In addition to author benefit nights yielding £329 5s and his managerial share of the profits, Steele was given £500 (making a total of c.£195,000 in current values) for dedicating the play to George I (T 52/32, p.265; *Document Register* no.3144).
18 i.e. the performance not of Banks's *Virtue Betrayed*, but Shakespeare's *Henry VIII*, on 26 October 1727, with Cibber as Wolsey, augmented to celebrate the coronation of George II on 11 October of the same year and satirized by Pope in 'The First Epistle of the Second Book of Horace Imitated' (Pope, *Poems*, p.646, lines 314–19). As a result of panic arising from overcrowding and a fire alert, a pregnant woman died in the crush to escape from the theatre (*The Daily Journal*, 28 October 1727, in LS2 940).

'To conclude, sir: if by our constant attendance, our care, our anxiety (not to mention the disagreeable contests we sometimes meet with, both within and without doors, in the management of our theatre) we have not only saved the whole from ruin (which, if we had all followed Sir Richard's example, could not have been avoided) – I say, sir, if we have still made it so valuable an income to him without his giving us the least assistance for several years past, we hope, sir, that the poor labourers that have done all this for Sir Richard will not be thought unworthy of their hire'.

How far our affairs being set in this particular light might assist our cause may be of no great importance to guess, but the issue of it was this: that Sir Richard not having made any objection to what we had charged for management for three years together, and as our proceedings had been all transacted in open day without any clandestine intention of fraud, we were allowed the sums in dispute, above mentioned; and Sir Richard not being advised to appeal to the Lord Chancellor, both parties paid their own costs and thought it their mutual interest to let this be the last of their lawsuits.[19]

And now, gentle reader, I ask pardon for so long an imposition on your patience. For though I may have no ill opinion of this matter myself, yet to you I can very easily conceive it may have been tedious. You are therefore at your own liberty of charging the whole impertinence of it either to the weakness of my judgment or the strength of my vanity, and I will so far join in your censure, that I farther confess I have been so impatient to give it you that you have had it out of its turn; for, some years before this suit was commenced, there were other facts that ought to have had a precedence in my history. But that, I dare say, is an oversight you will easily excuse, provided you afterwards find them worth reading. However, as to that point, I must take my chance, and shall therefore proceed to speak of the theatre which was ordered by his late Majesty to be erected in the Great Old Hall at Hampton Court,[20] where plays were intended to have been acted twice a week during the summer season. But before the theatre could be finished, above half the month of September being elapsed, there were but seven

---

19 After considering previous payments, Master of the Rolls Jekyll determined that Steele should pay his own costs and that £1,061 17s 6d (c.£200,000 in current values) was owed by Cibber, Wilks, and Booth to Steele's trustee, David Scurlock (C38/394; *Document Register* no.3426). The managers argued that their funds had been depleted by the South Sea Bubble crisis, but to no avail.

20 As early as 1715 there were plans to build a theatre at Hampton Court (*Weekly Journal*, 9 April 1715; *Document Register* no.2551).

plays acted before the court returned to London.[21] This throwing open a theatre in a royal palace seemed to be reviving the old English hospitable grandeur, where the lowest rank of neighbouring subjects might make themselves merry at court without being laughed at themselves. In former reigns, theatrical entertainments at the royal palaces had been performed at vast expense, as appears by the description of the decorations in several of Ben Jonson's masques, in King James and Charles the First's time; many curious and original drafts of which, by Sir Inigo Jones, I have seen in the museum of our greatest master and patron of arts and architecture, whom it would be a needless liberty to name.[22] But when our civil wars ended in the decadence of monarchy, it was then an honour to the stage to have fallen with it. Yet after the Restoration of Charles II, some faint attempts were made to revive these theatrical spectacles at court; but I have met with no account of above one masque acted there by the nobility, which was that of *Calisto*, written by Crowne, the author of *Sir Courtly Nice*.[23] For what reason Crowne was chosen to that honour rather than Dryden (who was then Poet Laureate and out of all comparison his superior in poetry) may seem surprising. But if we consider the offence which the then Duke of Buckingham took at the character of Zimri in Dryden's *Absalom, etc* (which might probably be a return to His Grace's Drawcansir in *The Rehearsal*), we may suppose the prejudice and recommendation of so illustrious a pretender to poetry might prevail at court, to give Crowne this preference.[24]

---

21 The *Original Weekly Journal* of 30 August 1718 reported that 'The King hath ordered the comedians of the Theatre Royal in Drury Lane to perform at Hampton Court during His Majesty's stay there', in return for £100 per performance. A performance of *The Beaux' Stratagem* on 24 September 1718 advertised 'The same entertainments that were performed yesterday before His Majesty at Hampton Court' (LS2 507). An order to specify costs was issued on 13 September 1718 (*Document Register* no.2890). Performances at Hampton Court continued into October with *Henry VIII* (1 October 1718), *Sir Courtly Nice* (6 October 1718), *The Constant Couple* (9 October 1718), and *Volpone* (16 October 1718); see LS2 507–10.

22 A reference to Richard Boyle, 3rd Earl of Burlington and 4th Earl of Cork (1694–1753), collector and patron. Burlington owned sketches by Palladio formerly in the possession of Inigo Jones. For an introduction to and selection of masques, see David Lindley, ed., *Court Masques: Jacobean and Caroline Entertainments 1605–1640* (Oxford: Oxford University Press, 1995).

23 John Crowne's *Calisto* was performed at Whitehall in 1675. The largely aristocratic cast included the future Queens Mary and Anne and the Duke of Monmouth, with coaching by members of the Duke's Company. For a detailed study, see Eleanore Boswell, *The Restoration Court Stage* (Cambridge, MA: Harvard University Press, 1932).

24 Dryden's *Absalom and Achitophel* was not published until 1681, six years after *Calisto*, and Dryden did contribute an epilogue for Crowne's play. Dryden's Zimri is 'Stiff in opinions, always in the wrong' (Dryden, *Poems*, p.204). Boswell, *The Restoration Court Stage*, p.179, argues that Rochester was responsible for the choice of Crowne and wanted to snub Dryden. In *The Rehearsal*, Drawcansir imitates Dryden's own bombastic heroes.

In the same reign, the King had his comedians at Windsor, but upon a particular establishment; for though they acted in St. George's Hall, within the royal palace, yet (as I have been informed by an eye-witness) they were permitted to take money at the door, of every spectator.[25] Whether this was an indulgence, in conscience I cannot say; but it was a common report among the principal actors when I first came into the Theatre Royal in 1690 that there was then due to the company, from that Court, about one thousand five hundred pounds for plays commanded, *etc*;[26] and yet it was the general complaint in that prince's reign that he paid too much ready money for his pleasures. But these assertions I only give as I received them, without being answerable for their reality. This theatrical anecdote, however, puts me in mind of one of a more private nature which I had from old solemn Bowman, the late actor of venerable memory.[27] Bowman, then a youth and famed for his voice, was appointed to sing some part in a concert of music at the private lodgings of Mrs Gwyn,[28] at which were only present the King, the Duke of York, and one or two more who were usually admitted upon those detached parties of pleasure. When the performance was ended, the King expressed himself highly pleased and gave it extraordinary commendations. 'Then, sir', said the lady, 'to show you don't speak like a courtier, I hope you will make the performers a handsome present'. The King said he had no money about him, and asked the Duke if he had any; to which the Duke replied, 'I believe, sir, not above a guinea or two'. Upon which the laughing lady, turning to the people about her and making bold with the King's common expression, cried, 'Od's fish! What company am I got into!'

Whether the reverend historian of his *Own Time*, among the many other reasons of the same kind he might have for styling this fair one the 'indiscreetest and wildest creature that ever was in a court' might know this to be one of them, I can't say;[29] but if we consider her in all the disadvantages

---

25 Boswell, *The Restoration Court Stage* p.59, notes a performance in St George's Hall in 1674.

26 Warrants for plays performed by royal command typically show sums owing of approximately £200 per three months (from the Lord Chamberlain's papers e.g. for the period 1685–90 and reproduced in Nicoll, *Restoration*, pp.312–14).

27 John Bowman or Boman (?1651–1739) is first noticed in the Duke's Company 27 the 1673–4 season, when the company's personnel was being comprehensively refreshed (see Downes, p.74). He then joined the United Company and moved with Betterton to Lincoln's Inn Fields in 1695. A regular in middle-ranking roles, he was more famed for singing in the lower range.

28 i.e. Nell Gwyn (see above, p.68 n.13).

29 Burnet began his *History of His Own Time* in 1683. Volume I was eventually published in 1724 and volume II in 1734. His summary of Nell Gwyn appears in I.262.

of her rank and education, she does not appear to have had any criminal errors more remarkable than her sex's frailty to answer for. And if the same author, in his latter end of that prince's life, seems to reproach his memory with too kind a concern for her support, we may allow that it becomes a bishop to have had no eyes or taste for the frivolous charms or playful badinage of a King's mistress. Yet if the common fame of her may be believed (which in my memory was not doubted), she had less to be laid to her charge than any other of those ladies who were in the same state of preferment. She never meddled in matters of serious moment, or was the tool of working politicians; never broke into those amorous infidelities which others in that grave author are accused of; but was as visibly distinguished by her particular personal inclination to the King as her rivals were by their titles and grandeur.[30] Give me leave to carry perhaps the partiality of my observation a little farther. The same author, in the same page (263),[31] tells us that, 'Another of the King's mistresses, the daughter of a clergyman, Mrs Roberts, in whom her first education had so deep a root, that though she fell into many scandalous disorders with very dismal adventures in them all, yet a principle of religion was so deep laid in her, that though it did not restrain her, yet it kept alive in her such a constant horror of sin that she was never easy in an ill course, and died with a great sense of her former ill life.'[32]

To all this let us give an implicit credit: here is the account of a frail sinner made up with a reverend witness! Yet I cannot but lament that this mitred historian,[33] who seems to know more personal secrets than any that ever writ before him, should not have been as inquisitive after the last hours of our other fair offender, whose repentance (I have been unquestionably informed) appeared in all the contrite symptoms of a Christian sincerity.[34] If therefore you find I am so much concerned to make this favourable mention of the one, because she was a sister of the theatre, why may not – but I dare not be so presumptuous, so uncharitably bold, as to suppose the other was spoken better of merely because she was the daughter of a clergyman. Well, and what then? What's all this idle prate, you may say, to the matter

30 Cibber refers to Barbara Palmer (Lady Castlemaine), Duchess of Cleveland (1640–1709), who was married during her affair with the King; and Louise de Keroualle, Duchess of Portsmouth (1649–1734), known for her attempts to influence policy.
31 I.263 in Burnet.
32 i.e. Jane Roberts, maid of honour to Catherine of Braganza, and the daughter of a clergyman.
33 A reference to Burnet's bishop's hat.
34 Gwyn's funeral at St Martin-in-the-Fields (17 November 1687) was conducted by Thomas Tenison, later Archbishop of Canterbury, whose sermon referred to Luke 15:7: 'there will be more joy in heaven over one sinner who repents …'. See DNB VIII.846.

in hand? Why, I say your question is a little too critical; and if you won't give an author leave now and then to embellish his work by a natural reflection, you are an ungentle reader. But I have done with my digression and return to our theatre at Hampton Court, where I am not sure the reader, be he ever so wise, will meet with anything more worth his notice. However, if he happens to read as I write (for want of something better to do), he will go on and perhaps wonder when I tell him that:-

A play presented at court or acted on a public stage seem, to their different auditors, a different entertainment. Now hear my reason for it. In the common theatre the guests are at home, where the politer forms of good breeding are not so nicely regarded. Everyone there falls to, and likes or finds fault according to his natural taste or appetite. At court, where the prince gives the treat and honours the table with his own presence, the audience is under the restraint of a circle where laughter or applause raised higher than a whisper would be stared at. At a public play they are both let loose, even till the actor is (sometimes) pleased with his not being able to be heard for the clamour of them. But this coldness or decency of attention at court, I observed, had but a melancholy effect upon the impatient vanity of some of our actors, who seemed inconsolable when their flashy endeavours to please had passed unheeded. Their not considering where they were, quite disconcerted them, nor could they recover their spirits till, from the lowest rank of the audience, some gaping John or Joan,[35] in the fullness of their hearts, roared out their approbation; and indeed, such a natural instance of honest simplicity a prince himself (whose indulgence knows where to make allowances) might reasonably smile at, and perhaps not think it the worst part of his entertainment. Yet it must be owned that an audience may be as well too much reserved, as too profuse, of their applause. For though it is possible a Betterton would not have been discouraged from throwing out an excellence, or elated into an error, by his auditors being too little or too much pleased, yet (as actors of his judgment are rarities) those of less judgment may sink into a flatness in their performance for want of that applause which, from the generality of judges, they might perhaps have some pretence to. And the auditor, when not seeming to feel what ought to affect him, may rob himself of something more that he might have had, by giving the actor his due who measures out his power to please according to the value he sets upon his hearer's taste or capacity. But however: as we were not, here, itinerant adventurers and had properly but one royal auditor to please, after that honour was attained to, the rest of our ambition had

35 See above, p.119 n.114.

little to look after. And that the King was often pleased, we were not only assured by those who had the honour to be near him, but could see it from the frequent satisfaction in his looks at particular scenes and passages; one instance of which I am tempted to relate, because it was at a speech that might more naturally affect a sovereign prince than any private spectator. In Shakespeare's *Harry the Eighth*, that King commands the Cardinal to write circular letters of indemnity into every county where the payment of certain heavy taxes had been disputed; upon which the Cardinal whispers the following directions to his secretary, Cromwell:

> A word with you:
> Let there be letters writ to every shire
> Of the King's grace and pardon: the griev'd Commons
> Hardly conceive of me. Let it be nois'd,
> That through our intercession this revokement
> And pardon comes. I shall anon advise you
> Farther in the proceeding – [36]

The solicitude of this spiritual minister in filching from his master the grace and merit of a good action, and dressing up himself in it while himself had been author of the evil complained of, was so easy a stroke of his temporal conscience that it seemed to raise the King into something more than a smile, whenever that play came before him. And I had a more distinct occasion to observe this effect, because my proper stand on the stage when I spoke the lines required me to be near the box where the King usually sat.[37] In a word, this play is so true a dramatic chronicle of an old English court – and where the character of Harry the Eighth is so exactly drawn, even to a humorous likeness – that it may be no wonder why His Majesty's particular taste for it should have commanded it three several times in one winter.[38]

---

36 *Henry VIII*, I.ii.114–20. Cibber had played Wolsey since 1716.
37 Cibber may be referring to the performance at Hampton Court either on 27 September or 1 October 1718 (LS2 507), when, according to the *Weekly Journal or British Gazetteer*, 'His Majesty, and their Highnesses the young Princesses were at the play.' A further royal command performance is listed at Drury Lane for 6 April 1719. Lowe cites Davies, I.365:

> Wolsey's filching from his royal master the honour of bestowing grace and pardon on the subject appeared so impudent a prevarication that, when this play was acted before George I at Hampton Court about the year 1717, the courtiers laughed so loudly at this ministerial craft that His Majesty, who was unacquainted with the English language, asked the Lord Chamberlain the meaning of their mirth; upon being informed of it, the King joined in a laugh of approbation.

38 See above, p.341 n.21.

This too calls to my memory an extravagant pleasantry of Sir Richard Steele, who being asked by a grave nobleman after the same play had been presented at Hampton Court, how the King liked it, replied, 'So terribly well, my lord, that I was afraid I should have lost all my actors! For I was not sure the King would not keep them to fill the posts at court that he saw them so fit for in the play'.

It may be imagined that giving plays to the people at such a distance from London could not but be attended with an extraordinary expense; and it was some difficulty, when they were first talked of, to bring them under a moderate sum. I shall therefore, in as few words as possible, give a particular of what establishment they were then brought to, that in case the same entertainments should at any time hereafter be called to the same place, future courts may judge how far the precedent may stand good, or need an alteration.

Though the stated fee for a play acted at Whitehall had been formerly but twenty pounds, yet (as that hindered not the company's acting on the same day at the public theatre) that sum was almost all clear profits to them.[39] But this circumstance not being practicable when they were commanded to Hampton Court, a new and extraordinary charge was unavoidable. The managers therefore, not to inflame it, desired no consideration for their own labour farther than the honour of being employed in His Majesty's commands; and, if the other actors might be allowed each their day's pay and travelling charges, they should hold themselves ready to act any play there at a day's warning. And, that the trouble might be less by being divided, the Lord Chamberlain was pleased to let us know that the household music, the wax lights, and a *chaise-marine* to carry our moving wardrobe to every different play, should be under the charge of the proper officers.[40] Notwithstanding these assistances, the expense of every play amounted to fifty pounds – which account, when all was over, was not only allowed us, but His Majesty was graciously pleased to give the managers two hundred pounds more for their particular performance and trouble, in

39 The Lord Chamberlain's warrants from 1666 onwards generally indicate £10 for a royal visit to the theatre and £20 for a court performance, with the higher figure applicable when a larger party (including the maids of honour, for example) attended the theatre (Nicoll, *Restoration*, pp.305–14). Whitehall performances took place in the evening and those in the theatres in the afternoon.

40 *Chaise-marine* indicates either a trolley with suspension springs to prevent damage, or a seat to be placed in a boat (i.e. from the city to Hampton Court) with devices to offset pitching and rolling. *Document Register* no.2892 notes a detailed account of the candles required for the 1 October 1718 performance of *Henry VIII*: 220 white quarter-pound candles, 16½ pounds of yellow wax candles, and 32½ pounds of tallow.

only seven times acting;[41] which last sum, though it might not be too much for a sovereign prince to give, it was certainly more than our utmost merit ought to have hoped for. And I confess, when I received the order for the money from His Grace the Duke of Newcastle, then Lord Chamberlain, I was so surprised that I imagined His Grace's favour (or recommendation of our readiness or diligence) must have contributed to so high a consideration of it, and was offering my acknowledgments as I thought them due; but was soon stopped short by His Grace's declaration that we had no obligations for it but to the King himself, who had given it from no other motive than his own bounty.[42] Now whether we may suppose that Cardinal Wolsey (as you see Shakespeare has drawn him) would silently have taken such low acknowledgments to himself, perhaps may be as little worth consideration as my mentioning this circumstance has been necessary. But if it is due to the honour and integrity of the then Lord Chamberlain, I cannot think it wholly impertinent.

Since that time, there has been but one play given at Hampton Court, which was for the entertainment of the Duke of Lorraine, and for which his present Majesty was pleased to order us a hundred pounds.[43]

The reader may now plainly see that I am ransacking my memory for such remaining scraps of theatrical history as may not, perhaps, be worth his notice. But if they are such as tempt me to write them, why may I not hope that in this wide world there may be many an idle soul no wiser than myself, who may be equally tempted to read them?

I have so often had occasion to compare the state of the stage to the state of a nation that I yet feel a reluctancy to drop the comparison, or speak of the one without some application to the other. How many reigns, then, do I remember from that of Charles the Second, through all which there

---

41 A warrant dated 15 November 1718 specifies a payment of £574 1s 8d for seven performances at Hampton Court, with £200 of that sum 'a present from His Majesty' (LC 5/157, p.154; *Document Register* no.2896).

42 Cibber perhaps seeks to repair the difficulties he and Steele would experience in 1719–20 with Lord Chamberlain Newcastle, holder of the office between 1717 and 1724 (see above, p.3 n.3 and p.332 n.2).

43 The company performed Farquhar's *The Recruiting Officer* at Hampton Court on 18 October 1731 for the visit of the Duke of Lorraine. According to *The Craftsman*, 11 September 1731, six plays had been planned but only one was given; *St James's Evening Post* of 21–3 September reports this was out of consideration for the strain on George II's eyes caused by candlelight. The Duke of Lorraine at this time was Francis I (1708–65), who held the title between 1728 and 1737, when he traded it for the Grand Duchy of Tuscany as part of the treaty to end the War of the Polish Succession. His visit to London was a diplomatic exercise following the signing of the Treaty of Vienna in March 1731, which had ended the Anglo-French alliance.

has been from one half of the people or the other, a succession of clamour against every different ministry for the time being? And yet, let the cause of this clamour have been never so well grounded, it is impossible but that some of those ministers must have been wiser and honester men than others. If this be true (as true I believe it is), why may I not then say, as some fool in a French play does upon a like occasion, 'Justement comme chez nous!'[44] 'Twas exactly the same with our management! Let us have done never so well, we could not please everybody. All I can say in our defence is that though many good judges might possibly conceive how the state of the stage might have been mended, yet the best of them never pretended to remember the time when it was better, or could show us the way to make their imaginary amendments practicable.

For though I have often allowed that our best merit as actors was never equal to that of our predecessors, yet I will venture to say that in all its branches, the stage had never been under so just, so prosperous, and so settled a regulation for forty years before, as it was at the time I am speaking of. The most plausible objection to our administration seemed to be that we took no care to breed up young actors to succeed us;[45] and this was imputed as the greater fault, because it was taken for granted that it was a matter as easy as planting so many cabbages. Now might not a court as well be reproached for not breeding up a succession of complete ministers? And yet it is evident that if Providence or Nature don't supply us with both, the state and the stage will be but poorly supported. If a man of an ample fortune should take it into his head to give a younger son an extraordinary allowance in order to breed him a great poet, what might we suppose would be the odds that his trouble and money would be all thrown away?

---

44 This phrase ('so it is with us') appears not in a play, but in a dialogue by Eustache Le Noble (1643–1711), *Les Diables au Palais; ou IV Entretien entre le Diable Boiteux et le Diable Borgne* (1707), p.11. Le Noble also wrote plays. His politics were the opposite of Cibber's: pro-Jacobite, some of his works were translated into English from the 1690s, and an English version of *Les Diables* appeared in 1708. Cibber may have come across the book during his visit to France in 1728. I am grateful to Dr Mark Darlow of Christ's College Cambridge for identifying the reference.

45 The ownership of leading roles by senior actors was largely endemic and had been a cause of tension within acting companies since the 1660s; the practice was, in different ways, partly responsible for the 1695 breakaway (see above, p.131) and the desertion of 1714 (see above, p.319 n.32). *The Daily Journal* of 5 January 1722 reported a disturbance at Drury Lane during which Cibber admitted the managers had been criticized for 'not pushing forward their young actors'. Yet his efforts to address the problem were not welcomed: on 13 January 1722, the *London Journal* reported that 'young comedians' assigned roles in Cibber's *The Rival Fools* (1709) were 'hissed and pelted off the stage'.

Not more than it would be against the master of a theatre, who should say, 'This or that young man I will take care shall be an excellent actor!' Let it be our excuse then for that mistaken charge against us, that since there was no garden or market where accomplished actors grew or were to be sold, we could only pick them up as we do pebbles of value: by chance. We may polish a thousand before we can find one fit to make a figure in the lid of a snuffbox. And how few soever we were able to produce, it is no proof that we were not always in search of them. Yet, at worst, it was allowed that our deficiency of men actors was not so visible as our scarcity of tolerable women. But when it is considered that the life of youth and beauty is too short for the bringing an actress to her perfection, were I to mention too the many frail fair ones I remember who, before they could arrive to their theatrical maturity, were feloniously stolen from the tree, it would rather be thought our misfortune than our fault that we were not better provided.[46]

Even the laws of a nunnery, we find, are thought no sufficient security against temptations without iron grates and high walls to enforce them – which the architecture of a theatre will not so properly admit of. And yet, methinks, beauty that has not those artificial fortresses about it, that has no defence but its natural virtue (which upon the stage has more than once been met with), makes a much more meritorious figure in life than that immured virtue which could never be tried.[47] But alas, as the poor stage is but the show-glass to a toyshop, we must not wonder if now and then some of the baubles should find a purchaser.

However, as to say more or less than truth are equally unfaithful in an historian, I cannot but own that in the government of the theatre I have known many instances where the merit of promising actors has not always been brought forward with the regard or favour it had a claim to. And if I put my reader in mind that in the early part of this work, I have shown through what continued difficulties and discouragements I myself made my way up the hill of preferment, he may justly call it too strong a glare of my

46 Cibber, Wilks, Oldfield, Porter, and Booth retired or died within a few years of each other, leaving a span of nearly a decade before the emergence of David Garrick from 1741; see letter from Aaron Hill on the effect on London Theatre, *Document Register*, no.3768. Cibber signally fails to associate any line of succession with his son Theophilus (in the company from 1720) or daughter-in-law Susannah (from 1732). On Cibber's reference to young actresses being 'stolen' (and by implication made pregnant), see wide fluctuations in the Drury Lane roster of actresses: for example, twenty in August 1708, ten in August 1709, fifteen in August 1710 (LS2a 447, 510, 599). On actresses leaving the stage during the Restoration period, see Howe, pp.91–107.

47 Cibber's *Love's Last Shift* contains echoes of Milton; here he may be recalling a famous passage from *Areopagitica* (1644): 'I cannot praise a fugitive and cloistered virtue.' John Milton, *Selected Prose*, ed. C.A. Patrides (Harmondsworth: Penguin, 1974), p.213.

13. 'Impatient to be foremost': Robert Wilks, by John
Faber, after John Ellys.

vanity. I am afraid he is in the right; but I pretend not to be one of those
chaste authors that know how to write without it. When truth is to be told,
it may be as much chance as choice if it happens to turn out in my favour.
But to show that this was true of others as well as myself, Booth shall be
another instance. In 1707, when Swiney was the only master of the company
in the Haymarket, Wilks (though he was then but an hired actor himself)
rather chose to govern and give orders than to receive them; and was so
jealous of Booth's rising that with a high hand he gave the part of Pierre, in
Venice Preserved, to Mills the elder, who (not to undervalue him) was out of
sight in the pretensions that Booth, then young as he was, had to the same
part.[48] And this very discouragement so strongly affected him that not long

48 Apparently a reference to the revival of Otway's play on 15 November 1707 (LS2a 388).
   Wilks played Jaffeir and Mills Pierre, while Booth was assigned the minor role of the
   conspirator, Bedamar. Cibber played Renault, as he had since 1700. Wilks did not assume
   formal management responsibility until March 1708 (as above, p.126 n.1).

after, when several of us became sharers with Swiney, Booth rather chose to risk his fortune with the old patentee in Drury Lane than come into our interest, where he saw he was like to meet with more of those partialities.[49] And yet again, Booth himself, when he came to be a manager, would sometimes suffer his judgment to be blinded by his inclination to actors whom the town seemed to have but an indifferent opinion of. This again inclines me to ask another of my odd questions, *viz.*, have we never seen the same passions govern a court? How many white staffs[50] and great places do we find in our histories have been laid at the feet of a monarch, because they chose not to give way to a rival in power, or hold a second place in his favour? How many Whigs and Tories have changed their parties when their good or bad pretensions have met with a check to their higher preferment?[51]

Thus, we see, let the degrees and rank of men be ever so unequal, Nature throws out their passions from the same motives; 'tis not the eminence or lowliness of either that makes the one, when provoked, more or less a reasonable creature than the other. The courtier and the comedian, when their ambition is out of humour, take just the same measures to right themselves.

If this familiar style of talking should, in the nostrils of gravity and wisdom, smell a little too much of the presumptuous or the pragmatical, I will at least descend lower in my apology for it by calling to my assistance the old, humble proverb, *viz.*, 'tis an ill bird that *—etc.*[52] Why then should I debase my profession by setting it in vulgar lights, when I may show it to more favourable advantages? And when I speak of our errors, why may I not extenuate them by illustrious examples, or by not allowing them greater than the greatest men have been subject to? Or why, indeed, may I not suppose that a sensible reader will rather laugh than look grave at the pomp of my parallels?

Now, as I am tied down to the veracity of an historian (whose facts cannot be supposed, like those in a romance, to be in the choice of the author to make them more marvellous by invention), if I should happen to sink into a little farther insignificancy, let the simple truth of what I have farther to say be my excuse for it. I am obliged, therefore, to make the experiment

49 As above, p.262.
50 Signifying membership of the Privy Council.
51 A tendency encouraged by royal appointments: William III and Anne in particular veered between balancing the interests of different political groupings in their governments and favouring one over the other. The careers of Robert Harley, 1st Earl of Oxford (1661–1724) and Robert Spencer, 2nd Earl of Sunderland (1641–1702) were particularly notable for their suppleness.
52 'It is a foul bird that defiles his own nest' (Tilley, B377); first recorded in 1509.

by showing you the conduct of our theatrical ministry in such lights as on various occasions it appeared in.

Though Wilks had more industry and application than any actor I had ever known, yet we found it possible that those necessary qualities might sometimes be so misconducted as not only to make them useless, but hurtful to our commonwealth;[53] for while he was impatient to be foremost in everything, he frequently shocked the honest ambition of others whose measures might have been more serviceable, could his jealousy have given way to them. His own regards for himself, therefore, were (to avoid a disagreeable dispute with him) too often complied with. But this leaving his diligence to his own conduct made us, in some instances, pay dearly for it. For example, he would take as much (or more) pains in forwarding to the stage the water-gruel work of some insipid author that happened rightly to make his court to him, than he would for the best play wherein it was not his fortune to be chosen for the best character.[54] So great was his impatience to be employed that I scarce remember, in twenty years, above one profitable play we could get to be revived wherein he found he was to make no considerable figure, independent of him. But *The Tempest* having done wonders formerly, he could not form any pretensions to let it lie longer dormant.[55] However, his coldness to it was so visible that he took all occasions to postpone and discourage its progress, by frequently taking up the morning stage with something more to his mind.[56] Having been myself particularly solicitous for the reviving this play, Doggett (for this was before Booth came into the management) consented that the

53 Lowe cites Davies, III.255:
> However Colley may complain in his *Apology* of Wilks's fire and impetuosity, he in general was Cibber's great admirer; he supported him on all occasions where his own passion or interest did not interpose; nay, he deprived the inoffensive Harry Carey of the liberty of the scenes, because he had, in common with others, made merry with Cibber in a song on his being appointed Poet Laureate; saying at the same time, he was surprised at his impertinence in behaving so improperly 'to a man of such great merit'.

54 Lowe cites John Dennis's Advertisement to *The Invader of his Country* (1720): 'I am perfectly satisfied that any author who brings a play to Drury Lane must, if 'tis a good one, be sacrificed to the jealousy of this fine writer, unless he has either a powerful cabal, or unless he will flatter Mr Robert Wilks and make him believe that he is an excellent tragedian.' The (ironic) 'fine writer' was Cibber.

55 A reference to the revival of Dryden and Davenant's adaptation on 7 January 1712, 'With new scenes, machines, and all the original decorations proper to the play'; LS2 266–8 lists a total of eight performances from then until 1 February. *The Tempest* appears to have 'lain dormant' since 10 July 1710 (LS2a 584), when Powell played Prospero with Elrington (see above, p.290 n.6) rather than Wilks as Ferdinand.

56 i.e. rehearsal time. See Stern, pp.227–33.

extraordinary decorations and habits should be left to my care and direction, as the fittest person whose temper could jostle through the petulant opposition that he knew Wilks would be always offering to it, because he had but a middling part in it – that of Ferdinand. Notwithstanding which, so it happened that the success of it showed (not to take from the merit of Wilks) that it was possible to have good audiences without his extraordinary assistance. In the first six days of acting it we paid all our constant and incidental expense, and shared each of us a hundred pounds: the greatest profit that in so little a time had yet been known within my memory! But alas, what was paltry pelf to glory? That was the darling passion of Wilks's heart, and not to advance in it was to so jealous an ambition a painful retreat, a mere shade to his laurels; and the common benefit was but a poor equivalent to his want of particular applause! To conclude, not Prince Lewis of Baden, though a confederate General with the Duke of Marlborough, was more inconsolable upon the memorable victory at Blenheim[57] (at which he was not present) than our theatrical hero was to see any action prosperous that he was not himself at the head of. If this, then, was an infirmity in Wilks, why may not my showing the same weakness in so great a man mollify the imputation, and keep his memory in countenance?

This laudable appetite for fame in Wilks was not, however, to be fed without that constant labour which only himself was able to come up to. He therefore bethought him of the means to lessen the fatigue, and at the same time to heighten his reputation; which was by giving up, now and then, a part to some raw actor who he was sure would disgrace it, and consequently put the audience in mind of his superior performance. Among this sort of indulgences to young actors, he happened once to make a mistake that set his views in a clear light. The best critics, I believe, will allow that in Shakespeare's *Macbeth* there are in the part of Macduff two scenes (the one of terror in the second act, and the other of compassion in the fourth) equal to any that dramatic poetry has produced.[58] These scenes Wilks had acted with success, though far short of that happier skill and grace which Mountfort had formerly shown in them.[59] Such a part, however, one might imagine would be one of the last a good actor would choose to part with.

57 Louis William, Margrave of Baden-Baden (1655–1707), military commander of the Holy Roman Empire during the War of the Spanish Succession; his victory in the Battle of Schellenberg (2 July 1704) drew Bavarian troops away from Blenheim (13 August 1704).
58 i.e. II.iii (the discovery of Duncan's murder) and IV.iii (Macduff learns of his wife and children's fate). Both scenes were performed in the adaptation by Sir William Davenant.
59 Wilks was probably playing Macduff by 21 November 1702, when he was awarded a benefit for *Macbeth* (LS2a 80); Betterton was presumably Macbeth and Elizabeth Barry Lady Macbeth. After Betterton's death in May 1710, Mills took over as Macbeth

But Wilks was of a different opinion, for Macbeth was thrice as long, had more great scenes of action, and bore the name of the play. Now, to be a second in any play was what he did not much care for, and had been seldom used to. This part of Macduff, therefore, he had given to one Williams, as yet no extraordinary (though a promising) actor.[60] Williams, in the simplicity of his heart, immediately told Booth what a favour Wilks had done him. Booth, as he had reason, thought Wilks had here carried his indulgence and his authority a little too far; for as Booth had no better a part in the same play than that of Banquo, he found himself too much disregarded in letting so young an actor take place of him. Booth, therefore, who knew the value of Macduff, proposed to do it himself and to give Banquo to Williams; and to make him farther amends, offered him any other of his parts that he thought might be of service to him. Williams was content with the exchange, and thankful for the promise. This scheme indeed (had it taken effect) might have been an ease to Wilks, and possibly no disadvantage to the play; but softly – that was not quite what we had a mind to! No sooner then, came this proposal to Wilks, but off went the mask and out came the secret! For though Wilks wanted to be eased of the part, he did not desire to be excelled in it; and, as he was not sure but that might be the case if Booth were to act it, he wisely retracted his own project, took Macduff again to himself, and while he lived never had a thought of running the same hazard by any farther offer to resign it.[61]

and Wilks continued as Macduff (LS2a 604 *passim*). Lowe cites *The Tatler*, no.68, 15 September 1709:

> In the tragedy of *Macbeth*, where Wilks acts the part of a man whose family has been murdered in his absence, the wildness of his passion, which is run over in a torrent of calamitous circumstances, does but raise my spirits and give me the alarm; but when he skilfully seems to be out of breath and is brought too low to say more, and upon a second reflection cry, only wiping his eyes – 'What, both my children! Both, both my children gone' – there is no resisting a sorrow which seems to have cast about for all the reasons possible for its consolation, but has no recourse. There is not one left, but both, both are murdered! Such sudden starts from the thread of the discourse, and a plain sentiment expressed in an artless way, are the irresistible strokes of eloquence and poetry.

Steele's Shakespearean quotations are inaccurately recalled from Sir William Davenant's version of *Macbeth* (London: P. Chetwin, 1674), p.55: 'Both, both my children / Did you say; my two?'

60 Charles Williams (d. 1731) appears to have joined the Drury Lane company in 1717 (LS2 462). He presumably had a lesser role in *Macbeth*, since he is listed as one of three beneficiaries for a benefit performance of the play on 1 May 1718 (LS2 493). When Cibber played Scipio in James Thomson's *The Tragedy of Sophonisba* on 28 February 1730 he was thought unsuitable for a tragic role and promptly gave up the part to Williams.

Here, I confess, I am at a loss for a fact in history to which this can be a parallel! To be weary of a post even to a real desire of resigning it, and yet to choose rather to drudge on in it than suffer it to be well supplied (though to share in that advantage), is a delicacy of ambition that Machiavelli himself has made no mention of;[62] or if, in old Rome, the jealousy of any pretended patriot equally inclined to abdicate his office may have come up to it, 'tis more than my reading remembers.

As nothing can be more impertinent than showing too frequent a fear to be thought so, I will (without farther apology) rather risk that imputation than not tell you another story much to the same purpose, and of no more consequence than my last. To make you understand it, however, a little preface will be necessary.

If the merit of an actor (as it certainly does) consists more in the quality than the quantity of his labour, the other managers had no visible reason to think this needless ambition of Wilks, in being so often and sometimes so unnecessarily employed, gave him any title to a superiority – especially when our articles of agreement had allowed us all to be equal. But what are narrow contracts to great souls with growing desires? Wilks therefore (who thought himself lessened in appealing to any judgment but his own) plainly discovered by his restless behaviour – though he did not care to speak out – that he thought he had a right to some higher consideration for his performance. This was often Booth's opinion as well as my own. It must be farther observed that he actually had a separate allowance of fifty pounds a year, for writing our daily playbills for the printer;[63] which

61 For occasional performances (e.g. 27 November 1718, LS2 516; 6 December 1728, LS2 1001), Macduff was played by Elrington, but Wilks continued in the role at least until May 1729 (LS2 1032). Booth is last recorded as playing Banquo on 5 October 1725 (LS2 834), after which Williams took over the role (16 November 1726, LS2 891). Lowe cites Davies, II.183, on the difference Booth might have made as Macduff:

> In the strong expression of horror on the murder of the King, and the loud exclamations of surprise and terror, Booth might have exceeded the utmost efforts of Wilks. But in the touches of domestic woe, which require the feelings of the tender father and the affectionate husband, Wilks had no equal. His skill in exhibiting the emotions of the overflowing heart with corresponding look and action, was universally admired and felt. His rising, after the suppression of his anguish, into ardent and manly resentment, was highly expressive of noble and generous anger.

62 Cibber's wording suggests a familiarity with Machiavelli's *Il Principe*, probably in the 1640 translation by Edward Dacres.

63 Apparently in addition to his total income for 1729 of £753 6s 8d, plus £60 benefit listed by the *Morning Chronicle and London Advertiser* in 1781 (see above, p.262 n.34). His total earnings were therefore equivalent to c.£166,000 in current values.

province, to say the truth, was the only one we cared to trust to his particular intendance, or could find out for a pretence to distinguish him. But
to speak a plainer truth, this pension (which was no part of our original
agreement) was merely paid to keep him quiet, and not that we thought it
due to so insignificant a charge as what a prompter had formerly executed.
This being really the case, his frequent complaints of being a drudge to the
company grew something more than disagreeable to us. For we could not
digest the imposition of a man's setting himself to work and then bringing
in his own bill for it. Booth, therefore, who was less easy than I was to see
him so often setting a merit upon this quantity of his labour (which neither
could be our interest, or his own, to lay upon him), proposed to me that we
might remove this pretended grievance by reviving some play that might
be likely to live, and be easily acted, without Wilks's having any part in it.
About this time, an unexpected occasion offered itself to put our project
in practice. What followed our attempt will be all (if anything be) worth
observation in my story.

   In 1725, we were called upon in a manner that could not be resisted to
revive *The Provoked Wife*, a comedy which, while we found our account in
keeping the stage clear of those loose liberties it had formerly too justly
been charged with, we had laid aside for some years.[64] The author, Sir John
Vanbrugh, who was conscious of what it had too much of, was prevailed
upon to substitute a new-written scene in the place of one in the fourth
act, where the wantonness of his wit and humour had originally made a
rake talk like a rake in the borrowed habit of a clergyman; to avoid which
offence, he clapped the same debauchee into the undress of a woman of
quality.[65] Now the character and profession of a fine lady not being so indel-
ibly sacred as that of a churchman, whatever follies he exposed in the petti-
coat kept him at least clear of his former profaneness, and were now innocently ridiculous to the spectator.

64 i.e. the revival of Vanbrugh's play on 11 January 1726 (LS2 850), with Cibber as Sir John
   Brute and Oldfield as his provoked wife. Cibber does not mention that the play had been
   a regular at the rival Lincoln's Inn Fields Theatre at least since 21 December 1715 (LS2
   381). Its 'loose liberties' had been a principal target of Jeremy Collier and its 'indecent
   expressions' were considered by the King's Bench in November 1701 (Luttrell, V.III).
65 Two previous revivals had advertised revisions to the play. The Queen's Haymarket
   performance on 19 January 1706 was 'with alterations' (LS2a 273), while the Lincoln's
   Inn Fields revival of 21 December 1715 stated (correctly) that the play had not been
   'acted these eight years' and had been 'carefully revised' (LS2 381). The revival Cibber
   refers to is described as 'revised by the author'. The changes Cibber refers to in IV.i
   and IV.iii were not published until 1743, when a Dublin edition announced 'an original
   scene, never before printed'. In 'was prevailed upon', Cibber implies he himself
   suggested the change.

This play being thus refitted for the stage, was (as I have observed) called for from [the] Court and by many of the nobility.⁶⁶ Now, then (we thought) was a proper time to come to an explanation with Wilks. Accordingly, when the actors were summoned to hear the play read and receive their parts, I addressed myself to Wilks before them all, and told him that as the part of Constant (which he seemed to choose) was a character of less action than he generally appeared in, we thought this might be a good occasion to ease himself by giving it to another (*here he looked grave*); that the love scenes of it were rather serious than gay or humorous, and therefore might sit very well upon Booth (*down dropped his brow, and furled were his features*); that if we were never to revive a tolerable play without him, what would become of us in case of his indisposition? (*here he pretended to stir the fire*); that as he could have no farther advantage or advancement in his station to hope for, his acting in this play was but giving himself an unprofitable trouble which neither Booth or I desired to impose upon him (*softly – now the pill began to gripe him*). In a word, this provoking civility plunged him into a passion which he was no longer able to contain. Out it came, with all the equipage of unlimited language that on such occasions his displeasure usually set out with, but when his reply was stripped of those ornaments, it was plainly this: that he looked upon all I had said as a concerted design not only to signalise ourselves by laying him aside, but a contrivance to draw him into the disfavour of the nobility by making it supposed his own choice that he did not act in a play so particularly asked for; but we should find he could stand upon his own bottom,⁶⁷ and it was not all our little caballing should get our ends of him. To which I answered (with some warmth) that he was mistaken in our ends. 'For those, sir', said I, 'you have answered already, by showing the company you cannot bear to be left out of any play. Are not you every day complaining of your being over-laboured? And now, upon our first offering to ease you, you fly into a passion and pretend to make that a greater grievance than t'other. But, sir, if your being in or out of the play is a hardship, you shall impose it upon yourself. The part is in your hand, and to us it is a matter of indifference now whether you take it or leave it'. Upon this, he threw down the part upon the table, crossed his arms, and sat knocking his heel upon the floor, as seeming to threaten most when he said least; but when nobody persuaded him to take it up again, Booth (not choosing to push the matter too far, but rather

<hr />

66 The performances on 17 and 18 January 1726 were advertised as being 'At the desire of
    several persons of quality' (LS2 851).
67 i.e. rest on his own secure foundations.

to split the difference of our dispute) said that for his part, he saw no such great matter in acting every day, for he believed it the wholesomest exercise in the world; it kept the spirits in motion, and always gave him a good stomach. Though this was, in a manner, giving up the part to Wilks, yet it did not allow he did us any favour in receiving it. Here, I observed Mrs Oldfield began to titter behind her fan. But Wilks being more intent upon what Booth had said, replied: everyone could best feel for himself, but he did not pretend to the strength of a pack-horse; therefore, if Mrs Oldfield would choose anybody else to play with her, he should be very glad to be excused.[68] This throwing the negative upon Mrs Oldfield was indeed a sure way to save himself; which I could not help taking notice of by saying it was making but an ill compliment to the company to suppose there was but one man in it fit to play an ordinary part with her. Here Mrs Oldfield got up and, turning me half round to come forward, said with her usual frankness, 'Pooh! You are all a parcel of fools to make such a rout about nothing', rightly judging that the person most out of humour would not be more displeased at her calling us all by the same name. As she knew, too, the best way of ending the debate would be to help the weak, she said she hoped Mr Wilks would not so far mind what had passed as to refuse his acting the part with her; for though it might not be so good as he had been used to, yet she believed those who had bespoke the play would expect to have it done to the best advantage, and it would make but an odd story abroad if it were known there had been any difficulty in that point among ourselves. To conclude, Wilks had the part and we had all we wanted, which was an occasion to let him see that the accident (or choice) of one manager's being more employed than another would never be allowed a pretence for altering our indentures, or his having an extraordinary consideration for it.[69]

However disagreeable it might be to have this unsociable temper daily to deal with, yet I cannot but say that from the same impatient spirit that had so often hurt us, we still drew valuable advantages. For as Wilks seemed to have no joy in life beyond his being distinguished on the stage, we were not only sure of his always doing his best there himself, but of making others more careful than (without the rod of so irascible a temper over them) they would have been. And I much question if a more temperate or better usage of the hired actors could have so effectually kept them to order. Not even Betterton (as we have seen), with all his good sense, his great fame

---

68 Constant, Wilks's role and a generic one of about 350 lines, is lover to Lady Brute, Oldfield's role.
69 Booth played Heartfree, Constant's cynical companion.

and experience, could, by being only a quiet example of industry himself, save his company from falling while neither gentleness could govern or the consideration of their common interest reform them.[70] Diligence, with much the inferior skill or capacity, will beat the best negligent company that ever came upon a stage. But when a certain dreaming idleness, or jolly negligence of rehearsals, gets into a body of the ignorant and incapable (which before Wilks came into Drury Lane, when Powell was at the head of them, was the case of that company),[71] then, I say, a sensible spectator might have looked upon the fallen stage as Portius in the play of *Cato* does upon his ruined country, and have lamented it in something near the same exclamation, *viz:-*

> O ye immortal bards!
> What havoc do these blockheads make among your works!
> How are the boasted labours of an age
> Defaced and tortured by ungracious action?[72]

Of this wicked doings, Dryden too complains in one of his prologues at that time, where, speaking of such lewd actors, he closes a couplet with the following line, *viz:-*

> And murder plays, which they miscall reviving.[73]

The great share therefore that Wilks, by his exemplary diligence and impatience of neglect in others, had in the reformation of this evil, ought in justice to be remembered; and let my own vanity here take shame to itself, when I confess that had I had half his application, I still think I might have shown myself twice the actor that in my highest state of favour I appeared to be. But if I have any excuse for that neglect (a fault which, if I loved not truth, I need not have mentioned), it is that so much of my attention was taken up in an incessant labour to guard against our private animosities, and preserve a harmony in our management that (I hope and believe) it made ample amends for whatever omission my auditors might sometimes know it cost me some pains to conceal.[74] But Nature takes care to bestow

---

70 As above, p.154.   71 As above, pp.161–2.

72 Cibber embellishes the end of the opening speech in Addison's *Cato*, I.i.11–12: 'Ye Gods, what havoc does ambition make / Among your works!'.

73 From Dryden's 'To Mr Granville, on his excellent tragedy called *Heroic Love*' (1698). Dryden refers to actors who 'Plot not on the stage, but on the town, / And in despair their empty pit to fill, / Set up some foreign monster in a bill: / Thus they jog on; still tricking, never thriving; / And murd'ring plays, which they miscall reviving' (lines 20–4; Dryden, p.510).

74 The professed harmony of the Booth–Cibber–Wilks partnership was doubtless aided by their common cause against Steele (as above, pp.333–40).

14. 'Too grave a dignity': Barton Booth,
by George White.

her blessings with a more equal hand than Fortune does, and is seldom
known to heap too many upon one man. One tolerable talent in an individual is enough to preserve him from being good for nothing; and if that was
not laid to my charge as an actor, I have in this light, too, less to complain
of than to be thankful for.

Before I conclude my history, it may be expected I should give some
farther view of these, my last contemporaries of the theatre, Wilks and
Booth, in their different acting capacities. If I were to paint them in the
colours they laid upon one another, their talents would not be shown with
half the commendation I am inclined to bestow upon them when they are
left to my own opinion. But people of the same profession are apt to see
themselves in their own clear glass of partiality, and look upon their equals
through a mist of prejudice. It might be imagined too, from the difference
of their natural tempers, that Wilks should have been more blind to the
excellencies of Booth than Booth was to those of Wilks; but it was not so.
Wilks would sometimes commend Booth to me, but when Wilks excelled,

the other was silent. Booth seemed to think nothing valuable that was not tragically great or marvellous. Let that be as true as it may, yet I have often thought that from his having no taste of humour himself, he might be too much inclined to depreciate the acting of it in others. The very slight opinion which, in private conversation with me, he had of Wilks's acting Sir Harry Wildair, was certainly more than could be justified: not only from the general applause that was against that opinion (though applause is not always infallible), but from the visible capacity which must be allowed to an actor that could carry such slight materials to such a height of approbation.[75] For though the character of Wildair scarce in any one scene will stand against a just criticism, yet in the whole there are so many gay and false colours of the fine gentleman that nothing but a vivacity in the performance, proportionably extravagant, could have made them so happily glare upon a common audience.

Wilks, from his first setting out, certainly formed his manner of acting upon the model of Mountfort,[76] as Booth did his on that of Betterton, but *haud passibus æquis*;[77] I cannot say either of them came up to their original. Wilks had not that easy regulated behaviour or the harmonious elocution of the one, nor Booth that conscious aspect of intelligence, nor requisite variation of voice, that made every line the other spoke seem his own natural, self-delivered sentiment. Yet there is still room for great commendation of both the first mentioned – which will not be so much diminished in my having said they were only excelled by such predecessors as it will be raised in venturing to affirm it will be a longer time before any successors will come near them. Thus, one of the greatest praises given to Virgil is that no successor in poetry came so near him as he himself did to Homer.[78]

75 A reference not to the play of that name by Farquhar but its predecessor, *The Constant Couple*, in which Wilks had starred as Sir Harry since its premiere in November 1699 (LS1 517). For Farquhar's praise of Wilks in the role, see above, p.210 n.46.
76 For Cibber's appreciation of William Mountfort's gentlemanly ease, see above, pp.94–5. Wilks was in London for up to two years before Mountfort's death in 1692; during his second stay, from 1698, he may have learned more from Cibber and others about the late actor's style in performance.
77 'With unequal steps': originally from Virgil, *Aeneid*, II.724 (*non passibus æquis*) but proverbial by 1740.
78 This judgment is first found in Marcus Fabius Quintilianus ('Quintilian'), *Institutione Oratoria* (c. AD 94): 'of all epic poets, Greek or Roman, [Virgil], without doubt, most nearly approaches Homer. I will repeat the words I heard Domitius Afer use when I was younger. I asked which poet he thought came closest to Homer, and he replied, "Virgil comes second, but is closer to first than third"'; translated from Quintilian, *De Institutione oratoria* (Oxford: Henry Cruttenden, 1693), p.510. There were reprints of the 1693 edition in 1714 and 1716, but no English translation until the twentieth century.

Though the majority of public auditors are but bad judges of theatrical action and are often deceived into their approbation of what has no solid pretence to it, yet (as there are no other appointed judges to appeal to, and as every single spectator has a right to be one of them) their sentence will be definitive, and the merit of an actor must in some degree be weighed by it. By this law, then, Wilks was pronounced an excellent actor; which, if the few true judges did not allow him to be, they were at least too candid to slight or discourage him. Booth and he were actors so directly opposite in their manner, that if either of them could have borrowed a little of the other's fault they would both have been improved by it. If Wilks had sometimes too violent a vivacity, Booth as often contented himself with too grave a dignity. The latter seemed too much to heave up his words, as the other to dart them to the ear with too quick and sharp a vehemence. Thus, Wilks would too frequently break into the time and measure of the harmony by too many spirited accents in one line, and Booth, by too solemn a regard to harmony would as often lose the necessary spirit of it; so that (as I have observed) could we have sometimes raised the one and sunk the other, they had both been nearer to the mark. Yet this could not be always objected to them. They had their intervals of unexceptionable excellence that more than balanced their errors. The masterpiece of Booth was Othello; there, he was most in character, and seemed not more to animate or please himself in it than his spectators.[79] 'Tis true he owed his last and highest advancement to his acting Cato, but it was the novelty and critical appearance of that character that chiefly swelled the torrent of his applause.[80] For let the sentiments of a declaiming patriot have all the sublimity that poetry can raise them to; let them be delivered too with the utmost grace and dignity of elocution that can recommend them to the auditor; yet this is but one light wherein the excellence of an actor can shine. But in Othello we may see him in the variety of Nature: there the actor is carried through the different accidents of domestic happiness and misery, occasionally torn and tortured by the most distracting passion that can raise terror or compassion in the spectator. Such are the characters that a master actor would delight in; and therefore in Othello, I may safely aver that Booth showed himself thrice the actor that he could in Cato. And yet his merit in acting Cato need not be diminished by this comparison.

79 Booth was playing Cassio at least from 28 January 1707, with Betterton as Othello (LS2a 340); he played Othello for Rich at Drury Lane at least from 21 January 1710 (LS2a 542) and for the triumvirate at the same theatre from 18 January 1711, with Cibber as Iago (LS2a 613).
80 Booth's 'advancement' was his elevation to shareholding manager, after playing Cato (see above, pp.302–6).

Wilks often regretted that in tragedy he had not the full and strong voice of Booth to command and grace his periods with. But Booth used to say that if his ear had been equal to it, Wilks had voice enough to have shown himself a much better tragedian. Now though there might be some truth in this, yet these two actors were of so mixed a merit that even in tragedy the superiority was not always on the same side. In sorrow, tenderness or resignation, Wilks plainly had the advantage, and seemed more pathetically to feel, look and express his calamity. But in the more turbulent transports of the heart, Booth again bore the palm, and left all competitors behind him. A fact perhaps will set this difference in a clearer light. I have formerly seen Wilks act Othello[81] and Booth the Earl of Essex,[82] in which they both miscarried. Neither the exclamatory rage or jealousy of the one or the plaintive distresses of the other were happily executed or became either of them, though in the contrary characters they were both excellent.

When an actor becomes and naturally looks the character he stands in, I have often observed it to have had as fortunate an effect (and as much recommended him to the approbation of the common auditors) as the most correct or judicious utterance of the sentiments. This was strongly visible in the favourable reception Wilks met with in Hamlet, where I own the half of what he spoke was as painful to my ear as every line that came from Betterton was charming.[83] And yet it is not impossible, could they have come to a poll, but Wilks might have had a majority of admirers. However, such a division had been no proof that the pre-eminence had not still remained in Betterton; and if I should add that Booth too was behind Betterton in Othello, it would be saying no more than Booth himself had judgment and candour enough to know and confess. And if both he and Wilks are allowed, in the two above-mentioned characters, a second place to so great

81 Wilks had played Othello at the Smock Alley Theatre before his first appearances in London. On 22 June 1710 he played it at the Queen's Haymarket in a benefit performance for Cibber, who played Iago (LS2a 581). Lowe cites *The Tatler*, no.188, 20–2 June 1710 on Steele's 'curiosity to observe how Wilks and Cibber touch those places where Betterton and Sandford so very highly excelled'.

82 John Banks's *The Unhappy Favourite; or, the Earl of Essex* was first performed by the King's Company in May 1681 (LS1 295–6); Wilks's role model, Mountfort, probably played the title role for the United Company in 1692 (LS1 416). The play remained popular throughout the period covered by the *Apology*. Wilks is first listed in the title role on 29 November 1706 (LS2a 325) but had probably been playing it for Christopher Rich at least since January 1703 (LS2a 85); *The Tatler*, no.14, 10–12 May 1709 singles out the role as one of his best. Booth played it on 25 November 1709 in a Drury Lane performance mounted '[a]t the desire of several persons of quality' (LS2a 524).

83 Wilks may have been playing Hamlet for Christopher Rich at Drury Lane from October 1703 (LS2a 125); he is first recorded in the role at the Queen's Haymarket on 11 January 1707 (LS2a 334), following Betterton's performance of it the previous month (LS2a 327).

a master as Betterton, it will be a rank of praise that the best actors since my time might have been proud of.

I am now come towards the end of that time through which our affairs had long gone forward in a settled course of prosperity. From the visible errors of former managements we had, at last, found the necessary means to bring our private laws and orders into the general observance and approbation of our society. Diligence and neglect were under an equal eye: the one never failed of its reward and the other, by being very rarely excused, was less frequently committed. You are now to consider us in our height of favour, and so much in fashion with the politer part of the town that our house, every Saturday, seemed to be the appointed assembly of the first ladies of quality. Of this too, the common spectators were so well apprised, that for twenty years successively on that day we scarce ever failed of a crowded audience; for which occasion we particularly reserved our best plays, acted in the best manner we could give them.[84]

Among our many necessary reformations, what not a little preserved to us the regard of our auditors was the decency of our clear stage; from whence we had now, for many years, shut out those idle gentlemen who seemed more delighted to be pretty objects themselves than capable of any pleasure from the play – who took their daily stands where they might best elbow the actor and come in for their share of the auditor's attention. In many a laboured scene of the warmest humour, and of the most affecting passion, have I seen the best actors disconcerted while these buzzing mosquitoes have been fluttering round their eyes and ears. How was it possible an actor so embarrassed should keep his impatience from entering into that different temper which his personated character might require him to be master of?[85]

84 By 'best plays', Cibber generally (but not exclusively) meant old ones. In the season 1726–7, for instance, Saturday performances at Drury Lane were of *Othello*, *The Old Batchelor*, *The Relapse* (twice), *The Constant Couple*, *Sir Courtly Nice*, *The Chances*, *Volpone*, *The Humorous Lieutenant*, *The Libertine Destroyed*, *Hamlet* (twice), *The Albion Queens*, *The Comical Revenge*, *The Man of Mode*, *The Way of the World*, *The Orphan* (twice), *The Mourning Bride*, *2 Henry IV*, *Mithridates*, *The Plain Dealer*, and *The History and Fall of Caius Marius*. The only eighteenth-century plays to appear on Saturdays in that season were Edmund Smith's *Phaedra and Hippolitus* (3 December 1726, LS2 895; again on 31 January 1727; LS2 900), James Moore Smythe's *The Rival Modes* (27 January 1727, LS2 905), Steele's *The Conscious Lovers* (11 February 1727, LS2 908), Addison's *Cato* (4 March 1727, LS2 911), Rowe's *The Fair Penitent* (11 March 1727, LS2 912) and *Tamerlane* (4 November 1726, LS2 889; again on 25 March 1727, LS2 915), and Cibber's *The Careless Husband* (14 January 1727, LS2 903; again on 19 March 1727, LS2 919).
85 The problem had required official intervention; Lord Chamberlain Kent's order dated 2 March 1708 commands the managers and shareholders to ensure 'no person whatever … come behind the scenes, or be upon the stage … excepting the the actors and servants necessary for the performance' (LC 5/154, p.320; *Document Register* no.1959).

Future actors may perhaps wish I would set this grievance in a stronger light; and to say the truth, where auditors are ill bred it cannot well be expected that actors should be polite. Let me therefore show how far an artist in any science is apt to be hurt by any sort of inattention to his performance.

While the famous Corelli, at Rome, was playing some musical composition of his own to a select company in the private apartment of his patron-cardinal, he observed, in the height of his harmony, his eminence was engaging in a detached conversation;[86] upon which he suddenly stopped short and gently laid down his instrument. The Cardinal, surprised at the unexpected cessation, asked him if a string was broke; to which Corelli, in an honest conscience of what was due to his music, replied, 'No, sir, I was only afraid I interrupted business'. His eminence, who knew that a genius could never show itself to advantage where it had not its proper regards, took this reproof in good part and broke off his conversation to hear the whole concerto played over again.

Another story will let us see what effect a mistaken offence of this kind had upon the French theatre, which was told me by a gentleman of the long robe then at Paris, and who was himself the innocent author of it. At the tragedy of Zaire, while the celebrated Mademoiselle Gaussin was delivering a soliloquy, this gentleman was seized with a sudden fit of coughing which gave the actress some surprise and interruption,[87] and his fit increasing, she was forced to stand silent so long that it drew the eyes of the uneasy audience upon him; when a French gentleman, leaning forward to him, asked him if this actress had given him any particular offence, that he took so public an occasion to resent it. The English gentleman, in the utmost surprise, assured him so far from it, that he was a particular admirer of her performance; that his malady was his real misfortune, and if he apprehended any return of it he would rather quit his seat than disoblige either the actress or the audience.

This public decency in their theatre I have myself seen carried so far, that a gentleman in their second *loge* (or middle gallery) being observed to sit forward himself while a lady sat behind him, a loud number of voices

---

86 Arcangelo Corelli (1653–1713), famed for his Op. 6 *Concerti Grossi* (hence, perhaps, Cibber's reference below); after his travels in Europe, Corelli settled in Rome from 1685, composing and playing in the service of Cardinal Pietro Ottoboni (1667–1740), who was both friend and patron. See Marc Pincherle, *Corelli: His Life, His Work*, trans. Hubert E. M. Russell (New York: W. W. Norton, 1956), pp.31–4.

87 Jeanne Catharine Gaussin (1711–67), leading actress at the Comédie Française, created the title role in Voltaire's 1732 *Zaïre*. Cibber's 'gentleman of the long robe' was a barrister or judge.

called out to him from the pit, 'Place à la dame! Place à la dame!'[88] When
the person so offending either not apprehending the meaning of the clamour (or possibly being some John Trott[89] who feared no man alive), the
noise was continued for several minutes; nor were the actors, though ready
on the stage, suffered to begin the play till this unbred person was laughed
out of his seat and had placed the lady before him.

Whether this politeness observed at plays may be owing to their clime,
their complexion or their government is of no great consequence; but if it is
to be acquired, methinks it is pity our accomplished countrymen, who every
year import so much of this nation's gawdy garniture,[90] should not in this
long course of our commerce with them have brought over a little of their
theatrical good-breeding too.

I have been the more copious upon this head, that it might be judged
how much it stood us upon to have got rid of those improper spectators
I have been speaking of. For whatever regard we might draw by keeping
them at a distance from our stage, I had observed while they were admitted
behind our scenes, we but too often showed them the wrong side of our
tapestry; and that many a tolerable actor was the less valued when it was
known what ordinary stuff he was made of.[91] Among the many more disagreeable distresses that are almost unavoidable in the government of a theatre, those we so often met with from the persecution of bad authors were
what we could never entirely get rid of. But let us state both our cases and
then see where the justice of the complaint lies. 'Tis true, when an ingenious indigent had taken perhaps a whole summer's pains, *invitâ Minervâ*,[92]
to heap up a pile of poetry into the likeness of a play, and found at last the
gay promise of his winter's support was rejected and abortive, a man almost
ought to be a poet himself to be justly sensible of his distress! Then, indeed,
great allowances ought to be made for the severe reflections he might naturally throw upon those pragmatical actors who had no sense or taste of
good writing. And yet, if his relief was only to be had by his imposing a bad
play upon a good set of actors, methinks the charity that first looks at home

---

88 Cibber visited France in the summer of 1728, with the last recorded Drury Lane
   performance of the 1727–8 season dated 13 June 1728 (LS2 981); the visit is reported in his
   daughter Charlotte's *A Narrative of the Life of Mrs Charlotte Charke* (1755) and reprinted in
   the edition by Robert M. Rehder (London: Routledge, 2016).
89 See above, p.119 n.114.
90 i.e. ornaments in the broad sense (costume, furniture etc.), but here also a reference to
   French actors and dancers, as above, p.209 n.43.
91 Cibber is either heedless of the parallel with the publication of the *Apology*, or confident
   of its discretion.
92 'Without inspiration' (literally, 'the muse Minerva being unwilling').

has as good an excuse for its coldness as the unhappy object of it had a plea for his being relieved at their expense. But immediate want was not always confessed their motive for writing. Fame, honour and Parnassian glory had sometimes taken a romantic turn in their heads; and then they gave themselves the air of talking to us in a higher strain. Gentlemen were not to be so treated! The stage was like to be finely governed when actors pretended to be judges of authors, *etc.* But dear gentlemen, if they were good actors, why not? How should they have been able to act, or rise to any excellence, if you supposed them not to feel or understand what you offered them? Would you have reduced them to the mere mimicry of parrots and monkeys, that can only prate and play a great many pretty tricks, without reflection? Or how are you sure your friend the infallible judge, to whom you read your fine piece, might be sincere in the praises he gave it? Or, indeed, might not you have thought the best judge a bad one if he had disliked it? Consider, too, how possible it might be that a man of sense would not care to tell you a truth he was sure you would not believe! And, if neither Dryden, Congreve, Steele, Addison, nor Farquhar (if you please) ever made any complaint of their incapacity to judge, why is the world to believe the slights you have met with from them are either undeserved or particular? Indeed, indeed, I am not conscious that we ever did you or any of your fraternity the least injustice![93] Yet this was not all we had to struggle with. To supersede our right of rejecting, the recommendation (or rather imposition) of some great persons whom it was not prudence to disoblige sometimes came in, with a high hand, to support their pretensions; and then, *cout que cout*,[94] acted it must be! So when the short life of this wonderful nothing was over,

---

93 Lowe quotes *The Laureate*, p.95, which recreates the experience of an unfortunate author at Cibber's hands:

> The court sitting, Chancellor Cibber (for the other two, like M——rs in Chancery, sat only for form's sake, and did not presume to judge) nodded to the author to open his manuscript. The author begins to read, in which if he failed to please the Corrector, he would condescend sometimes to read it for him; when, if the play struck him very warmly (as it would if he found anything new in it in which he conceived he could particularly shine as an actor), he would lay down his pipe (for the Chancellor always smoked when he made a decree) and cry, 'By God there is something in this: I do not know but it may do; but I will play such a part'. Well, when the reading was finished, he made his proper corrections, and sometimes without any propriety; nay, frequently he very much and very hastily maimed what he pretended to mend.

Lowe goes on to cite Genest's defence of Cibber's literary management (III.346): 'After all that has been said against Chancellor Cibber, it does not appear that he often made a wrong decree: most of the good plays came out at Drury Lane.'

94 i.e. whatever the cost.

the actors were, perhaps, abused in a preface for obstructing the success of it, and the town publicly damned us for our private civility.[95]

I cannot part with these fine gentlemen authors without mentioning a ridiculous *disgraccia* that befell one of them many years ago. This solemn bard (who, like Bayes, only writ for fame and reputation), on the second day's public triumph of his muse, marching in a stately full-bottomed periwig into the lobby of the house with a lady of condition in his hand, when raising his voice to the Sir Fopling sound that 'became the mouth of a man of quality', and calling out, 'Hey! Box-keeper! Where is my Lady such-a-one's servant', was unfortunately answered by honest John Trott (which then happened to be the box-keeper's real name), 'Sir, we have dismissed; there was not company enough to pay candles'; in which mortal astonishment it may be sufficient to leave him. And yet, had the actors refused this play, what resentment might have been thought too severe for them?[96]

Thus was our administration often censured for accidents which were not in our power to prevent – a possible case in the wisest governments. If, therefore, some plays have been preferred to the stage that were never fit to have been seen there, let this be our best excuse for it. And yet, if the merit of our rejecting the many bad plays that pressed hard upon us were weighed against the few that were thus imposed upon us, our conduct in general might have more amendments of the stage to boast of than errors to answer for. But it is now time to drop the curtain.

95 Lowe cites two examples of plays whose printed editions criticize the actors, neither of which was acted during Cibber's management: the anonymous *The Lunatic* (1705) and James Drake's 1697 *The Sham Lawyer: or the Lucky Extravagant*, the title page of which declares it was 'Damnably acted at the Theatre Royal in Drury Lane'. Cibber played Careless; Drake (1667–1707), although a Fellow of the Royal Society, was hardly a 'great person'. Bellchambers cites a further case, John Dennis's *The Comical Gallant* (1702), an adaptation of *The Merry Wives of Windsor*, in the preface to which the author claimed that 'Falstaff's part … was by no means acted to the satisfaction of the audience.' Cibber may also have been thinking of his adversary John Dennis's *Gibraltar; or, The Spanish Adventure* (1705), the preface to which complains of 'the calamities which attended the rehearsal'.

96 Assuming this was not an anonymous playwright (Cibber says he wrote for 'fame'), the circumstances do not entirely match any of the known writers of the period. It is possible Cibber was still thinking about Dennis's *Gibraltar* (1705), whose second and last performance was, Dennis complained in the preface, 'faintly and negligently acted, and consequently was not seen'. Dennis held a minor court post and may have qualified in Cibber's mind as a 'gentleman author'. In Etherege's *The Man of Mode*, III.iii.247–55, Loveit asks a footman his name. 'John Trott', he replies, and when Sir Fopling decides to call him 'Hampshire' instead, Loveit says the sound of Fopling's voice 'becomes the mouth of a man of quality'; from the edition by Michael Neill (London: Bloomsbury, 2019), p.86. John Trot the 'box-keeper' was dismissed by Cibber, Wilks, and Booth in September 1726 (memorandum in *Document Register* no.3324).

During our four last years, there happened so very little unlike what has been said before that I shall conclude with barely mentioning those unavoidable accidents that drew on our dissolution. The first, that for some years had led the way to greater, was the continued ill state of health that rendered Booth incapable of appearing on the stage.[97] The next was the death of Mrs Oldfield, which happened on the 23rd of October 1730. About the same time, too, Mrs Porter (then in her highest reputation for tragedy) was lost to us by the misfortune of a dislocated limb from the overturning of a chaise.[98] And our last stroke was the death of Wilks in September the year following, 1731.[99]

Notwithstanding such irreparable losses, whether, when these favourite actors were no more to be had, their successors might not be better borne with than they could possibly have hoped while the former were in being; or that the generality of spectators, from their want of taste were easier to be pleased than the few that knew better; or that at worst our actors were still preferable to any other company of the several then subsisting; or to whatever cause it might be imputed, our audiences were far less abated than our apprehensions had suggested. So that, though it began to grow late in life with me, having still health and strength enough to have been as useful on the stage as ever, I was under no visible necessity of quitting it. But so it happened that our surviving fraternity having got some chimerical and, as I thought, unjust notions into their heads (which, though I knew they were without much difficulty to be surmounted, I chose not, at my time of day, to enter into new contentions); and as I found an inclination in some of them to purchase the whole power of the patent into their own hands, I did my best, while I stayed with them, to make it worth their while to come up to my price; and then patiently sold out my share to the first bidder, wishing the crew I had left in the vessel a good voyage.[100]

---

97 A letter by Aaron Hill dated 2 October 1731 discusses the difficulties caused by Booth's illness (Document Register no.3594); he died on 10 May 1733.

98 As reported in the same letter by Aaron Hill (above, n.97). According to Davies, III.495, the accident happened in the summer of 1731; she returned to the company temporarily in January 1733.

99 Wilks died on 27 September 1732.

100 For Cibber's profit, see above, p.197 n.73. Lowe cites *The Laureate*, p.96:
> As to the occasion of your parting with your share of the patent, I cannot think you give us the true reason; for I have been very well informed it was the intention, not only of you, but of your brother managers, as soon as you could get the great seal to your patent (which stuck for some time, the then Lord Chancellor not being satisfied in the legality of the grant) to dispose it to the best bidder. This was at first kept a secret among you; but as soon as the grant was completed, you sold to the first who would come up to your price.

What commotions the stage fell into the year following, or from what provocations the greatest part of the actors revolted and set up for themselves in the little house in the Haymarket, lies not within the promise of my title page to relate;[101] or, as it might set some persons living in a light they possibly might not choose to be seen in, I will rather be thankful for the involuntary favour they have done me than trouble the public with private complaints of fancied or real injuries.

FINIS

---

101 Performances had been taking place at the Little Haymarket since 1721, but Cibber refers to the Drury Lane actors' rebellion of May 1733, led by his son Theophilus (see above, p.187 n.49), after which the company played at the Little Haymarket. A report of their return to Drury Lane is carried in the *Daily Advertiser* of 9 March 1734 (*Document Register* no.3807). A company led by Cibber's daughter Charlotte then occupied the Little Haymarket until they were evicted in September 1735 (report in the *London Daily Post*, 24 September 1735; *Document Register* no.3941). According to Davies's *Memoirs of the Life of David Garrick*, Cibber tried to secure a new licence for Theophilus, but to no avail (I.69–70).

ILLUSTRATIVE COLLATION

This text is based on the second edition, as published in octavo format (hence O1, the first octavo edition). Where errors were introduced into the text of the first edition (referred to below as Q1, that is, the first quarto), they have been corrected. Dodsley's edition of 1750 is listed as O2. Occasional changes to the spelling of proper names (e.g. Underhil/Underhill, Estcourt/Estcoart) have not been listed, nor have repeated instances of Cibber's distinctive spellings such as 'menagers' and 'cotemporaries'. All three texts switch between 'further' and 'farther'. 'Farther' is preferred here; it is both more frequent and echoes the Foppingtonian tones for which Cibber was mocked (see above, p.102 n.43). Page numbers are from the current edition.

Page number	Key words in this edition, as modernized (O1 variants in brackets)	As given in Q1 (not modernized)	As given in O2
13	of hasty head	of my hasty Head	
20	one of a more	the one of a more	
21	his acquaintance	one of his Acquaintance	
	butt (O1: But)	Butt	
22	everyone who has	every one that has	
	cannot	can't	
	time enough to	time to	
25	other conditions	other hard Conditions	
29	sat myself (O1: set myself	sate myself	
	here, when	here, where	
30	conversing, which is a	conversing; a	
31	among them	among 'em	
32	most a mind	most mind	
	contemporaries	Cotemporaries	
33	of his harp	to his Harp	
37	nothing I can say	nothing I say	
38	as what *you* say	as from what *You* say	
42	perhaps of	of perhaps	
43	eminent pleader (O1: eloquent pleader)	eminent Pleader	
48	commission	Cmission	
55	new honours of Lord Steward	new Honours of Duke of Devonshire	
57	no pretence	no great Pretence	

Page number	Key words in this edition, as modernized (O1 variants in brackets)	As given in Q1 (not modernized)	As given in O2
67	after the so long	after so long	
69	argument	Agreement	
	management (O1: Menagement)	Management	
78	be also tempted	be so often tempted	
	pronunciation (O1: Pronounciation)	Pronunciation	
79	powers at once united	Powers united	
95	had he not been (O1: he had not been)	he had not been	had he not been
96	make (O1: made)	made	
107	I have chosen	I have chose	
108	a Harlequin	an Harlequin	
123	any theatre	any one Theatre	
135	for erecting	for the erecting	
151	any share (O1: an Share)	any Share	
166	to be as much	to have been as much	
171	best they had done (O1: best They done)	best They had done	
185	His Majesty	his late Majesty	
	King George the First	King *George* I	
190	get money	get Mony	
194	not to suffer	not suffer	
	and misrule	or Mis-rule	
199	1707	1708	
202	At that time	At this time	
	what made (O1: what what made)	what made	
203	she got more	she grew more	
207	Mr Wilks	*Wilks*	
211	great disadvantages	greater Disadvantages	
212	ceiling	Cieling	
215	upon every other stage	upon any other Stage	
223	parts of them all	Parts of 'em all	
	must live	mustlive	
225	large elephant		fine Elephant

Page number	Key words in this edition, as modernized (O1 variants in brackets)	As given in Q1 (not modernized)	As given in O2
225	and acquaint	and acquainted	
231	chief characters	chie fCharacters	
240	the public money	our Publick Money	
242	eldest son	eldst son	
246	upon raising	upon the raising	
247	he were suffered	he was suffer'd	
249	laid aside	laid asider	
253	not an adept	but an adept	
	and exquisitely	and the exquisitely	
255	and probably make	and probably might make	
267	1714, which	1714, and which	
269	wanting nothing	wanted nothing	
	ceiling	Cieling	
270	stranger	stronger	
275	the support	theS upport	
277	judge of it by	judge of by	
289	submit	submi	
290	as well as a	as well as from a	
	the Dublin theatre (O1: *Dublin* Theatre)	the *Dublin* Theatre	
291	behaviour in Wilks	Behaviour of *Wilks*	
297	no patience	not patience	
308	conductor	chief Conductor	
	I most delighted in	I had most delighted in	
314	continued in it.	continued in it?	
315	acknowledgment	Acknowledment	
321	Member of Parliament	Member for the new Parliament	
326	Do not we	Do we not	
335	to say	to save	
	it is amazing	it seems amazing	
336	Upon this, sir	Upon this, Si	
337	as he had	as he has had	
344	had passed (O1: had pass)	had pass'd	
348	a court as well be	a Court be as well	
349	before we can find one	before we find one	
351	staffs (O1: Saffs)	Staffs	

Page number	Key words in this edition, as modernized (O1 variants in brackets)	As given in Q1 (not modernized)	As given in O2
363	and left all (O1: and all)	and left all	
365	advantage	Advanrage	
366	*Place à la dame!*	*Place à Dame!*	

SELECTIVE INDEX TO THE
APOLOGY AND FOOTNOTES

'Selective', because a comprehensive index to the *Apology* and the notes presented here would form a small book in its own right. In a small number of cases where a person had multiple roles, subheadings are used (actor, manager, personal, etc); where Cibber addresses matters of general significance, the subheading 'topics' is used. In general, however, entries refer to the events described rather than his commentary on them. Where Cibber refers to someone by occupation (e.g. 'the patentee'), an entry is given for the name (in that case, usually Christopher Rich); where he uses the subtitle of a play, the main title is given, and where he misidentifies a play, the actual play is listed.